WITHDRA

PROPERTY OF THE FRIENDS OF THE
EDWIN H. MOOKINI LIBRARY

Big Business
Economic Power in a Free Society

Big Business
Economic Power in a Free Society

Advisory Editor
LEON STEIN

Editorial Board
Stuart Bruchey
Thomas C. Cochran

A NOTE ABOUT THIS BOOK

By the time he wrote this book, Ripley (1867-1941) had instructed engineers at the Massachusetts Institute of Technology, served with the U.S. Industrial Commission, 1900-1901, and taught at Harvard University. He reached the conclusion that the movement of goods was the fundamental action of national economic life, with rates and routes crucially affecting prices and the cost of living. In his introduction, he writes that he is acting as advocate for the "helpless and unorganized general public." Ripley brings clarity, understanding, and masterful command of the facts to his examination of rebates, routing, discriminatory practices, basing point system, the Hepburn Act, the Mann-Elkins Act and a score of other abuses and proposed remedies.

RAILROADS

RATES AND REGULATION

BY

William Z[ebina] Ripley

ARNO PRESS
A New York Times Company
New York / 1973

Reprint Edition 1973 by Arno Press Inc.

Reprinted from a copy in
 The University of Illinois Library

BIG BUSINESS: Economic Power in a Free Society
ISBN for complete set: 0-405-05070-4
See last pages of this volume for titles.

Manufactured in the United States of America

Library of Congress Cataloging in Publication Data

Ripley, William Zebina, 1867-1941.
  Railroads: rates and regulation.

  (Big business: economic power in a free society)
  Reprint of the ed. published by Longmans, Green,
New York.
  Includes bibliographical references.
  1. Railroads--United States--Rates. 2. Railroads
and state--United States.   I. Title. II. Series.
HE1843.R6 1973   385.1   73-2532
ISBN 0-405-05110-7

RAILROADS
RATES AND REGULATION

RAILROADS

RATES AND REGULATION

BY

WILLIAM Z. RIPLEY, Ph.D.

Nathaniel Ropes Professor of Economics In Harvard University

WITH 41 MAPS AND DIAGRAMS

LONGMANS, GREEN, AND CO.
FOURTH AVENUE & 30TH STREET, NEW YORK
LONDON, BOMBAY, AND CALCUTTA
1912

COPYRIGHT, 1912, BY
LONGMANS, GREEN, AND CO.

THE·PLIMPTON·PRESS
[W·D·Q]
NORWOOD·MASS·U·S·A

PREFACE

THIS treatise is the outcome of a continuous personal interest in railroads, practically coincident in point of time with the period of active participation of the Federal government in their affairs. During these years, since 1887 when the Act to Regulate Commerce was passed, as the problem of public regulation has gradually unfolded, opportunity has offered itself to me to view the subject from different angles. At the Massachusetts Institute of Technology, as instructor of embryo engineers in the economic aspects of their callings; in service for the United States Industrial Commission in 1900-01, in touch alike with government officials and, travelling all about the country, with shippers and commercial bodies during a period of acute unrest; and finally ripening the practical experience, thus gained, in the favoring atmosphere of Harvard University, seeking to imbue future citizens with a sense of their civic responsibilities; through all these years, the conviction has steadily grown that, as one of the most fundamental agents in our American economic affairs, the subjection of transportation to public control was a primary need of the time. An earnest effort has been made to set down the facts concerning this highly controversial subject with scientific rigor and with fairness to all three of the great parties concerned, the owners, the shippers and the people. If bias there be, it will in all likelihood be found to favor the welfare of the "dim inarticulate multitude,"—that so inert mass of interests and aspirations, too indefinitely informed as to details and too much occupied in earning its daily bread, to be able to analyze its own vital concerns, to give expression to its will, and even sometimes, as it seems, wisely to choose its spokesmen and representatives.

It is this helpless and unorganized general public, always in need of an advocate, which, perhaps, most strongly appeals to the academic mind. If there be lack of judicial poise in this regard, it is, at all events, palliated by free confession in advance.

Nor is the history of the assumption by public authority of its inherent right to control railroads, as narrow an interest as it at first appears. Transportation, as a service, is the commodity produced by common carriers. The manner in which the price of this commodity has been brought under governmental regulation has a direct bearing upon another problem just beginning to open up; namely that of the control by the state of the prices of other things. It is not unlikely, in my judgment, that the final solution of the so-called Trust Problem in the United States, whether for good or ill, may ultimately contain as one important feature, the determination by governmental authority of reasonable prices for such prime necessities of life as milk, ice, coal, sugar and oil, when produced under monopolistic conditions. This view is shared by my colleague Professor Taussig in his "Principles of Economics." It is also distinctly set forth by President Van Hise of the University of Wisconsin, in his recent "Concentration and Control." When the seed of such an industrial policy is planted, as I believe it possible in time, the soil will have been richly prepared for its reception by our experience in the determination of reasonable charges for the services of railroads and other public utilities.

A word of explanation may also be offered to the reader who finds in these pages an almost exuberant mass of illustrative material. Possibly, even, it may be alleged that in places so thick are the circumstantial trees of evidence that one can scarcely perceive the wood of principle. But, under the circumstances, it is almost inevitable that this should be so. The method of inquiry adopted has been mainly inductive. Text books and theoretical treatises have been used only by the way. I hold them to be merely of secondary importance. The principal reliance has been upon concrete data, painstakingly gathered through many years from original sources. In this present excursion in the far more complex domain of the social sciences, an endeavor has been made to adhere strictly to the same scientific method pursued in the field of natural science in writing "The Races of Europe." A search far and wide for every possible bit of raw material had to be made at the outset. To this succeeded the classification and realignment of the concrete data thus obtained. The last step of all, was the formulation of the governing economic principles. But an almost indispensable result of this mode of work is a plenitude of reference and example. One might almost say that under such circumstances it becomes second nature to demand concrete illustration for every economic theory or principle laid down. Such a statement, however, would be fallacious. It would misrepresent the true sequence of events as above outlined. Rather should it be affirmed, that, inasmuch as the concrete examples are the sources of the reasoning, no theory can be held valid for which somewhere or somehow, positive illustration drawn from practice cannot be found. Such an ideal is, indeed, difficult to attain; but it may be stated as a cardinal principle to be always kept in mind. And it ought to excuse an author from the charge of over-elaboration of detail in illustration. The only crimes for which no verbal atonement will suffice are that the chosen illustration does not fit the principle, or else that the facts have been distorted to serve a preconceived idea.

References throughout this work to a second volume will be noted. This will deal primarily with matters of finance and corporate relations. The general subject of railroad combination was necessarily relegated to another set of covers. This, however, is quite fitting, inasmuch as the connection between matters of finance and organization is at all times so intimate and necessary. The development of inter-railway relationships has been, perhaps, next to the establishment of government regulation, the most striking phenomenon of the last decade. It is absolutely essential to a comprehension of present day financial problems, to understand the nature and extent of the consolidation of interests which obtains. This second volume, now nearly completed, will, it is hoped, appear early in 1913.

This volume is also frequently linked by means of cross references to a set of reprints of notable interstate commerce cases or special articles which was published some years ago as "Railway Problems." (Ginn & Co.) Much new material having accumulated since its original appearance in 1907, it is the intention to prepare a new and revised edition, particularly designed as an accompaniment to this treatise. But the same chapter numbers will be preserved for all material taken over from the first edition.

Many friends and specialists, who shall be unnamed, have been of assistance in various ways for which I am duly grateful. But a few have been so peculiarly helpful that it is fitting to make more particular mention of my personal obligation. Especially is this true of Hon. Balthasar H. Meyer of the Interstate Commerce Commission, from whom through many years of friendship and common interest in the subject, have come all sorts of aid and suggestion. Prof. F. H. Dixon of Dartmouth College, Statistician of the Bureau of Railway Economics at Washington, also a co-worker in the same field, has always without reserve freely shared the best he had to give. I have drawn liberally from his special contributions on transportation, particularly in the history of recent Federal legislation. Despite the difference in our point of view, the always friendly criticism of Frederic A. Delano, President of the Wabash Railroad, has been most welcome and serviceable. In matters of classification, Mr. D. O. Ives, Traffic Expert of the Boston Chamber of Commerce, has extended a helping hand. And I have profited greatly from the published work of Mr. Samuel O. Dunn, now Editor of the *Railway Age Gazette*. In this connection, acknowledgment should be made of my deep obligation to the other editors of that admirable technical journal, who have in series during a number of years afforded me an opportunity of reaching a class of readers and, it should be added, not infrequently of unsparing critics, whose intelligence and technical knowledge have held me to a strict accounting in all matters of fact or principle. Without this critical oversight, many statements, happily now tested, would have held less secure place. Then again, there is the entire staff of the Interstate Commerce Commission to whom I have been a care and trouble for so many years. Ungrudgingly have its members always given response to all sorts of requests, whether for documents, statistics or opinions. Without the official stores of information at Washington, this present volume would have been woefully incomplete.

CONTENTS

CHAPTER I

THE HISTORY OF TRANSPORTATION IN THE UNITED STATES

Significance of geographical factors, 1. — Toll roads before 1820, 2. — The "National pike," 3. — Canals and internal water-ways before 1830, 4. — The Erie Canal, 4. — Canals in the West, 6. — First railroad construction after 1830, 7. — Early development in the South, 9. — Importance of small rivers, 10.
The decade 1840–1860, 11. — Slow railway growth, mainly in the East, 12. — Rapid expansion 1848–1857; western river traffic, 13. — Need of north and south railways, 14. — Traffic still mainly local, 15. — Effect of the Civil War, 16. — Rise of New York, 17. — Primitive methods, 17.
The decade 1870–1880, 18. — Trans-Mississippi development, 18. — Pacific Coast routes opened, 19. — Development of export trade in grain and beef, 20. — Trunk line rate wars, 21. — Improvements in operation, 23. — End of canal and river traffic, 24.
The decade 1880–1890, 27. — Phenomenal railway expansion, 28. — Transcontinental trade, 28. — Speculation rampant, 29. — Growth of western manufactures, 30. — Rise of the Gulf ports, 31. — Canadian competition, 33. — General résumé and forecast, 34.
Public land grants, 35. — Direct financial assistance, 37. — History of state aid, 39. — Federal experience with transcontinental roads, 40.

CHAPTER II

THE THEORY OF RAILROAD RATES

Analysis of railroad expenditures, 44. — Constant $v.$ variable outlays, 45. — Fixed charges, 46. — Official grouping of expenses, 46. — Variable expenses in each group, 51. — Peculiarities of different roads and circumstances, 56. — Periodicity of expenditures, 61. — Joint cost, 67. — Separation of passenger and freight business, 68.

CHAPTER III

THE THEORY OF RAILROAD RATES (*Continued*)

The law of increasing returns, 71. — Applied to declining traffic, 73. — Illustrated by the panic of 1907, 75. — Peculiarly intensified on railroads, 76.
Growth of mileage and traffic in the United States since 1889, 77. — Increase of earnings, 79. — Operating expenses, gross and net income, 80. — Comparison with earlier decades, 85. — Density of traffic, 86. — Increase of train loads, 88. — Limitations upon their economy, 92. — Heavier rails, 93. — Larger locomotives, 94. — Bigger cars, 95. — Net result of improvements upon efficiency and earning power, 97.
The law of increasing returns due to financial rather than operating factors, 99.

CHAPTER IV

RATE MAKING IN PRACTICE

Evolution of rate sheets, 101. — Terminal *v.* haulage costs, 102. — Local competition, 104. — What the traffic will bear, 107. — Trunk line rate system, 111. — Complexity of rate structure, 113. — Competition of routes, 114. — Competition of facilities, 116. — Competition of markets, 118. — Ever-widening markets, 119. — Primary and secondary market competition, 121. — Jobbing or distributive business, 124. — Flat rates, 127. — Mississippi-Missouri rate scheme, 128. — Relation between raw materials and finished products, 134. — Export rates on wheat and flour, 135. — Cattle and packing-house products, 139. — Refrigerator cars, 140. — By-products and substitution, 142. — Kansas corn and Minnesota flour, 143. — Ex-Lake grain rates, 145.

CHAPTER V

RATE MAKING IN PRACTICE (*Continued*)

Effect of changing conditions, 147. — Lumber and paper rates, 148. — Equalizing industrial conditions, 148. — Protecting shippers, 149. — Pacific Coast lumber rates, 150. — Elasticity and quick adaptation, 152. — Rigidity and delicacy of adjustment, 153. — Transcontinental rate system, 154. — Excessive elasticity of rates, 155. — More stability desirable, 159. — Natural *v.* artificial territory and rates, 159. — Economic waste, 159. — Inelastic conditions, 161.— Effect upon concentration of population, 162. — Competition in transportation and trade contrasted, 163. — No abandonment of field, 165.
Cost *v.* value of service, 166. — Relative merits of each, 167. — Charging what the traffic will bear, 169. — Unduly high and low rates,

CONTENTS xiii

171. — Dynamic force in value of service, 177. — Cost of service in classification, 179. — Wisconsin paper case, 181. — Cost and value of service equally important, checking one another, 184.

CHAPTER VI

PERSONAL DISCRIMINATION

Rebates and monopoly, with attendant danger to carriers, 185. — Personal discrimination defined, 188. — Distinction between rebating and general rate cutting, 188. — Early forms of rebates, 189. — Underbilling, underclassification, etc., 190. — Private car lines, 192. — More recent forms of rebating described, 195. — Terminal and tap-lines, 196. — Midnight tariffs, 197. — Outside transactions, special credit, etc., 198. — Distribution of coal cars, 199. — Standard Oil Company practices, 200. — Discriminatory open adjustments from competing centres, 202. — Frequency of rebating since 1900, 204–6. — The Elkins Law of 1903, 205. — Discrimination since 1906, 207. — The grain elevation cases, 211. — Industrial railroads once more, 212.

CHAPTER VII

LOCAL DISCRIMINATION

Concrete instances, 215. — Hadley's oyster case not conclusive, 217. — Two variants: lower long-haul rates by the roundabout route, as in the Hillsdale, Youngstown, and some Southern cases, 221; or by the direct route, as in the Nashville-Chattanooga and other southern cases, 225. — Complicating influence of water transportation, 232. — Market competition from various regions, a different case, 234. — The basing point (southern) and basing line (Missouri river) systems, 238. — Their inevitable instability and probable ultimate abandonment, 242. — Postage-stamp rates, illustrated by transcontinental tariffs, 245. — Which line makes the rate? 255. — Cost not distance, determines, 256. — Fixed charges *v.* operating expenses, 257. — Proportion of local business, 259. — Volume and stability of traffic important, 261. — Generally the short line rules, but many exceptions occur, 263.

CHAPTER VIII

PROBLEMS OF ROUTING

Neglect of distance, an American peculiarity, 264. — Derived from joint cost, 265. — Exceptional cases, 265. — Economic waste in American practice, 268. — Circuitous rail carriage, 269. — Water and rail-and-water shipments, 273. — Carriage over undue distance, 277. — An outcome of commercial competition, 278. — Six causes of economic waste, illustrated, 280. — Pro-rating and rebates, 281. — Five effects of disregard of distance, 288. — Dilution of revenue per ton mile, 289. — Possible remedies for economic waste, 292. — Pooling and rate agreements, 293. — The long and short haul remedy, 295.

CHAPTER IX
FREIGHT CLASSIFICATION

Importance and nature of classification described, 300. — Classifications and tariffs distinguished, as a means of changing rates, 301. — The three classification committees, 304. — Wide differences between them illustrated, 305. — Historical development, 306. — Increase in items enumerated, 309. — Growing distinction between carload and less-than-carload rates, 310. — Great volume of elaborate rules and descriptions, 312. — Theoretical basis of classification, 314. — Cost of service *v.* value of service, 315. — Practically, classification based upon rule of thumb, 319. — The "spread" in classification between commodities, 319. — Similarly as between places, 320. — Commodity rates described, 322. — Natural in undeveloped conditions, 323. — Various sorts of commodity rates, 324. — The problem of carload ratings, 325. — Carloads theoretically considered, 326. — Effect upon commercial competition, 327. — New England milk rates, 329. — Mixed carloads, 331. — Minimum carload rates, 322. — Importance of car capacity, 334. — Market capacity and minimum carloads, 336.
Uniform classification for the United States, 337. — Revival of interest since 1906, 339. — Overlapping and conflicting jurisdictions, 340. — Confusion and discrimination, 341. — Anomalies and conflicts illustrated, 342. — Two main obstacles to uniform classification, 345. — Reflection of local trade conditions, 345. — Compromise not satisfactory, 346. — Classifications and distance tariffs interlock, 347. — General conclusions, 351.

CHAPTER X
THE TRUNK LINE RATE SYSTEM: A DISTANCE TARIFF

Conditions prevalent in 1875, 356. — Various elements distinguished, 358. — The MacGraham percentage plan, 360. — Bearing upon port differentials, 361. — The final plan described, 363. — Competition at junction points, 368. — Independent transverse railways, 370. — Commercial competition, 372. — Limits of the plan, 375. — Central Traffic Association rules, 376.

CHAPTER XI
SPECIAL RATE PROBLEMS: THE SOUTHERN BASING POINT SYSTEM; TRANSCONTINENTAL RATES; PORT DIFFERENTIALS, ETC.

Contrast between the basing point and trunk line systems, 380. — Natural causes in southern territory, 381. — Economic dependence, 381. —

CONTENTS

Wide-spread water competition, 382. — High level of rates, 382. — The basing point system described, 383. — Its economic defences, 384. — Early trade centres, 384. — Water competition once more, 385. — Three types of basing point, 387. — Purely artificial ones exemplified, 388. — Different practice among railroads, 390. — Attempts at reform, 391. — Western *v.* eastern cities, 391. — Effect of recent industrial revival, 392. — The Texas group system, 393. — An outcome of commercial rivalry, 394. — Local competition of trade centres, 395. — Possibly artificial and unstable, 395. — The transcontinental rate system, 395. — High level of charges, 396. — Water competition, 396. — Carload ratings and graded charges, 398. — Competition of jobbing centres, 398. — Canadian differentials, 400. — "Milling-in-transit" and similar practices, 401. — "Floating Cotton," 402. — "Substitution of tonnage," 403. — Seaboard differentials, 403. — Historically considered, 403. — The latest decision, 403. — Import and export rates, 404–409.

CHAPTER XII

THE MOVEMENT OF RATES SINCE 1870; RATE WARS

Contrast before and after 1900, 411. — Revenue per ton mile data, 412. — Their advantages and defects, 414. — Nature of the traffic, 416. — Low-grade traffic increasing, 416. — Growing diversification of tonnage, 418. — Present conditions illustrated, 419. — Length of the haul, 421. — The proportion of local and through business, 422. — Effect of volume of traffic, 424. — Proper use of revenue per ton mile, 425. — Index of actual rates, 426. — Its advantages and defects, 427. — Difficulty of following rate changes since 1900, 427. — Passenger fares, 429. — Freight rates and price movements, 430.
Improvement in observance of tariffs, 431. — Conditions in the eighties, 432. — The depression of 1893–1897, 433. — Resumption of prosperity in 1898, 436. — The rate wars of 1903–1906, 438. — Threatened disturbances in 1909–1911, 439.

CHAPTER XIII

THE ACT TO REGULATE COMMERCE OF 1887

Its general significance, 441. — Economic causes, 442. — Growth of interstate traffic, 442. — Earlier Federal laws, 443. — Not lower rates, but end of discriminations sought, 443. — Rebates and favoritism, 445. — Monopoly by means of pooling distrusted, 446. — Speculation and fraud, 447. — Local discrimination, 448. — General unsettlement from rapid growth, 449. — Congressional history of the law, 450. — Its constitutionality, 451. — Summary of its provisions, 452. — Its tentative character, 453. — Radical departure as to rebating, 454.

CHAPTER XIV

1887–1905. EMASCULATION OF THE LAW

Favorable reception, 456. — First resistance from unwilling witnesses concerning rebates, 457. — Counselman and Brown cases, 458. — The Brimson case, 459. — Relation to Federal Courts unsatisfactory, 460. — Interminable delay, 461. — Original evidence rejected, 461. — The Commission's court record examined, 462. — Rate orders at first obeyed, 467. — The Social Circle case, 468. — Final breakdown in Maximum (Cincinnati) Freight Rate case, 469. — Other functions remaining, 472. — The long and short haul clause interpreted, 474. — The Louisville and Nashville case, 474. — The "independent line" decision, 476. — The Social Circle case again, 478. — "Rare and peculiar cases," 479. — The Alabama Midland (Troy) decision, 481. — Attempted rejuvenation of the long and short haul clause, 483. — The Savannah Naval Stores case, 484. — The dwindling record of complaints, 485.

CHAPTER XV

THE ELKINS AMENDMENTS (1903): THE HEPBURN ACT OF 1906

New causes of unrest in 1899, 487. — The spread of consolidation, 487. — The rise of freight rates, 488. — Concentration of financial power, 490. — The new "trusts," 491. — The Elkins amendments concerning rebates, 492. — Five provisions enumerated, 493.
More general legislation demanded, 494. — Congressional history 1903–1905, 495. — Railway publicity campaign, 496. — President Roosevelt's leadership, 498. — The Hepburn law, 499. — Widened scope, 499. — Rate-making power increased, 500. — Administrative v. judicial regulation, 501. — Objection to judicial control, 503. — Final form of the law, 505. — Broad v. narrow court review, 506. — An unfortunate compromise, 507. — Old rates effective pending review, 508. — Provisions for expedition, 511. — Details concerning rebates, 512. — The commodity clause, 513. — History of its provisions, 514. — Publicity of accounts, 515. — Extreme importance of accounting supervision, 516. — The Hepburn law summarized, 520.

CHAPTER XVI

EFFECTS OF THE LAW OF 1906; JUDICIAL INTERPRETATION, 1905–'10

Large number of complaints filed, 522. — Settlement of many claims, 524. — Fewer new tariffs, 525. — Nature of complaints analyzed, 526. —

CONTENTS

Misrouting of freight, 527. — Car supply and classification rules, 527. — Exclusion from through shipments, 529. — Opening new routes, 530. — Petty grievances considered, 530. — Decisions evenly balanced, 532. — The banana and lumber loading cases, 532. — Freight rate advances, 534. — General investigations, 536.
Supreme Court definition of Commission's authority, 538. — The Illinois Central car supply case, 538. — Economic v. legal aspects considered, 540. — The Baltimore and Ohio decision, 541. — The Burnham, Hanna, Munger case, 542. — The Pacific Coast lumber cases, 543. — Decisions revealing legislative defects, 546. — The Orange Routing case, 546. — The Portland Gateway order, 547. — The Commission's power to require testimony affirmed, 549. — The Baird case, 549. — The "Immunity Bath" decision and the Harriman case, 550. — Interpretation of the "commodity clause," 552. — Means of evasion described, 553.

CHAPTER XVII

THE MANN-ELKINS ACT OF 1910

Prompt acquiescence by carriers, 557. — Opposition begins in 1908, 557. — Political developments, 558. — President Taft's bill, 559. — Three main features of the new law, 560. — Suspension of rate changes, 561. — Former defective injunction procedure remedied, 562. — The new long and short haul clause, 564. — Provision for water competition, 566. — The new Commerce Court, 566. — Congressional debates, 567. — Jurisdiction of the new Court, 568. — Its defects, 569. — Prosecution transferred to the Department of Justice, 570. — Liability for rate quotations, 571. — Wider scope of Federal authority, 572. — The Railroad Securities Commission, 573 — Its report analyzed, 574. — The statute summarized, 578.

CHAPTER XVIII

THE COMMERCE COURT: THE FREIGHT RATE ADVANCES OF 1910

The Commerce Court docket, 581. — The Commerce Court in Congress, 582. — Supreme Court opinions concerning it, 583. — Legal v. economic decisions, 586. — Law points decided, 586. — The Maximum (Cincinnati) Freight Rate case revived, 588. — Real conflict over economic issues, 590. — The Louisville & Nashville case, 590. — The California Lemon case, 592. — Broad v. narrow court review once more, 593.
The freight rate advances of 1910, 594. — Their causes examined, 595. — Weakness of the railroad presentation, 596. — Operating expenses and wages higher, 597. — The argument in rebuttal, 598. — "Scientific management," 598. — The Commission decides adversely, 599.

CHAPTER XIX

THE LONG AND SHORT HAUL CLAUSE: TRANSCONTINENTAL RATES

"Substantially similar circumstances and conditions" stricken out in 1910, 601. — Debate and probable intention of Congress, 602. — Constitutionality of procedure, 603. — Nature of applications for exemption, 604. — Market and water competition, 605.
The Intermountain Rate cases, 610. — The grievances examined, 611. — The "blanket rate" system, 611. — Its causes analyzed, 612. — Previous decisions compared, 615. — Graduated rates proposed by the Commission, 616. — The Commerce Court review, 620. — Water v. commercial competition again, 620. — Absolute v. relative reasonableness, 622. — Legal technicalities, 625. — Minimum v. relative rates, 624. — Constitutionality of minimum rates, 625.

CHAPTER XX

THE CONFLICT OF FEDERAL AND STATE AUTHORITY; OPEN QUESTIONS

History of state railroad commissions, 627. — The legislative unrest since 1900, 628. — New commissions and special laws, 629. — The situation critical, 630. — Particular conflicts illustrated, 631. — The clash in 1907, 632. — Missouri experience, 633. — The Minnesota case, 634. — The Governors join issue, 634. — The Shreveport case, 635.
Control of coastwise steamship lines, 638. — Panama Canal legislation, 641. — The probable effect of the canal upon the railroads, especially the transcontinental lines, 643.

INDEX...649

— # RAILROADS

CHAPTER I

THE HISTORY OF TRANSPORTATION IN THE UNITED STATES [1]

Significance of geographical factors, 1. — Toll roads before 1820, 2. — The "National pike," 3. — Canals and internal water-ways before 1830, 4. — The Erie Canal, 4. — Canals in the West, 6. — First railroad construction after 1830, 7. — Early development in the South, 9. — Importance of small rivers, 10.
The decade 1840–1860, 11. — Slow railway growth, mainly in the East, 12. — Rapid expansion 1848–1857; western river traffic, 13. — Need of north and south railways, 14. — Traffic still mainly local, 15. — Effect of the Civil War, 16. — Rise of New York, 17. — Primitive methods, 17.
The decades 1870–1880, 18. — Trans-Mississippi development, 18. — Pacific Coast routes opened, 19. — Development of export trade in grain and beef, 20. — Trunk line rate wars, 21. — Improvements in operation, 23. — End of canal and river traffic, 24.
The decade 1880–1890, 27. — Phenomenal railway expansion, 28. — Transcontinental trade, 28. — Speculation rampant, 29. — Growth of western manufactures, 30. — Rise of the Gulf ports, 31. — Canadian competition, 33. — General résumé and forecast, 34.
Public land grants, 35. — Direct financial assistance, 37. — History of state aid, 39. — Federal experience with transcontinental roads, 40.

THE possibility of a unified nation of ninety odd million souls, spread over a vast territory of three million square miles, — three-fourths of the area of Europe, — was greatly enhanced at the outset by the geographical configuration of the continent of North America. It was fortunate, indeed, that the original thirteen colonies were strictly hemmed in along the Atlantic seaboard, thus being protected against premature expansion. At the same time the north and south direction of this narrow coastal strip, with its variety of climates, soils, natural resources and products, brought about a degree of intercourse and mutual

[1] For authorities, see note at end of chapter.

VOL. I—1

reliance of the utmost importance. The mere exchange of the dried fish and rum of New England, for the sugar, tobacco, molasses and rice of the southern colonies, paved the way for an acquaintance and intellectual intercourse necessary to the development of national spirit. Throughout the colonial period, the protected coast waters and navigable rivers as far inland as the "fall line," rendered the problem of long distance transportation relatively easy. For everything went by water. Population was compelled to develop the country somewhat intensively, by reason of the difficulty of westward expansion. But this population after the Revolution began to press more and more insistently against the mountain barriers; so that the need of purely artificial means of transportation at right angles to the seaboard became ever more apparent.

The period from the Revolution down to 1829, when Stephenson's "Rocket" made its first successful run between Liverpool and Manchester, attaining a speed of twenty-nine miles per hour, was characterized in the United States by increasing interest in canals and toll roads as means of communication. As involving less expenditure of capital, the highways were naturally developed first. In 1756 the first regular stage between New York and Philadelphia covered the distance in three days, soon to be followed by the "Flying Machine," which made it in two-thirds of that time. Six days were consumed in the stage trip from New York to Boston. But by 1790 a considerable network of toll roads covered the northern territory,—systems which, as in Kentucky by 1840, attained a length of no less than four hundred miles. Post roads linked up such remote points as St. Louis, New Orleans, Nashville, Charleston, and Savannah by 1830. Pennsylvania had made an early beginning in 1806; and by 1822 had subscribed nearly two million dollars to fifty-six turnpike companies and wellnigh a fifth of that sum toward the construction of highway bridges. Most of these roads throughout the country, however, were private enterprises, and, even where aided by the state governments, were imperfectly built and worse maintained, disjointed and roundabout.

The need of a comprehensive highway system, especially for the connection of the coastal belt with the Middle West, early engaged the attention of Congress. Washington seems to have fully appreciated its importance. Ten dollars a ton per hundred miles for cost of haulage by road, necessarily imposed a severe restriction upon the extension of markets. The Federal Congress in 1802 appropriated one-twentieth of the proceeds from the sale of Ohio lands to the construction of such highways. Gallatin's interest in the matter five years later, led to his proposal of an expenditure of $20,000,000 for the purpose. The Cumberland Road or "National Pike" was the result. This great highway started from near the then centre of population in Maryland and cut across the Middle West, halfway between the lakes and the Ohio river. From the upper reaches of the Potomac it followed Braddock's Old Road to Uniontown, Pennsylvania, then by Wheeling over "Zanes trace" to Zanesville, Ohio. From that point on it trended toward St. Louis by way of Columbus and Indianapolis, ending at Vandalia, Illinois. During the space of thirty years about $10,000,000 was expended upon it, and it undoubtedly did much to promote the settlement of the country. But the success of canals and railroads in the meantime sapped the vitality of the movement for further turnpike construction before St. Louis was reached. By the close of the war of 1812, in fact, it had become apparent that highways were destined to serve only as feeders after all; and not as main stems of communication.

Improved riverways and canals constituted the next advance in transportation method. So far as the latter were concerned, although the initial expense was great, the subsequent cost of movement as compared with turnpikes was, of course, low. Especially was this cheapness of movement notable in river traffic. Whereas it was said to cost one-third of the worth of goods to transport them by land from Philadelphia to Kentucky, the cost of carriage from Illinois down to New Orleans by water was reputed to equal less than five per cent. of their value. Hence the steamboat, invented in 1807 and introduced on the Ohio river in 1811, opened up vast possibilities for enlarged markets. But it was not until the generation of sufficient power to stem the rapid river currents about 1817 that our internal water-ways became fully utilized.[1] From that period dates the rapid growth of Pittsburg, Cincinnati, and St. Louis. The real interest of the East in western trade dates from the close of the war of 1812. Even then, however, the natural outlet for the products of the strip of newly settled territory west of the Alleghanies, was still over the mountains to the Atlantic seaboard. Cotton culture in the South had not yet given rise to a large demand for food stuffs in the lower Mississippi valley. It was a long and wellnigh impossible way around by the Gulf of Mexico. Consequently the main attention of the people during the canal period between 1816 and 1840 was focussed upon direct means of communication between the coastal plain and the interior. A few minor artificial waterways, like the Middlesex canal from Boston to Lowell, completed about 1810, proved their entire feasibility from the point of view both of construction and profit. Even earlier than this the Dismal Swamp canal and one along the James river in Virginia had been projected and in part built. But the era of canal construction as such on a large scale cannot be said to begin until after the close of the war of 1812. The most important enterprise, of course, was the building of the Erie Canal to unite the headwaters of the Hudson river with the Great Lakes at Buffalo. This waterway, began in 1817, was completed in eight years and effected a revolution in internal trade. It was not only successful financially, repaying the entire construction in ten years, but it at once rendered New

[1] F. H. Dixon, Traffic History of the Mississippi river, prepared for the National Waterways Commission, 1909, is best on this.

York the dominant seaport on the Atlantic. Philadelphia was at once relegated to second place. Agricultural products, formerly floated down the Susquehanna to Baltimore, now went directly over the Hudson river route. Branch canals all over New York state served as feeders; and flourishing towns sprang up along the way, especially at junction points. The cost of transportation per ton from Buffalo to New York, formerly $100, promptly dropped to less than one-fourth that sum. By wagon it was said to cost $32 per hundred miles for transport, whereas charges by canal fell to one dollar. Little wonder that the volume of traffic immensely increased, and that, moreover, the balance of power among western centres was at once affected. The future of Chicago, as against St. Louis, was insured; and the long needed outlet to the sea was provided for the agricultural products of the prairie West.

The instant and phenomenal success of the Erie Canal immediately encouraged the prosecution of similar enterprises elsewhere. Philadelphia pushed the construction of a complicated chain of horse railroads, canals and portages in order to reach the Ohio at Pittsburg. In 1834 an entire boat and cargo made the transit successfully. The cost of this enterprise exceeded $10,000,000; but it was expected to provide a successful competitor for the Erie Canal. The latter in the meantime had been linked up with the Ohio river by canals from Cleveland to Portsmouth, from Toledo to Cincinnati, and from Beaver on the Ohio, to Erie on the Lake. By the first of these routes in 1835, no less than 86,000 barrels of flour, 28,000 bushels of wheat and 2,500,000 staves were carried by canal on to New York. Boston and Baltimore were prevented from engaging in similar canal enterprises only by the advent of the railway. Meantime the Chesapeake and Ohio Canal was started in 1828 as a joint undertaking of Maryland, Virginia, and the Federal government, to connect the Potomac with the Ohio. It was not completed in fact until 1850, long after its potential usefulness had ceased. Besides these through routes, canals for the accommodation of local needs were rapidly built in the East. Boston was connected with Lowell; Worcester with Providence; New Haven with the Connecticut river. In Pennsylvania, especially, the anthracite coal industry, developing after 1815, encouraged the building of artificial waterways. The Delaware and Hudson, the Schuylkill, Morris and Lehigh canals were built between 1818 and 1825 along the natural waterways leading out from the hard coal fields. New Jersey connected New York and Philadelphia by the Raritan Canal in 1834–1838 at a cost of nearly $5,000,000; and another canal to connect Delaware and Chesapeake bays was with difficulty, and only by the aid of the Federal government, finally completed about 1825 at a cost of nearly $4,000,000. Further south, many small canals and river improvements were made. The Dismal Swamp enterprise had already connected Chesapeake Bay and the coast waters and sounds of the Carolinas; but provision for slack water navigation of the Tennessee river at Mussel Shoals in Alabama, and of the various branches of the Ohio river in Kentucky was not made until the middle of the thirties.

The open prairies of the West offered the most inviting prospects for canal construction, both because of the dearth of roads and the ease of construction of artificial waterways. Not only through routes to the East, as already described, but local enterprises of various sorts abounded on every side. Chicago was connected with the Mississippi system by way of the Illinois and Michigan Canal; a route across the lower peninsula of Michigan, and many feeders in Indiana and Ohio were built. The demands upon the capital of the country for these purposes during the twenty years after 1815 were enormous; and it was only by resort to state subventions and grants from the Federal government out of the proceeds of sales of public lands, that so much was actually accomplished. State debts aggregating no less than $60,000,000 for canal construction were incurred prior to 1837. Much of this investment proved ultimately unproductive; extravagance and fraud were rife. But the economic results were immediately apparent and highly satisfactory, as witnessed in the higher prices obtainable for all the products of the interior for transportation to the seaboard. Flour, which could be had at three dollars a barrel at Cincinnati in 1826, rose to double that figure by 1835; and corn rose from twelve to thirty-two cents a bushel. The panic of 1837 and the subsequent depression, of course, put a severe check upon further canal building. But an even more potent force was the proved success of the newly invented mode of carriage by railroad. Before 1840 the era of canal construction was definitely at an end. Almost the only exception was the Erie Canal, which continued to prosper by reason of its strategic location. Rates were reduced in 1834; and two years later the canal was widened and deepened to accommodate the ever increasing traffic. Surplus revenues enabled the amortization of its debt; and by 1852 the revenue exceeded three million dollars annually. Although the pressure of railway competition was increasingly felt; as late as 1868, practically all the grain into New York was brought by canal barge. The movement of this canal tonnage, year by year, is shown by the diagram on page 25. As will be seen, it was not until the trunk line rate wars of 1874–1877 that the inferiority of the canal to the railroad, even in this favored instance, was finally demonstrated. The revival of interest in the Erie Canal which has occurred in recent years, leading to the expenditure of millions of dollars by the state of New York in still further enlarging it, is due to an effort to insure the supremacy of the port of New York in export trade against the growing competition of the Gulf ports, which it originally gained when the canal was constructed.

The first serious attempt at railroad operation in the United States was on the Baltimore & Ohio line in 1830. The company, although chartered in 1821, did not begin construction for seven years. It was three years later than this when Peter

Cooper's "Tom Thumb" made a trial run out from Philadelphia with a record of thirteen miles per hour. A road from Albany to Schenectady was opened in 1831; and a series of connecting links was rapidly pushed westward across New York state, finally reaching Buffalo in 1842. But prior to 1840, activity in railroad construction was most noticeable in Pennsylvania: partly because of its lack of so admirable a water route to connect it with inland markets as was enjoyed by New York, and partly because of the growth of the coal business which caused the main lines of the Reading Railroad to be laid down as early as 1838. The state of Pennsylvania was busily engaged in improving her existing route over the mountains by replacing the canal and portage portions with rail lines. Pittsburg, which formerly had been five and a half days distant, was thus connected by railroad in 1834. Cars built in the form of boat sections were to be transferred from the rails to canals along part of this route. The Pennsylvania Railroad aiming to provide continuous railway communication over the mountains, was not chartered until 1846; but, nevertheless, as early as 1835 Pennsylvania had over two hundred miles of railway, about one-quarter of the mileage of the United States. New York and New Jersey had about one hundred miles between them, while South Carolina had one hundred and thirty-seven miles. The Baltimore & Ohio during this time was being slowly pushed westward; although it did not reach the Ohio river until 1853, two years after the Erie had, by liberal state aid, been carried to the lakes at Dunkirk, Ohio. Thus it appears that during the decade to 1840 railroad building had progressed unchecked by the panic of 1837. This panic, in fact, by rendering the state construction of canals impossible, may actually have increased the interest in railroad building. The railways of this time were still mainly experimental. They were local and disconnected, serving rather as supplementary to, than as actual competitors of the existing water routes. In Massachusetts and Connecticut the lines radiating out from seaports were intended to serve only as feeders to coastwise traffic; just as short lines were built along the Great Lakes during the decade to 1850 to bring products out to a connection with the natural water routes. A notable exception was the continuous line which by 1840 was in operation lengthwise of the Atlantic coast plain from New York south to Wilmington, North Carolina. The Camden and Amboy between Philadelphia and New York was operated early in the thirties; about the same time that the Philadelphia, Wilmington & Baltimore was completed. Much interesting history centres about the first named road. It seems to have been a notoriously corrupting influence in New Jersey politics from the outset. Public opinion became so roused over its exactions, that a memorial from the merchants of New York to the Thirtieth Congress resulted. The enterprise was the most profitable of all the earlier companies, its net earnings in 1840 amounting to $427,000. In 1855 it paid a twelve per cent. dividend. From Washington south by way of Fredericksburg and Richmond, the southern states could be reached without undertaking the perilous passage round Cape Hatteras. By 1840 the only portions of the original colonies still isolated were New England, at one end, which was still obliged to depend upon Long Island transit to New York by boat; and in the Far South, the back country behind Charleston and Savannah.

Several important economic causes conspired to stimulate railroad construction at a very early time in the southern states.[1] They welcomed the new means of transportation even more eagerly than the wealthier, commercial and more densely populated North. Ever since the invention of the gin in 1793, the production of cotton had grown apace. Profits were so high that all interest in other forms of agriculture waned. Cotton production until about 1817 was mainly confined to

[1] U. B. Phillips, A History of Transportation in the Eastern Cotton Belt to 1860, 1908, is a standard authority in this field.

the long narrow strip of Piedmont territory, lying between the sandy "pine barrens" along the coast and the mountains in the rear. This fertile strip — the seat of the plantation system — thus geographically isolated, had only one means of communication with the outer world, namely the coast rivers debouching upon the sea at Charleston, Savannah, or, later on, upon the Gulf at Mobile. But these seaports were not conveniently situated to serve as local trade centres. They were separated from the cotton belt by the intervening pine barrens. The local business of buying the cotton from the planters, and in return supplying their imperative needs for supplies of all sorts, including even food-stuffs which they neglected to raise, was concentrated in a series of towns located at the so-called "fall line" of the rivers. From Alexandria and Richmond on the Potomac and James, round by Augusta, Macon, and Columbia to Montgomery, Alabama, such local centres of importance arose, each one just at the head of navigation. For some years profits were so large that heavy charges for transportation to the sea were patiently borne. But after the opening of the western cotton belt along the Mississippi bottom lands after 1817, the price of cotton experienced a severe decline, greatly to the distress of the older planters. For this reason an insistent demand for improved means of transportation had already brought about great interest in turnpike and canal building. South Carolina at a very early date had expended about two million dollars for these purposes. Steamboats on the smaller rivers were also used. Immediately upon the successful demonstration of traction by steam the aid of the states, cities and individuals was invoked; so that a well planned system of railroads resulted even as early as 1843. The South Carolina Railroad between 1828 and 1833 most successfully operated a pioneer line, its securities being quoted at twenty-five per cent. above par. The Charleston & Hamburg line opened in 1833, one hundred and thirty-seven miles long, was said to be the largest system under one management in the world. Augusta & Columbia were linked up with the coast. Savannah also penetrated inland to the Piedmont belt by a line finished in 1843 as far as Macon. The interest in a through route to connect Cincinnati and Louisville with Charleston was very keen; and had it not been for the tremendous fall in cotton prices in 1839–1840, the project might have succeeded. As it was, a great railroad convention at Knoxville in 1836 was attended by no less than four hundred delegates from nine different states. It was not so much the mileage of these roads which rendered them notable, as the fact of their intended reliance upon through freight instead of passenger business. Roads in other parts of the country were as yet depending in the main upon passenger traffic or upon the carriage of what we would now call local or parcel freight. These southern lines were built to accommodate traffic in great staple agricultural products — cotton out and food-stuffs in. Unlike the northern roads, also, they early adopted a uniform gauge and sought to promote long distance business. Later developments in the South especially in the direction of improved service were very slow. The northern states speedily outstripped them; but the enterprise of this region in railroad building and operation at the outset has not been fully appreciated.

The decade 1840–1850 was marked by slow growth of the railway net, — everywhere except in New England, where the main lines were being rapidly laid down. The doom of the canal as a competitor had been sealed, to be sure; but the dearth of private capital, except in New England, rendered progress slow until aid from the government was invoked. Until this time private enterprise had been the main reliance. Several important undertakings were now launched. The Pennsylvania Railroad was chartered in 1846, but was not completed to Pittsburg till 1852. The Boston & Albany line was built; and Buffalo had been reached. But neither the Baltimore & Ohio, nor the Erie had yet been pushed to completion. The possibilities of the great Northwest had not dawned upon the people. At the opening of the decade, St. Louis was still almost three times as large as Chicago. Cincinnati was the most important western centre, its prestige being enhanced by the first all-rail line to the Great Lakes at Sandusky, opened in 1848. The relative importance of these inland centres is indicated by their populations. In 1850 these were as follows: Cincinnati, 115,000; Chicago, 30,000; St. Louis, 78,000; and Louisville, 43,000. Cincinnati retained its preëminence until after the Civil War; but by 1880 had dropped to a low third in rank, only half the size of Chicago and two-thirds the size of St. Louis.[1] During the decade to 1850, the Ann Arbor line from Detroit also was pushed on to Chicago in 1852, to cut off the roundabout trip by lake;[2] but St. Louis was still isolated; Indianapolis was barely connected with the Ohio river. The river trade thus still dominated the western situation. In the South one important enterprise monopolized all attention, namely the construction by the state of Georgia of the Western & Atlantic road over the mountains from Atlanta to Chattanooga on the Tennessee river.[3] Atlanta was to become the western terminus of the coast roads, built, as has been said, to provide an outlet to the sea for the Piedmont cotton belt. This new enterprise was to open up a direct route, not alone to the new western South but to the entire Northwest by connecting with a navigable branch of the Ohio. It is an odd fact that at this time the southern ports were nearer the West than the cities of the North Atlantic. Part of the first rush of the Forty-niners to California was by way of Charleston and thence west over the Charleston & Hamburg line. From 1837 on, the Western & Atlantic line was under construction. In the meantime Atlanta had been reached from the east; so that at the beginning of the

---

[1] U. S. Report on Internal Commerce, 1880, p. 72 *et seq.*
[2] H. G. Pearson, An American Railroad Builder, John M. Forbes, 1911, for this field.   [3] *Yale Review*, 1906, pp. 259–282.

next decade, two at least of the main arteries of the southern net were ready for business.

The total mileage of the United States expanded in ten years after 1840 from 2,800 to upwards of 9,000 miles of line. For some time not over four or five hundred miles annually had been constructed; but suddenly the new mileage laid down in 1848 jumped to more than fourteen hundred miles. This was a presage of the great expansion to occur in the next few years, — an expansion made possible partly as a result of important mechanical improvements and inventions. Notable among these was the substitution of the solid iron rail for the primitive method of plating beams with thin strips of iron. The manufacture of rails in the United States, begun in 1844, did much to stimulate the subsequent growth. The repeal of the law of 1832 permitting free entry of railway iron which took place in 1843, marks the beginning of a new era. During these eleven years almost five million dollars in duties on rails was refunded.

The utmost activity in railroad building obtained from 1848 until the panic of 1857, interrupted only by a minor disturbance in 1854. The total mileage expanded more than threefold, attaining a total of 30,000 miles by 1860. A veritable construction mania prevailed in the states of Ohio, Indiana, and Illinois. Not very much, relatively, was accomplished in New York and Pennsylvania, and very little in New England, which was already well served. A dominant influence in promoting the new construction at this time was the imperative need of the South for food-stuffs. Cotton culture was in full swing in the lowlands of Alabama, Mississippi and Louisiana. An enormous steam and flat boat tonnage on the Ohio and Mississippi rivers had grown up to care for this trade.[1] By 1845 the river shipping amounted to nearly two million tons. Fifteen hundred out of four thousand steamboat arrivals at New Orleans in 1859, came from the Ohio river and

[1] Dixon, *op. cit.*

the upper Mississippi. The vessels had also greatly increased in size. The flat boats which in 1820 carried only thirty tons of freight, were enlarged tenfold in tonnage and threefold in length by 1855, and in that year first began to be towed back up the river. A rapid increase in coal shipments down stream from Pittsburg also took place during the forties. From 737,000 bushels in 1844, to 22,000,000 bushels in 1855 and 37,900,000 in 1860, represents an enormous development of internal commerce. The lead mines of Missouri shipping through St. Louis had become important after 1832 and quadrupled in volume by 1848, attaining a total of 42,400,000 pigs of sixty pounds each. This traffic steadily dwindled, however, falling away by one half within the next ten years. Memphis was rapidly growing, outstripping the city of Natchez which had formerly played a more important part in the southern trade. But the most important element in this Mississippi river business was the shipment down stream of food stuffs. Produce received at New Orleans was valued at $26,000,000 in 1830, $50,000,000 in 1841, and $185,000,000 in 1860. About thirty per cent. of this consisted of farm produce from the Northwest, together with horses, mules, implements, and clothing. The need of ampler transportation facilities to accommodate all this business was apparent. A response came in plans for new north and south lines of railway. The difficulty of financing these enterprises was solved in part by the expedient of land grants by the different states. These amounted to no less than eight million acres under President Fillmore, attaining a total of nineteen million acres under the Pierce administration. By 1861 these grants, mainly in aid of railroads, had reached a total of no less than 31,600,842 acres, — more than equal to the area of either of the states of Ohio, or New York.[1] The Illinois Central grant in 1851 was the largest among these. Congress in 1850 had made over a tract of 2,700,000 acres to the state of Illinois to be used for this purpose. This gift was

[1] *Cf.*, p. 36, *infra*.

soon followed elsewhere by grants to aid the building of the Mobile & Ohio and the Mississippi Central, together with smaller roads in Alabama and Florida. The Gulf of Mexico was thus reached by through lines from the west in 1858–1861. In other parts of the country railroads were pushed well out in advance of population. The Mississippi was reached by the Rock Island system in 1854, quickly followed by the Alton, the Burlington and the predecessor of the present Northwestern system. The Hannibal & St. Joseph was the first to reach the Missouri river in 1858. There is no doubt that the discovery of gold in California greatly stimulated interest in all these far western enterprises.

Despite this remarkable record of growth, a corresponding development of long-distance communication between different parts of the country had not yet taken place. While the all-rail routes were open, they still consisted in large part of disconnected local lines. The New York Central with difficulty in 1853, and in spite of intense local opposition, succeeded in effecting a consolidation of what were originally eleven separate lines; but the union with the Hudson River Railroad was not to follow until 1869. The Boston & Albany was still a local enterprise, although built with larger ends in view. At this time the possibility of long-distance carriage of grain was only very dimly appreciated. Fast freight lines to operate without breaking bulk over independent roads, constituted the first step in this direction. Such companies on the New York Central in 1855 and on the Erie two years later, were operating in the eastern trunk territory. The so-called Green lines were engaging in long distance business by way of Ohio river connections between the territory to the northwest and the great grain and pork consuming cotton belt. But railroad traffic as a whole was still relatively unimportant as compared with water carriage. The culmination of steadily increasing receipts on the Erie Canal did not occur until 1856. River tonnage went on steadily increasing for another twenty years. The years just before the war seem to have marked the turning point in respect of canal competition; but the total volume of railroad shipments, nevertheless, still appears insignificant by comparison with the present day. The total traffic in 1859 on the Pennsylvania Railroad was only 353,000 tons east bound and 190,700 tons west bound; while on the New York Central it was 570,900 and 263,400 tons, respectively. The important point was that the cost of shipment was steadily declining. According to H. C. Carey, the passenger rate from Chicago to New York had fallen from about seventy-five dollars to seventeen dollars in 1850; while the freight rate per bushel on wheat had fallen to twenty-seven cents; and per barrel of flour to eighty cents. Nothing but the development of a large surplus production in the West was needed to create a great traffic; and this was dependent upon the spread of population and improvements in agricultural production which had not yet occurred. Transportation as yet waited upon the progress of invention; not in instruments of transportation alone, but in all the other fields of industrial endeavor.

The panic of 1857 and the increasing bitterness of the slavery question, followed by the outbreak of the Civil War, quite diverted the attention of the country from internal development. Railroad construction had already declined from 3,600 miles in 1856 to 1,837 miles in 1860. It fell to less than 700 miles in 1861. Brisk recovery set in after 1865; but it was not until 1868 that any rapid growth again ensued, or even a resumption of the activity of the preceding decade. All of the southern lines were prostrated; the north and south roads, like the Illinois Central system, stood still. The western railway net alone was slowly expanding. The Burlington grew from 168 miles in 1861 to over 400 miles in 1865; and the Chicago & Northwestern then succeeded in bridging the Mississippi. The Erie was still a more important route by fifty per cent., measured by ton mileage, than the New York Central; although its evil days, under the control of Jim Fiske

HISTORICAL SURVEY 17

and Jay Gould in 1866–1869, were about to begin. The Mecca of trade from the Atlantic ports was still St. Louis, although Chicago outgrew it during the decade. The predominant direction of trade is shown by the widespread public interest in New York in the newly opened Western & Atlantic railroad, which by a spur from the Erie road at Salamanca, was to shorten the time of shipment of goods from New York to Cincinnati from one month to a week. The commercial star of New York was steadily rising. A great aid thereto was, of course, the progress of consolidation among the connecting links to Chicago. Vanderbilt and Scott were busily engaged in this constructive work. The former had shifted his interest from steamboats to railroads, and became dominant in the Harlem and Hudson River roads in 1863–1864. Three years later he secured control of the New York Central from Albany west, and consolidated it with the Hudson River line. These trunk line roads, the Pennsylvania and the New York Central, both finally secured connections with Chicago in 1869. A channel for new through currents of trade merely awaited the growth of business.

It is important to realize the relative primitiveness of transportation at the close of the Civil War.[1] The Bessemer steel process was not perfected until the latter half of the decade.[1] Iron rails still rendered light rolling stock necessary. But after 1868 the price of steel rails rapidly declined, from about $166 (currency) per ton in 1867 to $112 in 1872, and to $59 in 1876.[2] This doubtless gave a tremendous impetus to the developments of later years, although its effects were not evident for some time. One of the most troublesome features of the time were the differences of gauge which rendered through traffic difficult. In New York and New England, the standard gauge was four feet eight and one-half inches. West and south of Philadelphia

[1] E. D. Fite, Social and Industrial Conditions at the North during the Civil War, 1910, pp. 42–77.
[2] *Railway Age Gazette*, 1912, p. 125, reprints statistics since 1840 of all sorts concerning rails.

VOL. I—2

it was four feet ten inches. In the Far South it was five feet; and in Canada and Maine, either five feet six inches or six feet. Between Chicago and Buffalo five different roads still had no common gauge. Clumsy expedients of shifting car trucks, three rails or extra wide wheel flanges were adopted. Even as late as 1876 Albert Fink refers to the celerity with which trucks could be changed at junction points, not over ten minutes being requisite.[1] The first double tracking in the country, that of the New York Central, was not accomplished until the war period. There was not even a bridge over the Hudson at Albany until 1866, and no bridge at St. Louis, although the Northwestern had bridged the Mississippi higher up. No night trains were run generally. No export grain trade existed, although feeble beginnings had been apparent at New York for some years. Philadelphia did not even have a trunk line as late as the end of the war; and neither Boston nor Philadelphia had regular steamer lines to Europe. For the great staples of trade, the canals and rivers were largely utilized. The Erie Canal during the war, took twice as much freight as the Erie and New York Central together. Even in 1865 the ton mileage of the Erie Canal — 844,000,000 — compared with a ton mileage of 265,000,000 for the New York Central and 388,000,000 for the Erie Railroad. And in 1872, eighty-five per cent of the freight between New York and Philadelphia still went by water.

Railroad construction during the next decade to 1880 was extremely active. East of the Mississippi developments were confined in the main to building branches and feeders. One new through line in the East was opened, by the entrance of the Baltimore & Ohio into New York in 1873 and into Chicago in the following year. Another important enterprise was the building of the Air Line route to connect Atlanta with Richmond by a road traversing the fertile Piedmont belt. The

[1] U. S. Reports Internal Commerce, 1876, App. 31.

HISTORICAL SURVEY

completion by the state of Massachusetts of the Hoosac Tunnel line, providing a new outlet to the west from Boston, was also a notable achievement. This route was at last opened in 1874 after a painful experience extending over twenty years, involving an expenditure by the state of about $17,000,000. Most of the new railroad building of the seventies took place in the upper Mississippi valley. The states of Wisconsin, Minnesota, Iowa, (eastern) Nebraska and Kansas were rapidly gridironed with new lines. Much of this construction took place after 1868, activity culminating in 1872 with the building of no less than 7,379 miles of line. The panic of 1873 put an end to all this, except in California where expansion went on unabated. Nearly one thousand miles of new line were added to the systems of this state during the five years to 1878, — nearly doubling its mileage during this period. Elsewhere in the country little was accomplished during the protracted hard times. In 1875, for instance, only seventeen hundred miles were constructed. This cessation of development did not change for the better until the resumption of general prosperity in 1878. The net result of ten years building was, nevertheless, considerable, represented by an expansion from 53,000 to upwards of 93,000 miles of line. Railroad building, in fact, increased about two and one-half times as fast as population. So that by 1880 the United States was already more amply furnished with transportation mileage than any country in Europe.

Among the important events to be associated with this period was the opening of the first transcontinental route, marked by the joining of the Union and Central Pacific railroads in 1869. The history of its construction under liberal land grants from the Federal government belongs in another place. Aside from the political effect, the economic results were immediate. Population at once flowed over onto the Pacific slope. And a large volume of trade was at once deflected from the sea route round Cape Horn. The value of goods shipped by water between New York and San Francisco, which in 1869 amounted to $70,000,000, fell in the next year to $18,600,000, and in 1872 to less than $10,000,000. The success of the enterprise, together with growing interest in the Pacific states, doubtless led to the opening of construction of the Northern Pacific as a transcontinental route in 1870.

The rapid development of an export trade in grain to Europe between 1870 and 1874 was a direct result of improvements in agriculture and the opening up of a surplus grain-producing area. As yet this territory lay mainly east and south of Chicago. Even as late as 1882, over four-fifths of the eastbound trunk line traffic originated not further west than Illinois. Wisconsin and Iowa contributed less than ten per cent. of this business. The methods of handling wheat were still quite primitive. During the Civil War thousands of men were employed to unload the grain by hand, every tenth barrel being weighed. Elevators had been used in Chicago for some time but no eastern city had them until 1861. Prior to 1872, when the first grain elevator was set up at Baltimore, the cost of thus unloading grain by hand amounted to four or five cents per bushel. At Boston until 1867, all the export grain was still unloaded back of the city and hauled across to the waterfront.

The volume of exportable surplus products of the country rose rapidly after 1870. An increase from five or six bushels of wheat production *per capita* in 1860, to nearly nine bushels in 1879, left a large margin for foreign sale. The growth of such traffic, big with importance for the carriers, is indicated by the opposite diagram. The large total of $59,000,000 bushels of wheat and (equivalent) wheat flour reached in 1862, partly as a result of the closing of markets in the southern states, was not again surpassed for more than a decade. The most notable increase ensued after 1873, when the level rose about fifty per cent., to become established thereafter upon a permanently higher plane. A second sudden boost occurred again in 1877 when wheat exports rose rapidly to a total of 180,000,000 bushels within three years. The disastrous failure of European crops in 1879, with a coincident bumper yield in the United States, led to the immediate climax of the movement in 1881. These exports, moreover, which fifty years earlier, owing to the cost of carriage, were almost exclusively in the form of flour, were now in 1880 about three-fourths constituted of raw wheat. Examination of the diagram with its steep pyramid of development at this time is convincing as to the stimulus thereby given to the railway interests. Foreign trade in cattle and beef products also enormously increased during

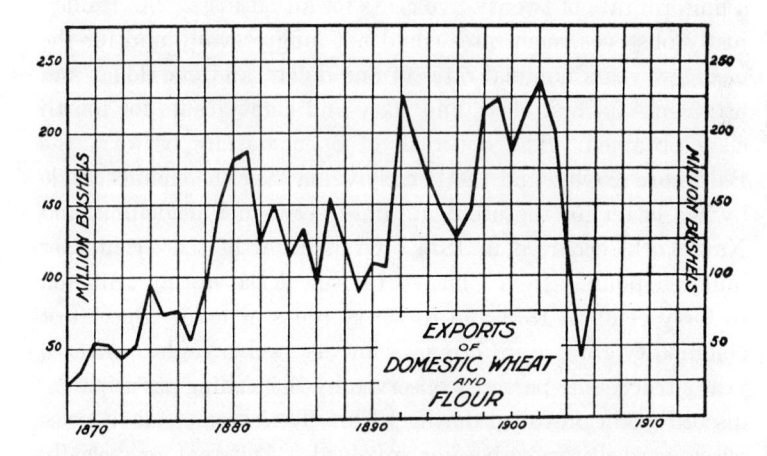

EXPORTS OF DOMESTIC WHEAT AND FLOUR

these years. In 1876 only 244 steers were exported, while in 1877, 71,794, and in 1881, 134,000 head were shipped abroad. The value of preserved meats exported quadrupled in one year after 1877, and grew eightfold by 1880. Doubtless part of this disposition of products abroad during the seventies was due to a cessation of demand at home owing to the prevalent hard times; but the important discovery was incidentally made that the demand abroad existed, and merely required cheap transportation for its successful development.

The second step necessary for permanently developing railroad business was a lowering of the charges. This was first brought about during the seventies through unregulated competition between the trunk lines. The fiercest warfare occurred during the years immediately following the entrance of the Baltimore and Ohio and the Grand Trunk railroads into Chicago in 1874. This was some five years after the Pennsylvania and the New York Central had consolidated their through lines to the same point. These two original rivals had already slashed rates indiscriminately. Charges of $1.88 and 82 cents for first- and fourth-class freight from Chicago to New York in 1868, had already for a brief period in the following year dropped to a uniform rate of twenty-five cents for all business. As Hadley justly observes, such rates could not long prevail; and for the next few years nominal rates of one dollar, and one dollar and fifty cents for first class, and sixty and eighty cents for fourth class obtained. The outbreak of open warfare between the Baltimore & Ohio and the Pennsylvania over the charges made by the latter for the use of its lines between Philadelphia and New York, occurred in 1874. Grain rates of sixty cents per hundred pounds from Chicago to New York during 1873 fell to forty cents in 1874 and to thirty cents in 1875. Special or commodity rates were often as low as twelve cents. After a year's truce, only partially observed by the leading participants, discord again prevailed during 1876. The commercial rivalries of seaboard cities now became involved. Different or specially favorable rates had been accorded to Baltimore and Philadelphia as compared with New York since 1869.[1] Rates finally fell lower than ever before. This was especially true of grain. The published rate in March, 1876, was forty-five cents per hundred pounds from Chicago to New York. In May it fell to twenty cents — a rate almost as low as prevails today with all modern improvements in methods of conducting the business. Westbound rates dropped correspondingly. Quotations from New York to Chicago at twenty-five cents per hundred pounds first class, and sixteen cents fourth class were freely given. Actual rates were often much lower than this.

[1] Pp. 361 and 404, *infra*.

Rival cities again intervened and finally the whole matter was of necessity referred for arbitration to a commission. Even then both the Erie and the Baltimore & Ohio roads were well advanced on the road to bankruptcy. For us, however, the immediate result of importance was a permanent reduction of the general level of freight rates, not alone for the trunk line territory but for the entire country. The diagram on page 413 shows this plainly. From an average revenue per ton of freight moved one mile of 1.92 cents in 1868, intermittently upheld until 1872, the fall of over one-third to about 1.1 cents in 1882 was sudden and continuous. The end was not yet. The renewed outbreak of a rate war between the trunk lines in 1881 and again in 1884 led to further reductions. The decision in 1882 of the Thurman Commission on Differentials settled nothing.[1] All kinds of traffic were affected. Immigrants were carried from New York to Chicago for $1.00 a head. Eastbound grain rates were as low as eight cents. At last, late in 1885, the warfare was terminated by an elaborate pooling agreement. These struggles brought about great reductions in the revenue of the carriers concerned; but declines in rates after this period were, in the main, more gradual, with short intervals of relief interspersed.

One immediate result of these lower freight rates was the impetus given to economy and systematic operation. This is the period when, as we have said, pooling as a device for restraint of competition first appeared in the "Evening" contracts on beef shipments in the West, in the notable Southern Railway & Steamship Association in 1874 and in the trunk line pool in 1877. Agreement between the anthracite coal roads began about 1872 and has continued with increasing effectiveness ever since.[2] This was also the heyday of the through freight lines which were now operating from every important western centre. In 1876 the first attempt at a systematic scheme of rate adjustment

---

[1] P. 404, *infra*.   [2] Pooling is discussed in vol. II.

between competing localities was made in trunk line territory.[1] Order was indeed emerging out of chaos. In respect of operation, larger locomotives and cars and longer trains were rapidly coming into use. On the Lake Shore the average train load in 1870 was 137 tons. Nine years later it had risen to 213 tons. The widespread substitution of steel for iron rails was not yet to follow for some time. For in 1880 only three-tenths of the mileage of the country was laid with steel. This proportion rose to eight-tenths in 1890. It was doubtless this change during the eighties which made possible the heavy decrease in operating expenses which occurred during the five years subsequent to 1881. It appears, indeed, as if the need of economy was enforced by the decline of rates in progress; but, as usual, the supply of economies waited upon the demand and, in fact, tarried well behind it. To this circumstance may be attributed some of the financial hardships suffered by the roads during the ensuing interval between the reduction of rates during the seventies and the mechanical improvements of the succeeding decade. An incidental result of the rate wars of this period, it may also be noted, was the readjustment of the relative shares of the great seaports in foreign business. Philadelphia, especially, increased its quota of exports from about eleven per cent. in 1860 to over twenty per cent. in 1880. Much of this was gained, however, from the southern ports, as the relative status of Baltimore, New York, and Boston remained about the same.

A second important consequence of the severe decline in railroad rates during the seventies, was the permanent supersession of canals and riverways in favor of railroads as means of transportation. The Erie Canal outlasted all the other artificial water routes, most of which had succumbed to rail competition by the close of the Civil War. But even as late as 1868, practically all of the grain arriving at New York came by canal. The change, when it occurred, came suddenly.

[1] Chapter X, *infra*.

No canal could meet the fierce slashing of rates which suddenly supervened on the rail lines. Since 1855, when the canal carried twice the traffic of all the trunk lines, until 1861–1862 when the rail and water lines were about even, the railroads had steadily gained in tonnage.[1] The turning point was reached in 1872 when the canal traffic actually began to decline. Between 1871 and 1876 the aggregate tonnage (both ways) on the New York canals fell away about half, spasmodically

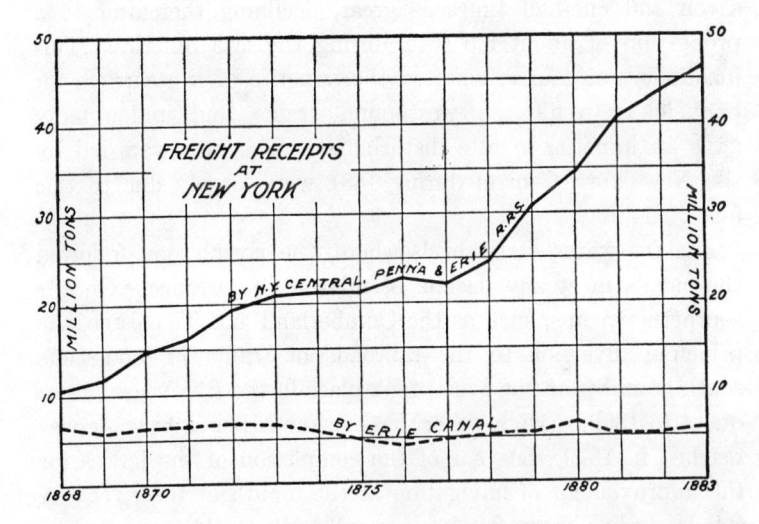

recovered during the great expansion of exports in 1879–1880, held constant for five years, and thereafter steadily dwindled away. As the accompanying diagram shows, the rise of railroad tonnage was rapid up to 1873. Thereafter for several years during the actual panic, despite the railroad wars and low rates, no great change occurred. But by 1876, eighty-three per cent. of all-grain receipts at Atlantic ports came by rail; and over nine-tenths of all the commerce between East and West had left the water routes. At New York the three

[1] Report of Committee on Canals of New York State, 1899, gives elaborate statistical data. *Cf.* especially table 14. Also Rep. U. S. Internal Commerce, 1881, p. 179, and 1884, p. 5.

main railroads carried six times the traffic of all the state canals in 1880. After that time the canal barges were loaded only with coal, lime, sand, cement, and similar low-grade traffic. So that in the rapid expansion of business, which, as our diagram shows, occurred after 1878, the canal shared not at all. The disparity between east- and westbound tonnage was notably great. In 1870 this eastbound traffic was about three times as great as the tonnage west bound. In 1881 it was seven and one-half times as great, declining thereafter to a proportion of about 6.5 to 1 during the late nineties. This inequality, of course, whetted the appetite of the carriers for back loads to fill the westbound trains, and undoubtedly gave an impetus to rate disturbance. The rate wars led by the New York Central during 1881 were largely due to this fact.

As for water carriage elsewhere, the rivers soon followed the canals in steady decline of relative importance. On the southern streams, such as the Cumberland and Tennessee, the principal diversion to the railroads of traffic in food-stuffs south bound from the West, took place in the five years subsequent to 1866.[1] High-water mark in the Mississippi trade was reached in 1879, the year of the completion of the jetties for the improvement of navigation at the mouth of the river. A steady decline thereafter has ensued down to the present day. New Orleans had then only recently engaged in foreign trade in grain. Exports of wheat and flour (equivalent) had suddenly risen from less than 1,000,000 bushels in 1875 to over 12,000,000 bushels in 1880. At this time this came principally by river. It was nearly ten years later before the Illinois Central actively engaged in such export business. But when the railroads finally seized upon it, the river trade was doomed. The only exception to this decrease of inland water transportation occurred on the Great Lakes. The carriage of coal, iron ore, and lumber rapidly increased. Through the Detroit river,

[1] U. S. Reports on Internal Commerce, 1876, App. p. 29.

the tonnage grew from 9,000,000 in 1873 to 20,000,000 tons in 1880; and through the St. Mary's Canal from 403,000 in 1860 to 1,734,000 tons in 1880. Inasmuch as a fair proportion of this rapidly growing business was ultimately destined to reach the seaboard either as raw material or in the form of manufactures, this water traffic contributed to, rather than lessened the prosperity of the trunk lines operating east of the lakes.

The growing importance of railroads during the seventies was accompanied by collateral developments, which deserve mention in a general preliminary survey. The abuses of personal discrimination and favoritism, constantly recurring rate wars and disturbances, the financial scandals of construction companies and subsidiary corporations, the frauds perpetrated by unscrupulous financiers like Gould and Fiske, coupled with the arrogance of railroad managements, aroused widespread public hostility. This led to an insistent demand for public regulation and control. The Granger movement formed its open expression in the western states. The searching inquiries of the famous Hepburn Committee of the New York legislature in 1879 voiced it in the East. The Windom report of 1874 was called forth on behalf of the Federal government. The first railroad commission, that of Massachusetts in 1869, was soon followed by others all over the country. And a campaign of education was set under way which finally led to the Federal inquiries of the Cullom Committee of 1886 and the Federal Act to Regulate Commerce of the following year.

The decade of the eighties, so far as common carriers are concerned, was primarily characterized by new railroad construction. Over 70,000 miles of line were built in ten years, — a mileage just about equal to the total new construction for both the ten preceding and the ten following years combined. The movement culminated in 1882, and again in 1887, in two veritable crazes of promotion and speculative activity, unequalled before or since in our railroad history. The first was suddenly stopped by a short, sharp railroad panic in 1884. Jay Gould's operations in Union and Kansas Pacific set a pace for manipulation and fraud, which could have no other sequel. The second craze was doubtless in part restrained by the moral effect of the passage in 1887 of the Act to Regulate Commerce; although, viewed in a larger way, it was more directly due to the exhaustion both of the supply of capital and of confidence among investors. These two outbreaks of railroad promotion are deserving of further comment, both by reason of their extent and character. Prior to 1880, new railroads constructed had averaged a little over two thousand miles annually. The figures for 1881–1882, respectively, were 6,711 and 9,846 miles, rising finally to a total of 11,569 miles in 1883. This record has never been surpassed but once: when, four years later at the height of the second "boom," 12,983 miles of new line were laid down. A large part of this building was in the Far West and Southwest, these regions being now opened up as the upper Mississippi valley had been developed between 1868 and the panic of 1873. A second transcontinental route was opened in 1881, through the joining of the Southern Pacific and Atchison Topeka and Santa Fé roads at Deming and El Paso. Within two years thereafter two direct routes to connect the Southern Pacific system with New Orleans were completed. The Pacific Northwest was admitted to rail connection with the rest of the country in 1883–1884, by two significant events. The Northern Pacific road was then opened, and the Oregon Short line to connect the Columbia river basin with the Union Pacific system. The Great Northern road reached the Pacific slope in the following year, accompanied by the Canadian Pacific, constructed just over the border. This activity in far western railroad building was mainly due to the growth of the Pacific slope; but it was also favored by the successful competition of railways with the water routes round Cape Horn. It was estimated that as late as 1878, not over one quarter of the total tonnage moved into California went by rail. But the railroads then inaugurated a system of special contracts by which shippers who agreed to use the railroads exclusively, were given considerably reduced rates. By 1884 when the plan was discontinued, the percentage of tonnage carried to California by rail rose from twenty-five to between sixty and seventy-five per cent.

In the eastern states, the eighties was the period of speculative "parallelling" of existing lines of road, in order to dragoon the older lines into purchasing the new ones at extortionate prices. This was done under the guise of affording satisfaction to the popular outcry for competition as a means of reducing rates. Two notable instances were the building of the West Shore road, paralleling the New York Central; and of the Nickel Plate line which similarly ran for miles within a few rods of the Lake Shore across northern Ohio. The fact was that the prolonged period of depression during the seventies had brought about an accumulation of surplus capital awaiting investment. The rapid repayment of its debt by the United States government, also released a large supply of funds. General prosperity prevailed and prices were everywhere rising. This increase of prices, extending from commodities to all issues of stocks and bonds, reduced the rate of return upon investment for these new supplies of capital in all the older enterprises. The only alternative, in seeking for a liberal return on investments, was to risk it in new ventures. Speculation ran riot. All sorts of projects were eagerly taken up, and among these, new railroads were most important. They were freely built, far in advance of population in the West or of prospective needs for enlargement in the East, not so much sometimes to develop the country, as to enrich the promoters. That they ultimately served the public interest was not the main concern in too many instances. This was also the heyday of the fraudulent construction company, already so ably utilized by the builders of the Pacific roads.[1]

[1] More fully treated in the chapters on speculation and finance in the second volume.

In short, speculation in every conceivable form ran riot in a way not repeated thereafter for nearly twenty years.

Aside from rampant speculation, American railroad history during the eighties must record various other economic events of importance. The city of New York and the New York Central Railroad were at the culmination of their relative importance in the export trade of the country. The volume of eastbound tonnage was enormous in the early eighties. In 1881, 2,500,000 tons of freight east bound were carried by the New York Central alone, a figure surpassed in only two years until 1896. Another event of importance was the general westward drift of population and agriculture. This was accompanied by a corresponding migration of manufactures inland from the Atlantic seaboard. The lines from the Central West to the South, such as the Illinois Central and the Cincinnati, New Orleans & Texas Pacific road, had formerly relied almost entirely upon the carriage of grain or flour and packing-house products from the farms of Ohio, Indiana, and Illinois to the cotton-raising South. During the latter half of the eighties they carried an ever increasing proportion of manufactured goods, such as boots and shoes, clothing, wooden ware, harnesses and groceries, — in fact everything denoted by the words general merchandise. More and more the supplies of grain, flour and packing-house products were being produced in Iowa, Nebraska, and Kansas, while larger quantities of general merchandise originated in the Middle West. The result was a need for new diagonal trunk lines from such points as Kansas City and Omaha into the lower Mississippi valley. The decline of Cincinnati as a great pork-packing centre dates from this time. Memphis and Vicksburg derived a new importance at the junction of such lines as the Kansas City, Memphis & Birmingham with the older Mississippi river roads. At about this time, in 1889, also, occurred the opening of the Gulf ports for the export of the surplus grain products of the territory west of the Mississippi. The significance of this for the eastern trunk lines did not appear until later; but the occurrence forms a part of that westward trend of population above mentioned. These years were all characterized by the increasing importance of long-distance through business, as distinguished from mere local trade. The markets of the country as a whole, the areas of commercial competition, were steadily expanding. Viewed in a large way, it was doubtless this economic phenomenon which at this time emphasized the need of centralized Federal control, instead of state regulation, if control there were to be. This found its expression in the passage by Congress of the Interstate Commerce Act of 1887.

A phenomenon of national importance was the rapid expansion of export trade in staple commodities, through New Orleans, Galveston and other Gulf ports. This began in 1889 when the Illinois Central first engaged in export business in grain. It soon assumed considerable proportions, with the growth of population and agriculture in the southwestern part of the United States; and, with the completion of the Panama Canal in 1913, will doubtless be even more notable in future. The opening of new railway connections with these Gulf ports about 1896 led to still further expansion of this trade. An immediate result was of course a decline in the relative importance of the great Atlantic seaports, particularly New York. A growing appreciation of this fact is accountable for the great interest in New York state in projects for enlarging the Erie Canal. A few figures, together with the diagram on the next page, illustrate the situation. A generation ago about nine-tenths of our exports of wheat and about seven-tenths of our exports of flour, went out through the port of New York. In 1899 less than one-half of our wheat and less than one-third of our flour was exported through the same city. The larger part of this loss ensued after 1896, with the opening of new lines to the Gulf ports as above mentioned. The New York Commerce Commission in its report for 1900 found that for 1899, while the nation's total foreign shipments of wheat was larger than at any time since 1892, New York actually exported twenty million bushels less than seven years earlier. Exports in 1900 were the smallest in her history, forming, that is to say, the lowest proportion of the total exports of the United States. They were actually about a million bushels of wheat less than went out through the two principal Gulf ports. An indirect result of this growth of New Orleans and Galveston was an intense competition between all the Atlantic trunk lines interested in the eastern seaports and the railroads tributary to the Gulf of Mexico. The part of the country most affected by this

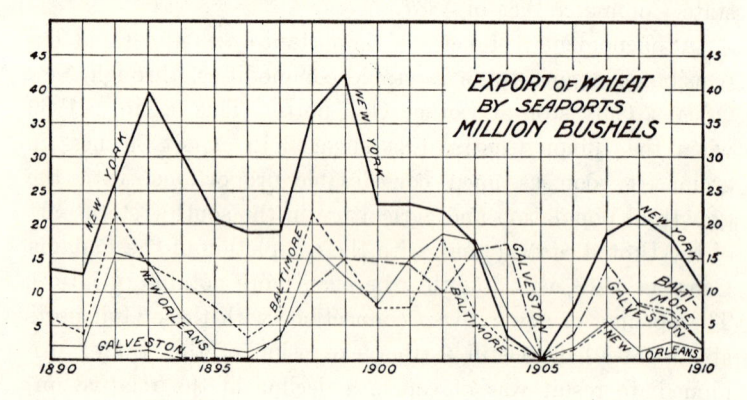

EXPORT OF WHEAT BY SEAPORTS MILLION BUSHELS

competition, of course, was that portion about equi-distant from the two sea coasts. This rivalry led to rate wars on a scale not witnessed before since the trunk line struggles during the seventies. St. Louis, Kansas City and all the region thereabouts, enjoyed the benefit of ruinously low rates as a consequence, — an advantage not accorded to other parts of the country. One cannot doubt that this factor was most influential in encouraging the growth of their population and trade.

The development of the Gulf ports more recently, together with the situation respecting rate wars on export grain, is still further indicated by the chart. When New Orleans in 1891 considerably increased its business through the activities of the Illinois Central Railroad, it speedily developed that climatic conditions led to saturation of the grain with moisture in the vessels' holds. This fact, together with other difficulties, discouraged progress. But, for a time, with the revival of foreign commerce in 1897, both the Gulf and Atlantic ports shared in the greatly increased business. Galveston had now come into the field; and at times surpassed New Orleans in importance by virtue of the development of wheat fields in the Southwest. But the over-weening ambition of these Gulf ports, threatening as they did the supremacy of New York, led to intense rivalry. All the lines to the Gulf became finally pitted against all the trunk lines serving the Atlantic seaboard. The advantage for two or three years seemed to lie with the southern lines; and, as the chart indicates, in 1903–1904 grain exports through New Orleans and Galveston actually exceeded those of any other ports. After the utter collapse of export business in 1905, trouble once more threatened to break out; but it was fortunately averted by a compromise effected in 1906. The Gulf lines on through freight demanded a substantial differential to offset certain disabilities, such as the longer haul, poorer service and climatic damage to which they were exposed. The trunk lines successfully met this contention in part, and finally brought about a peaceful settlement of the difficulty. Under this arrangement of a small differential in favor of the Gulf, New York, as the chart shows, has once more resumed its preëminence as compared with the rest of the country. But of late the ever-lessening volume of surplus American grain for export to Europe[1] has rendered the question of far less importance than at one time it threatened to assume.

The rapid growth and development of the Canadian railroads and ports has also been notable in recent years. The Grand Trunk Railway was a factor in Chicago business from the very first; and had to be reckoned with in all trunk line rate adjustments. The dressed beef rate war of 1887 proved

[1] *Cf.* the diagram on p. 21, *supra.*

this fact. But a new era of Canadian competition was inaugurated with the opening by the Canadian Pacific of the so-called "Soo" route in 1890, across the straits of Mackinac, thus opening a short line from St. Paul and Minneapolis to the East. Persistent rate wars during the next few years, particularly 1892–1893, finally led to recognition of the claims of this lien by the trunk lines. Much business was undoubtedly diverted from Chicago. Between 1884 and 1891 the flour shipped from Minneapolis increased over fifty per cent., yet the proportion going by way of Chicago largely declined. Much of this business, of course, ultimately reaches the seaboard by the combined Lake and rail routes; but a large part goes out through Canada during the open season. Yet, on the other hand, it is equally true that the wonderful development of the Canadian Northwest since 1905, contributes in many ways to the prosperity of American carriers and seaports.

As for new railroad construction since 1890, as shown by the statistical chart on page 78, it has been proportionately much slower than during the eighties. From about five thousand miles laid down in 1890, a drop ensued to less than two thousand miles in each of the four years of depression after 1893. And the former rate was not resumed until 1901, since which time construction has ranged about six thousand miles annually. This slackened rate of growth during the last fifteen years is an indication of a fact of great importance. The country as a whole with almost 250,000 miles of line in 1911 seems to be fairly well supplied with transportation routes. It seems as if the main trunk lines and systems had now been provided, leaving for the future the problem of constructing branches and feeders and of increasing facilities upon the main lines already built by duplication of tracks and enlargement of terminals. A comparison of the rates of growth of mileage and traffic, or of density of traffic, shows how new construction is lagging behind the development of business. Present conditions may best be shown by a few figures. The total mileage of the United States is nearly equal to a ten track railroad completely encircling the globe. The United States had already in 1900 about forty per cent. of the aggregate mileage of the world, considerably exceeding the total mileage of all the countries of Europe combined. The situation may be illustrated in another way, by reference to the relation of mileage to population and area. Europe in 1902 had about 7.4 kilometres of line to every 10,000 inhabitants, as compared with 41.4 kilometres (twenty-six miles) for the United States. This shows that proportionately to population the United States is about six times as well equipped with railroads as Europe. Similar results appear with reference to superficial area. As compared with Europe alone, we have about two-thirds as much mileage to every square mile of territory, despite the fact that our density of population is only about one-seventh of that of Austria Hungary — the most sparsely populated country in Europe. These figures show conclusively that our railroad problems for the future will be mainly concerned with accommodating the huge volume of existing traffic along the routes already built, rather than in seeking to develop new ones to parallel the old.

Several essential peculiarities of American railroad development stand out in sharp relief by comparison with the experience of Europe. The most significant, perhaps, is the large amount of public participation in construction, evinced through liberal grants of aid in lands, credit and cash by both the state and Federal governments. The huge aggregate of these state subventions is not generally appreciated. Because our railroads are now private concerns, so far at least as legal title is concerned, it is too often assumed in public discussion that they owe their existence solely to private initiative and enterprise. With all credit to their sturdy builders, to whose vision and courage so much is due, the plain historical fact remains that the people of the United States have had a large share in the great task of creating our present railway net, — not indirectly alone, through settlement of the virgin territory, but immediately and directly through land grants and subventions.[1]

The total of land grants by state and Federal governments in aid of railroads, according to the most careful estimates, is approximately, 155,000,000 acres, — that is to say, about 242,000 square miles. The United States alone is believed to have given about 26,000,000 acres or 40,000 square miles. For purposes of comparison, the following table of present-day areas is useful.

German Empire	208,000 sq. miles
France	204,000 sq. miles
Texas	265,000 sq. miles
New England States	66,000 sq. miles
Illinois	56,000 sq. miles
Belgium	11,000 sq. miles
Massachusetts	8,300 sq. miles

It thus appears that a gift of territory greater by about one-fifth than the entire area either of the German Empire or France, almost equal in size to the state of Texas or four times the New England states, has, at one time or another, been made in aid of railroad construction. The Federal grants

[1] The literature is considerable; in the form of special economic studies as well, of course, as in the standard histories and documents already named at the head of this chapter. The bibliography in Cleveland and Powell is to be commended. The long-promised Economic History of the United States in preparation by the Carnegie Institution will doubtless add much. Among special references, the following authors are typical; titles of others being given in the Catalogue of the Bureau of Railway Economics, 1912, under the names of states.
   Wisconsin. B. H. Meyer, *Bull. Univ. Wis.*, XII, 1892.
   Texas. C. S. Potts, *Bull. Univ. Texas*, No. 119, 1909.
   Missouri. J. W. Million, University of Chicago, 1896.
   Michigan. H. E. Keith, University of Michigan, 1900.
   Southern states. U. B. Phillips, History of Transportation, etc., 1908.
   Pennsylvania. A. L. Bishop, The State Works of Penn., 1907.
   Illinois. Davidson and Stuvé, History, etc.
   Nebraska. *Quarterly Journal of Economics*, VI, p. 337 *et seq.*
   On typical city participations; J. H. Hollander on the Cincinnati Southern, *Johns Hopkins University Studies*, 1894: U. B. Phillips, *op. cit.*, on the Western and Atlantic; on Philadelphia, Ringwalt, *op. cit.*: on municipal aid in Massachusetts, 2nd Ann. Rep. Mass. R.R. Com., etc.

equal about two-thirds of the area of the New England states, or, in other words, are about five times the size of the state of Massachusetts. A large proportion of the area of the newer commonwealths was offered as a bonus to railroads. Seven western states — including, for example, Minnesota, Iowa, and Wisconsin — gave away from a fifth to a quarter of their birthrights. Nebraska donated one-seventh, and California one-eighth. The Lone Star state discovered in 1882 that in her youthful ardor she had given away some 8,000,000 acres more than she possessed.[1] Shall it ever be said, in the face of such evidence, that these common carriers are private concerns, to be administered solely in the interest of holders of their securities?

As concerns aid in the form of funds or credit, that is to say, through subscription to railroad stocks or bonds, it is hazardous to venture statistics, particularly for the separate states and municipalities. But the statement[2] of direct appropriations and subscriptions to securities on the next page is as reliable as any. The amount of municipal and local aid can only be a matter of guess work, even nominally, to say nothing of its real cash value. Including everything from the heavy investments of such cities as Baltimore ($3,500,000) or Cincinnati ($10,000,000) down to those of little places like Watertown, Wisconsin,[3] with its railroad debt of $750,000 on a population of 7,553 souls ($100 *per capita*), the total for local aid as above stated seems conservative enough. For Massachusetts alone no fewer than 171 town and city bond issues for railroad construction were authorized in the forty years to 1871. The municipalities in Wisconsin by 1874, despite its later settlement, issued about seven million dollars in bonds for similar purposes. As long as the state legislatures were free to appropriate moneys, they did so with a lavish hand;

---

[1] Potts, *op. cit.*, p. 85.
[2] Thesis of Miss Ethel Jenney at Radcliffe College, under direction of Professor A. B. Hart. [3] B. H. Meyer, *op. cit.*, p. 362.

but when, as in Illinois in 1848, they were constitutionally prohibited from doing so, the enthusiasm shifted to the lesser governmental units. Forty-three counties in Nebraska, between 1869 and 1892, voted subsidy bonds to railroads to the amount of $4,918,000. In the case of towns and cities, also, it was possible to play off one against another. No ambitious community could stand idly by and see a new railroad go to a rival place. There was no option but to vote bonds. And farmers, as in Illinois, who had no cash, simply mortgaged their farms. It is clear that in the aggregate these local contributions greatly exceeded in amount those of the state and National governments.

Amounts granted to railroads

Alabama	$15,800,000
Arkansas	$7,100,000
Delaware	$600,000
Florida	$4,000,000
Georgia	$4,000,000
Illinois	$12,000,000
Indiana	$1,800,000
Kentucky	$200,000
Louisiana	$7,700,000
Maryland	$6,800,000
Massachusetts	$41,000,000
Michigan	$3,200,000
Minnesota	$2,200,000
Missouri	$31,700,000
New York	$5,400,000
North Carolina	$11,400,000
Ohio	$500,000
Pennsylvania	$12,700,000
South Carolina	$5,700,000
Tennessee	$34,100,000
Texas	$4,800,000
Virginia	$15,400,000
Total .... (approximately)	$228,500,000
United States:	
Bonds	$64,600,000
Interest to 1887	$114,000,000
	$400,000,000
Municipal and local	$300,000,000
	$700,000,000

A true estimate of the proportions of this public aid recognizes, of course, that many of these grants possessed only a nominal value. The eighty-mile line in Texas, cited by Potts as the recipient of 588,000 acres of land, was glad enough to dispose of them for sixteen cents an acre. Stickney mentions a Minnesota half-breed member of the legislature who took ten dollars in cash for his vote on a railroad bond subsidy, rather than $100,000 in capital stock. But, on the other hand, if the land or bonds had little value, the roads themselves were actually laid down at a very low cost. It was the proportion of public aid to total real investment which was significant. Wisconsin to 1874 had officially subsidized its roads to the amount of over $21,000,000, including lands at three dollars per acre. This sum was sufficient to have met one-half the legitimate cost of construction of the properties then existent. Reliable evidence [1] tends to show that the state and National governments, up to 1870, had pledged themselves one way or another for a sum equivalent to one-fifth of the cost of construction of the 47,000 miles of line then in the United States. And approximately another fifth, at the very least, must have been contributed from local and municipal sources.

In point of time, public aid by the states was quite unevenly distributed.[2] Massachusetts and Maryland, about 1826, were the first to take notice. But in the northern states most of the activity was confined to the period of 1837–1840; whereas, in the South, governmental subsidies did not become frequent until 1850. The whole movement, so far as the separate states were concerned, came to an end about 1870; after which time, with the exception of Massachusetts and Texas, little more financial encouragement of the sort is recorded. In many instances the hands of legislators were tied by constitutional prohibitions; and in other cases the railway net had been so far completed as to lessen the zeal of the public in the work. The centre of interest after the Civil War, in fact, is to be found in the activities of the Federal government.

[1] Miss Jenney, *op. cit.*   [2] Bogart, p. 219; Coman, p. 239.

More than a broad-line sketch of the land grants and subsidies to railroads by the United States would be out of proportion.[1] Sporadic grants in the South were made directly as early as 1835; but the first considerable transfer was made by act of Congress in 1850. This statute ceded to the state of Illinois the alternate, even-numbered sections of land for six sections in width on each side of the projected Illinois Central Railroad and its branches. The state then promptly turned over these lands to the promoters of the line. The Federal government lost nothing by the transaction. Rather did it gain, — the lands having been long in the market, — through the sale of the odd sections at a more than doubled price. Similar extensions of this grant soon followed down through Alabama and Mississippi. Then other states demanded recognition. Missouri, Arkansas, Iowa, Louisiana, Wisconsin and Minnesota were in turn appeased. The last direct grant to a state was made to Michigan in 1872. With the rise of interest in the Far West, the Federal government during the Civil War period inaugurated a new policy of direct charter and subsidy. Under this plan most of the transcontinental lines were built.

The Union Pacific Railroad was the most notable beneficiary of the Federal government. Its experience may be offered as typical. By an act of 1864, ten alternate sections of land per mile were granted, together with a subscription to junior bonds to the amount of $27,600,000. With this substantial encouragement the road was soon completed. The following table gives details concerning the succeeding grants to other companies.[2]

[1] For the Federal land grants, the standard works of Donaldson and Sanborn are best. Also, H. K. White, History of the Union Pacific Railroad, 1895: (The chapter on construction is reprinted in Ripley, Railway Problems, Chap. III.) E. V. Smalley, History of the Northern Pacific Railroad, 1883: etc.

[2] Details are in the Pacific Railroad Commission Report; 50th Cong., 1st sess., Exec. Doc. 51, 9 vols. The final settlement is described in *Quarterly Journal of Economics*, XIII, 1899, pp. 427–444.

Federal Aid to Railroads

	Bonds	Lands ($1.25 per acre.)
Union Pacific	$27,200,000	$14,100,000
Kansas Pacific	$6,300,000	$7,500,000
Central Branch (U.P.)	$1,600,000	$278,000
Sioux City and Pacific	$1,620,000	$54,000
Central Pacific	$25,800,000	$10,000,000
Western Pacific	$1,970,000	$567,000
	$64,623,000	(about) $32,536,000

The primary investment of the United States in this pioneer road was thus considerable. Despite elaborate sinking-fund provisions, the combination of speculation, fraud and mismanagement in its affairs, rendered even the payment of current interest charges impossible. Matters went from bad to worse, especially after 1883 when several new competitive routes were opened — the Southern and Northern Pacific roads, the Atchison and the Burlington. Bankruptcy ensued in 1893, a state of affairs which, as it soon appeared, could not be bettered until provision should be made for settlement of the government's claim.[1] Various proposals for partial payment proved unsuccessful. Until at last, in 1897, under threat of foreclosure proceedings, the banking interests in charge of reorganization agreed to a settlement in full — $27,200,000 principal and $31,200,000 interest. The outcome a year later on the Kansas Pacific, was less fortunate. The United States received payment of the principal of its lien, $6,300,000; but was obliged to forego the interest, amounting to about as much more. Then, in turn, in 1899, the Central Pacific claim, amounting to $27,855,000 principal and $30,957,000 interest was disposed of by being refunded in notes payable semi-annually over a period of ten years. Thus, with unexpected ease and despatch, was the direct interest of the United States in railroad affairs brought to a brilliant conclusion.

[1] A more detailed account of the rise of the Harriman system is in vol. II.

A striking characteristic of American transportation history, emphasized by the foregoing account of land grants and subsidies, is its essentially speculative character. Railroads were more often constructed in advance of population and settlement than to accommodate traffic already in existence. Speculation, as will appear in another volume, has permeated all of our railroad finance. In the early days the most extravagant visions of development were indulged in on all sides. In the words of a Wisconsin legislative committee in 1854 protesting against the passage of further laws for the encouragement of railroad construction: "In imagination every acre of land from Walker's Point to Snake Hollow has been plowed, sowed, fenced, and is bearing forty bushels of wheat. — Such estimates are quite delusive. — It takes money to make railroads. It takes money to make the mare go; much more the iron horse." True indeed, then and now! But a review of our transportation history makes it plain that without this national note of optimism and adventure, the vast capital creation in railroads of the present time could never have been called into being. Public aid and private enterprise and sagacity were alike needed to accomplish the great work in hand.

The dominating events in our later economic history, so far as railroads are concerned, have been the period of severe distress and prostration following the panic of 1893; a subsequent revival of prosperity, with unprecedented demands for transportation during the ten years thereafter until 1907; and a movement toward consolidation of the railroad net into great territorial systems, notably during the two years after 1898, as a result of which competition was practically eliminated from all railroad business. The long decline in freight rates was succeeded after 1900 by a steady rise of charges; the phenomenal prosperity and consolidations led to wild speculative outbreaks on the stock exchanges, especially in 1901 and 1906; and the spread of industrial consolidation enormously emphasized the evils and abuses of personal discrimination and favoritism. As a result of these influences there arose in turn, after 1900, an irresistible demand for greater governmental supervision, both of rates and of finance. Taken all in all, these later years have witnessed both a public and private interest in railroads, greater perhaps than at any earlier period of our history. But these later events, aside from being set in their proper relation to the whole in this preliminary general survey, require detailed analysis each one by itself. Where not considered within these covers, they will be treated in a second volume dealing primarily with matters of finance and corporate organization.

Note

No attempt at an exhaustive historical account is herein attempted. Except as specially noted, the main reliance has been placed upon the following standard works:—

Bogart, E. L. The Economic History of the United States, 1908.

Callender, G. S. Selections from the Economic History of the United States, 1765–1860, 1909.

Cleveland, F. A. (and Powell). Railroad Promotion and Capitalization in the United States, 1909.

Coman, K. Industrial History of the United States, 1909.

Gephart, W. F. Transportation and Industrial Development in the Middle West. Columbia University Studies, XXXIV, 1909. (Fine bibliography.)

McMaster, J. B. History of the People of the United States, 7 vols, 1883–1910.

Phillips, U. B. The History of Transportation in the Eastern Cotton Belt, 1908.

Poor, H. V. History of Railroads and Canals in the United States. 1860.

Ringwalt, J. L. The Development of Transportation Systems in the United States. 1888.

Tanner, H. S. Railways and Canals in the United States. 1840.

Many other authorities, such as the Annual Reports upon Internal Commerce (since 1876) have been consulted. The admirable Catalogue of Books on Railway Economics, 1912, gives an exhaustive list. Many special contributions to the forthcoming Carnegie Institution Economic History of the United States have also been utilized.

CHAPTER II

THE THEORY OF RAILROAD RATES

Analysis of railroad expenditures, 44. — Constant *v.* variable outlays, 45. — Fixed charges, 46. — Official grouping of expenses, 46. — Variable expenses in each group, 51. — Peculiarities of different roads and circumstances, 56. — Periodicity of expenditures, 61. — Joint cost, 67. — Separation of passenger and freight business, 68.

ANALYSIS of the theory of railroad rates begins naturally with a study of railroad expenditures. The examination of earnings is not feasible until a later time. For neither a railroad nor a factory can earn money until it has first liberally expended it. A physical plant must be provided, in the first place, which means the guarantee of interest on a large capital; and, secondly, it must often be operated unprofitably at the outset. This is especially true in a new and undeveloped country like the United States; where demand for transportation must be frequently created by the invasion of virgin territory, making it inviting for settlement. Twenty years ago such an analysis of railroad expenditures with any approach to precision, owing to the absence of scientific data, would have been impossible. A few companies, such as the Pennsylvania, the Union Pacific and the Louisville & Nashville, had indeed attempted to systematize their accounts; but there was no agreement as to details, despite a certain harmony in questions of principle. But since the passage of the Act to Regulate Commerce in 1887, and largely owing to the work of Prof. Henry C. Adams as statistician to the Interstate Commerce Commission, the matter may now be examined profitably in detail. The data is published annually in a volume entitled "Statistics of Railways in the United States." The amplified powers of the Interstate Commerce Commission since 1906 have considerably changed the system in force since the original law of 1887; but the general principles remain unchanged.[1] One feature of the new law, however, is important. Not only must detailed reports be periodically and promptly made; but no company is now permitted to keep its books in any other form than the one officially prescribed. This standard was adopted after extended conference with the Association of American Railway Accounting Officers, which body has, in fact, officially approved of the form adopted in most regards. These accounts, therefore, may be said to represent the combined intelligence of the practical and theoretical analysts, of the operating and financial staffs, and of the governmental supervisory board. A great impetus to scientific railroad economics has undoubtedly resulted from this co-operation between government officials and private managements.

The primary distinction in railroad expenses is between those which are constant and independent of the volume of traffic, and those which vary more or less directly in proportion to it. Thus, of the total outlay, it may at once be premised that for a time, at least, certain capital expenditures are entirely unrelated to the volume of business transported. Interest on bonded indebtedness is neither increased nor diminished, up to a certain point, by the number of tons of freight moved; whereas, on the other hand, other items of expenditure, such as wages of train hands and fuel cost, are more or less directly affected. The distinction above mentioned finds its clearest expression in the primary division of railroad accounts into so-called "operating expenses," which are variable; and "fixed charges," which, as the name implies, are constant. Much of the direct wear and tear of equipment belongs to the first class, while, as we have said, interest on its own funded or floating debt, together with capital obligations on leased lines, naturally fall into the second group. This second class of constant expenses, which along with taxes is often

[1] *Quarterly Journal of Economics*, XXII, 1908, p. 364 *et. seq.*

denominated in railway reports "Deductions from Income," is a relatively large one. Thus, in 1910, out of a total expenditure by all the operating railroads of the United States of $1,822,000,000, no less than $490,000,000, or about 27 per cent., consisted of interest on debt and taxes. This proportion of absolutely fixed expenditures, moreover, shows a remarkable constancy throughout a series of years. It reached highwater mark during the hard times in 1895, at 33.07 per cent. of all outlay. Indebtedness had accumulated unduly, while at the same time the volume of traffic was so small that mere operating expenses dwindled in proportion. But since that time, largely as a result of the financial reorganizations of 1893–1897, the percentage of fixed charges has reached its present low point. This improvement is also in part due to the growth of traffic, and thereby of operating expenses. The latter have indeed grown faster than the accumulation of debt, owing to the practice prevalent among American roads of paying for many improvements and additions out of surplus income, rather than by charging them to capital account, — that is to say, by borrowing money to pay for them.

Having at the outset deducted approximately one-quarter of our total expenditures to meet fixed charges, we may now proceed to analyze those outlays which remain. And this is to be done, always keeping in mind the fundamental distinction between constant and variable items. From 1887 until 1906 the operating expenses of American railroads were allocated in the four following groups:

(1) Maintenance of Way and Structures
(2) Maintenance of Equipment
(3) Conducting Transportation
(4) General Expenses

This grouping under the new law of 1906 has been somewhat re-distributed. But inasmuch as most of the statistical data as yet available is presented under the above-named heads, we shall adhere to that classification. This we may the more properly do, as our object is to show the general bearing of railroad expenditures upon rate making, rather than specifically to analyze cost accounts. For this simple purpose the above arrangement is entirely adequate.

The general nature of each of these above named groups is roughly expressed by its title. Under the first, Maintenance of Way, are segregated those outlays which have to do with the up-keep of the roadway and permanent structures in proper shape for the moving of trains. It includes, besides such obvious items as ballast, rails, ties and the wages of track men, every outlay on permanent structures, such as bridges and tunnels, stations, grain elevators, stock pens, gas, oil and water tanks, and even scrap bins and eating houses. To these are added scores of other minor items, such as maintenance of telegraph lines, fences and cattle guards, signal plants and docks and wharves. Every kind of tool or appliance used, and all wages paid in connection with the maintenance of this part of the property are included. Insurance and even the legal costs and damages incurred in connection with accidents, are all assigned to the appropriate property. The second group, Maintenance of Equipment expenses, includes, as the name implies, the proper care and preservation of all the rolling stock in good working order. Repairs and renewals of all locomotives, cars and vessels, form the largest single items. But all shop machinery and power plants are included, with specification in detail of every appliance needed in connection with the work, as, for example, over one hundred and fifty possible items from "adze handles, ammonia and auger bits" down to "wire brushes, wrenches and zincs." Conducting Transportation expenses, the third group, are supposed to provide for the actual movement of traffic. The two former classes of expenditure having put the fixed plant and rolling stock in condition, it remains to operate the property. Under this head is chargeable all costs of coal and supplies, wages of train hands from enginemen to car porters, yard, station, switch and signalmen and telegraph operators. To these are added such items as "purchased power," "cleaning cars," "clearing wrecks," and "losses and damages"; in short, every conceivable item of expenditure which can be assigned to the service as distinct from the mere property.

A fourth group of expenditures remains, denominated General Expenses. This includes all salaries of principal administrative officers from the president or receiver down to the real estate and tax agents, together with all their allowances for expenses, special cars or trains and the like. All clerical salaries in the general offices naturally belong here, as well as most of the legal expenses, outlay for pensions, relief departments and the like.

A distinct improvement in the matter of principle has been made in the revised classification of operating expenses under the new law of 1906, by the segregation of a fifth group, denominated Traffic Expenses.[1] These cover all the work of soliciting business, making rates and accounting for freight and passenger traffic. Such outlays were formerly grouped in the main under conducting transportation, but, as is quite evident, they are distinct in their nature from the expenses incidental to the actual handling of trains. Administrative railroad organization has long recognized the peculiar and important nature of this work by constituting it a separate department, usually headed by one of the vice-presidents of the road. The main items under this special head are salaries and expenses of a large staff of officers and clerks, such as general passenger and freight managers, agents and travelling solicitors; rents and care of offices at home or abroad; advertising, membership in traffic associations, immigration and industrial bureaus, expenses for experimental farms, field demonstrators, donations to expositions, fairs and stock shows — everything, in brief,

[1] U. S. Statistics of Railways, 1908, p. 165 (and annually thereafter), gives an outline of these expense accounts for all railways over five hundred miles long.

THEORY OF RAILROAD RATES 49

which tends to create or keep business, to be afterward actually handled by the transportation departments. In future the detailed official statistics will segregate these expenses; but at the present writing and in statistics down to 1906 they must be bulked in with conducting transportation. An important modification in accounting under the new law of 1906 has also been made in respect to depreciation charges. Heretofore the practice of companies varied widely, as will hereafter be shown. Under the new rulings a definite and uniform system of charging off for depreciation has to be provided, the details of which, however, need not concern us at this time.[1]

The following table based upon the returns for 1905 shows the relative importance of the principal items under railroad expenditures grouped under the proper headings:

	Per cent. of operating expenses	Per cent. of total expenditures
Maintenance of way and structures ..		19.78	14.39
Repairs of roadway	10.39	—
Renewals of rails	1.3	—
Renewals of ties	2.66	—
Repairs, etc., of bridges, etc.	2.32	—
Repairs, etc., of buildings, etc.	2.11	—
Maintenance of equipment	20.76	15.09
Repairs & renewals of locomotives .	8.29	—
Repairs & renewals passenger cars .	1.97	—
Repairs & renewals freight cars	8.20	—
Conducting transportation	55.49	40.36
Engine and roundhouse men	9.4	—
Fuel for locomotives	11.28	—
Train service (wages)	6.54	—
Switchmen, flagmen, etc.	4.34	—
Station service	6.44	—
General expenses	3.96	2.90
Total operating expenses	100	
Fixed charges		27.23
Total — all expenditures		100

[1] Treated in vol. II, chap. XV. Begins in U. S. Statistics of Railways, 1909, p. 76.

50 RAILROADS

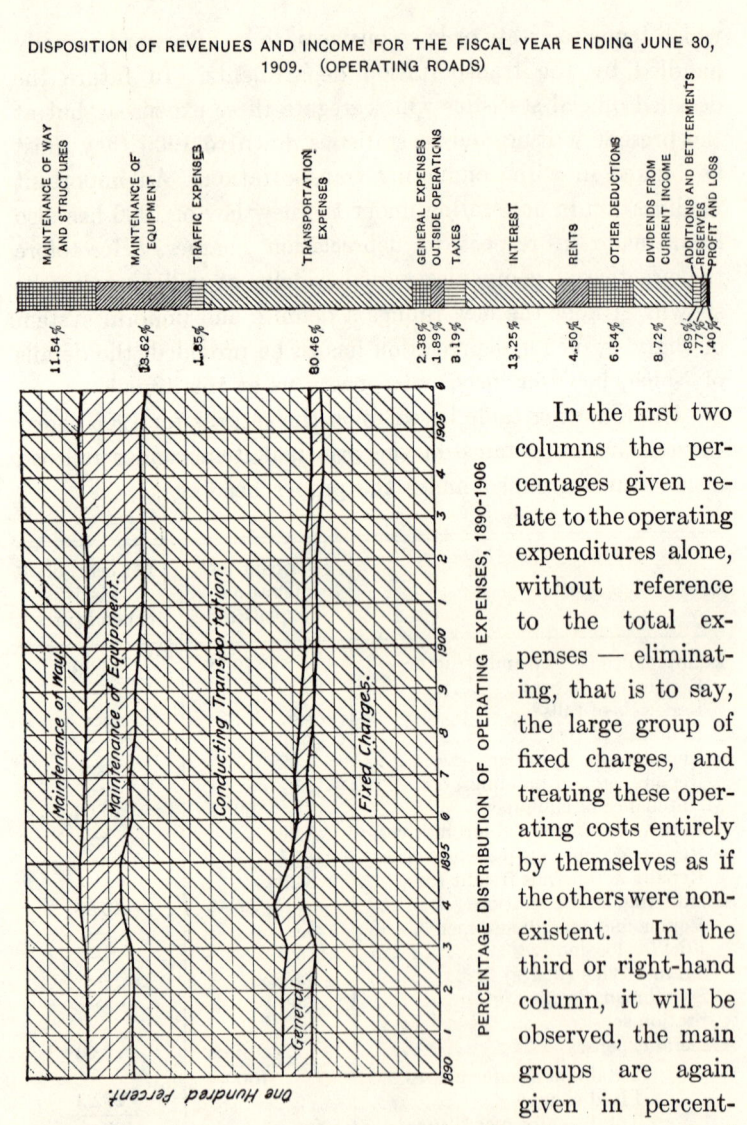

DISPOSITION OF REVENUES AND INCOME FOR THE FISCAL YEAR ENDING JUNE 30, 1909. (OPERATING ROADS)

MAINTENANCE OF WAY AND STRUCTURES	MAINTENANCE OF EQUIPMENT	TRAFFIC EXPENSES	TRANSPORTATION EXPENSES	GENERAL EXPENSES OUTSIDE OPERATIONS	TAXES	INTEREST	RENTS	OTHER DEDUCTIONS	DIVIDENDS FROM CURRENT INCOME	ADDITIONS AND BETTERMENTS RESERVES	PROFIT AND LOSS
11.54%	13.62%	1.85%	30.46%	2.38% 1.89%	8.19%	13.25%	4.50%	6.54%	8.72%	.89% .77%	.40

PERCENTAGE DISTRIBUTION OF OPERATING EXPENSES, 1890-1906

(chart showing: Maintenance of Way, Maintenance of Equipment, Conducting Transportation, Fixed Charges, General — One Hundred Percent)

In the first two columns the percentages given relate to the operating expenditures alone, without reference to the total expenses — eliminating, that is to say, the large group of fixed charges, and treating these operating costs entirely by themselves as if the others were non-existent. In the third or right-hand column, it will be observed, the main groups are again given in percentages, not of the operating expenses alone, but of the total outgo, including capital expenditures in the nature of fixed charges. It should also be noted, of course, that only a few

THEORY OF RAILROAD RATES

of the large or more important items are here included, and in the right-hand column no details, other than for the four main headings, have been computed. The constancy in the distribution of these groups of railroad expenditures over a term of years is graphically shown by the opposite diagrams.[1] The perpendicular line for each year is divided proportionately to the relative importance of each designated item of expense for that year. Thus the course of the horizontal lines, dividing the four main percentage zones, represents the ups and downs in the relative importance of each item. Occasionally, as in the years following 1895, the proportion of so-called general expenses decreased appreciably; but, in the main, all the items moved more or less in unison subject to the movements of wages and prices. This relative constancy proves how fundamental the arrangement of groups is.

The attempt to differentiate the constant from the variable expenses of railroads on the basis of the foregoing operating statistics may now be made. What proportion of each item in the table for each of the large groups is fixed in amount; and what proportion fluctuates more or less in connection with the volume of traffic?

Under the first category, Maintenance of Way and Structures, absorbing about one-fifth of operating expenses, over one-half is incurred for so-called "repairs of roadway." It is evident that a large part of this expense is due not to wear but to weather. A costly plant is exposed to every vicissitude of flood, fire, and waste. Reballasting and realignment may be somewhat more expensive where traffic is heavy; but certainly all general repairs, the wages of track walkers, the removal of snow, ice, and weeds, must be attended to entirely irrespective of the number or size of passing trains. Of the second item, renewals of rails, it is probable that this expenditure is directly traceable to wear and tear in large part. The more

[1] Changes in accounting rules in 1907 prevent its continuation to date; but the data for 1909 under the new system are reproduced alongside.

trains, the heavier the locomotive and cars or the higher the speed, the more rapidly must these rails be replaced. But even so, the proportionate amount is small, constituting generally between five and ten per cent. only of the group expenditure for maintenance of way. With ties, an item about twice as important as rails, the case is exactly the reverse. Ties rot out rather than wear out. They have a natural life varying from four to fourteen years, as influenced by climate, ballast, and drainage. The necessary expenditure per mile for them by different roads varies greatly, as might be expected; but it seems to bear little relation to the density of traffic. As for the principal remaining items under Maintenance of Way, such as repairs of bridges and buildings; if properly designed to withstand their loads and strains, most expenses of their upkeep such as repainting and reroofing should be practically independent of the volume of business. A recent elaborate discussion of these matters in 1907 in the Wisconsin Two-Cent Fare decision, reached the conclusion that all of the cost of rails, one-third of the ties and ten per cent. of expenditures for roadway, track and bridges, are all that can properly be charged to wear from traffic, as opposed to natural depreciation. Acworth illustrates this point by comparison of the Midland & Great Western Railway of Ireland and the Lancashire & Yorkshire Railroad. These two are of about equal length, approximately 530 miles. The latter carries forty times the traffic of the former road, and yet its expenses for maintenance of way are only eight times as much. It seems safe, in general, to conclude that in this first large group of expenditures for maintenance of the fixed plant, probably not over one-third are variable to any considerable degree. Acworth for England estimates this proportion at about two-fifths.

The proportion of variable expenditures for Maintenance of Equipment—the second group—is probably higher than in that of maintenance of way. This is due to two causes. Rolling stock is, of course, subjected more directly to wear and tear

THEORY OF RAILROAD RATES 53

in service than are bridges, cuts and fills and buildings. Rolling stock, moreover, is susceptible to change of type and improvement. Its effective life is thus shortened both by use and by replacement. Before being worn out it may have become antiquated. More powerful locomotives and larger cars suited to new requirements of the business may necessitate scrapping otherwise good equipment. This very fact, however, imposes upon the management the need of intensive service while it lasts. All the mileage possible must be extracted from each vehicle before it goes out of date, and this implies a higher proportion of wear-out than of mere rust-out. Yet the fact is still true that many of the items in this class are unaffected by the mileage or tonnage performance. There is little difference in wear on a freight car as between light and moderately heavy loads; and as for passenger cars, the actual wear assignable to the paying load is a negligible quantity. We may, at all events, risk an estimate in the statement that probably not over half of all the expenditures of a railroad for maintenance of equipment vary with the volume of the business.

The direct effect of a changing volume of business is most clearly seen in the third group of operating expenses, having to do with Conducting Transportation. This is very important, comprising as shown by the table on page 49, no less than fifty-five per cent. of operating outlay and forty per cent. of total expenditures including fixed charges. At first glance it would appear as if, at last, one had here to do with a direct relativity between cost and volume of business. Surely the cost of fuel for motive power will vary with the tonnage moved! This item, amounting in 1905 to no less than $156,000,000 for the railroads of the United States, was the largest in the budget, constituting eleven per cent. of all operating expenses. Yet brief consideration shows that even here much of this expense is constant and invariable. A locomotive will burn fully one-third as much coal merely to move its own weight as to haul a loaded train. Five to ten per cent. of its total daily consumption is required merely for firing up to the steaming point. Twenty-five to fifty pounds of coal per hour go to waste in holding steam pressure while a freight train is waiting on a siding. Every stop of a train going thirty miles per hour dissipates energy enough to have carried it two miles along a level road. In brief, expert evidence shows that of this important expenditure for coal, from thirty to fifty per cent. is entirely independent of the number of cars or the amount of freight hauled. The largest wage items in this group of conducting transportation expenses are for engine and roundhouse men, and conductors and brakemen. This expense is, of course, even more independent of the volume of business than the cost of coal. No more engine men or conductors are needed for a heavy through express or freight train than for a single car train on a branch line. And the extra cost for service of more brakemen as the size of the train increases, is relatively unimportant when modern equipment with air brakes is used. Appreciation of this fact is largely responsible for the great increase in train loads in recent years. Train-mile costs can be economized most effectively by distributing the wages of a train crew over as large a tonnage as possible of paying freight. As for the wages of station men, switch and flag men, they are largely, and often entirely, independent of the amount of business. From all these considerations, it appears that at a conservative estimate, no less than fifty per cent. of the cost of conducting transportation constitutes a fixed charge upon the property once it is in operation, irrespective of the volume of business transacted.

The group of general expenses, which alone remains for analysis, is relatively small in amount. It is obvious that these outlays are a constant burden but slightly influenced by the variation in traffic. Salaries may indeed be reduced somewhat during hard times — a few clerks may be laid off; but, on the other hand, this being an expense of organization, the general staff must be maintained at about a certain standard of efficiency regardless of business.

Summarizing our estimates thus far, we may reconstruct a table, distributing expenditures theoretically according as they are constant or variable in somewhat the following way:

	Per cent. of operating expenses			Per cent. of total expenses		
	Both	Constant	Variable	Both	Constant	Variable
Maintenance of way.......	20	13.4	6.6	15	10	5
Maintenance of equipment..	20	10	10	15	7.5	7.5
Conducting transportation..	56	28	28	40	20	20
General expenses..........	4	4	—	3	3	—
	100	55.4	44.6			
Fixed charges.................................				27	27	—
				100	67.5	32.5

Thus one arrives at the general conclusion that approximately two-thirds of the total expenditure of a railroad and more than one-half of the actual operating expenses are independent of the volume of traffic. The remaining third of all expenditures, or what amounts to the same thing, the other half of the operating expenses, are immediately responsive to any variation in business. Applied to the railroad net of the United States, this means that only about one-third of the $2,000,000,000 disbursed in 1905 — an amount equal to about two and one-half times the national debt — was susceptible of variation according as the traffic expanded or decreased. This provisional estimate, defective principally because of inadequacy of the returns as to depreciation and replacement, agrees in the main with computations based upon other data. The Vice-President of the Southern Pacific Railroad, in 1892, after extended investigation, arrived at precisely the same general conclusion. The great German authority, Sax, estimates that one-half of a road's operating outlay is constant and that this operating outgo equals about half the total expenditure, the other half being capital cost and hence constant. This calculation places the constant factors even higher than ours, viz., at about three-fourths of the total expenditure. Eaton states that half of the operating expenses respond to changes in the volume of traffic. Our estimate, above detailed, seems to be in accord therefore with good authority, and differs but little from any of the reliable writers.

It should be observed in passing that the relative distribution of outgo above mentioned, varies greatly both as between different railroads and, on the same road, as between different years.[1] During lean seasons the imperative need of reducing expenses generally induces the heaviest inroads on expenditure for maintenance of way. Nearly one-third of these expenditures can probably be postponed for short periods without serious detriment to operation; but, of course, there is for each property an irreducible minimum at which economy must halt. On the other hand, the cost of moving each train, that is to say, the outlay for fuel and wages, cannot be greatly cut, although some discontinuance of freight trains may take place. The most readily postponable outlay is therefore found in the department of maintenance of way. Two hundred ties per mile may be annually renewed instead of twice that number for a year or two. Heavy decreases in the wage account for road and track men may be effected, sometimes at the cost of public safety perhaps, but none the less effectively from an immediate fiscal point of view. A series of hard years thus always results in heavy proportional curtailments of maintenance of way expenses. In 1895, for instance, midway between the two worst years of the depression of 1893–1897,

[1] U. S. Statistics of Railways, 1908, p. 165, and annually thereafter gives data for all large roads.

only 19.82 per cent. of operating expenses was devoted to maintenance of way, with 15.76 per cent. expended for maintenance of equipment.[1] Six years later, in the full tide of prosperity, the outlay for maintenance of way had risen to 22.27 per cent. With over 350,000 freight cars idle on sidings, as during the spring of 1908, expenditures on repairs of equipment may temporarily be postponed. Depreciation rather than wear takes place. An economy of about five per cent. may temporarily be effected in this wise. It is only with the return of prosperity that the temporary postponement of this expenditure makes itself felt. Economy at the expense of efficiency is poor business policy in the long run. With the revival of activity on the other hand, as in 1898, there may be witnessed a sudden concentration of the postponed expenditures of the preceding years. The Illinois Central was spending $1,400 per mile on maintenance of way in 1905, as against only $1,150 in 1897. A succession of fruitful years may, however, find the property so thoroughly kept up that some measure of relaxation in expenditures may ensue. During these good years with heavy traffic, it is the maintenance of equipment charges which tend to rise. Locomotives and cars are constantly in need of repair owing to hard usage. This was a noticeable feature during the four years after 1900. The Illinois Central, expending only $866 per mile for maintenance

[1] The sharp decline in traffic in 1911, especially after the suspended advance of rates, as affecting maintenance expenditures per mile of road, is shown as follows:

	1911	1910
Baltimore & Ohio	$5931	$6336
Union Pacific	3296	3363
Great Northern	2375	2653
New York Central	8681	8087
Northern Pacific	2451	3413
Pennsylvania	9088	9792

Multiplying these differences into thousands of miles of line shows the great economy resulting.

of equipment in 1897, laid out $2,200 per mile for the same purpose in 1907.

Sometimes, as in January, 1903, or November, 1906, general wage increases all along the line take place. These, of course, affect all branches of the service. Supplies of all kinds may also enhance in price. It was doubtless the rise in the price of coal which increased the proportionate importance of the fuel item in the railroad budget of the United States from 9.8 per cent. in 1900 to 11.8 per cent. in 1904. The tremendous rise in expenses of all kinds in 1907 was not at first appreciated because of the large volume of traffic. It was only when the sharp decline in business following the panic in October of that year took place, that the full influence of this factor became apparent.

As between different roads also, the relative proportion of the various elements of cost will vary according to circumstances. Northern lines are exposed to heavy maintenance of way charges, owing to snow, ice, and frost. In rugged districts or with heavy grades, expensive operation is apparent in high conducting transportation expenses. On the Pennsylvania trunk line, rising to 2,100 ft. above sea level and with many curves, the distribution of expenditures is quite different from that on the New York Central, which operates a straighter line at about water grade. On the Union Pacific, movement expenses have been at times over fifty per cent. higher than on the St. Paul road, which operates in level country. It is a combination of high grades and poor equipment, which undoubtedly keeps the relative cost of conducting transportation so high on the Erie. The proportion of local to through business is of importance in this connection.[1] Railroads like the Boston & Maine or the St. Paul system before 1908, because they have so much local business, contrast strongly with others like the Chicago Great Western, the Erie or the old Fitchburg Railroad. On the latter roads the distribution of expenses is

[1] *Cf.* pp. 259 and 422, *infra.*

THEORY OF RAILROAD RATES

different, because their large volume of through traffic carried in bulk is so much cheaper to handle. Obviously, the expense incident to frequent stops and loss of time, as well as in loading and unloading local business, will be much greater than in long haul trainload traffic. The cost of large items like fuel will vary greatly in different parts of the country from perhaps $1.25 per ton for coal in Pennsylvania up to $7 or more on the Pacific coast. Since the recent discoveries of petroleum in Texas and California, economies have been effected upon the Southern Pacific, which by comparison with Northern Pacific, still using coal, may be of great importance. More than six-tenths of the cost of locomotive service is for fuel, so that a reduction of cost from $4 a ton to an oil equivalent at $1 per ton may aggregate a large sum. It has been estimated that such a saving on 1,600,000 tons of coal would pay five per cent. on an additional capital of $100,000,000. Similarly the character of the freight, whether it be like coal, iron ore or grain, cheaply handled, or merchandise which must be carefully housed and treated; its regularity, whether it flows evenly the year round like the dressed beef business, or as on the cotton and cattle range roads, is concentrated in a short season and all moves in one direction;[1] the relative proportions of freight and passenger business — in New England about on an equality, while in the West and South nearly nine-tenths freight; and, finally, the efficiency of management, in the use of rolling stock, making up trainloads and keeping all equipment busy; all of these factors will influence the proportionate distribution of expenditures. The operation of each road thus constitutes an interesting problem in statistical analysis by itself.[2]

[1] The provision of plant and equipment to carry the "peak of the load" is often a serious handicap.

[2] For an instance of detailed analysis of cost, the general investigation of soft coal rates to the lakes in 1912 is highly suggestive. Two-thirds of revenue went for operation and maintenance, one-third for return upon plant. This was the first attempt to justify an advance in rates for a large volume of traffic on the ground that it did not contribute its proportionate share of earnings. 22 I.C.C.Rep., 604.

The relation of course between density of traffic and the distribution of expenditures is direct. Heavy and frequent trains increase the wear and tear as distinct from mere depreciation from age and weather. This is demonstrated graphically by the following diagram.[1] The solid black horizontal

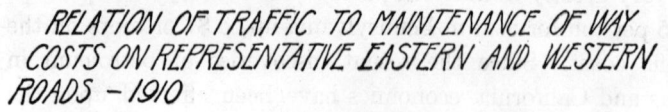

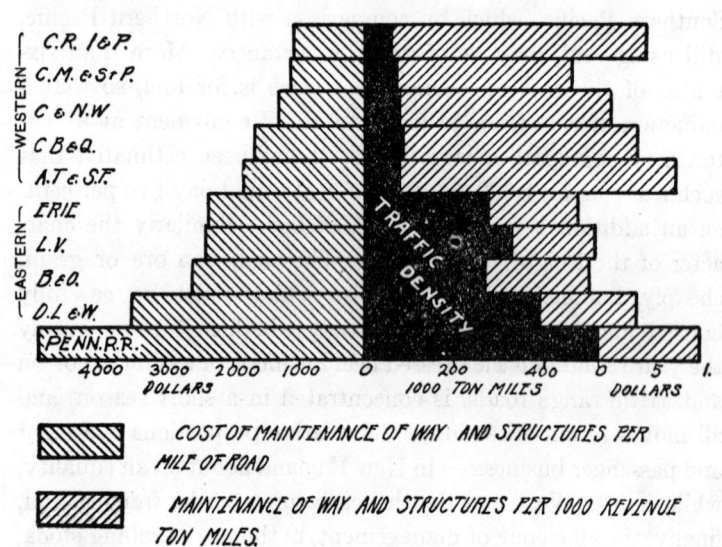

RELATION OF TRAFFIC TO MAINTENANCE OF WAY COSTS ON REPRESENTATIVE EASTERN AND WESTERN ROADS – 1910

WESTERN:
- C.R.I.&P.
- C.M.&St.P.
- C.&N.W.
- C.B.&Q.
- A.T.&S.F.

EASTERN:
- ERIE
- L.V.
- B.&O.
- D.L.&W.
- PENN.R.R.

4000 3000 2000 1000 0 DOLLARS | 0 200 400 1000 TON MILES | 0 5 DOLLARS

▨ COST OF MAINTENANCE OF WAY AND STRUCTURES PER MILE OF ROAD

▨ MAINTENANCE OF WAY AND STRUCTURES PER 1000 REVENUE TON MILES

belts to right of the centre show how low is the density of traffic on the five upper western roads by contrast with the five carriers in trunk line territory. The left hand horizontal belts show proportionally in dollars the outlay per mile of road for maintenance. Naturally the expense of such maintenance is likewise less on the western lines. But when stated, not absolutely in dollars per mile of road but in terms of utilization, as by the shaded belts to right of the centre, the true state

[1] From Railroad Operating Costs; by Suffern & Co., New York, 1911.

of things appears. Density considered, in other words, the western roads are all as well kept up as those in the East. The necessity at all times of interpreting such expenditures, not in absolute figures but in terms of utilization, is obvious; and yet it is not always done in practice.

Up to this point it has appeared as if, in making distinction between the constant and variable expenditures of a railroad, it was the latter only which grew as the volume of traffic increased. This is not absolutely, but only relatively true, not only of the so-called constant operating expenses, but of fixed charges as well.[1] Everything depends upon the length of time under consideration. Many expenses follow the fluctuations of business, not evenly but by jerks. Up to the full limit of utilization of the existing plant, each increment of traffic seems to necessitate but a very small increase in the so-called variable expenses, with hardly any change at all in the constant ones. A branch road can haul more and more tons of freight with a given outfit of cars and locomotives by merely increasing slightly its outlay for fuel, train service, wages and supplies. But after a certain point more rolling stock must be provided to accommodate the growing business. As each of these additions to property occur, they contribute new quotas to the fixed charges and to the so-called constant expenses of operation, such as maintenance of roadway and the like. Nor can these new expenses be allocated to the new business alone. The moment the old traffic has outgrown the existing plant, the new expenditure becomes chargeable to all the business alike. The new outgo must be distributed evenly over the entire volume of traffic thereafter handled. Each ton, both of old and of new traffic, beyond the haulage capacity of the locomotives then in service, is equally responsible for the expense of new equipment purchased. Although the old business could have been handled without a million dollars

[1] Lorenz in *Quarterly Journal of Economics*, XXI, pp. 283-292, is suggestive.

spent for double-tracking or terminal enlargement, this addition to the expense of maintenance of way or to the fixed charges is equally attributable to every ton of traffic hauled.

A concrete example may aid in making this important principle clear. The new through-freight trunk line built by the Pennsylvania Railroad since 1900, paralleling its old four-track one, represents both in the cost of maintenance and capital charges, a sudden jump in the expense of transporting each ton of freight on *both* lines, until such time as the new business grows to a point where it can support the new line by itself alone. The relation between increasing returns and density of traffic is well illustrated in this instance. With six tracks in operation nearly all the way from Pittsburg to Philadelphia, the four old tracks are sometimes almost fully utilized for passengers and fast freight. The extraordinary density of traffic appears in the statement that this road in 1911 on 3534 miles of track handled one-third more ton miles than the Union Pacific — by far the most worked of all the western lines — handled on 13,674 miles of track. The two new low-grade Pennsylvania freight tracks are used only for slow traffic; largely coal and west-bound steel empties. Notwithstanding the extraordinary density of traffic on this extra two track line, it probably does not meet the fixed charges on cost of construction of the line. Yet the new double track was absolutely necessary, regardless of its profitableness, in order to relieve congestion on the old four tracks. In other words, the demands of the service forced an expenditure which in and of itself was not financially self-supporting. But the profit from the old lines would be sufficiently enhanced to take care of the whole. The bearing of such cases upon the capital needs of the future is obvious. A resolutely conservative policy of finance becomes imperative under such circumstances.

In much the same way, the general condition of congestion reached in 1903–'05 on the eastern trunk lines and in the West and South in 1906–'07, manifested mainly in the need for more tracks and terminals, represented the permanent outgrowth of the old plant; and necessitated a readjustment of capital expenses for the purpose of enlargement. Viewed in a large way over a term of years, nearly every expenditure, even the fixed charges which appear constant or independent of the volume of business, thus become in reality imbued with more or less variability.

The preceding considerations hold good not alone of increased facilities, but of their curtailment as well. This point is often neglected in respect of capital outlay, which once made cannot be recalled. Rotting of ties we have held to be a constant expense of operation. It goes on steadily, whether traffic conditions be good or bad. But, on the other hand, those ties, if they be under a third or fourth track, would never have been laid had not there been a promise of business sufficient to render the added investment profitable. As Lorenz observes, "the question is not, What expenditures would disappear if a certain proportion of the traffic should be discontinued? but What expenditure would not now be incurred if that traffic had never been called forth?" Viewed in this way, even the necessary replacement of ties under a (temporarily) little used extra track, is an expense determined at some time, even if not always, by the volume of the business. In the long run, therefore, the percentage of total cost which we may assign to an increase in the volume of traffic, is higher than appears from a cross-section of expenses, taken, as was at first had, in a given year. Lorenz has illustrated this steady expansion of all groups of expenditure in relation to expansion of traffic by the following table, in which the actual figures for each year [brought down to date] are replaced by an index number based upon 100 for the year 1895. It would have been highly suggestive to continue all of this data alike to the present time; but, as noted on the table, certain items have been so modified by changes in accounting practice, that this could not be done.

RAILROADS

	Gross earnings from operation	Ton miles	Passenger miles	Total operating expenses	Maint. of way and structures	Maintenance of equipment	Conducting transportation	Gen'l expenses
1895	100	100	100	100	100	100	100	100
1896	107	111.8	107	106	111.2	117.9	103.1	99.4
1897	104	111.6	100.5	103	108.5	106.4	99.8	98.4
1898	116	133.8	109.7	113	120.4	124.9	109.1	101.1
1899	122	145.1	119.7	118	126.8	134.6	115.6	110.0
1900	138	166.1	131.5	132	150.4	164.2	126.9	112.7
1901	147	172.5	142.3	142	164.6	173.2	135.5	121.8
1902	160	184.5	161.5	154	185.2	200.2	151.7	131.4
1903	176	203.2	171.6	173	198.6	225.6	174.7	142.1
1904	184	204	179.8	184	194.8	250.7	188.6	153.5
1905	193	219	195	191	191	253	179	154
1906	216	254	206.5	212	216	288.8	194	166
1907	240	277	227	241	—[1]	—[1]	—[1]	—[1]
1908	222	256	238	230	—	—	—	—
1909	224	256	238	220	—	—	—	—
1910	256	300	265	251	—	—	—	—

According to this showing, maintenance of equipment, which we held in our analysis to be about one-half a constant expense and independent of traffic, especially after 1900, appears to have actually outrun the expansion of ton-mileage and passenger business. How largely this is due to actual purchases for the sake of future growth is not determinable. And maintenance of way outlay — one of our largely constant expenses — has increased, in fact, more rapidly than conducting transportation, which we held to be mainly variable. But these figures are confused by the failure to differentiate in the accounts, mere maintenance from actual improvements and additions to plant. Expenditures for these latter purposes, charged to operating expenses rather than to capital account, have been so enormous during these years of prosperity that they confuse the true facts utterly. It is to be hoped that now

---

[1] Change of accounting methods vitiates further comparisons of operating costs after 1907.

with the revised statistics since 1906, which will permit a clearer definition of these expenditures in detail, an analysis covering a series of years will bring out the real relationships. Equally important is the fact that these years have been characterized by rapid and extensive rises, both of prices and wages. Had our table covered a longer series of years the results would have been more clear. Until such an analysis be made, it will suffice for our purpose, viz., the analysis of the principles of railroad rate making, that we adhere to our first general conclusion, namely — that of the total expenditures of a railroad *at any given time* about two-thirds of them are constant, while only one-third vary with the ups and downs of the volume of traffic. Comprehending in survey a long period of years, it might happen, as Acworth concludes, that nearly one-half of the total expenditures were entirely fixed in character, leaving the other half as dependent upon the amount of transportation effected.

The manner in which heavy capital outlay for maintenance accompanies as well as partly accounts for a decline in the cost of conducting transportation on American roads, is graphically shown by the diagram on the next page.[1] During ten years a steady decline in direct operating costs has accompanied an equally marked upward tendency in expense of maintenance. The bearing of this on the problem of rate advances in future is direct. Profitableness results from two separate sources; economical operation such as longer trains and better loading, and also from far heavier capital investment in plant, by which such operation is rendered possible.[2] Both alike, however, attend upon increased volume of business. Heavy capital investment may lessen immediate maintenance charges, — lower grades and straighter alignment naturally wearing less; but, on the other hand, the burden of interest and other fixed

[1] From Railroad Operating Costs, by Suffern & Co., New York, 1911.
[2] *Cf. Yale Review*, 1910, pp. 268–288; with reference to the rate advances of that year.

expenses steadily grows. How will they stand toward one another by 1925 on the eastern trunk lines? Will growth of business bring lower rates or not? A fine field for further analysis is as yet unworked.

RATIO OF MAINTENANCE OF PROPERTY AND CONDUCTING TRANSPORTATION TO TOTAL OPERATING EXPENSE.

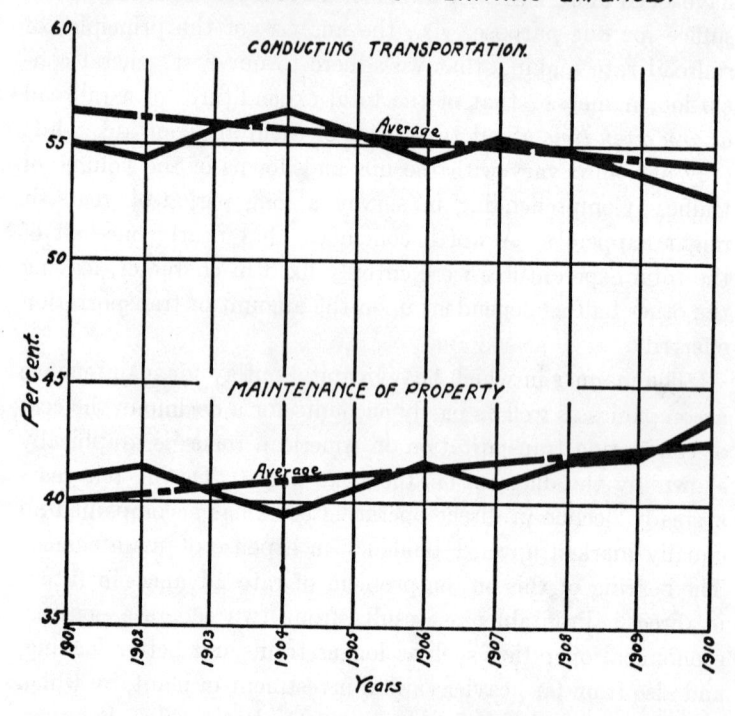

One final relation between operating and fixed expenses is left for consideration. It is so well put by J. Shirley Eaton in an unpublished paper, that it can best be stated in his own words:

"It is impossible to have an absolute and universal line of demarcation between the direct and the fixed expense, that shall be the same on all roads. One road chooses to reduce a grade and thereby increase the capital account in order to save in the current expense of a helper at a hill or the lost margin of efficiency of the loaded train on the level.

The relation between a current expense and the annual charge of the capitalized cost on a fixed plant that performed the same service, was well illustrated in a case arbitrated by Mr. Blanchard in New Orleans. One road which did not have access to the heart of the city undertook to compensate its disadvantage by trucking to and from its depot. The hire of a public truckman to perform the service for its patrons was very soon commuted to the practice of paying the amount of the truck expense to the consignee by deducting it from the freight bill rendered, the consignee or shipper performing the service. This, known as 'drayage equalization,' was claimed by competitors to be in the nature of a rebate to secure business. The arbitrator decided that the first roads had elected to buy their right of way into the heart of the city; and the road that had not built into the city elected to pay the expense of the same service in the shape of a current drayage bill instead of in the shape of interest on money invested in right of way. Therefore he decided there was no cause for complaint." [1]

Railroad expenditures, as Taussig clearly pointed out a number of years ago,[2] afford a prime illustration of the production of several commodities by a single great plant simultaneously at joint and indistinguishable cost. The classic economists illustrated this law by the joint production of wool and mutton and of gas and coke. In both of these instances neither commodity could conceivably be produced alone. Nor was either one, so to speak, a by-product of the other. So nearly of equal importance are the two, in fact, that the cost of production for each may approximately be determined by dividing the total cost according to the relative worths of the two or more products. The law of joint cost with reference to the production of transportation is somewhat different. Compare, for instance, the carriage by a railroad of thousands of passengers and different commodities in every direction, under varying conditions, singly or by wholesale, slowly or by express, over a given set of rails every day; with the operation of a great refinery producing simultaneously kerosene,

[1] *Cf.* the Free Cartage case, 167 U. S., 633.
[2] *Quarterly Journal of Economics*, V, 1891, pp. 438–465; reprinted in Ripley, Railway Problems.

gasolene, lubricating oils and greases as well as various odd chemicals. Both are examples of production at joint cost, but with various important contrasts. In the refinery all the costs are joint. All the processes are interlocked. Every increase in the output of kerosene produces *pari passu* an increase of the other commodities. On the railroad not all, but only a part of the costs are joint, in such manner as has been shown. For, from the joint portion of its plant—roadway rails and locomotives—the railroad may produce transportation of different sorts quite independently. It may choose to especially cultivate its passenger traffic, or its cotton or coal business. After a certain point of congestion is reached, the various sorts of traffic on the railroad may even become actually competitive with one another so far as the joint use of the plant is concerned. It is plain that this could never happen in the refinery. The use of more stills for making kerosene would automatically produce more by-products of every sort. But on a railroad it might well happen that the coal and passenger business might come to interfere with one another. A choice of emphasis as between fast refrigerator beef or fruit traffic, and limited express service, may have to be made on a long single track line. Nevertheless, in spite of these peculiarities of transportation, the general law of joint costs holds good, in that it is a demand for each service rather than its cost which finally determines the chargeable rate.[1] This must be so, because of the fact that the cost of each shipment is so largely joint and indeterminate, and that a large part of the entire plant is indistinguishably devoted to the general production of transportation without reference to particular units of business. One concrete example may serve to illustrate this point.

For years attempts have been unsuccessfully made by accountants to effect the primary separation between expenses of passenger and freight business, in order to determine the

[1] Two important qualifications of this law, however, are set forth at p. 265, *infra*.

cost of transportation per unit in each case. Some companies like the Louisville & Nashville and the Burlington system, still divide up the two, usually on the basis of the engine mileage for each class of traffic. This may be serviceable enough for comparisons of costs from year to year in the same company, but it has no general value and it may, moreover, become highly misleading. The most absurd conclusions may result. Thus at one time it appeared from such data, compiled by the Interstate Commerce Commission, that the New York Central, with five times the density of traffic of the Illinois Central, was actually conducting its freight business at a much higher cost per ton mile. Such inconsistencies induced the Interstate Commerce Commission in 1894 to abandon the attempt at any such primary separation of accounts.[1] It has since been reattempted, in special cases, as by the Wisconsin Railroad Commission in its notable "Two-cent Fare" decision in 1907, the division being made according to a number of different criteria.[2]

But it is plain that a very large proportion — probably over half — of the expenditures for freight and passenger business are entirely joint, however distinct the revenues from each service may be. We have seen that approximately two-thirds of the outgo is incurred on behalf of the property as a whole. Certain expenses, to be sure, such as train wages, coal consumption and the maintenance of rolling stock, are readily divisible; but with respect to the maintenance of way and structures — about forty per cent. of the total outgo — all guides fail. Even in respect of the cost of rails, due to wear and tear of train movement, we are quite at sea in the allocation of expenses. Freight trains may indeed be four times as heavy as passenger trains; but, on the other hand, they move at far slower speeds. And then, finally, how about the large

[1] The first successful attempt, as to soft coal rates to the lakes, is in 22 I.C.C. Rep., 613. *Cf.* 13 *Idem*, 423.
[2] Wisconsin Railroad Commission Report, 1907, p. 101. Compare also Woodlock, p. 91; U. S. Statistics of Railways, 1894, p. 70; *Yale Review*, 1908, p. 382; and Record, Cincinnati Freight Bureau Case, II, p. 941.

item of capital cost, the proportion of outgo for fixed charges? This equals about twenty-seven per cent. of the total expenditures for the United States as a whole. We may, of course, divide these expenses arbitrarily on the basis of the relative gross revenue from freight and passenger business respectively. And yet how absurd it would be to attempt to allocate an expense of a million dollars for the abolition of grade crossings in this way. As between the New Haven road, with passenger and freight revenues about equal, and a western road with only one-tenth of its income derived from passengers, the apparent cost of freight business on the eastern road would be absurdly reduced by any such process. The facts are plain. So many expenditures are incurred indiscriminately on behalf of the service as a whole — being an indispensable condition for operation of the property at all — that no logical distinction of expense even as between passenger and freight traffic is possible. This being so, how futile it is to expect to be able to set off the expenses due to any particular portion either of freight or passenger service, and especially to any individual shipment. It may oftentimes be possible to determine the *extra* cost due to individual shipments. This, of course, mainly applies to what are called movement expenses. Thus the haulage cost of a 2,000-ton grain train from Chicago to New York has been estimated at $520. But how small a part this is of the total cost, the preceding analysis must have made clear. In the Texas Cattle Raisers' case, detailed analysis of the extra cost for the traffic in cattle was presented.[1] The starting point in this attempt was necessarily an allocation of freight and passenger expenditures, which, if defective, would vitiate the entire subsequent calculation as to costs. In this instance, it was the judgment of the Interstate Commerce Commission in its final decision in 1908, that no such separation of expenditures was possible as a basis for the determination of cost of service.

[1] 13 I.C.C. Rep., 423. Compare 9 *Idem*, 423; and *Yale Review*, 1908, p. 287.

CHAPTER III

THE THEORY OF RAILROAD RATES (*Cont'd*)

The law of increasing returns, 71. — Applied to declining traffic, 73. — Illustrated by the panic of 1907, 75. — Peculiarly intensified on railroads, 76.
Growth of mileage and traffic in the United States since 1889, 77. — Increase of earnings, 79. — Operating expenses, gross and net income, 80. — Comparison with earlier decades, 85. — Density of traffic, 86. — Increase of train loads, 88. — Limitations upon their economy, 92. — Heavier rails, 93. — Larger locomotives, 94. — Bigger cars, 95. — Net result of improvements upon efficiency and earning power, 97.
The law of increasing returns due to financial rather than operating factors, 99.

A railroad theoretically presents a clear example of an industry subject to the law of increasing returns — that is to say, an industry in which the cost of operation grows less rapidly than the volume of business done. Each ton of freight added to the existing traffic costs relatively less to haul. From this it follows, obviously, that the net returns increase more than proportionately with the expansion of traffic. This may be demonstrated by a simple calculation. It has already been shown that only about two-thirds of the total expenditures of a railroad are applied to operation, the remaining third being devoted to capital account. Moreover, of these two-thirds of the total applied to operating outlay, only about one-half responds to any change in the tonnage, the other half being constant up to a certain point. Otherwise expressed, an increase of one per cent. in traffic and, therefore, of revenue, produces an increase in expense of only one-half of two-thirds of one per cent.[1] Two-thirds of the entire increment of revenue

---

[1] Illustrated by the seasonal variation of business. *Vide* appendix to this chapter at p. 100.

goes to profit. Carry this increase further and the effect is more striking. Suppose traffic to grow tenfold. The former outlay being $100 for a given volume of business, would be divided according to our rule as follows: one-third for fixed charges, one-third for constant operating outlay and one-third for variable expenses. With ten times as much traffic, only the last group of outgoes will expand. One thousand dollars revenue would therefore become available under the new conditions, to pay the same fixed charges as well as constant operating costs. The total outgo would thus become $33 plus $33 plus $330, or $396 in all. Almost two-thirds of the increment of revenue still remains as profit. It might well happen that such an expansion could not ensue without large increases in the capital and plant, as has already been noted; but up to that point this calculation would hold good. The following statement varying but slightly from our foregoing assumptions, illustrates the principle.[1] Let the distribution of expenditures for given conditions, producing $100 of revenue, be these, viz.:

Operating expenses	$ 67
Fixed charges	$ 28
	$ 95
Profits for dividends	$ 5
	$100

Now assume an increase of ten per cent. in the traffic and consequently in the revenue; but assume also that the average *extra* cost per unit, of the new business, is only forty per cent. as much as for the preëxisting tonnage. Were the added cost of each ton mile as great as before, the operating expenses would rise by the full ten per cent. of $67. But on Webb's assumption, they will rise by only forty per cent. of ten per cent. The new account would then stand thus:

[1] Webb, Economics of Railway Construction; originally in Wellington's Economic Theory of the Location of Railways.

Operating expenses ($67 plus forty per cent. of ten per cent. of $67)	$ 69.68
Fixed charges as before	$ 28.00
	$ 97.68
Income, increased by ten per cent	$110.00
Balance for profit or dividends	$ 12.32

By an increase of ten per cent. in tonnage, balance for dividends has more than doubled.

In this connection it will be noted that a constant rate of return per unit of business newly acquired has been assumed. Attempts were made on behalf of the railroads, during the long period of decline of ton mile revenue down to 1900, by Newcomb and others, to show that this is an unreasonable assumption; in that increased traffic is presumably to be had only by a progressive lowering of the rates charged. This contention has been effectively demolished by the steady and remarkable growth of traffic since 1900, even in the face of a substantial rise of rates all along the line. A necessary corollary to our proposition, beside that of the maintenance of a constant scale of charges, is, of course, also of the continuance of a given grade of service and of costs of operation. If more luxuriously appointed passenger trains or quicker freight service have to be given in order to produce the growth of business, the added costs of operation must, naturally, be taken into consideration. If widespread rise of wages follows an increase in the general cost of living, that too is an entirely extraneous factor. But with a given grade of service, constant rates and steady wage scales, there can be no question, up to the point of full utilization of the existing plant, that the operation of railroads affords clear demonstration of the law of increasing returns.

The obverse side of the law of increasing returns is also of great importance. For the same reason that when traffic increases, only a portion of the expenses are affected, it follows that, when business declines, only a part of the costs can be lopped off. In other words, a reduction in the volume of traffic does not in itself alone lead to a corresponding reduction in the operating expenses. Of course, many of these latter may, as we have seen, be temporarily postponed, as they were in 1893–1897, especially in the group of maintenance-of-way expenses. In such an event they must ultimately be made good by extraordinary outlay at some later time. But, unless they be thus postponed and unless the rates charged for service be reduced in order to stimulate traffic, it is inevitable that the margin of profit will drop as rapidly as it tends to rise with increased volume of business. This may be illustrated by the following computation.[1] Assume the total revenue from a given business to be $100, and assume it to be distributed as before, viz.:

Operating expenses	$ 67
Fixed charges	$ 28
	$ 95
Leaving profit	$ 5
Total	$100

A positive decline of ten per cent. in the tonnage, if the cost for operation per unit of the portion lost was the same as the rest, would obviously reduce the operating expenses also by ten per cent. Let it next be assumed, as was done previously, that the average extra cost per unit of the latest increment of business was only forty per cent. as much as for the remainder of the tonnage. How closely this will approximate the facts in any particular instance will depend upon the density of traffic attained in relation to the capacity of the existing plant. If the addition of the last ten per cent. of business did not increase the large proportion of fixed expenses at all, and only added forty per cent. per unit more to the variable expenses; *per contra*, the loss of it would merely reduce the variable expenses and still leave the constant outlay the same. On this assumption, by the loss of ten per cent. of business the total amount of operating expenses under the new conditions would

[1] Webb, *op. cit;* originally from Wellington.

be lessened, not by ten per cent. of $67, but by only forty per cent. of ten per cent. of $67. The income would, however, decline by the full amount of ten per cent. The account, after a loss of ten per cent. of business, would then stand somewhat as follows:

Operating expenses ($67 less forty per cent. of ten per cent. of $67)	$64.32
Fixed charges, as before	$28.00
	$92.32
Income, reduced by ten per cent.	$90.00
Leaving a deficit of	$2.32

Or, in other words, a decline of ten per cent. in tonnage has transmuted a five per cent. dividend condition into one involving an actual deficit nearly half as great as the former profit.

The sudden reversal from apparent prosperity to very real distress, such as occurred during the fall of 1907, is thus explained. Its suddenness may be shown by the following table of monthly gross and net earnings, promulgated by the Interstate Commerce Commission.[1] The acute panic occurred during October, but its effect was not apparent until the following month. The total mileage included is shown by the first column:

		Mileage	Earnings per mile Gross	Net
1907	July	223,900	$1,022	$304
1907	August	224,100	$1,079	$345
1907	September	224,300	$1,045	$314
1907	October	224,700	$1,116	$337
1907	November	224,800	$981	$261
1907	December	224,400	$861	$197
1908	January	198,700	$746	$148

[1] *Wall Street Journal*, March 25, 1908.

This table shows that whereas under full prosperity, up to and including the month of October, the net revenue was about thirty per cent. of gross; after the sharp decline in traffic, it dropped in November to twenty-six per cent., and progressively thereafter to twenty per cent. in January. In other words, a decline of about one-fourth in the gross revenue within four months, entailed a loss of over fifty per cent. in net earnings. Higher operating expenses in the winter may have exaggerated this tendency, but, on the other hand, drastic economies were put into effect, which would more than offset the difference.

The urgent need of at once meeting any loss of business by prompt reduction of operating expenses is apparent. But there is comfort to be found at this point in the fact that each one per cent. saved in operation at any given time, results in saving two per cent. for the net earnings. According to our estimates, and as a rule practically, operating expenses equal about two-thirds of gross revenue, leaving one-third to meet charges and pay dividends. Every reduction from this two-thirds of gross revenue, therefore, transferred to the balance, increases the latter proportionately twice as much. This fact in turn explains the urgent pressure always brought to bear at such times to effect economies all along the line. These are too often indiscriminately made.[1] Such paring down of expenses should always be made with an eye to their ultimate effect upon the operating efficiency of the property in the long run. To postpone much-needed repairs of equipment during a period of depression, like that of 1907–1908, when repair shop costs are at a low ebb, only to hamper operations and to effect repairs under pressure when business revives, is an instance of such wasteful economy.

The qualification of the law of increasing returns as applied to railroads, arising from the distinction between long and short term production of its commodity — transportation —

[1] Eaton, Railroad Operations, etc., pp. 44–58.

as above described, is of course by no means confined to carriers alone. It holds good of a factory or mercantile establishment as well. But in the case of railways, it is emphasized by the abruptness with which the condition of congestion of plant arises. The limit of full working capacity in a factory is elastic, by reason of the fact that under the "peak of load" — in busy seasons — it may prolong operations beyond the daylight hours or, at worst, work all night by double shifts. But a railroad, customarily working by night as well as by day and thus distributing its operations over the entire twenty-four hours, enjoys no such expansible limits upon utilization of its plant. When such full utilization is attained, the end comes suddenly. No postponement to a more favorable time for raising funds for better terminals or four tracking the main line is possible; nor does its character as a public servant permit a railroad to curtail service. The dead wall of congestion cannot be gotten around by either path. A crisis is presented, calling for the most heroic measures. This, of course, still further emphasizes the need for a long look ahead into the future with respect to railroad finance; not for the management alone, but for the government as well, charged as it is at present with control over rates for service.

The application of the law of increasing returns to railroads in actual practice is beset with difficulties. In order to make these clear, it will be necessary first to describe the phenomenal development of this country which has taken place during the last two decades.

The freight service of the railroads of the United States, measured by weight, in 1910, amounted to 1,026,000,000 tons. Only since 1899 when the corresponding figure given by the Interstate Commerce Commission was 501,000,000 tons, have accurate data been obtainable. This would indicate a growth in ten years of about one hundred per cent. But this figure takes no account of the distance each ton of freight travels.

This factor is included in what is known as ton mileage — that is to say, the equivalent of the number of tons of freight carried one mile. Obviously, so far as the amount of service rendered is concerned, one ton carried a hundred miles is the equivalent of one hundred tons transported one mile. Every carrier totalizes in this way each ton of freight movement by multiplying it into the distance transported. For the United States as a whole, this ton mileage in 1910 was 255,016,000,000 — that is to say, the service rendered would be represented by the carriage of that number of tons one mile. The appended diagram shows the phenomenal rapidity with which this transportation service has grown since 1899. The scale on the left hand side of the chart serves this purpose. The right hand scale indicates the miles of line in operation.

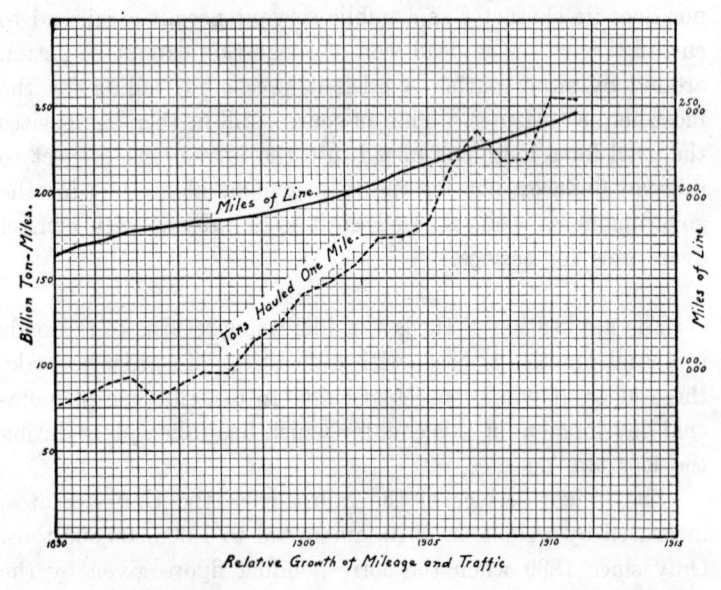

Relative Growth of Mileage and Traffic

The rapid growth up to 1893 was suddenly interrupted by panic and subsequent industrial depression lasting for about four years. Recovery began in 1897, since which time the freight movement has increased by leaps and bounds from about 95,000,000,000 ton miles to 255,016,000,000 ton miles in 1910. It is obvious that the growth of transportation in any country is bound to be more rapid than the increase either in population or in wealth. It appears, indeed, almost as if the volume of transportation in the United States increased more nearly as the square of population than in direct proportion. It has been estimated that we forward two and a half times as much freight *per capita* as some of the leading European countries like France. Our domestic population from 1890 to 1910 increased about fifty per cent. The railroad mileage grew at about the same rate. Yet the freight service surpassed this rate of growth more than six times over; and the passenger service augmented nearly as much. Both alike in 1910 were practically three times as great in volume as twenty years before. The diagram on page 78 is intended to illustrate the relative rapidity of this development. While population and mileage increased about one half, the railroads in 1910 hauled the equivalent of three times the volume of freight traffic handled in 1890. At the beginning of this period, the railroads had to seek the freight. Now it appears that traffic normally will seek the railroads. At times, even, as in 1906–1907, the railroads have actually sought to escape the flood of business presented.

The magnitude and importance of the growth of tonnage, as above described, is revealed by the rapid increase in railroad earnings. The course of these is shown by the succeeding chart on page 82. Gross revenues of American railroads in 1889 were about one billion dollars. In 1910 they amounted to $2,750,000,000. Thus it appears that gross earnings almost equalled three times the amount of twenty years ago. The net income available for dividends has grown even faster. The increase was, roughly speaking, about five fold; namely, from 101 millions in 1889 to 515 millions in 1910. Nearly three and one-half times as much money went annually to the owners of railroad securities as dividends and interest, besides leaving surplus earnings for 1910 of about 222 millions available for improvements and surplus. But the limit of utilization seems to have been about reached on many roads in 1906; and an era of extensive new capital outlay to increase the existing plants and facilities ensued. Indications are not lacking to show that at the height of activity before the industrial collapse of 1907–1908, such a point of saturation had been reached, especially in trunk line territory and on the northern transcontinental lines.[1] On the Northern Pacific, for instance, the ton mileage increased from 2.2 billions to 5.2 billions between 1900 and 1906. The Northwest was suddenly confronted at that time with the new issue of enlarging facilities, which had been slowly becoming apparent elsewhere in the country during the preceding decade. Grain actually rotted on the ground, and an acute coal famine occurred, because of sheer inability of the roads to care for the new traffic. Changes in methods of business also somewhat exaggerated this strain upon the carriers. Merchants now expect quick delivery to order. They object to stocking up months ahead, even when conditions are auspicious; therefore, business, when especially stimulated, comes with an irresistible rush. All these causes, coupled with undiscriminating attempts by inadequately bedded roads to imitate the methods of progressive ones by prematurely increasing their train loads, led to a practical breakdown of the transportation business of the country in the autumn of 1906. To the student of transportation, this congestion denoted the attainment of a point of saturation for the then-existing physical plant. The analogy to the case of the Pennsylvania Railroad, previously described, is obvious. Such a predicament is bound to arise in the development of any carrier in a rapidly growing country. Its fiscal significance will appear in due time.

A comparison of the growth of business and of operating expenses for the entire railroad system of the United States

[1] Investigation in 12th Ann. I.C.C. Rep., 561.

over a series of years is given in the following table. The results are expressed by means of index numbers based upon the year 1880, taken as 100.[1]

RELATIVE INCREASE IN TRAFFIC ITEMS, OPERATING EXPENSES AND REVENUE FROM 1880 TO 1906, INCLUSIVE

Items	1880	1881 to 1885	1886 to 1890	1891 to 1895	1896 to 1898	1904 to 1906
Ton miles of freight	100	134.36	203.23	264.90	313.81	595.0
Passenger miles of passengers	100	138.12	189.46	233.15	224.65	412.0
Operating expenses	100	132.75	174.39	215.30	221.42	394.0
Gross income from operation	100	—	—	183.0	190.0	346.0

(Average, from and inclusive)

From this table it appears that between 1880 and 1906 the ton mileage of freight increased about six fold, and the passenger business more than four fold. Operating expenses, on the other hand, were in 1906 less than four times as great as in 1880. Increasing returns are quite evident. The period from 1880 down to 1896–1898, before the recent general increases in prices and wages took place, shows this even more strikingly. In order to transport more than three times as much freight and two and one-quarter times as many passengers, it required a direct outlay for operation of little more than twice as much money.[2] On the other hand, owing to the rapid rise of all operating costs since 1898, a comparison of expenditures confined to the last ten years by themselves, affords an apparent contradiction. The results for this period have already been

[1] From Report of Commission to Investigate the Postal Service, 1901, p. 220; brought down to 1906 when local disturbances in wages, other costs of operation and rates outweigh all general considerations.

[2] Between 1890 and 1910 freight ton mileage rose three times over. Operating expenses grew by about two and one-quarter times.

given, classified in greater detail. And yet, despite this disturbing factor and the one earlier mentioned that these later operating expenses have been heavily loaded with improvement expenditures, it appears by comparison of 1895 with 1905, that passenger business has more than doubled, and freight business is two and a half times as great, while operating expenses in 1905 were not much over twice their amount ten years before.

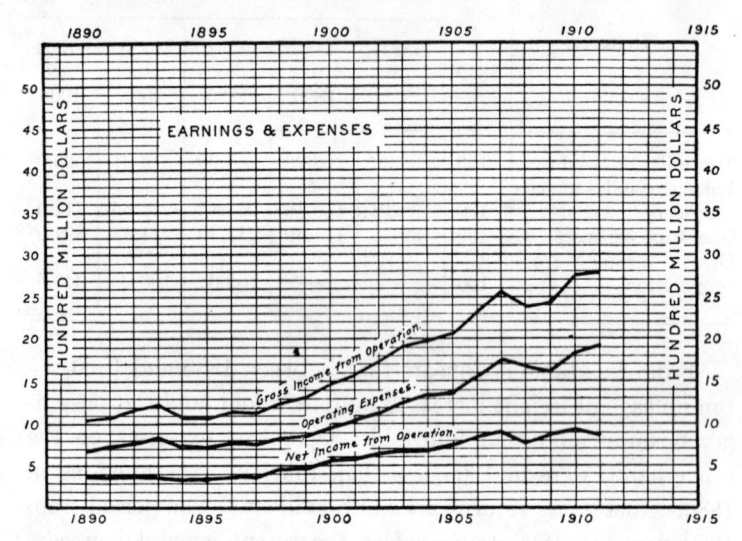

EARNINGS & EXPENSES

Gross Income from Operation.
Operating Expenses.
Net Income from Operation.

A comparison of the movement of gross earnings with operating expenses introduces still another disturbing factor, namely, the changes from year to year in the level of freight rates as well as in the character of the traffic handled. The effect of fluctuating costs of production of transportation having just been considered, we may now turn to the fiscal returns as affected by the price obtainable for the service given. Any long-time comparison of results reflects the influence of the steady decline of freight rates during the generation prior to 1900. Thus comparing 1880 with 1898, as shown by the preceding table, operating expenses grew in the ratio of 100 to 221, while gross income grew from 100 to only 190. Three fold the freight business produced less than twice the revenue. Pushing the comparison later, down to 1906, operating expenses grew after 1880 from 100 to 394, while gross income rose to only 346. This reflects the influence during the last few years of the rapid rise in prices and wages.

According to the opposite diagram, comparing 1890 with 1910, both operating expenses and gross income from operation seem to have moved together; the curve of gross revenue rising proportionately only a little faster than that for operating expenses. The latter have risen from a general figure of about $800,000,000 before the depression of 1893–1897, to $1,822,000,000 in 1910; the former from about $1,200,000,000 to over $2,750,000,000. Both alike somewhat more than doubled, therefore, in twenty years. At times, especially during the rapid revival of business after 1897, before rising prices began to affect costs of operation, extraordinary increases in earnings appeared, out-stripping the growth of expenditures. Comparing the year 1899 with 1895 we find that the gross earnings of the railroads of the United States increased by twenty-two per cent. This involved an increased expense of operation, however, of only eighteen per cent. Similar comparison year by year, there having been an enormous expansion of business, shows an increase in gross earnings somewhat more rapid than the growth of operating expenses. This differential advantage has progressively lessened since 1902, and especially since the let-up in 1907. The official returns for 1911 with the marked decline in gross, show an even more distinct drop in net earnings. Whether the need of an increase of rates commensurate with the augmented operating costs is imperative, can only be ascertained after a return to more normal business conditions.

These relationships would be the more striking could we exclude the enormous expenditures for betterments which have been charged to operating expenses during these years. Comparisons of net earnings are vitiated by uncertainty upon this point. Working over these results by comparison per mile of line, it appears that the rate of increase in earnings per mile of line for five years prior to 1900, was approximately double the rate of increase of operating expenses per mile of line. The greatly lessened cost of performing additional business becomes at once apparent. But these latter conclusions, as has been said, cover only a brief period of time. Judging by the results over many years, it appears that changes both in the level of freight rates and of wages and prices have operated to leave the railroads not much better off than they were some time ago. The only thing which has saved them whole in the face of rising prices and wages since 1900, and especially since 1907, has been the rise of freight rates and the enforced improvements in operation. With the methods of transportation, such as size of cars and locomotives and train loads, as they were a decade ago, very real distress would be more widely apparent than it is. On the whole, the public seems to have shared in the benefits of these improvements to a considerable degree. This statement, however true for the entire railroad system of the country as a whole, does not by any means represent the facts for any single system. Moreover, it is not by any means clear how fully the railroad system of the country has been enlarged and improved out of surplus earnings. There is reason to think that foundations in some cases — the Pennsylvania road, for example — have been laid during these prosperous years, for largely increased tonnage in the immediate future without a corresponding growth of expenses chargeable to plant; in other words, that the transition to a distinctly higher grade of operation has been effected out of surplus earnings.

The comparison of gross and net earnings from operation, if expenditures have grown almost as fast as gross income, confirms the preceding conclusions. Surveying the chart for the period since 1890, it appears that net earnings for the railroads of the United States have more nearly trebled than doubled; the increase having been 177 per cent. up to 1910. This takes no account whatever of the immense volume of new capital added to the system. The entirely distinct question of the relative rate of return upon the investment will engage our attention at a later time. Examination of the years of rapid revival after 1897 by themselves, however, especially for individual companies, shows striking results. This is especially true of roads, not then developed up to a fair working capacity for their plants.

An interesting comparison with the previous decade, 1870 to 1880, exemplifies this relation still further. The gross earnings of the trunk lines of the United States decreased very greatly per mile of line from $7,211 in fact to $6,636 during the decade; but at the same time the net earnings steadily increased. This was due primarily to the great volume of business developed, — the ton mileage increasing more than three fold during these ten years. It happened despite the fact that the miles of line during the same period had more than doubled. The following decade, 1880 to 1890, was represented by an increase of only 82.7 per cent. in mileage, while the number of tons of freight hauled one mile increased by 132 per cent. Density increasing in this way, a corresponding ability to carry at a lower rate per ton was a necessary result. So indisputably has this law — that an expanding volume of business up to a certain point, may profitably be carried at a continually lowered cost — been proved, that it is estimated by so competent an authority as the *Engineering Review* that, provided sufficient tonnage be available for 2,000-ton freight train loads, a cost of one mill per ton mile can be attained. Its significance may be realized from the fact that the lowest revenue per ton mile reported for the United States is 2.21 mills per ton mile for the long haul soft coal business of the Chesapeake & Ohio.[1] This, of course, does not imply that any railroad in actual operation, carrying all kinds of freight including a large pro-

[1] *Cf.* data as to revenue per ton mile on p. 413, *infra*.

portion of local traffic, can in the immediate future hope to attain this result. It is intended only to show that, provided the volume of traffic be large enough, the cost of operation tends to decline as a matter of course, until a condition of congestion for the existing plant has been reached. At this point a new cycle of costs of operation and of profits makes its appearance.

The most important single factor in the production of increasing returns upon a railroad is the density of traffic; that is to say, the amount of business which can be conducted with a given set of rails, terminals and rolling stock. In other words, it is the degree of effective utilization of the plant and equipment. It is too obvious to need demonstration, after what has been set forth concerning the nature of railroad expenditures, that economy of operation and, consequently, profits are more or less directly dependent upon this fact. Such effective utilization of the property may be secured in two ways: either by a large tonnage per mile of its line, or else by a concentration of such traffic as it may have into large train loads, which can individually be transported at low cost. The first of these economizes the fixed expenses for roadway and line which respond but slowly to enlargement of traffic, by distributing them thinly over a large tonnage; the second economizes the mere movement expenses which tend to grow less rapidly than the size of the trains. For neither fuel consumption nor wages of train crews expands *pari passu* with the paying load. Fortunate the lot of the railroad which enjoys both these advantages, of density of traffic per mile of line and of tonnage capable of such concentration in heavy train units.

Traffic density — the tons of freight carried one mile per mile of line — is readily computed. The ton mileage, representing the total transportation service, is merely divided by the number of miles of line operated. The following graded table illustrates the wide range of this figure, according to the

THEORY OF RAILROAD RATES

location of different companies and the nature of their business, as well as the change in the last few years.[1]

	1902–3				1910
	Traffic density	Agric'l products	Products of mines	Manu- factures	Traffic density
		Percentage of tonnage			
Rock Island Company	428,116	25	29	14	581,000
C. M. & St. P.	605,139	23	24	17	709,000
Great Northern	657,102	—	—	—	814,700
N. Y., N. H. & H.	802,954	—	—	—	1,057,000
Wabash	885,208	24	32	9	1,322,000
Baltimore & Ohio	2,181,518	6	62	8	2,711,000
New York Central	2,163,000	16	44	12	2,548,000
Lake Shore ('05)	3,355,209	—	—	—	3,911,000
Penn'a Railroad ('05)	6,337,625	—	—	—	5,139,000

The first of these companies operates in a sparsely settled agricultural territory. The St. Paul system lies nearer Chicago, but is still largely dependent upon a local and rural constituency. The Great Northern — a great transcontinental trunk line — despite its sparsely settled western area, exchanges a large volume of through freight for the Pacific Coast for lumber and other bulky products carried east. The New Haven serves perhaps the most densely settled area in the United States, but much of its traffic is on branch lines and is of a retail character. The Wabash lies in well settled territory and hauls a heavy tonnage of low-grade freight. The last two are not only great trunk lines to the seaboard, but also tap the coal and iron fields. Much of their tonnage is consequently of low grade. The Pennsylvania enjoys a still further advantage, super-adding a rich local traffic in manufactures and merchandise. As compared with its rival trunk line, the New York Central, it hauls relatively little grain; but, on the other hand,

[1] Other data as to density on p. 413, *infra*.

the New York Central has a much smaller coal and iron business. Some one has aptly characterized the difference between the two roads, describing the New York Central as "operating between good points, but not through a good country" so far as local business is concerned. On the one, through traffic is supplementary to local business, while on the other it is the reverse. The high density of trunk line traffic is such that about two-thirds of all the tonnage of the United States is transported east of the Mississippi and north of the Ohio river.

Traffic density has enormously increased during the last two decades, as a result of the filling up of the country and the relative cessation of new construction. This is manifested by the growth since 1890. In that year the density was less than 500,000 ton miles per mile of line, and during the depression of 1893 it fell well below that figure. The total of 1,053,000 reported for 1911 represents, therefore, more than a doubling of the density in twenty years. This growth during 1898 and 1905–'06 was notable. The latter period, especially, was a time when congestion upon all the roads of the country occasioned much distress. The fact is evident that the country has well grown up to the measure of its existing transportation facilities.

The second measure of effective operation for the production of increasing returns, is concentration in the trainload. This is regarded by many as the supreme test of efficiency in management. Great progress has been made during the past years in this regard in the United States — an improvement which has largely enabled the carriers to bear up under an increasing burden of expenditure. The trainload is generally adopted today as the unit of operation, measuring the cost of service.[1] It is a fact that, within certain limits, the cost of handling a train does not vary greatly with its capacity. Since the first application of air-brakes to freight trains in 1887,

[1] Also known as "average tons per train mile." Obtained by dividing the ton mileage by the sum of the freight and mixed train miles.

THEORY OF RAILROAD RATES

a train crew sufficient to handle fifteen cars can care for thirty about as well in long haul wholesale business. Fuel cost, also, as has been shown, lags well behind the rate of increase of the load. Eaton in his Railroad Operations, concludes that from thirty to fifty per cent. of cost is independent of the trainload. The effect is that any increment in the paying load very materially decreases the cost of operation per ton.

Progress in the United States in increasing the average train load is shown by the lowest curve on the diagram on page 97. The scale applicable is along the left hand side of the chart. From 175 tons per train in 1890 to an average figure of 383.10 in 1911 is certainly a remarkable showing. The most rapid increase seems to have occurred after 1897, with the first resumption of general prosperity. As for individual roads, the following table of average train loads is suggestive, as showing the gradation between roads of different type, as well as progress from year to year:

AVERAGE NUMBER OF TONS OF FREIGHT PER TRAIN (TONS PER TRAIN MILE)

Road (Fiscal Years)	1901	1905	1910
Pennsylvania Railroad (East of Pittsburg)..	478	498	649
Pennsylvania Company (West of Pittsburg)	382	420	511
Pennsylvania System (Both)	454	476	607
Chesapeake & Ohio	511	557	701
Great Northern	347	541	520
Erie Railroad	379	416	497
New York Central & Hudson River	365	381	413
Northern Pacific	324	367	429
Atchison, Topeka & Santa Fé	238	265	298
Chicago & Northwestern	255	259	261
New Haven	208	222	293
Southern	190	194	237

The great coal and iron roads, the trunk lines and the transcontinental lines all concentrate their business; while the granger roads, like the Atchison and North Western, the roads with much local business like the New Haven or the Southern, operating in sparsely settled regions, all have of necessity smaller trainloads. But all alike betray remarkable progress in this regard. In 1870 the average for the best roads was little above 100 tons, — such as 103 tons reported for the New York Central and 137 tons on the Lake Shore. From this level to results of 400 or 500 tons on the average represents a notable achievement. The Lake Shore for 1911 reports a revenue train load of 635 tons. It should be observed, however, that such results come from longer trains, not, apparently, so much from larger cars. To raise the average trainload on the Wabash from 196 tons in 1890 to 386 tons in 1908 is also worthy of note. The significance of these recent figures can be realized from the fact that the London & North Western, one of the leading railroads in Great Britain, reports recently an average freight train load of only 68 tons. This represents probably a fair average for European railroads as a whole, although in England the general practice of privately owned cars, of light locomotives, short freight sidings, etc., may reduce the figure slightly below the continental average. Statistics not only show the notable improvement in recent years; they at the same time show how the trainload performance is affected by trade conditions. For nearly every road the trainloads for 1904 were distinctly lower than in the preceding years. This was a year of acute business depression. The movement of great staple commodities, such as iron ore, coal, steel and iron and lumber, was greatly curtailed. All business was conducted on a narrower basis. Smaller trainloads were an almost inevitable consequence. The revival in the following year, however, immediately improved the conditions of operation, as the figures indicate.

It will be noted that the figures for the American roads above given represent averages. These are compounded from local and through traffic taken together. It is apparent at once that local trains must average far lighter loads than are customary upon long hauls without breaking bulk. Thus New England railroads report for 1906 an average trainload of only 220 tons, while other parts of the country, such as the North Central group, report 426 tons of paying load. Only by separation of local from through business can we adequately appreciate the enormous advances which have taken place in railroad operation in the United States, with corresponding reductions in the cost of transportation. While the New York Central at one time reported an average trainload of 322 tons, the average load of its through trains on the main line rose as high as 750 tons. More than twice this figure is attained upon the Pittsburg, Bessemer & Lake Erie road in hauling ore from the lakes to the furnaces at Pittsburg. The Illinois Central, for its low grade and long haul to the Gulf, has recently built locomotives capable of hauling 2,000 tons of net paying load. A standard grain train on the Lake Shore in 1903 consisted of fifty cars holding forty tons each. Even this figure has recently been surpassed by the New York Central, which, with its monster new "mogul" engines, hauls eighty loaded 30-ton cars, giving 2,400 tons of revenue freight. The Mallet locomotives with a tractive effort of 100,000 lbs., at present seem to have reached the limit of size and weight. Seventy-five grain cars holding 1,000 bushels apiece are equivalent to the production of twenty bushels per acre of an area of six square miles. This is an ordinary trainload. It is not infrequent to transport a fifth more than this. Eighty and even one hundred cars in a train since 1900 often bring the load up to 3,600 and even 4,000 tons of freight. Such a train is over four-fifths of a mile long. From these figures it certainly appears that trainloads for long haul are standardized at not less than 2,000 tons, a figure which would have seemed absolutely impossible to railroad managers of fifteen or twenty years ago. The maximum trainload in Germany on coal traffic, which, of course, greatly exceeds any general average for trains of all classes, is about five hundred tons. It has been regarded as a notable achievement that this represents an increase of about one hundred tons in the last decade.

On the other hand, the extravagant promises of economy from large trainloads have been considerably abated of late. It has been effectively demonstrated that there is a limit to such growth. Only low-grade and long haul carload traffic can profitably be concentrated. In 1903, for instance, a general decrease in trainloads followed a reduction in the relative amounts of low as compared with high grade tonnage. Less iron, coal, and raw materials and more merchandise and manufactures offered for carriage, necessitated a positive reduction in the trainloads as already mentioned. Nor can local business in less than carload lots profitably be concentrated beyond a certain point. Grades must be uniform to attain such economy. The trainload must not exceed the traction power on the heaviest inclines, or else expensive pusher engines or breaking up of trains will offset all other savings. Moreover, too great trainloads even on the best roadbeds involve slower speeds. Not only is other traffic thus impeded, but the economy in wages vanishes after a certain point with such slower movement. The fashion had been set by James J. Hill, the master mind in the transcontinental field. His notable results, due to a careful working out of every detail, led to a frenzied imitation on all sides. Many roads then discovered to their loss that while they had provided rolling stock for heavy loading, ampler terminals, longer sidings and heavier bridges also were a necessary accompaniment. Part of the congestion of traffic in 1906–1907, already mentioned, and a portion of the financial embarrassments of recent years, were undoubtedly due to too great haste in seeking economies of this sort in rolling stock, without at the same time making provisions for enlargement of other portions of the plant. A more discriminating policy has consequently resulted of late. Traffic is being sorted according to its availability for concentration. The best utilization of the rails and terminals is being more considered. Business demands for quick delivery also enter into the calculation. Instead of a few huge slow-moving leviathans blocking other trains, the line may perhaps better be kept full of many smaller trains moving more nearly together. Such are certain of the details now being worked out. None of them, however, weaken the main proposition that a discriminating concentration of traffic conduces very greatly to economy of operation.

This concentration of traffic units is largely due to technical improvements of various kinds. Foremost among these has been the development of the steel rail. In 1880 more than seven-tenths of our mileage was still equipped with iron rails. Rapid progress ensued during the next ten years, upward of eighty per cent. being in steel rails by 1890. At the present time, the proportion is above ninety-eight per cent. In fact, no iron rails have been made for many years, except for repairs and on insignificant branch lines in remote parts of the country. A steady increase in the weight of the rails has ensued. The standard rail for main lines until the Civil War weighed fifty-six pounds to the yard. In the seventies this was increased to sixty-three and above; in the latter eighties the best practice was to use seventy-five pound sections. Since 1900, they frequently run as high as one hundred pounds, in regions of dense traffic. Few main lines of track now average less than seventy-five pounds. It is this increase in the use and size of steel rails which has permitted improvements in rolling stock. But, on the other hand, grave dissatisfaction with the quality of the rails manufactured of late years, particularly since the establishment of practical monopoly under the United States Steel Corporation has become manifest. Numerous accidents due to breakage of rails, especially since 1905, have revealed either defects in manufacture or an undue load imposed by heavier rolling stock, too high speed, or both. The matter has become steadily worse. In 1902 the Interstate Commerce Commission ascribed seventy-eight accidents to broken rails.

Nine years later the number had risen to 249. The need of improvement is now fully recognized on all sides.

The power and efficiency of locomotives has increased, perhaps, more since 1890, and particularly since 1895, than in any previous period. Superior materials particularly have contributed to this result, such as the substitution of cast steel for cast iron and of nickel steel for wrought iron in axles, crank pins, etc. Some of the improvements which may be mentioned are, for instance, an increase in the average heating surface from 2,000 in 1890 to nearly 3,000 square feet at the present time, and an increase in the average steam pressure from 160 pounds to 210 pounds per square inch in the same period. The maximum weight has also increased very rapidly. The average weight of a locomotive at the close of the Civil War was approximately 90,000 pounds. This has increased in somewhat the following proportions: To 1881, 102,000 lbs.; to 1893, 135,000 lbs.; to 1895, 148,000 lbs.; to 1898, 230,000 lbs.; rising in 1900 to 250,000 lbs. Passenger locomotives since 1892 have almost doubled in weight, and freight engines have more than done so. Compound and double or Mallet locomotives are also supplanting those of simpler type for peculiarly heavy service. The first compound engine was built in 1899, only one being constructed in that year. In 1900 a single locomotive works turned out 500 — a number constituting two-thirds of the entire output of that company — for use in the United States. Such locomotives cost more in first instance; but the greater weight and steam capacity, together with the considerable saving in fuel, amounting to perhaps twenty per cent., more than offset this objection. The traction efficiency of these improved locomotives may be shown by the statement that in 1885 the decapod Baldwin locomotives, made to haul 3,600 tons on a level, represented the maximum capacity. Five years later the same company built locomotives to haul 4,000 tons, not only on a level, but on any ordinary grade. As indicative of late advances in locomotive construction, we may instance those built about 1900 for the Illinois Central and the Union Railroad at Pittsburg, both low-grade roads, carrying exceedingly heavy train loads. The first of these weighed, including its tender, 365,000 lbs., the Union Railroad consolidation engines weighing 334,000 lbs. Such locomotives are stated to be twice as powerful as the best which were manufactured twenty-five years ago. This record is surpassed by engines which have just been built for pusher service on the soft-coal Virginian Railway. They are of the Mallet type, weighing 540,000 pounds; with a train capacity of 4,230 tons. The evaporative surface is 6,760 square feet. As summarizing the increased efficiency of American locomotives, we may instance the figures of the Interstate Commerce Commission, showing the average performance of locomotives for the United States. Whereas in 1894 the average number of tons of freight carried per locomotive was about 32,000 tons, this rose to 46,000 tons in 1899, and to 54,600 tons in 1906. At the same time the number of tons of freight hauled one mile for each freight locomotive in the United States increased from 4,000,000 in 1894 to approximately 6,000,000 in 1899, and to 7,300,000 in 1910. In other words, the average performance of each freight locomotive in the United States has increased by more than fifty per cent. in the last decade.

The economy of large freight cars has been amply demonstrated. Marked advances in the average capacity have taken place in the last few years. In the sixties a 15,000 pound freight car represented about the normal capacity. This has increased, as measured by maximum load, to 28,000 pounds in 1873; to 40,000 pounds in 1875; to 60,000 pounds in 1885; to 70,000 pounds in 1895; while at the present time 80,000 to 100,000 pound cars are in everyday use. Cars of this latter type, built to carry forty to fifty tons, are necessarily of pressed steel construction, and are mainly useful for the carriage of coal and ore and similar low-grade commodities. It seems to be questionable whether a maximum capacity has not been about reached, in view of the exceedingly great wear and tear imposed upon track, bridges, etc. Up to this point the economy of heavy loading is indisputably proved. Increased size of cars far more than proportionately increases the paying load. Thus, for instance, an 18,000-pound car will carry 20,000 pounds load, while a 22,000-pound car will carry a load twice as great. It is stated on good authority, for example, that a car of forty tons capacity can be built which will weigh but 3,000 pounds more than a thirty-ton car, and cost hardly fifty dollars more. This is undoubtedly the reason why at the present time the average load per car is at least one hundred per cent. greater than the maximum which was possible twenty years ago.

A steady increase in the freight performance of American equipment is shown by official data of the Interstate Commerce Commission. Whereas in 1894 it required on an average 1,888 freight cars for every 1,000,000 tons of freight transported their capacity has so increased that the same amount of traffic in 1906 was carried by only 1,127 cars. In other words, an enormous increase in the freight service had been attained. On the other hand, the actual mileage performance of much of this equipment is extraordinarily low. It averages only about 9,000 miles annually or an equivalent of thirty miles a day. At a speed of fifteen miles an hour, this means that actual movement under a paying load, allowing for one-third of its journeyings empty, occupies but little over an hour and a quarter a day. The actual performance is, however, not quite as poor as appears. For, of course, this average includes the non-movement of all cars in bad order (sometimes one-tenth of the total); and also all idle equipment. This latter consideration is of great moment. Special cars, suitable only for seasonal business; and especially demurrage delays, often forty-eight hours or more, adversely affect the result. Where separate mileage records of "foreign" cars are kept, as on the Wabash system, it appears that their mileage is twice as high as for "home" cars. The difference is due to the fact that cars off their own rails, mainly are in actual demand and are kept moving. Probably the daily performance of loaded cars is not less than 150 miles. But a journey of this length, with two days' delay at each end at terminals, would bring the average down to about thirty miles. The public does not always appreciate these facts; and is often querulous. It is certain that the problem how to secure greater efficiency in the use of this equipment is as yet imperfectly solved.[1]

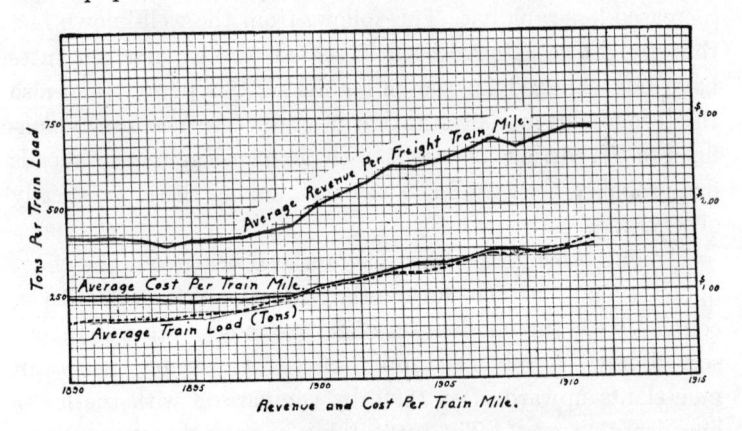

Revenue and Cost Per Train Mile.

The discussion of the nature of railroad expenditure may be concluded by a comparison of the net effects of the developments of the last few years; that is to say, of steadily expanding costs of operation and of slowly and tardily rising rates chargeable for service on the one hand, as over against the results obtained by mechanical improvements and increasing economy of operation coupled with growth of tonnage, on the other. The average cost of transportation has greatly increased. This, according to the statistics of the Interstate Commerce Commission, is shown upon the diagram herewith

[1] *Cf. Quarterly Journal of Economics*, XVIII, p. 299; on *per diem* reform. Also, *Railway Age*, 1903, p. 136; 15th Ann. Rep., I.C.C., p. 79; and Circular Letters, 1901, Chicago Bureau of Car Performances.

by the middle curve.[1] The average cost of running all trains per mile, which had fallen from 96 cents in 1891 to 91.8 cents in 1895, rose to $1.07 in 1900, and in 1911 increased by more than one-third, to $1.54 per mile. Against this should be set the fact that while the trains thus cost more to haul per mile, their paying load has increased in somewhat smaller proportion. This is shown by the upper curve on the diagram above mentioned. For freight trains the increase has been from $1.65 to $2.89 per mile. Passenger revenues per train mile have increased less rapidly. This follows from the well-known fact that freight rates have been increased, while passenger rates have not changed for the better during this period; and also that economies in concentration of traffic are necessarily confined to the carriage of freight. The immense gain in trainloads has probably been the main element, among these, as already observed.

Among other things this diagram also brings out the effect upon revenue of the substantial rate increases after 1900, coupled with the elimination of rebate losses. It will be observed how sharply the upper curve of revenue per train mile slants upward after 1899, by comparison with the lower line denoting cost. The same thing apparently occurs again after the set-back of 1907.

The interrelation between these various factors may be more readily shown by confining our attention to the period during which a practically uninterrupted development of business ensued, thus eliminating the confusion due to the four years of depression after 1893. The data on our various charts for the years 1898–1906 demonstrate that during this period the ton mileage, measuring the freight traffic handled, has practically doubled. To transport this doubled tonnage, a growth in freight train mileage of only eighteen per cent. was necessary. This was due, of course, to the notable concentration of train loading, already described, as well as to a density of traffic

[1] Using the right hand scale.

per mile of line almost sixty per cent. greater. As a consequence of these economies in operation, the revenue per freight train mile has increased by about fifty per cent.; while the average cost of running all trains per mile has grown less rapidly, namely, by 42 per cent. Had we data for freight trains alone it would surely be lower than this. In the meantime during this period of eight years, the rate of return in revenue per ton mile received, remained practically unchanged.[1] From all of which it would appear that even despite all these confusing factors, the law of increasing returns, so far at least as 1898 –'06 was concerned, was making itself appreciably felt.

Attentive consideration of the available figures, especially as shown by diagram on page 97, shows apparently that the various economies in operation, heavier trainloads and the like, have not since 1906 yielded any greater profit from mere operation, with the ever increasing volume of business. In other words, the increase in the margin between cost of operation and revenue per train mile, — measuring profitableness per unit of movement — has not kept pace with the augmentation of the size of that unit, — the trainload. Thus it follows, as one would expect, even making allowance for all changes in rates, wages and other expenses, that the law of increasing returns as applied to railroads, does not arise primarily from economic considerations as to mere physical operation. The law originates primarily in the fiscal conditions attaching to the heavy capital investment, — the fact, namely, that fixed charges up to a given point of saturation tend to remain constant, absolutely; but become proportionately less, therefore, as the volume of business expands. From this fact, therefore, rather than because of any marked economies of large-scale production, may it be affirmed that railroads offer a notable example of the law of increasing returns. The important bearing of this distinction will appear in due time in connection with the problem of the determination of reasonable

[1] Diagram on p. 413, *infra*.

rates. Added significance, also, is given to the relation between the cost of new capital, measured by the rates of interest on bonds and dividends on stocks, and the supply necessary to provide adequate extensions and improvements in future.

Appendix:

The subjoined chart, reproduced by the *Railway Age Gazette* from a bulletin of the Bureau of Railway Economics, brings out forcibly the manner in which, within the short time limits of full utilization of plant, a large increase of business can take place without a commensurate growth of expenses. The phenomenon for railroads is of course cyclical. Annually, as here indicated for 1911, the second half of the year is marked by a much heavier movement of traffic, principally, of course, the crops. But expenses never rise in proportion. This is most evident for the eastern group of roads, as here shown. This causes the net revenue curve, also, to vary much more than in proportion to the volume of traffic, in consequence.

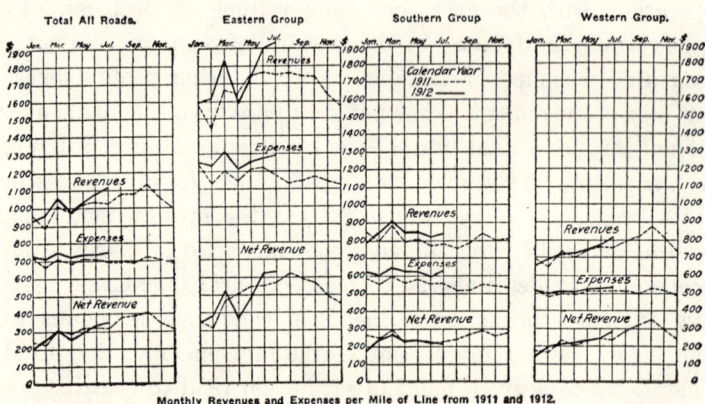

Monthly Revenues and Expenses per Mile of Line from 1911 and 1912.

CHAPTER IV

RATE MAKING IN PRACTICE

Evolution of rate sheets, 101. — Terminal *v.* haulage costs, 102. — Local competition, 104. — What the traffic will bear, 107. — Trunk line rate system, 111. — Complexity of rate structure, 113. — Competition of routes, 114. — Competition of facilities, 116. — Competition of markets, 118. — Ever-widening markets, 119. — Primary and secondary market competition, 121. — Jobbing or distributive business, 124. — Flat rates, 127. — Mississippi-Missouri rate scheme, 128. — Relation between raw materials and finished products, 134. — Export rates on wheat and flour, 135. — Cattle and packing-house products, 139. — Refrigerator cars, 140. — By-products and substitution, 142. — Kansas corn and Minnesota flour, 143. — Ex-Lake grain rates, 145. —

THE task of constructing a freight or passenger tariff is an eminently practical one. The process must be tentative and experimental. Little can be calculated in advance. Tariffs are not made out of hand; they grow. Not until a rate has been put into effect, can its results be known. The lower limit of charges, however, is more or less fixed. Obviously the rate must not be less than that portion of the variable expenses incident to each particular unit of business. This variable expense is divisible into two parts, one for loading and unloading, and the other for actual movement. The first step in constructing a tariff, therefore, is to separate these two portions of the variable outgo. General experience fixes the terminal outlay for loading and unloading at an average figure of about twenty or twenty-five cents per ton at each end of the line; that is to say, at an average of about two and one-half cents per hundred pounds as the total terminal cost.[1] Just where, above or below this average, the figure for any particular tariff will lie, depends upon a multitude of details.

[1] Testimony before the Hepburn Committee, in 1879, p. 2921, is interesting on this point.

This terminal expense is obviously quite independent of the length of the haul. It costs no more to load for a carriage of 3,000 miles than for one between two adjoining stations. It is the second portion of the specific costs, namely, the movement expense, which varies with the distance. This movement cost is more difficult of determination, as affected by a multitude of variable factors, such as the grades, curvature, number of stops, the size of train load, and above all, the volume of the traffic. Assuming the simplest physical conditions, one would expect the movement expense, aside from the initial cost of getting up steam in order to move at all, to rise proportionately to the distance traversed. Graphically represented, the tariff would appear somewhat as follows:

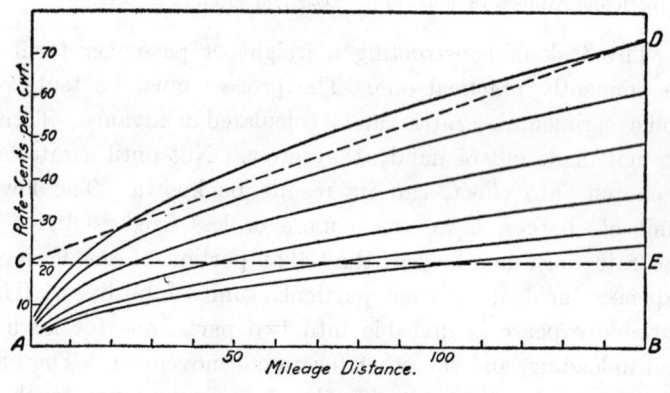

Relation of Cost of Carriage to Distance.

In this diagram the distances of carriage are represented along the horizontal line, A B; while the rate charged is laid off vertically. The distances A C and E B represent the constant terminal cost; while the steadily rising rates with increasing distance, due to movement expenses, are shown by the sloping dotted line C D. This chart at once demonstrates why under the very simplest physical conditions a straight mileage tariff is unscientific and unreasonable. For the constant terminal expense, spread evenly over the mileage traversed as the movement expenses grow, becomes progressively less and less in proportion to the total of the two, which constitutes the real rate. The longer the haul, the lower the ton-mile cost as a matter of necessity. As Chanute calculated on the New York Central a generation ago,[1] while the average cost per mile of hauling a ton ten miles was 4.062 cents, it descended progressively to less than one cent per mile for distances over five hundred miles. A common rule is that the rate rises as the square root of the distance, rather than in proportion to it. A hundred-mile haul represents a cost approximately only twice as great as one of twenty-five miles, instead of being four times as much. For thrice a given cost the haul may be increased nine times. The course of such a tariff with increasing distance would be represented by the parabolic curved lines on the preceding diagram.[2]

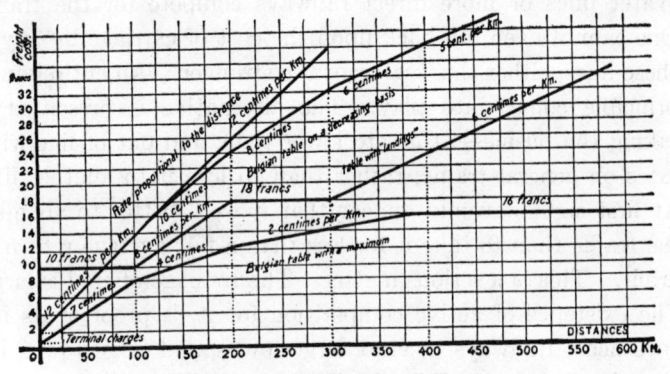

Diagram of Belgian Tariff Sheets.

The particular curve would depend upon the commodity and local physical conditions. In territory where movement expenses were heavy or operation difficult, the curve would obviously rise more rapidly. Such a mathematical tariff does

[1] U. S. Reports on Internal Commerce, 1876, p. 25.
[2] U. S. Industrial Commission, 1900, IX, p. 631. *Cf.* also diagram of European tariffs in Senate (Elkins) Committee, 1905, V, App. p. 271.

not depart widely from the one traced by the heavy dotted line C D first described. The progressive decline of the per mile rate with increasing distance may be illustrated by the rough estimate of allowing two and one-half cents per hundred weight or fifty cents per ton for terminal cost, with one-half cent additional per mile for movement expenses. For a ten-mile haul this would cost fifty-five cents, or an average of 5.5 cents per mile. Were the distance 500 miles, the average cost would be only $\frac{50+250}{500}$ cents or 0.6 cents per ton mile.

Thus far the problem has been seemingly simple. The next step introduces new complications. Our hypothetical railway line at a point one hundred miles out, may cross a navigable river or canal, or may intersect another railway. Engineering considerations of absolute cost of operation now no longer predominate. Relative costs by rival lines enter into the case. Water lines or more direct railways compete for the traffic. One cannot even fall back upon the cost of carriage by any of these lines, either the weaker or the stronger. An entirely new principle comes into play. The alternative is presented of taking the business at a rate lower than, and out of line with, rates on general traffic, rather than to lose it to another line. At first sight it would appear that it were better to abandon the traffic than to take it for less than a fair average return or profit. This is a serious matter. The tonnage offered is large. The existence of active competition for it, is proof of its importance. Railways meet at large towns, and large towns become larger because the roads meet there. The main reason for not abandoning the traffic, however, arises from that primary fact, to which one constantly recurs, that all expenses are not alike in their nature. A concrete example will make this plain.

Suppose, for instance, the normal rate to yield a fair average return, all expenses considered, be thirty cents per hundredweight. Two-thirds of the cost of this, or twenty cents, would not cease as outgo, were this business abandoned. The rails would rust, the ties would rot, and trains would move but with lighter loads, and the fixed charges would still go on inexorably night and day. Ten cents per hundredweight will meet the variable and extra cost incident to this particular business. A fifteen-cent rate would at least repay these extra outlays. It would do more. It would contribute five cents per hundred pounds to the twenty cents outgo per hundredweight, which, without the traffic, would have to be borne *in toto*. Even a rate of eleven cents would contribute something to this end. For it would leave a surplus of one cent per hundredweight to lighten the other burden. Adopting Hadley's phraseology,[1] if you take at eleven cents, freight that costs you thirty cents to handle, you lose nineteen cents on every hundredweight. If you refuse to take it at that rate, you lose twenty cents on every hundredweight you do *not* carry. For your constant expenses go on, while the other road gets the business. There is only one course open. The rate at the competitive point must be cut; if not to make a profit, at least to stop a greater loss. And one comfort may be uncovered in so doing. The lowered rate may so stimulate new business and enlarge the volume of traffic, that it may be handled at much lower cost. In fact, this consideration alone in absence of all competition, may induce a lowering of rates at certain points out of line with the general schedule. This incentive, conditioned by the fact of increasing returns, is always in the background. The destiny of many places is manifested in terms beyond the control of the carrier. Soil may be poor, climate or population adverse to progress. But some particular places enjoy peculiar advantages for growth. Not to stimulate new business at these points where traffic might be cultivated, even without rivals in the field, is little better than allowing it to escape over a competitor's line of rails, were they present.

Cutting the normal rate at competitive points or at important points in order to stimulate traffic, in conformity with the principle above stated, transforms our tariff diagram as

[1] P. 165, *infra*.

shown herewith. The rate rises steadily with the increasing distance from A, except at E and F. At these points it is fixed at a lower point, determined not primarily by the cost of service at all, but by the available demand for it. Traffic at these points is charged what it will bear; not as much but as little as it will bear: which, being translated, means that the charge is set as high as possible, still holding the volume of business constant, or even increasing it if that can be accomplished. The total profit is constituted of the profit per unit of freight multiplied into its volume. The centre of interest is here

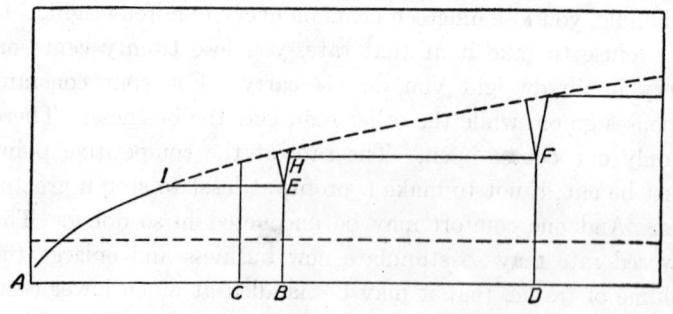

Effect of Competition at Certain Places on Rates.

shifted from the average profit per unit considered alone, to the total profit thus obtained. At this point another difficulty presents itself. Although, as set forth elsewhere, local discrimination, — charging a lower rate for a more distant point, — may sometimes not only be not injurious but actually beneficial to all parties concerned, it is the exception, not the rule.[1] Ordinarily to accord a remote point a lower rate without patent cause, is an economic anomaly, and, moreover, a political blunder. It violates the democratic principle of cost of service as underlying rate schedules. Most legislative bodies have prohibited it by law. The United States and most of the American commonwealths do not permit it, other than in ex-

[1] *Cf.* chap. VII, *infra.*

ceptional cases. The result is that on our hypothetical tariff, the rates from A to points intermediate between A and B and B and D must be cut to the levels, E and F, fixed for those latter places. Such was the action taken by the trunk lines in 1887 in conformity with the requirements of the long and short haul clause of the Federal Act to Regulate Commerce. An original progressively rising tariff is thus at once transformed to a series of level grades or platforms, the shifts of level corresponding to the location of large towns or competitive centres; and the grade of each platform being fixed by the rate determined under competition at those points.[1] This ascending series of grades may be most irregular, as conditioned by local circumstances. The general steepness of the gradation is low on eastern roads like the New York Central, with a large volume of traffic and easy operating conditions. On western lines like the Denver and Rio Grande, in rugged territory, with a sparse population and light tonnage, the per mile rate rises rapidly and the gradation of the general tariff is steep. But always it will be found that the changes in rates occur at competitive points, with transition to a new level of rates determined by the conditions at the next competitive point beyond.

An important fact concerning this tariff thus far developed, is that, of course, the height of the upper level at the most remote point must never exceed what the particular traffic will bear. In other words, supposing that the traffic consist of grain or coal, not more than a certain amount could ever be charged, no matter how great the distance, without so far diminishing the profit in the transaction as to render the business impossible. This is shown by the diagram opposite the next page, whereon it appears that each commodity, coal, wheat, cement, lumber, or oil, having attained a certain level of rates, never rises thereafter, no matter what the distance. Each attains the maxi-

[1] Such a tariff on the Illinois Central is charted in Reports, U. S. Industrial Commission, IX, p. 295.

mum of what it will bear. That level it can never exceed. This immediately leads to another consideration. No single tariff is applicable to any large number of commodities. Each one must be regarded as a law unto itself. Not only does the ultimate amount which each is able to bear depend upon the value of that commodity, but also the conditions determining competition with respect to it must be different all along the line.[1]

Thus it appears that the height of the extreme upper level in our diagrammatic series of rates is fixed by the highest charge which that particular traffic will bear.[2] Beyond a certain point, no matter how great the distance, the rate cannot be increased above this level. This maximum varies, of course, with each commodity. On cotton it may be fifty-five cents per one hundred pounds; on grain or coal it will be much lower, and on sand or cement lower still. The problem of the traffic manager is to attain this highest rate as speedily as possible with increasing distance, and to grade his rates with distance up to this level as quickly as possible, consistent, of course, with maintenance of a full volume of business. But not only may the final limit of what the traffic will bear be different for each commodity; the steps or stages by which the rate progresses up to this maximum, are quite independently determined. The actual tariffs of local class rates in general are much simpler than the commercial conditions of rate making often warrant. Probably the major portion of tonnage on American railways moves under special or commodity rates. Even in Prussia over three-fifths of the traffic is of this exceptional sort. These special rates are made with a view to particular circumstances prevalent at the time. Bids from a quarryman in Vermont on stone for a public building in Chicago, may be dependent upon

---

[1] Such are commodity as distinct from class rates, described in connection with classification in chap. IX.

[2] Tapering rates are discussed by J. M. Clark in Columbia University Studies in History, etc., XXXVII, 1910, chaps. IX and X. *Cf.* also Hammond, Railway Rate Theories, etc., 1911, p. 70.

RATE MAKING PRACTICE

the grant of a low rate on his marble in competition with a quarry in North Carolina, also able to supply the particular stone required. The various ascending series of rates are thus rendered bewilderingly complex. This is also shown by the foregoing diagram of rates between St. Paul and Chicago.[1] The rate on a cheap, heavy commodity like coal, probably rises rapidly at first, and soon attains a maximum beyond which it can never go. On this diagram, for instance, the freight rate on soft coal for points up to 180 miles out is higher than that on flour. Beyond that point the flour rate in turn exceeds that on coal. Cement is higher than lumber for the first 150 miles; but after that point the relatively greater value of lumber holds it steadily above cement. On heavy cheap commodities the relatively high cost of cartage in competition enables the railway to reap the full measure of its advantage and to charge well up to the maximum of what the traffic will bear, within a comfortably short distance. Furthermore, variable costs for terminal charges have to be considered. Wherever they are high the rate must rise at once sufficiently to cover these, no matter how short the distance; but thereafter the rate may not need to be increased greatly for some time. On light higher-grade goods the wagon is an effective competitor for longer distances.[2] Moreover, the competitive points at which rates rise from stage to stage are seldom the same for all classes of goods. A river crossing brings competition for coal, lime, or cement, but does not affect the rates chargeable on high-class freight which seldom goes by water in any event. A railway specially interested in the development of some particular industry, wherever it crosses our hypothetical line, effectively holds down the rate on the product of that business. Junction points with other railways having no such interest may have no influence upon that rate, but may cause modifications in other directions. Another rail-

[1] From A. B. Stickney, Railroad Problems, p. 69.
[2] *Cf.* note on p. 375.

way being in need of back loads over its line, as the result of a predominant movement, let us say, of beef cattle at certain seasons of the year, may introduce competition in all the tonnage capable of being carried on cattle cars. Such a road holds down the rates on this traffic wherever it happens to cross, but has no effect upon any other rate. Thus it comes about in practice, as the last diagram well illustrates, that the tariff lines cross and recross one another, generally rising with increasing distance, but at all sorts of different times and places.

Few generalizations are possible in this connection. Rate making must in a growing country ever be a matter of infinite detail. It is generally true, however, that beyond a certain point the tariff on different grades of commodities will separate more and more widely with increasing distance. For, obviously, after the low-grade goods have reached the maximum which they can bear — and this they tend to do speedily — they must remain practically constant; while those of higher grade continue progressively rising. And for very short distances the rate on the low-grade goods may even exceed that imposed upon higher-class tonnage. The coal rate for a ten-mile haul may exceed that upon some commodity worth twice as much; but for a 200-mile haul the coal rate may be only one-eighth of the rate on the other goods. Long experience on the part of the carriers has, however, enabled them to arrange their tonnage in classes; for each of which the conditions are more or less uniform. By reserving the exceptional traffic for special treatment under commodity rates, a fairly consistent scheme of charges, rising by stages with increasing distance may be evolved.

Few standard railway tariffs in the United States develop beyond the point covered by the preceding paragraph. Many of them are unable even to reach this stage of logical growth. In the South, for instance, they have never got beyond the stage of progressively rising local rates, with independent and often radically reduced charges at all large towns or competitive points.[1] Each traffic manager, particularly since the effective prohibition of working agreements between competing lines by the Trans-Missouri Freight Association decision of the Supreme Court in 1896, has been left to work out his own salvation, not aided by, but in spite of, the efforts of his rivals. There is, nevertheless, one example of further development in the so-called trunk line territory, lying east of the Mississippi and north of the Ohio and Potomac rivers. Conditions here, in general, are most favorable by comparison with the West and South. Both population and traffic are dense, and the state legislatures are conservative in making grants for the construction of new lines. The companies are historically mature. The good fruits of coöperation had already appeared in the evolution of a scientific and logical scheme, long before such coöperative action had been frowned upon by the law and the courts. All the railways in trunk line territory have worked in harmony, so far as general classified local tariffs are concerned — however much they may have fought one another over differentials to seaboard cities, or export and import rates. Their system is comparatively simple in principle, although it has required the experience of many years to work out in detail. Fully described elsewhere,[2] it will suffice for present purposes to say that all rates from intermediate points between Chicago and New York, are fixed at a definite proportion of the Chicago-New York rate both for east- and westbound shipments. Thus, for instance, as shown by the map of trunk line rate distribution, at page 365, the rate from Detroit to New York is seventy-two per cent. of the Chicago-New York rate. The percentages from the following points are as indicated, namely: Cincinnati, eighty-seven per cent.; Indianapolis, ninety-three per cent.; Grand Rapids, ninety-six per cent.; Peoria, Ill., one hundred and ten per cent.; Louisville, Ky., one hundred per cent.; Milwaukee, one hundred per cent.; and even points in Canada, such as

[1] P. 380, infra.   [2] Chapter X, p. 360, infra.

Toronto, seventy-eight per cent., etc. Every place, no matter how small, has a certain percentage of the New York-Chicago rate assigned to it. This rate changes with any variation of the standard or basic charge. Thus when the Chicago-New York rate, first-class, is seventy-five cents, the rate from Indianapolis is ninety-three per cent. of that figure. Any change of Chicago-New York first-class rates modifies every intermediate rate in exactly the same proportion. This was well exemplified in the rate wars of 1893. These percentages have been fixed after a long process of compromise among conflicting interests. Another point of special interest is that these rates are adjusted on the basis strictly of the long and short haul principle, namely, that all intermediate points enjoy a somewhat lower rate than the terminal points, although the percentage may not be exactly upon a mileage basis. Consideration of the distribution of these percentages points to many apparent inequalities in the adjustment; but, as a matter of fact, it will be found that the existence of competing routes, of water transportation or of other factors, offers a partial explanation in most instances.

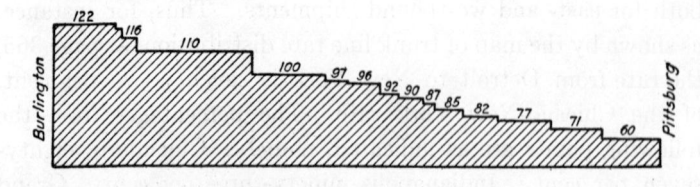

Such being the general character of this comprehensive trunk line system, the relation of it to the tariffs described heretofore is not difficult to demonstrate. Each separate railway having developed a well-ordered rate schedule, they have all met and agreed upon a unified scheme; which as far as possible harmonizes all conflicting interests. The gradation of rates rising with increasing distance from New York on each separate road, is adjusted to the corresponding gradation of rates of its neighbors on either side. The result is a series of rate zones, lying more or less concentrically about the terminal point. These zones are highly irregular in width and area, but possess one feature in common. Each remoter zone is one stage higher in rates than its predecessor. This relationship is indicated by the cross section diagram herewith. This cross section, of course, differs from the diagrams heretofore shown. It is purely geographical, being taken, not along one single railway but as the crow flies — straight across the whole trunk line territory. But in order to appreciate the significance of this elaborate scheme, one should imagine a whole series of such progressively rising rates, radiating out along the different lines of railway. Connecting the corresponding levels or stages upon each one with those of its neighbors, the concentric zones are immediately outlined. The advantage of such a broad scheme is that it generalizes the single line tariff; taking into view every place, no matter how small and irrespective of its location whether upon a through line or merely a local transverse one. Every town, no matter how insignificant, is assigned a place in a logically evolved plan. Such would seem to be the ideal of rate construction, toward which all traffic managers should strive.

The foregoing description of the development of a mileage tariff is applicable to only a part of the traffic. A very large volume of tonnage, — said to be not less than seventy-five per cent. in America, sixty-three per cent. in Prussia and fifty per cent. in the United Kingdom, — moves under special rates made in quite another way in response to the exigencies of commercial competition. The making of these freight rates in practice is an extremely complicated matter. No single road is independent of rates made by its rivals — rates applicable not only to competing commodities and markets, but also as affected by apparently the most remote and disconnected contingencies. Thus railway rates, as has well been said, are not a set of independent threads; they form a fabric. They are

VOL. I—8

so interwoven everywhere that if one thread be shortened, it will cause a kink in the fabric that may run almost anywhere. In order to understand this it will be necessary to describe somewhat in detail the nature of competition as applied to transportation; and then to show by a few concrete illustrations, the various factors which actively enter into the determination of specific rates. Laymen and legislators do not sufficiently appreciate the extremely delicate nature of the work. Much discussion relative to railway competition seems to be based upon the assumption that it consists in the main of the competition of railway lines more or less parallel or else operating under substantially like conditions. As a matter of fact competition in transportation is to a large degree far more complex.

Railway competition is of three entirely distinct sorts. These may be denominated, respectively, competition of routes, competition in facilities and competition of markets.[1] The first of these, competition of routes, as the name suggests, is limited to the activities of the carriers alone. It occurs whenever two railways are exposed to identical commercial conditions both at the point of origin and of destination. The rivalry is direct and physical. The only competition possible is that concerning the route by which traffic may move between those two points. Such competition is most likely to arise between more or less parallel lines, as for instance between the various trunk roads from New York to Chicago. The classic instances in our history are of the rate wars due to the West Shore and the Nickel Plate, which were built for the express purpose of engendering competition with the then existing lines,— the New York Central and the Lake Shore, respectively. The same sort of simple competition prevails, of course, between a railway and a parallel canal or other waterway,

[1] The voluminous record in *U. S.* v. *Union Pacific*, etc. (The Merger case), U. S. Supreme Court, October term, 1911, No. 820 abounds in concrete illustrations of all three. *Cf.* esp. Appellant's Brief of Facts, p. 34.

as, for instance, between the Erie canal and the trunk lines, or the Illinois Central and the Mississippi river. Such simple competition as this, where confined to railways alone, almost inevitably leads to one of two results: the roads may remain independent, preventing ruinous rate wars by pooling; or else, as a result of long continued cut-throat competition, the bankrupt road may be bought up and merged with the solvent one. This was the fate of the old New York and New England railway, finally purchased by the New Haven system; of the West Shore and Nickel Plate lines; and of the Kansas Pacific, unloaded on the Union Pacific by Jay Gould. The nature of railway competition is indeed such that no other result than consolidation or pooling can ensue. Weyl is right in his observation that, — "Strictly speaking, permanent competition can exist, not between railroads struggling for the same traffic; but solely between those railroads which have no territory in common."

This first form of competition of routes or, as it has been called, of alternative routes, often obtains where conditions of competition are more obscure than in these simple instances above named. In the rivalry for the imported plate glass or crockery traffic between the trunk lines and the Gulf roads, the competition is none the less of routes between Liverpool and Chicago, although the water carriage by way of New Orleans or Galveston is so much more roundabout. Freight actually moves from Boston to Chicago by a line 1786 miles long, *via* Asheville, N. C., while the direct distance is only 1004 miles.[1] From St. Louis to Meridian, Miss., is 512 miles by direct rail line; yet traffic may move over 2000 miles going to New York and then around.[2] The map on p. 271, showing the various rail and water lines concerned in traffic between New York and the little town of Troy, Ala., shows how widespread are the ramifications of competition of this sort. Mani-

[1] Senate (Elkins) Committee, 1905, Digest, App. II, p. 10.
[2] Cincinnati Freight Bureau case, 1910, p. 447.

fold instances of such roundabout carriage have been elsewhere described in full.[1] They differ from the competition of parallel routes, however, in the important regard that absorption of the long lines by the short ones becomes both physically and financially impossible. Whenever a large area like the Pacific slope is devoid of manufactures, and wherever the source of supplies is sufficiently concentrated, as, for instance, in the manufacture of agricultural implements which are almost exclusively made in or about Chicago, we still have to do with a clear case of competition of routes, although a great number of carriers may participate in the business. When molasses or rice are only to be had from New Orleans, the centre of such business, the carriers to all tributary consuming points compete for the routing of it over their own respective lines. These carriers may operate either by land or sea or by a combination of both; and they may transport commodities by the most roundabout ways.[2] The determinant feature, however, distinguishing this class of competition is neither the mode or carriage nor its length; but is found in the fact that the commercial conditions at both ends of the line, points of origin and destination, are identical for each participant in the business. Direct competition of routes, therefore, has to do with pure transportation, — the creation of place values, — and this being the case, the relative cost of service is always a factor of moment.

Competition of facilities, the second of the three phases of railway competition above mentioned, deals, as its name implies, not at all with the rates charged but with the facilities or conveniences afforded. Such competition is confined solely to rivalry for business at the established rates. Immediately on the appearance of any departure from these conditions the

[1] Chapter VIII, *infra*. *Cf*. also p. 255. Which line has the advantage?
[2] Albert Fink's detailed description of the numberless alternative routes by which traffic moved into the South, is perhaps one of the best instances in print. U. S. Reports Internal Commerce, 1876, App. pp. 1–16. The Danville, Va., case is an admirable instance. 8 Int. Com. Rep., 409; reprinted in Railway Problems, chap. XVI.

question becomes one of competition of either of the other two sorts. An instance of competition of facilities would be the introduction of reclining chairs or of a superior service in passenger business. When the Rock Island system offered such facilities without an extra charge, it became necessary at once for others to meet this competition in the same way that they would meet a reduction of rates. Any reduction in time of transit for freight business between two given points without extra charge, would in the same manner give rise to competition of facilities. Such facilities, however, as might have a distinct money value, as, for instance, free storage, cartage, demurrage or milling-in-transit, any one of which practically amounts to giving value without charge, are, of course, equivalent to a reduction of the rate; and do not belong in this class of considerations at all. Only those conveniences or facilities, which, while attempting to secure business may not be compounded for money, should be classified in this group. It should also be observed that competition of facilities may as readily arise between parts of the same railway system or under pooling agreements to maintain rates, as between distinct and independent companies.[1] And such competition between parent and child often arises. Thus, for instance, business was as actively solicited as ever by the Pennsylvania and the Baltimore & Ohio in competition during the several years of financial control of one by the other prior to 1907. The New Haven railway may compete with its own water lines around Cape Cod or on Long Island Sound. But in all of these instances the cardinal feature to note is that the competition is always at the established rate. For New England, although the New Haven system and the Boston and Maine do not compete on rates at their points of contact, there is constant rivalry in respect of facilities or service. The same thing is undoubtedly true of the

[1] A notable instance between the Southern and Union Pacific roads since their combination. *Cf.* Appellant's Brief of Facts, *U. S.* v. *U. P.*, etc., Supreme Court, Oct. term, 1911, No. 820, p. 34 *et seq.*

Atchison and the Southern Pacific in the carriage of California fruits. Although operated under pooling agreements, yet they were competitors in the matter of the service offered. Each sought an enlarged volume of tonnage, but not by cutting the agreed rate.

The third form of competition in transportation is dependent upon the competition of markets; and is not in reality direct competition between carriers at all. This is the most difficult of all forms to understand.[1] It is certainly in many cases more than a "euphemism for railway policy."[2] Yet although indirect and often obscure, it is of fundamental and conclusive importance in the determination of freight rates. Commercial competition deals not with a mere choice of routes, but with alternative markets. The carriers act, not independently and of their own volition, but only as agents or representatives for their constituents, the shippers. They may become tools or weapons in the hands of merchants or manufacturers who are the real contestants. It is largely in this sense that it is so often alleged, and rightfully, that railway traffic managers oftentimes do not *make* rates at all. Their energies are bent to the analysis of those circumstances by which their rates are made for them.

The production or preparation of commodities for final consumption falls naturally into two distinct parts; the creation of form value, succeeded by the conferring of place value. Transportation is concerned alone with the latter process. Of these two operations, the latter, the creation of place values, is by far the more elastic and adaptable process. The grower, the miner or the manufacturer has his first costs more or less rigidly fixed by natural or human conditions; such as the fertility of the soil, the grade of ore, the prevailing scale of wages,

---

[1] Albert Fink's description in U. S. Reports Internal Commerce, 1876, App. p. 38, is a classic.
[2] *Cf.* p. 621, *infra*. Also the dialogue in 21 I.C.C. Rep., 356–359; and *Ibid.*, 414.

and so on. His proximity to the status of a marginal producer depends upon his relative position in these respects. With the carrier, matters are more contingent. Including within its reach, as it does, many grades of producers and consumers, each more or less rigidly held bound by his own circumstances and conditions, as above said, the carrier is able to exercise a wide range of choice in fixing that margin of value created which it reserves for itself. And at all times, by reason of the factors set forth elsewhere, primarily its subjection to the law of increasing returns, this intermediate share of the carrier tends to adjust or accommodate itself to the end that it may discover or produce a wider margin between values in the hands of producer and consumer, respectively. This may be best accomplished by a progressive widening of its field of activities, that is to say, by an enlargement of its physical reach and scope. It is always striving to lower the cost of production made by the marginal producer. Its motto must ever be, to get more business, if not right at home by search for it abroad — and this always with the chance that the greater the distance between the producer and the consumer, the greater the possible margin of place value remaining as its individual share.

This ever-present incentive to widen the market carries with it a direct consequence. A market is a commercial area characterized by a prevalent equality of prices. Phenomenal development in this respect is characteristic of the United States. For many commodities the market is coextensive with the national domain. It is the chosen function of transportation agents, by rail and water, to ensure this result; to preserve an equality of prices, despite the variety of producing and consuming conditions. The railway is the agent by which the market is thus widened and rivalries are thus equalized. In railway parlance this is what is known as "keeping everyone in business." The following quotation from the Senate Committee Hearings of 1905 adequately describes the process: "I am interested in the erection of a mill that has just been completed, and sometime since I was figuring on the question of a smokestack. I wanted to have that stack built out of brick that is burned in New Jersey, and that is several hundred miles away. It is a long way to ship freight from New Jersey to North Carolina. A quotation was made me by the stack builder, whose office is in New York, and I remarked to him, 'That price is prohibitive; I cannot pay that price for that stack.' He said, 'That is the best I can do; but if you will tell me what you can afford to pay for that stack, in competition with home-burned brick, I will see what I can do with the railway people.' He said,'All right; I will take it up with the railway people.' His quotation included the delivery of the brick and the erection of the stack at my plant. It would require something like about fifty carloads of brick to build that stack. Within a week he had his price revised, and gave me a satisfactory quotation and took my contract for the stack. Of course he had to get a special rate from the railway people, because there is no regular tariff on brick from New Jersey to North Carolina." In this instance the railways actually created this new business by so adjusting the margin between the minimum cost of making brick in New York and in North Carolina, as to make it possible for the traffic to move. The special rate here mentioned, however, should be carefully distinguished from a secret rebate offered to one contractor as against another in the same place. This commodity rate, while special to meet a particular contingency, was open to any other shipper similarly circumstanced. The student cannot too carefully discriminate between these two sorts of special rates. They are constantly confused in the public mind. The effect of these open commodity rates, is not to create difference of opportunity between individuals, but to generalize economic conditions and equalize prices throughout wide areas.

The most satisfactory way to describe commercial competition as applied to carriers is by concrete illustrations. There are two distinct varieties or degrees of it, which may

RATE MAKING PRACTICE

be denominated primary and secondary. These might as properly, perhaps, be called simple and complex, or direct and indirect. Of these, the first concerns those cases wherein a commodity undergoes no physical transformation between producer and consumer. Shipments are usually direct. Only one rate is involved. Shall St. Louis and the South, for example, be supplied with salt from the Kansas or Michigan fields?[1] This is a case of pure transportation, — the creation of place value, alone. The Aroostook farmers of Maine compete in prices with the potato growers of Michigan in the New York market. Each district is usually represented by a railway, dependent upon the prosperity of its particular constituency. Competition of markets is usually more keen where a number of carriers are concerned, each representing its own clients; but it may conceivably arise as between several markets served by the same company, especially with the growth of great railway systems. The Southern Pacific must insure a rate from California on oranges to eastern markets, as compared with the rates over the southern roads from Florida, sufficiently low to warrant the venture of capital in the industry.[2] Marble from the quarries of Vermont and North Carolina, and paving blocks from the Lithonia district in Georgia and from Wisconsin or South Dakota, must meet in Chicago on even terms. Such competition, although simple and direct, recognizes no national bounds. Copper from Montana must be laid down in Liverpool at rates to permit of meeting the price on Chili bars from South America. Our entire grain and cotton crops must be transported at rates which will enable them to hold their own in European markets. The California raisin has, in this manner, had to make its way into Eastern markets in the United States against the pressure of importations from Spain, as described in another place.[3] The cotton mills in New England and in the South must have their output carried to

[1] 5 I.C.C. Rep., 299; or 22 *Idem*, 407.   Reprinted in Railway Problems.
[2] 14 I.C.C. Rep., 476.   [3] P. 178, *infra*.

China under conditions which will enable them to meet the price made by the British manufacturer. This last instance, however, introduces us to the second form of competition; inasmuch as a double transportation is involved first from the fields to the mill, and thereafter from the mill to the consumer.

Secondary or indirect forms of commercial competition in transportation, concerning, as has been said, not one but two distinct carriages of entirely different goods, needs to be in turn subdivided still further. The products of agriculture and mines afford the best instances. The lumber business is peculiarly suggestive in this connection, owing to the fact that in the United States a vast treeless area in the Middle West is surrounded with forest tracts available for development. The market again in this case is limited only by our national frontier. Omaha is supplied with yellow pine and cypress from Louisiana after a 1,200-mile haul; Oregon fir brought 1,800 miles in each instance for fifty cents per hundred pounds; and with Michigan hemlock and pine transported less than 500 miles for eleven and a half cents. These various sorts of lumber are all more or less competitive. And in each case the final cost of laying down the product in Omaha is determined; first, by the rate from the stump to the mill, and then, as sawed lumber, thence on to destination. The Eau Claire, Wisconsin, lumber case [1] before the Interstate Commerce Commission, fully describes the intricacies of adjustment needed to hold a number of such producers on a parity. In this instance Eau Claire, "next the stump," as an important lumbering centre was shown to be declining in importance relatively to Mississippi river towns, which received their logs by raft down stream. A differential of a few cents was threatening the welfare of a considerable population. The Wichita, Kansas, cases are suggestive in a similar way.[2] Sugar is laid down at this market from every point of the compass. From Hawaii

---

[1] 5 I.C.C. Rep., 264; reprinted in our Railway Problems.
[2] Discussed on p. 232, *infra*.

it is shipped in the raw state to San Francisco, and then brought East, like the Oregon lumber, cheaply, as a backload to counterbalance westbound shipments of grain and manufactures. From New Orleans refineries comes the Louisiana product, and from the Atlantic sea ports the Cuban sugar; but in each case the carriage is broken at an intermediate point, at which manufacture or jobbing ensues. A large class of operations analogous to this, known as "milling in transit" and "floating cotton," elsewhere described in detail, involve the same complexity and inter-relation of rates.[1] The point to carry forward is that commerical competition demands that in every case not single rates but the sums of all the interlocked rates for each competing person or region shall be properly adjusted. If this be not done, some one will be excluded from the market and "put out of business."

By this time in our ascending scale of complexities, it will be observed that manufacture now begins to outweigh mere transportation in importance. With low-grade products, like salt or sugar, the increment of value due to transportation is relatively high as compared with manufacturing costs. As the grade of product rises, however, the differences in value and in form between the raw and the finished product, render the problem of location of the manufacture more difficult as affected by the relative adjustment of rates of transportation for the two. According to the data of the Federal Bureau of Corporations, the cost of refining crude petroleum, worth three to four cents a gallon at the wells in Pennsylvania, should not exceed one-half cent a gallon. This sum would barely pay for the first hundred miles of its carriage by rail, as ordinarily shipped. The market is, of course, extraordinarily extensive; hence the persistent flagrancy of the practices of secret rebating by the Standard Oil Co.[2] To obtain such special favors in transportation outweighed in importance the incentive to introduce economies in production. In this in-

[1] Chapter IX.   [2] Details in chap. VI.

dustry, where little waste occurs in manufacture, the refineries may well be located at the consumers' door. The manufacture of furniture for the Pacific states, on the other hand, must be located "next the stump," in North Carolina or New England. The long carriage must be applied, not to the bulky lumber but to the finished product. The freight rate on lumber from Oregon to Pittsburg is just about equal to the value of the logs at the mill. Obviously, the large proportion of waste or common lumber will not bear a high addition to its cost by carriage to any distance. In the manufacture of fur hats a shrinkage of weight occurs of one-half between the fur scraps and the finished product. In such a case it is imperative, either that the factory be near the source of supply or that the rate on the two distinct commodities be nicely adjusted. The decision of the United States Steel Corporation to build a large plant at Duluth for supplying the northwestern market is the outcome of such considerations. The main point is that the adjustment of a number of rates may determine, not only the general welfare of the industry but even its specific geographical location with reference to the raw material on the one side and the market on the other.

The jobbing or wholesale business of the United States exemplifies the most highly involved and complex details of commercial competition.[1] In this field it appears most clearly that, as is so often alleged, railway traffic managers hold the welfare of entire communities, as it were, in the palms of their hands. In all the cases heretofore cited, great natural forces outweighed the purely personal and human ones. Soil, climate and mineral resources more or less completely determined the final outcome

[1] *Cf.* Carload Minimum in chap. IX and the Texas system on p. 393, *infra.*

The following cases best illustrate these principles: Burnham, Hanna, Munger, etc., 14 I.C.C., 299; and 20 *Idem*, 141; later in 218 U. S. Rep., 88. (P. 442, *infra.*) Greater Des Moines Committee, 14 *Idem*, 294. Indianapolis, Kansas City and Fort Dodge, 16 *Idem*, 57, 195, and 572. Warnock, 21 *Idem*, 546 and 23 *Idem*, 195. St. Louis Business Men's League, 9 *Idem*, 318. And the Wichita cases in chap. VII, p. 232, *infra.*

of commercial competition. But the distributive business of a country is more largely artificial. It is more subject to human control, and may be influenced by personal considerations. Shall the economically dependent southern planter be supplied with manufactures of all sorts, — from harnesses to tin dippers — from mid-western cities like Cincinnati and Chicago or from eastern centres, such as New York and Baltimore? This is the underlying economic issue raised in the notable Cincinnati Freight Bureau Case in 1894; in the course of whose determination the Supreme Court of the United States raised the more immediate and pressing question of the authority of the Interstate Commerce Commission to regulate rates at all. In the dust raised by the controversy over this purely legal question, the basic economic dispute was lost to view.[1] Shall the people of the Pacific slope be supplied with hardware and analogous products from their own large cities which buy at wholesale from the East, break bulk at San Francisco or Seattle and ship out to smaller towns in less than carload lots; or shall the distribution take place at the hands of jobbing houses located several thousand miles away at Chicago or St. Louis? This is the economic dispute raised in the St. Louis Business Men's League case.[2] The very existence of San Francisco as a commercial centre may depend upon it. For the primary and secondary operations of commerce are often complementary. At the large cities, concentration of raw staples moving inward naturally entails back loads outward at low rates for manufactured goods distributed by jobbers. Or, taking the smaller places, the farmer will of necessity buy his cotton cloth, sugar and coal in the town to which he drives by wagon to deliver his cotton, corn or wheat.[3]

The entire puzzling class of cases dealing with the southern

[1] Pp. 248, 392, and 588. Both cases are reprinted in our Railway Problems.
[2] Pp. 125, 241, 398. Also in Railway Problems.
[3] I.C.C. Rep., No. 861; decided Aug. 23, 1906.

basing point system are primarily concerned with such issues as these.[1] Three distinct classes of cases arise. There is, first, the competition between cities of equal size, be they large or small, such as Memphis, Tenn., and Little Rock, Ark.; Danville, Va., and Lynchburg; or Cleveland, and Cincinnati, Ohio: secondly, the rivalries between large cities and what may be called secondary local centres in the same part of the country, — such as Seattle, Wash., v. Spokane; Chicago v. Burlington or Dubuque, Iowa; or Atlanta, Ga., v. Macon: and thirdly, the intense rivalries between the great first-class cities, like New York, Philadelphia, and Chicago, and the rest of the field, big and little.[2] The mail order houses, the express business and the parcels post intervene at this point. But in all of these issues, series of no less than three separate transportation costs have to be totalized and kept more or less on a parity. The intricacy is increased by reason of the fact that shipments must be made, first at wholesale to the jobbers, and thereafter usually in less-than-carload lots to retailers. If the carload rate be relatively too low, with reference to the rate on small lots, the jobbers near the market will be upbuilt and the jobbers at a distance cannot compete. If the opposite relation obtains, the jobber in a distant great city will be able to ship out small orders cheaper than the local dealer can obtain them by carload and, breaking bulk, peddle them from his own town. So narrow is the margin of profit on staple goods that a difference of a fraction of a cent per pound may exclude a dealer from the field entirely. This question of carload ratings is, however, treated elsewhere; impinging, as it does upon matters of freight classifications.[3]

The rivalries of jobbers and middlemen in different cities are inevitably borne into the offices of traffic managers. Were all railways equally interested in all cities alike, the matter need not go further, engendering railway rivalries. But such

[1] Chapters VII and XI. [2] Read testimony on p. 278, *infra*.
[3] P. 325, *infra*.

is seldom the case. Hardly a road can be named, whose interests are not more or less identified with some particular city. Commercial rivalry thus at once leads to railway competition. Four or five railways, like the Chicago and Northwestern, radiate out to the west from Chicago, and have no interest in St. Louis. Almost as many, like the Missouri Pacific, go out from St. Louis without entering Chicago. Others, like the old Union Pacific and, formerly, the Atchison system, only come to the Missouri river, and consequently wish to upbuild their eastern termini, Omaha or Kansas City. Only a few, like the Illinois Central, reach them all. Such a road is usually called upon to act as a mediator in all disputes. "It is a continual struggle between the line from Kansas City to St. Louis with no interest in Chicago, and the line from Kansas City to Chicago with no interest in St. Louis," as one witness before the Industrial Commission phrases it. Compromise is the only outcome. And in this manner an involved structure of differentials is built up, oftentimes top heavy and always susceptible of collapse on the defection of any party to the agreement. When a truce was patched up between the trunk lines and the Gulf roads after the sugar rate war of 1905, it is said to have taken twenty experts three entire days merely to "line up" rates on a parity between the competing jobbing centres.

The simplest compromise in any dispute over rates between competing centres is the concession of absolute equality or, as it is called, of flat rates between all points irrespective of distance. This shifts the burden from the carriers and places competition entirely upon the shoulders of the merchants. Oddly enough, also, this result of equal rates regardless of distance between various competing centres, especially when they are secondary distributing or concentrating points rather than original sources of traffic, may sometimes evolve naturally out of commercial conditions imposed by tariffs built up upon the basis of distance. The accompanying theoretical diagram, based upon actual traffic conditions prevalent in Missouri river territory, serves to illustrate the way in which, under certain circumstances, such equalization of rates may take place. Two groups of cities are here represented as though lying respectively along two river valleys north of their separation at a point G. Let us call them the Mississippi and the Missouri for purposes of identification. The starting point is equality of rates from such a distant point as New York (O) to all places along the Mississippi from A to G. Such equality properly

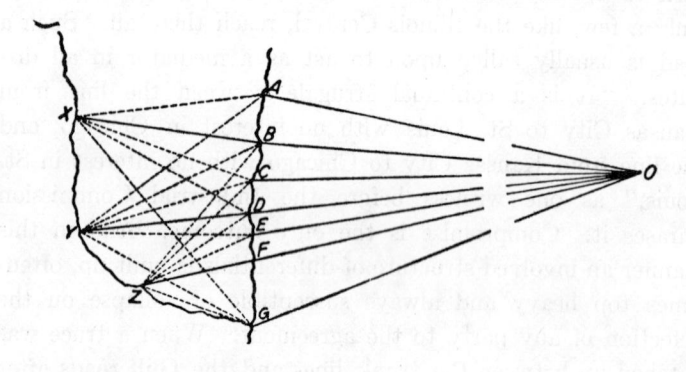

arises in theory from the substantially equal distance from New York. In practice also, under the trunk line rate system,[1] such equality prevails, inasmuch as the rates from New York to such a series of Mississippi river crossings is fixed at 125 per cent. of the rate from New York to Chicago. By a similar course of reasoning, namely, the approximately equal distance from New York (O), rates from that place to a second series of points along the Missouri river should be and are in effect made equal. From these two facts it logically follows that the balances of the rates from all points on the Mississippi river out along an extension of their lines from New York toward the west should also be equal. This is obviously in conformity with the mathematical principle that equals subtracted from

[1] Described in chap. X.

equals leave equal balances. Thus the rates B X, D Y and F Z are compelled to equality. From this relationship in turn follows still another. All rates from any point on the inner series of towns to any point whatsoever on the outer western series of places along the Missouri river must remain equal regardless of distance. For each line from New York to A, B, C, D, etc., wishes, of course, to participate in business not only on the direct extension of its own line, but to as many other points as possible.[1] Without some agreement, however, it would normally enjoy traffic only on the direct extension of its own line. The point Y would most naturally be reached by way of C, D or E, over the shortest routes. Competitors on either side would similarly enjoy an advantage in more direct lines from New York to the places immediately beyond them. Thus for business from New York to Z, the more direct lines through E, F or G would obviously have an advantage over lines which passed around through A, B, C or D. An almost irresistible incentive to cut-throat competition would exist. The only way the lines east of the inner circle can peaceably partition business to the outermost western points is by an agreement to make *all* rates between the inner and outer circles the same. In this manner the rates from A to Z or from G to X are reduced to an equality with the rates offered by the shortest route between the two rivers, which, in this case, is E Z. The rate for this shortest line then becomes the basic one, upon which all the others depend.

The foregoing economic reasoning underlies the actual tariff system prevailing in what is known as Missouri river territory.[2] Two great streams separating at St. Louis form the eastern and western boundaries of Missouri and Iowa. All along the two edges of these states are located important river

[1] Procedure is described at p. 282, *infra*.
[2] Admirably described in *Annals Amer. Acad. Pol. Science*, April 11, 1908; reprinted in our Railway Problems, rev. ed.

cities, each of which has more or less direct communication with every other crossing on the other river, over a complicated system of interlaced lines. There are no physical barriers, the country being plain and open. The starting point and basis of the whole scheme is the shortest direct distance between the two nearest points, namely Hannibal on the Mississippi, and St. Joseph and Kansas City on the Missouri. The situation is shown by the map herewith. At these points

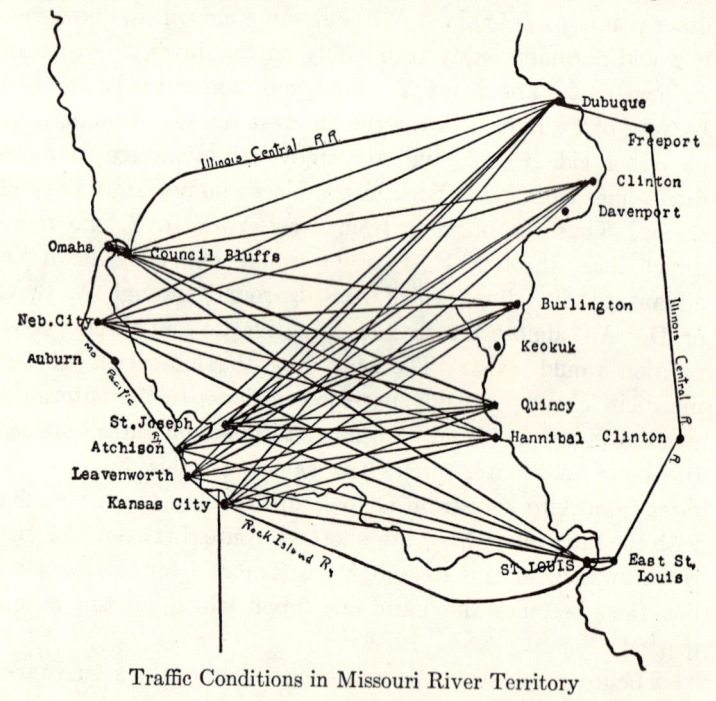

Traffic Conditions in Missouri River Territory

the two rivers are approximately two hundred miles apart. For this distance the base rate of sixty cents per hundred pounds, first class, is fixed by common agreement. Were local business only to be considered, and were the railways not competing, the rate between other points on the two rivers at greater distances apart, such as for instance, Burlington on the Mississippi and Omaha on the Missouri, might be determined on a relative distance basis, as in trunk line territory. But the commercial fact is that a large proportion of the business between all these points consists of long-distance traffic from the eastern seaboard which may cross the Mississippi at any one of these gateways between Dubuque and St. Louis on its way to the cities on the Missouri river. All of these through long-distance shipments must, of course, enjoy the same competitive rate to the ultimate western destination on the Missouri river. And, inasmuch as the rate from the east to the Mississippi crossings is everywhere the same, namely 125 per cent. of the New York-Chicago rate, it follows that the balance of the rate from these points on to the Missouri river across Iowa and Missouri, irrespective of distance, must likewise be the same. In other words, the rates between all these Mississippi and Missouri river points must be equalized, irrespective of the length of the intervening route, whether it be two hundred miles by the shortest direct line from Hannibal to Kansas City across Missouri, three hundred and fifty miles from Burlington to Omaha across Iowa, or even seven hundred miles by the roundabout line of the Illinois Central skirting both states. In brief, every railway which touches both rivers, however circuitous its route, is compelled to quote the same rate from every point on the Mississippi river to every other point on the Missouri. This rate must be the one fixed, as already described, for the shortest direct line, namely sixty cents per hundred pounds first class. Furthermore, in precisely the same way that these rates to Missouri river points from the eastern seaboard are built up and equalized, the rates from Chicago to the same Missouri river points must be kept even. The rate through from any one of the long chain of Mississippi gateways must be the same irrespective of distance. This figure, by common agreement, has for many years been twenty cents per hundred pounds higher than the rate across Illinois to the Mississippi river gateways from Chicago alone. The dominant note of this whole tariff is equalization of rates between all points in competition with one another over all possible routes. Freight thus moves freely in every direction and all markets are held on an absolute parity.[1] It is one of the most remarkable features of American commercial organization, this practical elimination of the element of distance from interstate trade over wide areas.

The possible evil lurking in too widespread an acceptance of the principle of the flat rate is clearly apparent in the reasoning of the Eau Claire, Wisconsin, lumber case.[2] This town complained of the disability under which it labored in shipping lumber to Missouri river points by comparison with other places round about. It appeared in the evidence that as early as 1884, under arbitration, all the rates from competing centres had been adjusted on the basis of differentials; and that, as interpreted by the carriers, the purpose of these differentials was to even up the differences between competing towns; to the end that all manufacturers should be put upon an equality in the consuming territory. But this necessarily involved the practice of penalizing or nullifying in a way the advantages of location. "If Eau Claire could produce lumber cheaper than Winona or La Crosse, then the latter points were to have a lower rate in order to enable them to compete." This practice the Interstate Commerce Commission condemned at that time; and it has consistently adhered to the precedent then laid down. Obviously, any other general course of action would be analogous to hobbling the fleetest horse in a race to bring him down to the rate of progress of the slowest laggard. The principle of the handicap applied within moderate limits makes for an exciting athletic contest; but if it be overdone, it eliminates all interest from the contest whatever. The race becomes one, not of skill or endurance in running, but of securing a sufficiently liberal handicap. Competition to

[1] Similarly in the South, p. 246; and also Texas rates on p. 393.
[2] 5 I.C.C. Rep., 264; reprinted in Railway Problems, chap. VIII.

be of advantage in the way of progress must always have in view the survival of the fittest and the elimination of the unfit.

The vast extent of the United States, the necessity of transporting commodities great distances at low cost and the progressiveness of railway managers, has led to an extraordinary development of the phase of rate making above-mentioned. The principle of the flat rate, based upon the theory that distance is a quite subordinate, if not indeed entirely negligible, element in the construction of freight tariffs under circumstances of competition, was fully accepted twenty-five years ago.[1] J. C. Stubbs, traffic manager of the Harriman lines, speaking of transcontinental business in 1898, clearly expressed it as "the traditional policy of the American lines as between themselves to recognize and to practise equality of rates as the only reasonable and just rule ... regardless of the characteristics of their respective lines, whether equal in length or widely different." It is the theory upon which the southern basing-point system is founded; and it is the common practice in making rates into and out of New England — being in fact vital to the continued prosperity of this out-of-the-way territory.[2] President Tuttle, of the Boston & Maine, has most ably supported this principle of equality of rates irrespective of distance. "It is the duty of transportation agents," he says, "to so adjust their freight tariffs that, regardless of distance, producers and consumers in every part of this country shall, to the fullest extent possible, have equal access to the markets of all parts of this country and of the world, a result wholly impossible of attainment if freight rates must be constructed upon the scientific principle of tons and miles." This is the principle of the blanket rate attacked in the famous

[1] Theoretical explanation of the flat rate is offered in Chapters I and X.

[2] Best described in McPherson, Railroad Freight Rates, 1909, pp. 67-70. The bitter opposition by New England senators in 1910 to amendment of the long and short haul clause is thus explained.

Milk Producers' Protective Association case in 1897;[1] and it is the practice which has been so fully discussed of late, as generally applied to lumber rates from the various forest regions of the United States into the treeless tract of the Middle West. The principle, while applied thus generally in the construction of tariffs, is of far greater applicability in the making of special or commodity rates. Wool rates afford one of the best examples. Under such rates the bulk of the tonnage of American railways is at present moved. The essential principle of such special rates, constituting exceptions to the classified tariffs, is that of the flat rate; namely, a rate fixed in accordance with what the traffic will bear, without regard to the element of cost, that is to say, of distance. But a noticeable trend away from the flat rate is evident in recent decisions of the Interstate Commerce Commission; especially in the Intermountain case,[2] revision of the wool and cattle rates,[3] and the general disposition to lessen special tariffs all along the line.

The intricacy of freight rate adjustment in response to the subtleties of commercial competition depends only in small measure upon the absolute freight rate imposed. The main problem is really that of relativity. But this does not mean mere relativity as between directly competing commodities or places. A strict relativity based upon commercial conditions must often obtain as well between the rates on raw materials and their own finished products; between all the various by-products in an industry; and, of course, always as between goods capable of substitution one for another. A few illustrations will serve to make these details clear.

The matter of properly correlating the freight rate on raw materials and the finished products made from them, is more far-reaching than it seems. The location and development of manufacturing depends upon it. The country may be

[1] 7 I.C.C. Rep., 92. [2] P. 610, *infra*.
[3] 23 I.C.C. Rep., 151 and 657. Also *ibid.*, 404.

broadly divided into agricultural and manufacturing sections. The first of these is ambitious to develop its resources; not only to feed, but to clothe itself and make other provision for its needs. No sooner does it seek to develop local manufacturing than it finds itself exposed to competition from the older established manufacturers at a distance. Sometimes, even, these remote manufacturers draw their supplies of raw material from its own fields and forests. These supplies are then shipped long distances as raw material; manufactured and thereafter returned to sell in competition with the local product. The local market in relatively undeveloped areas is probably insufficient to provide support for manufactures on a profitable scale. It is essential to dispose of the surplus product over a wider area. Thus there arise two classes of manufacturers: one "next the stump," manufacturing at the source of the raw material and desiring to ship the finished product; the other, remote perhaps from supplies of raw material, but favored by long experience, by abundant supplies of capital and of skilled labor and by other advantages.[1] Neither class of producers can prosper without overflowing into the domain of the other. The outcome of this competition depends in part upon the policy of the carriers. If the rate on the raw material be relatively low, the remote manufacturer is aided. Cotton mills and shoe factories in New England prosper in competition with establishments in the South or the Middle West. If, on the other hand, the rate on raw materials be inordinately high, while at the same time low on outward-bound shipment of manufactures from the seat of the raw materials, the tendency is in favor of the upbuilding of manufactures, not near the historic centres of population and consumption, but near the sources of natural wealth, which are the potential homes of manufacturing.

The long-standing controversy over relative rates on wheat and flour for export affords an interesting illustration of the dif-

[1] *Vide* chapter on Localization of Industry in the Twelfth Census of Manufactures, I, pp. 190–214.

ficulties of properly correlating charges of this sort.[1] Originally the rates on wheat and flour — the raw material and the manufactured product — were the same. In 1890 the railways leading to the Gulf ports began to discriminate by giving lower rates on wheat, but the trunk lines until 1899 held to the original equality between the two. Finally, however, the struggle between the trunk lines and the Gulf roads for business forced the former to lower their rates on wheat, leaving the flour rates — not subject to Gulf competition — undisturbed. At times the rate on wheat for export was as much as nine cents per hundred pounds lower than the rate on flour. Thus the rate on wheat for export from the Mississippi river to the seaboard was frequently twelve cents, while the rate on wheat from the same points to Chicago added to the rate on flour there manufactured and sent on in barrels or bags to New York, was twenty-two cents — a clear discrimination against the domestic manufacturer in this instance of ten cents per hundred pounds. For his American-made flour, sent abroad in competition with flour made in Liverpool from American wheat, would evidently cost that much more at delivery. In other words, wheat could be transported to England and there ground much cheaper than it could be ground here and then shipped. This bore with particular severity upon small millers, partly because their costs of manufacture were relatively high, and also because any limitation of export business forced the large millers to bid more keenly for local domestic trade. Inasmuch as a fair margin of profit to the American manufacturer would not exceed two cents per hundredweight, it is apparent that this discrimination operated severely against the American miller. Minneapolis fortunately was unaffected by this discrimination, much of its exports going out by Canadian lines

[1] Int. Com. Rep., 214; reprinted in Railway Problems. A typical later one is 15 I.C.C. Rep., 351 and Opin. 817, 1909, p. 363. Also Ann. Rep., I.C.C., 1901 and 1902. Hammond, Railway Rate Theories, etc., 1911, p. 21; also, p. 160.

to the Lakes. The carriers defended this difference in rates on the ground of water competition by the Lakes or combined rail and water routes, which were alone open to wheat, and which thereby unduly lowered the rate on that commodity; and also on the basis of the lower cost of service in moving the raw material as compared with the finished product. It is apparent that issue was really raised in such a case between the interests of the farmer and of the manufacturer. The United States, producing a surplus of wheat the price of which is made on the Liverpool market in competition with the world, is compelled to find an outlet for this product. It is obvious that any reduction of the freight rate — the prices in Liverpool remaining fixed — would inure to the benefit of the farmer, who would thereby receive a higher price for his product. Viewed in this way the railways by discriminating in favor of the rate on wheat were helping the farmers. But, at the same time, by moving this wheat more cheaply than flour the railways were encouraging the location of flour milling abroad and rendering it impossible to manufacture flour for export at a profit in the cities of the Middle West. In these export cases it does not appear clearly why the rate on flour for export might not have been reduced somewhat. The Interstate Commerce Commission finally rendered a decision to the effect that the existing difference in rates constituted an undue preference in favor of the foreign manufacturer, adding at the same time that these discriminations seemed to be due primarily not to a desire of the railways to aid the American farmer in disposing of this surplus wheat, but to the bitterness of competition between the Gulf and trunk line railways.[1] They decided that any discrimination greater than two cents per hundred pounds in favor of wheat for export as against flour was unreasonable. This difference was permitted, however, on account of the greater cost of handling the manufactured product. It is significant of the then state of the

[1] *Cf.* p. 31, *supra.*

law that the railways paid no attention to this order, and, although conditions improved somewhat, there is still great complaint.

The relative rates on wheat and flour, even when for domestic consumption, illustrate the same difficulty of commercial competition — the necessity of adjusting the rate on raw materials to that on the finished product.[1] The rate on wheat from Wichita, Kan., for example, to California is fifty-five cents per hundred pounds, while the rate on flour between the same points is sixty-five cents. Is this difference in rates economically justifiable? California wheat is soft, so that flour produced from it is much improved by the admixture of hard wheat, such as may be obtained in Kansas. California, formerly a large wheat exporting state, has of late years relied to a considerable degree upon the Middle West for part of its supplies. Kansas flour sells for seventy-five cents a barrel more than California wheat flour. Shall this Kansas wheat, to be consumed in California, be ground in Wichita or in California? Here is material for controversy, not between one particular railway and another, but in reality between the millers in Kansas and the millers in California. It is quite analogous to the issue raised over export wheat and flour between the miller in Chicago and his rival in Liverpool. In this instance, if milled in Kansas, the railways enjoy the carriage of flour; while, if ground in California, the railways carry the commodity in the form of wheat. Owing to certain practical conditions, such as the percentage of waste and relative differences in labor costs, the Kansas miller appears to enjoy a certain advantage over his far western competitors. At this point the interest of particular railway companies appears. The Rock Island, if the milling industry in Kansas develops, obtains the haul not only of the flour but also of the fuel and of supplies for the communities engaged in the business. On the other

---

[1] I.C.C. Rep., No. 917; decided June 24, 1907. Later ones are in 10 *Idem*, 35 and 16 *Idem*, 73.

hand the Southern Pacific is more largely interested in the local development of manufactures in California. The Rock Island by maintaining a higher rate on flour than on wheat, would tend to hold its clients in the field. The Southern Pacific, on the other hand, by securing the reduced rate on the wheat from Kansas would materially advance the welfare of its constituents. Thus the rivalries of the competing localities immediately become the direct and immediate concern of rival railways.

Cases precisely analogous in principle to those concerning the relativity of rates on grain and grain products have troubled the carriers for years in respect to the rates upon cattle and packing house products.[1] A low rate on cattle as compared with beef favors Chicago today as against Missouri river points, the latter being nearer the cattle ranges; just as a generation ago it enabled cattle to be brought to New York and Boston to be there slaughtered and sold on the spot. The history of this controversy throws much light upon the difficulties of rate making in practice. Originally the railways encouraged cattle raising by a rate which was only about one-third of the rate charged for beef. Slaughtering was carried on in the East adjacent to the great markets. To this policy the western packers objected strenuously. They demanded a relatively low rate on their finished product in order to enable them to bid against the local eastern slaughter houses. The stockmen, on the other hand, naturally desired a continuance of the low rate on cattle, as it perpetuated competition between eastern and western buyers. The controversy between the stock raisers and the packers was thus shifted onto the shoulders of the traffic managers of the railways. The dispute culminated in 1883 when the Trunk Line Association appointed a special committee to consider what the proper adjustment should be.

[1] Older cases in Hammond Railway Rate Theories, etc., 1911, p. 45; such as 10 I.C.C. Rep., 428, etc. Later are 11 *Idem*, 296; 21 *Idem*, 491; 22 *Idem*, 77 and 160; and 23 *Idem*, 656.

This committee in turn referred the matter to Commissioner Albert Fink, "Seeking a relativity of rates so as to make the charges for transportation, including the expenses incident to the transportation of dressed beef, the same per pound as the charges per pound of dressed beef transported to the East in the shape of live stock." A difficult task this, considering the variety of by-products emerging into value year by year. Cattle rates had been for some time fifty-two per cent., and then later sixty per cent. of the dressed beef rates. This was relatively higher for cattle than had been charged during the seventies. But the western packers demanded that the relativity in favor of the finished product be still further advanced until cattle rates should equal seventy-five per cent. of the rates on beef. This would effectually discourage the shipment of cattle to eastern centres, and would tend to upbuild Kansas City and Chicago at their expense. In 1884, the matter being still in dispute, was referred to Hon. T. M. Cooley, afterward chairman of the Interstate Commerce Commission. He decided that a fair compromise would be forty cents on cattle from Chicago to New York with coincident rates of seventy cents on beef. This would make the cattle rate about fifty-seven per cent. of the beef rate. It was a victory for the stockmen as against the western packers, who at once raised a great outcry.

It would have been difficult to predict the final outcome had not an entirely new factor appeared, which transformed the conduct of the beef packing industry.[1] Specially constructed stock cars owned by private companies began to be built. These favored the perpetuation of competition between eastern and western packers. To checkmate this, the western packers had already embarked in 1879 upon the ownership of privately owned refrigerator cars for the carriage of their finished products. The custom was adopted by the railways of paying for the use of these cars by making an allowance of

[1] The best accounts are in connection with the history of private car abuses. *Cf.* references on p. 192, *infra*.

so much a mile as a deduction from the established tariffs. This at once opened the way to secret rebates of all sorts. The refrigerator traffic in these private cars was large in volume, very regular and highly concentrated as to source. A large tonnage could be diverted at any time to that road which could best show its appreciation of the favor. The Grand Trunk, for instance, in 1887 swept the board, monopolizing this entire business for a brief time, obtaining it by secret and discriminating rates. The railways, jointly, sought to free themselves from the domination of the large packers; but the phenomenal growth of their business, both domestic and export, rendered them too powerful to resist. According to expert data, during nine months to May 1, 1889, three shippers alone received from one line of road $72,945 for the use of their cars. This about equalled the initial cost of eighty new cars. For the fiscal year 1895, $8,744,000 was paid by the railways of the United States for the use of these cars — about $4,000,000 of this being in the form of rental. At this rate, profits of from twenty-five to fifty per cent. upon the investment accrued to the great packers. These virtual rebates, of course, drove all competitors from the field. The story of the gradual extension of this system of private cars to include fruit and produce business belongs in another place. Suffice it to say that the bondage was broken only by the passage of the Hepburn Act of 1906. The growth of these private refrigerator car lines caused the disappearance of live stock shipments. Packing and slaughtering on a large scale at the seaboard, either for domestic consumption or export, was doomed. Meantime, however, the controversy over the relative rates on beef and cattle continued just as if anything really depended upon it. The issue was again submitted to the commissioner of the Trunk Line Association in 1887. In the following year a select committe of the United States Senate was appointed at the urgent request of the cattle raisers. Testimony before this committee showed in detail how eastern packers were striving to build up establishments near the points of consumption, but were driven out of the business by the relatively high costs of shipping cattle, as compared with the rates at which dressed beef could be actually delivered from Chicago and Missouri river points. This entire history, aside from its significance as a study of personal discrimination, illustrates the effect of a relatively increasing differential rate, partly open and partly secret, against the raw material of an industry as compared with the finished product. The result, at all events, has been to concentrate the packing industry in the Middle West. Nor is the controversy closed even yet.[1] But this time it is a question, not between the seaboard and Chicago, but between Chicago and Missouri river points, or those still nearer the southwestern ranges. Fort Worth and Oklahoma City now become complainants against the Missouri river points.[2] Always and everywhere the manufacture seeks to develop at or near the source of the raw material. Whenever this tendency does not appear in an industry it is pertinent to inquire how far the relative adjustment of rates is responsible for the phenomenon.

Complexities in rate adjustment often arise from the fact that in the manufacture of many commodities the marketing of by-products is of increasing importance. The rate on the whole series of related commodities must be taken into account at once. Thus in lumbering, a large amount of waste or very low-grade lumber is necessarily produced. This common lumber cannot bear long transportation; it must be utilized locally, if at all. On the other hand, the choicest specialties will command a price even in remote markets. A monopoly price is enjoyed in such a case. The Pacific coast lumbermen can market their long timbers anywhere in the United States; but the demand for the common lumber, restricted to a sparsely

---

[1] U. S. Supreme Court decision in the Chicago Live Stock Exchange case in 1908; 209 U. S. 108.
[2] 22 I.C.C. Rep., 160; 22 *Idem*, 656.

RATE MAKING PRACTICE 143

populated region, tends to be exceeded by the supply.[1] The real competition between the southern, the Michigan, the Wisconsin and the Pacific coast manufacturers thus narrows down to the sale of the medium-grade product. And the cost of production of this is, of course, in part dependent upon the profit made upon the other two sorts, each of which in its own field appears to be a monopoly. A wide market and a good price for medium-grade lumber may so lessen the cost of the cheapest by-products that they in turn may be so reduced in price as to widen their reach to the consumer. Each rate reacts upon the others. The situation can be successfully controlled only by adjusting them all at once.

Not only are rates competitive as between raw materials and the finished product made from them, but the circle of competition immediately widens to include all commodities capable of substitution one for another.[2] Coal rates, of course, are partly determined by rates on cordwood, and *vice versa*. During the great coal strike in Pennsylvania in 1903, soft coal rates and hard coal rates were sadly disturbed. Such substitutions are always likely to occur. But the conditions are not always so simple as this. An instance in point is given by a witness before the Senate (Elkins) Committee on Interstate Commerce in 1905.[3] This shows how a reduction in the rate for transportation of corn from Kansas to Texas brought about a corresponding reduction in the rate on flour from Minneapolis to Chicago. There was a large crop of corn in Kansas; and the Chicago lines anticipated brisk business in the carriage of this product. The traffic managers of lines from Kansas to Texas, however, discovered a large demand for corn in Texas at a price higher than then prevailed in Kansas. Any rate less than the difference in prices between

---

[1] 14 I.C.C. Rep., 1–74.
[2] *Cf.* Hammond, Railway Rate Theories, etc., 1911, pp. 14–17, mainly with reference to classification, however.
[3] Testimony, vol. II, p. 1676. 11 I.C.C. Rep., pp. 212 and 220.

the two districts would cause shipments of corn to flow from Kansas to Texas, just as inevitably as water flows down hill. This rate would needs be low; but the corn could be loaded on empty southbound cars which had been used to haul cotton out of Texas to the north. This, of course, entailed a diversion of corn from the Chicago railways, which promptly reduced rates in order to hold their traffic. For years the rates upon wheat and corn had been fixed in a definite relation to one another, based upon commercial experience. Any reduction of the corn rate compelled a reduction of the wheat rate. A fall in the wheat rate brought about a drop in the rate on flour. These reductions in corn started in southern Kansas; but parallel lines in northern Kansas were compelled to follow suit. Grain in the territory between the two roads could be hauled by wagon either north or south corresponding to a fraction of a cent per bushel difference in the price. Thus the reduction in rates spread from one line to another all over Kansas, throughout Nebraska up into Dakota and finally to Minnesota. It not only affected the corn rate everywhere but it caused a reduction in the rate on flour from Minneapolis to Chicago.

The reliance of Texas for a portion of its corn supply upon the surplus product of Kansas sometimes leads to odd results. This commodity is sometimes shipped as corn meal and sometimes transported as corn to be afterwards ground in Texas. The Texas millers at one time demanded a relative reduction of the rate on grain as compared with corn meal, and the railway commission of that state upheld them in that demand. For ten years down to 1905 the differential in favor of the raw product had been three cents a hundred pounds. Then the railways, in connection with a general advance of rates, increased the charge on corn meal until it amounted to about nine cents per hundred pounds more than the rate on corn. One cent a hundred pounds being a good profit in grinding corn meal, this change shut the Kansas millers out of Texas business. Application was made to the Interstate Commerce

Commission for relief. It then appeared on investigation that the carriers had made use of the Texas millers in order to prevent a general reduction of *both* grain rates and rates on grain products. The Texas millers on general principles had favored both these reductions. What happened is best described in the evidence before the Senate Committee on Interstate Commerce of 1905. "The railways went to the millers of Texas and they said to them, 'Is there anything you want here?' 'Why,' said the [Texan] millers, 'yes; we would like to have that differential between corn and corn meal increased; we think you ought to put the rate on corn meal up.' The railway said, 'All right; you just stay away from that meeting down at Austin so that there will not be any excuse for the Texas commission, and if it undertakes to reduce these rates we will raise this differential; we will raise the rate on corn meal to the rate on flour.' The millers kept away from Austin — they kept their part of the bargain — and they stayed away, and the Texas commission was left without any support for their proposition to reduce the corn rates, and the railway kept their part of the bargain and lifted up the rate on corn meal so that the differential was from nine to seven and one-half cents, and that put the Kansas mills out of business."

Apparently insignificant details often determine the outcome of commercial competition. Thus in the milling business, where the margin of profit in the manufacture of flour may not be over three cents per barrel, an infinitesimal change in the freight rate may mean success or failure to long-established industries. And the conditions vary indefinitely. Thus, as between flour milling in Duluth and Buffalo, Duluth can buy its wheat from the farmer direct during the entire winter, but must ship its product mainly during the period of open water navigation on the lakes. The reverse is true with the Buffalo miller who can ship out his flour during the entire season, but who must accumulate his whole stock of wheat before navigation closes. And then Minneapolis as a milling centre has to be taken into account. Eighty per cent. of the spring wheat grown in the United States is in territory from which the freight rates to Minneapolis and Duluth are the same. But the basic rate to the East and Europe, fixing the all-rail rates, is the combined lake and rail. By this route Duluth is one hundred and fifty miles nearer the market than is Minneapolis, and consequently enjoys a lower rate on its flour shipped out. A three-cornered competitive problem exists, in which any change at one point entirely upsets the commercial equilibrium.

The obligation on the part of a railway to protect its constituency, not only in respect of particular rates, but in general conditions as well, introduces still further complications. The freight business of New England, for example, consists, first, of the carriage of raw materials and supplies inwards; and, secondly, thereafter of the transportation of the finished product out to the consuming markets. Narrowly considered, it may seem expedient to crowd the rate on coal as high as the value of service probably will permit; but viewed in a large way, it may prove to be a far better business policy to maintain the rate on coal, cotton, and other staple supplies so low, that the growth of population and production may in the long run yield far greater returns on the high-grade manufactures which the territory produces. Turning to the southern field, where the economic conditions are reversed, it may be the better policy to hold down the rate on raw cotton in order thereby to stimulate this great basic industry and thereby enhance the demand for the merchandise and foodstuffs which depend upon general prosperity. A free hand afforded for the suitable adjustment of such apparently independent services may contribute far more to the general welfare than an insistence upon a petty and near-sighted policy of extorting from each individual service all the rate it can possibly endure. American railway managers are gradually but surely coming to take a more liberal view of these great possibilities and to consider the economic development of their territories, not narrowly, but in a generous way.

CHAPTER V

RATE MAKING IN PRACTICE (*Continued*)

Effect of changing conditions, 147. — Lumber and paper rates, 148. — Equalizing industrial conditions, 148. — Protecting shippers, 149. — Pacific Coast lumber rates, 150. — Elasticity and quick adaptation, 152. — Rigidity and delicacy of adjustment, 153. — Transcontinental rate system, 154. — Excessive elasticity of rates, 155. — More stability desirable, 159. — Natural *v.* artificial territory and rates, 159. — Economic waste, 159. — Inelastic conditions, 161.— Effect upon concentration of population, 162. — Competition in transportation and trade contrasted, 163. — No abandonment of field, 165.
Cost *v.* value of service, 166. — Relative merits of each, 167. — Charging what the traffic will bear, 169. — Unduly high and low rates, 171. — Dynamic force in value of service, 177. — Cost of service in classification, 179. — Wisconsin paper case, 181. — Cost and value of service equally important, checking one another, 184.

NOT only must rates of all sorts be delicately adjusted to suit the immediate exigencies of trade; they must be constantly modified in order to keep pace with its ever changing conditions. This is peculiarly true of a rapidly growing country like the United States. An admirable instance is afforded by the complaint of the Lincoln Commercial Club before the Interstate Commerce Commission.[1] Lincoln, Nebraska, lies about fifty-five miles southwest of Omaha. Originally all its supplies came from the East, as both cities were for a time outposts of civilization. The coal supply came from Iowa and Illinois, and the salt from Michigan. On these and most other commodities the rates to Lincoln were made up of a through rate from the East to the Missouri river, plus the local rate on to destination. The city of Lincoln thus paid considerably more than Omaha for all of its supplies. Gradually conditions

[1] 13 I.C.C. Rep., 319. The general investigation of wool rates is another admirable instance. 23 *Idem*, 151.

have changed; until in 1907 it appeared that over half the soft coal consumed in Lincoln was brought from Kansas and Missouri; four-fifths of the lumber from the South and nearly all the rest from the Pacific coast; glass and salt from the gas belt and salt beds of Kansas; and a great deal of beet sugar from the western fields. For a large proportion of these and other supplies, Lincoln was actually as near or nearer the point of production than Omaha, and yet the difficulties of effecting an adjustment between rival carriers had prevented any modification of rates corresponding to these changes in economic conditions. On every one of these commodities the rate to Lincoln remained steadily higher than to Omaha, regardless of the source of supply. Unanimous consent was necessary for readjustment. So long as any single road refused assent, a general rate disturbance might be precipitated by any independent action. The beneficent effect of the exercise of governmental authority, powerful enough over all interested parties to compel acquiescence, has been clearly apparent in affording relief.

A similar instance in the state of Wisconsin is afforded by the compulsory readjustment of the freight rate on wood pulp, lumber and sawed logs.[1] On investigation it appeared that, despite a very much lower commercial value for the raw material used in paper manufacture, the rates on pulp wood were more than double those on logs to be sawed up for lumber. It appeared, furthermore, that this apparent anomaly was due not so much to high rates on the pulp wood as to very low rates on sawed logs. These latter rates for many years had been fixed at a very low figure because originally the bulk of such logs, cut in the river bottoms, was floated down stream to mills along the Mississippi river. Competition with lumber raft rates originally determined the charges on lumber by rail. The paper industry did not begin until these conditions of water competition had quite disappeared. Gradually, with the progress of deforestation, all the timber is now found on the

[1] Wisconsin Railroad Commission, 1908. *Cf.* p. 181, *infra*.

uplands far from navigable water courses; so that the rates today are not at all influenced by competitive rates on the lumber rafts down river. Nevertheless the old tariffs on lumber remained in force despite the changed conditions, while the new rates on pulp wood were fixed independently of any rates by water. It was only after careful investigation that the injustice to the paper manufacturers from the disparity in charges appeared. Here again it was the rigidity and interlocked complexity of adjustment which placed it in the power of one road to block change of any sort.[1] The compulsory exercise of governmental authority cut the Gordian knot with the result that substantial justice now obtains.[2]

From the preceding statements it will be observed that carriers have another important commercial function beside that of equalizing industrial conditions.[3] They also act in a protective or insurance capacity to the merchant or manufacturer. The policy of "keeping everyone in business" implies not only variety but variability of conditions. Capital is proverbially timid. It will not venture into a new and uncertain enterprise unless either profits are immediate and high or, if moderate, likely to endure. In any event some guarantee of permanence is required. This guarantee the carrier is often able to offer. It may assume the obligation of protecting its clients; that is, of saving them harmless against the intrusion or irruption of hurtful competition. It thus exercises in a certain sense the function of an insurance company, but with this important difference: that while it has the strongest interest in protecting its established industries against ruinous

[1] The diverse interests to be reconciled must also include the lumbering centres once "next the stump," but now placed at a relative disadvantage. The Eau Claire lumber case [reprinted in Railway Problems, pp. 203–233] should be read in this connection.
[2] The remarkable rise of the sash, door and blind industry in the South, as prejudiced by comparison with Chicago under an outworn schedule of rates, is given in 23 I.C.C. Rep., 110.
[3] On the parity cases, consult Hammond, Railway Rate Theories, etc., 1911, pp. 120 and 149.

competition from abroad, it may desire to share in some degree in their development and prosperity by way of reward. In this latter sense the relation of the carrier to its clients partakes of a profit-sharing arrangement. One of the broadest issues between American railways and the public at the present time is precisely this: whether the carriers are to share in business profits; or merely, in addition to furnishing transportation, are to collect a fixed fee for a service in the nature of industrial insurance. That it lies in their way to furnish such protection under modern economic practice is an indisputable fact.

This nice question is almost daily pressing for solution at the hands of the Interstate Commerce Commission. It arises every time an increase of freight rates occurs. Take, for example, the Pacific coast lumber cases of 1908. The dissenting opinions of the Commission show how debatable the proposition is.[1] Up to about 1893 the lumber interests of the Pacific coast were quite undeveloped and entirely dependent upon water transportation for reaching markets. At this time low rates of forty to sixty cents per hundred pounds on forest products to markets in the Middle West were introduced, partly to build up the industry and partly to create a back loading for the preponderantly westbound tonnage of all transcontinental lines. Under these rates the business has enormously developed until, on the Northern Pacific road in 1906, the shipments of lumber east bound amounted to one-third of its entire traffic both ways, and yielded nearly one-fifth of its freight revenue. So greatly had this traffic expanded that it aided, if not actually produced, a reversal of the direction of transcontinental empties. Practically all these roads now have an excess of tonnage to the east whereas ten years ago much the larger volume of freight was moving westward. Meantime the lumbermen under the stimulus of these lower rates, and of the phenomenal rise in the price of lumber, had been wonder-

[1] 14 I.C.C. Rep., 1–74 and Ann. Rep. I.C.C., 1911, p. 46. The later judicial history will be found at p. 443, *infra*.

fully prosperous. The price of logs had risen since 1893 from about $2.50 per 1,000 feet to $13.50 in 1906; partly in consequence of the extraordinary demand consequent on the Valparaiso and San Francisco earthquakes. The mills had moved in from the rivers and the coast, and had become absolutely dependent upon rail transportation for reaching markets. At this stage, and most unfortunately in November, 1907, just at a time of industrial panic, the carriers raised their rates by about ten cents per one hundred pounds. The market price of logs had already dropped from $13.50 per thousand by approximately one-third. These two causes, commercial depression and the increased freight rate, brought about a complete collapse in the industry. And the increased freight rates were contested before the Interstate Commerce Commission in the hope that, as in the southern field the rate increases from Georgia points had been annulled,[1] these might also be found unreasonable. The broad question concerns the obligation of carriers, once having brought about an investment of capital in the industry, to continue to give the same rates as those under which the ventures had been undertaken, due regard being had, of course, to such changes in costs of service as might have ensued. The lumbermen demand that all the increment of profit due to prosperous developments shall remain unto them; in other words, that the carriers' share of the increased values shall remain fixed. On the other hand, the railways defend their increases, partly upon the ground of increasing expenses of operation, and partly upon the broader ground that the freight rate being proportioned to the price of the product, should rise in harmony with it. Upon this question the Commission was divided, the majority holding in favor of annulling the increase, while the chairman and one other member decided that the increase was justifiable.[2]

[1] P. 489, *infra*.
[2] Rates must not vary with profits. 13 I.C.C. Rep., 429; and consistently held ever since.

Elasticity and quick adaptation to the exigencies of business are peculiarities of American railway operation. Our railway managers have always been most progressive in seeking, in and out of season, to develop new territory and build up traffic. The strongest contrast between Europe and the United States lies in this fact. European railways more often take business as they find it. Our railways *make* it. Much of this business is made possible only by special rates adapted to the case in hand. These need not be secret or discriminating, as has already been observed. For although offered with reference to particular cases, they may be open to all comers. The economic justification lies in the fact that the railway can afford to make a low rate, leaving a bare margin of profit above the *extra* cost of adding this traffic to that which is already in motion. Such rates cannot exceed a definite figure based upon what the traffic will bear. A higher rate than this would kill the business. Something is contributed toward fixed charges by the new traffic, so far as the railway is concerned; and at the same time the shipper on his part is enabled to enlarge his operations. Yet such a scale of rates if applied to the whole traffic of the railway might be ruinous in the extreme. The domestic shipper of wheat may conceivably be helped, rather than injured, by a special rate on grain for Liverpool without which the railway would lose the business entirely. To transport California fruit for a mere fraction of the rate per ton mile which is laid upon other traffic may actually enable those other goods to be carried more cheaply than before. Of course, if the other traffic be directly competitive, as for instance in this case, oranges from Florida, that is an entirely different matter. Railway representatives rightfully insist upon these special rates to develop new business as a boon to the commercial world. They contrast them with the hard and fast schedules of European railways. They allege that such elasticity loosens the joints of competition, "keeps everyone in business," equalizes prices over large areas, and is in fact the life of trade. One of the stock objections to railway regulation is that it may lessen this elasticity, "substitute mile posts for brains," and produce stagnation in place of activity.

Paradoxical as it may seem, a certain rigidity of rate schedules is a natural consequence of the very delicacy with which individual rates are adjusted to meet the demands of trade. Each road is jealously and aggressively alert to protect its own constituency regardless of the rights of others. No single traffic manager is free to grant reductions of rates, even when considered to be just, by reason of the opposition of competing lines. The consent of every one of these interests is necessary in order to insure stability, and the penalty for acting independently may be a rate war, disastrously affecting relations with connecting lines. Thus, for example, in the South the Southern Railway for some time was willing to concede, as a measure of justice, a reduction of rates on cotton from Mississippi river points to the mills in North and South Carolina.[1] The growth of the textile industry had resulted in a demand for cotton far exceeding the production of the Carolinas. At the same time the increasing attention devoted to manufacturing of a higher grade had forced the manufacturers to draw upon the long-staple supplies of the Mississippi bottom lands. The Piedmont cotton was too short in fibre for the finer sort of goods. The Carolina mills were, however, compelled to pay a higher rate upon cotton from such points as Memphis than was paid for the long haul up to New England. Thus, for instance, as late as 1900, rates were fifty-nine cents to South Carolina, while they were only fifty-five and one-half cents per hundred pounds from the same points to New England mills. This was obviously unjust. But the Southern Railway alone, interested in the welfare of its Carolina clients, was powerless to act without the consent of its competitors operat-

---

[1] Arbitration of Cotton Rates, etc., Nov. 15 and 16, 1900; pamphlet arguments of Southern v. Illinois Central Railways. Wool rates are the same. 23 I.C.C. Rep., 151.

ing from Memphis west of the Alleghanies. These latter lines, having no interest in the southern mills and a unity of interest in the long haul traversed to New England, sought to prevent an equalization of the differences. Controlling rates also on cotton for export to various seaports, they were for a long time able to prevent a change. On the other hand, in the same territory the railways operating south from Cincinnati and Louisville desired to reduce rates on manufactured products from the Central West.[1] These were the very lines which in the former instance prevented the reduction of cotton rates on the Southern Railway to Carolina points, by threats to meet such reductions by cutting their own rates on cotton going north through the Ohio gateways. Yet a reduction of their rates on manufactures for building up western trade threatened the business of the Southern Railway, which had been mainly interested in the traffic from Atlanta seaboard points. It may readily be seen that this situation, extending to practically every important point, "jacked up" all these rates, not because of their inherent reasonableness and not even because the railways independently acknowledged them to be just, but simply and solely because any disturbance of this house of cards might lead to a general downfall of the whole system.

Another interesting example of the difficulty of bringing about a change in rate adjustment is afforded in the transcontinental field. For some years a general agreement seems to have been adopted as a sort of a compromise between the various conflicting interests. Under present conditions Chicago and all points east of the Mississippi from Maine to Florida enjoy precisely the same rate to the Pacific coast.[2] Chicago has at various times contended before the Interstate Commerce Commission for graded rates which should recognize, for instance, that being 1,200 miles nearer San Francisco than

[1] This was the gist of the complaint in the Cincinnati Freight Bureau case; pp. 248, 392 and 588, *infra*.   [2] Chapters XI and XIX, *infra*.

RATE MAKING PRACTICE 155

Boston on the basis of distance, it should have proportionately lower freight rates. Apparently some of the transcontinental roads, such as the Great Northern, have been willing to make this concession. They could not, however, take any action without first obtaining the consent of every railway and steamship company with which they compete. Inasmuch as almost every railway in the country participates in transcontinental business, an agreement was practically impossible. Entirely aside from the merits of this particular intricate question, it must be borne in mind that there is no such thing as independence of action on behalf of any single carrier. It becomes exceedingly easy for one road to play a dog-in-the-manger part. The shipper may be subjected to an extortionate policy, not dictated by the road over which he ships, as a matter of fact, but by roads operating perhaps a thousand or more miles away.

Praiseworthy as is the elasticity of railway rates in the United States, there is, nevertheless, much to be said in support of the contention that at times this has been carried to an extreme. Stability and certainty have been treated as of secondary importance. Particular shippers have been aided, but the general interests of trade have suffered some injurious consequences. It is not entirely clear whether the advantage gained from elasticity has at all times been worth the cost. Certain of the disadvantages of instability of rates seem to have been overlooked.

In the first place railway tariffs have in the past undoubtedly been too voluminous and complex. The number of these filed with the Interstate Commerce Commission is extremely large. Eleven railways alone during the year to November 30, 1904, filed 30,125. The total schedules of all American railways filed during the year to November 30, 1907, was 220,982. One single carrier had 15,700 tariffs in force at the same time. The New York Central & Hudson River in December, 1899, had no less than 1,370 special commodity rates in force. There were endless contradictions and conflicts. Secret rates were hidden in devious ways in this mass of publications. Special tariffs "expiring with this shipment"; rates quoted not numerically but by numbered reference to tariffs of other carriers and applicable by different routes; agreements to meet rates of any competing carriers, were among the irregular methods of concealment adopted. Although literally complying with the law by publicly filing all tariffs, conditions were often such that not even an expert in rates could discover in this maze of conflicting evidence what the rate at any time actually was. The door was opened wide to personal discrimination and abuses of all kinds.[1] Those conditions are not necessary. They do not obtain on the best roads in other parts of the world. Nor is such instability found in respect of some important lines of trade. No agricultural product fluctuates in price more abruptly or widely than raw cotton,—from five to seventeen cents a pound. Yet the rates on that commodity have remained quite undisturbed throughout the southern states for many years. But the best proof of all that rates have been unduly numerous, is the great reduction in volume which has taken place since 1910 under compulsion of law. This feature will be especially considered in another connection.[2]

The second disadvantage of too great elasticity in freight rates is that it may, at times, promote rather than lessen that state of economic unrest inevitable in all business, especially in a new country. Under a continual disturbance of rates, the merchant is unable with security to enter into long-time contracts. Rates are sometimes changed, not to suit the shipper but to serve the railway's interests. Sometimes traffic may be diverted from its natural channels. The spirit of initiative and self-reliance on the part of shippers may be undermined. Persistent titillation of competition may be pleasant for a time, but its final results may be injurious. Constant appeal to the traffic manager of his road for aid and comfort may quite

---

[1] Now covered by law since 1910. Pp. 512 and 571, *infra*.
[2] Pp. 324 and *infra*.

naturally divert the shipper's attention from an aggressive commercial policy which would render him independent of minor changes in freight rates. The more responsibility the traffic manager assumes, the more may be put upon him. And it must always be remembered that each move by one road to protect a client, will probably be checkmated by the tactics of rival lines. Economic peace, not warfare, should be encouraged by the services of common carriers. One of the positive advantages of governmental regulation of railway rates is that it contributes to stability. That this view is shared by experienced railway men, appears from the following testimony of President Mellen of the New Haven road.[1] "I think that great trouble comes to the business of this country through the fact of these little breaks in rates. During November two new railways were opened into the city of Denver. They sought to make themselves popular by lowering rates, and rates went down very low. They went down legally, but they went down very low. Just before the rates went down the merchants of the city had stocked Denver with goods and the lowering of the rates demoralized their prices; they lost a large amount of money, and dissatisfaction was caused from Chicago to Denver. Lowering of rates demoralized business generally. I think if those roads had known that the rates which they made had to remain in force thirty days they would have hesitated before they lowered them. I would increase the time required before rates could be reduced."

The foregoing consideration suggests still another argument in favor of stability of freight rates, even at the expense of a certain amount of flexibility. Special rates which create new business should be carefully distinguished from special rates which merely wrest business from other carriers or markets. Any expedient which will make two blades of grass grow where one grew before; which puts American wheat into Liverpool

[1] Senate Committee on the Transportation Interests of the United States and Canada, 1890, p. 362.

in competition with India and Argentina; which cheapens California fruit on the eastern markets; which offers a wider choice of building stone for Chicago; which will establish new industries for the utilization of local raw materials, deserves the greatest encouragement. Our country has been unprecedently developed in consequence of the energy and progressiveness of its railway managers. But thousands of other special rates have no such justification, even where they are public and open to all shippers alike. These are the expression of railway ambition to build up trade by invading territory naturally tributary to other railways or traders. A significant feature of commercial competition is the utilization of distant markets as available "dumping grounds" for the surplus products left over from the local or natural market. In the St. Louis Business Men's League case [1] the Pacific coast jobbers complained that the large distributing houses in the Middle West thus invaded their territory. Having met their fixed charges from their own natural territory, they invaded the remotest districts by cutting prices to the level of actual production cost per unit of new business. The Florida orange growers protest against the relatively lower rate on California fruit, which is carried twice the distance for less money per box. This, it is urged, enables the western grower, having glutted his natural market in the Middle West, to "dump" his surplus into the eastern field, to which alone the Florida orange is restricted. This line of argument is the same as that which upholds the systems under which lower rates are given for exported or imported commodities than those on goods for domestic consumption. It is always alleged that such sales at long reach actually benefit the consumer or producer near at hand, inasmuch as they contribute something toward the fixed expenses of the business, which must be borne in any event. This raises at once the much broader question as to what constitutes a "natural market" or the "natural territory"

[1] 9 Int. Com. Rep., 318; in our Railway Problems, chap. XVII.

which rightfully belongs to any given economic agent. It is, however, too extended an issue to be discussed at this time.¹

Too many special commodity rates, intended to meet the needs of particular shippers instead of increasing new business, may merely bring about economic waste through exchange between widely separated markets or by causing an invasion of fields naturally tributary to other centres.² Whenever a community producing a surplus of a given commodity supplies itself, nevertheless, with that same commodity from a distant market, economic loss results. Numerous instances could be cited where identical products are redistributed after a long carriage to and from a distant point in the very area of original production. Dried fruits may be distributed by wholesale grocers at Chicago in the great fruit-raising regions of the West and South. Cotton goods made by southern mills may be shipped to New York or Chicago, and then sent back again for final distribution with the addition of a middleman's commission and a double freight rate. The Colorado Fuel & Iron Company seeks special rates in order to sell goods over in Pittsburg territory; while its great competitor, the United States Steel Corporation, has an equal ambition for the trade of the Pacific Slope. In another case it appeared that a sash and blind manufacturer in Detroit was seeking to extend his market in New England. Manufacturers of the same goods in Vermont were simultaneously marketing their product in Michigan. The Detroit producer did not complain of this invasion of his home territory, but objected to the freight rate from Boston to Detroit, which, probably because of back loading, was only about one-half the rate on his own goods from Detroit to the seaboard. Is not this an economic anomaly? Two producers, presumably of equal efficiency, are each invading the territory naturally tributary to the other and are enabled to do so by reason of the railway policy of "keeping

[1] Hammond, Railway Rate Theories, etc., 1911, p. 82, cites cases.
[2] Chapter VIII, *infra*.

everyone in business." The New England railways are compelled by reason of the remoteness to their territory to defend this policy. As President Tuttle, of the Boston & Maine, expresses it, "I should be just as much interested in the stimulating of Chicago manufacturers in sending their products into New England to sell as I would be in sending those from New England into Chicago to sell. It is the business of the railways centering in Chicago to send the products from Chicago in every direction. It is our particular business in New England to send New England products all over the country. The more they scatter the better it is for the railways. The railway does not discriminate against shipments because they are east bound or west bound. We are glad to see the same things come from Chicago into New England that are manufactured and sent from New England into Chicago." No one questions for a moment that the widening of the sphere of competition by transportation agencies is a service of incalculable benefit to the country. But it should also be borne in mind that superfluous transportation is economic waste. The industrial combinations in seeking to effect a strategic location of their factories in order to divide the field have apparently come to a full recognition of this fact.

A fourth objection to undue development of special commodity rates is that they may entail increased burdens upon the local constituency of each railway. The proportion of such special rates is fifty per cent. greater in America than in the United Kingdom. It is plain that each shipment which fails to bear its due proportion of fixed charges, even though contributing something thereto, leaves the weight of interest and maintenance charges upon the shoulders of the local shipper. To be sure, those special rates which permanently create new business, operate otherwise. But in the vast complex, each railway often wrests from competing carriers only about as much tonnage as it loses. It invades rival territory, but its own constituency is invaded in retaliation. Thus there is rolled up an inordinately large proportion of such special traffic, leaving the regular shipments and the local trade to bear the brunt of fixed charges. Momentous social consequences may result. Not only the cost of doing business, but the expense of living in the smaller places is increased. One of the most dangerous social tendencies at the present time is the enormous concentration of population and wealth in great cities. Increased efficiency and economy in production are much to be desired; but social and political stability must not be sacrificed thereto. Is it not possible that a powerful decentralizing influence may be exerted by checking this indiscriminate and often wasteful long-distance competition, through greater insistence upon the rights of geographical location?

Finally, an abnormal disregard of distance, which is always possible in the making of special rates to meet particular cases, may bring about a certain inelasticity of industrial conditions. This may occur in either one of two ways. The rise of new industries may be hindered; or the well-merited relative decline of old ones under a process of natural selection may be postponed or averted. The difficult problem of fairly adjusting rates on raw materials to finished products in order that the growth of new industries may take place, while at the same time the old established ones shall not be cramped or restricted, has already been discussed. It is equally plain that at times there may be danger of perpetuating an industry in a district, regardless of the physical disabilities under which it is conducted. One cannot for a moment doubt the advantages of a protective policy on the part of railways; safe-guarding industry against violent dislocating shocks. An inevitable transition to new and perhaps better conditions may perhaps be rendered easier to bear. To New England, constantly exposed to the competition of new industries rising in the West, this policy has been of inestimable value. On the other hand, it is incontestable that in the long run the whole country will fare best when each industry is prosecuted in the most favored location, conditions of marketing as well as of mere production being always considered. If Pittsburg is the natural centre for iron and steel production, it may not be an unmixed advantage to the country at large, however great its value to New England, to have the carriers perpetuate the barbed wire manufacturers at Worcester. If California can raise a finer or more marketable variety of orange, and at a lower cost, than Florida, it would be a backward step to counteract the natural advantage of the western field by compelling the southern railways to reduce their rates to an amount equal to the disability under which the Florida grower works. The principle laid down by the so-called "Bogue differentials" in the lumber trade[1] bears upon this point. In order to equalize conditions between a large number of lumbering centres sending their products to a common market, certain differentials between them were allowed under arbitration, "to enable each line to place its fair proportion of lumber in the territory." Did this mean that the disability of any place in manufacturing cost, should be compensated by a corresponding reduction in the ensuing transportation cost? This was the view of some of the carriers who were zealous to keep the market open to all on equal terms. Yet it is evident that, carried beyond a certain point, such a policy would not only nullify all advantages of geographical location, but it would also reverse the process of natural selection and of survival of the fittest, upon which all industrial progress must ultimately depend. Each particular case, however, must be decided on its merits. Our purpose is not to pass judgment on any one, but merely to call attention to the possible effect of such practices upon the process of industrial development.

Centralization, or concentration of population, industry and wealth is characteristic of all progressive peoples at the present time. Great economic advantages, through division of labor and cheapened production, have resulted; but, on the other

[1] 5 Int. Com. Rep., 264; in our Railway Problems, chap. VIII.

hand, manifold evils have followed in its train. Sometimes it appears as if American railway practices, in granting commodity and flat long-distance rates so freely, operated in some ways to retard this tendency. But the influence is not all in that direction. Many staple industries, utilizing the raw material at their doors, might supply the needs of their several local constituencies, were it not that their rise is prevented by long-distance rates from remote but larger centres of production. Denver, in striving to establish paper mills to utilize its own Colorado wood pulp, is threatened by the low rates from Wisconsin centres. Each locality, ambitious to become self-supporting, is hindered by the persistency of competition from far away cities. This is particularly true of distributive business. The overweening ambition of the great cities to monopolize the jobbing trade, regardless of distance, has already been discussed. And it follows, of course, that the larger the city the more forcibly may it press its demands upon the carriers for low rates to the most remote hamlets. The files of the Interstate Commerce Commission are stocked with examples of this kind. The plea of the smaller cities and the agricultural states — Iowa, for example — for a right to share in the jobbing naturally tributary to them by reason of their location, formed no inconsiderable element in the recent popular demand for legislation by the Federal government.

The marked difference between competition in transportation and trade has long been recognized in economic writing, but has not as yet been accorded due weight in law. The most essential difference arises from the fact, already fully set forth, that a large proportion of railway expenditures are entirely independent of the amount of business done. This involves as a consequence, the exemption of carriers from the fundamental law of evolution. Survival of the fittest does not obtain as a rule in railway competition. The poorest equipped, the most circuitous and most nearly insolvent road is often able to dictate terms to the standard and most direct trunk lines. This has been exemplified time and again in the history of rate wars the world over.[1] The bankrupt road having repudiated its fixed charges has nothing to lose by carrying business at any figure which will pay the mere cost of haulage. The indirect line having no business at the outset has nothing to lose, and everything to gain. The Canadian Pacific, for example, was perhaps originally built without any expectation of being able to participate in San Francisco business; and yet, like the Grand Trunk, it has always been an active factor in the determination of transcontinental tariffs.

The fact is that cost of production, while in trade fixing a point below which people may refuse to produce or compete, in transportation may merely mark the point at which it becomes more wasteful to stop producing than to go on producing at a loss. Hadley's classic statement is so admirable that it cannot be improved upon. "Let us take an instance from railway business, here made artificially simple for the sake of clearness, but in its complicated forms occurring every day. A railway connects two places not far apart, and carries from one to the other (say) 100,000 tons of freight a month at twenty-five cents a ton. Of the $25,000 thus earned, $10,000 is paid out for the actual expenses of running the trains and loading or unloading the cars; $5000 for repairs and general expenses; the remaining $10,000 pays the interest on the cost of construction. Only the first of these items varies in proportion to the amount of business done; the interest is a fixed charge, and the repairs have to be made with almost equal rapidity, whether the material wears out, rusts out, or washes out. Now suppose a parallel road is built, and in order to secure some of this business offers to take it at twenty cents a ton. The old road must meet the reduction in order not to lose its business, even though the new figure does not leave it a fair profit on its investment; better a moderate profit than none at all. The new road reduces to fifteen cents; so does the old road.

[1] *Cf.* p. 255 *et seq.*, *infra*.

A fifteen cent rate will not pay interest unless there are new business conditions developed by it; but it will pay for repairs, which otherwise would be a dead loss. The new road makes a still further reduction to eleven cents. This will do little toward paying repairs, but that little is better than nothing. If you take at eleven cents freight that cost you twenty-five cents to handle, you lose fourteen cents on every ton you carry. If you refuse to take it at that rate, you lose fifteen cents on every ton you do not carry. For your charges for interest and repairs run on, while the other road gets the business." [1]

Another peculiarity of railway competition, distinguishing it from competition in trade, is that there is no such thing as abandonment of the field. This is tersely expressed by Morawetz in his Corporation Law. "It should be observed that competition among railway companies has not the same safeguard as competition in trade. Persons will ordinarily do business only when they see a fair chance of profit, and if press of competition renders a particular trade unprofitable, those engaged in that trade will suspend or reduce their operations, and apply their capital or labor to other uses until a reasonable margin of profit is reached. But the capital invested in the construction of a railway cannot be withdrawn when competition renders the operation of the road unprofitable. A railway is of no use except for railway purposes, and if the operation of the road were stopped, the capital invested in its construction would be wholly lost. Hence it is for the interest of the railway company to operate its road, though the earnings are barely sufficient to pay the operating expenses. The ownership of the road may pass from the shareholders to the bondholders, and be of no profit to the latter; but the struggle for traffic will continue so long as the means of paying operating expenses can be raised. Unrestricted competition will thus

[1] A carload of bamboo steamer chairs from San Francisco to New York for $9.40 in the course of a rate war, would seem to be rather below bedrock. 21 I.C.C. Rep., 349.

render the competitive traffic wholly unremunerative, and will cause the ultimate bankruptcy of the companies unless the operation of their traffic which is not the subject of competition can be made to bear the entire burden of the interest and fixed charges." So profoundly modified in short are the conditions of railway competition by contrast with those in industry, that it is clear beyond a shadow of doubt that a railway is essentially a monopoly. This requires no proof so far as local business, in distinction from through or competitive traffic, is concerned. It is equally true in respect to all traffic of sufficient importance to bring about pooling agreements or a division of the business, in order to forfend bankruptcy and consolidation. To attempt to perpetuate competition between railways by legislation is thus defeating its own end. The prohibition of pooling agreements which refuses to recognize the naturally monopolistic character of the business, can have but one result, namely, to compel consolidation as a measure of self-preservation. Such legislation defeats itself, bringing about the very result it was intended to prevent.

Two general theories governing the rates chargeable by railways are entertained, known respectively as cost of service and value of service. According to the first, the proper rate for transportation should be based upon the cost for carriage of the persons or goods, with an allowance for a reasonable profit over and above the expenses of operation involved. This line of argument is commonly advanced by representatives of shippers and the public, who reason by analogy from other lines of business. In several European countries when railways were first built, and afterward, especially in Germany in 1867, attempts were made to apply this principle widely in the construction of tariffs. Practical railway men, on the other hand, usually adhere to the second principle of value of service. This argument maintains that, while theoretically cost of service should determine minimum rates, owing to the nature of commercial competition, as a matter of fact rates must be based upon the principle of charging what the traffic will bear. This is accomplished by proportioning the rate to the commercial value of the service. Practically the rate is found by charging as much as the traffic will stand without evidence of discouragement. Thus if the price per bushel of wheat in New York is twenty-five cents higher than in Chicago, it would obviously be absurd to charge a rate which would absorb all of that increment of place value due to transportation. Enough margin must be left to the shipper who buys wheat in Chicago and sells it in New York, to permit a reasonable profit on the transaction, after payment of the freight rate.

These two principles of cost of service and value of service are directly opposed in one regard; inasmuch as the cost of service theory harks directly back to railway expenditure; while the value of service principle contemplates primarily the effect upon the railway's income account. Any charge is justified according to the latter view, which is not detrimental to the shipper as indicated by a positive reduction in the volume of business offered. No charge, on the other hand, may be deemed reasonable according to the cost of service principle, which affords more than a fair profit upon the business, regardless of its effect upon the shipper. As a matter of fact neither of these views is entirely sound by itself. Both have large elements of truth in them. Each qualifies the other. In the first place, it is to be noted that between them they fix the upper and lower limits of all possible charges. Less than the cost of service cannot be charged; else would a confiscatory rate result. This was the plea set up by the railways in the now celebrated Texas Cattle Raisers' Association case against the cancellation by the Interstate Commerce Commission of an extra charge of $1 per car for switching charges at Chicago. At the other extreme, more than the traffic will bear cannot be charged without a disproportionate decline in volume of tonnage. This would be bad business policy, as it could at once entail loss of revenue. The railway could not submit to the former alternative; it would not conceivably resort to the latter.

Attempts have been made by various authors to account for the phenomena of rate making on other grounds. The German author, Sax, has sought to trace an analogy between the imposition of taxes and railway charges, alleging that both should be proportioned to what the shipper "can afford to pay," from an ethical rather than an economic point of view. Acworth interprets the phrase "charging what the traffic will bear" to mean something analogous to this. His allegation is that rate schedules are built up upon the principle of "equality of sacrifice," otherwise characterized as "tempering the wind to the shorn lamb." High class traffic contributes liberally of its abundance of value, while third class passengers and low grade tonnage are let off lightly on the ground of their poverty. Taussig in his memorable contribution to the subject [1] has, however, shown how untenable this theory of "equality of sacrifice" is. Not ethical but purely economic considerations are applicable in such circumstances except, of course, in so far as common carriers, enjoying privileges by grant of the state, may be considered as imposing taxes for the performance of a quasi-public duty. This latter test of a reasonable rate has underlaid a long line of Supreme Court decisions since the Granger case.[2] Nevertheless, as so frequently happens, legal and economic bases of judgment seem to be lacking in harmony.

There can be no question that for an indispensable public service like transportation, conducted under monopolistic conditions, the ideal system of charges would be to ascertain the cost of each service rendered and to allow a reasonable margin of profit over and above this amount. To the application of this principle alone, however, there are several insuperable objections both theoretical and practical. Such cost is practi-

[1] *Quarterly Journal of Economics*, V, 1891, pp. 438–65; reprinted in Railway Problems, chap. V.
[2] *Cf.* Int. Com. Reports, 1903, p. 436.

cally indeterminate, being joint for all services in large part, as we have seen: it is highly variable, being perhaps never twice the same, as circumstances change from time to time; cost is unknown until volume is ascertained, and volume is ever fluctuating; the cost of service, obviously, could never be ascertained until after the service had been rendered, while, of course, the schedule of rates must be known in advance, in order that the shipper may calculate his probable profits; and finally the principle of increasing returns, flowing from the dependence of cost upon volume of traffic, imposes such an incentive for development of new business, which in turn depends for its volume upon the rate charged, that cost of service is subordinated at once to other considerations in practice.

Of these objections to rate making upon the principle of cost of service alone, it would indeed appear as if the first should be conclusive. If the cost is simply indeterminable, why bother about any further refutation of the principle at all? But the persistency of the idea that somehow railway operations are analogous to the business of an ordinary merchant; and that cost and profits are ascertainable; renders it necessary to pile proof upon proof of the limitations upon its applicability to real conditions in service.

Not only is the mere cost of service indeterminable; if it could be ascertained, it would not establish the chargeable rate in many instances. The freight service of a railway comprises the carriage of all kinds of goods simultaneously, from the most valuable high-priced commodities, such as silks and satins, down to lumber, coal, cement, and even sand.[1] To compel each of these classes of goods to bear its proportionate share of the cost of carriage, would at once preclude the possibility of transporting low-priced goods at all. One dollar a hundred pounds may not be too much to add to the price of boots and shoes for transportation from Boston to Chicago.

[1] The Hepburn Committee testimony in 1879, p. 2893, is eloquent upon this aspect of the question.

It would still form only a small part of the total cost of producing and marketing them. But to add anything like that sum to the cost of one hundred pounds of salt or cement would put an end to the business at once. Only about so much can in practice be added to the price of any given commodity for freight without widely limiting the area of its available market. Thus raw cotton seems to be able to bear an addition of about fifty cents per hundred pounds for freight to its total cost. Experience demonstrates that anything more than this one-half cent per pound charged on cotton, entails more loss than gain. In the case of fancy groceries or fine furniture, there may be no considerable demand in any event above a certain ascertainable level of prices. For boots and shoes or cut building stone it may be that competition from some other centre of production nearby, precludes any great addition to the price for freight. The business simply will not bear more than a certain proportion of charge. Not only would the rigid application of the cost of service principle hinder all transportation of low-grade traffic; it would also prevent any development of long distance business. It is indubitable that sole reliance upon cost of service as a basis for rate making is theoretically unsound, and impossible of practical application.[1]

Cost of service, while unsound as a sole reliance, nevertheless affords an important check upon the value of service principle. Without it there is always grave danger that traffic managers, seeking to enlarge their revenues, may push rates unreasonably high. At first sight it would appear as if this could not occur, inasmuch as an inordinately high rate would immediately reduce the volume of business offered. It is constantly alleged by railway men that this must of necessity occur. And it would indeed follow, were it not that the incidence of the rate is rarely upon the actual shipper. He merely pays it, and at once shifts it to the consumer. For low-grade

[1] 1st Annual Report, I.C.C., 1888. *Cf.* Strombeck, Freight Classification, pp. 35–60.

or staple goods like cement or kerosene, where transportation charges form a large part of the total cost of production, it is conceivable that higher freight rates might so far increase the price as to check consumption. Five cents a hundredweight higher freight means $1.25 per 1,000 ft. added to the price of soft lumber, $2 to hard lumber; three cents per bushel added to the price of wheat, and $1 to the ton of pig iron or coal. Such substantial additions might readily reduce the demand. Yet even this would not be true of necessities of life like anthracite coal or sugar, on which latter the freight rate amounts to about one-half cent per pound. Is five cents a barrel added to the price of flour likely to decrease the consumption of that staple commodity? Yet the enhancement of railway revenues would indeed be enormous from such an increase of freight rates. For these necessities of life, an increased freight rate might become an actual charge upon the people, without reducing their consumption, like a tax upon salt. Only upon goods the use of which might be freely lessened, would higher freight rates be reflected in a corresponding decline in the volume of business. Moreover, with all high grade traffic, the value of service principle fails utterly by itself alone to prescribe the upper level of a reasonable charge. Competent testimony is ample upon this point. Thus from the commissioner of the Trunk Line Association;[1] "The tonnage of the higher class articles is an extremely difficult matter for transportation companies to increase or decrease. . . . In that class of articles the carrier can do but little to increase the transportation." And the reason in part lies in the almost immediate diffusion of the burden in the processes of distribution. That no complaints are made — a defence often brought forward for higher rates — proves by itself the uncertain incidence of the burden imposed.

That the principle of charging what the traffic will bear affords no protection to the consumer against exorbitant rates

[1] C., N. O. & T. P. case, testimony, vol. II, pp. 332–333.

on many commodities, follows also from the relative insignificance of transportation charges as compared with the value of the goods. This, in fact, is naïvely conceded by railway managers themselves; when, as in the case of the widespread freight rate advances of 1908–1909, publicity agents flooded the country with calculations as to the infinitesimal fraction which would be added to the price of commodities by a ten per cent. rise in rates.[1] The rate from Grand Rapids to Chicago on an ordinary dining room set of furniture, being $1.60, a ten per cent. increase would add only sixteen cents to the cost. A harvester transported one hundred miles would be enhanced seventeen and a half cents in price; a kitchen stove carried from Detroit to the Mississippi would only cost twenty-five cents more; and the price of a Michigan refrigerator sold in New York, would be only seven and one-half cents higher; were freight rates to be increased by ten per cent. in each instance. On wearing apparel the proportions were represented as even more striking. An ordinary suit of clothes transported three hundred miles, under similarly enhanced rates, would, it was alleged, cost only one-third of a cent more. For all their apparel, made in New England, consisting of everything from hats to shoes, each wearer in the Middle West would be affected by a ten per cent. rise of rates by less than one cent apiece. True enough all this; and a striking testimonial to the effectiveness of the railway service of the country! But at the same time, if a ten per cent. increase of rates is inappreciable to the consumer, why not increase them by twenty per cent.[2]

[1] *Cf.* The Freight Rate Primer, bearing no authors or publishers name, but largely compiled from addresses by President W. C. Brown of the New York Central & Hudson River. Similar arguments and computations occur in the testimony before the Senate (Elkins) Committee of 1905, pp. 1162 and 2276.

[2] Now who will say that it is unreasonable to charge $7\frac{1}{2}$ cts. to carry a suit of clothes from Chicago to New York. . . . Railways could charge three or four times the cost of transportation for a pair of drawers and the rates would still be reasonable. . . . But all the first-class rates are of that nature. — Albert Fink, testimony, C., N. O. & T. P. case, p. 290.

And what becomes of the argument that charging rates according to what the traffic will bear, is an ample safeguard against extortion? Many of these small changes in price are diffused in the friction of retail trade;[1] some of them are unfortunately magnified to the consumer, especially under conditions of monopoly. When freight rates on beef go up ten cents per hundredweight, the consumers' price is more likely than not to rise by ten times that amount. But even assuming the final cost to follow the range of transportation charges closely, is it not evident that, so small relatively are many freight charges by comparison with other costs of production, that consumption is not proportionately affected by their movement one way or the other? And yet the entire argument that the value of service principle is a self-governing engine against unreasonable rates, is based upon this assumption. Surely the increased income to the carriers when rates are raised must come from someone. Because it is not felt, is no reason for denying its existence as a tax. But the very fact that it is not felt, undermines the argument that a safeguard against extortion obtains. The theorem that value of service in itself affords a reliable basis for rate making, pre-supposes that freight rates and prices move in unison; a supposition which a moment's consideration shows to be untenable in fact.[2] Such cases must be finally settled by some reference, indefinite though it be, to the cost of conducting that particular service; or rather, as Lorenz puts it, to the *extra* cost incident to that service. This extra cost may oftentimes be segregated, where the total cost could not be ascertained.[3]

[1] Senate (Elkins) Committee, 1905, p. 1162.
[2] In *re* Proposed Advances in Freight Rates, I.C.C., April 1, 1903.
[2] An interesting illustration of such determination of separable or extra cost was the computation by which the movement expenses of a train load of 50 cars of grain, 80,000 lbs. to the car, from Buffalo to New York were fixed at $520. I. C. C. Reports, 1903, p. 397. Or again in the estimation of the costs of operation in the express service from New Orleans to Kansas City in the banana trade. I. C. C. Rep., No. 1235, 1908. The able Wisconsin Railroad Commission has carefully studied a number of such cases, notable in its Two-Cent Fare decision of 1906.

That the problem is, however, a most difficult one is evidenced by the periodic controversies over railway mail pay.[1]

Of course in order that any change of rates should be reflected in prices, all carriers must of necessity agree upon the matter. The price is made by the least expensive source of supply. So that any carrier refusing to raise rates, might aid in the continuance of an already established price. Under conditions of transportation prevalent in the United States twenty years ago, the likelihood of an increased freight rate becoming a tax upon the community, was lessened by the probability that either by means of secret rebates, or by special and perhaps open commodity rates, some roads might choose to protect their clients against enhancement of prices. Markets were local — not reached by great systems operating from remote sources of supply. The policy of the northern transcontinental lines in making lumber rates from Oregon to the Middle West, might be quite independent of any policy in force on the southern hard pine carrying roads. But under present day conditions, the entire area of the United States is one great market. Hence, with rebates eliminated and with practical monopoly established through actual consolidation, control or harmony of policy, the carriers have the consumers much more completely at their mercy. Only two safeguards for the public interest remain. One is government regulation, or at all events supervision, of charges. The other is "enlightened self-interest" — which in transportation matters means a full appreciation of the possibilities and limitations in the application of the value of service principle to the determination of rates.

Considerations of cost of service afford protection, not only against unreasonably high rates, but also against unduly low charges. The evil in such cases is not only that the carriers operate at a loss, but that inequality and discrimination are inevitable concomitants of too low rates. No railway con-

[1] *Cf.* Tunell, Railway Mail Service, Chicago, 1901.

RATE MAKING PRACTICE   175

ceivably, of course, will charge unremunerative rates for a long time. But it sometimes happens that managements may be led to the adoption of policies of temporary expediency, not compatible with the long-time welfare of stockholders. During the presidency of Charles Francis Adams on the Northern Pacific in 1890 an unaccountable and unnatural diversion of traffic from this road to the Atchison, Topeka & Santa Fe suddenly occurred.[1] A large volume of freight from the East to Oregon was diverted to the round-about route *via* Southern California. On investigation it appeared that the English banking house of Baring Brothers, having become involved in unfortunate Argentine speculation, and being obliged to force a market for its investments in Atchison securities, demanded an immediate showing of large gross earnings regardless of the net profits. Orders to get traffic at any price went forth. A market was made for Atchison stock; although it was powerless to prevent the firm's final bankruptcy. In such a case the only safeguard against unreasonably depressed rates by the Atchison road, which, of course, immediately compelled corresponding reductions by the natural routes to the Northwest, should have been consideration of the actual cost of moving traffic by so long and round-about a route. And yet this consideration was entirely ignored. Another illustration of the same danger occurred in April, 1903.[2] A gang of western speculators unobtrusively acquired control of the Louisville & Nashville road, by taking advantage of the issue by that company of a large amount of new stock. This they did by the use of borrowed money. They had no intention, even had they been sufficiently well financed to do so, of permanently controlling the road as an investment. They bought the stock merely in order to resell it at a higher figure. They threatened the railway world with a general disturbance of rate conditions throughout the South. Their plan was to cut rates and steal traffic from other roads in order to make a large show

[1] Personal correspondence.   [2] Details in vol. II.

of gross earnings; and to unload their stock holdings on the market thus made, before the public learned the truth. This was prevented only by repurchase of their stock at very high prices. In such a case, what guidance would the principle of charging what the traffic would bear, afford? Cost of service must be invoked in order to determine the reasonableness of the low rates in force.

In any industry where rates are made under conditions of monopoly rather than of free competition, it is imperative that cost of service be constantly held in view. Under conditions of free competition it is bound to obtrude itself automatically; but under monopoly it must oftentimes be forcibly invoked. The shipper whose manufacturing plant has once been located in a certain place is no longer free to accept or reject a certain rate. He can afford neither to move nor to abandon his works. In order to continue in business he must meet the prices made by competitors. This price may be made elsewhere under more favored circumstances. To a manufacturer an increase of freight rates instead of curtailing output, may lead to attempts to lessen the costs of production per unit by an enlarged output sold at cut prices. Under such conditions an enhanced freight rate is a positive deduction from profits without any gain to the consumer. It is impossible to trace any safeguard against extortion in the operations of a value of service law under such circumstances. An instance in point is afforded by a complaint of the Detroit Chemical works in 1908.[1] This company imported iron pyrites through Baltimore from Spain; that being the source of the bulk of the material used here in the manufacture of sulphuric acid. The Detroit Company sold its product throughout the West in competition with companies at St. Louis, Chicago and Buffalo. The companies at Chicago and St. Louis enjoyed low import rates by way of the Gulf ports. The Buffalo concern used to be favored by a low rate said to be due to canal competition on

[1] 13 I.C.C. Rep., 357.

shipments from New York. Since 1903, however, the rate on pyrites from Baltimore to Detroit had been steadily increasing, from $1.56 to $2.72 per long ton. Even this latter rate by itself does not seem absolutely excessive, yielding a revenue of less than four mills per ton mile. But here again, it was not the absolute but the relative rate upon which the continued welfare of the industrial concern depended. The question had to be decided, not on the basis of cost, but from the point of view of the value of the service to the user. The carriers after this petition was filed voluntarily reduced the rate fifty-one cents per ton in January, 1908. The relative rate as compared with that to other competitive points was thus more equitably adjusted. The Interstate Commerce Commission on a review of the evidence held that this increase to $2.72 was unreasonable and unjust so long as it had been in effect; and awarded reparation to the amount of fifty-one cents per ton on all shipments made during its continuance.

It is indisputable that the great dynamic force in railway operation inheres in the value of service idea. The traffic manager who is always considering how much it will cost to handle business, will seldom adventure into new territory. The United States, as a rapidly growing country, is consequently the field in which charging what the traffic will bear, has been most ardently upheld as the only practicable basis for rate making. A few detailed illustrations will serve to show the results of its application in practice. Not infrequently does it happen that rates are different over the same line for shipments between two given points in opposite directions. Where this is due to a preponderance of traffic in one direction, and a consequent movement of "empties" which invite a back loading at very low rates, the difference of charges according to direction may actually be due to differences in the cost of carriage.[1] An empty train, which must be returned from New York to Chicago for another loading of grain, or to Georgia or Oregon for ship-

[1] 5 I.C.C. Rep., 299.

VOL. I—12

ments of lumber, if loaded with merchandise, can be moved with no allowance for dead weight of cars or locomotives; inasmuch as the train must move in any event, whether loaded or empty. But even where this defence of difference in the cost of service fails, the practice may be entirely proper from every point of view. By increasing the total tonnage a special rate may ultimately contribute to lower charges all along the line. Raisin culture began in California in 1876. Prior to that time the Spanish product had supplied the American market. The first thing to do was to find a market for the California raisins in the East. They would not bear the freight rate which had previously been charged for Spanish raisins moving over the transcontinental lines westward. A very low rate was all that the new traffic would bear. During the year 1876 therefore 70,000 lbs. of California raisins were carried east at one and three-fourths cents per 100 lbs., while simultaneously 1,000,000 lbs. of Spanish raisins were carried west over the same lines at a rate of three cents. No such difference in the cost of service in opposite directions existed, although a preponderance of empties moving eastward undoubtedly cheapened the service from California. The aim of the commodity rate was to upbuild a new industry. How far this succeeded appears from the fact that in 1891, no Spanish raisins were carried west at all; while the eastbound shipments amounted to 37,600,000 lbs.[1] The preceding illustration leads us then to this further conclusion. The cost of service principle might most conceivably be applied to a railway in a purely static state. But, dynamically considered, as involving the growth and development of business, it fails utterly by itself to meet the necessities of the case.

At times it is inevitable that cost of service and value of service considerations come flatly into opposition. Usually, as in the California raisin case or in the grant of low rates on Oregon lumber east bound about 1893, they reinforce one

[1] On raisins compared with citrus fruits: 22 I.C.C. Rep., 1.

another; that is to say, the lower rate given to build up business obtains on a service given at lower cost. But it sometimes happens that shipments of the same commodities over a line in opposite directions may occur and that the lower rate applies to the (presumably) more costly service. In 1906 a manufacturer in Menasha, Wis., complained to the Interstate Commerce Commission [1] that his rates on woodenware to the Pacific slope were ten cents per 100 lbs. higher than were rates on the same goods between the same points east bound, *notwithstanding* the fact that the empty car mileage west bound was then three times as great as in the contrary direction. The movement of empties west bound would certainly seem to justify as low if not lower rates on the basis of comparative cost of operation, supposing that there was coincidence in time. Only one satisfactory explanation for this apparent anomaly suggests itself; viz., that this low eastbound rate was given to build up a new industry in the West. In other words, the cost of service, a dependable guide for a road in a static condition, failed of effect upon a line possessed of great dynamic possibilities. Occasionally opposition of principles like this may occur in questions of classification. It may temporarily be worth while, in order to build up a new industry, to accord a lower rating to a commodity actually more valuable or more expensive to handle than others. Here again the dynamic force in the value of service principle outweighs all other considerations of relative cost of service.

The value of service principle in general fails, not only in the determination of absolutely reasonable rates, but it is inadequate also to the solution of perhaps the more difficult problem of relative rates. This question of relativity is twofold; first as between different places, and secondly as between different commodities. These are, in other words, the problems respectively of distance tariffs and of classification. The manner in which distance tariffs evolve, has already been dis-

[1] Interstate Commerce Commission, No. 797.

cussed, and it is evident that the cost of service principle is of fundamental importance, even though it be tempered by considerations of commercial expediency, that is to say, by the necessity of at all times under stress of competition, charging only what the traffic will bear. But while the value of service principle — charging according to demand in other words — applies at the competitive points, the other principle of relative cost should be the fundamental one in fixing upon the scale of local non-competitive rates.

The second phase of the problem of relativity arises in connection with classification.[1] How shall goods be graded in respect of their freight charges for identical services in carriage? Besides illustrating the interplay of the two fundamental principles, this topic serves also to clear up another possible confusion of terms. Proportioning transportation charges to the value of the service must always be clearly distinguished from basing them upon the mere value of the goods. Nothing is more certain than that no direct causal relation between freight rates and the intrinsic value of commodities is traceable. On wire the freight rate between two given points may be about one-fourth of the commercial value; on sheet iron one-third; on lumber somewhat more, and on hay two-fifths; while on cattle and hogs the freight rate may range as low as one-tenth to one-eighth of their commercial value. On coal, on the other hand, the freight rate often more than equals the price of the coal at the mine, and on very low grade commodities like bricks, the transportation charges may equal two or even three times the worth of the goods.[2] For each locality or even direction, these percentages will change. Positive reasons for these varying relationships are discernible in local trade conditions. While in general cheap goods are rated lower; if for any reason — bulkiness or risk — they cost relatively

[1] More in detail in chap. IX.
[2] Senate (Elkins) Committee, 1905, testimony of Mr. Bird, Traffic Manager of the St. Paul road. This is best measured, of course, by revenue per ton mile, chap. XII, *infra*.

more to transport, they may very properly be advanced in grade. Normally, raw products move at lower rates than finished products — for instance, wheat and flour or cattle and beef. This is in accord with charging what the traffic will bear in relation to value. But in the making of export rates, it may be to the interest of the carrier to reverse this order, actually according to the finished product the lower rate, thereby encouraging the development of manufactures at home rather than abroad.[1] Classification committees and regulative commissions are thus compelled to waver between the two opposing considerations of cost and value. One cannot avoid the conclusion, however, that, contrary to the usual rule, in this field of classification undue weight is often accorded by railway managers to that small element of total cost of service arising from risks of damage in transit — insurance cost, in other words — to the neglect of the financially more important consideration of what the traffic will bear. This emphasis upon the cost side of the account by classification committees, oddly enough is peculiarly characteristic of ratings in the higher class commodities. Among low grade goods, like grain, lumber or coal, the risk of damage is small, so that insurance cost becomes almost negligible. The insistent consideration among these low grade commodities is much more apt to be that of relative demand; arising from the necessity of close and constant adjustment to the behests of trade. Special or commodity rates, based directly upon what the traffic will bear, rather than upon the element of cost, are likely to prevail in these cases. But the very large revenue which could be obtained from increasing the rates upon the higher grade of goods seems not to be fully appreciated.

A valuable instance of the play of opposing considerations of cost and value of service in the classification of freight rates is afforded by the complaint in 1908 of the pulp paper makers in Wisconsin, already cited in another connection.[2] It appeared

[1] Flour v. wheat, p. 135, *supra*. [2] P. 148, *supra*.

that for similar service over the same roads, the rates per carload on saw logs for lumber were only about one-half those charged for carriage of logs to be ground into paper pulp. Judged on the basis of commercial value, hemlock and spruce bolts, too short and often otherwise unfit for lumber, were worth much less than saw logs; and yet they paid double the freight rates. This was not because the pulp wood was less desirable as traffic. In many ways it was more so. The haul was twice as long as for saw logs. The paper mills brought relatively more supplementary tonnage in the form of coal, food stuffs and supplies for workmen and their families. Fully as much of the finished product to be reshipped to consumers resulted. While smaller in volume, the pulp wood business was far more permanent. It was growing rapidly while the lumber business was declining. Moreover, the actual cost of service in hauling pulp wood was fully as low as for lumber logs. Carloads were much heavier, and were more regular in movement. In practice they involved no milling-in-transit obligation, that is to say, no obligation to re-ship the finished paper out over the same road; while all the saw log rates carried this obligation — a matter of some moment to the railways. And finally the value of the service to shippers of pulp wood was less than to mere lumbermen; in other words, the paper makers were operating under closer margins of profit; their plants were more costly, and depreciated more rapidly. The defence of the carriers in this case was not that the rates on pulp wood were too high in themselves, but that the rate on saw logs was perhaps unduly low — the latter having been crowded down to a minimum figure by competition in the early days of the business by the lumber raftsmen who floated the saw logs downstream from the forest to the saw mills. But of equal importance probably in perpetuating the higher rates on pulp logs, was the assumption that while the value of the bolts themselves was perhaps even less than that of saw logs, the value of the resultant product, paper, was much greater than that of lumber. But the Wisconsin Railroad Commission, in entire harmony with the principle repeatedly laid down by the Federal commission, held that the carriers must be guided by real distinctions of cost from a transportation standpoint and not by gradations of value. If the goods were bulky, awkward, or risky to handle, perhaps requiring special appliances or equipment, relatively high classification was permissible. But if they were substantially similar for purposes of carriage, no gradation in rates based upon differences in the ultimate uses to which the commodity might be put would be upheld. Such was the reasoning of the Interstate Commerce Commission in a decision, holding that fire, building and paving brick must be accorded equal rates, regardless of their differing values.[1] That the element of value is, however, not negligible is brought out in a later Federal case,[2] wherein it was recommended that cheap china, to be given away as premiums in the tea trade, be rated nearer ordinary crockery or earthenware, even though shipped in the same manner as high grade chinaware. Under the official classification, chinaware is rated first class if in boxes, and second class in casks. Earthenware or crockery is carried at twenty per cent. less than third class, in small packages (L. C. L.). On the basis of mere cost of service, it would seem as if boxes of chinaware should have a lower rating than casks. Boxes stow better than casks, with less risk of breakage. But the commercial practice being to ship the finer grades of chinaware in boxes, such shipments are graded higher because the traffic will usually bear a higher rate. Thus considerations of cost of service yield to those of value. The Interstate Commerce Commission, however, noting the exceptional circumstances under which the tea company distributed its cheap chinaware, recommended a revision of the classification to

---

[1] More in detail at p. 318, *infra*. Also Hammond, Rate Theories of the I.C.C., 1911, p. 32.
[2] U. P. Tea Co.; I.C.C. Rep., No. 1569, 1908.

meet the needs of the case; in other words ordering a greater emphasis upon the elements of the value of the service, even at the expense of relative cost of operation.

Our final conclusion, then, must be this: That both principles are of equal importance; and that both must be continually invoked as a check upon each other. The tendency to the elevation of cost of service to a position of priority — rather characteristic of regulative bodies and of legislators — is no less erroneous than the marked disposition of railway managers to insist upon the universal applicability of the principle of charging what the traffic will bear. Neither will stand the test of reasonableness alone. Whether the one or the other should take precedence can only be determined by a careful study of the circumstance and conditions in each case; and in practice, the instances where either principle becomes of binding effect to the entire exclusion of the other, are extremely rare.

CHAPTER VI

PERSONAL DISCRIMINATION

Rebates and monopoly, with attendant danger to carriers, 185. — Personal discrimination defined, 188. — Distinction between rebating and general rate cutting, 188. — Early forms of rebates, 189. — Underbilling, underclassification, etc., 190. — Private car lines, 192. — More recent forms of rebating described, 195. — Terminal and tap-lines, 196. — Midnight tariffs, 197. — Outside transactions, special credit, etc., 198. — Distribution of coal cars, 199. — Standard Oil Company practices, 200. — Discriminatory open adjustments from competing centres, 202. — Frequency of rebating since 1900, 204–6. — The Elkins Law of 1903, 205. — Discrimination since 1906, 207. — The grain elevator cases, 211. — Industrial railroads once more, 212.

THE philosophy of rebating has perhaps never been better described than in the following quotation from the Cullom Committee investigation of 1886:

"Mr. WICKER. I am speaking now of when I was a railroad man. Here is quite a grain point in Iowa, where there are five or six elevators. As a railroad man, I would try and hold all those dealers on a 'level keel,' and give them all the same tariff rate. But suppose there was a road five or six or eight miles across the country, and those dealers should begin to drop in on me every day or two and tell me that that road across the country was reaching within a mile or two of our station and drawing to itself all the grain. You might say that it would be the just and right thing to do to give all the five or six dealers at this station a special rate to meet that competition through the country. But, as a railroad man, I can accomplish the purpose better by picking out one good, smart, live man, and, giving him a concession of three or four cents a hundred, let him go there and scoop the business. I would get the tonnage, and that is what I want. But if I give it to the five it is known in a very short time. I can illustrate that better by a story told by Mr. Vanderbilt when he and his broker had a deal in stocks. The broker came in and said, 'Mr. Vanderbilt, I would like to take in my friend John Smith.' Mr. Vanderbilt said, 'Let us see how this will work. Here are you and myself in this deal now. We take in John Smith; that makes a hundred and eleven. I guess I won't do it.' When you take in these people at the station on a private rebate you might as well make it public and lose what you intend to accomplish. You can take hold of one man and build him up at the expense of the others, and the railroad will get the tonnage."

"SENATOR HARRIS. The effect is to build that one man up and destroy the others?"

"Mr. WICKER. Yes, sir; but it accomplishes the purposes of the road better than to build up the six."

The force of this description of the underlying motive for personal discrimination, so far as the carrier is concerned; namely to build up one man at the expense of his competitors and to attach him in interest indissolubly to the company, is well exemplified in a case which occurred in 1908 at Galveston, Texas.[1] Practically all railway traffic entering Galveston was destined for export. Wharfage facilities were limited to two concerns, one of them being the Southern Pacific Terminal Co. A uniform charge of one cent per hundredweight for cotton seed meal and cake passing over the wharves of both companies had been the rule for a long time. Yet it appeared on complaint that one merchant had been granted wharfage space under discriminatingly favorable conditions. Exemption from demurrage charges, free storage room and other favors and a fixed rental of $15,000 per year irrespective of the amount of his shipments, had enabled him, having been in business only since 1898, to build up a very large traffic. The export of cotton seed cake instead of meal had greatly increased since 1904. The business of all other competitors since this contract was made had shrunk to insignificant proportions by comparison with that done by this favored merchant. The margin of profit in the business was so small that the difference between the charges and privileges enjoyed by this individual and his competitors, was forcing them all out of business. It was estimated by the Interstate Commerce Commission that if the customary wharfage charges had been paid, the rental would have been nearly $30,000 for the year 1907, irrespective

---

[1] 14 I.C.C. Rep., 250. Upheld by the Supreme Court in 1911; 219 U. S., 498. Also 23 *Idem*, 535.

of other favors. The cotton planters complained also that this monopoly limited their market and depressed business. It is clear that the larger the business, that is to say the more nearly it became a monopoly, the smaller became the wharfage charges per hundredweight under this system of a fixed rental; and, in consequence, the greater was the disability of the other shippers. The advantage to the railroad appeared in a contract entered into, which provided that all traffic for this individual should be routed over the Southern Pacific or its connecting lines. As he had practically gathered in all the cotton seed export business of Texas and the adjoining states within two years, it is evident that this consideration was of great value to the railroad. The economic motive in this case and in the one previously cited was the same. It will be found in fact to underlie almost all cases of personal favoritism and discrimination.

The supreme disadvantage in building up a great monopoly in order to win traffic for a railroad is, of course, that the moment the shipper becomes sufficiently powerful, he can play off one road against another, thus becoming practically master of the situation. Sindbad is soon overwhelmed by the old man of the sea. And the weaker the road financially, the more powerful is the appeal, to which at last even the strongest lines must succumb. The history of the Standard Oil Company during the eighties clearly exemplifies this. The rapid rise of the cattle "eveners" yet earlier, until, as the private refrigerator car companies they controlled the situation, was primarily traceable to the same causes. The late J. W. Midgly[1] gives a forcible illustration in the attempt in 1894 of ninety-five railroads to reduce the mileage allowance paid for use of oil tank cars owned by private companies from three-fourths to one-half cent per mile, loaded and empty. The Union Tank Line promptly replied that it would in that event at once con-

[1] Circular Letters of the Chicago Bureau of Car Performances; undated.

centrate all its vast tonnage to points north and west of Chicago, upon the single line — presumably the weakest one — which would continue the old rate. This argument was irresistible; and in the old days of unregulated competition was in the nature of things bound to be so.

Careful distinction must ·be made at this point, between personal discrimination and general rate cutting. Rebating, — that is to say, departure from published tariffs,—occurs in both cases. The difference between the two is that in the one case it is special, particular and secret; while in the other it is so general, if not indeed universal, as to be matter of common knowledge. Rebating, in other words, is a common feature of rate wars. But, on the other hand, general harmony in the rate situation by no means implies the absence of personal favoritism. During a wide-open rate war, indeed, the most iniquitous aspect of rebating, — inequality of treatment as between rival shippers, — may be quite absent. All may be getting the same rate, namely a cut rate; although the chances are of course that the bigger the shipper, the more substantial the concessions offered. It is important to keep this distinction clear, especially since the railways have awakened to the losses to themselves attendant upon rate wars.

All parties concerned are probably agreed in the hope of eliminating the rate war forever. But there is not the same evidence of either an intent or desire on the part of railway officials to get rid of what, from a public point of view, is even more insidious and unjust; that is to say, the secret concession of favors to a few chosen large shippers. General rate wars, as will later appear, are probably a thing of the past.[1] But secret rebating seems, on the other hand, to be an evil which must be combatted vigorously and unintermittently in order to uproot it as a feature of American industrial life. And of course it must cease. For it is the most prolific source of evil known in transportation. It has probably had more to do

[1] The latter half of chap. XII.

with the creation of great industrial monopolies than any other single factor. The first feature of any reform of our intolerable "trust" situation, must be to keep the rails open on absolutely even terms to all shippers, large or small.

The keynote of discrimination is, as we have said, the creation of monopoly, or, at all events, of so large an aggregation of shipments, that a profitable partnership between the shipper and the railroad results. This is clear in recent indictments which charge that the railroads concerned, having selected one large firm of forwarders in New York and Chicago are giving them a monopoly in respect of all imports. In the case of the great beef packers, the railroad having once built up a shipper by favored rates, may continue in the enjoyment of this concentrated tonnage with greater security and profit than if it moved in a multitude of small shipments by numerous competitors. Of course there is another less common form of rebating which, so far as its profit is concerned, is limited to the particular dishonest railway official who arranges the matter. Such favoritism as this, however, represents a loss to the company; and has always been stamped out by the carriers when discovered. The principal form above described, is much more difficult to uproot. And yet for some reason, it is a distinctively American abuse. European countries seem never to have suffered from it, to any such degree as has the United States. It is, as has just been said, perhaps the most iniquitous, the most persistent and until very recently the most nearly ineradicable evil connected with the great business of transportation.

Rebating in the early days consisted in simply refunding by direct payment to the favored shipper, a certain proportion of the freight bill. This refund might be in cash, in presents to himself or his family, in salary allowances to clerks, in free passes, or in free transportation of other goods. In a recent case in New York it has taken the form of importer's "commissions." But, since 1887 at least, an inconvenience in all such transactions is their necessary entry in some form or other upon the books of the company. Of course such rebates could be covered up as a fictitious charge to operating expenses; or, as in the case of the Atchison in 1893, might be carried as an asset, as if such refunds would ever be paid. Nearly $4,000,000 was thus entered as padding in Atchison assets, when it went into a receiver's hands at that time.[1] Much of the flagrant Standard Oil rebating in the eighties was almost openly, and certainly boldly, carried on by these means. But public sentiment was always against it; and of course, it was a breach of good faith as between the railways themselves, in their endeavor to maintain agreed rates. Secrecy, therefore, always attaches to these transactions; and the most ingenious devices were invented to confer favors without detection.

Underclassification of freight was a very common device in the old days. It has reappeared again since 1907 in much the same form. There is a great difference between the freight on a keg of nails and of fine brass hardware or cutlery. Who is to know whether a shipment be billed as one or the other? Is every box of dry goods to be examined in order to discover whether it contains silks or the cheapest cotton cloth? A carload of lumber or cordwood might easily by prearrangement be filled inside with high grade package freight. The utmost vigilance is in fact necessary on the part of carriers, to prevent such fraudulent practices by shippers. Under the Joint Rate Trunk Line Inspection Bureau in 1893, 183,575 such false descriptions or underweighings were detected on westbound shipments from seaboard cities alone.[2] What the amount of such underclassification of freight by collusion between agent and shipper was, can only be conjectured. Even more difficult to detect was the practice of underbilling.[3] At a certain

[1] The chapter on reorganizations in vol. II will afford other instances with full references. Com. & Fin. Chron., LIX, p. 232.

[2] 55th Cong., 1st Sess., Sen. doc., 39, p. 29.

[3] Ann. Rep., I.C.C., 1896, p. 82: and 1897, p. 53. Fine cases in 1 I.C.C. Rep., 633–656.

PERSONAL DISCRIMINATION

time, the rate on flour from Minneapolis to New York was thirty cents per hundredweight, divided between connecting roads in the proportion of ten cents from Minneapolis to Chicago, and twenty cents from there on to destination. In the meantime, as against this ten cent proportion of the through rate to New York, the local rate from Minneapolis to Chicago was twelve and one-half cents. As between two rival shippers, the one sending to Chicago on a New York through rate instead of a local one, would enjoy a clear advantage of twenty-five per cent. over his competitor. And who was to know whether a car billed through to New York, was really going beyond Chicago or not? In one period of three months, 1098 cars thus through billed to New York were turned over at Chicago to a belt line road; and only 468 actually went on to that destination. About sixty per cent. of the traffic was being rebated by this means. Very complicated arrangements of this sort were rife in the Missouri river rate wars on grain in 1896. This was known as the "expense-bill" system; or "carrying at the balance of the through rate." [1]

Many services or facilities are worth as much to a merchant as a direct refund in cash. He may be given free cartage. This was a very common expedient in the early days; being fully considered by the Interstate Commerce Commission.[2] Or free storage on wheels or in freight houses may be utilized as a cover for favoritism. A low carload rate might be given, and then the goods be held, storage free, by the railway at some central point; to be subsequently delivered piecemeal as sold. The dealer would be relieved of all expense for warehousing as well as of high less-than-carload rates from the initial point of shipment. The competitor who paid the less-than-carload rate on an equal volume of business would be sadly handicapped. Cases are on record where fish was thus

---

[1] Investigation of grain rates at Missouri river points; 54th Cong., 2nd Sess., Sen. doc. 115, pp. 17–22, etc.
[2] 167 U. S. Rep., 633.

stored free from November to February, being reshipped on order in small lots. Or an excessive allowance might be made by the railway for some service or facility afforded by the shipper. The beef interests first got their hold upon the carriers by demanding liberal rebates in return for acting as "eveners" in the partition of traffic between the trunk lines about 1873. Complaint against excessive allowances to favored grain elevator owners, was common all through the West for years. The elevator allowance cases before the Interstate Commerce Commission in 1906–1910 concerning practices on the Union Pacific lines illustrate the delicacy of the issues involved.[1]

Deductions from the full tariff for the use of special equipment owned by shippers, has been one of the commonest means of building up great monopolies.[2] The allowances to the Standard Oil Company for the use of its tank cars, before the construction of pipe lines, and especially prior to 1888, were a source of great unrest.[3] But the construction of pipe lines has not lessened their importance. It is on record that the use of private cars in other lines of business has led to grave abuses. When stock cars and beef refrigerator cars, owned by private shippers, first began to be used about 1883–1884, they were much sought after by the railroads as traffic. They moved regularly, not by seasons; the volume of business was large and rapidly growing; it was concentrated at a few large initial points; much of it was high class and very remunerative. With the enormous extension of refrigeration to cover the long-distance movement of fruit and vegetables, a still more powerful encouragement came into play. These latter businesses were highly seasonal. Few roads could afford to maintain

[1] P. 211, *infra*.

[2] On private car lines, Columbia University Studies, etc., LXXXI, 1908, p. 185. J. W. Midgley's Circular Letters as chief of the Bureau of Car Performances in 1901, costing him his position, by the way, are most significant. Car service reform resulted nevertheless. *Cf. Quarterly Journal of Economics*, 1904, p. 299. See pp. 96 and 140, *supra*.

[3] U. S. Bureau of Corp., Rep. on Trans. of Petroleum, pp. 36, 60, 81, 88.

highly specialized equipment to care for a business of a few weeks length. But a private company operating all over the country, could utilize its cars first for early vegetables and fruits from the south, then from the middle west or the Oregon-Washington region, and finally in winter for oranges from California or Florida. The number of these cars rapidly increased until by 1903 there were 130,000 in service, — in fact about one-eleventh of all the freight cars in the United States were privately owned. The so-called Armour interests, primarily engaged in the packing business, were by far the largest single concern.

The system of payment for the use of these cars consisted of an allowance, based upon the mileage performed. This used to be one cent per mile, loaded and empty, for refrigerator cars. In 1894 a determined effort was made by the carriers to reduce this below the point then reached of three-fourths of a cent per mile. But the extraordinary concentration both of ownership and traffic, rendered it easy for the car companes to defeat the proposition. In the meantime the steady increase in volume of traffic, making whole trainloads possible, together with the growth of very long distance business, made it imperative that these trains be operated at high speed with few stops. This at once enormously enhanced the earning power of each car, as based upon mileage. The performance was often as high as four times that of the ordinary freight cars.

Under these new conditions, at the current rate of earnings, a car would pay for itself in three years, besides paying all expenses of maintenance. The burden of these allowances became very great. The situation some years ago is well described by a former member of the Interstate Commerce Commission, as follows: —

"Investigations made by the Interstate Commerce Commission at different times have disclosed to some extent the very large sums received by shippers as mileage for the use of such cars.

"By an investigation made in 1889 it appeared that on a single line of road between Chicago and an interior Eastern point — a distance of 470 miles — refrigerator cars owned by three shipping firms made in nine months, from August 1, 1888, to May 1889, 7,428,406 miles, and earned for mileage $72,945.97, being about $8,112 a month or substantially at the rate of $100,000 a year.

"By another investigation, made in 1890, it appeared that private stock cars to the number of 250 had been used upon a line made up of two connecting roads between Chicago and New York, beginning with 150 cars on September 1, 1880, increased 30 more a month later, 20 more another month later, and reaching the total of 250 in June, 1890; that the cars altogether had cost $156,500, and had earned for mileage in two years, from September 1, 1888, to September 1, 1890, $205,582.68; that the entire expense to be deducted during that period for car repairs and salaries for their management was $34,050.48, leaving net revenue to the amount of $171,532.20, being an excess of $15,032 above the whole cost of the cars. The cars were, therefore, paid for and a margin besides in two years, and, thereafter, under the same management and with a corresponding use of the cars, an income of upward of $100,000 a year was assured on an investment fully repaid, or, in effect, on no investment whatever."

By 1903 the railroads were paying over $12,000,000 annually for the use of such equipment.

With the growth of their power, the extortionate demands of these private car lines, both upon the railroads and the shipper, steadily enlarged. From the roads they often compelled fictitious mileage allowances; and from the shipper the most outrageous charges were made for icing and other services en route. The reports of the Interstate Commerce Commission for 1903–1904 and of the Senate (Elkins) Committee of 1905 deal fully with these abuses. Moreover the Armour company gradually forced other competitors out of business, and with the growth of monopoly, its exactions became even more extreme. The following instance is typical.

"In 1898 the Armour Car Lines Company was furnishing cars for the movement of Michigan fruits from points on the Pere Marquette Railroad to Boston in competition with other private car companies, and its charge for refrigeration to Boston was $20 per car. Its present charge to Boston is $55 per car. Before the present exclusive contract was entered into between the Armour Car Lines and the Pere Marquette

Railroad Company the actual quantity of ice required was charged for at $2.50 per ton. Under this system the cost of refrigerating cars from Pawpaw, Mich., to Dubuque, Iowa, averaged about $10 per car, while the present schedule of the Armour Car Lines is $37.50. The cost of icing from Mattawan, Mich., to Duluth was $7.50, as shown by an actual transaction in the year 1902, while the present refrigeration charge between those points is $45. The cost of icing pineapples from Mobile to Cincinnati under an exclusive contract with the Armour Car Lines is $45, while the cost of performing the same service from New Orleans to Cincinnati over the Illinois Central is $12.50 per car."

Fortunately the progressive enlargement of Federal powers of supervision has tended to check these exactions. But the system of special allowances for the use of privately owned equipment, is one which needs the most careful watching by the authorities.

With the passage of time, and especially since 1896, new and even more elaborate schemes for rebating have come to light. One of the most ingenious, which was discovered about 1904 to be very widespread, was the use of terminal or spur track railway companies.[1] In Hutchinson, Kansas, for example, were salt works having a capacity of some 6000 barrels a day. Two railways were available for shipments. A new company was incorporated, all its stock being held by the salt works owners, which constructed sidings to both railroad lines. The spur track was less than a mile long and cost only about $8000 to build. But the company was chartered as the Hutchinson and Arkansas River Railroad. Its officers were the owners of the salt mills. It owned neither engines nor cars. Yet it entered into a traffic agreement with the Atchison road for a division of the through rate to many important points, its share being about twenty-five per cent. So substantial a prorate was this, that in a few months the H. and A. R. R. received back some fifteen thousand dollars as its share of the through

[1] 10 I.C.C. Rep., 1, 148, 385 and 661: 18th Ann. Rep., I.C.C., 19 and 42: Senate (Elkins) Committee, 1905, pp. 2424–2495. Later cases discussed at p. 212, *infra*.

freight rates. And every dividend declared by it was, of course in effect a rebate enjoyed exclusively by this particular mill, as against less favored competitors.

Obviously, rebates assuming the above-described form are open only to very large shippers, to whom it is worth while to incur the considerable expense. But many concerns have already such trackage in or about their works. Nothing is needed except to incorporate them separately, and then to enter into suitable traffic agreements with standard roads. Many of the so-called trusts were implicated in such transactions, about 1904–1905. The International Harvester Company at Chicago had for years performed much of its own terminal service; and until 1904 was allowed as high as $3.50 per car for switching charges by connecting railroads. It then incorporated the Illinois Northern Railroad, which was promptly conceded twenty per cent. of all through rates, with the Missouri river rate as a maximum. On this traffic it would be allowed as high as $12 per car, instead of $3.50 as before. The Illinois Steel Company afforded in 1905 an even more flagrant example. Apparently it had enjoyed extra-liberal proportions of through rates since 1897, by means of its separately incorporated and, in fact, really important terminal road. But an allowance of $700 to $1000 for hauling a trainload of coke some seven miles, yielded a profit on the business of perhaps ninety per cent. It was an advantage which no competitor could hope to equal. No doubt the practice of switching allowances was properly used at the start. But the large crop of cases discovered in 1904–1905 proved that they had come to be very widely used as a cover for rebating. It is not always easy, however, to decide when such an allowance ought to be made to a privately owned terminal company. The Anheuser-Busch case, decided in June, 1911, with a dissenting opinion by Commissioner Harlan, shows how intricately involved such issues may become.[1]

The so-called "midnight tariff" was a strictly legal way of

[1] P. 212, *infra*.

conferring favors upon certain shippers. It was much in evidence during the grain wars between lines serving the Gulf ports about 1903. And it seems to have been a device used at times all over the country. A traffic manager wishing to steal all the business of a large shipper from some competing road, and to build him up at the expense of his rivals, secretly agrees to put into effect a low rate on a given date. The shipper then enters into contracts calling for perhaps several hundred carloads of grain to be delivered at that time. This reduction is publicly filed, perhaps thirty days in advance, with the Interstate Commerce Commission at Washington. But who is to discover it, in the great medley of new tariffs placed on file every day? Yet this is not all. A second tariff, restoring the full rate, is also filed to take effect very shortly, — perhaps only a day, — after the reduction occurs. All these are public, and open to all shippers alike. But only the one who was forewarned is able to take advantage of them. He rushes all his shipments forward while the reduced rates are in effect. Before other competitors can assemble their grain or other goods, the brief reduction has come to an end; and rates are restored to their former figure.

The President of the Chicago Great Western Railway has concisely described the commercial effect of one of these midnight tariffs.

"A clean profit, he says, over all expenses of one half of a cent per bushel is a satisfactory profit to the middleman; and a guaranteed rate of transportation of even so small a sum as one-quarter of a cent per bushel less than any other middleman can get, will give the man possessing it a monopoly of the business of handling the corn in the district covered by the guaranty. Why? Such are the facilities of trade by means of bills of lading, drafts, telegraphs, banks, etc., that to do an enormous corn trade, the middleman requires only a comparatively small capital to use as a margin. A capital of $50,000 is ample thus to handle 15,000,000 bushels, and with activity, double that amount, per annum. One quarter of a cent per bushel profit on 15,000-000 bushels would amount to $37,500 which is equal to .75 per cent. per annum on the capital employed."

A similar device was used by the Burlington road in its dealings with the Missouri river packing houses on export traffic. They signed an agreement making a rate to Germany of twenty-three cents per hundred to last until December 31, 1905. Before the expiration of this time, however, the roads concerned, publicly filed an amended tariff presumably for all shippers of thirty-five cents per hundred. They nevertheless continued the old rate to the packers. This case went to the Supreme Court which decided in 1908 that the device was unlawful and discriminatory.[1]

And then again there are all the possibilities of the printer's art to be used, in connection with the preparation of elaborate tariffs.[2] The tariff of "33 cents per hundredweight" may conceivably be a typographical error, to be speedily corrected in a supplementary hektograph sheet filed the next day. Involved and elaborate rate sheets may be reprinted with only one little change among a thousand items left as before. Different tariffs may interlock with complicated cross references. In one case in 1902 it took seven different tariffs to enable one to compute the rate for a given shipment. In twelve months, to December 1907, there were filed with the Interstate Commerce Commission 220,982 such tariffs, each containing changes in rates or rules. Some "expire with this shipment," — and some agree to "protect" any rate of any competing carrier, that is to say, to meet it if it happen to be lower.

An entirely different plan of rebating, — and a most effective one, — has to do with apparently unrelated commercial transactions.[3] Many shippers are large sellers of supplies to the railroad. How easy then to make a concession in rates to an oil refinery for example, by paying a little extra for the lubricating oil bought from a subsidiary concern. The Federal authorities in recent years and especially in connection with the prosecution of the Standard Oil Company in 1908–1911,

---

[1] P. 209, *infra*.
[2] 11th Ann. Rep., I.C.C.; 16th *Idem*, p. 13; and 21st *Idem*, p. 14.
[3] Bureau of Corp., Rep. on Trans. of Petroleum, 1905, p. 105 *et seq.*

have discovered the most extraordinary variations in the prices paid by railroads for supplies. Independent concerns were often not allowed to compete in the sale of lubricants at all. It would be difficult to prove any connection between so widely separate sets of dealings; and yet it is clear that rebates are often given in this way. Or even more fruitful as an expedient, especially in these later days when rebating is a serious offence, why not confer a favor by extra liberality in allowances for damages to goods in transit? In 1909 the so-called Beef Trust was specifically ordered by the Attorney General of the United States to desist from such practices. Positively the only way to detect such fictitious allowances for damages, is to ferret out each case by itself. This is a slow and necessarily expensive process. Damage allowances and *quid pro quo* transactions in the purchase of supplies, are indeed almost "smokeless rebates," as they have aptly been termed.

Personal discrimination may be as effective upon competition through denial of facilities to some shippers, as through conferring of special favors upon others. Practices of this sort have been quite common in the coal business, especially in the matter of furnishing or refusing to furnish an ample supply of cars or suitable spur tracks to mines. In the well known Red Rock Fuel Company case in 1905,[1] the railroad definitely announced its policy, "not to have a lot of little shippers on its line who would ship coal when prices were high and then shut up shop and go home and let the large shippers have the lean years." The development of over 4,000 acres of coal lands was thus denied in favor of the large companies, until the Interstate Commerce Commission took the matter up. A year later came the startling revelations upon the Pennsylvania Railroad as to the practice of discrimination in furnishing cars to coal mines.[2] A comprehensive investigation by the com-

---

[1] 11 I.C.C. Rep., 438; *Cf.* 13 *Idem*, 70; and 19 *Idem*, 356.
[2] Report on Discriminations and Monopolies in Coal and Oil; Jan. 25, 1907, pp. 1–81.

pany itself resulted in the discharge of a number of high officials. It appeared, for example, that the assistant to President Cassatt had acquired $307,000 in stock of coal companies without cost; that a trainmaster for $500 had purchased coal mine stock which yielded an annual income of $30,000; and that one road foreman was given three hundred shares of the same company stock for nothing. In all these cases the object was to secure not only an ample supply of cars for the favored companies, but perhaps even the denial of suitable service to troublesome competitors. In this regard, the old practices of the Standard Oil Company in the eighties are recalled. Not only, as in the celebrated Rice case,[1] did it demand heavy refunds on its own shipments, but it also compelled the imposition of a surtax on its competitors' traffic which was to be added to its own special allowance.

Yet other means of favoring large shippers at the expense of small ones, are almost impossible to eradicate. Certain of these may be illustrated by recently discovered practices of the Standard Oil Company. They are fully described in a special report of the United States Commissioner of Corporations in 1905. Upon the basis of this evidence, extraordinary efforts were made by the Federal authorities to secure convictions and to impose heavy fines for violation of the Elkins law. But the company escaped heavy penalties, in the main, by reason of legal technicalities. The prosecutions of 1906–1909, however, cannot be regarded as valueless, merely because the company escaped the imposition of fines aggregating millions of dollars. The moral effect of it was thoroughly good; and it is now clear that laws can be so drawn as to apply in future. Nor can any student of the evidence doubt for a moment, that, whether strictly an infraction of the law or not, the net result of these practices was to confer an advantage upon this large shipper, not open to its smaller competitors. Certain of its advantages, such as the ownership of pipe lines

[1] Ripley, Railway Problems, chap. II, fully described.

from the wells to the seaboard refineries and the strategic location of its plants, are the fruit of great resources and keen business acumen. But other advantages, particularly the relative rates on refined oil from Standard Oil plants and from centres of independent refining, are, according to the report of the Bureau of Corporations, due to pressure brought to bear upon the carriers. Whether they are or not, the result is discriminatory just the same.

The reason for the persistent pressure for low rates on petroleum products is, of course, that the cost of manufacture is so low relatively to the expense of transportation. An ample manufacturing profit is one-half cent per gallon of crude oil; and the average cost of refining does not exceed that amount. Yet a half cent will scarcely pay freight for more than one hundred miles. Hence it follows that for distances greater than this, the question of profit or loss may entirely depend upon the delicate adjustment of the freight rate. In this regard, a great company shipping all over the country has a great advantage over smaller competitors with a strictly local market, in that it can play off one rate against another. Thus, in one notable case, cited by the Bureau of Corporations, the Burlington road gave an absolutely unremunerative rate from the Standard refinery at Whiting near Chicago to East St. Louis, thereby enabling troublesome competition to be subdued; but it was recompensed by the payment of heavier charges on shipments to other points on the Burlington system, where, there being no competition, the high freight rate could be shifted on to the consumer. The Commissioner of Corporations gives one instance on the Northwestern road of a carload rate from Whiting to Milwaukee in order to meet water competition from independents at Toledo, which netted the carrier just ninety-two cents for the carriage of 24,000 pounds of oil a distance of eighty-five miles, with free return of the empty car.

The peculiarity of many of these rate adjustments of the

Standard Oil Company of late years was that they were publicly filed; and hence not open to legal attack. This does not however detract in the least from their discriminatory character. One example, right here in New England, now happily corrected, may be cited from the records of the Interstate Commerce Commission for 1906.[1] The southern half of New England was mainly supplied with kerosene from the great Standard refinery at Bayonne, New Jersey. The oil was brought there from the fields by pipe line; and, being refined, was distributed by tank vessels all along the coast, with a short rail haul thereafter to inland points. The total cost to the Standard company was estimated by the Bureau of Corporations at between fourteen and sixteen cents per hundredweight. To meet this, the independent western refiners had to ship all the way by rail. This was more expensive in any event; but for some years they found their handicap greatly increased by the refusal of the New Haven road to join in any joint through rate. The western independents, therefore, had to pay the sum of two local rates, up to and beyond the Hudson river, thereby bringing their transportation up to approximately thirty cents per hundred pounds. In other words, their cost of carriage per gallon was enhanced more than enough to constitute a fair refining profit in itself. The result was the practical exclusion of competition from this source. Fortunately, however, after this investigation the New Haven was ordered to pro-rate with the western roads, thereby overcoming about half of this disability. This case clearly evinces the necessity of effective Federal regulation of such matters as joint rates; and it also shows how possible it may be to so adjust tariffs, openly and even legally, as to favor one shipper over another.

Unlike the preceding instance, most of the Standard's rebates have been, in fact if not technically, secret. Perhaps the most flagrant case occurred in the rates from Whiting to the southeastern states. The Bureau of Corporations estimated

[1] 11 I.C.C. Rep., 558; U. S. Bureau Corp'ns Rep., p. 148.

that $70,000 a year was saved by this device; and all competition from independent sources was eliminated within that territory. The Illinois Central and Southern roads cross at an obscure point in Tennessee known as Grand Junction. This was made a centre of distribution for the entire South.[1] But the rate under which the oil moved, — and in one given month 169 carloads were thus carried, — was given on a special tariff, publicly filed at Washington, to be sure, but prescribing the rate, not from Whiting but from Dalton, Illinois, to Grand Junction, Tennessee. Dalton was an almost unknown station, near the refinery. Of course any other shipper who happened to know of it, and who happened to have oil to ship from Dalton to Grand Junction, could have had the same rate of thirteen cents a hundred pounds. But he would find it moved over a roundabout route, over four different connecting lines, instead of over the rails of a single company. As against this rate of thirteen cents, the only routes known to the Ohio independent producers charged from nineteen to twenty-nine and one-half cents per hundred pounds. Meantime the Standard's oil was by this devious means reaching every point in the South at prices which no competitor could hope to meet. In one case, the oil going by way of Grand Junction, travelled over one thousand miles when the direct route from Chicago was only a little over five hundred miles. The adjustment was everywhere such that, even on the commonly known tariffs, Whiting enjoyed a special advantage over the sources of independent oil. Atlanta, Georgia, is only 733 miles by short line and 1003 miles by way of Grand Junction from Whiting. Toledo, with its independent refineries, is distant only 687 miles. Yet despite this fact, the commonly known rates were shown to be, from Whiting, 33.2 cents as against 47.5 cents from Toledo. So, even without the Grand Junction contrivance, the Standard was seemingly favored more than enough. It should be added, in conclusion, that while the Grand Junction rate was publicly filed, its discriminatory

[1] Routes shown by the map on p. 647, *infra*.

character stands proven by the fact that all the actual shipments were "blind billed;" that is to say, no local agent knew what was the rate actually paid. Such blind bills of lading are photographically reproduced in the report above named. Moreover the ill repute of the transaction was indicated by the prompt cancellation of the rate when discovered in 1905. But in the meantime it had done its work, and fixed monopoly prices for an indispensable product over a quarter of the territory of the United States.

Aside from the palpably dishonest secret rebating, the real root of the difficulty with many of the other big shippers beside the Standard Oil Company, — and an abuse moreover exceedingly hard to correct, — is the open adjustment of rates from competing centres of manufacture or distribution in such a way as to confer favors. The Bureau of Corporations' report on the Transportation of Petroleum Products deals fully with this. Relative rates, as above stated, always seem to favor Chicago (Whiting) as against the centres of independent refining such as Cleveland, Pittsburg, or Toledo. Formerly, before the great refinery was established in 1890 at Whiting, — which, by the way, produces one-third of all the kerosene used in the United States, — the roads from these centres made joint through rates all over the country. They still do so on many other commodities. But on petroleum products they have been withdrawn. The result is that everywhere, except where they can secure entrance by water, the disability in rates against the independent refiner is most effective. That much the same conditions prevail in other lines of business is affirmed on the highest authority. The *Railway Age Gazette* has repeatedly protested against the pressure which is now brought to bear against the carriers by such organizations as the Illinois Manufacturers' Association to substitute open but discriminatory local rates for the old secret favors upon which the great shippers throve for so many years. Fortunately, however, this situation in some cases relieves the Federal government of the burden of detection of mal-adjustments of this sort. For the communities aggrieved are constantly on the watch to protect their interests against rival cities. This factor clearly appears in the sugar and cement lighterage cases in 1908.[1] Carriers at New York in order to equalize rates with carriers serving Philadelphia refineries, grant "accessorial allowances" for the use of lighters or for cartage, in order, as they aver, to overcome the disability against their clients. But Philadelphia shippers are ever on the alert to detect such favors given at New York; and substantially aid the government in eradicating the evil. In the grain elevator allowance cases, likewise, at Omaha and Council Bluffs in 1906–1909, not only unfavored shippers at these points but St. Louis grain merchants as a body, intervened as complainants against the system. The powerful motive of self-interest thus invoked is of great service.

Before dismissing these recent and widely "muck-raked" oil cases, it may not be out of place to mention the new interpretation of the Elkins law which has resulted therefrom. One concerns the definition of separate offences. In the notorious $29,000,000 fine case, the Federal Circuit judge applied the maximum penalty of $20,000 for each offence to each separate carload in a large aggregate of shipments. On review of the case, each separate settlement of freight rates was defined as the unit of an offence. As entire train loads had been forwarded or paid for at one time, this materially reduced the aggregate of possible penalties. And, in the second place, the question of legally provable intent was raised. The turning point in the $29,000,000 fine case, was the ruling of the judge on review, that it was necessary to prove that a standard rate, higher than the one actually paid, had actually been filed at Washington; and that the defendant had knowingly accepted

[1] 20 I.C.C. Rep., 200, with dissenting opinion. Reviewed by the U. S. Commerce Court 1912; *Railway Age Gazette*, chap. LII, p. 1550. P. 586, *infra*.

a concession from this figure. These points the government was unable in fact to establish; and this ended the case.[1]

While general rate cutting has been less common since 1900, partly also because the roads were rapidly forming great combinations especially in order to eliminate it, subsequent developments have proved that personal and secret favoritism to large shippers was still very common. Despite all they could do to withstand pressure, traffic managers seemed powerless without the aid of the law. Perhaps the greatest revelation of the extent of personal rebating was afforded by the great Wisconsin investigation under the leadership of Governor La Follette in 1903.[2] The original purpose of this inquiry was fiscal; namely, to examine into the subject of railroad taxation. But its scope speedily widened, and at last skilled accountants were put into the books of all the railroads traversing Wisconsin.

The facts elicited by the Wisconsin investigation were startling. For the years 1897–1903, the direct rebates appearing in the accounts of the Wisconsin lines alone, — taking no account of other forms of rebates such as excessive damage allowances and the like, — were $7,000,000. The Chicago and Northwestern alone had allowed more than half of this amount. And from what is now known of other forms of allowance, the total must have been indeed very great. In one year recently, there was evidence to the effect that rebates on the New York Central lines amounted to $1,000,000. According to its own admission, the Michigan Central road, in 1902–1903, made allowances of $586,000. The rebating to the beef packers, especially on export business during 1902, was notorious. No wonder the progressive railroad leaders desired to put an end to this leakage of revenue. And at their request,

[1] U. S. Circuit Court of Appeals, decided March 12, 1902. The history is in Ann. Rep., I.C.C., 1907, p. 114; 1908 pp. 26 and 36; and 1909, p. 26.
[2] Never published. Outlined in Wisconsin *Assembly Journal*, 1905, chap. II, pp. 1463–1497.

the wise legislation known as the Elkins Amendments to the Act to Regulate Commerce was passed in 1903.[1]

The Elkins law of 1903 not only came at a time when the carriers were in need of every cent of revenue to tide over a hard year, but it also followed demonstration under the test of judicial procedure, that convictions for rebating were practically impossible under the old law. To convict for unjust discrimination it was necessary to show, not merely the allowance to one favored shipper, but the fact also had to be proved that no such allowances were made to others on the same sort of traffic under similar conditions. This could scarcely ever be done. In fact, during almost twenty years, there had been less than a score of convictions. Most of the prosecutions had failed utterly. Both government and carriers pressed for legislation. This was promptly given in the Act of February 19, 1903. There were four important features of this law. Railway corporations, not merely individuals as before, were now made directly liable to prosecution and penalties. The tariff filed became the lawful standard. The fact that all shippers got the same low rate was, therefore, no longer a defence. In the third place, the shipper as well as the carrier could be held accountable. In other words, accepting as well as giving rebates, became unlawful. And, finally, jurisdiction was conferred upon the Federal courts to restrain any departure from published rates or any "discrimination forbidden by law" by writ of injunction. This fully legalized a rather doubtful course of procedure to which the Interstate Commerce Commission had been compelled to resort as a last weapon in the rate wars on grain and beef since 1901. It also abolished the penalty of unjustment; imposing fines instead. But this action was subsequently rescinded in the law of 1906.

The record of the vigorous prosecutions against rebating under the Elkins law,[2] affords conclusive evidence, not only as

[1] *Cf.* p. 492, *infra.*
[2] *Cf.* 59th Congress, 1st Session, Senate Doc. 526.

to the widespread extent of the evil, but as to its identification with many of the large industrial combinations. The history of the activities of the Interstate Commerce Commission is to be found in its file of annual reports. But little seems to have been done for the first two years; but great activity was displayed during 1905. The ensuing year was rather notable by reason of the success in securing convictions. Besides the Standard Oil cases, there was collected in fines for rebating between October, 1905, and March, 1907, the sum of $586,000. Several men were sent to jail, for from three to six months. Among the trusts implicated were the beef packers, who have been indefatigable in concocting rebating devices; the tin plate combination; and, most notable of all, the American Sugar Refining Company. Nearly $300,000 in fines was imposed upon this concern alone. The secret allowances in these cases were most ingeniously arranged. Some were "refund of terminal charges;" some were "lighterage demurrage;" some were allowances for damages. Many were paid by drafts instead of checks so as to preclude identification of individuals; some were by special bank account; but the sums involved were very large. Shipments of sugar on which rebates of four to six cents per hundred were given, amounted within a relatively brief period to upwards of 70,000,000 pounds on one line alone. As sugar shipments westbound from New York constituted nearly one-third of the total tonnage, the importance of these prosecutions appear. The following quotation from a letter from an agent of the sugar trust accompanying a claim for overcharge of $6,866 on shipments of syrup, introduced in evidence in one of these cases, aptly describes the situation, both then, now, and always. "We hope to devise some means to enable us to conduct our freight matters with the transportation companies satisfactorily even under the new conditions imposed by the Elkins bill; but there may be some cases that cannot be taken care of, in the event of which we will, like all other shippers, have to take our medicine and look pleasant." The Interstate Commerce Commission reported as to the conditions in 1908 that "many shippers still enjoy illegal advantages." Many convictions were, however, secured. And investigations in California showed the existence of an extensive system of preferential rates.[1] A list of 108 firms was discovered on the Southern Pacific road alone, who were enjoying "special inside rates" which often aggregated $50,000 per month. Many of these assumed the form of refunds upon claims for damages.

Thus the rebate as an evil in transportation, even since amendment of the law in 1906–1910, while under control, is still far from being eradicated. Favoritism lurks in every covert, assuming almost every hue and form. Practices which outwardly appear to be necessary and legitimate, have been shown to conceal special favors of a substantial sort. Among the latest forms, undue extension of credit may be mentioned. It appeared, for instance, in 1910 that the Hocking Valley Railroad was favoring the Sunday Creek Coal Company to the extent of credit for transportation on its books to the amount of $2,400,000.[2] Another device which amounted to favoritism whether so intended or not, has been brought into court upon prosecution of the so-called Beef Trust. Substantial concessions in the rate from Kansas City to various foreign countries prevailed by reason of the fact that long time contracts for shipments at an established rate continued after a new higher general tariff had been put into effect. This increase of rates in general, leaving the trust rates at the old figure, of course created an undue and unlawful preference.[3] The chapter might be further amplified by details concerning "substitution of tonnage at transit points;"[4] excessive allowance for claims, and, as in a recent important case against the New York Cen-

[1] 13 I.C.C. Rep., 123.
[2] Ann. Rep., I.C.C., 1910, p. 10.
[3] *Idem*, 1909, p. 32. Circuit Court of Appeals decision, April 29, 1911, Ann. Rep., I.C.C., 1908, p. 32.
[4] 18 I.C.C. Rep., 280. *Cf.* p. 401, *infra*.

tral, exorbitant rates paid for advertising in a theatrical publication, in order to secure transportation for an itinerant troupe of travelling players.[1]

The extreme subtlety of personal favoritism was recently brought to light in connection with the selling price of coal in the little town of Durham, North Carolina.[2] Complaint was entered that a certain retailer was charging but five dollars a ton while his competitors were unable to dispose of theirs at a profit for less than six dollars. The explanation offered, that this person employing no bookkeeper and, paying no rent, was enabled to do this because of these savings, proved inadequate. Investigation developed the fact that no direct preference from railroads existed, but that there were, nevertheless, various peculiar features as to division of rates which invited further examination. Thus, for example, while the Norfolk & Western received $30.80 for hauling a carload of coal 160 miles, the Durham & South Carolina Railroad received $24.80 for hauling the same car one mile. This little railroad was owned by a lumber company which seemed in effect to have set up the defendant coal merchant in business. An arrangement between this little switching road and the Seaboard Air Line, as well as the Norfolk & Western, also favored the Durham & Southern. The key to the situation lay in the fact that the Dukes,—powerful financial interests controlling the American Tobacco Company, the Southern Power Company and large cotton mills, — also controlled the Durham & Southern through the lumber company. The Seaboard Air Line, therefore, when it gave to this little switching road for a twenty-mile haul, about forty per cent. of its division on through business, surreptitiously conferred a heavy bonus upon its little connection. It must have lost money under such a division of rates. The only conclusion possible is that this little railroad was specially favored in order to purchase the goodwill of financiers controlling a large traffic in other lines of

[1] *Boston Transcript*, Feb. 20, 1912.   [2] 22 I.C.C. Rep., 51.

business. The rebate, however, was not given to the American Tobacco Company, but constituted a comfortable profit "on the side" for powerful interests in its management.

The elevation cases concerning the legitimacy of a special payment for unloading grain in private elevators, have been under dispute for years. Their validity has recently been affirmed by the Supreme Court in an important decision in 1911.[1] This litigation illustrates the difficulty of defining rebates as an expression of personal favoritism. In 1899, the Union Pacific Railroad made a contract with Peavey & Company at Council Bluffs to erect an elevator and to transfer grain for a charge of one and one-quarter cents a hundred pounds. This arrangement was objected to by competing railroads on the ground that it gave compensation to a private concern, engaged in general grain business for the handling of its own property. The Union Pacific insisted that the expedient was necessary and proper as a means for promptly unloading its cars at Omaha. The Commission, after investigation, sanctioned the contract. In 1907, the matter again came before the Commission upon complaint of other railroads competing with the Union Pacific along the Missouri river. It was alleged that the continuance of the elevator allowance by the Union Pacific would virtually compel all other roads to make similar allowances. Still the Commission adhered to its former conclusion that undue discrimination did not result. The practice, however, gradually spread until all the roads at Missouri river points put in an allowance of three-fourths of one cent as an elevator charge. This brought forth a complaint from the lines at St. Louis that traffic was being diverted from that point as a result; and the Commission, once more considering the matter, held that the practice was prejudicial to public interest. Conditions, in fact, had changed, mainly through the increase of through shipments to the East without transfer at the Missouri

[1] 222 U. S., 42. The system is described in the *Railway Age Gazette*, June 4, 1909.

river. The Commission, therefore, held that when such transfer took place, it was for the accommodation of local grain merchants, who ought to pay for the service rendered. At this stage of the proceedings, the matter went to the Supreme Court of the United States upon appeal. The decision finally upheld the Commission, in holding that the payment of an elevation allowance was not unlawful, but that if paid to one elevator, it must be paid to all. The bearing of this case upon the larger issue, of payments by railroads for special services rendered by, shippers cannot fail to be of great importance in the future.

The use of the industrial railroad as a means of preferential treatment still occasions difficulty.[1] The case is simple where but one shipper makes use of the terminal plant; but where a number of shippers may utilize it jointly, it becomes difficult to draw the line between pro-rating allowances and actual rebates. The Manufacturers' Railroad Company, with twenty miles of track, four locomotives and one hundred and ten employees, serves a considerable manufacturing section in South St. Louis. A majority of the stock of this terminal railroad is held by persons controlling the Anheuser-Busch Brewery. The enormous traffic of this concern, equal to about one-thirtieth of the total tonnage of St. Louis, is handled over the line of the Manufacturers' Railway. Almost nine-tenths of its business consists of shipments of beer; but in 1910 some 5,424 carloads belonging to other patrons moved over its rails. For this terminal service the Anheuser-Busch Company, through the Manufacturers' Railway, got a very substantial allowance for the service rendered. For example, in one month on ten carloads of beer, the Louisville & Nashville allowed

[1] 21 I.C.C. Rep., 304. Compare also before the U. S. Commerce Court; the Stock Yards case, 192 Fed. Rep., 330; the California Switching case, 188 Fed. Rep., 229; and the Crane Iron Works case, No.55, April session, 1912. The tap-line decision, 23 I.C.C., 277, most fully discussed the general policy to be observed toward industrial roads in the lumber business. *Cf.* also the use of boat lines. 23 *Idem*, 358.

$45 out of a total revenue of $391.60 for moving the traffic something less than four thousand feet. The disparity is obvious between this allowance and the balance remaining as compensation for moving the traffic 477 miles, including three first-class railroad tolls and terminal charges at the other end.[1]

A prime difficulty is to determine whether unduly low commodity rates amount practically to special favors granted to large shippers. Much evidence recently tends to show that the trusts enjoy advantages of this sort not extended to other competitors. The Steel Corporation, through its ownership of railroads and steamships, certainly has a great advantage over its rivals.[2] But other trusts not controlling common carriers of their own, are also accorded what seem to be unduly low rates upon their products. Recent evidence before the Interstate Commerce Commission seems to show that sugar, beef, and coffee do not bear their proper share of transportation costs.[3] Copper, the product of a powerful trust, enjoys a lower ton mile rate than grain, — a rate, despite its high intrinsic value, actually below that on soft coal.[4] The discrimination is too palpable to be passed over without explanation.

From the survey of rebating and rate wars, — which latter of course afford the most favored soil in which personal favoritism may flourish, — one cannot avoid the conclusion that a great improvement in conditions has been brought about. The strengthened arm of the Federal government has come to the support of the carriers; and has assisted them to a material enhancement of their revenues, by putting a stop to serious leakages in income. But the carriers could undoubtedly do much on their own account, could they be granted the right to make traffic agreements, subject always, of course, to the

[1] *Railway Age Gazette*, LII, pp. 269 and 340.
[2] Evidence before the Stanley House Committee on Steel Corporation, Feb. 28, 1912, p. 3667; and Bureau of Corporations on U. S. Steel Corporation, II, p. 72.
[3] *American Economic Review*, 1911, p. 789.
[4] S. O. Dunn, American Transportation Question, pp. 62, 81.

approval and supervision of the Interstate Commerce Commission. Whether Congress will ever permit this, remains to be seen. The most important result of all this Federal activity so far, has been the moral stimulus toward fair business dealing which has been given. Thousands of shippers today, quite apart from the fear of fines or imprisonment, would disdain to ask or accept favors which a decade since would have been regarded as entirely proper. No one can doubt that the *morale* of business is distinctly higher than it used to be. Could such higher standards become universal, the Department of Justice would be relieved of a substantial part of its present duties.

CHAPTER VII

LOCAL DISCRIMINATION

Concrete instances, 215. — Hadley's oyster case not conclusive, 217. — Two variants: lower long-haul rates by the roundabout route, as in the Hillsdale, Youngstown, and some Southern cases, 221; or by the direct route, as in the Nashville-Chattanooga and other southern cases, 225. — Complicating influence of water transportation, 232. — Market competition from various regions, a different case, 234. — The basing point (southern) and basing line (Missouri river) systems, 238. — Their inevitable instability and probable ultimate abandonment, 242. — Postage-stamp rates, illustrated by transcontinental tariffs, 245. — Which line makes the rate? 255. — Cost not distance, determines, 256. — Fixed charges *v.* operating expenses, 257. — Proportion of local business, 259. — Volume and stability of traffic important, 261. — Generally the short line rules, but many exceptions occur, 263.

ANY unreasonable departure from a tariff graded in some proportion according to distance is known as local discrimination. It constitutes one of the most difficult and perplexing problems in transportation. Personal discrimination now happily having been practically eliminated since the enactment of the Elkins Amendments to the Act to Regulate Commerce, this issue of local discrimination under the rehabilitated long and short haul clause, has recently assumed an added significance.

A merchant of Wilkesbarre, Pennsylvania, purchased a carload of potatoes at Rochester, New York, and had the freight bill made for a delivery to Philadelphia, because the freight to Philadelphia was less than it was to Wilkesbarre, which is 143 miles nearer. He stopped the potatoes at Wilkesbarre, unloaded them, and paid the freight. A few days later he received a bill from the Lehigh Valley Company for twelve dollars additional freight. If the potatoes had gone to Philadelphia, he would have paid forty-eight dollars freightage.

As they stopped at Wilkesbarre, he had to pay sixty dollars; that is, twelve dollars for not hauling the carload 143 miles.[1]

A merchant in Montgomery, Alabama, shipped two carloads of fruit jars from Crawfordsville, Indiana, to Montgomery. He shipped them to Mobile and then paid the local rate from Mobile back, those fruit jars going through Montgomery on the way out. By having them hauled 350 miles farther, he saved seventy-five dollars on the two carloads.

On first-class goods, at one time, the rate from Louisville to Montgomery, was $1.26 per hundredweight. On to Mobile, 180 miles further south, it was only ninety cents. In the same territory the rate on kerosene oil from Cincinnati at times has been three times as much to interior points as to New Orleans, three times as far. West of the Missouri river and in the Rocky mountain area similar complaints are common. Denver, Colorado, pays $1.79 per hundredweight on cotton piece goods, in small lots, hauled 2,000 miles from Boston; while the rate to San Francisco, 1,400 miles further away, on the same line, is only $1.50. This discrepancy is even greater in wholesale rates. No carload rating is given to Denver; while for similar shipments to the coast the rate is only one dollar per hundredweight. In the opposite direction, sugar is carried from San Francisco through Denver to Kansas City for sixty-five cents per hundredweight, as compared with a rate of one dollar if the sugar is stopped at Denver. Smaller places in the West afford equally striking instances. The rate on rope from San Francisco to Independence, Kansas, is seventy-five cents; while the same goods are hauled on through Independence, Kansas, much farther, to Missouri river points for sixty cents per hundred pounds. Wichita, Kansas, complains that cotton piece goods from New York by way of Galveston are rated at $1.36; while by the

---

[1] Cullom Committee, Report, Testimony, p. 532. *Cf.* instances in Hudson's Railways and the Republic; and Parson's Heart of the Railway Problem as showing popular misunderstanding.

same route Kansas City, 225 miles longer haul by that route, the charge is only ninety-three cents. The Southwestern Lumberman's Association complains, —

"that a train of cars of lumber starts from Camden or other common point in Texas via Atchison, Topeka and Santa Fe Railway, and one car is dropped off in Oklahoma at 27½ cents per 100 pounds; one each also at Wichita and Emporia, Kansas, at 27½ cents per 100 pounds; one at Kansas City at 23 cents, and two cars also set off this same train at Kansas City, destined for Omaha and Lincoln, Nebraska, at 23 and 24 cents per 100 pounds, respectively. The balance of this train, now at Kansas City, runs on to Chicago, and 24 cents per 100 pounds is the charge then for most of the train which is left there. . . . Why should builders of homes in Wichita and Emporia, Kansas, pay higher freight than builders in Kansas City, Omaha, and Chicago when using yellow pine from Texas?"[1]

Such instances as these might be multiplied indefinitely. They are often striking in character. The first impression is of intolerable abuse. The simplest tenets of justice and fair dealing appear to be violated. Careful analysis should, however, always be made before drawing such conclusions. Railroad practice seldom departs so flagrantly from the fundamental consideration of cost of service without very substantial economic justification.

The reasoning underlying local discrimination is admirably set forth by President Hadley in the following passage from his *Railroad Transportation*: —[2]

"On the coast of Delaware, a few years ago, there was a place which we shall call X, well suited for oyster-growing, but which sent very few oysters to market, because the railroad rates were so high as to leave no margin of profit. The local oyster-growers represented to the railroad that if the rates were brought down to one dollar per hundred pounds, the business would become profitable and the railroad could be sure of regular shipments at that price. The railroad men looked into the matter. They found that the price of oysters in the Philadelphia market was such that the local oystermen could pay one dollar per hundred pounds to the railroad and still have a

[1] Senate (Elkins) Committee Report, 1905, p. 1892.
[2] Pp. 116–117.

fair profit left. If the road tried to charge more, it would so cut down the profit as to leave men no inducement to enter the business. That is, those oysters would bear a rate of one dollar per hundred, and no more. Further, the railroad men found that if they could get every day a carload, or nearly a carload, at this rate, it would more than cover the expense of hauling an extra car by quick train back and forth every day, with the incidental expenses of interest and repairs. So they put the car on, and were disappointed to find that the local oyster-growers could only furnish oysters enough to fill the car about half full. The expense to the road of running it half full was almost as great as of running it full; the income was reduced one-half. They could not make up by raising the rates, for these were as high as the traffic would bear. They could not increase their business much by lowering rates. The difficulty was not with the price charged, but with the capacity of the local business. It seemed as if this special service must be abandoned.

"One possibility suggested itself. At some distance beyond X, the terminus of this railroad, was another oyster-growing place, Y, which sent its oysters to market by another route. The supply at Y was very much greater than at X. The people at Y were paying a dollar a hundred to send their oysters to market. It would hardly cost twenty cents to send them from Y to X. If, then, the railroad from X to Philadelphia charged but seventy-five cents a hundred on oysters which came from Y, it could easily fill its car full. This was what they did. They then had half a carload of oysters grown at X, on which they charged a dollar, and half a carload from Y on which they charged seventy-five cents for exactly the same service.

"Of course there was a grand outcry at X. Their trade was discriminated against in the worst possible way — so they said — and they complained to the railroad. But the railroad men fell back on the logic of facts. The points were as follows: 1. A whole carload at seventy-five cents would not pay expenses of handling and moving. 2. At higher rates than seventy-five cents they could not get a whole carload, but only half a carload; and half a carload at a dollar rate (the highest charge the article would bear) would not pay expenses. Therefore, 3. On *any* uniform rate for everybody, the road must lose money, and 4. They would either be compelled to take the oyster car away altogether, or else get what they could at a dollar, and fill up at seventy-five cents. There was no escape from this reasoning; and the oyster men of X chose to pay the higher rate rather than lose the service altogether."

The logic of this oyster case seems convincing in its simplicity. But it presents more complications than appear at the outset.

LOCAL DISCRIMINATION 219

First of all, what is the nature of the competition at the more distant point which is alleged to "compel" the lower rate? Is it merely of rival routes or of competing markets? It will be advisable to keep the two distinct so far as possible. Under the first heading, competition of routes, the subjoined sketches represent two possible situations. In both instances, however, Y, enjoying the lower rate, is more distant from

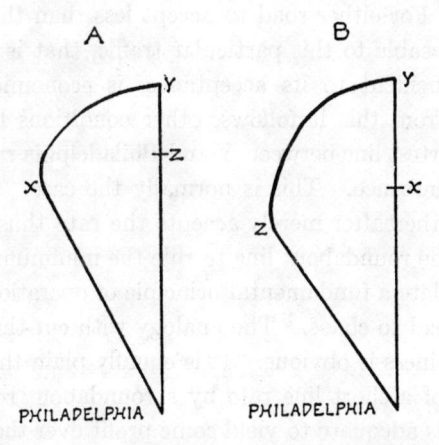

```
        A                    B
        Y                    Y
       /|                   /|
      / |                  / |
   X-+  |                  |  +-X
     \  +-Z             Z-+  |
      \ |                  \ |
       \|                   \|
  PHILADELPHIA         PHILADELPHIA
```

Philadelphia than X. The difference between the two arises from the fact that in the one case X is nearer Philadelphia than Y on a roundabout line; while in the other X is actually nearer than Y by the shortest direct route. We may safely assume that the compelling competition alleged at Y as justifying the lower rate is by rail; as, the commodity being a marine bivalve, both places presumably enjoy equal facilities for water carriage. At all events, assuming that we have to do with competing rail routes alone, what differences obtain between the two sets of circumstances above sketched? Not insignificant inequalities in the length or power of the two routes are implied by the diagrams. They are supposed to represent substantially different lines, which may, for the purpose of the argument, be denominated strong, natural, or standard, and weak, unnatural, or abnormal, respectively, so far as the particular traffic in hand is concerned. That this distinction is not irrelevant, but frequently of determinant force, is shown by an analysis of concrete cases which have arisen for adjudication.

This proposition is clear beyond dispute. The actual cost of service, which fixes an irreducible minimum rate between Y and Philadelphia, is less on the short line than by the roundabout one. For either road to accept less than the portion of the cost traceable to this particular traffic, that is to say, the *extra* cost incident to its acceptance, is economically inconceivable. From this it follows, other conditions being equal, that the shortest line between Y and Philadelphia rules the rate in the last instance. This is normally the case. The roundabout route thereafter merely accepts the rate thus compelled. To permit the roundabout line to rule the minimum rate would not only violate a fundamental principle of operation: it would inevitably lead to chaos. The analogy with cut-throat competition in business is obvious. It is equally plain that the mere acceptance of a short line rate by a roundabout road, so long as this rate is adequate to yield some profit over the extra cost, while of advantage to some, may not work positive injury to any one. This condition normally corresponds to the state of affairs represented by diagram A. The nearer point, X, as Hadley avers, has no just grievance against Y because the latter has the good fortune to have a direct service to Philadelphia at a low rate. For Y to withdraw shipments from the line *via* X might even destroy the only chance of X for a market. It would also deprive Y of whatever benefit it might have derived from competition either of routes or of facilities. Of course, we have expressly omitted market competition as a factor, reserving it for separate treatment. Yet one objection arises. Normally, the direct line ought to maintain a tariff conforming in some ·degree to the distance principle. The roundabout line can compete at Y only by a violation of it, unless, indeed, its local tariffs be graded much more gradually.

In other words, its progression towards the maximum must be distributed over a much longer line. Even this would, on Hadley's statement of fact, eliminate X from the Philadelphia market. Such reduction of local rates upon the roundabout route would in turn discriminate against places like Z on the direct line, equally distant with X from Philadelphia. For the latter places would necessarily be assessed at a higher rate per ton-mile.[1] This would constitute another form of local discrimination, which will be discussed in due time. There is, therefore, at best, only a choice of adjustments, either of which leads to some form of inequality. But, upon the whole, balancing the evil with the good, the first variant of our oyster case appears to be best solved by according all shippers at Y a somewhat lower rate than X enjoys.

Conditions corresponding to diagram A have frequently given rise to complaints before courts and administrative tribunals. An interesting illustration is afforded by the Hillsdale ice case in Michigan.[2] Ice was moved from this town to Springfield and Columbus, two neighboring Ohio cities, over several different routes. (See map on next page.) To Columbus the shortest road was by the Hocking Valley Railroad directly through Toledo. Another route by way of Sandusky existed; and even a third through Sandusky, thence over to Springfield, and in by the side door, so to speak, to Columbus. This last routing was due to the fact that the Big Four road from Sandusky diagonally across to Springfield had no access to Columbus except through a branch line from Springfield. This last-named zigzag route was 295 miles in length as against 190 miles by the direct line through Toledo. To Springfield, on the other hand, no direct route from Hillsdale existed; but freight might move either *via* Sandusky by the Big Four road

[1] Another instance is afforded by the Savannah Freight Bureau case: 7 Int. Com. Rep., 458. See our Railway Problems, chap. XII.
[2] Interstate Commerce Commission Reports, decided May 14, 1903. *Cf.* the extraordinary diversion of traffic over the long route in Troy-Chatham, N. Y. case: 23 I.C.C. Rep., 263.

or through Sandusky and around by way of Columbus. The shortest of any of these lines to Springfield, however, was twenty-nine miles longer than the shortest line to Columbus. This established Columbus, therefore, as normally the nearer point. Complaint arose from the fact that ice carried over the zigzag route to Columbus actually passed through Spring-

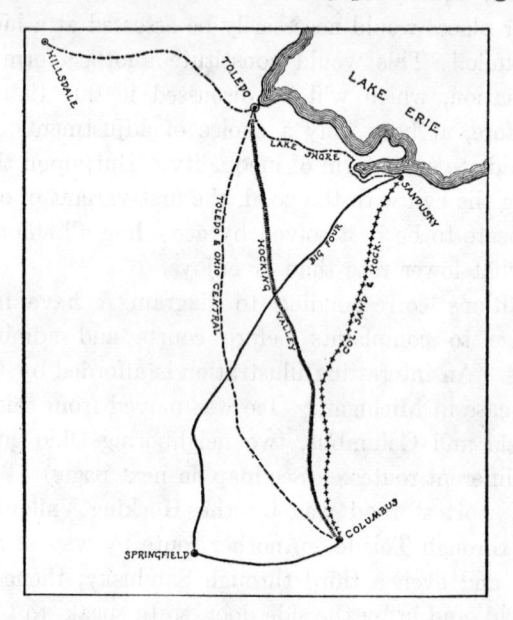

field and forty-five miles beyond to reach its destination. For such shipments over the Big Four road, Springfield instead of Columbus was the nearer point. But, contrariwise, for ice coming to Springfield through Columbus, the latter in turn became the intermediate point.[1] The specific complaint was that the rate by all routes to Springfield was one dollar per ton, while to Columbus it was only eighty cents. Originally, the rate was higher ($1.25 per ton), but was the same to both points. Is this a case of local discrimination or not?

[1] This recalls Traffic Manager Bird's testimony relative to Wisconsin controversies before the Senate (Elkins) Committee, 1905.

The Big Four road operating through Springfield answered that it was not responsible for the eighty cent rate to Columbus; that this was made by the direct line; and that it obviously must meet this rate or withdraw from the ice business. It alleged, moreover, that the rate of one dollar was reasonable in itself as compared with other rates in the same territory, and was in fact substantially less than it formerly was; nor would its withdrawal from Columbus ice business evidently be of any advantage whatever to Springfield, but would indeed deprive it of some small contribution to joint expenses of operation on all its tonnage. No evidence being offered that Springfield was positively injured by this adjustment, the Commission properly dismissed the complaint.

The distinctive feature of this class of cases, as has been said, is that the intermediate point preferring the complaint is always on a roundabout route.[1] St. Cloud, Minnesota, and Wichita, Kansas, whose contentions are described hereafter in detail, were thus situated. The so-called "rare and peculiar" case of Youngstown, Ohio, cited in the original Louisville and Nashville decision of 1889, was in no sense different. It was a case of pure competition of routes.[2] Traffic to New York was starting its journey from Pittsburg, over the rails of the same company, in exactly opposite directions. Some of it went east by the direct line; while other freight first moved due west, thence north, by way of Youngstown, Ohio, until it reached the main line of the Erie, which took it on to New York. This traffic, therefore, described three sides of a rectangle in reaching its destination, traversing a route 172 miles longer than by the direct line. The issue was raised by a demand for as low a rate to New York from Youngstown as Pittsburg enjoyed, on the ground that it was nearer New York by this indirect line;

[1] Using this term technically as described on p. 256, *infra*.
[2] Chapter XIV, p. 480, *infra*. The original correspondence setting forth these conditions is reprinted by the Senate (Elkins) Committee, 1905, Digest, App. III, p. 46. 21 I.C.C. Rep., 64, and 17 *Idem*, 335 are analogous cases.

Pittsburg traffic, in other words, passing through it *en route* to the seaboard. The reply, of course, was that, although nearer by an indirect road, it was more distant by the natural and shortest route, and consequently should pay more for the service. What the roundabout line was really demanding was permission to compete at Pittsburg for New York business, without being compelled to reduce its local rates from intermediate points like Youngstown. In other words, the long line was demanding exemption from the long and short haul clause, while the direct short line conformed to it. Without such exemption it could not continue to reach out for Pittsburg business, as the loss incident to reduction of its local rates would outweigh the profit in the competitive tonnage.

One side of the Savannah Freight Bureau Fertilizer case [1] — namely, the complaints of local stations on a roundabout road — brings it within our first category. The roundabout line from Charleston to Valdosta, shown upon the map at p. 648, was 413 miles long as against a direct route of only 273 miles. Kathleen, Georgia, is only 288 miles out from Charleston on this indirect line, — approximately the same distance as Valdosta, which thus corresponds to Y in the oyster case. Yet Kathleen paid a rate of $3.32 per ton on fertilizer from Charleston as against $2.48 charged to Valdosta, 125 miles beyond. But this excess distance is by an indirect route. Most of the notable English cases concerning local discrimination appear to be of the same stamp.[2] The complaints of a number of smaller places in the St. Paul-Milwaukee territory, like Cannon Falls, Lacrosse, and Northfield some years ago, reduce in part to the same thing.[3] Whether the Troy, Alabama, and Wichita, Kansas, cases belong here or in the next group is indeterminate, owing to the difficulty of comparing conditions of carriage by rail and by water, respectively.

[1] 7 Int. Com. Rep., 458: reprinted in our Railway Problems, chap. XII.
[2] Brief of Ed. Baxter, Alabama Midland Railway case, U. S. Supreme Court, p. 71; and Acworth, p. 83. Details in chap. XIV and XIX, *infra*.
[3] 14 I.C.C. Rep., 299.

On the other hand, the set of circumstances shown in diagram B (page 219, *supra*) is of quite a different sort. The justification for the local discrimination is much less clear. Here, as before, the distant point Y enjoys a lower rate than X because of the presence of competition; but it is important to inquire both as to the nature and the amount of it. In the first case, competitive traffic from Y was *extra* rather than normal in character, so far as the line serving X was concerned. It was relatively small in amount. Whatever surplus revenue resulted from it aided the local tariffs, including those at X, in supporting the burden of fixed expenses. This burden they were bound to bear entirely in the absence of competitive business picked up at Y. The distant point Y of course had no complaint in any event, and the chances are that X was benefited, as we have seen. But in the second case the great bulk of the traffic from Y belongs naturally to the direct line through X. It constitutes the mainstay of its business. The direct line, unlike the roundabout one, cannot withdraw from the field when rates become unremunerative. It is in this business passing directly through X to stay. Nine-tenths of the Y traffic, perhaps, moves through X in this latter case; in the former one, one-tenth would perhaps measure the proportion of the indirect line. Under this assumption, it is obvious that the question of the level of rates at Y, as determined by the presence of competition, assumes a ninefold greater importance in the eyes of X, so far as the effect upon local rates in supporting the fixed and joint expenses of the road is concerned. In any event, even the line operating under a disability supposedly earns some small net return on competitive traffic, else it would withdraw from the field. This it is in fact free to do at any time; and, however small the net return, it is at least all gain. On the other hand, when the net return on a large volume of its natural business becomes unduly small, the financial stability of the direct line is put in jeopardy. The danger of local rates (as at X) being actually enhanced or at least prevented from reduction, because of an unduly low level of competitive rates at more distant points, is thus much greater when X is a way station on a direct line than when, as in our first instance, it is an intermediate point on a roundabout route. For this reason the direct line through X is at the outset put to a justification of its local tariffs, as to whether they are inherently reasonable or not; first, by comparison with the general level throughout the surrounding territory; and, secondly, as yielding a return on the capital actually invested. This seems to have been the line of reasoning which the Interstate Commerce Commission adopted in the recent important Spokane, Washington, cases.[1] The low through rates to the Pacific coast were established as reasonable by the competition of sea routes round the Horn, and especially by the newly-opened Tehawntepec Railroad. The only ground for finding there was discrimination against Spokane was an inherent unreasonableness in its rate. This was, in fact, the outcome; the decision being rendered notable, further, by reason of the prominence given to the valuation of the railroads' property as a basis of judgment.

The first important point to be established, then, in this second variety of the oyster case was as to the relative distribution of traffic from the more distant competitive point by the several lines open to it. The next concerned the absolute reasonableness of the rate at the intermediate point. In the third place, we must inquire whether the rate at the more distant point may not be unreasonably low. This was a contingency not possible, as we have just seen, in the Spokane case. But others may be different in this regard. One is thus forced to consider the effect of the presence of roundabout competitive lines upon the level of rates at the more distant point. An indirect rival road may, as in the St. Cloud case, carry only seventy-three carloads a day as compared with a daily movement of one thousand cars by the direct lines. On the other

[1] Details at pp. 245 and 610, *infra*.

LOCAL DISCRIMINATION 227

hand, as in the Savannah Freight Bureau case, Valdosta, Georgia, may receive nine-tenths of its supply of fertilizer by indirect roads. But in any event it is the potential, not the actual, movement of tonnage, which may count in the long run. It is indisputable that the short line between two points never pares its rates down to an irreducible minimum except under compulsion. The presence of a roundabout route affords just this pressure to reduction. Even allowing that in the last analysis the long line will strike bed-rock of no profit first, it is indisputable that such lines frequently, instead of merely meeting rates made for them by the direct routes, seek to divert business by actually undercutting those rates. Having only a small share of the tonnage, they take risks which would be fatal to others. To transport at an absolute loss is of course no more defensible than the argument of the merchant that the only way to compensate for selling goods below cost was to enlarge the volume of his business. But, of course, there is always the chance that, by enlarging this volume sufficiently, operating expenses may be so far cut down that a loss may be transformed into a profit. The diversion of enough traffic from the direct railroad line to accomplish this end would, of course, reduce the volume of its traffic and thereby unduly burden it, to the manifest injury of all local points like X.

Suggestive illustrations of lower rates at the more distant point than are under the circumstances actually "compelled" by competition of routes are to be had. In a recent case[1] the rates on bananas from Charleston, South Carolina, to Danville and Lynchburg, Virginia, respectively, were called in question. The traffic moved through Danville on its way to Lynchburg, sixty-six miles beyond, at a rate of forty-three cents to Danville as compared with a rate of twenty cents to Lynchburg. The reason for the low rate at Lynchburg was the presence of a rival route, — bananas, coming in through Baltimore. But the lowest rate "compelled" by this competition was in fact

[1] Interstate Commerce Reports, No. 696, decided June 25, 1904.

thirteen cents higher than the Danville line charged at Lynchburg. In other words, the long-distance rate was that much lower than it need have been. This instance is analogous in another way to our oyster case, inasmuch as the demand at Danville being limited, one-half of the same carload paid the Danville rate of forty-three cents, while the other half went on at the lower rate of twenty cents enjoyed at the more distant point. It is in this connection, of rates unduly low at so-called competitive points, that the partial weakness in the railroad arguments in many of the Southern basing point cases appears. Since the Supreme Court of the United States has held that competition at the more distant point justifies its lower rates, the Interstate Commerce Commission is powerless to give effect to whatever opinion it may entertain that at times it is neither water nor commercial competition which actually brings about the low rate at the basing point; but merely a consensus of opinion among carriers that that place will respond quickly enough to favors granted, to make it worth while to try the experiment.[1] This conviction is vastly strengthened, of course, since entire monopoly among all the southern railroad lines has become an established fact. It is an absurdity to speak longer of any competition between rail carriers existing in a large part of this territory.[2]

Actual illustrations of this second variant of the oyster case, free still from the complications of competition of markets, are not common, but occasionally arise. Chattanooga, which aspires to be the commercial and industrial centre of eastern Tennessee, is about 150 miles southeast of Nashville, as shown by the accompanying sketch map. Owing to the southwestern trend of the Appalachian Mountain valleys, it is only 846 miles from New York by rail, almost as the crow flies; while Nashville has access to the North principally through Ohio river

[1] *Cf.* the opinion in the Savannah Fertilizer case in our Railway Problems, chap. XII.
[2] Chapter XI, *infra*, also in volume II.

gateways, over lines, at the best, 1,058 miles in length. By these lines, therefore, the latter is 212 miles further from New York than Chattanooga. But the two competitive places are only 151 miles apart; whence it follows that the shortest possible all-rail line from New York to Nashville, swings around to the south by way of Chattanooga. The situation is complicated

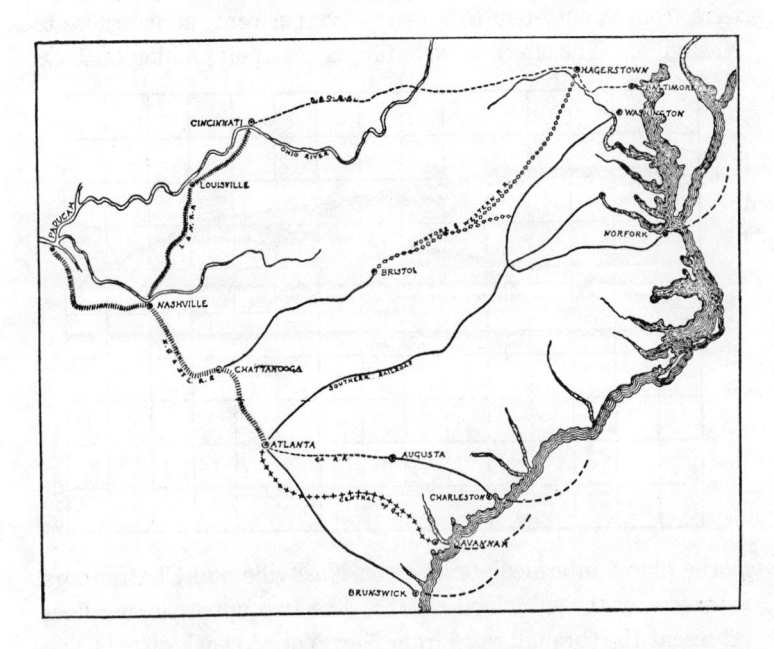

by other combined rail and water routes from New York through Norfolk, Savannah, and Charleston. But all these lines also reach Nashville by coming up through Chattanooga. From every point of view, therefore, Chattanooga, on the basis of mileage, is the nearer point to New York — 151 miles nearer by the direct line, all rail; equally nearer by all combined rail and water routes: and 212 miles nearer than is Nashville by the roundabout all-rail lines through Louisville or Cincinnati. Its location corresponds to X in our second variation of the oyster case; namely, an intermediate point on the direct line to

230   RAILROADS

another more distant point Y, which latter enjoys the competition of more roundabout routes.

The disability against Chattanooga, against which it protested, was substantial.[1] Its first-class rate from New York was $1.14 per hundred pounds, while Nashville paid only ninety-one cents. On various commodities the Chattanooga rates were from twenty-five to seventy-five per cent. above those to Nashville. The effect of such differences upon jobbing business

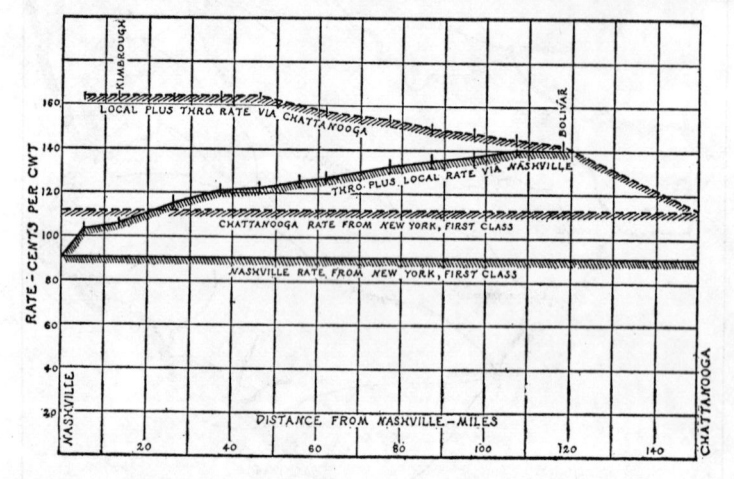

at the places intermediate between Nashville and Chattanooga is shown by the subjoined chart. The two upper sloping lines represent the through rates from New York to each distributing centre, plus the local rates out to way stations. Even at Bolivar, the nearest place to Chattanooga, the Nashville combination is slightly lower than that based upon Chattanooga. This disability steadily increases as Nashville is approached, rates from Chattanooga rising while those from Nashville fall, until at Kimbro the jobber located at Chattanooga — the nearer point to New York on the direct line — must lay down his New York goods at a rate of sixty-three cents a hundred

[1] 10 Int. Com. Rep., 111; reprinted in full in our Railway Problems, chap. X. Also the Commerce Court decision in chap. XVI, *infra*.

pounds higher than his competitor in Nashville enjoys. This adjustment is partly an historical product. Nashville, by the old river routes from Pittsburg down the Ohio and up the Cumberland, was formerly nearer the Eastern cities than Chattanooga. Then, the trunk lines through Cincinnati with heavy traffic and low rates shortened the distance; and, finally, the Louisville & Nashville Railroad, supplanting the river routes, undertook to build up Nashville as against Cincinnati and Louisville. Historically, on the other hand, Chattanooga was long an unimportant point. It took, as it still does, the same rate from the North as prevailed at some twenty-three other southern cities from Atlanta to Memphis. Here is the crux of the difficulty. The rates at Nashville must be assumed as historically fixed. Whatever remedy may apply must come from a reduction of the rates to Chattanooga, the nearer point. This place has now become an important centre, the meeting point of a number of rail and water lines. The long prevalent grouping of all the southern cities with equal rates from the North must be replaced by a system of differentials, if the discrimination against Chattanooga is ever to be ameliorated.

By this time it will be observed that in the discussion of the Chattanooga case we have drifted far beyond the mere competition of rival routes. Commercial competition, which affords the justification for grouping all these twenty-three important southern cities together, is a topic to be treated elsewhere by itself. The difficulty in many of these cases is to distinguish between the really strongest line and the one which is merely the shortest. Upon this point one's decision of the Chattanooga case might actually depend. The Louisville & Nashville contends that Nashville even today is, from an operating point of view, nearer New York than Chattanooga, although the distance is 212 miles more. All the trunk lines compete at Ohio river points, and bring them relatively much closer to New York. The density of traffic on these lines is far heavier than on the air line to Chattanooga.

It happens that Chattanooga meets this allegation of greater trunk line density and cheapness by proof of the still greater economy of operation by the coastwise steamers to southern ports, traffic coming thence north by rail through Chattanooga. The appearance of water competition in any of these cases always introduces an almost insuperable difficulty in the way of comparison of long and short lines. Shipment by vessel differs from rail carriage, primarily in the relatively high terminal costs, the absence of all maintenance of way costs, and the low cost of actual propulsion. With a cargo once securely stowed, the distance traversed by a vessel is of relatively little importance, much less so than in the case of carriage by rail. A powerful factor in determining water rates, moreover, especially by sea, is the absence of local traffic. Wharves and terminals being expensive to build and maintain, and the method of loading in a ship's hold not being conducive to ease in access or assortment, vessels are confined largely to bulk traffic at a few important points. The expenses of operation must be more uniformly distributed over the cargo than in the case of a trainload. The water line, therefore, is deprived of one advantage in cutting rates. It cannot, so readily as a railroad, recoup itself for losses on competitive business or at competitive points by falling back upon its earnings from way stations.

From all these considerations it not infrequently comes about that, unlike carriage by rail, the longest way round may indeed be the shortest way home. This is clear in the highly involved Wichita, Kansas, cases.[1] Wichita, a commercial centre of southern Kansas, is 200 odd miles south-west of Kansas City. Its all-rail rates from the East are higher than to Kansas City. Yet by the water route from New York to Galveston and thence up by rail, as compared with

---

[1] The leading Wichita cases are as follows: 9 I.C.C. Rep., 507, 534 and 558. — 10 *Idem,* 460. (Lehmann Higginson Co.). — 13 *Idem,* 389. Also 189 U. S. Rep., 274. — Also Senate (Elkins) Committee, 1905, IV. p. 2874 *et seq.*

Kansas City, it is a nearer and intermediate point. The Interstate Commerce Commission well expresses the difficulty:

"It is quite probable that the actual cost of transporting cotton piece goods from New York to Wichita *via* Galveston does not exceed that of carrying them from New York to Kansas City *via* the cheapest route. The all-rail haul is to the latter point 1,300 miles and over. The ocean and rail movement involves a rail carriage of from 1,100 to 1,300 miles, depending upon the route selected. If the goods move through some Gulf port, there is a rail carriage of not less than 850 miles. If, therefore, the rate were to be measured by the expense of the service, it is probable that Wichita would today enjoy as low a rate as the Missouri river."

The Wichita complication, moreover, works both ways. Wichita and Kansas City form two angles of a narrow triangle with its apex at the Gulf ports; but the distance from Kansas City is longer than from Wichita. Railroad competition brought it about, however, that the rate on export grain from Wichita *via* Kansas City to the Gulf came to equal the rate from Kansas City to the Gulf *via* Wichita. But the former was a much longer and more roundabout haul; and, moreover, was less than the shorter haul rate from Wichita to the Gulf direct. The analogy to the Hillsdale case, above-described, will appear clearly on inspection of the map.

Summarizing the results so far reached, in all that concerns the two sorts of cases considered in the preceding paragraphs, our conclusion is that, when competition by rail at the distant point is alone present, and when the nearer point is on a roundabout route, a railway "is entitled to carry the traffic past X to Y (Philadelphia) for considerably less than nothing"; but, when the nearer point is on a direct line, the case is debatable. Proof that normal competition compels the lower rate at the remoter station must be uncommonly clear and conclusive. In other words, the facts that the rate at Y is not unduly low and also that the rate at X is not unreasonably high must both be firmly established.

A distinct class of cases of local discrimination is suggested by the recent case of Montgomery, Ala., in the United States Commerce Court.[1] These like other cross line cases, akin to that of Wichita, Kansas, above-mentioned, arise in connection with practices as to the division of joint rates. They will be discussed in connection with pro-rating in our second volume.

The question has forced itself forward constantly as to whether the existence of the alleged discrimination in rates is merely a matter of relativity in cost of operation or whether it inflicts positive injury upon the nearer point. Would it benefit the nearer point if the lower rate beyond were withdrawn? It is here that the complexity of some of these cases of local discrimination becomes apparent. To understand this phase of the matter, the factor of commercial competition, as distinct from mere rivalry of routes, must be introduced. Hadley's analysis of the oyster case is quite inadequate on this point. Rates in that instance were on commodities (oysters) produced at practically uniform cost at both X and Y. They were, moreover, rates *from* two places out to a common market. Would it, however, make any difference if the controversy concerned the rates in the opposite direction; or, in other words, from a common centre of distribution out to two competing consuming points? Would it make any difference whether the goods were to be consumed at X and Y; or were to be used as raw material in manufactures at those two points; or were to be distributed throughout the countryside from X and Y as jobbing centres? It is at once evident that these issues are more complicated than in the first case. The two points X and Y being commercial and industrial rivals, is it not possible that the growth of one may take place at the expense of the other? At any given time there is only a fixed demand for the goods consumed, manufactured in or redistributed from the two places. Trade won by one is quite lost to the other. Of course, in a measure, this might also have been true of the oyster production. But, inasmuch as in that

[1] Chapter XVIII, p. 590, *infra*.

case the rate from Y was not affected by the entry of X, its prosperity would not probably be disturbed. The Hillsdale ice case, above described, is also one where the commodity (ice) is of relative unimportance for Columbus and Springfield, respectively. How would matters stand if the rates in question were on lumber or coal for manufacturing purposes? The difference, no doubt, is merely of degree and not of kind. Magnitudes, however, must not deceive us. The rights of Kathleen or Danville are just as sacred as those of Youngstown and Pittsburg.

St. Cloud, Minnesota, is located upon a line of the Northern Pacific Railroad, seventy-six miles northwest of St. Paul.[1] It is a competitor not only with St. Paul, but with other local centres in the vicinity, like Elk River, Princeton, and Anoka, either for flour milling or for distributive jobbing business. It is about the same distance as these other places from Duluth or Superior; through which the entire district obtains its supplies, such as coal from the East by lake boats; and by way of which its flour must be shipped to the Eastern markets and to Europe. And yet the rate on flour made at St. Cloud to New York in 1899 was twenty-eight and a half cents per hundredweight, as against a rate of twenty-one and a half cents from St. Paul, this latter rate being enjoyed also by Milaca, Princeton, Elk River, and Anoka. The rates on coal and other supplies from the East were likewise proportionately higher than to St. Paul and these neighboring towns. The specific complaint in this case is of local discrimination. The Northern Pacific Railroad operates the long line between St. Paul and the head of Lake Superior by way of Brainerd. On this business, passing through La Crosse, it has to meet a rate compelled at St. Paul by the competition of no less than three direct lines to Duluth. It avers that this business, taken either way for longer distances and at lower rates than are accorded

[1] 8 Int. Com. Rep., 346; reprinted in full in our Railway Problems, chap. XI.

to La Crosse, in no way affects the rates at that point; and that whatever it can earn as a contribution to joint expenses decreases the burden of these upon La Crosse rates. This is all entirely true from the transportation point of view; but,

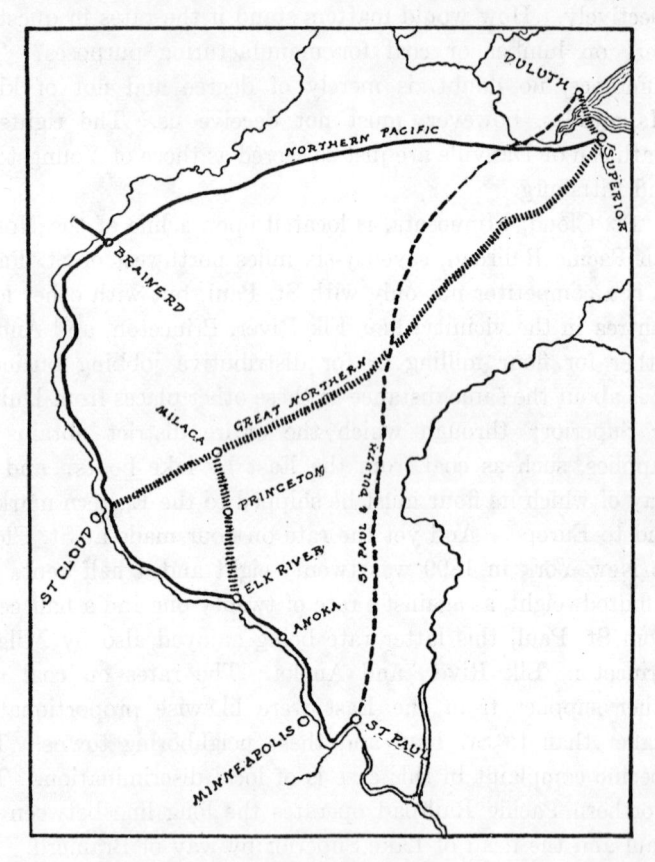

viewed in a large way, the situation is altered. Wheat of local production about La Crosse is rendered of less value by practically the excess of the La Crosse rate per hundredweight over the rate enjoyed from St. Paul. The Interstate Commerce Commission found that this was equivalent to a difference of fully $1 per acre in the value of wheat lands tributary to La

Crosse. And on the other hand, of course, the cost of all its supplies is enhanced above the level of rival manufacturing centres. On soft coal this equalled no less than eighty-five cents per ton. To this the Northern Pacific replied that the discrimination against La Crosse was not of its creation, but had existed before its entry into any St. Paul business by its indirect route. The Commission found, however, that in fact the participation of this indirect line on St. Paul-Duluth business did affect the short-line rate; and that its withdrawal would at least tend to prevent any further reduction of the St. Paul and related rates. If the withdrawal did not remove the discrimination against La Crosse, it would not at all events aggravate it. The vital point, differentiating this case from that of the Savannah Freight Bureau, previously stated, was the actual damage to the intermediate point due to the existence of commercial competition between it and the place more distant.

An important feature in commercial competition is its entire dissociation from all considerations of cost of service by long or short routes. Neither strong nor weak lines make the rate. The business is there. Market conditions are fixed. The carriers are free to take traffic or leave it. Single-handed, at least they cannot rule the price of transportation. The price of sugar at Kansas City is made by competition of Louisiana sugar coming from New Orleans, of beet sugar and Hawaiian sugar from Colorado and San Francisco, and of the world's sugar from New York. This is why Kansas City, in the complaint stated in the opening paragraph, enjoys a lower rate on sugar from San Francisco than the transcontinental lines can accord to Denver. The only possible justification for the apparent anomaly in lumber rates from Texas points, cited in the same paragraph, is that, as the heart of the Middle West is approached, lumber supplies from every point of the compass converge upon common markets. As is so frequently averred in such cases, no carrier makes the rate. The rate is made for all of them by conditions beyond their control. The only rates, therefore, which it is in their power to fix in some accordance with average costs of operation, are the rates at local stations. For these rates alone can they be brought to book.

Just here another characteristic of commercial competition as distinct from rivalry of routes is to be noted. Local discrimination, wherever it is alleged to occur, frequently assumes the form of complaint against rates to various places, not on the same line but by different and often widely separated lines. Complaints of this class might arise, for instance, referring back to our diagrams of the oyster cases, between X and Z. Philadelphia, we will assume, as before, to be the common market. A multitude of different varieties of protest are distinguishable. Point X equally distant from Philadelphia with Z may pay a higher rate than Z. Or X may be less distant than Z, and yet be called upon to pay the same rate. It may even be less distant than Z and yet actually be charged a higher rate than Z. But in all these instances the two points (X and Z) are not on the same route, but on divergent routes. The issue remains the same. The conditions imposed at the point of convergence being fixed, each line must exercise its own ingenuity in conforming thereto. Methods in each case must differ, according to the length of line, the direction and composition of the traffic, and other factors.

Three general schemes of rate-making are distinguishable in American practice. The most satisfactory one is that which obtains in trunk line territory, of zone tariffs with a gradation in some degree corresponding to distance.[1] At the other extreme is the system of the flat or postage-stamp rate, exemplified in the Missouri-Mississippi river territory,[2] and in Pacific coast rates from all points east of the Mississippi.[3]

[1] Chapter X, *infra*. [2] Chapter IV, *supra*, p. 128.
[3] Chapters XI and XIX, *infra*.

Intermediate between the two are the systems of basing lines and basing points. The first of these, the basing line system, prevails throughout the country west of the Missouri river. The second, the basing point system, is found throughout the southern states east of the Mississippi. In both the principle is the same. The two differ only in detail. Through rates are made to certain designated places; and from there on, a local rate to all other places, large or small, is added. This local charge rises, of course, with distance. Thus the first-class rate to Denver, Colorado, is made up of a rate of eighty cents from Chicago to the Missouri river, plus $1.25 for the balance of the haul. From Chicago to a point in central Nebraska the only difference would be a lower local. In southern territory the rate to Troy, Alabama, equals the sum of the through rate to the nearest basing point, Montgomery, and of the local rate from there on to destination. The only difference in detail between these two systems is that in the western territory, all competing lines being parallel (until the routes around by sea and back from the Pacific coast are met), rates rise in all cases progressively with distance. The complaint of local discrimination rests merely on the allegation that the rate of progression with increasing distance is too rapid. In the South, on the other hand, owing to the encircling seacoast with deeply penetrating navigable rivers, the competing routes from the East or North converge from different and even from directly opposite directions. Hence it is impossible to base rates upon extended boundary lines, like the Missouri river. Rates must be based upon certain designated points. This introduces a serious complication. Points, instead of lines, being used for basing purposes, in the South, local rates rise outward in every direction around each basing centre until the sphere of the next basing point is met. And local rates to points even back on the same line, through which the traffic has already passed to reach the basing point, are thus of necessity higher than rates to points beyond.

240   RAILROADS

The economic anomaly of rates actually falling progressively as the length of the haul increases is graphically well illustrated in the accompanying diagram, based upon data in the Georgia Railroad Commission cases.[1] The charges from

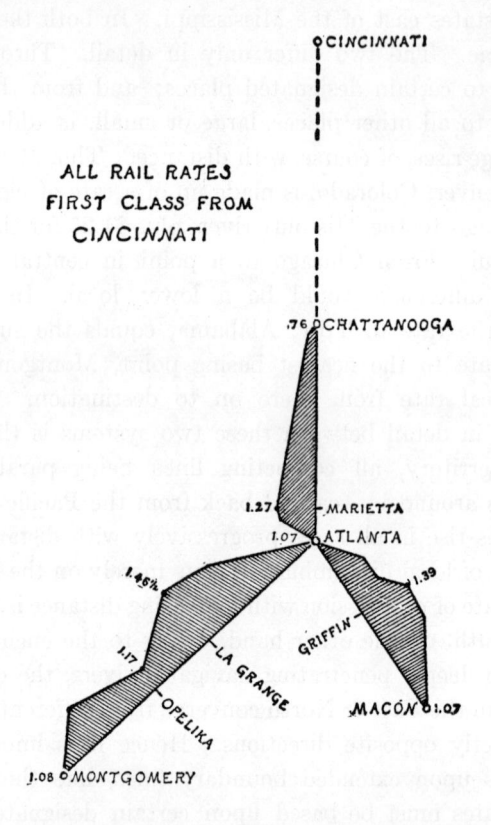

```
                    ○ CINCINNATI



        ALL RAIL RATES
        FIRST CLASS FROM
          CINCINNATI

                  .76 ○ CHATTANOOGA


                    1.27  ╱ MARIETTA
                      1.07 ○ ATLANTA
              1.45%              1.39
                ╱  LA GRANGE  GRIFFIN
            1.17                     
                  OPELIKA      MACON ○ 1.07

        1.08 ○ MONTGOMERY
```

Cincinnati to local points on all lines converging upon Atlanta equal the sum of the rates to Atlanta plus the local charges out. This holds good even on the direct line from Cincinnati through Chattanooga, as the diagram shows; yet of course it also follows that rates must again decline as the next basing point is approached in any direction; be it Montgomery to the west,

[1] 5 I.C.C. Rep., 324; p. 483, *infra*.

Macon to the south, or even Chattanooga to the north. The only condition analogous to this in the Far West appears in those places whose rates are made up by a combination of the low water rates to the coast plus a local back eastward into the mountains. The transition from this Pacific coast combination to the system based upon the Missouri river occurs at those places where the aggregate charges from either direction become equal. Viewed as a large matter of principle the whole western system is analogous to the southern system. It is inevitable in both that intermediate points should in all cases be assessed at a higher rate than those adopted as bases.[1]

The reason advanced in support of these basing point or basing line systems is that they are an outgrowth of commercial competition; in other words, that they are compelled by conditions beyond the carriers' control. Sometimes it may be the competition of widely encircling water routes — as from New York around to Galveston and up to Kansas City in the southwestern field, or to Mobile and up to Montgomery, Alabama, in the southeastern states. But, in many other cases, market competition from other centres of supply set the limit to the rate at the basing point. Missouri river cities enjoy a great advantage over all competitors, as meeting places of the ways. Generally, the low rates to the base points have been originally accorded in order to build up local distributive or industrial centres in the face of competition from older places. Nashville undoubtedly owes a large measure of its present prominence to the fact that in the old days its principal railroad gave a foothold and made a clientage for its merchants as against older rivals in Cincinnati and Louisville. Nor can it be said that this was an injury to that clientage, composed of consumers all through the adjacent countryside. Rates for these consumers were not put up, in order to build up Nash-

---

[1] *Cf.* Commissioner Fifer's dissenting opinion in the St. Louis Business Men's League case, 9 Int. Com. Rep., 318; reprinted in our Railway Problems, chap. XVII.

ville. On the contrary, Nashville was given perhaps inordinately low rates, in order that the sum of these low rates and of the local rates out to Four Corners should be at least as low as those from Cincinnati and Louisville direct. This last argument is the main economic defence of the southern basing point system.[1] It applies equally to the advocacy of a low basing line at Missouri river cities for rate making to points beyond.[2]

The main difficulty with any system of basing points or lines, which so flagrantly violates the distance principle, is first of all to determine at what points to base; and thereafter to accommodate the system to the normal growth and development of the country. The system is inelastic. It tends to break down of its own weight. It must enlarge, if at all, by fits and starts, in each case with violent dislocation of trade. A generation ago towns in Iowa complained that the Mississippi river was a basing line. Then, when the Missouri river line was substituted, an outcry rose from all the points in Nebraska. The persistent complaint from Denver against its rate adjustment as compared with Kansas City, — a competitive distributing centre, — well exemplifies it. The Denver Chamber of Commerce intervenes, and proposes that the basing line be moved from the Missouri river out to Colorado common points (like Denver). Indeed, in each case the argument in favor of the change is identical. Each tier of complainants — thriving cities which have recently come to more or less commercial maturity — plead their inability to compete with the centres adopted some years ago for basing purposes. Denver, for example, wishes to sell goods throughout Utah. But its total charges there on goods purchased in the East amount to eighty cents from Chicago to the Missouri river, plus $1.25 on to Denver, plus $1.64 on to destination, — a sum of

[1] Chapter XI, *infra*.
[2] 11 I.C.C. Rep., 495; 15 *Idem*, 555; U. S. Industrial Commission, IV, p. 264 and IX, p. 287. Also pp. 129, *supra*, and 442, *infra*.

$3.69 per hundred pounds. The Kansas City dealer, on the other hand, gets a low base rate of only eighty cents with a single additional rate directly out to Utah of $2.05. In other words, the latter can lay down his goods in Utah for $2.85 as against $3.69 paid by the Denver competitor. The point to be carried forward, however, is not so much the disparity against Denver, as the fact that the moment Denver is promoted to be a basing point it becomes defendant in a complaint of precisely the same sort, brought by the places still further west. This inelasticity of basing point schemes, together with their inability to expand without abrupt dislocations of trade, is apparent everywhere in the South. Just as Chattanooga complains against Nashville, so the little intermediate stations between Chattanooga and Atlanta, as our diagram on page 240 showed, become restive under rates of $1.27 as compared with a rate twenty-one cents lower charged on to Atlanta. The system of basing points or lines may be an inevitable concomitant of industrial immaturity; but it is none the less difficult to defend as a permanent system or as one inherently just. And its final relegation to the scrap heap, in favor of a system of rates graded more or less according to distance, is ardently to be desired.[1]

Does a constant rate applied over a long stretch on the same line constitute local discrimination? May the nearer points rightfully protest against the fact that equally low rates are accorded to remoter points? This is the gist of the controversy in the very suggestive Milk Rate cases in 1897.[2] Here the conflict of interest between producer and consumer

[1] The feasibility of doing this in the South could all parties concerned be whipped into line, is demonstrated by the ingenious adaptation of the trunk line system to local conditions by a special committee of the Southern Railway and Steamship Association in 1880. Report of meeting August 12, 1880, in Proceedings, VII.
[2] 7 I.C.C. Rep., 92. The report and opinion is reprinted in full by the Senate (Elkins) Committee, 1905, as Appendix H.

is obvious. The city of New York naturally desires a wide market from which to draw its supply. On the other hand, the near-by producers wish to enjoy the advantages of nearness to the market to the fullest degree. Study of the evolution of rate sheets clearly shows how such grouping of charges over long distances may be in the nature of a compromise to avoid actual violation of the long and short haul principle. Oftentimes places scattered along over a hundred miles of railroad enjoy absolute equality of charges. Obviously, the ton-mile rate steadily falls within such a group with progressive remoteness. Yet it is an inevitable feature of tariff building.[1] It is the kernel of the admirable trunk line rate system. Such an equalization of rates between points unequally distant from a given centre, not infrequently arises in connection with mere competition of transportation routes. Referring back to the diagrams on page 219, it may happen that a complainant at X, the nearer point, recognizing the inevitableness of a low rate at Y, may succeed in securing an agreement that, while its charges cannot be less than at Y, at least they shall not be more. This was all that was asked in the "rare and peculiar" case of Youngstown, Ohio.[2] But it is apparent that such a solution differs only in degree from those previously discussed. The question of principle remains the same. The roundabout route to New York up back by way of Youngstown could continue to compete at Pittsburg for as low a rate as on direct shipments, even if it observed the long and short haul principle to which the Pennsylvania direct route was committed, only by charging much lower rates per ton mile on Pittsburg traffic through Youngstown than was levied on business there originating. This raises precisely the same question of distribution of joint expenses between local and competitive traffic, already discussed. In certain contingencies under the second variety of the oyster cases, such a solution might apply. Would Chattanooga, for example, assuming it to belong in the second

[1] P. 103, *supra*.   [2] Pp. 223, *supra;* and 296, *infra*.

class of oyster cases, be contented with an equality of through rates with Nashville, leaving its local rates out to smaller towns as they are?

The most extreme instance of uniform or postage-stamp rates applied over long distances occurs in the transcontinental tariffs from different points in the East. These differ radically from the adjustment of rates between different points on the Pacific slope, already described. At the far western end the lowest rates are accorded to coast cities, because of water competition by sea. Rates to interior points progressively rise by the addition of locals inward toward the interior. The rates thus compelled by water competition are accepted by the all-rail lines. Thus the Pacific coast end is practically built upon a basing line. It might be expected that in consequence of water competition by sea a similar system would prevail at the eastern end of the line; that rates to the Pacific coast from interior cities would rise progressively according to distance inland, until at all events the direct all-rail charge became as low as by the combined rail-and-water rates. But such is not the case, and for two reasons. The first is that in the East interior cities are large and powerful factors in trade. There were no such interior cities in the Far West, until Spokane came into its own. These inland eastern cities, Pittsburg, for example, demanded equality of opportunity with the seaboard cities in Pacific coast trade. They succeeded in obtaining it by a grant of as low rates as New York or Boston enjoyed. In the second place, all the Pacific coast carriers enjoy monopoly as far east as the Missouri river. But east of that line there are many routes interested in middle western cities, but having no interest in those in the East. They, too, have insisted upon giving their clients in such places as St. Louis and Chicago as low rates as Philadelphia or New York. Little by little the equality of rates was extended until for many years the blanket rate has covered the entire United States east of the Mississippi river.

Does not this constitute local discrimination against the middle western cities? This was one of the main contentions in the St. Louis Business Mens' League case. Being one thousand miles nearer San Francisco, it demanded recognition of that fact in its tariffs. The difficulty is accentuated when both eastern and western point rates are considered together. St. Louis enjoys no lower rate than New York, although one thousand miles further east; and inland points in the Rocky mountain area may be one thousand miles further east than San Francisco and yet pay a higher rate. Thus it is possible to lop off one thousand miles at each end of the line without affording any recognition of it in the tariffs. The situation is too involved to discuss in detail in this place; but one finds it difficult to avoid the conclusion that the whole system will demand revision before long. Geographical conditions are immutable. Trade conditions are not. Perhaps it was inevitable that the former should by force of circumstances have been somewhat overlooked during a period of rapid growth. But, as commercial affairs approach a condition of stability and permanence, the matter will call for most careful examination.

Constant rates applied over long distances on the *same* line almost inevitably tend to pass over into a system of equality of rates over *different* lines.[1] The necessity was evident enough in the Milk Rate case. This phase of the matter may theoretically best be discussed by reference to the following diagram. Suppose A, B, C, and D to represent any four inland "common points." It remains to show how it comes about that they all finally enjoy equal rates to all four seaports, regardless of location. Each appears to be naturally tributary to some one of the seaports by a dominant or short-line route. In each in-

[1] Similar cases are 12 I.C.C. Rep., 564; 14 *Idem*, 476 on oranges; 16 *Idem*, 276; 22 *Idem*, 93 and 115; and 23 *Idem*, 195; are local but identical problems of distances. Also the Superior Commercial Club case, just handed down June 25, 1912, on grain rates. *Cf.* also Hammond, Railway Rate Theories, etc., p. 94.

stance this route properly rules the rate. Moreover, the four seaports may be considered for traffic purposes as equally and interchangeably distant from one another without regard to location. This follows from the fact that, except in extreme instances, rates by water do not vary according to distance, so small is the cost of mere propulsion by comparison with the terminal costs. In other words, the rate is the same from

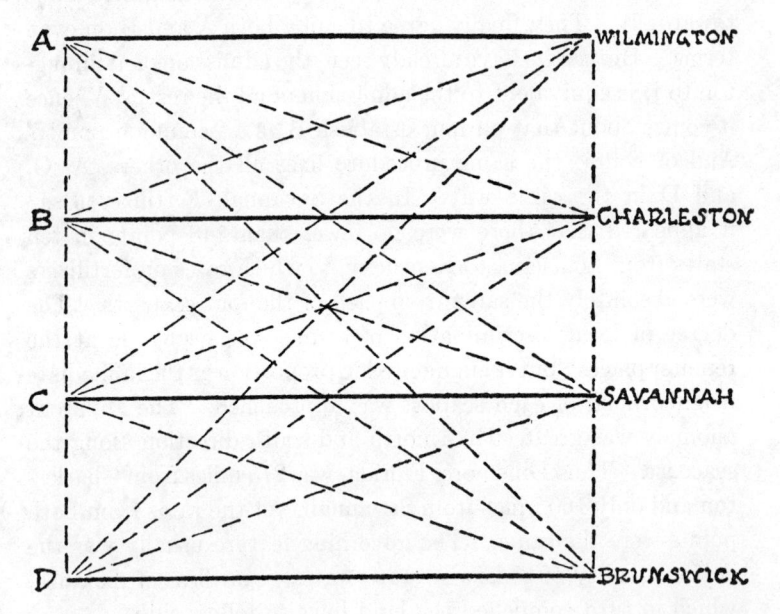

Wilmington to Brunswick or Savannah as to its next neighbor Charleston. From this it follows, further, that Wilmington, Savannah, and Brunswick can all reach B — the point to which Charleston is nearest — on even terms. They may each have a direct line to B; but, as compared with a possible combined low water rate to Charleston and a low direct rail rate inland to B, the Charleston route may be at least able to hold its own. All three outside competitors, then, are on even terms with one another in respect of access to B. But how does Charleston stand towards B as against the field? We have already concluded that a roundabout route must be allowed to meet, though not to undercut, the ruling rate. Such a roundabout route from Wilmington on this diagram to its own natural tributary A could be, and as a matter of fact is, made by passing around by way of Charleston or any other seaport. Charleston wishes to share in this trade at A, and may reach it by similar tactics. It stands towards A precisely as Wilmington stands towards B. They finally agree to enjoy both A and B on even terms. But, as we have already seen, the admission of Wilmington to B is equivalent to the admission of all the rest. Whence it comes about that all four establish B as a "common point." And of course the same procedure fixes all the others, A, C, and D in the same way. In the Savannah Fertilizer case [1] it appeared that there were no fewer than 148 points in ten states from Louisiana to Kentucky, to which rates on fertilizers were absolutely the same from each of the four seaports. The degree of local discrimination of course was negligible at the remoter places; but it augmented in proportion as the immediate neighborhood of each seaport was approached. The apparent anomaly was greatest in a north and south direction along the seacoast. Thus Dinsmore, Florida, was 275 miles from Charleston and only 160 miles from Savannah, yet the rates from both points were the same. The governing feature usually was the entire equality of coastwise water rates, regardless of distance, which in turn compelled the land lines to follow suit.

The Cincinnati Freight Bureau case, otherwise known as the Maximum Freight Rate case,[2] affords the best example of the difficulty in practice of adjusting rates over different and widely separated lines on a distance basis, in order to satisfy the demands of commercial competition. Atlanta, Georgia, the key to the southern market, is 876 miles by rail from New York, but only 475 miles from Cincinnati and 733

[1] 7 Int. Com. Rep., 458; reprinted in our Railway Problems, chap. XII.
[2] Chapter XIV, *infra*, discusses its legal aspect. Reprinted in full in our Railway Problems, chap. VI.

from Chicago. In other words, Cincinnati is fifty-four per cent. as far from Atlanta as is New York; and even Chicago is only eighty-four per cent. as remote. In general, this valuable southern territory, on the basis of mere distance, is really nearer to the leading middle western cities than to those on the Atlantic seaboard. Yet this geographical situation is not reflected in the railway tariffs. Rates from the West, especially on manufactures, were much higher, always relatively and often absolutely. Thus first-class goods in 1894 paid $1.47 per hundred from Chicago (733 miles), while from New York (876 miles) the rate was only $1.14. At points like Chattanooga the disparity was even greater. This city is only 595 miles from Chicago as against 1,060 miles from Boston. Yet the rates were actually lower ($1.14) from New England than from Chicago ($1.16). The principal reason for this of course was the cheap coastwise water competition by way of Charleston and Savannah. The eastern all-rail routes could charge no more than the combined rail-and-water lines. The difference in relative cost of operation by water was recognized by means of so-called "constructive mileage." From New York to Savannah by sea is about 750 miles; yet the allowance to the steamers was proportioned upon a distance of only 250 miles. Water cost was thus fixed by comparison with rail cost in the proportion of one to three. Yet, even with this allowance in favor of eastern cities, New York remained more distant from Atlanta than Cincinnati; the "rate-making" distance from the former being 538 miles as against only 475 miles from Cincinnati. The arbitrary reduction of the New York distance left Chicago more remote (733 miles), but not in so great degree as its tariffs implied. These tariffs were also peculiar in another regard. The handicap against the western cities was much higher in respect of manufactures and high-class freight than upon foodstuffs and raw produce. This in turn was clearly due to a long-established agreement between the lines east and west of the Alleghanies, as to a division of the field. Originally each set of lines was harassed by roundabout competition from the other. Western foodstuffs and raw produce were reaching the South by way of the Atlantic seaboard; and eastern manufactures from New York, for instance, were rambling about over western lines in order to reach places like Atlanta and Augusta, naturally served by direct routes from the East. The agreement to divide the field, dating from 1878, steadily became more irksome, however, to the West, with the development of manufactures of its own. The problems raised by this change are too large to be considered here. The main question for the present inquiry is as to the relative fairness of rates from two widely separated centres to a common market, those rates not being proportioned to distance.

The final settlement of this knotty question is suggestive of the extreme difficulty of attempting to apply mileage or distance rates over different railroads too rigidly. The complaint being as to relativity, there were only two possible solutions.[1] One was to increase the eastern rates, the other to order a reduction of the charges from the West. The former course was impossible, owing to the presence of water competition by sea, not under control. The latter alternative was, therefore, chosen by the Interstate Commerce Commission in its decision in 1894. The rates from western cities were always composed of two parts. The charge from the Ohio south was kept distinct as a local rate. The other portion of the rate applied from Chicago, for example, down to the Ohio river. Of these two parts, the trunk line portion appeared reasonable enough. It was the southern local, often one hundred per cent. higher than the other, which seemed most unreasonable; and which, according to all appearances, had been used to bring about a closure of the market to western manufactured goods. Consequently the Commission ordered a reduction of the southern local rates, cutting them drastically,

[1] *Cf.* testimony in Elkins Committee Report, 1905, p. 2726. The Commerce Court case on page 588, *infra*, brings it to date.

but leaving the northern locals unchanged. This decision was never carried into effect; as the Supreme Court of the United States held the Commission to have no such rate-making power. Nothing was done apparently to remedy the disparity in charges against the West, although the railroads serving that territory urgently pressed for action. Every time they threatened a reduction of their western rates, the eastern line came down in proportion. This left the relative rates as before, although the general scale would be lower all round.

At last, in 1905, the eastern lines from Baltimore south agreed to permit a reduction of five cents in the rates from western cities by lines *north* of the Ohio river; but they refused to accede to any change in the rates from the Ohio south. This was the exact opposite of the Interstate Commerce Commission's proposition, although both plans were intended to compass the same object; namely, to place western shippers more nearly on a parity with the East. The Commission, in 1894, laid all reduction upon the southern portion of the rate; the railroads, in 1905, placed it all upon the northern part. This obviously afforded no relief to the original complainant, Cincinnati. In fact, it actually operated to its great disadvantage, inasmuch as it let its two powerful rivals, Chicago and St. Louis, into the southern field on distinctly more favorable terms. Such was the outcome as a result of the friction of railroad competition. The reasonableness of some reduction was clear. But to the layman, the fairness of laying the reduction entirely upon the northern locals, already relatively low, instead of upon the extremely high southern part of the rate is not by any means so clear.[1]

One further detail of this adjustment of southern rates raises a question:

"Rates between Richmond, Virginia, and Atlanta, Georgia, are less than the rates between Richmond, Virginia, and Greenwood,

[1] *Cf.* Answer of Receivers' and Shippers' Association of Cincinnati to statement of W. J. Murphy, etc., March 15, 1907.

South Carolina (an intermediate point). This is due to indirect competition between Richmond and Western jobbing points; and in order to permit the jobber or manufacturer in Richmond to do business as against his competitor in Cincinnati, it has been necessary to fix the rates from Richmond to Atlanta with some reference to the rates from Cincinnati to Atlanta. At Greenwood, South Carolina, we find that the Cincinnati shipper pays a very much higher rate than to Atlanta, and that the rates from Richmond are already sufficiently low to enable the Richmond shipper to compete at Greenwood with the Cincinnati shipper."[1]

Is this not in a measure well described in the passage, "unto him that hath shall be given; but from him that hath not, shall be taken away even that which he hath"? This railway argument contains dangerous possibilities. In effect, upon the theory of charging what the traffic will bear, it means that a railway (in this case the Seaboard Air Line) may increase its own local rates, not in proportion to the length of its own haul (from Richmond to Greenwood), but according to the remoteness of that local point from another competing market. The inevitable effect of the general adoption of such a policy must be to erect arbitrary barriers to the free and wide-spread movement of commerce. The great advantage of the flat rate or of commodity rates is that, placing all competing centres upon an absolute parity irrespective of distance, they encourage the utmost freedom of trade.

Certain general conclusions seem to be warranted by the analysis of these cases of local discrimination. The first is that they all show the extreme delicacy of commercial adjustment and the existence of conditions well beyond the control of the carriers, jointly or singly. Trade jealousies in particular — the rivalry of producing and consuming centres — render relativity of rates of paramount importance to shippers. This class in the community is interested comparatively little in the absolute level of rates, that being more directly the concern

[1] Senate (Elkins) Committee Report, 1905, Digest, Appendix III., p. 231.

of the general consuming public. To the public, as represented by State and Federal legislatures, it is difficult to make these complicated matters of commercial competition clear. The only basis of rate making that is easily understood is one founded in general upon the distance principle, or, in other words, correlated with considerations of cost of operation. Any departure from this basis is apt to breed suspicion, and at all events puts the carrier upon the defence. It is bad policy, in their own interest, for railroads to permit a continuance of such violations of the distance principle in their general tariffs (commodity rates as a special resource to meet the special needs of commercial competition may be set aside), except in extreme cases. This was recognized by the trunk lines when they almost unanimously acquiesced in the long and short haul provisions of the Act of 1887. The people of the United States have the same right that they had then, to expect that at the earliest possible moment the wise provisions of the trunk line rate adjustment shall be widely accepted in the West and South. Whether those regions, and the railways that reach them, have yet sufficiently developed to warrant the change is a matter requiring careful consideration in detail.

The necessity of some exercise of governmental control over these carriers of the country, in order to mitigate, if not to eliminate, local discrimination as far as possible, is evident. Many of the instances previously cited have clearly shown how impossible it often is for any railroad, single-handed, to deal with an involved situation in a large way. Take the Cincinnati Freight Bureau case, for instance. Conceding, as many would, the claim of western cities to some readjustment of tariffs in their favor, is it not an anomaly that the lines south from Baltimore, several hundred miles away, should finally dictate the means to be employed to remedy the situation at Cincinnati and Chicago? Who else but the Federal government could ever hope to disentangle the almost hopeless snarl of competition involved in the controversy over differentials to and from the Atlantic seaboard?[1] This controversy is at bottom one of local discrimination. And yet how is the Interstate Commerce Commission to aid in the solution of these intricate problems under present conditions? Its hands formerly doubly tied, are now in part freed by rehabilitation of the long and short haul clause. But it cannot yet deal with minimum rates, nor is it clear that it can prescribe differential rates.[2] True, the commission may, in some cases, accomplish by indirection its purpose of establishing a proper relativity between rates through the exercise of its newly granted power to fix maximum rates. This, as we shall see, was done in the recent Spokane and Denver decisions. Holding that the charges at interior points were out of line with through rates to the Pacific coast; and being unable to govern the long-distance tariffs, it simply ordered a reduction of certain rates at Spokane and Denver as inherently unreasonable. This solution is not, however, always practicable. Not infrequently the lower rate at the remoter point will drop as soon as the intermediate rate is lowered. Thus the former relativity of charges is re-established on a generally lower scale. The complaint in the Eau Claire lumber case required the exercise of such power over minimum rates, in order to remove the disability against a particular centre. And then, finally, it is indubitable that commercial competition as a "compelling" factor has been somewhat over-emphasized by the railroads. Too often conditions in part brought about by themselves, or in which at least they have acquiesced, have been set up as a defence for rates favoring certain points. This is especially true of the southern basing point cases.[3] Whether any further grant of powers to the Interstate Com-

---

[1] 22 I.C.C. Rep., 99 is a case of conceded injustice for fourteen years; yet of a complete deadlock between carriers, broken only by Federal intervention.
[2] *Infra.*   [3] Chapter XI, *infra.*

merce Commission by Congress is necessary at this time in order to enable progress to be made in this connection, it is as yet too soon to predict. The course of affairs for the next few years will at all events bear attentive watching.

In the case of competition between a direct and a longer, more roundabout line, which one "controls" or fixes the rate? It is an important matter, involving as it does the economic, if not the legal, right of a carrier to participate in any given traffic. Concerning this question the greatest diversity of opinion prevails. On the one hand, both writers [1] and practical railway men [2] aver that the short line makes the rate, while the long line merely meets the rate thus made. This is probably the more prevalent opinion. Yet expert evidence of an opposite sort is to be had for the seeking. The Interstate Commerce Commission has repeatedly held that the short line is at the mercy of the longer line under certain circumstances; [3] and traffic managers not infrequently plead their inability to control rate situations in the face of irrepressible, roundabout competition.[4] There is evidently a confusion of thinking, or else a loose use of terms where statements are so conflicting. As a matter of voluntary agreement among roads, or of prescribed rates under government regulation, the issue often assumes the form of controversy as to whether a road operating under a physical disability shall be permitted to participate in a given business by a concession in rates or not. Thus in the notable Milk Rate cases it was a question whether roads with heavy grades should be allowed to make concessions in rates. This

[1] Acworth, "Elements of Railway Economics," p. 125.
[2] Testimony of J. J. Hill, Senate (Elkins) Committee, 1905, p. 1507; certainly in the Missouri-Mississippi river territory, the Hannibal-St. Joe distance rules.
[3] Especially in the Danville and St. Cloud cases; 8 Int. Com. Rep., 357 and 429. *Cf.* the Vermont Central case, 1 *Idem*, 182 and 82: and 7 *Idem*, 481.
[4] An especially notable instance was the Canadian Pacific differential arbitration in 1898. Proceedings, etc., p. 73, argument of J. C. Stubbs.

issue really also underlies the question of enforcement of the long and short haul clause. In the recent Spokane case the Harriman lines to St. Paul asked that they, being long lines, should not be compelled to reduce their rates to the figure prescribed for the direct Hill roads.

It is clear in the first place that "short line" and "long line" are merely used as convenient terms to designate differences in the cost of operation. This was well put by James J. Hill before the Elkins Committee of 1905.

"We will say that the distance from Cincinnati to New York is 800 miles, and that they haul 800 tons behind one locomotive on one per cent. ruling grades. Now somebody else builds a road with a 0.3 grade, and he can haul 2,000 tons — twice and a half the amount; but that line is 200 miles longer. You can see readily that to move a given number of tons the second road runs less than half the train miles, so that the farthest way round is the nearest way home in that case."

The problem should really be stated thus in terms of cost not of distance. Suppose the roundabout line to be in part or wholly by water, as in competition between the transcontinental roads and the Isthmian or Cape Horn routes, or as between the direct all-rail line from Boston to Nashville, Tenn., and the steamer line from Boston to Savannah, and thence up to Nashville by rail. In such cases the rail lines allow the water routes a differential or constructive mileage in recognition of their relatively cheaper per mile expenses of operation. The differential may sometimes exist, where, judging by the bulk of traffic, the advantage, irrespective of the differential, lies with the line giving the lower rate. In other words, as measured by volume of business, the stronger line and not the weaker one enjoys the benefit of the differential. This is the case in the coastwise traffic between Atlantic and Gulf ports; where the bulk of the tonnage goes by steamer and at lower rates than by all-rail lines. The difficult point to settle in all such cases is whether the allowance is made as a voluntary *concession* to the roundabout line because it *costs* more to operate; or whether it is a toll or tribute, because, irrespective of the cost, the long line rate is made on the basis of value of service. The problem, then, resolves itself into this: how far in practice does cost of operation really "control" the rate in cases of competition between two lines differently circumstanced in this regard? If cost is of fundamental importance, the "short line," using the term as above said in a figurative sense, "controls" the rate. If cost is an entirely secondary matter, rates being made in accordance with considerations of value of service, the "long line" holds the upper hand, and the short one is at its mercy.

It is important, moreover, in the comparison of costs of operation, to keep in view the inter-relation between fixed charges and operating expenses. This point is often neglected. Any well-considered outlay upon permanent improvements, of course, increases fixed charges according to the extent of the new capital investment; but at the same time it presumably lessens the direct cost of operation. The interest upon funds spent for heavier rails, reduction of grades, straightening of curves, better terminals or heavier rolling stock, must be set over against the direct economies resulting from heavier train loads, lessened expenditure for wear and tear, for accidents and claims or for wages. This relation between current expense and capital cost was clearly emphasized in an arbitration decision by the late S. R. Blanchard, already cited in another connection. Two roads were in competition for business at New Orleans. One had costly but convenient terminal facilities. The other was so far from the heart of the city that the drayage expenses were an important item. This second railway began by offering free cartage to shippers in order to even up with its more favored competitor; but this soon gave way to the practice of private teaming by shippers with an allowance on the freight bill for "drayage equalization." The other road objected to this on the ground that it constituted a virtual rebate; that in other words the weaker line was taking business at an abnormally low rate. The arbitrator, however,

VOL. I—17

upheld the practice, on the ground that the heavier operating expense for cartage was merely an alternative for increased interest charges, had the road elected to construct costly and more convenient terminals. One road virtually paid money for team hire, the other paid it in interest on bonds.

Analyzing the main question two propositions are certain. Firstly, the long line can never charge *more* than the short line; whence it follows that as the short line reduces its rate, the long one must accept that rate as made; and, secondly, the long line, costing more to operate, is, in the process of reduction of rates, bound to be the first to strike the bed-rock of cost incident to that particular service. To go below this point of particular cost would obviously be indefensible from every point of view. The general rule, then, is that "the short line rules the rate." This is accepted widely in practice, as for example throughout trunk line territory and between the so-called Missouri-Mississippi river points, where the short line from Hannibal to St. Joseph determines all rates by longer routes.[1] But the problem yet remains unsolved. The long line may never be able to charge *more* than the short line — may it, however, charge *less* under certain conditions? The moment it is enabled to do so, the long line and not the short line, for the moment, "controls the rate." If, now, we use the technically proper terms, the question becomes this: Under what circumstances is average cost of service in railway competition set aside in favor of other considerations; or, otherwise stated, when may a line, operated under a disability as to cost, properly give a lower rate than its competitors notwithstanding? Does disability justify a handicap or the reverse? This was the form which the question assumed in the notable Milk Rate case: as to whether the weaker lines in respect of distance or grades should be allowed compensation therefor by permission to charge higher rates.

[1] It is also the rule in France. Senate (Elkins) Committee, V, p. 273. *Cf.* the Superior grain case. I.C.C., decided June 25, 1912.

One of the common instances of rate control by a line operating under a disability as to distance or normal cost is the competition of a bankrupt with a solvent property. The "roundabout" line, like the Erie or the old New York and New England, having repudiated its fixed charges, undoubtedly "makes" the rate which the other roads must meet or lose the traffic. Usually they prefer to absorb or control it otherwise, financially, thus substituting monopoly for a ruinous condition of competition. Yet such instances resolve themselves, evidently, into questions of relative cost of operation after all. The bankrupt road holds the whip hand, because, having repudiated its fixed charges, its average costs of operation are correspondingly reduced. The validity of operating cost as a basis of charges is surely not shaken by this exceptional case.

The relative proportions and the distribution of local and through traffic upon two lines of differing length in competition with one another are primary factors in determining the ability of either one to "make the rate." This is, of course, especially true under the operation of any long and short haul law, under which any reduction of the competitive rates would necessitate a lowering of the charges at intermediate points. No road is going to sacrifice lucrative rates upon a large volume of local traffic unless it can gain either a large volume of business or a very long haul from a competitive point. Many of the notorious rate disturbers in our industrial history have been "short cut" roads — the shortest lines between given important points, regardless of the nature of the intervening territory — like the old New York and New England, the Erie or the Canada Southern. Other roads, like the Chicago Great Western or the Central Vermont, were more roundabout, and yet enjoyed but little local business, depending almost exclusively for their livelihood upon long hauls between termini. On the Central Vermont at one time, through business constituted seventy-nine per cent. of the total; and only five per cent. was strictly local in origin. On the other hand, the Louisville & Nashville, in its original petition for exemption from the long and short haul clause, stated that eighty per cent. of its income was derived from local business. This consideration, as applied to competition between the two primary trunk lines, may not be without significance. As compared with the Pennsylvania Railroad, rich in local business, the New York Central, running along the narrow Mohawk and Hudson valleys, has not inaptly been described as operating "between good points, but not through a good country." Under a strict enforcement of the long and short haul clause, the dilemma on the former road would be more serious than on the latter. To choose between its rich local traffic in iron and steel or coal and the long haul business from the West, would be a more difficult matter for the Pennsylvania, than for the New York Central management to weigh its through grain business against the local traffic from interior New York points.

In one way the persistence of locally high rates in the South and West, irrespective of the low charges at competitive points, is defensible on the ground that local business is scanty.[1] The roads cannot live upon it. Their mainstay is the long-distance traffic from important points.[2] On the other hand, where there is no obligation to maintain a distance tariff, of course the road with rich local business enjoys a great advantage in making rates at competitive points. It can practically subsist upon its revenue from its own particular constituency, meeting all its fixed charges thereby; and can afford to cut rates on the competitive tonnage down to the bone. Such a road, quite irrespective of the length of its line, would obviously "control" the rate at competitive points, as against any rival without such a subsidiary and independent source of income.[3]

[1] *Cf.* Mr. Fink's testimony in Hearings Senate Committee on Interstate Commerce, 51st Cong. 1st session, Sen. Rep., 847, p. 29.
[2] Solution of transcontinental dilemma depends upon this choice. *Railway Age Gazette*, Nov. 25, 1910. *Cf.* chaps. XI and XIX, *infra*.
[3] 19 I.C.C. Rep., 218 affords an excellent example as between the Union

Volume of traffic is another fundamental element in the determination of cost of operation. No matter how short the line or how easy its curves and grades, unless it can handle its tonnage in large bulk it will operate at a disadvantage. Hence a most important factor to be reckoned with, in deciding which of two competing lines is in a commanding position as to rates, is the volume of traffic, both in gross and as susceptible of concentration on either line. In the notable Chattanooga case, for example, although the line from New York to Nashville, passing around to the south by way of Chattanooga, is 212 miles shorter than the lines *via* Cincinnati or Louisville, the latter, by reason of the density of traffic in trunk line territory, seem to stand at least on an even footing. On the other hand, the enjoyment of the bulk of the tonnage sometimes places its possessor at the mercy of a petty rival. The Fall River water line to New York, carrying an overwhelming preponderance of the business, obviously could not afford to cut rates to prevent the Joy Line from stealing a small portion of the traffic. The same principle holds good in other lines of business. The Standard Oil Company can better afford permanently to concede a small fraction of business to a small independent dealer, so long as he knows his place and refrains from ambition to enlarge, rather than to attempt to drive him out entirely by cutting prices on a huge volume of business. Occasionally independents are shrewd enough to take advantage of this; and so to distribute their business that they shall in no single place menace a powerful rival, and yet comfortably subsist on the gleanings over a wide area.[1] In no single locality are they important enough to exterminate, at the cost of cut rates applied to a large volume of business; and yet in the aggregate they may make quite

Pacific and the Denver and Rio Grande. Also the Montgomery, Ala., case in the Commerce Court, p. 590, *infra*. Also the Union Pacific Merger case, Brief of Facts for Appellants, 1912, p. 276.

[1] For an instance in the tobacco business: *Cf. The Atlantic Monthly*, 1908, p. 487.

a fair livelihood. The only difference between the status of a railway and other lines of business in this regard is that the railway may not be quite so free to deploy its forces. Its territory and tonnage are more definitely circumscribed by physical conditions of location.

A point to be noted in this same connection is the relative stability of the traffic. Is it concentrated in a few hands or does it arise from many scattered sources? In the former case either road by making a bold stroke may so entirely capture the business that, by reason of the enhanced volume, a handicap in operation may be overcome. Thus, in the notable instance of trunk line competition for the beef traffic some twenty years ago, the Grand Trunk, although much more roundabout, besides being handicapped in other ways, by securing *all* the business, could afford to make rates impossible under other circumstances.

Whether the business in question is natural or normal to a road, or is an extra, diverted from other more direct lines, is still another factor of importance affecting ability to compete successfully for any given traffic. The best statement of this is found in the argument of J. C. Stubbs before the Arbitration Board on Canadian Pacific Differentials in 1898.[1] "These are differentials in favor of weaker lines — lines which upon the merits of their service cannot successfully compete for the business, but claim a share of it as the reward of virtue, the price of maintaining reasonable rates. . . . For example, the Canadian Pacific road was not projected or built for the purpose of developing, fostering, or sharing the carrying trade between San Francisco and the eastern part of the United States. . . . After they were built and the various connections made, then, and not until then, it was seen that there was a business opened. The route having been opened, the newer and longer lines entered the field of competition against the older, shorter, and more direct lines by cutting the latter's

[1] Page 72.

rates. . . . In a fight of this kind, paradoxical as it may seem, the stronger line always got the worst of it. . . . The weaker or longer line, not having any business at the outset, had nothing to lose. Everything was gain to it, which appeared to show an earning above the actual cost of handling the particular lot of freight. Quite a distinction between that and the average cost of handling all business. Such an unequal warfare could not long continue, and the common result was that the stronger line sought for terms, and ultimately bought the weaker line off, . . . this class of differentials is and always has been obnoxious."

Our final conclusion must therefore be that the outcome in cases of unequal competition in respect of cost of operation can seldom be predicted with certainty. Everything depends upon local circumstances and conditions. Sometimes the long line and sometimes the short line will dominate. Careful analysis of every feature of the business must be made before positive affirmation is possible. This result is at all events worth noting. A due appreciation of the complexity of the business of rate making may safeguard us against the cocksure statements of the novice, who has never closely examined into the subject. President Taft has recently emphasized the need of expert service in the field of customs and tariff legislation. It is greatly to be hoped that a similar appreciation of the care with which railway legislation should proceed may prevail at Washington during the present session of Congress.

CHAPTER VIII

PROBLEMS OF ROUTING

Neglect of distance, an American peculiarity, 264. — Derived from joint cost, 265. — Exceptional cases, 265. — Economic waste in American practice, 268. — Circuitous rail carriage, 269. — Water and rail-and-water shipments, 273. — Carriage over undue distance, 277. — An outcome of commercial competition, 278. — Six causes of economic waste, illustrated, 280. — Pro-rating and rebates, 281. — Five effects of disregard of distance, 288. — Dilution of revenue per ton mile, 289. — Possible remedies for economic waste, 292. — Pooling and rate agreements, 293. — The long and short haul remedy, 295.

THE general acceptance, both in practice and theory, of the principle that distance is a relatively unimportant element in rate making [1] is significant at this time, in connection with the recent amendment of the Act to Regulate Commerce. It is important also because of the marked tendency toward the adoption by various state legislatures of the extreme opposite principle of a rigid distance tariff. The old problem of effecting a compromise between these two extreme theories by some form of long and short haul clause — the original section 4 of the act of 1887 having been emasculated by judicial interpretation — is again brought to the front. For these reasons it may be worth while to consider certain results which inevitably follow the widespread acceptance of this principle of the blanket rate. Its benefits are indeed certain; namely, an enlargement of the field of competition, and an equalization of prices over large areas, and that too at the level of the lowest or most efficient production. But these advantages entail certain consequences — of minor importance, perhaps, but none the less deserving of notice.

[1] P. 133, *supra*.

The subordination of distance to other factors in rate making is a logical derivation from the theory of joint cost. This theory justifies the classification of freight, namely, a wide range of rates nicely adjusted to what the traffic in each particular commodity will bear, while always allowing each to contribute something toward fixed and joint expenses. In the same way it explains a close correlation of the distance charge to what each commodity will bear. It assumes that any rate, however low, which will yield a surplus over expenses directly incidental to the increment of traffic and which thus contributes something toward indivisible joint costs, serves not only the carrier by increasing his gross revenue, but at the same time lightens the burden of fixed expenses upon the balance of the traffic. This principle of joint cost, so clearly set forth by Professor Taussig,[1] is fundamental and comprehensive. It pervades every detail of rate making. But it rests upon two basic assumptions which, while generally valid, are not universally so. In the first place each increment of traffic must be *new* business, not tonnage wrested from another carrier and offset by a loss of other business to that competitor. And secondly, each increment of traffic must be *economically suitable* to the particular carriage in contemplation.

The first of these assumptions fails wherever two carriers mutually invade each other's fields or traffic. Each is accepting business at a virtual loss, all costs including fixed charges on capital being taken into account, in order to secure the increment of business. Each gain is offset by a corresponding loss. It is the familiar case of the rate war. A less familiar aspect of the matter is presented when traffic is disadvantageously carried by two competing roads, each diverting business from its natural course over the other's line. The sum total of traffic is not increased. Each carries only as much as before but transports its quota at an abnormal cost to itself. This may, perhaps, swell gross revenues; but by no process of leger-

[1] *Quarterly Journal of Economics*, V, 1891, p. 438.

demain can the two losses in operating cost produce a gain of net revenue to both. And each increase of *unnatural* tonnage, where offset by a loss of natural business, instead of serving to lighten the fixed charges, becomes a dead weight upon all the remaining traffic. The commonest exemplification of this is found in the circuitous transportation of goods, instances of which will be given later.

The second case in which the principle of joint cost fails to justify charges fixed according to what the traffic will bear may arise in the invasion of two remote markets by one another; or, as it might be more aptly phrased, in the overlapping of two distant markets. A railroad is simultaneously transporting goods of like quality in opposite directions. Chicago is selling standard hardware in New York, while New York is doing the same thing in Chicago. Prices are the same in both markets. Of course if the two grades of hardware are of unequal quality, or if they are like goods produced at different cost, an entirely distinct phase of territorial competition is created. But we are assuming that these are standard goods and that there are no such differences either in quality or efficiency of production. What is the result? Is each increment of business to the railroad a gain to it and to the community? The goods being produced at equal cost in both places, the transportation charge must be deducted from profits. For it is obvious that the selling price cannot be much enhanced. The level of what the traffic will bear is determined not, as usual, by the value of the goods but by other considerations. The traffic will bear relatively little, no matter how high its grade. The result is that the carrier, in order to secure the tonnage, must accept it at a very low rate, despite the length of the haul.

This is the familiar case of the special or commodity rate granted to build up business in a distant market. Special rates confessedly form three-fourths of the tonnage of American railways, as has already been said. The assumption is usually made that such traffic is a gain to the railways, justified on the principle of joint cost as already explained. But does it really hold good in our hypothetical case? There is a gain of traffic in both directions, to be sure. But must it not be accepted at so low a rate that it falls perilously near the actual operating cost? It is possible that even here it may add something to the carriers' revenue, and thereby lighten the joint costs in other directions. But how about the community and the shipping producers? Are any more goods sold? Perhaps the widened market may stimulate competition, unless that is already keen enough among local producers in each district by itself. The net result would seem to be merely that the railroads' gain is the shippers' loss. There is no addition to, but merely an exchange of, place values. Both producers are doing business at an abnormal distance under mutually disadvantageous circumstances. It may be said, perhaps, that the situation will soon correct itself. If the freight rates reduce profits, each group of producers will tend to draw back from the distant field. This undoubtedly happens in many cases. But the influence of the railway is antagonistic to such withdrawal. It is the railway's business to widen, not to restrict, the area of markets. "The more they scatter the better it is for the railroads." "Keep everyone in business everywhere." And if necessary to give a fillip to languishing competition, do so by a concession in rates. Is there not danger that with a host of eager freight solicitors in the field, and equally ambitious traffic managers in command, a good thing may be overdone, to the disadvantage of the railway, the shippers and the consuming public?

An objection to this chain of reasoning arises at this point. Why need the public or other shippers be concerned about the railways' policy in this regard? Is not each railway the best judge for itself of the profitableness of long-distance traffic? Will it not roughly assign limits to its own activities in extending business, refusing to make rates lower than the actual incidental cost of operation? And are not all low long-distance rates, in so far as they contribute something toward joint cost, an aid to the short haul traffic? The answer will in a measure depend upon our choice between two main lines of policy; the one seeking to lower *average* rates, even at the expense of increasing divergence between the intermediate and the long distance points, the other policy seeking, *not so much lower rates as less discriminatory rates* between near and distant points. In the constant pressure for reduced rates in order to widen markets it is not unnatural that the intermediate points, less competitive probably, should be made to contribute an undue share to the fixed sum of joint costs. The common complaint today is not of high rates but of relative inequalities as between places. It is a truism to assert that it matters less to a shipping point what rate it pays than that its rate, however high, should be the same for all competing places. This immediately forces us to consider the consumer. What is the effect upon the general level of prices of the American policy of making an extended market the touchstone of success, irrespective of the danger of wastes arising from overlapping markets? That the result may be a general tax upon production is a conclusion with which we shall have later to do. Such a tax, if it exists, would go far to offset the profit which unduly low freight rates in general have produced. In short, the problem is to consider the possible net cost to the American people of our highly envolved and most efficient transportation system. Our markets are so wide, and our distances so vast, that the problem is a peculiarly American one.

Having stated the theory of these economic wastes, we may now proceed to consider them as they arise in practice. Concrete illustration of the effect of disregard of distance naturally falls into two distinct groups. Of these the first concerns the circuitous carriage of goods; the second, their transportation for excessive distances. Both alike involve economic wastes, in some degree perhaps inevitable, but none the less deserving of evaluation. And both practices, even if defensible at times,

PROBLEMS OF ROUTING 269

are exposed to constant danger of excess. It will be convenient also to differentiate sharply the all-rail carriage from the combined rail and water transportation. For as between railroads and waterways, the difference in cost of service is so uncertain and fluctuating that comparisons on the basis of mere distance have little value.

Recent instances of wasteful and circuitous all-rail transportation are abundant. A few typical ones will suffice to show how common the evil is. President Ramsay of the Wabash has testified as to the roundabout competition with the Pennsylvania Railroad between Philadelphia and Pittsburg by which sometimes as much as fifty-seven per cent. of traffic between those two points may be diverted from the direct route. "They haul freight 700 miles around sometimes to meet a point in competition 200 miles away." [1] Chicago and New Orleans are 912 miles apart, and about equally distant — 2,500 miles — from San Francisco. The traffic manager of the Illinois Central states that that company "engages in San Francisco business directly *via* New Orleans from the Chicago territory, and there is a large amount of that business, and we engage in it right along." [2] Wool from Idaho and Wyoming may move west 800 miles, to San Francisco; and thence *via* New Orleans over the Southern Pacific route to Boston.[3] This case, therefore, represents a superfluous lateral haul of nearly a thousand miles between two points 2,500 miles apart. The Canadian Pacific used to take business for San Francisco, all rail, from points as far south as Tennessee and Arkansas, diverting it from the direct way *via* Kansas City.[4]

Goods moving in the opposite direction from San Francisco

[1] Senate (Elkins) Committee Report, 1905, III, pp. 2152–2153. The transverse Buffalo, Rochester and Pittsburg seems to be the feeder for the New York Central and the Reading.
[2] *Ibid.*, IV, p. 2849.
[3] U. P. Merger case: Supreme Court, October term, No. 820, Appellant's Brief of Facts, pp. 135–193 and also p. 493.
[4] Question of Canadian-Pacific Differentials, Hearings, etc., Oct. 12, 1898, p. 115. Privately printed. *Cf.* also the Sunset Route, *ibid.*, p. 116.

have been hauled to Omaha by way of Winnipeg, journeying around three sides of a rectangle by so doing, in order to save five or six cents per hundred pounds.[1] Between New York and New Orleans nearly one hundred all-rail lines may compete for business. The direct route being 1,340 miles, goods may be carried 2,051 miles *via* Buffalo, New Haven (Indiana), St. Louis and Texarkana.[2] A generation ago conditions were even worse, the various distances by competitive routes between St. Louis and Atlanta ranging from 526 to 1,855 miles.[3] New York business for the West was often carried by boat to the mouth of the Connecticut river, and thence by rail over the Central Vermont to a connection with the Grand Trunk for Chicago. To be moved at the outset due north 200 miles from New York on a journey to a point — Montgomery, Alabama — south of southwest seems wasteful; yet the New York Central is in the field for that business.[4] The map herewith, prepared in connection with the Alabama Midland case, shows the number of lines participating in freight carriage between New York and the little town of Troy, Alabama. It is nearly as uneconomical as in the old days when freight was carried from Cincinnati to Atlanta *via* the Chesapeake and Ohio, thence down by rail to Augusta and back to destination.[5] It was common for freight from Pittsburg to go by boat down to Cincinnati, only to return by rail *via* Pittsburg to New York at a lower rate than on a direct shipment.[6] Even right in the heart of eastern trunk line territory, such things occur in recent times. The Cincinnati, Hamilton and Dayton prior to its consolidation with the Pere Marquette divided its

[1] 51st Congress, 1st sess., Sen. Rep., No. 847, p. 176.
[2] *Pubs. Amer. Stat. Ass.*, June, 1896, p. 73.
[3] Reports Internal Commerce, 1876, pp. 54–59.
[4] Map in Brief of Ed. Baxter, U. S. Supreme Court in the Alabama Midland case.
[5] Windom Committee, II, p. 795.
[6] Cullom Committee, p. 530. Hudson also cites similar cases from the Hepburn Committee. *Cf.* also Report on Internal Commerce, 1876, App. p. 57.

eastbound tonnage from the rich territory about Cincinnati among the trunk lines naturally tributary. But no sooner was it consolidated with the Michigan road than its eastbound

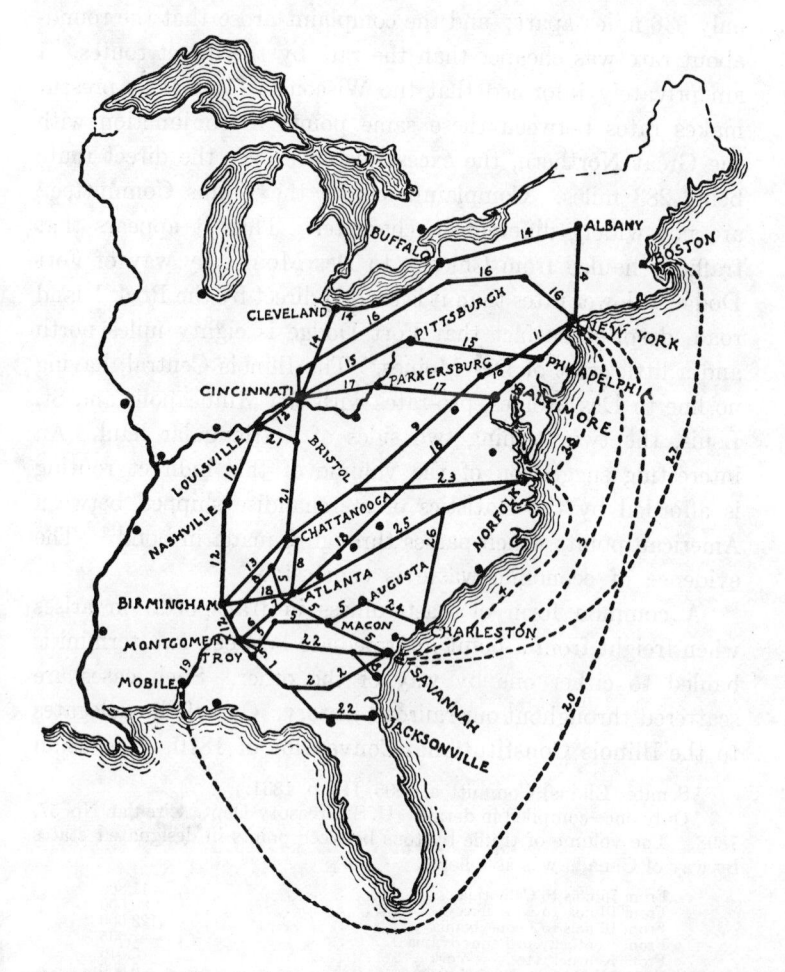

freight was diverted to the north — first hauled to Toledo, Detroit and even up to Port Huron, thence moving east and around Lake Erie to Buffalo.[1] In the Chicago field similar

[1] New York *Evening Post*, Sept. 30, 1905.

practices occur. Formerly the Northwestern road was charged with making shipments from Chicago to Sioux City *via* St. Paul. This required a carriage of 670 miles between points only 536 miles apart; and the complaint arose that the roundabout rate was cheaper than the rate by the direct routes. I am privately informed that the Wisconsin Central at present makes rates between these same points in conjunction with the Great Northern, the excess distance over the direct route being 283 miles. Complaints before the Elkins Committee [1] are not widely different in character. Thus it appears that traffic is hauled from Chicago to Des Moines by way of Fort Dodge at lower rates than it is carried direct by the Rock Island road, despite the fact that Fort Dodge is eighty miles north and a little west of Des Moines. The Illinois Central, having no line to Des Moines, pro-rates with the Minneapolis and St. Louis, the two forming two sides of a triangular haul. An interesting suggestion of the volume of this indirect routing is afforded by the statistics of merchandise shipped between American points which passes through Canada in bond.[2] The evidence of economic waste is conclusive.

A common form of wastefulness in transportation arises when freight from a point intermediate between two termini is hauled to either one by way of the other. Such cases are scattered throughout our railroad history. One of the delegates to the Illinois Constitutional Convention of 1870, cites, as an

[1] Senate (Elkins) Committee, 1905, III, p. 1831.
[2] Only once compiled in detail. U. S. Treasury Dept., Circular No. 37, 1898. The volume of traffic by tons between points in designated states by way of Canada was as follows:

From Illinois to California	11,800
From Illinois to New Jersey	80,000
From Illinois to Pennsylvania	123,000
From Kentucky to Pennsylvania	1,005
From Kentucky to New York	5,516
From Missouri to Pennsylvania	5,000
From Pennsylvania to Missouri	13,824
From New York to Kentucky	3,357
From New York to Missouri	12,869
From New York to Tennessee	609
From Ohio to Pennsylvania	26,801
From Pennsylvania to Ohio	5,251
From Ohio to New York	211,657
From New York to Ohio	55,243

instance of local discrimination, the fact that lumber from Chicago to Springfield, Illinois, could be shipped more cheaply by way of St. Louis than by the direct route.[1] And now a generation later, it appears that grain from Cannon Falls, forty-nine miles south of St. Paul on the direct line to Chicago, destined for Louisville, Kentucky, can be hauled up to St. Paul on local rates and thence on a through billing to destination, back over the same rails, considerably cheaper than by sending it as it should properly go.[2] The Hepburn Committee reveals shipments from Rochester, New York, to St. Louis, Minneapolis or California, all rail, on a combination of local rates to New York and thence to destination.[3] Presumably the freight was hauled three hundred miles due east and then retraced the same distance; as New York freight for southern California is today hauled to San Francisco by the Southern Pacific and then perhaps three hundred miles back over the same rails. Even if the rate must be based on a combination of low through rates and higher local rates, it seems a waste of energy to continue the five or six hundred miles extra haul. Yet the practice is common in the entire western territory. From New York to Salt Lake City by way of San Francisco is another instance in point.[4] Of course a short haul to a terminal to enable through trains to be made up presents an entirely different problem of cost from the abnormal instances above mentioned.[5]

Carriage by water is so much cheaper and as compared with land transportation is subject to such different rate-governing principles, that it deserves separate consideration. Mere distance, as has already been said, being really only one element

[1] Debates, II, p. 1646, cited in University of Illinois Studies, March, 1904, p. 21.
[2] Senate (Elkins) Committee, 1905, I, pp. 32-34. *Cf.* also 10 I.C.C. Rep., 650. Another good instance on Arizona is in 16 *Idem*, 77.
[3] Page 2031.
[4] Senate (Elkins) Committee, 1905, II, p. 921.
[5] Cullom Committee, II, p. 101.

in the determination of cost, a circuitous water route may in reality be more economical than direct carriage overland. Yet beyond a certain point, regard being paid to the relative cost per mile of the two modes of transport, water-borne traffic may entail economic wastes not incomparable to those arising in land transportation. In international trade, entirely confined to vessel carriage, a few examples will suffice for illustration. Machinery for a stamp mill, it was found, could be shipped from Chicago to San Francisco by way of Shanghai, China, for fifteen cents per hundredweight less than by way of the economically proper route. Were the goods ever really sent by so indirect a route?[1] It would appear so when wheat may profitably be carried from San Francisco to Watertown, Massachusetts, after having been taken to Liverpool, stored there, reshipped to Boston, thereafter, even paying the charges of a local haul of nearly ten miles;[2] or when shipments from Liverpool to New York may be made *via* Montreal to Chicago, and thence back to destination.[3] I am credibly informed that shipments of the American Tobacco Company from Louisville, Kentucky, to Japan used commonly to go *via* Boston. Denver testimony is to the effect that machinery, made in Colorado, shipped to Sydney, Australia, can be transported *via* Chicago for one-half the rate for the direct shipment; and that on similar goods even Kansas City could ship by the carload considerably cheaper by the same roundabout route. Conversely straw matting from Yokohama to Denver direct must pay $2.87 per hundred pounds; while if shipped to the Missouri river, five hundred miles east of Denver, and then back, the rate is only $2.05.[4]

As a domestic problem, water carriage confined to our own territory has greater significance in the present inquiry. Purely coastwise traffic conditions are peculiar and in the United

---

[1] 10 I.C.C. Rep., 81.
[2] Senate (Elkins) Committee, 1905, II, p. 919.
[3] *Ibid.*, p. 1624.   [4] 11 I.C.C. Rep., 508.

PROBLEMS OF ROUTING 275

States, as a rule, concern either the South Atlantic seaports or transcontinental business. As to the first-named class, the volume and importance of the traffic is immense. Its character may be indicated by a quotation from a railroad man.

"Now a great deal has been said, chiefly on the outside, about the Canadian Pacific Railway seeking by its long, circuitous and broken route to share in a tonnage as against more direct and shorter lines all rail, and I propose to show to you gentlemen that not only have we a precedent on which to claim differentials, many of them, and that we also have numerous precedents to show that there are numerous broken, circuitous water and rail lines operating all over the country that are longer and more circuitous than ours, and still they do operate with more or less success. . . . In saying this I do not wish to be understood as criticising the right of any road to go anywhere, even with a broken and circuitous line, to seek for business, so long as they are satisfied that taking all the circumstances into account such business will afford them some small measure of profit. * * *

"The distance by the Chesapeake & Ohio Road, Boston to Newport News, is 544 miles by water; Newport News to Chicago, 1071 miles, total 1615 miles from Boston to Chicago, against 1020 miles by the shortest all-rail line from Boston, showing the line *via* Newport News, 58 per cent. longer. The distance by the Chesapeake and Ohio from New York to Newport News in 305 miles, to which add 1071 miles, Newport News to Chicago, total 1376 miles, against the shortest all-rail line of 912 miles, 50.87 per cent. longer. Again the distance between Boston and Duluth by all-rail is 1382 miles, against 2195 miles *via* Newport News and Chicago, 58.82 per cent. longer by the broken route.

"The Southern Pacific Co., or System rather, in connection with the Morgan line steamers, carries business, *via* New York, New Orleans and Fort Worth, to Utah points at a differential rate. The distance from New York to Denver *via* water to New Orleans thence rail to Fort Worth is 3155 miles, against 1940 miles by the direct all-rail line, showing it to be longer *via* New Orleans 62.61 per cent.[1]

Allowing a constructive mileage of one-third for the last named water haul,[2] many of these even up fairly well with the all-rail carriage; although a route from New York to Kansas

[1] Question of Canadian Pacific Freight Differentials, Hearings, etc., Oct. 12, 1898, p. 17. Privately printed. See also pp. 72 and 116 on the same point.
[2] Record Cincinnati Freight Bureau case, II, p. 306.

City by way of Savannah, Georgia, would appear to be an extreme case, owing to the relatively long haul by rail.[1] The increasing importance of Galveston and the necessity of a back haul to compensate for export business make it possible for that city to engage in business between New York and Kansas City, although the roundabout route is two and one-half times as long as the direct one.[2] As compared with these examples, it is no wonder that the competition for New York-Nashville or New England-Chattanooga business by way of Savannah, Mobile, or Brunswick, Georgia, is so bitter. The roundabout traffic thus reaches around by the southern ports and nearly up again to the Ohio river.[3]

The second great class of broken rail and water shipments consists of transcontinental business. Goods from New York to San Francisco commonly go by way of New Orleans or Galveston,[4] as well as by Canadian ports and routes.[5] In the opposite direction, goods are carried about 1000 miles by water to Seattle or Vancouver before commencing the journey east. But more important, as illustrating this point, is the traffic from the Central West which reaches the Pacific coast by way of Atlantic seaports. As far west as the Missouri, the actual competition of the trunk lines on California business has since 1894 [6] brought about the condition of the "blanket" or "postage stamp" rate. The same competitive conditions which open up Denver or Kansas City to New York shippers by way of New Orleans or Galveston, enable the Southern Pacific Railroad or

[1] Hearings, Question of Canadian Pacific Freight Differentials, Oct. 12, 1898, p. 55.
[2] U. S. Industrial Commission, IV, p. 134.
[3] 55th Cong., 1st sess., Sen. Doc. No. 39, p. 88.
[4] By water from New York, 1800 miles to New Orleans, with 2489 miles by rail. Or to Galveston 2300 miles with 2666 miles by rail, a total of 4966 miles. The direct line, all rail, is about 3300 miles. Allowing constructive mileage of 3 to 1 for water carriage, they are far from equal.
[5] Texas cotton bound for Yokohama by way of Seattle.
[6] On these matters the Record of the Business Men's League of St. Louis case before the Interstate Commerce Commission, 9 Int. Com. Rep., 318; and the Hearings on Canadian Pacific Differentials are illuminating.

Cape Horn routes to solicit California shipments in western territory to be hauled back to New York, and thence by water all or part of the way to destination. How important this potential competition is — that is to say, what proportion of the traffic is interchanged by this route — cannot readily be determined.

Transportation over undue distances — the carriage of coals to Newcastle in exchange for cotton piece goods hauled to Lancashire — as a product of keen commercial competition may involve both a waste of energy and an enhancement of prices in a manner seldom appreciated. The transportation of goods great distances at low rates, while economically justifiable in opening up new channels of business, becomes wasteful the moment such carriage, instead of creating new business, merely brings about an exchange between widely separated markets, or an invasion of fields naturally tributary to other centres. The wider the market, the greater is the chance of the most efficient production at the lowest cost. The analogy at this point to the problem of protective tariff legislation is obvious. For a country to dispose of its surplus products abroad by cutting prices may not involve economic loss; but for two countries to be simultaneously engaged in "dumping" their products into each other's markets is quite a different matter. In transportation such cases arise whenever a community, producing a surplus of a given commodity, supplies itself, nevertheless, with that same commodity from a distant market. It may not be a just grievance that Iowa, a great cattle raising state, should be forced to procure her dressed meats in Chicago or Omaha;[1] for in this case some degree of manufacture has ensued in these highly specialized centres. But the practice is less defensible where the identical product is redistributed after long carriage to and from a distant point. Arkansas is a great fruit raising region; yet so cheap is transportation that dried fruits, perhaps of its own growing, are distributed by

[1] Senate (Elkins) Committee, 1905, III, p. 1830.

wholesale grocers in Chicago throughout its territory. The privilege of selling rice in the rice-growing states from Chicago is, however, denied by the Southern Railway Association.[1] An illuminating example of similar character occurs in the Southern cotton manufacture, as described by a Chicago jobber:

"Right in North Carolina there is one mill shipping 60 carloads of goods to Chicago in a season, and a great many of these same goods are brought right back to this very section. . . . I might add that when many of these heavy cotton goods made in this southeastern section are shipped both to New York and Chicago and then sold and reshipped South, they pay 15 cents to 20 cents per hundred less each way to New York and back than *via* Chicago. This doubles up the handicap against which Chicago is obliged to contend and renders the unfairness still more burdensome."[2]

The overweening desire of the large centres to enter every market is well exemplified by recent testimony of the Chicago jobbers.[3]

"A few years later, when the railroads established the relative rates of freight between New York and Philadelphia and the Southeast, and St. Louis, Cincinnati and Chicago and the Southeast, giving the former the sales of merchandise and the latter the furnishing of food products, the hardware consumed in this country was manufactured in England. At that time we, in Chicago, felt that we were going beyond the confines of our legitimate territory when we diffidently asked the merchants in western Indiana to buy their goods in our market. Today, a very considerable percentage of the hardware used in the United States is manufactured in the Middle West, and we are profitably selling general hardware through a corps of travelling salesmen in New York, Pennsylvania and West Virginia, and special lines in New England.

"What we claim is that we should not have our territory stopped at the Ohio river by any act of yours. It is not stopped, gentlemen, by any other river in America. It is not stopped by the greatest river, the Mississippi. It is not stopped by the far greater river, the Missouri. It is not stopped by the Arkansas; it is not stopped by the Rio Grande.

[1] Record before the I.C.C.; Cincinnati Freight Bureau case, I, p. 166.
[2] Senate (Elkins) Committee, 1905, III, pp. 2540–2541.
[3] Senate (Elkins) Committee, 1905, III, pp. 2538 and 2550.

It is not stopped even by the Columbia; and, even in the grocery business, it is not stopped by the Hudson. There are Chicago houses that are selling goods in New York city, groceries that they manufacture themselves. Mr. Sprague's own house sells goods in New York city, and Chicago is selling groceries in New England. As I say, even the Hudson river doesn't stop them."

All this record implies progressiveness, energy, and ambition on the part of both business men and traffic officers. Nothing is more remarkable in American commerce than its freedom from restraints. Elasticity and quick adaptation to the exigencies of business are peculiarities of American railroad operation. This is due to the progressiveness of our railway managers in seeking constantly to develop new territory and build up business. The strongest contrast between Europe and the United States lies in this fact. European railroads take business as they find it. Our railroads make it. Far be it from me to minimize the service rendered in American progress. And yet there are reasonable limits to all good things. We ought to reckon the price which must be paid for this freedom of trade.

One further aspect of economic waste may be mentioned, especially as bearing upon Federal regulation so far as it affects carload ratings and commercial rivalry between remote middlemen in the large cities and provincial jobbing interests. The actual cost of handling small shipments being about one-half that of carriage by carloads, the cheapest way in which to supply, let us say, the Pacific slope or Texas territory, is to encourage the local jobber who ships by carload over the long haul. For, obviously, distribution by less-than-carload lots from New York, or even Chicago direct, direct to the crossroad store, is bound to be a wasteful process by comparison.[1] But in addition there are also, of course, the social factors to be considered, which are of even greater weight.

[1] Briefly discussed in the St. Louis Business Men's League case: 9 Int. Com. Rep., 318.

The causes of economic waste in transportation are various. Not less than six may be distinguished. These are: (1) congestion of the direct route; (2) rate cutting by the weak circuitous line; (3) pro-rating practices in division of joint through rates; (4) desire for back-loading of empty cars; (5) strategic considerations concerning interchange of traffic with connections; and (6) attempts to secure or hold shippers in contested markets. These merit consideration separately in some detail.

Congestion of traffic upon the direct line is a rare condition in our American experience. Few of our railways are overcrowded with business. Their equipment may be overtaxed, but their rails are seldom worked to the utmost. Yet the phenomenal development of trunk line business since 1897 sometimes makes delivery so slow and uncertain that shippers prefer to patronize railways less advantageously located, even at the same rates. The congestion on the main stem of the Pennsylvania railway between Pittsburg and Philadelphia is a case in point.

Special rates or rebates often divert traffic. The weak lines, in that particular business, are persistently in the field and can secure tonnage only by means of concessions from what may be called the standard or normal rate. The differential rate is an outgrowth of this condition. The present controversy over the right of the initial line in transcontinental business to route the freight at will involves such practices. The carriers insist that they can stop the evil only by the exercise of choice in their connections. An interesting recent example is found in the Elkins Committee testimony. It appears that lumber from points in Mississippi destined for Cleveland instead of going by the proper Ohio river gateways was diverted to East St. Louis. The operation was concealed by billing it to obscure points, — Jewett, Ill., near East St. Louis, and Rochester, Ohio, — and there issuing a new bill of lading to destination:

Senator Dolliver. And these people carry it up to this little station near St. Louis and then transfer it to another station near Cleveland?

Mr. Robinson. Oh, no; to any point on the Central Traffic Association territory. In other words, it may go to Cleveland.

Senator Dolliver. Why do they bill it to Rochester?

Mr. Robinson. In order to get the benefit of keeping it in transit fifteen days without any extra cost, first.

Senator Dolliver. I do not see how that would affect the question of billing it to Rochester.

Mr. Robinson. Because that enables the wholesaler to have fifteen days extra time in which to sell the lumber.

The Chairman. Why haul it all around the country and then reduce the rate on that long haul?

Mr. Robinson. In order that roads that are not entitled naturally to this traffic may by this process get the traffic.

Senator Dolliver. What roads from Mississippi to East St. Louis?

Mr. Robinson. Any of the trunk lines — the Illinois Central, the Louisville or the Southern Railway lines. The roads in Mississippi south of the river are not parties to this arrangement, you understand. In fact, as fast as they find it out they break it up, or try to. They do not want their traffic diverted.

Senator Kean. Does it not come down to this, that some road is trying to cheat another on the use of its cars?

Mr. Robinson. Not only that, but it is trying to get traffic that does not belong to it.[1]

Wherever a large volume of traffic is moving by an unnatural route, the first explanation which arises therefore is that rebates or rate-cutting are taking place.[2]

A third cause of diversion of traffic is akin to the second; and concerns the practices in pro-rating. Much circuitous transportation is due to the existence of independent transverse lines of railway which may participate in the traffic only on condition that it move by an indirect route. This situation is best described by reference to the following diagram. Let us suppose traffic to be moving by two routes passing through

[1] Testimony, III, p. 2495 *et seq.*
[2] The Report of the U. S. Commissioner of Corporations on the Transportation of Petroleum, 1906, affords admirable examples. *Vide*, pp. 5, 7, 14 and the map at p. 256.

points B and C, and converging on A, which last-named point might be Chicago, St. Louis, New York or any other railroad centre. Cutting these two converging lines of railway, we will suppose a tranverse line passing through B and C. Obviously the proper function of this railway is as a feeder for the through lines, each being entitled to traffic up to the half-way point, D. But over and above serving as a mere branch, this road, desirous of extending its business, has a powerful incentive to extend

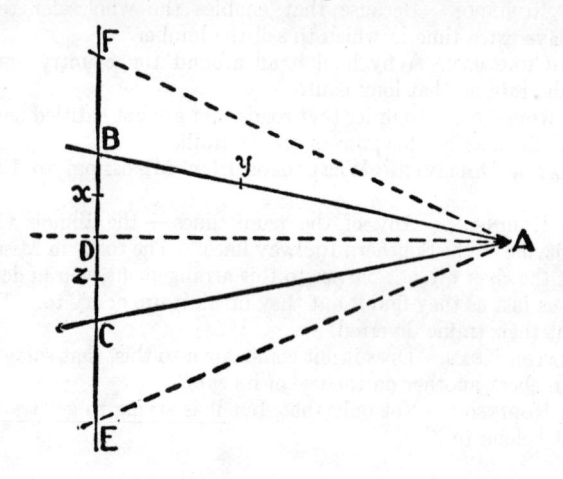

operations. The longer the tranverse haul, the greater becomes its pro-rating division of the through rate with the main line. Traffic from C is of no profit to the tranverse road so long as it is hauled directly to A. But if hauled from C to the same destination by way of B, the profit may be enhanced in two ways. In the first place the pro-rating distance is greater; and secondly, such traffic from C not being *naturally* tributary to the main line B A but merely a surplus freight to be added to that already in hand, the main line A B is open to temptation to shrink its usual proportion of the through rate in order to secure the extra business. This same motive may on proper solicitation induce the other main line C A to accept traffic from B and its vicinity. The result is a greatly enhanced profit to the cross line and circuitous carriage of the goods in both directions around two sides of a triangle. Only recently in a case in Texas the Interstate Commerce Commission found that two roads thus converging on a common point were each losing to the other traffic which rightfully was tributary to its own line. In a recent case, ninety-nine per cent. of the business from Chatham to New York was moving over a route 249 miles long, when it might have gone directly only 144 miles, by prorating with another road.[1] Our illustrative examples are not fanciful in any degree.[2]

This roundabout carriage becomes of course increasingly wasteful in proportion to the width of angle between the main lines converging on the common point. And several cases indicate that in extreme instances the two main lines may converge on a common point from exactly opposite directions, while the transverse or secondary road or series of roads forms a wide and roundabout detour. The well known Pittsburg-Youngstown case, cited in the original Louisville & Nashville decision in 1887, serves as illustration. The Pennsylvania was competing from Pittsburg directly eastbound to New York with certain feeders of the New York Central lines which took out traffic bound for the same destination but leaving Pittsburg westbound.[3] Other instances of the same phenomenon occur at Chattanooga, where freight for New York may leave either northward or southward, at Kansas City and in fact at almost any important inland centre.

Another extreme form may arise even in the competition between two parallel trunk lines cut transversely by two independent cross roads. One of these latter may induce traffic to desert the direct route, to cut across to the other trunk line, to move over that some distance and then to be hauled back

[1] 23 I.C.C. Rep., 263.
[2] Similar triangular cross-road competition is in evidence in the Wichita, Kan., cases on export grain, p. 232, *supra*.
[3] 1 I.C.C. Rep., 32; and Industrial Commission, XIX, p. 442.

again to a point on the first main line where it may find a "cut" rate to destination. Grain sometimes used literally to meander to the seaboard in the days of active competition between the trunk lines. Wheat from Iowa and northern Illinois finally reached Portland, Maine, by way of Cincinnati in this manner, with a superfluous carriage of from 250 to 350 miles:

"Starting within 90 miles of Chicago, though billed due northeast to Portland, wheat has travelled first 97 miles due southwest to avail of the connection of the Baltimore and Ohio Railroad for Cincinnati, and thence north to Detroit Junction, a total of 716 miles to reach the latter point and save 5 cents in freight. The direct haul through Chicago would have been 340 miles less, or a total of 376 miles only." [1]

Another witness describes the route as follows:

Property billed for Portland, Me., started 90 miles below Chicago, although Chicago is on a direct line, and took a southeasterly course, then to Springfield, from Springfield to Flora, then to Cincinnati, and then over the Hamilton and Dayton system to Detroit, there to take the Grand Trunk road to Portland. This was owing to the billing system adhered to here with great tenacity. Property ran around three sides of a square, and I lost money on some of that property.[2]

This ruinous diversion of freight seems to have been dependent upon the existence of active competition at Detroit and ceased when the Grand Trunk came to an agreement with the American lines. But there can be no doubt that wherever these cross lines exist there is a strong tendency toward diversion. In the recent hearings of the Senate Committee on Interstate Commerce on railway rate regulation, a railroad witness again describes the operation:

Mr. VINING. Well, for instance, take the time when I was on the Grand Rapids and Indiana Railroad. Its connection at the south was at Fort Wayne, with the Pittsburg, Fort Wayne and Chicago Road. We took lumber out of Michigan and wanted to send it east. We had to

[1] Statements taken before the Committee on Interstate Commerce of the U. S. Senate with respect to the Transportation Interests of the U. S. and Canada. Washington, 1890, p. 616. *Cf.* chap. X, p. 363, *infra;* also the Wichita cases, in chap. VII, p. 232, *supra.*
[2] *Ibid.*, p. 631.

compete with lines that went by way of Detroit, that went perhaps through Canada and that in some cases were shorter. Of course, if we wanted to send lumber from Grand Rapids to New York we had to make at least as low a rate as was made by other lines leading from Grand Rapids to New York. That rate might be just the same from Fort Wayne as from Grand Rapids, so that we could not get any more than the low rate from Fort Wayne. We had to go in that case to the Pittsburg, Fort Wayne and Chicago Railway and say: "Here are so many carloads of lumber, or so much lumber, at Grand Rapids, a part of which could be shipped to New York if we had through rates that would enable us to move it. These other lines are carrying it for 25 cents a hundred pounds to New York. You join us in a through rate of 25 cents and we can give you some of that business." . . . But if I were with a short line and wanted to negotiate with a long one, I should try to put my case just as strongly as possible before the long line. I should say to them: "We can not take 5 per cent. of a rate of 25 cents. It would not pay us. You know that; you can see that"; and they, as business men, would admit it. "Well," I would say, "give us 5 cents a hundred pounds and we will bring the business to you, and if you do not, we can not afford to do it."

SENATOR CULLOM. I think in some instances they have stated before us that they gave 25 per cent.

Mr. VINING. They might.[1]

Whenever the cross road was financially embarrassed, the tendency to diversion was increased. For then, of course, having repudiated fixed charges, the cross line could accept almost any rate as better than the loss of the traffic. And that this was in the past almost a chronic condition in western trunk line territory appears from the fact that eighteen out of the twenty-two roads cutting the Illinois Central between Chicago and Cairo have been in the hands of receivers since 1874.[2]

It not infrequently happens that the initial railroad may entirely control a roundabout route, whereas shipments by the most direct line necessitate a division of the joint rate with other companies. In such a case the initial line will naturally favor the indirect route, at the risk of economic loss to the community and even to its own shippers. An interesting

[1] Senate (Elkins) Committee, 1905, II, p. 1706.
[2] Quoted from Acworth, 55th Cong., 1st sess., Sen. doc. 39, p. 33.

illustration is afforded by a complaint of wheat growers at Ritzville in the state of Washington concerning rates to Portland, Oregon.[1] By direct line with low grades along the Columbia river the distance was 311 miles. This was composed of several independent but connecting links. The Northern Pacific on the other hand had a line of its own, 480 miles long, which moreover crossed two mountain ranges with heavy grades. It based its charges upon the cost of service by this roundabout and expensive line; and insisted upon its right to the traffic despite the wishes of the shippers. The Commission upheld the shippers' contention for the right to have their products carried to market in the most efficient manner.[2] Another instance on the Illinois Central is suggestive, concerning shipments from Panola, Illinois, to Peoria, a distance of about forty miles by the shortest line of connecting roads. Yet the Illinois Central having a line of its own *via* Clinton and Lincoln transported goods round three sides of a rectangle, a distance of 109 miles, presumably in order to avoid a pro-rating division of the through rate.[3] Of course elements of operating cost enter sometimes, as in the case of back-loading;[4] but in the main, the pro-rating consideration rules.

Rebates may or may not be given in connection with circuitous routing. Sometimes the same result may be obtained when one carrier merely shrinks its proportion of a joint through rate, leaving the total charge to the shipper unaffected. Of course it goes without saying that an implication of improper manipulation of rates does not always follow the diversion of freight from a direct line. The rate may be the same by several competitive routes, shipments going as a reward for energy, persistency, or personality of the agent. A recent case, concerning rates on lumber from Sheridan, Indiana, to New York illustrates this

---

[1] *Newlands v. Nor. Pac. R. R. Co.;* 6 Int. Com. Rep., 131.
[2] *Cf.* the case of the C. H. & D. R. R. on p. 271, *supra*.
[3] Record, Illinois Railroad Commission, concerning Reasonable Maximum Rates, 1905, p. 165. [4] *Cf.* p. 287, *infra*.

point.¹ Sheridan is twenty-eight miles north of Indianapolis on the Monon road. Quoting from the decision:

"In the division of joint through rates on percentages based on mileage, the defendant line naturally prefers arrangements with connections giving it the longest haul and largest percentages. Therefore, it carries this freight at rates based on a carriage through Indianapolis by a direct line eastward, while in fact it carries it in an opposite direction north and west by a longer route, the reduced ton mileage being accepted to secure the traffic."

The Iowa Central, cutting across the four main lines between Chicago and Omaha, derives a large revenue from such diversion. Coal from Peoria west, instead of moving by the shortest line to Omaha, is hauled across the first three to a connection with the devious Great Western line.² The motive is obvious.

A fourth cause of diversion of traffic has to do rather with the operating than the traffic department. An inequality of tonnage in opposite directions may make it expedient to solicit business for the sake of a back load. The Canadian Pacific may engage in San Francisco-Omaha business by way of Winnipeg, because of the scarcity of tonnage east bound. The traffic to and from the southeastern states is quite uneven in volume. The preponderance of bulky freight is north bound to the New England centres of cotton and other manufacture; while from the western cities, the greater volume of traffic is south bound, consisting of agricultural staples and food stuffs. To equalize this traffic it may often be desirable to secure the most roundabout business. A disturbing element of this sort in the southern field has always to be reckoned with. A good illustration elsewhere occurs in the well known St. Cloud case.³ The Northern Pacific accepted tonnage for a most circuitous haul to Duluth, but seems to have done so largely in order to provide lading for a preponderance of "empties." In

---

[1] 10 I.C.C. Rep., 29. [2] *Boston Transcript*, Oct. 14, 1905.
[3] 8 Int. Com. Rep., 346; reprinted in our Railway Problems, chap. XI.

this case it did not lower the normal rate but accepted it for a much longer haul.

Not unlike the preceding cause, also, is a fifth, the desire to be in position to interchange traffic on terms of equality with powerful connections. Mr. Bowes, traffic manager of the Illinois Central, justifying the participation of this road in Chicago-San Francisco business by way of New Orleans, well stated it as follows: [1]

"Of course the Southern Pacific Railroad, as you gentlemen know, originate and control a very large traffic, which they can deliver at various junctions; at New Orleans, where they have their long haul to the Missouri river, and we naturally want some of that business, a long haul traffic to New Orleans, and in giving it to them we place them under obligations to reciprocate and give us some traffic. That is one of the things that occurs to a railroad man as to increasing the volume and value of his traffic for the benefit of his company."

A sixth and final reason for diversion of traffic from the direct line may be partly sentimental, but none the less significant. It concerns the question of competition at abnormal distances. We may cite two railroad witnesses, who aptly describe the situation. "We can haul traffic in competition, and we frequently do, as I stated, at less than cost, or nearly so, in order to hold the traffic and our patrons in certain territory — Kansas City for instance — but we do not like to do it." [2] Or again, "The Charleston freight is not legitimately ours. . . . We make on these through rates from Chicago to Charleston, for instance, scarcely anything. But it is an outpost. We must maintain that or have our territory further invaded." [3] In other words, the circuitous or over-long distance haul is a natural though regrettable outcome of railroad competition.

What are the effects of this American practice of unduly disregarding distance as a factor in transportation? Not less

---

[1] Senate (Elkins) Committee, 1905, IV, p. 2850.
[2] President Ramsey of the Wabash; Senate (Elkins) Committee, 1905, III, p. 1971.   [3] Windom Committee, II, p. 796.

than five deserve separate consideration in some detail. It inordinately swells the volume of ton-mileage; it dilutes the ton-mile revenue; it produces rigidity of industrial conditions; it stimulates centralization both of population and of industry, and it is a tax upon American production.

One cannot fail to be impressed with the phenomenal growth of transportation in the United States, especially in recent years. It appears as if its volume increased more nearly as the square of population than in direct proportion to it.[1] But do these figures represent all that they purport to show? Every ton of freight which moves from Chicago to San Francisco over a line one thousand miles too long adds 1000 ton miles to swell a fictitious total. Every carload of cotton goods hauled up to Chicago to be redistributed thence in the original territory and every ton of groceries or agricultural machinery exchanged between two regions with adequate facilities for production of like standard goods contribute to the same end. How large a proportion of this marvellous growth of ton mileage these economic wastes contribute can never be determined with certainty. That their aggregate is considerable cannot be questioned.

These practices must considerably dilute the returns per mile for service rendered by American carriers — in even greater degree than they enhance the apparent volume of transportation. Long-distance rates must always represent a low revenue per ton mile, owing to the fixed maximum for all distances determined by what the traffic will bear. Furniture made in North Carolina for California consumption[2] cannot be sold there in competition above a certain price. The greater the distance into which the possible margin of profit is divided, the less per mile must be the revenue left for the carrier. Yet this is not all. Such would be true of simply over-long distance carriage. But to this we must add the fact that some of this long-haul tonnage reaches its remote destination over a round-

[1] P. 78, *supra*. [2] Senate (Elkins) Committee, 1905, III, p. 2008.
VOL. I—19

about line, which increases the already over-long carriage by from twenty-five to seventy-five per cent. It is apparent at once that a still greater dilution of the average returns must follow as a result. From 1873 down to 1900 the long and almost uninterrupted decline of rates is an established fact. Has the volume of this economic waste increased or diminished in proportion to the total traffic throughout this period? If it is relatively less today, at a time when ton mile rates are actually rising, it would be of interest to know how far such economies offset the real increases of rates which have been made. Rates might conceivably rise a little, or at all events remain constant, coincidently with a fall in ton mile revenue produced through savings of this sort.

The third result of undue disregard of distance is a certain inelasticity of industrial conditions. This may occur in either of two ways. The rise of new industries may be hindered, or a well-merited relative decline of old ones under a process of natural selection may be postponed or averted. The first of these is well set forth as follows: [1]

"It is always considered desirable to have a long haul, and the rates on a long haul should be much less, in proportion to distance, than on a short haul. This is a principle of rate-making which has grown up as one of the factors in the evolution of the railroad business in this country, and it has greatly stimulated the movement of freight for long distances, has brought the great manufacturing centres in closer touch with the consumer at a distance and the producer in closer touch with centres of trade. It has been of undoubted benefit to both, though it may oftentimes retard the growth of new industries by a system of rates so preferential as to enable the manufacturer a long distance from the field of production of raw material to ship the raw material to his mills, manufacture it and return the manufactured goods cheaper than the local manufacturer could afford to make it, and thus, while building up the centres of manufacture, have retarded the growth of manufacturing in the centres where the raw material is produced."

The other aspect of industrial rigidity is manifested through the perpetuation of an industry in a district, regardless of the

[1] Senate (Elkins) Committee, 1905, IV, p. 3115.

physical disabilities under which it is conducted. Another quotation describes it well.[1]

SENATOR CARMACK. Is it the policy of the roads, wherever they find an industry established, to keep it going by advantages in the way of rates regardless of changes in economic conditions?
Mr. TUTTLE. I think in so far as it is possible for them to do so. It has not been possible in all cases. We could not keep iron furnaces running in New England; they are all gone.

One cannot for a moment doubt the advantages of such a policy as a safeguard against violent dislocating shocks to industry. It may render the transition to new and better conditions more gradual and easier to bear. It has been of inestimable value to New England, as exposed to the competition of newer manufactures in the Central West. But on the other hand, it is equally true that in the long run the whole country will fare best when each industry is prosecuted in the most favored location — all conditions of marketing as well as of mere production being considered. If Pittsburg is the natural centre for iron and steel production, it may not be an unmixed advantage to the country at large, however great its value to New England, to have the carriers perpetuate the barbed wire manufacture at Worcester.[2] Each particular case would have to be decided on its merits. My purpose at present is not to pass judgment on any of them but merely to call attention to the effect of such practices upon the process of industrial selection.

In the fifth place, every waste in transportation service is in the long run a tax upon the productivity of the country. More men may be employed, more wages paid, more capital kept in circulation; but it still remains true that the coal consumed, the extra wages paid and the rolling stock used up in the carriage of goods, either unduly far or by unreasonably roundabout routes, constitute an economic loss to the community. In many

[1] *Idem*, II, p. 976.
[2] Specifically described in Senate (Elkins) Committee, 1905, II, p. 923.

cases, of course, it may be an inevitable offset for other advantages. In the Savannah Freight Bureau case [1] (map, p. 648, *infra*) Valdosta, Georgia, was 158 miles from Savannah, while it was 275 and 413 miles by the shortest and longest lines respectively from Charleston. Valdosta's main resource for fertilizer supplies, other things being equal, would naturally be Savannah, the nearer city. Yet in the year in question it appeared that nine-tenths of the supply was actually drawn from Charleston; and much of it was hauled 413 instead of a possible 158 miles. No wonder the complainants alleged "that somebody in the end must pay for that species of foolishness." Whenever the Colorado Fuel and Iron Company succeeds in selling goods of no better grade or cheaper price in territory naturally tributary to Pittsburg, a tax is laid upon the public to that degree.[2] When Chicago and New York jobbers each strive to invade the other's field, the extra revenue to the carriers may be considerable; but it is the people who ultimately pay the freight. The analogy to the bargain counter is obvious. The public are buying something not necessary for less than cost; while the carriers are selling it for more than it is worth. Economies would redound to the advantage of all parties concerned.

What remedy is possible for these economic wastes? Both the carriers and the public have an interest in their abatement. The more efficient industrial combinations have taken the matter in hand, either by strategic location of plants or, as in the case of the United States Steel Corporation, by the utilization of a Pittsburg base price scheme, with freight rates added.[3] But probably the large proportion of tonnage is still shipped by independent and competing producers. To this traffic the rail-

[1] 7 Int. Com. Rep., 458; reprinted in our Railway Problems, chap. XII.
[2] "Practically it may be declared that the public, considered as distinct from railway owners, must pay for all the transportation which it receives." . . . H. T. Newcomb in *Pubs. Am. Stat. Ass.*, N. S. Nr. 34, p. 71.
[3] Agreements for a scale of cross freights by wholesalers' or jobbers' associations as in Ohio for groceries or hardware are equally effective.

ways must apply their own remedies. Either one of two plans might be of service. The right to make valid agreements for a division either of traffic or territory, if conceded to the carriers by law under proper governmental supervision, would be an effective safeguard. This would mean the repeal of the present prohibition of pooling. Or a reënactment of the long and short haul clause, now emasculated by judicial interpretation, would do much toward accomplishing the same result.

Agreements between carriers previous to 1887 were often employed to obviate unnecessary waste in transportation. The division of territory between the eastern and western lines into the southern states is a case in point. Thirty years ago competition for trade throughout the South was very keen between the great cities in the East and in the Middle West. Direct lines to the northwest from Atlanta and Nashville opened up a new avenue of communication with ambitious cities like Chicago, St. Louis and Cincinnati. The state of Georgia constructed the Western and Atlantic Railroad in 1851 for the express purpose of developing this trade. As western manufactures developed, a keen rivalry between the routes respectively east and west of the Alleghany mountains into the South was engendered. A profitable trade in food products by a natural, direct route from the Ohio gateways was, however, jeopardized by ruinous rates made by the warring trunk lines to the northern seaboard. Corn, oats, wheat and pork came down the coast and into the South through the back door, so to speak, by way of Savannah and other seaports. On the other hand the eastern lines into the South were injuriously affected by the retaliatory rates on manufactured goods made by the western lines for shipments from New York and New England. Freight from each direction was being hauled round three sides of a rectangle. Finally in 1878 a reasonable remedy was found in a division of the field and an agreement to stop all absurdly circuitous long hauls into one another's natural territory. A line was drawn through the northern states from Buffalo to Pittsburg and Wheeling;

through the South from Chattanooga by Montgomery, Ala., to Pensacola. Eastern lines were to accept goods for shipment only from their side of this line to points of destination in the South also on the eastern side of the boundary. Western competitors were to do the same. The result was the recognition of natural rights of each to its territory. This agreement has now formed the basis of railway tariffs into the southern states for almost a generation. Similar agreements, on a less extensive scale, are commonly used to great advantage. Thus in the "common point" territory formerly tributary to Wilmington, Savannah and Charleston, the first named city insisted upon its right to an equal rate with the other two, no matter how great the disparity of distance. The Southern Railway and Steamship Association arbitrated the matter, fixing a line beyond which Wilmington was to be excluded.[1] Obviously such agreements have no force in law at the present time. The only way to give effect to them is for connecting carriers to refuse to make a joint through rate. This effectually bars the traffic. Moreover entire unanimity of action is essential. Every road must be a party to the compact. Otherwise the traffic will reach its destination by shrunken rates and a more circuitous carriage even than before.

One cannot fail to be impressed in Austria and Germany with the economic advantages of an entirely unified system of operation. No devious routing is permitted. Certain lines are designated for the heavy through traffic, and concentration on them is effected to the exclusion of all others. Between Berlin and Bremen, for example, practically all through traffic is routed by three direct lines. No roundabout circuits occur because of the complete absence of railway competition. No independent lines have to be placated. The sole problem is to cause the tonnage to be most directly and economically transported. And this end is constantly considered in all pooling or through-traffic arrangements with the railway systems independently operated.

[1] 7 Int. Com. Rep., 458; in our Railway Problems, chap. XII.

The Prussian pooling agreements with the Bavarian railways are typical. Each party to the contract originally bound itself not to route freight over any line exceeding the shortest direct one in distance by more than twenty per cent. Compare this with some of our American examples of surplus haulage of fifty or sixty per cent! And within the last year, the renewal of these interstate governmental railway pools in Germany has provided for a reduction of excessive haulage to ten per cent. The problem of economical operation in Austria-Hungary with its mixed governmental and private railways is more difficult. But no arrangements are permitted which result in such wastes as we have instanced under circumstances of unlimited competition in the United States.

A more consistent enforcement of the long and short haul principle might provide a remedy almost as effective as pooling. The Alabama Midland decision nullified a salutary provision of the law of 1887 by holding that railway competition at the more distant point might create such dissimilarity of circumstances as to justify a higher rate to intermediate stations. Turn to our diagram on page 282 and observe the effect. Traffic around two sides of a triangle from A to C by way of B is carried at a rate equal to the charge for the direct haul from A to C; or it may be even at a lower differential rate. Complaint arises from the intermediate points y and x of relatively unreasonable charges. The roundabout route replies with the usual argument about a small contribution toward fixed charges from the long haul tonnage, which lessens the burden upon the intermediate rate. This is cogent enough up to a certain point. It might justify a lower rate to D, on the natural division of line territory. It might be defensible on principle to accord D a lower rate than x or possibly even than y. To deny the validity of lower rates to z or C would however at once follow from the same premises.

Under the new long and short haul clause, what may be done by the Interstate Commerce Commission? This body roughly determining the location of D, a natural division point, would then refuse to permit A B, B C to charge less to either z or C than to any intermediate point, x, B or y. Coincidently it would bar the other road A C, C B from any lower through rate to points beyond D, such as x, B or y than to any intermediate station. Two courses would be open to the roads. They must either mutually withdraw from all business beyond D or reduce their rates to all intermediate points correspondingly. In a sparsely settled region with little local business, they might conceivably choose the latter expedient. But in the vast majority of cases the roads would prefer to withdraw from the unreasonably distant fields.[1] Simultaneously taken by each line, such action would put an end to the economic waste. At the same time it would terminate one of the most persistent causes of rebates and personal favoritism. To be sure it would generally operate in favor of the strong, direct lines as against the weak and roundabout ones. Great benefit would accrue to the Pennsylvania, the Illinois Central or the Union Pacific railroads. The activities of the parasitic roads and the scope of parasitic operations by the substantial roads would inevitably be curtailed. Much justice would be done and much local irritation and popular discontent would be allayed.

[1] This problem is involved in the Youngstown-Pittsburg case already mentioned. In the original Louisville and Nashville decision the Commission apparently preferred to encourage competition even at the risk of its being roundabout and "illegitimate." But after the railway attorneys expanded the "rare and peculiar" cases to cover all kinds of competition, the Commission apparently regretted its earlier position. *Cf.* 1 I.C.C. Rep., 82; 5 *Idem*, 389; and especially the brief of Ed. Baxter, Esq., in the Alabama Midland case, U. S. Supreme Court, Oct. term, 1896, No. 563, p. 118.

CHAPTER IX

FREIGHT CLASSIFICATION [1]

Importance and nature of classification described, 300. — Classifications and tariffs distinguished, as a means of changing rates, 301. — The three classification committees, 304. — Wide differences between them illustrated, 305. — Historical development, 306. — Increase in items enumerated, 309. — Growing distinction between carload and less-than-carload rates, 310. — Great volume of elaborate rules and descriptions, 312. — Theoretical basis of classification, 314. — Cost of service v. value of service, 315. — Practically, classification based upon rule of thumb, 319. — The "spread" in classification between commodities, 319. — Similarly as between places, 320. — Commodity rates described, 322. — Natural in undeveloped conditions, 323. — Various sorts of commodity rates, 324. — The problem of carload ratings, 325. — Carloads theoretically considered, 326. — Effect upon commercial competition, 327. — New England milk rates, 329. — Mixed carloads, 331. — Minimum carload rates, 322. — Importance of car capacity, 334. — Market capacity and minimum carloads, 336. Uniform classification for the United States, 337. — Revival of interest since 1906, 339. — Overlapping and conflicting jurisdictions, 340. — Confusion and discrimination, 341. — Anomalies and conflicts illustrated, 342. — Two main obstacles to uniform classification, 345. — Reflection of local trade conditions, 345. — Compromise not satisfactory, 346. — Classifications and distance tariffs interlock, 347. — General conclusions, 351.

IMAGINE the Encyclopædia Britannica, a Chicago mail-order catalogue and a United States protective tariff law blended in a single volume, and you have a freight classification as it exists

[1] 1901. Ripley, W. Z.; Report U.S. Industrial Commission, XIX, pp. 383–397.
1902. Interstate Commerce Commission, Railways in the U. S. in 1902. Part II. [Fine data.]
1905. Acworth, W. M.; Elements of Railway Economics, pp. 99–118.
1909. Dunn, S. O.; Uniform Classification, *Railway Age Gazette*, XLVII, pp. 413, 462, 497, 552.
1911. Hammond, M. B.; Railway Rate Theories of the Interstate Commerce Commission.
1912. Strombeck, J. F.; Freight Classification. (Limited to classified schedules.)

EXCERPTS FROM THE FREIGHT CLASSIFICATIONS

OFFICIAL (Trunk Line) A	Subject to Uniform Bill of Lading Conditions. L.C.L. / C.L.	WESTERN A	C. L.	SOUTHERN A	Item No.	Classif Released
1 Academy or Artists' Board, in cases (C. L. min, weight, 36,000 lbs.)	2 / 5	1 ADVERTISING MATTER printed, N. O. S. (exclusive of signs and show cards), boxed or in bundles, prepaid (not otherwise specified) 1		1 Accoutrements, Military 1		1
2 Acetone, in iron drums	3 / 5	2 Advertising Matter consisting of Almanacs, Circulars and Pamphlets, for advertising purposes only and so stated on shipping ticket and bill of lading, value not exceeding 5c. per lb. and so receipted for, in bundles or boxes prepaid or guaranteed.........2	3 Min. wt. 24,000 lbs.	2 ACIDS (Carriers' Option) viz:		
3 ACIDS:				3 Acetic, liquid, in bbls., or drums, L. C. L.		3
* * * * * *	*			Same, C. L., min. wt. 30,000 lbs.		5
4 Acetic, liquid:				5 Carbolic, crude, in bbls. or drums		3
In carboys, boxed (C. L., min. weight 24,000 lbs.) (subject to Rule 27 and Note 2)	1	3 Chinese, Japanese and Palm-leaf Fans, with advertisements printed on the face, and Catalogues, boxed or in bundles, prepaid...1		6 Carbonic, liquid, in drums or tubes		
In bbls. or iron drums (C. L., min. weight 36,000 lbs.)	3 / 5					
In tank cars (see Note 1)	.. / 5	4 Advertising Racks (sheet iron) nested solid, boxed or crated, min. C. L. wt. 30,000 lbs. ..2.........4				
5 Boracic, in bags, boxes, bbls. or casks (C. L., min. weight 36,000 lbs.)	3					
* * * * * *	*	* * * * * * *	*	* * * * * *		
7 AGRICULTURAL IMPLEMENTS AND MACHINES:		6 AGRICULTURAL IMPLEMENTS:		44 AGRICULTURAL IMPLEMENTS, C.L., owners to load and unload, viz:		
8 Agricultural Implements and Machines, N. O. S.:		Except Hand:		45 Cleaners, Tobacco, min. wt. 15,000 lbs.		3
S. U.	D1	Barrel Carts:		46 Fodder Shredders and Corn Huskers, min. wt. 12,000 lbs.		4
K. D. flat	1	7 Set up, on wheels..............1½		47 Fodder Shredders and Corn Huskers, in mixed C. L. with other agricultural implements, min. wt. 20,000 lbs.		6
Min. weight 24,000 lbs. subject to Rule 27)	.. / 5	8 K. D. flat...................1½				
9 Axes or Hooks, Bush:		9 Bean Pickers, S. U. crated......1½				
In bundles	1	10 Beet Harvesters:		48 Harvesters and Pickers, Cotton, min. wt. 15,000 lbs.		3
In boxes	.. / 3	11 Set up....................A	Min.			
Min. weight 24,000 lbs. (subject to Rule 27)	.. / 5	12 K. D., in bundles..............2	wt.			
		13 K. D., boxed or crated.........3	24,000			
		14 Boll Weevil Machines K.D. flat 3	lbs.			
		15 Blue Grass Strippers:				
		16 S. U.......................D 1				
		17 K. D., small parts boxed....3				
* * * * * *	*	* * * * * * *	*	* * * * * *		

CLASSIFICATION

23	ZINC:	
24	Pig or Slab (C.L., min. weight 36,000 lbs.)	4 6
25	Plates (not Engravers' Plates) boxed (C. L., min. weight 36,000 lbs.)	4 5
26	Scrap:	
	In bags	2 ..
	In bales	3 ..
	In boxes, kegs, bbls. or casks (see Note)	4 ..
	Min. weight 36,000 lbs	6 ..
	* * * * * *	*
	* * * * *	*
34	ZINC, SULPHATE OF:	
	In boxes or kegs	2 ..
	In bbls. (C. L.), min. weight	4 5
35	Zylonite Goods, in packages	1 ..

42	ZINC:	
43	Ashes, min. C. L. wt. 40,000 lbs. ...4........D	
44	Batts or Wainscoting enameled ...2	
45	Concentrates, in sacks, min. wt. 40,000 lbs. C	
46	Dross, min. C. L. wt. 40,000 lbs. ...4........D	
47	Flue dust, min. C. L. wt. 40,000 lbs. ...4...5	
48	Pigs or slabs ...4 ⎱ Min.wt.	
49	Sheet, in casks ...4 ⎰ 36,000 lbs.	
50	Shavings, min. C. L. wt. 36,000 lbs. ...2........R	
51	Sheets, perforated for screens, boxed, min. C. L. wt. 36,000 lbs. ...4...5	
52	Sheet or roll, not packed ...1	
53	Strips (for weather strips), boxed or crated ...3	
54	Sweepings, min. wt. 40,000 lbs. ...4........E	

14	ZINC, viz.:	
15	In boxes, casks, sheets or rolls	4
16	In blocks or pigs, L. C. L.	5
17	Same, C. L., min. wt. 30,000 lbs.	6
18	Scrap, packed	5
19	ZINC, CHLORIDE OF, viz.:	
20	In boxes, or in glass jugs, or carboys, packed, L. C. L.	1
21	In kegs, or bbls., L. C. L.	4
22	Same, packed, or in tank cars, C. L. (see General Rule 3)	6
23	Zinc Ashes or Residue, L. C. L.	4
24	Same, C. L.	6
25	Zinc Dust and Zinc Flue Dust; same as Paints	5
26	Zinc Oxide	
27	Zinc Paints; same as Paints.	
28	Zinc, Sulphate of, in boxes	1
29	Same, in kegs, bbls. or drums	4
30	Zincs, Battery, in crates, boxes, or bbls., L. C. L.	3
31	Same, C. L.	6

299

in the United States at the present time! A few selections from the first and last items of such a document are reproduced on the preceding pages. They give some idea of the amazing scope of trade. Such a classification is, first of all, a list of every possible commodity which may move by rail, from Academy or Artist's Board and Accoutrements to Xylophones and Zylonite. In this list one finds Algarovilla, Bagasse, "Pie Crust, Prepared"; Artificial Hams, Cattle Tails and Wombat Skins; Wings, Crutches, Cradles, Baby Jumpers and all; together with Shoo Flies and Grave Vaults. Every thing above, on, or under the earth will be found listed in such a volume. To grade justly all these commodities is obviously a task of the utmost nicety. A few of the delicate questions which have puzzled the Interstate Commerce Commission may give some idea of the complexity of the problem.[1] Shall cow peas pay freight as "vegetables, N. O . S., dried or evaporated," or as "fertilizer" — being an active agent in soil regeneration? Are "iron-handled bristle shoe-blacking daubers" machinery or toilet appliances? Are patent medicines distinguishable, for purposes of transportation, from other alcoholic beverages used as tonics? What is the difference, as regards rail carriage, between a percolater and an every-day coffee pot? Are Grandpa's Wonder Soap and Pearline — in the light of the claims put forth by manufacturers, suitable either for laundry or toilet purposes — to be put in different classes according to their uses or their market price? When is a boiler not a boiler? If it be used for heating purposes rather than steam generation, why is it not a stove? What is the difference between raisins and other dried fruits, unless perchance the carrier has not yet established one industry while another is already firmly rooted and safe against competition?

The classification of all these articles is a factor of primary importance in the making of freight rates both from a public and

[1] 10 I.C.C. Rep., 281; 13 *Idem*, 111; 4 *Idem*, 32; 9 *Idem*, 264; 17 *Idem*, 511; 23 *Idem*, 242; 2 *Idem*, 1.

private point of view. Attention has been directed of late to its significance and importance to the private shipper, by reason of the use made of it in the advances of freight rates which have taken place throughout the country within the past decade. Its public importance has not been fully appreciated until recently as affecting the general level of railway charges. So little was its significance understood, that supervision and control of classification were not apparently contemplated by the original Act to Regulate Commerce of 1887. The anomaly existed for many years, therefore, of a grant of power intended to regulate freight rates, which, at the same time, omitted provision for control over a fundamentally important element in their make-up. The Interstate Commerce Commission, however, assumed jurisdiction over the matter: and for more than twenty years, despite doubts expressed by the Department of Justice as to its legality, passed upon complaints as to unreasonable classification without protest even from the carriers themselves. Control over it has now been assured beyond possibility of dispute by the specific provisions of the Hepburn Act of 1910.

The freight rate upon a particular commodity between any given points is compounded of two separate and distinct factors: one having to do with the nature of the haul, the other with the nature of the goods themselves. Two distinct publications must be consulted in order to determine the actual charge. Although both of them usually bear the name of a railway and are issued over its signature, they emanate, nevertheless, from entirely different sources. The first of these is known as the Freight Tariff. It specifies rates in cents per hundred pounds for a number of different classes of freight, numerically designated, between all the places upon each line or its connections. Thus the tariff of the New York Central & Hudson River Railroad gives rates per hundred pounds from New York to several hundred stations, for first, second, third, etc., classes. This freight tariff, however, contains no mention whatever of commodities by name. The second publication which must be consulted supplies this defect. This is known as the Classification. Its function is to group all articles more or less alike in character, so far as they affect transportation cost, or are affected in value by carriage from place to place. These groups correspond to the several numerical classes already named in the freight tariff. Thus dry goods or boots and shoes are designated as first class. Turning back to the freight tariff, the rate from New York, for example, to any particular place desired, for such first-class freight, is then found in cents per hundred pounds. It thus appears, as has been said, that a freight rate is made up of two distinct elements equal in importance. The first is the charge corresponding to the distance; the other is the charge as determined by the character of the goods. Consequently, a variation in either one of the two would result in changing the final rate as compounded.[1]

A concrete illustration or two may emphasize the commercial importance of classification. So far as it may be used to effect an increase of rates, the following case is typical, as given by a Boston manufacturer, in evidence before the Senate Committee on Interstate Commerce in 1905:

"From July 15, 1889, to January 1, of this year, the classification (of carbon black, basis of printers' ink) continued to be once and a half first class in less-than-carload lots, third class in carload lots, approximately twice the freight required between 1887 and 1889. Meanwhile, the price had declined. . . . On January 1 the classification was again raised, to class 2, rule 25, an increase of about ten per cent. in carload lots. Numerous efforts have been made by myself and others to have this commodity classified where it belongs, as dry color, but the only result has been the reverse of what we desired; and the industry

[1] Railways in the United States in 1902, by the Interstate Commerce Commission, 1903. Part II, p. 24, gives much data on changes of classification of specific articles since 1886.

has been and is in a somewhat precarious condition, as we have contracted for millions of pounds of black at prices fixed at the point of delivery, and had no notice of the raise in freight rate until subsequent to its going into operation." [1]

The Spokane Chamber of Commerce, in these same Senate Committee hearings, gave an illustration of the use of classification to bring about a change of rates without modifying the individual railway tariff. "The Pacific Coast Pipe Company started to make wired wooden pipe in the spring of 1900. . . . There was at that time but one factory of the kind on the North Pacific coast, located at Seattle. . . . The Seattle factory, backed by the big lumber firms on the coast, finding a serious competitor in the Spokane field, got the railways to put manufactured pipe under the lumber classification, thus reducing the rate from Seattle to Spokane from forty-six to twenty cents per 100 pounds. . . . The Spokane factory at once filed a vigorous protest, with the result that the railways put back the rate from Seattle to Spokane to forty-six cents, but established a maximum rate of fifty cents for Seattle pipe, which, of course, shut off all territory east of Spokane from the Spokane factory. . . . The remnant of the Spokane factory . . . has been compelled to shut down, and the entire plant is being removed to Ballard." Whether these facts are exactly as thus informally stated or not, is by the way. If not done at this time, it is certain that similar manipulation of classification rules often enters into commercial competition.[2]

Freight tariffs and classifications are as distinct and independent in source as they are in nature. Tariffs are issued by each railway, by and for itself alone and upon its sole authority. Classifications, on the other hand, do not originate with particular railways at all; but are issued for them by coöperative bodies, known as classification committees. These committees

[1] For the rate advances of 1900, mainly effected by this means; U. S. Industrial Commission, IX, p. 859, and XIX, p. 282.
[2] *Cf.* underclassification as a means of rebating; p. 190, *supra*.

are composed of representatives from all the carriers operating within certain designated territories. In other words, the United States is apportioned among a number of committees, to each of which is delegated by the carriers concerned, the power over classification; that is to say, the right to assign every commodity which may be shipped or received to any particular group of freight ratings. This delegation of authority is always subject, however, to the right of filing whatever exceptions to the classification any railway may choose independently to put in force. These exception sheets contain the so-called commodity tariffs, to be subsequently described, which stand out in sharp relief against the so-called class rates. Such exceptions are independently filed by each railway at Washington and do not generally form integral parts of the volume issued by the classification committee, except in the southern states. New editions of these classifications are published from time to time as called for by additions or amendments, the latest, of course, superseding all earlier ones. Thirty-seven such issues have already appeared in series in trunk line and southern territory, while fifty have been put forth in western territory, since the practice was standardized in 1888.

At the present time freight classification for all the railways of the United States is performed mainly by three committees, known as the Official, the Southern and the Western, with headquarters, respectively, in New York, Atlanta and Chicago. Each of these three committees has jurisdiction over a particular territory. Thus the Official Classification prevails east of Chicago and north of the Ohio and the Potomac; the Southern, over the remaining part of the country east of the Mississippi; and the Western, throughout the rest of the United States. In addition to these three primary classifications there is also another, issued by the Transcontinental Freight Bureau, with headquarters at Chicago. This committee has supervision over classification upon the Pacific coast business. A number of the states also, notably Illinois, Iowa and most of the southwestern commonwealths, promulgate state classifications having relation, however, only to local business within their several jurisdictions. These are prescribed by law and represent modifications to suit peculiar exigencies or to foster local trade ambitions. There are also a number of other coöperative local railway committees, each dealing with the special concerns of its own territory, and representing the joint interests of the railways therein included to all the world outside. Thus, for instance, Southern Classification territory is subdivided into local units, known, respectively, as the Southeastern Mississippi Valley Association, the Southeastern Freight Association, and the Associated Railways of Virginia and the Carolinas.[1] But for all practical purposes, so far as the larger problems of classification are concerned, our attention may be concentrated upon the three principal committees above mentioned.

Some impression of the wide differences between these three main classifications in different parts of the country may be derived from the set of excerpts at the head of this chapter. In three parallel columns the alpha and omega of each are reproduced, together with bits of one of the most complicated schedules, viz., that dealing with agricultural implements. Even where the same commodities occur in each classification, the diversity in description, mode of packing, carload and other requirements, renders any direct comparison almost impossible. The mere fact that the class assignment, as shown at the right in each column, happens to be the same, as in the case of acetic acid in barrels or drums which moves both in Official and Southern Classification territory, third class in less-than-carload lots (*L. C. L.*) and fifth class in carloads (*C. L.*), shows nothing at all as far as equality of charges is concerned. For, as has been said, this is only half the statement of the rate. The spread between charges for different classes yet remains to be

[1] The Official Railway Guide of the United States gives the personnel of scores of these associations annually, with a definition of the territory of each.

determined. The actual relativity between third-class and fifth-class rates, moreover, may be very different in the two places. In the New York Board of Trade case[1] this point was well exemplified. Comparative conditions as to rates in the three main sections of the country, as they then existed, were as follows:

RATES IN CENTS PER HUNDREDWEIGHT

	Miles	Class I.	Class IV.	Canned goods L.C.L.	Canned goods C.L.
New York to Chicago (Official class'n)	912	75	35	65	30
Chicago to Omaha (West'n class'n)	490	75	30	28.5	25
Louisville to Selma (South'n class'n)	490	98	63	63	52

On the trunk lines fourth-class rates were thus less than half those charged for the first class; in the West they were even lower, relatively; while in the South fourth-class rates were about two-thirds as high as the first-class rates. These differences in the spread between classes, as will be seen, interlocking as they do with a multitude of other considerations, are a serious bar to any partial modification in the direction of uniformity for the United States as a whole. Only by consideration of every factor entering into any given rate may comparisons safely be entertained.

Historically considered, the development of freight classification has been much the same in England and the United States. Early railway practice was an outgrowth of the tariffs in force upon canals and toll roads.[2] In America, freight charges were at the outset often arbitrarily fixed by the state legislatures, as conditions precedent to the grant of charter. In many instances they were based upon the customary performance by wagon, distinguishing between light-weight articles paying by the cubic foot, and heavy ones for which

[1] 3 I.C.C. Rep., 473.
[2] Acworth's Elements of Railroad Economics, p. 104, is best on England. *Cf.* McPherson's Railroad Freight Rates, p. 148.

the tariff was based upon weight. Thus in 1827 the charter of the South Carolina Railroad established its tolls at one half the usual wagon charge. The Southern Pacific in local rates on ore into San Francisco followed along just below the charges by ox cart. The freight was proportioned also according to the length of haul by an arbitrary mileage rate. It soon developed, however, that railway rates were unique in the fact that not only was there a great increase in the volume of trade, but also in the diversity of articles offered for transportations as well. Far more elaborate classifications were soon seen to be necessary.

The South Carolina Railroad tariff of 1855, described by McPherson,[1] exemplified the primitive traffic conditions then prevalent. Goods were divided into four classes. The first consisted of articles of light weight or high value, including, for example, such incongruities as bonnets, tea, and pianos. The remaining three classes paid by weight with a descending scale of charges. It is difficult to explain why coffee and sugar should be rated lower than stoves and feathers; or why dry hides and rice should be charged a higher rate than cotton yarn and bacon; but it is evident that a rough classification according to weight, value, use and cost of service was being attempted. There was in addition a considerable collection of special rates on chosen commodities according to the method of packing them, whether by barrel, bale or case. And there were also what corresponded to modern commodity rates upon cordwood, lumber, bricks, and similar goods. This tariff, though primitive, including no less than three hundred items, was far more elaborate than those commonly used at the time. The Louisville & Nashville originally distinguished but three classes: one by bulk, another by weight and a third applicable to live stock. Poultry was rated by the dozen long after the Civil War, with a higher charge for Muscovy than for ordinary ducks. The traffic manager of the Chicago, Mil-

[1] *Op. cit.*, p. 149.

waukee & St. Paul testified before the Elkins committee in 1905, that the classification in Illinois in his youth was printed on the back of a bill of lading no greater than the size of an ordinary sheet of letter paper, and the page was not full.

From these modest beginnings the development of classification in the United States was rapid, responding to the ever-increasing intensity of competition and the spread of markets, particularly after 1875. By the middle of the eighties most of the large railways were working under six or eight different classifications. It began to be apparent that some check must be placed upon such increasing complexity. For conditions were well-nigh intolerable, with one set of rules for Illinois, and yet another west of Buffalo, divided into eastbound and westbound sections, with still a third on westward shipments local to territory between Chicago and the Missouri river. The first attempt at a systematic scheme was made in 1882, but the agreements then made proved unstable. By 1887 conditions had become insupportable, so great was the number and the diversity of the classifications throughout the country.[1] Some applied to local business only, and were peculiar to each road. Some applied only to westbound business, others to eastbound traffic. The traffic manager of the New York Central & Hudson River testified before the Interstate Commerce Commission that there were at one time 138 distinct classifications in trunk line territory alone. The case of the Wabash in 1883 was typical. A shipper desiring to determine freight rates over that road might be compelled to consult a classification for the middle and western states in six classes; one for the Southern Railway & Steamship Association territory in eighteen classes; one for Mississippi valley business in five classes; one known as the Revised Western in nine classes; the Trunk Line East in thirteen classes; the Trunk Line West in five classes; a classification for Texas points in eight classes; and two for the Pacific coast, according to di-

[1] Cullom Committee, Testimony, p. 759.

rection, in eight and nine classes, respectively. This situation, rendering it almost impossible for any shipper to determine in advance what his freight rates were going to be, as well as what his competitor was paying, early impressed itself upon the Interstate Commerce Commission. And it was doubtless due in part to its initiative that classifications were shaken down into substantially their present general form in 1888.

The natural growth of classification in a rapidly developing country like the United States, has manifested itself in three distinct ways: there has been a steady increase in the number of items of freight separately enumerated; a growing distinction in rates between carload and less-than-carload shipments; and a steadily enlarging volume of the most elaborate special rules and descriptions. As for the mere increase in distinct commodities enumerated, in the East in 1886 there had come to be about 1,000. The first Official Classification in the following year increased to 2,800 items; and by 1893, in the eleventh issue, there were twice that number. The latest Official Classification, No. 34 in 1909, contained approximately 6,000 separate enumerations — not many more, in fact, than fifteen years earlier. The point of saturation, or else the limit of human ingenuity, seems to have been about reached some years ago. The same thing was true of the Western Classification. In 1893 this contained 3,658 items, representing an increase of about 2,000 over the number of commodities classified by name in 1886. By 1909, as the

NUMBER OF RATINGS IN 1909 [1]

	Less than Carload	Carload
Southern Classification	3,503	703
Western Classification	5,729	1,690
Official Classification	5,852	4,235

above figures show, it comprehended 5,729, almost as many separate items, in fact, for less-than-carload lots as were recog-

[1] *Railway Age Gazette*, September 8, 1911, p. 458.

nized in trunk line territory. Only in carload ratings is the Western Classification less extensive. The Southern Classification reflected somewhat simpler trade conditions prevalent south of the Ohio river, by the relatively smaller number of articles enumerated; but it should be added that the number of exceptions — filling no less than 160 pages in the latest issue — is indicative throughout of a lesser degree of standardization than is found elsewhere. Perhaps the most striking feature of the southern system is the very small proportion of carload rates. But it should be noted in this connection that the basing point system afforded preference to market towns in any event; so that jobbers in such places did not need wholesale rates to the same degree. This phase of the matter will be elsewhere discussed.[1]

The second natural tendency in the development of classification above mentioned, is an increase in the number of separate ratings for large and small shipments. The normal growth of trade ought to make possible a steady increase in shipments by the carload, rather than by the box, barrel, or case; and the increase in the number of separate carload ratings — always, of course, at a reduced rate by comparison with less-than-carload lots — conforms territorially to the growth in the volume of trade. In 1877, even in trunk line territory, only twenty-four commodities were accorded a special carload rate.[2] By 1880 the number had increased to 50, and seven years later to 160. Just before the passage of the Act to Regulate Commerce there was no distinction between carload and small lots in eighty-five per cent. of the articles enumerated. A sudden change supervened in the first Official Classification issued after the Federal Act. The number of carload ratings was suddenly raised to 900, provoking a storm of protest from eastern shippers who resented this advantage accorded to jobbers in the West and South, because it enabled the latter to buy their supplies directly at wholesale.

[1] P. 385, *infra*.   [2] 3 I.C.C. Rep., 473.

CLASSIFICATION

The dispute between dealers in the older and newer commercial centres came to a head in the so-called New York Board of Trade and Transportation case of 1888, elsewhere discussed. Yet notwithstanding this protest of jobbers and manufacturers in eastern trade centres, who insisted that they should be permitted to compete on even terms with provincial jobbers by making their shipments direct from New York or Boston in small lots as cheaply as the local jobber could buy them by the carload, the number of separate carload ratings steadily augmented year after year. By 1893 more than half of the articles enumerated in the Official Classification were allowed a lower rate for large shipments. Present conditions are set forth by the statistics in the preceding paragraph. From these it appears that in trunk line territory nearly three-fourths of the commodities now enjoy carload ratings; while in the South, on the other hand, only about one-fifth of them make such distinction between carload and less-than-carload lots.[1] One reason is evident; namely, that throughout a large part of the South few jobbers command a business of sufficient magnitude to make use of carload shipments. It is but recently, to take a specific illustration, that business has developed in volume sufficient to permit of the shipment of fly paper in carload lots. Until such time no distinction between large and small shipments could well be made.

Conditions in the West, according to these figures, are intermediate between those in the East and the South. On the other hand, transcontinental business, as carried on in competition with ocean steamers, is almost entirely confined to shipment by the carload. The Transcontinental Classification is unique, therefore, in offering but very few opportunities for shipment by package, except under specially onerous con-

---

[1] Railways in the United States in 1902, I.C.C., 1903, Part II, p. 39; In the South in 1876 only 6 per cent. of items had carload ratings; while in 1902, 65 per cent. were so favored, as compared with 82 per cent. in trunk line territory and 81 per cent. in the West.

ditions. The spread, in other words, between the two sorts of carriage operates most unfavorably by contrast upon the intermountain centres. Denver, for example, under the Western Classification enjoys no carload rates, while competitors at San Francisco have a large number.[1]

A much more elaborate code of rules and regulations having reference to local practices and conditions is the third accompaniment of the growth of trade.[2] Prior to 1887, and again before the recent revival of interest in uniform classification, conditions had become intolerable in this regard. All sorts of details, covering relatively unimportant differences in conditions of carriage, bill of lading contracts, marking and packing, led to constant confusion and annoyance, especially in cases of shipment from one classification territory to another. An eastern shipper of iron bolts, having in mind that a gunny sack is equivalent to a box or barrel in the East, orders a small shipment in a bag to a far western point. He finds that bolts in bags under the rules of the Western Classification, are specially enumerated only for carload lots, and that he must pay a rate one class higher for such shipment than if contained in a barrel, box or keg. This difference in classification may more than absorb his profit. Recent evidence before the Interstate Commerce Commission,[3] contained a striking illustration of such local diversity in rules and descriptions as applied to furniture.

"*Western class:* 'Bank, store, saloon and office furniture, consisting of arm rails, back bar mirrors, bottle cases, chairs, counter-fittings, desk, foot rails, metal brackets for arm and foot rails, refrigerators, tables and work boards. Note — Door, window and bar screens, partitions, prescription cases, patent medicine cases, show cases, wall-cases wainscoting, office railing and wooden mantels may be shipped with bank, store, saloon or office furniture in mixed carloads at third-class, minimum weight 12,000 lbs.

[1] The Intermountain Rate cases are fully discussed at p. 610, *infra*.
[2] Samuel O. Dunn, *Railway Age Gazette*, September 10, 1909, p. 462, is best on this. *Cf.* 8 I.C.C. Rep., 368.
[3] Proposed rate advances November 29, 1910.

"There is no such provision as this in the Official Classification. On the contrary, a shipment of that kind can only be made by figuring out the less-than-carload rate on each article, many of which take first, double first and even three times first ratings.

"For example, mirrors over five feet in length are classified double first class in the official classification, while show cases, set up, take three times first. The natural result of this difference in classification has been to shut out competition of eastern dealers in these articles entirely in Western Classification territory."

Only in a customs tariff of the United States would one expect to find any such complexity as is discoverable in railway documents of this sort.

The mere interpretation of such classification rules is often difficult; especially with reference to the mode of packing. Suppose a tariff provides a certain rate on stamped metal ware in boxes, barrels or crates and, furthermore, fixes the charge fifty per cent. higher for shipment in bales, bags or bundles. If the consignment is encased in corrugated strawboard, which of the two rates applies? The difference in rates being so great, it becomes quite an item on a shipment of fifteen carloads from Buffalo to the Pacific coast.[1] Or it may be a question as to whether a crate for Colorado cantaloupes is actually of such dimensions as to come in under a specially favorable commodity rate.[2]

The growing diversification of manufactures and trade is, of course, responsible for all three of the developments above indicated. Not only the increasing refinement of commerce, but the technical nomenclature or trade jargon, necessary for the specific and accurate description of so many thousands of articles, have conspired to render these documents extremely cumbersome in the absence of a general revision and simplification. It is but natural that one item after another should be added, each bearing a particular name or being classified

[1] 22 I. C.C. Rep., 565.
[2] 22 I.C.C. Rep., 585. *Cf.* also 23 *Idem*, 395, on articles too large to be loaded through the side door or too long to be loaded through the end window.

upon some new basis. A striking example of this increase of complexity was afforded by the cotton goods schedule in the Southern Classification. By 1900 there were upwards of thirty different names under which cotton cloth might be shipped. Great complaint was occasioned, as well as the possibility of fraud, by underclassification, etc. Most of these thirty names did not represent different values of goods, but in many instances were merely trade-marks of particular manufacturers. At the urgent request of the shippers this complicated schedule was superseded in 1900 by one comprehensive title of "cotton goods in the piece" irrespective of color, particular method of weaving or other subordinate details.

From the point of view of economic theory, the warrant for a differentiation of charges between various classes of commodities offered for transportation, may be considered primarily from two distinct points of view. The first is that of operation, which determines cost. The second is from the standpoint of traffic whereby the value of service, so-called, is measured. The reasonableness of making a distinction in freight rates according to the character of goods is easily apparent, as judged on the basis of cost of service. A multitude of factors enter into consideration at this point. The railway ought in self-protection to charge more for hauling a thing, if it actually costs it more in the long run to perform that service. Some of the factors which enter into this cost were well put by the Interstate Commerce Commission in 1897.[1]

"Whether commodities were crude, rough, or finished; liquid or dry; knocked down or set up; loose or in bulk; nested or in boxes, or otherwise packed; if vegetables, whether green or dry, desiccated

[1] Hammond, Railway Rate Theories, etc., 1911, p. 42, analyzes interstate commerce decisions as to these. Strombeck, Freight Classification, 1912, pp. 35–60, also discusses the various factors entering into cost.

CLASSIFICATION 315

or evaporated; the market value and shippers' representations as to their character; the cost of service, length and direction of haul; the season and manner of shipment; the space occupied and weight; whether in carload or less-than-carload lots; the volume of annual shipments to be calculated on; the sort of car required, whether flat, gondola, box, tank, or special; whether ice or heat must be furnished; the speed of trains necessary for perishable or otherwise rush goods; the risk of handling, either to the goods themselves or other property; the weights, actual and estimated; the carrier's risk or owner's release from damage or loss."

Instances of approval of classification on the basis of such cost of operation are frequently found in the decisions of the Interstate Commerce Commission. For example, special service or equipment, as in the rapid transport of fresh vegetables and fruit from the South, justify the carriers in a specially high classification.[1] Rates on live hogs by comparison with rates on hog products, as well as on live cattle and dressed beef, have likewise been adjusted in terms of cost of carriage. A classification on hogs yielding a rate equal to two-thirds of that on hog products has been held equitably to represent the relative expense.[2] Even the indefinite element of risk has been accepted as justifying a higher classification for live stock as compared with other commodities.[3]

Classification is less easy to defend from the standpoint of the traffic manager alone, than from that of the vice-president in charge of operation. Value of service is at times difficult to understand. It is not at first sight reasonable, that of two commodities which cost the railway exactly the same amount to transport, one should be charged twice as much as the other. For example, the rate on anthracite coal is very much higher than upon soft coal; the rate upon wheat is higher than the rate upon some other foodstuffs; the rate upon fine woollen

---

[1] 6 I.C.C. Rep., 295; 10 *Idem*, 255.
[2] 4 I.C.C. Rep., 611; 9 *Idem*, 382. But compare 23 *Idem*, 663, fixing the rate on stock cattle at 75 per cent. of that for beef or fat cattle. How about cost of service here?
[3] 10 *Idem*, 327.

goods is very much higher than upon coarse cotton cloth, etc.[1] It has been urged frequently that any discrimination in the freight rate on the basis of difference, either in the value of the commodity itself or in the value of the service rendered, is unreasonable and unjust. The case, however, is entirely analogous to that of discrimination between a long and short haul of the same goods. The principle is perfectly defensible in both cases, and has been accepted in legal decisions as well as by economic writers for many years. It is based upon the fact, which confronts one at every turn in a discussion of railway economics, that a large proportion of the expenses of a railway is independent of the amount of traffic. These fixed expenses must be met at all cost if the road is to remain solvent. They constitute a charge upon the entire traffic of the line, and are not susceptible of apportionment to each unit of transportation. Any rate which will contribute a surplus, small or large, above the mere cost of transportation, — that is to say, above the expenses incident to this particular carriage, — and which thereby lessens by the amount of that excess the burden of the fixed charges remaining upon other traffic, is justifiable. But it is defensible only under two conditions. The first is that the goods at any higher rate will go by another route or not at all; and the second is that the effect may not be detrimental to the general course of business,— that is to say, that it is not opposed to the public welfare. Thus a long haul at a lower rate than the rate charged for a shorter haul, if it must be lower in order to secure the business, constitutes no injustice to the local shipper; for the surplus remaining above the cost of haulage of that particular increment of freight lessens thereby the charge which must be made upon local freight for meeting interest on bonds, maintenance of way, and equipment expenses, etc., all of which charges, as we have seen, go on more or less independently of the traffic. On precisely the same grounds a discrimination of freight rates

---

[1] *Cf.* revenue per ton mile by commodities, p. 421, *infra*.

in favor of the cheaper commodity or the less valuable service may be defended. Coal or sand may reasonably be carried at two and one-fourth mills per ton mile, while the road is coincidently charging three or four times as much for hauling dry goods or fine hardware. For if a quarter of a mill per ton mile can be earned above the expenses incident to hauling that sand or coal, it enables the rates on the dry goods or hardware to be maintained at a lower point than they otherwise would be. It is unnecessary to elaborate this principle further. It is everywhere accepted as valid. And it in a measure substantiates Mavor's statement that "freight rates, like rent, are rather the effect of price movements than the cause of them." When tariffs are high because prices are high, we are afforded a fair illustration of value of service as an element in rate making.

Value of service, therefore, as affording a warrant for classification, has also been recognized in a number of Interstate Commerce decisions since 1887. A relation between the grade of the charge and fluctuations in the market price of the commodity — in other words, charging what the traffic will bear — is at times discernible. It is to the interest of the public that carriers should be satisfied with relatively smaller profits from the transportation of commodities of low price which are in general demand.[1] Under these circumstances changes in price of such staple commodities as iron and steel or the lower priced grains, should be reflected in a corresponding modification of rates.[2] Akin to this is recognition of a relation in general between the value of a commodity and its classification. Where, for example, articles representing different stages of manufacture have to be graded, it is but fair that the raw material, or the partly-made product should be graded

---

[1] *Cf.* p. 412, *infra*, on the significance of revenue per ton mile.
[2] 6 I.C.C. Rep., 88; 9 *Idem*, 382; 4 *Idem*, 48. On freight rates and prices compare Rep. U. S. Industrial Commission, XIX, p. 366, and chap. X, *infra*.

lower than the finished article.[1] Similarly, articles which may fairly be substituted for one another ought to be classified with reference to their common market value.[2] The relative value of commodities, as controlling classification, clearly governs the treatment of hard and soft coal.[3] The practical difficulty, of course, is to know where to stop in admitting such considerations. Shall "small-vein" soft coal, because it cannot compete on even terms with the "big-vein" product, be accepted for carriage on a more favored basis?[4] Some rather nice questions, both of business and public policy, would be suggested by such a precedent.

Different classification of the same commodity according to the use to which it may be put, is evidently an attempt to grade according to value rather than cost of service. Automobile parts may come in from the wheelmaker at second-class rates, but when they go out to jobbing houses they are rated three times first class.[5] A number of cases of this sort have come before the Commission. Shall cow peas, for example, be classed with corn and oats as agricultural products in one case, while according them a rating with commercial fertilizers in another, inasmuch as they may become an active agent in nitrogenizing soil?[6] More recently the Commission has declined to recognize the validity of classification on this basis. Thus brick is always to be charged the same without regard to whether it is for fire, building or paving purposes.[7] Unusually low rates for steam coal used by carriers and open only to certain shippers for this or other particular purposes, likewise have been forbidden.[8] The carriers have attempted

[1] Hammond, Railway Rate Theories, p. 14 *et seq.*
[2] *Ibid.*, pp. 27 and 36.
[3] *Ibid.*, p. 29.
[4] 14 I.C.C. Rep., 127.
[5] *Freight*, February, 1905, p. 61.
[6] 10 I.C.C. Rep., 281.
[7] 17 I.C.C. Rep., 197. But compare 23 *Idem*, 7, on stock and fat cattle; and 14 *Idem*, 127, on "big-vein" and "small-vein" coal, as above.
[8] 20 I.C.C. Rep., 426; 21 *Idem*, 41.

to distinguish in grade between dried fruit and raisins. For the two industries call for relatively different protection against old-established competitors.[1]

As actually effected in practice, classification of freight seems to have been largely empirical — the result of long experience in sympathetically feeling the pulse of the business community. In the main, despite their denial of the validity of cost as an element in rate making, traffic managers and the Interstate Commerce Commission seem to have been swayed more commonly by this consideration in the make-up of schedules. Nevertheless, charging what the traffic will bear, as a principle, will suffice alone to explain many of the details of classification now in force. Rates have been adjusted so as to secure the largest amount of business possible at the highest rate compatible with that volume. In other words, traffic managers have been mainly influenced by the consideration well stated by a witness before the United States Industrial Commission: that, "a freight tariff is made as it is, not because it ought to be that, but because it must be that." The procedure of classification committees seems, in other words, to have been mainly based upon considerations of revenue, and that, too, without any very positive evidence as to details.[2] Rule-of-thumb experience, therefore, is mainly represented in classifications of the present time; that is to say, an adjustment of freight rates upon different commodities to suit the commercial conditions which have happened to prevail at any given time. All of which emphasizes still further the need of scientific revision of these most important schedules, preferably by the carriers themselves, but by public authority if commercial inertia be too powerful to be overcome.

The spread of a classification, — that is to say, the graduation of rates as between all kinds of goods, from fine silks

[1] 2 *Idem*, 1.
[2] Evidence before the Interstate Commerce Commission and the Industrial Commission as to freight rate advances in 1900 proves this point.

to lime and sand, or from aeroplanes, "set up," to pig iron, "knocked down," — is not constant. How shall this be theoretically justified? At first sight it would appear as if the relativity of charges between different things, as determined by cost or value of service, ought to remain fixed; that is to say, for example, that rates on raw hides fairly standing at one-half of the charge for shoes, ought to remain always and everywhere at this ratio. Advocates of a rigid classification prescribed by public authority seem often to assume that this could be brought about. But a moment's consideration of the nature of a tariff as it has already been described will show that this is impossible. The spread or gradation, far from being fixed, must in the nature of things ever vary from place to place with change of trade conditions. The rate on raw hides relatively to that on shoes in New England — the centre of manufacture for footwear — should be very different at Kansas City or Chicago, whence the raw hides are derived: different alone, if for no other reason than because hides, moving east, progressively add the cost of carriage the farther they go; while with shoes the augmentation of value goes on in the opposite direction, geographically. True as between commodities, the same inconstancy of ratio also holds good as between different points along a given line. The rate from New York to Durham, North Carolina, for example, on first-class freight may be fifteen per cent. above that for freight of the second class; the second class may be twenty per cent. above that of third class for this distance, etc.; yet the divergence between these same classes for another distance, as between New York and Jacksonville, Florida, may be quite different, — twenty per cent. between first and second class, twenty-seven per cent. between second and third, and so on. This is indeed rather a difficult matter to understand.

This ever-changing spread of rates from place to place, as between different commodities and with all possible combinations of the two, may be clearly explained by reference to the diagram at page 108, showing the gradation of charges by distance for different goods. Is it not plain that the spread between commodities at any given place is indicated by taking a vertical cross section of the diagram at that point? We have already seen that the curves, rising with increase of the distance, do so by different degrees. They cross and recross, making an intricate lace work of lines, because of the fact that while cost, in general, may increase more or less proportionately to distance, competition in its ever-varying forms, plays all sorts of pranks with the rates from point to point. The rate at any station is shown by the height of the curve on the vertical line for that place. Even, however, if the curves never crossed, but rose by evenly spraying out from the point of shipment at one end of the line, as in the case of those for the three upper classes, their relative heights would constantly change with distance. But owing to the complexities of competition the onward and upward movement of the curves for particular commodities is usually much more erratic than this. Some goods, like children, "get their growth" early. They soon attain the level of all the charge they can ever bear. Others distribute their development over a much greater distance. Sometimes, as we have observed, the coal curve will be above the wheat curve; sometimes it will be below. In other words, the vagaries of these sloping lines cause the vertical cross sections, indicative of spread, to vary from point to point all along the line. Such a thing as constancy of ratio between classes or particular goods is, in the nature of transportation things, impossible. This is a matter of fundamental importance, especially in its bearing upon the proposition, soon to be considered, of substituting a single uniform classification under government authority for the present threefold system. Moreover, it demonstrates the great commercial disturbance which might ensue from a general advance of freight rates by an indiscriminate transfer of commodities from lower to higher classes, such as was attempted in 1900. Such procedure is altogether illogical, and economically as upsetting to trade as a general "horizontal" increase or reduction of a customs tariff.

Commodity rates as a means for enabling shippers to reach beyond their immediate territory and gain an entrance to new markets, form an entirely distinct variety of charges from those quoted in the classified tariffs. These are special rates made to suit particular contingencies,[1] although, of course, under the law they must be filed with the Interstate Commerce Commission in the same manner. Such commodity rates, however, do not apply to persons but to localities. Although granted to shippers in a particular place to build up an industry, the privilege of shipment under the same conditions is theoretically open, of course, to all others at that point. Such commodity rates naturally apply to three sets of commercial conditions: they either govern large shipments for long distances, as in the case of live stock; or, if for short distances, they are confined to commodities of the very lowest grade, such as lime, sand or paving blocks; or else they are introduced to meet special conditions, such as an irregular market or rapidly fluctuating competitive circumstances, as in the case of goods for import or export. Such special rates are almost invariably granted for carload lots alone. The reason is, naturally, that it would not be worth while to make an exception to the classified schedules for less than that amount. Moreover, it should be observed, special rates of this sort are often introduced in order to meet changeable competition, such as by steamship lines engaged in export or import business. The classified ratings change but little, and oftentimes remain the same for many years. But in all cases where fluctuating conditions have to be met, commodity rates by the carload are likely to appear. This is one reason why the transcontinental tariffs, exposed to competition either by the Cape Horn

[1] Pp. 108, 118, etc., *supra*.

or Panama water routes, contain so large a proportion of commodity or carload ratings.[1]

Exceptional or commodity rates are also commonly found in a territory like the southern states, where manufactures are struggling to maintain a foothold. If it appear that a new industry can maintain itself in competition with already established industries elsewhere only by a concession in charges, the traffic manager may elect to grant a commodity rate until such time as the industry has been placed firmly upon its feet. The tonnage moving under commodity rates in such circumstances may be much greater than that included under the classified schedules. Attention has already been drawn to this fact, but it merits still further comment. Probably three-fourths of the business of American railways is done under such special rates. This is apparently a higher proportion than rules in foreign countries with the possible exception of England. Yet it is important to notice that the revenue obtained from such traffic is relatively much less than the tonnage, inasmuch as most commodity rates are confined to low-grade goods. Whether such exceptions to the classified tariffs are on the increase or not is open to question. The evidence tends to show that special rates granted in connection with industrial development tend to increase up to a certain point. Commodity rates, for example, are said to be much more important in the West than they were fifteen years ago.[2] But, on the other hand, industrial conditions having once become standardized and assured, the natural disposition of the railways is to substitute regular schedules for a multiplicity of special rates. The dilemma is that such a special rate once allowed, is exceedingly difficult to withdraw. An earnest attempt was made by the trunk lines in 1899 to retire a large number of these commodity rates. It then appeared that the New York

[1] Sixteenth Annual Report I.C.C., 32; 19 I.C.C. Rep., 244; 21 *Idem*, 349 and 418.
[2] 18 I.C.C. Rep., 459.

Central & Hudson River Railroad had no less than 1,370 on file. Opposition naturally arose to the cancellation of these — an opposition less easily overcome because of the complication that the withdrawal of commodity rates meant practically the abolition of carload ratings. Such action, therefore, looking toward simplification of tariffs, threatened substantially to disturb all the existing commercial adjustments. Nevertheless it is encouraging to note that a distinct reduction in the number of separate and independent rates put into effect is apparent since the recent extensions of Federal authority. The following table, covering the tariffs officially filed at Washington since 1906, is proof positive of great improvement in this regard:

FREIGHT SCHEDULES FILED WITH THE INTERSTATE COMMERCE COMMISSION

1896	131,597
1906	193,995
1907	187,041
1908	161,584
1909	129,294
1910	109,550
1911	93,821

A reduction of more than one half within five years is matter for public congratulation.[1]

Special or commodity rates for the maintenance of equilibrium between competing markets fall naturally into several distinct groups.[2] In the first of these, concerning commodity rates on grain and grain products and cotton, production takes place over a vast extent of territory and the products are marketed in places widely remote from one another. The problem under such circumstances is mainly that of securing equalization through different gateways.[3] In the case of wheat it is a question first of concentration at primary markets,

[1] *Cf.* Annual Report, I.C.C., 1909, p. 11.
[2] McPherson, Railroad Freight Rates, pp. 117–148, is good on this.
[3] Cotton pools in the South; *cf.* vol. II.

such as St. Paul, Kansas City, or Chicago; and thereafter of carriage by competitive routes whether by the way of the Gulf, by any of the various Atlantic seaports or by the St. Lawrence River. Commodity rates are thus determined in this first class of cases mainly with references to competition of routes. On the other hand, when production is spread over a considerable territory, but when transportation is thereafter effected along converging lines to a fairly localized centre of manufacture, the problem of equalizing conditions, competitively, by the resort to commodity rates, has mainly to do with competitive conditions at the place of production. Rates on wool to the highly localized markets of the world afford illustration of this second type of commodity rate problem.[1] Commodity rates upon fruits and vegetables to common markets from such widely separated sources of supply as Florida and California or the equilibration of conditions of production for coal or lumber from the most widely scattered sources of supply, are perhaps the most difficult of all to settle satisfactorily.

The amount of reduction to be allowed on shipments by carload as against consignments in small lots is a nice and most perplexing problem in classification. Attention has already been directed to the great increase in distinct carload ratings which has accompanied the development of trade. As affecting the interests of shippers in different parts of the country, the question came up almost immediately after the passage of the Act to Regulate Commerce. In the so-called New York Board of Trade case,[2] complaint was entered by eastern merchants against a great increase in the number of wholesale ratings in 1888. More than five times as many commodities as before were abruptly given lower rates when shipped out of New York

---

[1] 23 I.C.C. Rep., 151, investigating the transportation of wool affords a fine example.
[2] 3 I.C.C. Rep., 473.

by the carload. Inasmuch as a vey large proportion of groceries and other supplies went by box or package, this reduction accorded on carload shipments greatly benefited the jobbers all through the West and South. Under new conditions provincial middlemen could buy in carloads; and then re-distribute from local centres much more advantageously than before. The Commission, called upon to decide as to the relative rights of these two classes of jobbers, attempted to bring about an adjustment which should, in the main, conform to the existing trade conditions; and yet should take into consideration the relative cost of service in the two cases. The competitive struggle between eastern and both southern and western dealers revealed in these early proceedings, has cropped out continually in official proceedings ever since that time. In a modified form the same question came to the front in connection with the general advance of freight rates in 1900.[1] The changes at this time were twofold — not only modifications in the number of carload ratings, but also an altered differential or spread between the charges for the two sorts of shipments. The question is a vital one to all the shipping interests of the country. It is one of the most troublesome elements in the establishment of a uniform classification for the United States as a whole. For inability to standardize reasonable differences between carload and small shipments, under the widely different trade conditions and practices in various sections of the country, is an almost insuperable difficulty in the way of that reform.

The economic justice of allowing a carload shipper lower rates than one who ships in small lots is apparent, on account of the difference in the cost of such service to the railways. This has been recognized by the Interstate Commerce Commission and the courts as beyond question. Not only the amount of paying freight in relation to dead weight; but the cost of loading and unloading, of billing or collection and of adjusting

[1] United States Industrial Commission, XIX, 1901, p. 281.

damages — all of these elements of cost are noticeably less in the case of a full carload. Turning from these considerations of cost to those prescribed by what may be called traffic principles, the difficulty in arriving at a just determination may be easily appreciated. Glass battery jars in less-than-carload lots were at one time charged from New York to Atlanta, Georgia, second-class rates, namely ninety-eight cents per one hundred pounds. The same commodity when in carload shipments (not less than 20,000 pounds) was rated as fifth class; in which case the charge from New York to Atlanta became sixty cents. Here was a plain difference of thirty-eight cents per one hundred pounds — upward of sixty per cent. greater charge — to the small shipper whose business or capital was insufficient to warrant shipments to such an amount. Two results of such discrimination are possible. In the first place, the large shipper is enabled to undersell his smaller competitor and perhaps to drive him out of that class of business. This may take place as between two dealers, both located in the South and buying their supplies from New York. The second result is that under such rates it is impossible for the manufacturer or northern jobber to sell direct from New York to the retailer in the South in competition with the provincial jobber there located, who ships his goods in at the cheap carload rate and distributes them thereafter. The problem thus concerns at the same time both the small local shipper or dealer, as against a more formidable provincial competitor; and also the remote jobbers as a class against the whole group of local middlemen. In the latter case, sometimes, as in the South, the question is still further complicated by a basing point system, under which the provincial jobber re-distributes to the country stores the goods which have already been shipped in on a low carload rate.[1] And, locally, there is also the immanence in the South of water competition by sea and river to be kept in mind. Boat charges are based upon space requirements rather than

[1] P. 387, *infra*.

weight. This introduces further important considerations in fixing the spread of charges.

The problem as it affects the manufacturer is akin to that concerning the jobber. Originally, as a matter of fact, the carload reduction was essentially a manufacturers' rating, especially for goods in which the cost of raw material formed a large part of the price of the finished product. The relations of the carload rate on the former to the less-than-carload rate on the latter, it is obvious, may readily become an important element in industrial success. It is plain enough that carload charges under such circumstances should be substantially less than those upon small consignments; but that is far from affording a satisfactory answer to the question as to the proper spread or difference in charge to be allowed between the two.

Obviously, in any representation as to the reasonableness of the discount which shall be allowed on carloads, either on the basis of cost or of traffic principles, the interests of localities are commercially pitted one against another. The New York or Chicago jobbing house desiring to sell its goods directly to the retailers throughout the West, wishes to have a relatively low rate on such small shipments as the retailers in lesser places alone can afford to purchase. Participation in this distributing business, however, is resented by the middlemen located in western centres — Omaha, Denver, Kansas City, etc. — who all insist that there should be so wide a difference between carload and less-than-carload rates that they may ship in their wholesale purchases at a low rate, and thus compete in their own territory with the manufacturer in the East or the jobber in New York who desires to sell direct.[1] Comparison of the classifications in different parts of the country reveals the influence of these local interests. The railways in Official Classification territory desire, of course, to build up the manufacturing and jobbing cities tributary to them. This can best

[1] *Cf.* testimony of Wicker before the Cullom Committee in 1886.

be done by encouraging the growth of eastern jobbing centres, stimulated by as low rates for retail as for wholesale shipments. The railways in the western and southern territory, on the contrary, are obliged to consider the claims of their constituents, and to correspondingly minimize the advantages which foreign competitors of their local wholesale dealers enjoy. Another consideration must also be kept in view, namely, that carload ratings can only be accorded when business has developed a magnitude sufficient to permit shipments of that size. The growth of the volume of business in general, therefore, might be normally expected to produce an increase in the proportion of carload ratings. Experience, as we have seen, confirms this view. The normal development, then, is toward an increase in the number of lower rates quoted for carload lots. This is retarded only by the influence of the jobbers and manufacturers in the eastern trade centres, who insist that they shall be permitted to compete on even terms with provincial middlemen by making their shipments direct in small lots at rates approximately as low as the local jobbers pay on carload lots. This question is an exceedingly important one, requiring the balance of opposing interests to a nicety.

Not unfamiliar aspects of the problem of carload rating are revealed in a recent case before the Interstate Commerce Commission, concerning milk rates in New England.[1] And yet the normal order is reversed. Usually, complaint is made of the denial of carload ratings. In this instance a plea was entered for a useable small unit rate as against the wholesale charge. The dispute was precipitated by a deadlock in 1910 between the three large Boston milk contractors and the farmers' associations of several states. The producers, failing in their demand for an increased price, declined to furnish milk at the old figure. A famine resulted, which drew the attention of the public sharply to the system under which the Metropolitan district of Boston was supplied. The belief prevailed that the

[1] 22 I.C.C. Rep., 303.

peculiar transportation conditions known as the "leased car system" which had existed for half a century, was mainly responsible for the tight monopoly of the milk supply. Under this arrangement specially low charges were allowed to those who made shipments regularly by the carload. The Massachusetts legislature, after an investigation, finally passed a law providing that no carrier should charge more for the transportation of milk by the can than was charged for larger quantities; and also that the same facilities, icing, for example, should be furnished in the one case as in the other. This settled the intra-state charges; but it left matters as before for all the other New England states contributing to the market. In this form the controversy was brought before the Federal authorities, which exhaustively considered the methods of transportation as affecting all parties concerned. The contrast with the older elastic situation as to milk ratings in New York was sharp in many respects.[1] This earlier controversy had to do mainly with the relative rights of nearby and distant producers. It was a question of the element of distance as affecting a local or territorial monopoly. The Boston case, on the other hand, was rather a matter of carload ratings than of graduation of charges according to the length of the haul. The monopoly in this instance was that of contractors who had succeeded in getting entire control of the business by reason of the wide spread between charges for milk by the can and by the "leased car." Shipments by the can from the independent farmer were rendered practically impossible since they had to be carried in the baggage car and were liable to spoil through lack of refrigeration.

By contrast with the New York "open car system," the New England plan from the standpoint of cost of service alone seemed to offer several advantages. A caretaker, hired by the milk contractor and in constant personal touch with the farmers, exercised supervision both over milk and cans; this

[1] 7 I.C.C. Rep., 92.

insured a heavier loading and more prompt service at terminals; resulted in the operators providing the best facilities for handling the supply; and allowed surplus milk to be directed to other uses without waste. A large investment had been made under this system, dependent upon its continuance for a reasonable return. On the other hand, denial of equally low rates with the same facilities for refrigeration to the single-can shipper, had undoubtedly fostered monopoly. The railways, conforming to the new Massachusetts law above mentioned, offered to furnish and operate a car suitable for independent shippers on condition that six hundred cans should be tendered for shipment. But they denied obligation to furnish icing facilities, which latter, of course, were absolutely necessary for the success of the competitive service. To be sure, the leased car controlled by the contractors had been theoretically open to all, on condition of a small charge for icing; but the farmers contended that independent shippers ought not to be compelled thus to deliver over their property into the hands of competitors, with the accompanying exposure of their business relations. In the light of all these complications the Commission decided that a *per* can rate with the necessary refrigeration, and bearing a proper relation to the carload rate, ought to be established. And there the matter rests at this time.

The problem of mixed carloads, also, is a difficult one to adjust to the needs of primary and secondary distributing points.[1] It is oftentimes of vital importance to a small jobber to be able to make up a carload of miscellaneous packages. His business may not be large enough to permit him to enjoy the advantage of a carload rate on any single commodity. Or the independent meat packer may be greatly benefited by a rule which permits him to bulk his soap and other by-products

[1] Samuel O. Dunn, *Railway Age Gazette*, September 10, 1909, p. 463. *Cf.* 12 I.C.C. Rep., 510; 9 *Idem*, 440; and 23 *Idem*, 504.

with other goods in securing a wholesale rate. Why may a paper manufacturer not combine paper bags and wrapping paper in one territory as well as another? In this regard the rules in the West and South are naturally much less liberal than in the East. The privilege of mixture has been given only to a limited extent to jobbing and manufacturing centres by means of commodity tariffs. Such mixture is usually restricted to analogous articles, such as agricultural implements, furniture or commodities intended to serve a joint purpose. The recent bitter protest against the discontinuance of the right to ship binder twine with agricultural implements is a case in point. On the other hand, eastern railways are a unit in opposing the bulking of separate shipments in carloads when owned by different shippers. The western and southern roads do not specially forbid it. All such differences come to the fore in any attempt to unify the practice of all the carriers of the country under a single set of regulations.

Assuming the reasonableness of a difference in charges between carload and small shipments, where shall the dividing line as to size be drawn? This is the important and perplexing problem of minimum carload rates. Turning to our excerpt from the Western Classification on page 298, it appears that 24,000 pounds of advertising matter, N. O. S. (not otherwise specified), must be shipped at one time in order to warrant a carload rate. Under such circumstances a consignment of 20,000 pounds would be classified first instead of third class — the difference in rate varying according to distance, but in all cases being substantial. Between St. Louis and St. Joseph, Missouri, for example, the charge would be sixty instead of thirty-five cents per hundredweight. Were the minimum weight for carloads but 15,000 pounds, as in the case of harvesters under the Southern Classification, this particular shipment of advertising matter would have enjoyed the full benefit of wholesale charges.[1] From this instance it is apparent that the point at which the minimum carload weight falls, is of great importance in the determination of the actual rate — an importance also dependent, of course, upon the spread between carload and less-than-carload charges. It is also evident that minimum carload ratings may readily be used as a means of advancing charges. If, as appeared in a recent case,[2] the minimum carload for wool in sacks was advanced between 1896 and 1912 from 15,000 to 20,000 pounds, the effect upon the shipper of a consignment of 18,000 pounds, for example, would be as truly an increase of charges as if the freight rates themselves had been actually advanced. For under the new schedule, he would be compelled to pay less-than-carload charges instead of the lower carload rates formerly granted. Moreover, it is apparent that minimum carload weights may enter seriously into commercial competition in a number of ways. If 45,000 pounds of raw cotton by a special round-bale process can be loaded upon a standard car; when but 25,000 pounds of the ordinary square bales could be carried by the same equipment; it is evident that tariffs based upon the higher minimum would especially favor one set of competitors as against another.[3] They might, in fact, be sufficient to turn the scale entirely in

---

[1] The following wide variations as between the different classifications appear in these excerpts alone, varying from 40,000 to 12,000 lbs, in the Southern Classification, for instance.

    Official Classification —
        Scrap zinc..............................36,000 lbs.
        Acetic acid in carboys ....24,000 lbs.
    Western Classification —
        Advertising matter ....24,000 lbs.
        Advertising racks, iron...................30,000 lbs.
    Southern Classification —
        Zinc concentrates ....40,000 lbs.
        Fodder shredders ....12,000 lbs.
        Harvesters ....15,000 lbs.

Search through the entire list would doubtless disclose a far wider range, with coal or iron at 90,000 lbs. or more, and feathers at the foot of the list.

[2] 23 I.C.C. Rep., 158.   [3] 11 I.C.C. Rep., 328.

favor of the round-bale system throughout the South. Granted, however, that such heavy loading makes for economy in operation, it is clear, nevertheless, that the carload minima must be so established as not to discriminate against the great bulk of shipments of the more common sort. All along the line one meets with such illustrations of the bearing of the minimum carload upon rivalry in business. Large shippers are continually striving for a high minimum. The small shippers oppose it for the same reasons. In a similar way the interest of the manufacturer distributing his goods direct, in competition with middlemen, is vitally affected.[1]

Car capacity, both as regards ability to load and carry economically, is the principal factor in the determination of minimum carload rates. It is largely a question of relative cost of operation.[2] Reference has already been made to the great economy incident to the use of large cars, whereby the paying load becomes less in proportion to the dead weight. This, of course, largely accounts for the steady increase in carload capacity in recent years. But the question is even more complicated. An adjustment must be made between two main groups of freight: first, that which is sufficiently heavy to be readily loaded to the minimum weight in ordinary cars; and, secondly, light and bulky goods of which the common car will contain but a small proportion in bulk of its truck capacity by weight. Fortunately, we may evade the moot point, theoretically, as to whether a carrier is entitled to the same revenue from a given vehicle, whether it be loaded with heavy or light goods; that is to say, whether the rate ought properly to decrease per pound with increase in the density of the lading. This is a technical matter as to cost. But it carries certain implications of considerable importance commercially, as will shortly appear.

[1] Changes in minimum carloads since 1887 by commodities are fully described in "Railways in the United States in 1902," I.C.C., 1903, Part II, p. 17. Their relation to rate increases is evident.

[2] Strombeck; Classification, p. 35 *et seq.; Railway Age Gazette*, June 30, 1911, p. 1696.

CLASSIFICATION

The difficulty of conforming carload minima upon light and bulky articles to those on heavier goods has appeared with each attempt to standardize equipment. Widely divergent rules in the three main classification territories still cause great confusion in this regard. There is a constant temptation to construct extra long or wide cars, particularly in the western states, in order to assist the manufacturers of such light and bulky products as furniture and agricultural machinery in their competition with dealers in the East, shipping under Official Classification requirements. In other words, the penalty carried under the rules as to minimum carloads, for the use of cars larger than the standard, has been much less in the West than in the East and South. The situation has been further complicated in some instances by the arbitrary action of state railway commissions. The experience in this regard is illuminating, as again showing the extreme delicacy of adjustment in such matters under the stress of commercial competition. The short-line distance between the Missouri and Mississippi rivers lies entirely within the state of Missouri. It governs, as we have already seen,[1] the entire rate structure in this part of the country. This commonwealth some years ago by law fixed a carload minimum of 20,000 pounds for furniture, agricultural implements and wagons.[2] As it is not practicable to attain this minimum load on an ordinary standard car, the Missouri shipper was stimulated to demand larger equipment in order that he might avail himself of the lower rate for carload lots. The local railways, accordingly, built such cars, which, of course, travelled far beyond the limits of this single commonwealth. This forced other western roads, in order to protect their clients in the same markets, to adopt a similar policy. The result is that extra large equipment is relatively more common throughout this territory; thereby conferring a distinct advantage over

[1] P. 128, *supra*.
[2] *Railway Age Gazette*, September 24, 1909, p. 553, Samuel O. Dunn, best treats this topic.

their eastern competitors upon western shippers of such light and bulky freight. In pursuance of this same protective policy, the western roads have also enforced distinctly favorable rules as to carload lots applied to several small cars instead of one large one.[1] These troublesome details are given in the hope that they may show how far the ramification of trade competition extends. They re-enforce the conviction that any reform of classification is a matter of extreme difficulty; and, if undertaken at all, must be done under governmental compulsion and by a single universal reform, rather than by any attempt at piecemeal improvement.

Next to ability to load and carry, as a determinant factor in fixing minimum carload weights, the consuming capacity of the market must be considered. A reasonable minimum carload in the East might well be unfair in the West or South. An old-established factory in New England might satisfactorily use a quantity of raw material which in a carload lot would overwhelm a western or southern plant. Thus it comes about that minimum weights on the same goods quite properly vary widely in different territories; being higher in the East than in the West, and least of all in the South. The problem, therefore, of standardizing carload rates throughout the country, unfortunately becomes exceedingly difficult. A compromise will fail to satisfy anybody; and, moreover, such a change of minimum carload weights at once necessitates a remodelling of the particular distance tariff to which it applies. This point was well illustrated in a recent case.[2] A railway accepted for the same carriage at different times two carload shipments of lime from a given concern. On the one, a rate of thirty-four cents per one hundred pounds was based upon a minimum carload weight of 24,000 pounds. On the other twenty-nine cents was assessed upon a minimum of 30,000 pounds. The carrier alleged that these differences in rates per pound were entirely compatible in

---

[1] *Cf.* the "two-for-one" rule in the Indianapolis case; 16 I.C.C. Rep., 254. [2] 23 I.C.C. Rep., 259; also 23 *Idem*, 226.

view of the difference in carload minima. It then appeared that these minima, especially with a perishable commodity like lime, varied considerably according to destination. Large distributing centres were given low rates on high minima, while small towns, consuming relatively less, were best served by a lower carload minimum to which a higher rate per pound was applied. In other words, the close interrelation between the rate and the minimum was a matter of great commercial importance.

The relation of carloads to consuming capacity of the market is an element in the trade policy of protection to clients extended by the railway. The difficulty of properly relating rates upon raw and finished products has already been discussed. Carload minima must also be considered in this connection. Why should 50,000 pounds be prescribed as the carload limit on corn to Texas points, when the limit on corn-meal is only 30,000 pounds? Evidently differences in loading capacity are inadequate as an explanation. Nor can this be accounted for on the ground of any difference in mere cost of carriage. The explanation is purely commercial — springing from the competition between northern mills and mills located in Texas, both making use of raw material from the same fields. A heavy carload minimum is entirely practicable on corn for the Texas miller; but an equally heavy carload requirement on corn-meal would shut out the northern miller entirely from many local points. For the market at these small places is, of course, relatively restricted.[1] There can be no doubt that every feature of classification, even down to the last minute details of carload minima, stands in such intimate relation to commercial competition, that to disturb it in one regard may entail the most far-reaching consequences.

Ever since 1888 the constantly increasing elaboration of the three main classifications in force, with all the resulting incon-

[1] 11 I.C.C., 223. *Cf.* also p. 395, *infra.*

sistencies and overlappings, has led to a persistent demand for the introduction of a single uniform classification for the entire country. Soon after the passage of the original Act to Regulate Commerce in 1887, a resolution passed the House of Representatives directing the prescription of such a classification. Apparently the Interstate Commerce Commission was fully alive to the difficulties of such an undertaking. The railways were induced to move in the matter, but to no purpose.[1] This first abortive attempt reflected the mutual jealousies of competing roads, as well as the difficulties of suiting a single classification to the variety of local conditions existing throughout the country. All that was done was the recommendation of a "Board of Uniform Freight Classification," comprising two members from each of the important territorial bodies and including both the Mexican and Canadian carriers. Changes were to be made by a two-thirds vote. Jurisdiction over the tripartite division of territory, east, south and west, was to be assigned to district chairmen. Final authority for the country at large was to be vested solely in the whole board. The absolute refusal of the New York Central & Hudson River to accede to this plan prevented its acceptance. Apparently too many special or commodity rates were in force upon its line, in order to hold its powerful clients in markets all over the country, to make it practicable to adopt the scheme. Efforts toward uniformity were renewed in 1890, confined this time, however, to an attempt to merge the Official and Western Classifications. But the same jealous regard of local interests in each territory, especially with reference to the treatment of carload ratings, once more proved an insuperable obstacle. The trunk lines insisted upon such specially low charges on small shipments as would enable manufacturers and jobbers in the East to hold their markets in remote districts in competition with rivals in the Middle West. The issue raised in the New York Board

[1] Nothing was accomplished, beyond the preparation of a comprehensive report, under the chairmanship of J. W. Midgley in June, 1890.

of Trade case, previously discussed, led to the defeat of this plan.

A notable revival of interest in uniform classification under governmental authority has taken place since the enactment of the Mann-Elkins amendments to the Interstate Commerce Law in 1906. An independent bill in Congress to authorize the enforcement of such a schedule failed. The railways were stimulated, however, to make a further attempt to solve the difficulty.[1] Protracted sessions during 1907-1908 by a conference of five representatives from different parts of the country, known as the Uniform Classification Committee, led to many concessions and compromises in favor of harmony. The committee expressed its belief that a uniform classification could be drawn up in time; but it emphasized the important point that all changes in classification must be accompanied by such advances or reductions in the distance tariffs as to insure the prevailing commercial adjustments.

The latest advertisement of the difficulties of uniform classification took place in connection with the attempted introduction in 1912 of various amendments and reforms proposed by this Uniform Classification Committee.[2] Acting in conjunction with the National Association of Railway Commissioners, an earnest attempt seems to have been made to eliminate differences between the three great schedules. Few articles were actually shifted from one class to another, the effort being concentrated upon the establishment of more uniform rules and descriptions. It was alleged by shippers that more often than otherwise, these changes had brought about an advance rather than a reduction of charges. It is difficult to decide as to this. But it is clear that progress in the direction of uniformity is

---

[1] *Railway Age Gazette*, May 10, 1907, p. 727; 1909, p. 415. The whole movement is reflected in the Proceedings of the National Convention of State Railroad Commissioners year by year.

[2] *Railway Age Gazette*, 1912, pp. 211, 224, 252 and 370.

taking place. For example, the minimum carload weight for paper, once varying greatly in different parts of the country, was fixed at an intermediate figure which fairly satisfied conflicting interests. Many opportunities for personal discrimination were also eradicated. Grading according to value, for instance, has in the past been a prolific source of abuse. Candy at less than fifteen cents a pound rated third class, but if of higher value moving on first-class rates, offered an incentive to false declaration on the part of unscrupulous shippers which was very properly eliminated. Abolition of the distinction between finished stationery and flat paper, put an end to possible under-classification in the same way. Naturally the carriers in abolishing such fine distinctions, grade upward rather than downward. Much objection was also made at this time to beneficial modification of the rules for mixed carload shipments. Binder twine had for years been classified with ploughs and harvesters rather than with ropes and cordage. Half a carload of agricultural machinery, therefore, with half a carload of twine, formerly moving under carload rates, was no longer, as proposed, to be allowed the privilege of mixing. Similarly, abolition of the right to bunch wood-working and iron-working machinery naturally aroused protest. Such details are here offered, not because of their intrinsic importance, but as illustrating the opposition on behalf of shippers to any movement toward uniformity, even in these minor details. What the force of this opposition would become, were propositions advanced for shifting thousands of articles bodily from one class to another, may be readily imagined. The experience thus far obtained, emphasizes the point that any considerable improvement must be carried through, if at all, by direct pressure from governmental authority, not upon the carriers alone *but upon the shippers as well.*

The degree of complexity at the present day incident to overlapping and conflicting jurisdiction of the several state and railway classification committees and associations, may be best described by means of a few examples.[1] Traffic originating in Southeastern Freight Association territory, except Florida, destined to cities in trunk line territory is governed by the Southern Classification all the way if moving on through rates; if on local rates, the Official Classification applies north of the Ohio river. From "Green Line territory"[2] to Pacific coast terminals, the Southern Classification governs to the Mississippi or other gateways; the Western Classification beyond. But if it originate in Louisiana or Mississippi, the Western Classification governs all the way. From most places in Tennessee, Western Classification rules govern all the way, "subject to commodity rates or less-than-carload consignments, classified not lower than fourth class." To Wisconsin from points throughout the South, the Southern Classification governs all the way. But to Minnesota, generally, Southern rules govern to the Ohio river crossing, while Western rules apply to the balance of the trip; unless the goods move through trunk line territory by way of the Virginia gateways, in which case the Official Classification is effective. These are only a few samples chosen from a large collection. Is it any wonder that to the uninitiated, rate making under such conditions appears to be almost a superhuman task; and is it surprising that to the unscrupulous, such complicated conditions give rise to more or less successful attempts at evasion of published rates?

The present threefold territorial division of the country, for the purposes of classification, naturally affords all sorts of possibilities in the way of veiled discrimination, not merely as between persons but as affecting the interests of different competing markets. Not only is there liability to confusion, but the way is paved for all sorts of favoritism. Wherever shipment is made from one classification territory to another, it is always possible to adjust the rates with a view to local advantage. For instance, one of the principal causes of complaint in the

[1] Lectures by O. M. Rogers, La Salle Extension University, Chicago, 1910. [2] P. 12, *supra*.

South is the advantage which Nashville, Tennessee, enjoys through having all of its rates from eastern and northern centres made upon the Official Classification. Inasmuch as the rates under the Southern Classification are considerably higher, this operates to place other competing cities in the South under a distinct disability in competition with Nashville. It is possible, therefore, for the Louisville & Nashville by this means to build up one community at the expense of another. The same device gives Richmond, Norfolk and the other Virginian cities a great advantage over their competitors.[1] Again, rates from New York to Memphis and New Orleans are made upon the Official Classification, by whatever route; while to intermediate points, such as Vicksburg, Natchez, and Baton Rouge, they go on the rates prescribed by the Southern Classification, which are considerably higher. From New York to St. Paul through Chicago, shipments are made on the low rate basis of the Official Classification; while from Chicago to St. Paul they go under the Western Classification. From Birmingham, Alabama, to St. Paul, the rates as far as Chicago are based upon the Southern schedule, and from thence on under the Western. From San Francisco to St. Paul, the Western Classification prevails, unless the freight is carried under the commodity rates of the Transcontinental schedule. The peculiar situation of Nashville on shipments from the Northeast has already been stated. This immediately complicates the rates from so-called Cook County Junctions — that is to say, from Chicago territory. All consignments for the entire distance are governed by the Southern Classification. This, in face of the low Official Classification rates from trunk line territory, operates as a discrimination against Chicago. Even more complicated still are the combinations by which rates are made from local points in the North into the Far Southwest. And still farther complexity results from the existence, as already mentioned, in

---

[1] Well brought out in the Danville case, 8 I.C.C. Rep., 409 and 571; and in the complaint of Wilmington, 9 *Idem*, 48.

several parts of the country, such as Iowa, Illinois, Georgia, etc., of state classifications, prescribed by the railway commissions. These, to be sure, are intended for application only to local rates. But by this means, the jobbing interests of the localities are protected, without at the same time giving consideration to an equitable adjustment as between all the remoter interests concerned.[1] One of the primary advantages, therefore, from the unification of the three systems now existing, would be the possibility of readjusting not only definitely, but also equitably, the conflicting interests of various shippers and communities now tied up by these local arrangements.

A recent case[2] illustrates the bearing of classification rules upon competition in trade as between rival cities. Chicago and most of the Ohio river gateways enjoy a so-called "two-for-one-rule," permitting the application of carload rates on part carloads in excess of full car ladings. The complaint alleged that the denial of this privilege to Indianapolis, whereby less-than-carload rates were charged on excess fractional carloads, unjustly discriminated against this city in the transportation of various light and bulky articles, such as vehicles and furniture, in competition for trade throughout the Southwest. The difficulty arose from a conflict between rules in the Western Classification and the Southwestern Tariff Committee, the latter being a subordinate body having jurisdiction over local practices in Texas and the neighborhood. The rule in one case provided that where a car of sufficient capacity to accommodate light and bulky shipments could not be promptly furnished, two smaller cars would be provided, subject to wholesale rates, however the consignment was divided between the two cars. The Commission declined to interfere in this case, anticipating the necessity for a thoroughgoing revision of all such rules

---

[1] Notable recent instances are afforded in the State Rate cases now pending before the U. S. Supreme Court, and in the Shreveport case, 23 I.C.C. Rep., 31; both discussed in chapter XX.
[2] 16 I.C.C. Rep., 254.

which, it is obvious, almost invite manipulation of rates and improper discrimination.

Even a cursory examination of the classification a few years ago would bring to light all sorts of petty anomalies and inexplicable conflicts both of description and rates. Most of these doubtless had some warrant originally, but it seems, indeed, as if many differences might be eliminated.[1] For instance, "excelsior spring beds K. D. (knocked down), sawdust, and leather belting, are all in the second class of the Official Classification, when shipped in less-than-carload lots. In the Western, only the belting and beds are in the second class, excelsior is third and sawdust fourth; while in the Southern, beds are first class, belting second class, excelsior fifth class, and sawdust sixth." The recent complaint of the Greater Des Moines Committee[2] disclosed an odd state of affairs under which old shoes were given a carload rating to Des Moines — an advantage not extended to new and unused footwear. Why should axes be given carload rating in trunk line territory when the freight rate on hatchets is the same whether the shipments are in 100 pound or 20,000 pound lots? Is it logical that cotton piece goods from Atlanta to Boston should be differently classified from the same commodity exchanged between the same two cities in the opposite direction; or that goods should enter Richmond, Virginia, on one classification and go out on another? Such anomalies are sometimes difficult to account for. Their existence, however, despite the efforts of the carriers to eliminate them and to keep them eliminated, emphasizes strongly the need for such continual revision as shall more generally standardize practice. Few carriers alone are able to withstand pressure from powerful shippers. It is difficult, in fact, even for the classification committees to oppose them. The strong hand of the government should enforce

[1] Some are described in the Reports of the U. S. Industrial Commission, 1900; and the Senate (Elkins) Committee, 1905.
[2] 14 I. C.C. Rep., 294.

harmonious action to the fullest degree compatible with the growth of trade and conflicting commercial interests. It would help the railways even more than the shippers.

And yet, bearing in mind all the disadvantages and evils of the present threefold system, the obstacles incident to the substitution of a single uniform classification for the United States grow more impressive as one examines them in detail. Our vast territory and the extreme diversity of agricultural and industrial conditions render the problem far more difficult than in the compact and more homogeneous communities abroad. The primary advantage of the present system is that each of the three existing classifications more or less clearly reflects local trade conditions in its own territory. From the point of view of transportation, the same commodity may well be able to yield widely different proportions of the total revenue levied upon the traffic of that section. For example, cotton piece goods may be rated first class in Western territory, fourth class in Southern, second class less fifteen per cent. in Official territory, and one-third of first class in the transcontinental tariffs. The reason for this diversity of treatment is that such cotton piece goods both in the South and the East are a staple product of the district. The rates, therefore, in each case are intended to foster the manufacture of cotton by according a relatively low freight rate upon its output. In the West, on the other hand, where no cotton is raised and no cotton mills exist, these goods become much more valuable, as classified, relative to other commodities. Oranges or lemons in southern California are favored by almost commodity rates in order to foster the industry in that locality. But these citrus fruits reaching New England as a luxury, may consequently there be made to contribute a much larger proportion of the railways' revenue. The East, as a rule, classifies manufactured products relatively low, inasmuch as it is the home territory for industry of this sort. But these products, when they pass beyond the Mississippi, rise almost automatically to a higher class as they increase in value to the community in which they are consumed. How different are the commercial conditions under which wool is rated east and west! In one territory it is distributed to manufacturers in small lots at way stations; in the other it moves long distances in solid carload lots.

One further illustration may make our point clear. At first sight it is anomalous that in the East the rates on cattle and shoes between New York and Boston are not widely different, namely nineteen cents and twenty-five cents, respectively, per one hundred pounds; while as between Montana and Chicago, the rate on shoes west bound is almost four times as great as the rate on cattle over the same haul eastward. In other words, rates on shoes in the East are at bedrock, whereas in the West it is the cattle rates which are held at the lowest possible point. Ton-mile rates on shoes, in other words, increase progressively toward the west, while ton-mile rates on cattle rise, contrariwise, in the direction of the stronghold of manufactures. The difference between the two, however, is in the fact that the upper level of what the traffic will bear is very much greater in the case of one than of the other. Cattle, possibly, may never support more than seventy-five cents per hundredweight; while shoes can be moved under rates four times as high.

Obviously any mere compromise between divergent classifications, each based upon the protection of a local constituency against competition from outside its own territory, can hardly prove satisfactory. Cotton piece goods, already instanced in this regard, if grouped as first class in the West, second class less fifteen per cent. in the East, and fourth class in the South, would hardly be adequately treated in a uniform classification for the entire country by averaging these different figures. For neither the West nor the South would be satisfied — the rating being too high to fully protect the southern mills against competitors in New England; nor, on the other hand, would the classification be sufficiently high in the West to yield the roads proportionately the revenue which goods of that character ought properly to contribute. The East, alone, lying intermediate between the other two, would not be greatly disturbed. The necessary outcome, it is predicted, of the adoption of any such average or uniform classification would be the quotation of exceptional commodity rates wherever the uniform classification was at variance with local interests. The increase in commodity ratings after 1887 — now happily reversed — may perhaps be in part accounted for in this way. Any such stimulation of exceptional ratings would be a primary objection to any uniform classification for the United States as a whole. As one witness before the Interstate Commerce Commission testified, "If ever there is a uniform classification, it will take a warehouse to hold the commodity tariffs." Were such the case, far greater complexity and possible discrimination might exist than at the present time.

A second equally important disadvantage of the prescription of a uniform classification arises from the fact, already noted, that classifications and distance tariffs are interlocking and interdependent. Any change of the one involves a change of the other. Therefore, a unification of the three existing classifications would render it necessary to overhaul from top to bottom the distance tariffs under which it was to be applied all over the country. For example, the rate from New York to Atlanta, first class, being $1.14, while the rate from New York to Chicago, about the same distance, first class, was 75 cents; to choose a first-class rating which should apply on both these lines would involve, not only a re-classification of the commodities, but also that the new rates applying upon first-class goods should be somewhere between $1.14 and 75 cents. Inasmuch as it had taken many years to reach the present adjustment, it seems hardly possible that a new arrangement could be made which would yield the railways a satisfactory return upon their traffic. The difficulty herein suggested was clearly instanced in the case of a comparison made between the Southern Classification and the Uniform Classification proposed in 1890. The difficulty, and always a prominent one, was that the Uniform Classification was largely for carload lots, while the practice was entirely different in the old Southern Classification. Moreover, most of the Southern rates were given for goods "released"; that is to say, at the owner's risk. Cotton piece goods, non-released, in less-than-carload lots from New York to Atlanta, were charged sixty cents a hundredweight under the old Southern Classification. As reclassified in the suggested Uniform Classification, the rate was ninety-eight cents; and was given only for "released," that is to say, at owner's risk. The difference for the same commodity from Louisville to Atlanta was as fifty-six cents in the old Southern, to ninety-two cents under the Uniform. Canned goods, not otherwise specified, "non-released," in less-than-carload lots from Louisville to Atlanta, were charged sixty-eight cents under the old Southern Classification. The new Uniform Classification, in order to yield the same revenue, made it necessary to charge a rate of eighty-one cents. Differences of this kind were manifest in every one of the thousands of commodities. In other words, the adoption of a uniform classification meant to abolish by a stroke of the pen all the old rates which formerly existed. An entirely new schedule of rates would have had to be worked out; with the most uncertain results upon revenue and upon the rival commercial interests concerned. The magnitude of such a task can be scarcely appreciated. Years would be required to reach a condition of relative stability once more.

The close interdependence of classification and distance tariffs, as well as, incidentally, the differing spread of rates between various groups of goods under the three existing classification systems, are so fundamental in their bearing on reform that yet another illustration may not be out of place. It is given in the following table. This shows the rates from St. Louis — standing at the meeting point of the main classification territories — for approximately equal distances out in three different directions.

CLASSIFICATION

Rates	Cents per 100 lbs.

Southern Classification —
St. Louis to Nashville
(323 miles)

1	2	3	4	5	6	A	B
61	52	45	35	28	23	22	26

Official Classification —
St. Louis to Louisville
(317 miles)

1	2	3	4	5	6
41	34½	25½	17½	15	12

Western Classification —
St. Louis to St. Joseph
(320 miles)

1	2	3	4	5	A	B	C	D	E
60	45	35	27	22	24½	19½	17	13½	11

Illinois Classification —
St. Louis to Chicago
(284 miles)

1	2	3	4	5	6	7	8	9	10
43.3	35.2	27.5	22	17.6	16.6	15.1	13.5	10.7	9.6

One line penetrates Southern territory 323 miles to Nashville; another goes eastward 317 miles to Louisville under Official ratings; and the third extends westward 320 miles to St. Joseph, according to the schedules of the Western Classification. To these three there is also added a set of rates north bound under the Illinois Classification which applies between St. Louis and Chicago, 284 miles. This last schedule, of course, is prescribed by the state railway commission. The first point to notice is the widely different number of groups in the four schedules. One is divided into eight classes; another into six; while the last two are each spread over ten subdivisions. Secondly, bearing in mind that the three upper schedules govern approximately the same mileage, it will be noted that the Official rate, first class, is only about two-thirds of that in the other two classes. If one then compares the sixth group in each case, an even greater divergence appears — the Official rate being only about one-half of that in the other two cases. Or, taking the lowest rates of all in the three upper schemes — always, be it noted, for equal mileages — it now appears that the Official and the Western descend to about the same figure, while the Southern is arrested at a point more than twice as high. The primary significance of this showing is, of course, that a single uniform classification in which all of these three systems should be merged, means not merely a re-assignment of all possible commodities in a given number of classes; but also a complete recasting of the distance tariffs as well. In other words, as aforesaid, freight rates being compounded of the two factors, distance charge and classification, all the delicate adjustments based upon commercial competition throughout the country, would be thrown into utter confusion; unless every modification of the grouping of classes were accompanied by a corresponding change in the rates per mile. A task sufficient indeed to appall the best of traffic experts!

To complete the demonstration of the complexity of present arrangements, and yet of the danger incident to rudely disturbing them, one should apply the classified rates in the preceding paragraph for these equal hauls to particular commodities. Take household goods in carloads, for example: —

	Cents per 100 lbs.	Per Cent. of first-class rate.
St. Louis to Nashville	23	38
St. Louis to Louisville	34.5	83
St. Louis to St. Joseph	19.5	33
St. Louis to Chicago	15.1	35

Examination of the classification volumes thus assigns these the following rates in the three directions for equal distances out of St. Louis. Going east the charge would be 34.5 cents, going west 19.5 cents, and going south 23 cents per 100 pounds, respectively. The hodgepodge is made more manifest by the right hand column in this table, in which the percentage of first-class rates levied upon household goods in carloads under the four classifications is shown. Under the Official system, with the lowest first-class rates, as above noted, the rate on household goods is higher than under any of the other three. The result is that the relation between the rate on household goods and first-class goods is eighty-three per cent.; whereas in the other two cases it is substantially less than half this percentage. This single illustration, it is hoped, may drive home the conclusion that there is an immense mass of fortuitous and utterly unreasonable allocation under the classification systems as they are at present established.[1] But whether that may be used as an argument in favor of substituting a single uniform classification is open to serious doubt. Rather does it serve to emphasize the fact that rigid revision of the present scheme under Federal control, perhaps, is more necessary than an experiment in uprooting the entire system.

A few general conclusions may be drawn from this rather over-elaborate description of present conditions as to classification in the United States. It has been necessary, however, to reiterate details in order to make clear the extremely unsatisfactory situation at the present time. In fact, in this domain of classification, standardization of practice so characteristic of American rate making and operation in general, has noticeably lagged behind. Whether it will be possible, in view of the wide extent of the country and the diversity of its climatic and commercial conditions, ever to devise a single uniform classification is open to serious doubt. Even the Interstate Commerce Commission, once a leader in the demand for uniformity, now concedes this fact in particular instances.[2] Thus: — "wool east of the Mississippi is taken up at numerous points and is carried

---

[1] "In the Southern Classification plate glass, all sizes, in carloads, is rated third class; window glass and rough or ribbed glass, fifth class. In the Western Classification plate glass, outside measurement not exceeding 100 united inches (that is, length and width added), is rated fourth class in carloads; window glass, and rough, rolled, or ribbed glass, fifth class. In the Official Classification plate glass, outside measurement not exceeding 80 united inches, is rated fourth class in carloads; window glass and rough and ribbed glass, fifth class. Thus it appears that in Southern Classification territory plate glass of ordinary size is rated higher than in Official or Western Classification territories; and while in the two latter territories plate glass is rated one class higher than window glass, or rough or ribbed glass, in Southern Classification territory, plate glass is rated two classes higher than rough, ribbed, or window glass. As applied to the transportation from St. Louis territory to Memphis it results in payment by the consignee at Memphis of rates on plate glass which are 50 per cent. higher than the rates on window glass." — 21 I.C.C. Rep., 113.

[2] 23 I.C.C. Rep., 169.

under comparatively light loading. What would be a fair classification there, would not be just in the Far West, where the movement is almost entirely in carloads and where the actual loading is from two to three times that in Official Classification territory. We are of the opinion that wool should be classified under the Western Classification as second class, l. c. l., and fourth class, c. l.," etc. The experience of England is, of course, commonly cited as a precedent.[1] In that little country the ever-increasing complexity of classification was precisely parallel to our own. From simple schedules for a few hundred articles, the number of items steadily increased until there were over 4,000. At this point the government intervened; and after tedious and protracted sessions under the auspices of the Board of Trade in 1888 the whole schedule was brought down to 1,400 separate items. All the complicated and confusing rules were harmonized and many anomalies were cut out. Certain it is that matters should be firmly taken in hand in this country in the same manner. The separate state classifications and hundreds of conflicting rules and jurisdictions should be eradicated. Even if a single uniform classification be proved impracticable, as seems to me likely, it might still be possible to greatly simplify the present intolerable mix-up. There should be a representative of the Interstate Commerce Commission on each of the classification committees, ready at all times to exert pressure for simplification and uniformity.[2] The three main classification committees, supposing that they shall continue to exist, should interlock by exchange of representatives. The greater the reform flowing from the initiative of the carriers themselves, the better. Thus, in time, matters may become sufficiently standardized as between the three main committees so that, under legal compulsion or otherwise, the final problem of uni-

---

[1] Acworth, Elements, etc., p. 99; McDermott, Railways, p. 29; Ripley, Railway Problems, chap. XXV.

[2] 22 I.C.C. Rep., 103, is a fine instance of rectification of unjust classification rules on vehicles into the South from Toledo, Ohio.

formity may be tackled by recasting the whole body of tariffs and classifications together. But such a task at this writing appears almost superhuman. Conditions may, of course, so shape themselves ultimately that it may be brought about. But, in the meantime, steady and persistent pressure should be exercised in the direction of this final goal. Reform of classification practice is certainly the greatest need of the time in the transportation field.

CHAPTER X

THE TRUNK LINE RATE SYSTEM: A DISTANCE TARIFF

Conditions prevalent in 1875, 356. — Various elements distinguished, 358. — The MacGraham percentage plan, 360. — Bearing upon port differentials, 361. — The final plan described, 363. — Competition at junction points, 368. — Independent transverse railways, 370. — Commercial competition, 372. — Limits of the plan, 375. — Central Traffic Association rules, 376.

THE trunk line freight rate system effectively demonstrates certain principles in railway economics which are of great importance. The danger of arbitrary administrative interference without a full understanding of the intricacies of rate making, and at the same time the essential soundness of American railway practice in seeking independently to solve these complex problems by equitable means, are amply illustrated. The fallacy of certain objections to governmental control, on the other hand, is revealed with corresponding clearness. Three principles in particular deserve mention in this connection. These are: (1) that the element of distance should be a prime factor in the final adjustment of rates as between competing localities;[1] (2) that coöperation and agreement between competing carriers are essential to any comprehensively fair system; and (3) that permanency and stability of rates are of equal importance with elasticity. That all three of these results have been voluntarily worked out in practice by the trunk lines is a tribute at once to the ability and fairness of their traffic officials. Standards are thus established toward which the carriers in the West and South should strive, as soon as their local traffic conditions will permit, in an endeavor to promote good relations with the shipping and consuming public.

[1] Compare chap. IV, p. 102, *supra*.

That distance tariffs, modified in part to suit commercial conditions, are not only theoretically sound, but entirely practicable, this study aims to prove. The bogey of German rate schedules vanishes into thin air when it appears that the greatest railway companies in the United States have for years adopted the same principles in working out their tariffs. The long and short haul rule is here enforced, not alone as between various points on the *same* line, but also as between points equally distant from a common destination on *different* roads. Thirty years ago the trunk lines conceded the principle, for the recognition of which the shippers of the West and South are now so vociferously clamoring before Congress and the Federal courts.

This desirable end could never have been attained if the several competing companies had not been able to act in cooperation. The erroneous popular opinion that railway competition must be preserved in the public interest, had it been legally enforced in this territory a generation ago, would have prevented absolutely any comprehensive solution of the problem. Until Congress abandons this theory, and treats railways as essentially monopolistic, thereafter to be protected and maintained as *beneficent* monopolies through adequate governmental supervision, the lesson of trunk line experience will not have been learned. And, finally, the interesting fact that for almost thirty years it has not been necessary to change either the main system or, in many instances, the actual rates charged thereunder, is an offset to the contention that success in railway operation is to be judged by the instability of rates, seeking to follow constantly the ups and downs of commercial conditions. Certain modifications, especially in export and import traffic, or wherever water rates have to be made or met, are, of course, inevitable. But it is absurd to reason from this that railway tariffs in the main need to be continually jostled about at the behest of the shipping public. Of course, if one railway changes its rates, all the rest must follow. That is the principal reason why many of our rate schedules have been as uncertain as the weather. But there is no reason why, if all parties in competition keep good faith and observe their tariffs, a schedule of class rates for domestic shipments should not remain practically constant.

Take the rates on raw cotton from Mississippi river points like Memphis to New England cities, for example. Was any staple product ever subject to greater fluctuations in price than raw cotton, varying as it has in the last few years, from five to fifteen cents a pound? Yet through it all, good years and bad, whether for the planter or the manufacturer, the freight rate has stood unchanged at fifty-five cents per hundredweight. In the same way, within the limits hereafter to be described, the trunk line rate system has endured for a generation. Founded upon sound and, consequently, defensible principles, it has promoted good feeling between railway and shipper. And, if the changes of classification since 1900 had not been made, one may reasonably doubt whether the demand for Federal legislation would have been any more insistent throughout the eastern central states than it now is in New England.

The causes leading to the adoption of a systematic rate scheme by the trunk lines acting jointly [1] can be understood only in the light of the conditions existing about 1875. The Baltimore & Ohio Railroad had entered Chicago in 1874,

[1] The literature on the subject is scanty. Much of the material has necessarily been gathered in the field by conference with traffic officials and others. My hearty thanks are due primarily to Paul P. Rainer, Esq., chief of the Joint Rate Inspection Bureau at Chicago, for his willingness to impart such explanation of this complicated matter as the delicate responsibilities of his important post permit. The map published herewith, while in part prepared from the actual percentage tables, with his permission and that of several important trunk line officials concerned, has been checked and corrected by his official copyright map of January 1, 1899. While the scheme of graphic representation is entirely different, the facts represented are the same. I am also especially indebted to H. C. Barlow, Esq., formerly president of the Terre Haute & Evansville Railroad and now director of the Chicago Commercial Association, and to J. W.

after which time the most furious rate wars between the four trunk lines had been in progress. The main dependence of all these lines was still upon the grain traffic, and all of this was moving in one direction toward the seaboard. As late as 1882, seventy-three per cent. of the trunk line tonnage east bound consisted of such commodities.[1] Moreover, — and this is a point of especial importance, — the bulk of this grain originated in the territory east of the Mississippi and south of Chicago. Over four-fifths of the eastbound traffic came from the states of Illinois, Indiana, Ohio, Michigan, and Pennsylvania. The great northwest and trans-Mississippi territory was not yet opened up. Wisconsin and Iowa contributed only about ten per cent. of the eastbound tonnage, while over two-thirds of the westbound business did not pass beyond Illinois.[2] Nor was the traffic concentrated as yet in the larger cities. Mr. Fink makes it clear that most of the business was gathered up by the trunk lines and their connections from small towns along the way. The modern problem of the great city in competition with the small towns was as yet unknown.

Midgley, Esq., for many years one of the Trunk Line Commissioners, for assistance in many ways.

The principal references consulted are included in the following list:

1874. Windom Committee Report, officially known as Report of the Select Committee on Transportation Routes to the Seaboard, 43d Congress, 1st Session, Senate Report No. 307, vol. I, pp. 24–30; vol. II, pp. 7, 80, 283.
1879. Hepburn Committee Report, New York State, Special Committee on Railroads, 8 vols., pp. 3001–3006, 3102–3111.
1886. Cullom Committee Report, 49th Congress, 1st Session, Senate Report No. 46, vol. II, p. 101.
1887. Typewritten Record, Opinion, etc., of the Interstate Commerce Commission in Detroit Board of Trade v. Grand Trunk, etc., Railways. Also the Toledo case (1889) and that of Pratt Lumber Company (1905), I.C.C. Reports, vol. II, p. 315; vol. V, p. 166; and vol. X, p. 29.
1890. Senate Report on the Transportation Interests of the United States and Canada, 51st Congress, 1st Session, Senate Report No. 847, pp. 497, 611–636.
1892. Cincinnati Freight Bureau case. Copy of Record before the Interstate Commerce Commission, etc., United States Circuit Court for Southern District of Ohio, In Equity No. 4748, vol. I, pp. 42–53. (Reprint.)
1900. Report of United States Industrial Commission, vol. IV, pp. 556–562.
1905. Elkins Committee, officially known as Hearings before the Committee on Interstate Commerce, United States Senate, 5 vols., vol. II, p. 1569, and vol. III, p. 2271.
1905. Record of Proceedings before the Illinois Railroad and Warehouse Commission in the Matter of Revision of the Schedule of Reasonable Maximum Rates, etc., Springfield, especially pp. 31 et seq. (Reprint.)
1876–1905. Proceedings and Circulars, Joint Executive Committee and Joint Rate Committee of the Trunk Line, etc., Associations.

[1] Fink, Adjustment of Railroad Transportation Rates, etc., p. 16.
[2] *Ibid.*, pp. 19 and 52.

The trunk lines had few feeders. Only the main stems to Chicago had been built. Consequently these central states were served by a host of little cross lines, built as local enterprises, many of them radiating from Chicago, Cincinnati, Toledo, or Cleveland at right angles with the trunk lines, and, for the main part, engaged in an endeavor to open up their territories to water communication with the East by way of the lakes and the Erie Canal. Rail rates, nominally at least, were still high, the rate first-class Chicago to New York, for example, being about double its present figure; and the conditions of railway operation were such that water competition was a matter for grave concern. Every change in the lake situation was at once reflected in the rail rates, violent dislocations at the opening and closing of navigation in the spring and fall being of especial importance.

Among these confusing elements in the problem of trunk line rate adjustment five distinct phases were prominent. In the first place the four trunk lines were a unit in opposition to the diversion of traffic to the Great Lakes and the Erie Canal. However much they might bicker with one another afterward, — apportionment of the rail business being a distinct feature of the problem, — their interests at the outset were identical respecting the necessity of holding the business on land. Water competition by way of the lakes or the Ohio river was a danger common to them all. The intensity of this pressure may be understood from the statement that the trunk lines were not even consulted in making the Chicago-New York rate on which the western lines pro-rated. They had no voice in it, merely accepting the figure offered them by their connections into Chicago.[1] The second feature of the problem, namely, the division of the all-rail traffic among the competing carriers, is immaterial to the main question before us. Thirdly, it was essential to the trunk lines to restrict and control the activities of the

[1] Windom Committee Report, II, p. 7.

subsidiary cross lines and feeders, most of which, as has been said, were independent. Many of these, aside from having a direct interest in their longest haul to a terminus on the lakes or the Ohio river, had been built by local capital, and were administered in the interests of the lake cities or Cincinnati and Louisville. There was no unity whatever in their policies, and the most ridiculous wastes of transportation resulted. Grain was literally meandering toward the East instead of moving by a direct route.[1] Joint through rates would be made by the most extraordinary chain of connecting links leading to the seaboard by very circuitous ways.[2]

A fourth evil, akin to this, consisted of the difficulty of maintaining through rates, not as among the trunk lines who might be made parties to a pool, but by reason of cut-throat competition between their western connections.[3] The agents of these western lines would indiscriminately cut rates to or from points on their lines, and then expect their trunk line connections to accept a proportionate shrinkage of the joint through rate for their part of the haul. The weaker companies would, of course, be susceptible to such temptations in order to secure the business. No stable apportionment of this western traffic among the eastern lines would be possible until they could agree upon a fair rate for the trunk line haul, and rigidly adhere to it. And, finally, water competition, causing constant fluctuations in the lake and Ohio river rates, while directly potent only at waterway points, was continually putting the through rates from these points out of line with the local rates from non-competitive inland centres. Or, perhaps, the Ohio river and lake rates would be out of joint with one another. The Chicago basis, if applied to Paducah, would make a rate on tobacco that would send it *via* New Orleans.[4]

[1] Waste of transportation as an economic problem has already been discussed in chap. IX, *supra*.
[2] This persisted even in 1890. Consult 51st Cong., 1st sess., Sen. Rep., No. 847, p. 616.   [3] Hepburn Committee, pp. 3006–3010.
[4] Hepburn Committee Report, p. 318.

Products would go down the Mississippi after the lakes had been closed by ice. A considerable amount of corn was certainly moved to New York by that route.[1] Some device for coördination of the through and local rates — or, as one might put it, for the distribution of the localized shock of water rate changes — was imperatively necessary.

An ingenious rate clerk named MacGraham, in the offices of the Pennsylvania Railroad, proposed a comprehensive scheme for meeting these difficulties which was first used for westbound rates on December, 15, 1871. The Chicago-New York rate was to constitute a basis, upon which all other rates were to be made in percentages, according to their relative distance from New York.[2] Thus, assuming Chicago to be 900 odd miles from New York, the rate from a point 600 miles inland would be about sixty-six and two-thirds per cent. of the Chicago rate, whatever that might be. Whenever the lake rate at Chicago changed, every other rate throughout trunk line territory would vary in due proportion. Relativity of charges would thus be preserved. Moreover, the shortest route, "worked or workable," was to be used in calculating the rates, the basic distance being about 920 miles by the Lake Shore from Chicago to Dunkirk, Ohio, and thence by the Erie to New York. This would give compelling effect to distance as a factor, and would tend to penalize the roundabout carriage of goods. More than this, however, it would render the inland territory directly tributary to New York. From a point, for example, fifty or one hundred miles south of Chicago, Toledo, or Cleveland, the local rate into those towns plus the through rate east to New York would always exceed the rate by a direct route east. For the hypothenuse of a triangle is clearly always shorter than the sum of the other sides. All shipping points equidistant from New York would enjoy equal rates, those rates at any time being determined by the state of water

[1] Windom Committee Report, II, p. 287.
[2] This was adopted officially by the trunk lines April 13, 1876.

competition. This was a manifest advantage to the small inland centres, while the rate on the lake front was not affected. The trunk lines lost something, perhaps, through lower rates at intermediate points; but the gain through diversion of traffic from the lake to the rail lines more than compensated. For conditions were such in the summer of 1875 that the lake boats were prepared to carry grain for almost nothing. The railroads were helpless in such cases.[1] The only real sufferers were the short, independent cross lines and the lake and river cities. Of these, the former were reduced to a status of mere feeders or branches of the trunk lines. They were compelled to accede to the plan, however, by threatened refusal of the trunk lines to turn over business to them west-bound, unless they reciprocated with their grain shipments east-bound.[2] Many of these lines became bankrupt later, and were absorbed by the larger companies.[3] And, as for the cities unfavorably affected, the scheme based upon distance was so obviously fair that their protests were of no avail.[4]

The great contest between the trunk lines over the granting of differentials to Philadelphia and Baltimore, as against New York and Boston, played a not unimportant part in the diplomacy leading to the acceptance of the MacGraham system. The New York Central, the Lake Shore, and the Boston & Albany roads, of course eagerly accepted it, because it promised aid in meeting the lake competition to which they were peculiarly exposed. The Pennsylvania and the Erie, lying considerably further from Lake Erie, would also be benefited,

[1] Hepburn Committee Report, p. 3112.
[2] Record Proceedings Railroad Commission of Illinois in Revision of Maximum Freight Rates, 1905, pp. 32 and 88.
[3] 55th Cong. 1st ses., Sen. Doc. No. 39, p. 33. The Hepburn Committee (p. 3111) describes the local jealousies which prevailed.
[4] Chicago has never become reconciled to it, however, alleging that it injures her commercially. Compare Windom Committee, 1874, vol. i, p. 24; 51st Cong., 1st ses., Sen. Rep. No. 847, 1890, p. 611 *et seq.;* Elkins Committee, 1905, pp. 1433, 2538 *et seq.;* and Record Proceedings Illinois Railroad Commission on Revision of Maximum Rates, 1905. *Cf.* p. 378, *infra.* Seaport differentials are discussed in chap. XI, *infra.*

operating as they did in a territory naturally tributary to them, but exposed to drainage to the lakes by lateral lines. But the Baltimore & Ohio, ever since its entry into Chicago in 1874, had been a thorn in the flesh of the others. The territory along its line was so far from the lakes that it had little to fear from water competition at intermediate points between Chicago and the seaboard. Would it accept a plan primarily intended to meet a danger which, while injuring its powerful rivals, was of less consequence to itself? Fortunately for the scheme, it was based upon the solid principle that distance was of preponderating influence in the adjustment of rates. The entire contention of the Baltimore & Ohio and the Pennsylvania for a differential rate to Baltimore and Philadelphia below New York rested upon this same principle. The distance from Chicago to the southern ports was less. Consequently, they insisted, they were entitled to offer a lower rate. The MacGraham scale and the port differentials were thus logically connected. They stood or fell together. The MacGraham plan materially aided the Baltimore & Ohio in making good its demands.[1] It was acceptable, therefore, by reason of this collateral advantage.

Another factor in the situation appealed to the Pennsylvania and the Baltimore & Ohio. Their lines to tide water were about seventy-five and one hundred miles shorter, respectively, than the shortest line to New York.[2] In the division of the joint through rate between a chain of connecting railway lines this was of great advantage. It always aids the shorter line if pro-rating is based upon mileage. A feeder one hundred miles long pro-rating with a trunk line one thousand miles in length would be entitled to only one-eleventh of the total rate. Were the trunk line only eight hundred miles long, the neutral road might claim one-ninth. This seemingly slight difference

[1] Hepburn Committee, p. 3104.
[2] Distances are given in the Thurman-Washburne-Cooley Advisory Commission on Differentials, etc., of 1882.

might mean several hundred thousand dollars more earnings to the neutral road or feeder, if it turned over its business to the short line.[1] Any emphasis upon distance as a general principle strengthened the Baltimore & Ohio in securing patronage from other roads by this means. The other trunk lines, through acceptance of the MacGraham scale, conceded the distance principle, and with it, coincidently, the pro-rating practice.

After three years' experience, the MacGraham scale was readjusted to conform more closely to the cost of service principle. The plan, as thus revised, is the one still in force.[2] It recognizes that railway charges should be proportioned to the length of haul, so far as actual costs of haulage are concerned; but it first eliminates those constant elements in cost which do not vary with distance. The original MacGraham scale made no such distinctions. The expenses at terminals, such as loading and unloading, are, of course, entirely independent of the distance covered by the shipment. These, being determined roughly by experimentation, are first deducted from an assumed Chicago rate. From the remainder the rate per mile by the shortest route to New York (920 miles) is then calculated by simple division. This rate per mile is then applied to the distance to any intermediate point, and the terminal charge is again added. Thus a rate is found which is reduced to a percentage of the original Chicago base rate.

[1] Hepburn Committee, pp. 3188, 3195. "Taking the Indianapolis & St. Louis Railroad, for example, running to Indianapolis, where they can connect with all the trunk lines. . . . Assume that company had only 100 cars of business per day; if the property went to Baltimore, that company would receive $800 per day more than if it came to New York, pro-rating the rates by mileage to both places; now $800 a day, there being 300 working days in the year, is a difference of $240,000 a year."

[2] The revised table of percentages is reprinted in full in Hepburn Committee Report, p. 3107 et seq.

364 RAILROADS

	Cents per 100 lbs.
For Illustration [1]	
Chicago to New York	25
Less fixed charges on both ends of the line	6
The basis of rate for computation being the remainder, or	19
Using short line mileage 920 miles, Chicago to New York, would yield a rate per mile	00.0206
Short line mileage Indianapolis to New York, 833 miles, yields a rate of	17.2
Plus six cents fixed charges, as above, makes	23.2
The percentage of New York rate being	93 per cent.
Which is the present percentage basis Indianapolis to New York	
Short line mileage Frankfort, Indiana, to New York is 881 miles, which would yield at the rate of 00.0206 cents per mile	18
Plus terminal charges	6
Which is 96 per cent. of 25 cents	24

The revised system provides in theory for an absolutely constant rate per ton mile. It is a rigid mileage tariff in every

---

[1] The official rule from Proceedings of the Joint Executive Committee, June 12 and 13, 1879, is as follows:

"First. — That from all points being less distant from New York than Chicago new percentages be adopted for making up rates on eastbound freight upon the following basis: the percentages from points of the same, or no greater distance than Chicago, to continue as heretofore.

"Second. — That six cents per 100 pounds be first deducted from an assumed rate of 25 cents per 100 pounds, Chicago to New York, said deduction to represent the fixed charges at both ends of long or short hauls.

"Third. — That, after such deduction, the rate per mile, which the remainder, or 19 cents per 100 pounds, produces from Chicago to New York, shall be charged per mile from all common points named in the first section, according to the percentages of distance shown by the table adopted at Chicago, April 30, 1876, to which result so computed the 6 cents per 100 pounds of fixed charges first above deducted shall be again added, and the percentage of the Chicago rate of 25 cents, produced by such additions, shall thereafter constitute the percentage of the Chicago rate, which shall be subsequently charged from the points named in first section.

For Illustration

Chicago to New York, per 100 lbs.	25c.
Less fixed charges, per 100 lbs.	6
Basis of rate for computation	19
Columbus, Ohio, as at present 70 per cent. of Chicago net rate, will be	13.3c
To which add the fixed charges	6
And the new percentage from Columbus will hereafter be $77\frac{2}{10}$ per cent. of Chicago, in lieu of 70 per cent., as at present.	19.3c

respect. The original MacGraham scale had been so in theory, but not in practice. As amended in conformity with a sound economic principle, it had, moreover, one important practical advantage over the original scale. It yielded more revenue at all the intermediate points.[1] Local rates would be higher as thus calculated than they were originally. It would be unjust to ascribe undue importance to this motive on the part of the roads in the adoption of the new system. That the plan yielded additional revenue, while obviously more just in theory, was naturally no objection to its acceptance.

The fruits of all this process of adjustment are depicted upon the accompanying diagram. Viewing it in a large way, and reserving details for later consideration, we may compare it to a topographical contour map. The several rate zones are thus analogous to a series of levels or steps rising from east to west. Our cross section of these along a line from Pittsburg to Burlington, Iowa, makes this relation plain. Another cross section at right angles to the first from Louisville, Kentucky, to Lansing, Michigan, and beyond, shows how these levels are arranged in a plane from north to south. These steps form a sort of irregular amphitheatre opening toward the east, with its main axis lying in a direction slightly south of west toward St. Louis. Or, more correctly, these rate zones, pursuing our analogy to a topographical contour map, indicate a broad valley opening toward the east. Along the bottom of this freight-rate valley lie the great direct trunk lines converging from Chicago and St. Louis. Throughout the State of Illinois the valley opens up onto a plateau, somewhat grooved in the middle at Peoria, where the direct lines from the west cross a neutral field tributary neither to Chicago nor St. Louis exclusively.

[1] Hepburn Committee, p. 3104. A hypothetical instance will serve as illustration. Suppose a point with an 80 per cent. rate on the old schedule. When Chicago paid 25 cents, the rate to this point would be 20 cents. Under the new scheme the intermediate rate would be 80 per cent. of 19 cents, or 15.2 cents, plus 6 cents terminal charge, making a total of 21.2 cents. This is 84.8 per cent. of the Chicago rate instead of 80 per cent. as before. Compare table, p. 373, *infra*.

CROSS-SECTION THROUGH LOUISVILLE AND LANSING

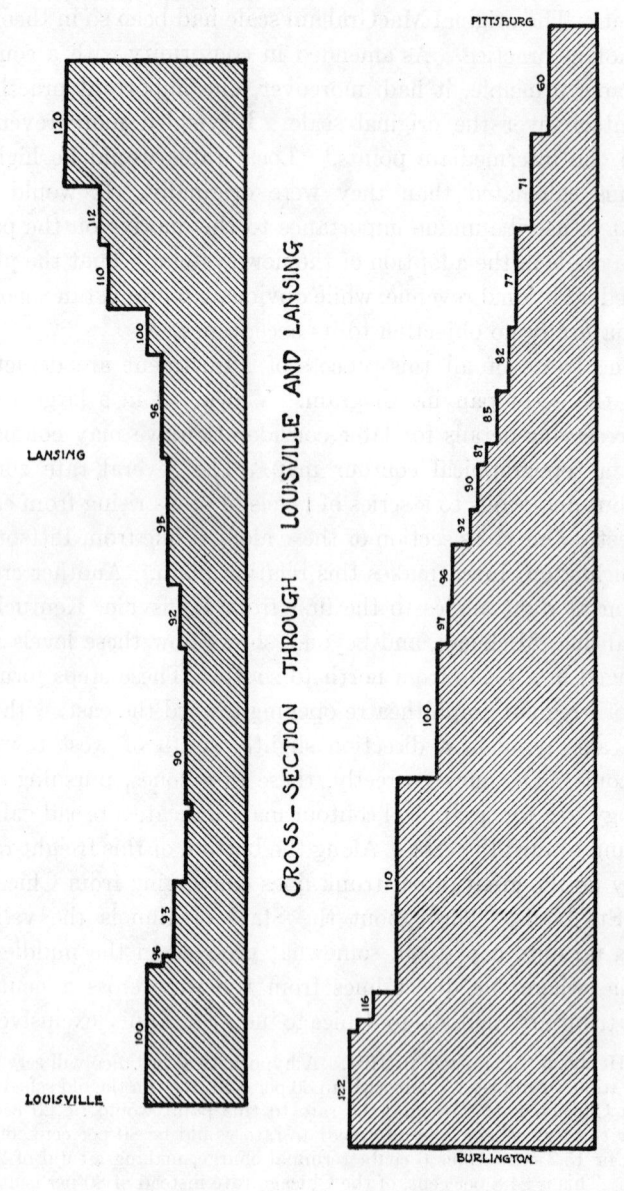

CROSS-SECTION FROM BURLINGTON TO PITTSBURG

This general description harmonizes with the apt figure used by that master mind in railway economics, Albert Fink. Speaking of this situation, he says, "The trunk lines are nothing but great arteries of commerce, like rivers, only with this difference: the rivers never run across each other, the territory from which they draw their supplies is distinct and well defined." Since his time, by reason of co-operative action for a generation, the confusing maze of railway lines has now been reduced to a single comprehensive system. Cross-currents of trade hither and thither have been united or articulated in such a way as, speaking in terms of freight charges, to cause the great internal commerce of the country to flow downhill toward the seaboard in an orderly and reasonable way. The inequalities incident to commercial competition have been modified, or, to revert to our original figure, eroded; so that one may literally speak of the products of the country as flowing, like rivers, in more or less natural channels over the railway lines from the great interior basin towards the Atlantic seaboard.

The mathematical precision of the method of computation heretofore described, while theoretically applicable to a series of parallel roads in a flat country, free from either water competition, the competition of cross railway lines, or the competition of towns and cities of unequal size and importance, obviously requires modification to suit the actual traffic conditions in this densely populated trunk line territory. The process of adjustment has been gradual and necessarily tentative. Every influence brought to bear has been subversive of systematic arrangement, tending, that is to say, to amend the scheme out of all semblance to mathematical order. After reading volumes of the Proceedings of the Joint Rate Committee, filled with petitions of railways, towns, and individuals for exception to the general rules, one is surprised to find that, after all, the scheme is so well ordered as it is. It has been held true only by rigid adherence to the rule that by the shortest "workable and worked route" no intermediate place shall be charged more than is charged to any point beyond. In other words, the long and short haul principle is consistently observed. Space does not permit a discussion of all of the factors which have tended to modify the original simple scheme. Three alone may be considered as illustrative of the rest. These are: (1) the effect of railway competition at the important junction points; (2) the influence of the independent cross lines of railway; and (3) commercial competition between producing or distributing centres.

The effect of railway competition at junction points is revealed at once, upon inspection of the map, by the general law that the boundary line of zones lies immediately west of the large cities. Notice the location of Cleveland; Warren, Pennsylvania; Newark, Ohio; Dayton, Fort Wayne, Detroit, Port Huron, Cincinnati, Indianapolis, Louisville, Lansing, Logansport, Terre Haute, Peoria, and Decatur. Columbus, Toledo, and Evansville, Indiana, are about the only exceptions. In nearly every case the theoretical zone boundary has been shifted in such a way that the rate rises just west of the important competitive point. The reason is obvious. Rates being held down at these points, and no greater rate being possible at any other point further east, conditions must be equalized *upwards*, immediately the depressing influence of competition is removed. Each zone level is of necessity an average of a theoretic constantly rising scale from east to west. Places immediately west of an important junction point are raised somewhat above their theoretical grade as a compensation for those places on the westerly side of each zone whose rate is held down below their theoretical level by the exigency of competition at the next large town. Or, to be specific, Indianapolis may hold down the rate to ninety-three per cent. of the Chicago rate farther west than otherwise would be the case. In fact, by reason of its paramount importance as a railway centre, it has held down the rate so far west that for purposes of equalization the rate west of it immediately jumps to one hundred per cent. For, as will be observed, on inspection of the map, the 96-97 per cent. zone is interrupted at this point; the 92-95 per cent. zone being extended unduly far west and the one hundred per cent. zone being extended inordinately far east, until the two meet just west of Indianapolis. Detailed study of the schedules and maps will reveal many similar instances.

The converse of the proposition that important junction points lie near the western zone boundaries is found in the fact that, where competition is absent, the zones sweep much farther east than mathematically would be prescribed. In other words, wherever competition is less keen, the percentage rates remain high. Were competition entirely uniform in its geographical distribution, the several zones would be parallel, sweeping evenly clear across the map. Illustration of this circumstance will be found in the extension of the 87 per cent. zone far to the east, along the Ohio river, in fact nearly to Parkersburg, West Virginia; or, again, in the 110 per cent. territory which extends nearly to Louisville. This latter rate has been recently amended, as will be shown later; but for many years continued, as here represented, abnormally far to the east. In both these instances the railway facilities along the river are monopolized by the Baltimore & Ohio as a trunk line. The only competition is due to the Cincinnati, Hamilton & Dayton and Norfolk & Western, both of which work their traffic from New York north. The population and traffic density being at the same time low, a relatively high level of rates has resulted. Sometimes, also, it may happen that in these outlying regions the shortest line "workable and worked" to the seaboard may not be due east, but may proceed north until a junction with a trunk line can be effected.[1]

[1] Thus from Ironton, in the 87 per cent. zone south of Columbus, Ohio, the distance to Columbus is 127 miles, added to 638 miles from Columbus to New York makes a total of 765 miles. Multiplying this by 00.0206 makes it 87 per cent. of the Chicago rate.

VOL. I—24

The influence of independent transverse lines of railway has been of great importance in shifting the zone boundaries from their theoretical location to conform to practical requirements. Study of the map permits a second important generalization. Not only does the boundary of the zones usually lie just west of large cities, the course of the boundary at the same time frequently follows the location of important independent transverse railways. The zone boundary, in other words, lies just west of the cross railway line. For example, the western boundary of the 100 per cent. Chicago zone, after leaving a point on the Illinois Central, is defined from north to south by the course of the Chicago & Eastern Illinois Railroad, and below Terre Haute by the line of the Terre Haute & Evansville. Similarly, practical exigencies determined the odd shape of the 110 per cent. zone, formed like a great distorted boot leg. The western boundary of this 110 per cent. zone from Peoria south closely follows the Peoria, Decatur & Evansville road nearly to the Ohio river. Similarly conditioned by railway lines are the boundaries north and south of Indianapolis, and especially north and south of Fort Wayne, Indiana. In other cases where the transverse lines do not cross nearly at right angles with the trunk line, the zone boundary will follow one railway for some distance, and then skip across to another railway whose general direction is more nearly perpendicular to the trunk lines. Thus, from Toledo to Lima, Ohio, the western boundary of the 76–80 per cent. zone follows the Cincinnati, Hamilton & Dayton, cutting the Baltimore & Ohio and Pennsylvania trunk lines at right angles; and then it jumps across to the east until it strikes the sweep of the Toledo & Ohio Central, which carries it down almost to Columbus. Similarly, the western boundary of the $66\frac{1}{2}$ per cent. zone follows the line of the Pittsburg & Western north from Warren, in order that that line may participate in New York business by working its line north *via* Painesville on the Lake Shore.

TRUNK LINE SYSTEM 371

Why is it apparently necessary that these zone boundaries should follow along just west of the cross railway lines? The reason may be made clear by a concrete instance. Originally and until about 1891, Louisville, Kentucky, instead of having the 100 per cent. Chicago rate, as at present, enjoyed, on the base of its distance from New York, about 96 or 97 per cent. of the Chicago rate. In other words, the 96-97 per cent. zone shown on our map as interrupted at Indianapolis, partly for reasons already mentioned, originally swept across the map all the way from Grand Rapids to the Ohio river. This territory from Chicago south is served by the Monon Railway (Chicago, Indianapolis & Louisville), whose line, not fully indicated on the map, thus lay partly in 100 per cent., partly in 96 per cent., and partly in 97 per cent. territory. An important part of the traffic of the Monon, as well as of the other independent north and south lines, consists of business coming in from the east at the north and worked south, or coming in from the east at the south and worked north. Or, in other words, this line subsisted in part upon indirectly routed tonnage from New York, let us say, destined for Louisville, but reaching it by way of Chicago junction points. Freight thus hauled around two sides of a triangle, instead of by a direct line, as described in Chapter VIII,[1] constitutes one of the important sources of waste of transportation energy. The Monon by such tactics is able to participate in, and to profit by, a much larger volume of through business. That is to say, its proportion of the entire haul is much greater than it would be if the business moved by the shortest line. Moreover, when indirectly routed, the Monon, often securing for its trunk line connections tonnage for the east which would naturally go to other competitive trunk lines, is able to exact a higher pro-rating than even its extended lateral haul would justify on a strictly distance basis. Such circumstances always greatly enhance the profitableness of lateral hauls to minor connecting roads. It is obvious that

[1] Page 264, *infra*.

much of this transverse haulage would be impossible wherever the lateral railway lines traverse different zones of rates. It might haul traffic from its 100 per cent. end to connect at its 96 per cent. end with a trunk line for the east, but not in the opposite direction. The Monon, always in a position to disturb the rate situation, through connection with all the competing trunk lines, insisted upon equality of rates all along its lines. To do this, the 100 per cent. zone had to be extended east to Indianapolis. Thereafter the Monon could profitably "work its line in both directions." This illustration will serve to show why ordinarily the zone boundaries conform as closely as possible to the course of the lateral roads. The confusion which would be engendered, were the Peoria, Decatur & Evansville to be partly in the 110 per cent. and partly in higher percentage territory, while still insisting upon its right to work its line both ways, can readily be imagined. To avoid such difficulties, the present modification of strictly distance percentages had to be adopted.

The third dominant influence, above mentioned, in modifying the mathematical precision of percentages based alone upon the distance from New York, has been the commercial competition of traders and cities one with another. The aim of all rate adjustment should be, and in fact, so far as possible in American railway practice, is to equalize conditions, so that the widest possible market shall result. Producers or traders in each city demand access on even terms to all territory naturally tributary to them by reason of their geographical location. Each particular railroad sees to it that its own patrons and cities are "held" in all parts of these markets, as against the efforts of competing railways to promote the welfare of their own constituencies. Consequently, the Proceedings of the Joint Rate Committee are filled with discussions as to the advisability of amending general rules here and there to suit local conditions. Minor changes are continually being effected. Grand Rapids, Michigan, once in 100 per cent. territory, asked for a 90 per cent. rate, and in 1891 secured a reduction to 96 per cent.[1] Louisville, once in 97 per cent. territory, is now a 100 per cent. point. Shifts in both directions have frequently occurred, as the following table of percentages shows:[2] —

Basis	Detroit	Toledo	Sandusky	Cleveland
April 13, 1876	85	78	71	65
June 23, 1879[3]	81.5	81.5	78	73.5
April 14, 1880	75.5[4]	75.5	75.5	70
Present (1900)	78	78	78	71

A number of changes were made in 1887 in order to conform to the long and short haul clause. Flint, Michigan, for example, was reduced from 95 to 92 per cent.; Ashtabula, Ohio, from 71 to 67; while Springfield, Ohio, was raised from 82 to 83 per cent.[5] Detroit has been most active in prosecuting its claims for a reduced percentage.[6] But the Interstate Commerce Commission in 1888 upheld the present status. A recent minor change is indicative of the forces which must be dealt with. Evansville, Indiana, on the Ohio river, according to our map, is a 110 per cent. point. Vincennes, Indiana, lies just north of it in the 108 per cent. triangular zone. Since this plate was made, Evansville has been reduced to 105 and Vincennes to 103 per cent., respectively. This is substantially, I am told, on a mileage basis. The reason for the amendment is that certain important industries are located at these points. Either to favor them specially or to remove a pre-existing disability in competition with other towns, this change was

[1] *Cf.* Industrial Commission, IV, p. 556.
[2] Record, Detroit Board of Trade case.
[3] Consult p. 195, *supra*.
[4] Computed apparently by regular rules, but on the basis of only 4 cents terminal charges instead of the usual 6.
[5] Joint Rate Circular, No. 815.
[6] Demanding a 70 per cent. rate on a strict mileage basis, and also, because the pro-rating basis with Western lines is that figure.

insisted upon by the railways interested in their prosperity. By tentative processes of adjustment like this the present general relations have been established.[1] They have been kept constant only by the steady resistance of the majority of carriers to action which is in the interest of a few. Judged by results, it would appear that the broad view has, in the main, prevailed.

The actual situation resulting from the above-named causes, it should be observed, is not quite as simple as our map makes it appear. Most of the zones are in fact subdivided into minor gradations. Thus the closely dotted zone designated "86–90 incl." is constituted of an 87 per cent. area up as far as the railway from Dayton to Indianapolis; while the rest of it is broken up into little 88, 89, and 90 per cent. areas, respectively. The same thing occurs elsewhere. Our map generalizes the results, in an effort to bring out the zone relationships as fully as is technically possible in a single diagram. Certain of the zones, however, such as the 60, 66½, 100, and 110 per cent. territories, are bounded exactly as here represented.

As for direction, the original scale was intended only for eastbound traffic. Westbound rates were lower and more regular. But the system worked so well that it was soon extended to cover the westbound business. Owing to difficulties of routing, in order to transport by the shortest line into Chicago, these westbound percentages were often quite different from those in the opposite direction.[2] Detroit, for instance, for some time prior to 1886, enjoyed a 70 per cent. rate west bound, while its percentage in the opposite direction was 78.[3] But, after the passage of the Act to Regulate Com-

---

[1] 23 I.C.C. Rep., 684, on wool from Detroit, for example. 13 *Idem*, 300 concerns Evansville rates and those across in Kentucky.

[2] Trunk Line Association Circular No. 523, issued July 26, 1883, gives tables of these percentages in each direction. Present westbound percentages are given in *ibid.*, No. 751, issued April 3, 1899.

[3] Typewritten record, Detroit Board of Trade case, 1887-88, Interstate Commerce Commission Office, pp. 244–251.

merce in 1887, efforts were made to harmonize the differences.[1] At the present time the rates east and west are in most cases the same.

At this point it is essential to understand the limitations within which this percentage system is confined. It does not necessarily determine the exact rate to be applied in practice from every little station in trunk line territory. For, in the first place, it concerns only the so-called common points; that is to say, points where competition of two or more carriers is effective. Purely local stations are charged an "arbitrary" into the nearest common point.[2] But, inasmuch as throughout this much be-railroaded country most shippers are less than twenty miles from the next line,[3] and since, moreover, the arbitrary can never raise the local rate above the rate to the next common point beyond,[4] the scale is practically effective everywhere. A more important consideration is the fact that this scale, even for common points, does not positively fix the rate. It merely provides a minimum below which rates shall not be reduced, except by authority of the roads acting jointly. It is a minimum, not a maximum, schedule in every sense. Its provisions are never promulgated in the form of tariffs as such. They are rarely known to shippers, but serve only as a guide to traffic officials. The Interstate Commerce Commission, in sanctioning the system, has expressly recognized this fact.[5] Moreover, these percentage rates applied at first to "classified" tonnage. They were soon, however, extended to

[1] Under a committee headed by the late J. T. R. McKay, of Cleveland. The Official Classification and the 75 cent New York-Chicago rate first-class were then adopted for good.

[2] 12 I.C.C. Rep., 186, on points about New York, for example.

[3] I am told that rivers intervening, to cut off cartage by wagon to competing lines, have sometimes effectively influenced the charges.

[4] The long and short haul principle has always been given great weight here. All exceptions to it were removed in good faith by the carriers when the Act of 1887 was passed. *Cf.* Windom Committee, vol. I, p. 26; vol. III, pp. 42, 134, and 283.

[5] *G. C. Pratt Lumber Co. v. Chicago, Ind. & Louisville Railway Co.*, decided January 27, 1904.

include the great bulk of commodity or special rates which are independently made. And I am informed by the chairman of the Trunk Line Association that the MacGraham table was applied to special rates — such as sugar, coffee and molasses — as early as 1871.

Other exceptions to the applicability of this percentage system deserve mention, although they are of relative unimportance. Principal among these is the confusion engendered in Illinois territory through the entry of the western lines into Chicago. Throughout their constituencies, by reason of the sparse population, freedom from competition, inequality of east, and westbound tonnage, and low-grade freight, western railroad rates per ton mile are very much higher than on the trunk lines. Moreover, they are naturally desirous of as long a haul as possible, namely into Chicago. To turn over their local Illinois traffic to the trunk line feeders exposes them financially to the same losses as those above mentioned in the case of lateral independent lines further east. But these western lines, being stronger, have insisted upon recognition of their claims to a proportion of the through rate which would at least "pay for their axle grease."[1] The result is that throughout Illinois, especially in the north and toward the Mississippi, the distance principle is considerably distorted, as our map clearly shows. The percentage system practically excludes freight "from beyond," the rates on that being determined by other rules.[2]

East of the Central Traffic Association territory shown on our map the same percentage system is extended to points in New York and Pennsylvania.[3] Suppose, for example, the rate were desired from Columbus, Ohio, to Albany, New York, or any other point between Buffalo and New York City. The

[1] U. S. Industrial Commission, vol. IV, p. 562.

[2] *Cf.* 8 Int. Com. Rep., 169, on grain rates from Minnesota and trans-Missouri points; as also 23 I.C.C. Rep., 195.

[3] *Cf.* Joint Committee Information No. 298 of January 13, 1900, giving all these rules in detail.

rate from Columbus to New York City would first be determined as a percentage of the Chicago-New York rate, under the system already described. Then from Columbus to Albany the rate would be prescribed as a new percentage of this percentage. The initial western points, however, are not determined individually, but are comprehended in large groups. Thus the rate from all points in the 72–78 per cent. territory, shown on our map, to Albany, New York, is 96 per cent. of what the rate would be from those points to New York City. Syracuse has 76 and Utica 87 per cent., respectively, of the rate from any point in this 72–78 per cent. territory. From points beyond Chicago, taking, that is to say, more than 100 per cent. of the New York-Chicago rate, the percentages of the rate to New York City applying to Albany, Syracuse, and Utica are correspondingly modified to 96, 84, and 91, respectively. Other complications, such as the addition of arbitraries to Boston and New England points or the subtraction of differentials to Baltimore and Philadelphia, follow. But, in the main, conforming always to the long and short haul principle,[1] rates to all local stations are prescribed within narrow limits by means of a small number of these fixed points. The system is the same, although details may vary. Everything interlocks and is harmoniously related on the distance basis.

Rates from one point to another within the Central Traffic Association territory shown on our map now alone remain for consideration. These cannot, of course, be adjusted on a percentage basis, inasmuch as such traffic may not be east or west bound at all, but may consist of shipments in any direction. There is no logical reason why they should interlock with east or westbound through rates when the traffic is, perhaps, moving locally north and south. Nevertheless, the long and short haul principle is observed with the same fidelity. A rigid distance tariff for short hauls, the limits of which are prescribed by the rates for long hauls under the MacGraham schedule,

[1] *Cf.* Windom Committee, vol. II, pp. 42 and 134.

prevails.[1] For distances up to 75 miles this conforms closely to the rates originally prescribed by the Ohio legislature. For greater distances it is much lower than the Ohio tariff.[2] Thus the Ohio rate for 350 miles is 87.5 cents, while the C. F. A. (Central Freight Association) scale is only 42 cents. The Ohio scale for 200 miles is 50 cents, the C. F. A. rate for the same distance is only 33 cents. Thus it appears that this C. F. A. tariff, applicable to interstate business and beyond control of any state legislature, has, in reality, been voluntarily adopted by the interested railroads. The tariff is only a minimum scale, below which the roads agree not to reduce rates, and above which the actual rates often rise.[3] Nevertheless, the fact remains that these rates, according to distance, are so much lower than the Illinois Railroad Commission's tariff that Chicago and other distributing centres throughout the State of Illinois claim that it works great hardship to them. The situation in Illinois is geographically peculiar. Its great commercial centre is in the extreme northeastern corner, while, at the same time, the greatest extension of the state is north and south. These circumstances, coupled with an interstate (C. F. A.) tariff lower than the Illinois official tariff under which Chicago merchants must ship out their goods, enable Detroit, Indianapolis, and Cincinnati to undersell Chicago in its own state. Chicago can be equalized there only by special or secret rates.[4] Other local centres, like Quincy, Illinois, joined with Chicago in this complaint to the Illinois Railroad Commission that their rates were too high.[5] Think of it! Shippers complaining that a government rate was too high, and requesting

[1] Known as the C. F. A. scale. Full text is printed in Illinois Railroad Commission Proceedings in Maximum Freight Rate case, Record, etc., 1905, p. 43. See also p. 97.
[2] Detailed comparison is made in *ibid.*, p. 45. See also p. 17.
[3] Illinois Railroad Commission Proceedings in Maximum Freight Rate case, Record, etc., 1905, p. 152.
[4] Exhibit A 15, *ibid.*, shows this by means of a map. See also Senate (Elkins) Committee, 1905, vol. III, p. 2271.
[5] The double disability of these smaller places is stated in *ibid.*, p. 7.

that the railway tariff (C. F. A. schedule) be adopted in its place! Is that not evidence that reasonable treatment of its shippers by railway companies is appreciated by the public? Without undue extension further details of this interesting controversy cannot be given. It will suffice to state that in December, 1905, the Illinois Railroad Commission ordered a reduction of its official schedule by 20 per cent., in an attempt to reduce its rates to conform more nearly to the C. F. A. railway tariff.

The evils incident upon two conflicting governmental authorities, State and Federal, each attempting to regulate rates independently, are clearly indicated in the preceding paragraph. The Interstate Commerce Commission has been brought flatly up against them in one of its recent Texas cases.[1] Local and interstate rates must inevitably be adjusted with reference to one another, so complex are the conditions of commercial competition. While the plain people remained unsatisfied that any real Federal regulative power existed, it was inevitable that the number of arbitrary state tariffs, like those of Illinois and, more recently, of Missouri, should tend to increase. But now since the amplified Federal powers under the laws of 1906 and 1910, any clash between the two must result in limitations placed upon state activity.

[1] Chapter XVIII, *infra*.

CHAPTER XI

SPECIAL RATE PROBLEMS: THE SOUTHERN BASING POINT SYSTEM; TRANSCONTINENTAL RATES; PORT DIFFERENTIALS, ETC.

Contrast between the basing point and trunk line systems, 380. — Natural causes in southern territory, 381. — Economic dependence, 381. — Wide-spread water competition, 382. — High level of rates, 382. — The basing point system described, 383. — Its economic defences, 384. — Early trade centres, 384. — Water competition once more, 385. — Three types of basing point, 387. — Purely artificial ones exemplified, 388. — Different practice among railroads, 390. — Attempts at reform, 391. — Western v. eastern cities, 391. — Effect of recent industrial revival, 392. — The Texas group system, 393. — An outcome of commercial rivalry, 394. — Local competition of trade centres, 395. — Possibly artificial and unstable, 395. — The transcontinental rate system, 395. — High level of charges, 396. — Water competition, 396. — Carload ratings and graded charges, 398. — Competition of jobbing centres, 398. — Canadian differentials, 400. — "Milling-in-transit" and similar practices, 401. — "Floating Cotton," 402. — "Substitution of tonnage," 403. — Seaboard differentials, 403. — Historically considered, 403. — The latest decision, 403. — Import and export rates, 404–409.

THE rate system in the southern states contrasts sharply with that of trunk line territory.[1] Its most unsatisfactory feature is its complete violation of the distance principle. Public

[1] Among the best references on the subject are the following: McPherson, Railway Freight Rates, pp. 85–92, especially on the Virginia-Carolina cities; Rep. U. S. Internal Commerce, 1876, App., pp. 1–20; U. S. Senate (Elkins) Committee Hearings, 1905, Digest, App., III. The principal I.C.C. cases are as follows: 1891. Social Circle; 4 I.C.C. Rep., 744. — 1892. Georgia R. R. Com.; 5 *Idem*, 324. — 1893. Troy, Ala.; 4 Int. Com. Rep., 348. In Railway Problems. — 1894. Summerville, Ga.; 4 *Idem*, 521. — 1894. Cordele, Ala.; 6 I.C.C. Rep., 343. — 1895. Tifton, Ga.; 6 Int. Com. Rep., 343. — 1897. Lagrange, La.; 7 *Idem*, 431. — 1897. Griffin, Ga.; 7 *Idem*, 224. — 1899. Dawson, Ga.; 8 *Idem*, 142. In Railway Problems. — 1899. Aberdeen, S. C.; 10 I.C.C. Rep., 289. — 1899. Wilmington, S. C.; 9 *Idem*, 118. — 1900. Piedmont; 6 Int. Com. Rep., 588. — 1900. Hampton, Fla.; 8 *Idem*, 503. — 1900. Danville, Va.; 8 *Idem*, 409. In Railway Problems.

dissatisfaction was long voiced by a large number of complaints before the Interstate Commerce Commission in the early days, — a cessation of these complaints since 1900, however, was the result of the nullification of the law by judicial interpretation, rather than an indication of any acquiescence of the public in the scheme. Next to settlement of the problem of transcontinental rates, a reasonable adjustment of the southern situation is one of the important tasks confronting the Federal authorities.

Certain natural features of southern territory are connected with its peculiar rate system. The first of these is its scattered and relatively thin settlement. Density of population varies between one-third and one-fourth of that in the northern states. This greatly limits the volume of local business. In the second place, the largely agricultural character of the country, yielding a traffic predominantly of low grade, has had a great effect. Much attention being devoted to cotton, there is little local interchange of freight. The business, moreover, is largely seasonal in character. In the early days, at least, practically all of the profits of the carriers had to be made between September and January. This concentration of interest in the movement of the cotton crop is now rapidly being supplanted by a much more general movement of traffic; but the rate system in force is an outgrowth of the conditions prevalent in the early days.

The entire dependence of this territory for manufactured goods upon the northeastern states, and for foodstuffs upon the West, has had a profound effect, we have seen, upon its railway development.[1] The predominant direction of traffic is rendered quite peculiar by contrast with trunk line territory. In the North, the principal railroads lie parallel, east and west; in the South, they are radially distributed outward from Atlanta like the spokes of a wheel. Imagine a triangle with its apex at this

[1] Chapter I affords a historical review of railway development in the United States.

city, — the focus of all transportation interests in the South, — and with its other two angles lying at New York and Chicago respectively. The hollow centre of this triangle, as appears by the accompanying map, is occupied by the Allegheny mountain chain. The movement of traffic historically along the western side of this triangle has been overwhelmingly southward; at one time the disproportion south-bound from western territory being as thirteen to one.[1] Along the eastern side of this triangle, — that is to say parallel with the Atlantic seaboard, — the preponderance of tonnage, by bulk and probably by value as well, has been toward the north. In this direction cotton in the early days, and latterly lumber, have moved from southern fields and forests to northeastern markets. In Virginia-Carolina territory, today, about three-fifths of the loaded mileage is north bound. The uneven distribution of traffic is still further complicated by the excess of tonnage east-bound in trunk line territory along the northern side of our triangle, above mentioned. This general description explains many of the abnormalities in freight rates throughout this territory. Bulky staples moving one way, while manufactured goods, high in value but more concentrated in weight, go the other, greatly complicate the problem of economical operation.

Another omnipresent complication in the southern states is the widespread existence of water competition. The situation in the South in this regard is not unlike that of England. Its entire territory is threaded with a series of more or less navigable watercourses which penetrate from the seaboard or the Mississippi river, far into the interior. Here again is a physical peculiarity of the southern territory, which historically explains, even if it does not fully justify, as we shall see, certain peculiarities of its freight rate system.

The first general characteristic of the southern system is the relatively high level of freight rates. Bearing in mind that the

[1] Rep. Internal Commerce, 1876, App., p. 28; Senate (Elkins) Committee, 1905, Digest, App. III, p. 71.

distance from New York to Chicago is practically the same as from New York to Atlanta, the freight rate, first-class, on the trunk lines was, in 1900, 75 cents per hundredweight as against $1.14 to Atlanta. Sixth-class rates then stood to one another as 25 cents and 45 cents respectively, the relatively high ones being in the South. Reference, for example, to the table on page 349, will bring out this contrast at the present time in another way. According to this the rates in the South are not higher than in the West for the same distance. The disproportionately high charges in the South, however, occur mainly in the field of local rates. And it is the local, rather than the through, charges, which cause the present dissatisfaction. The principal complaint concerning through rates is that they are made up principally as the sum of locals based upon Ohio or Mississippi gateways.[1] Whenever such sums of locals have given place to unbroken through rates, a large measure of satisfaction to shippers has resulted. And then, finally, it should be observed that certain peculiarities of the classification system somewhat increase the relatively high grade of charges throughout this territory,[2] tending to support the allegation that rates are unreasonably high.

The so-called basing point system is the second fundamental peculiarity of southern rate adjustment. It has already been discussed in connection with local discrimination.[3] This basing point system, although not absolutely confined to the South, has been more highly developed here than elsewhere. In principle it is simply this: certain cities are established as basing points,[4] and rates to all other places in that neighborhood are

[1] *Cf.* the Commerce Court case; February session, 1912, No. 40. Also *cf.* p. 251, *supra*.
[2] Page 311 *supra*.   [3] Pp. 239–252, *supra*.
[4] A list of these on the Louisville and Nashville R. R. is given in U. S. Senate (Elkins) Committee, 1905, Digest, App. III, pp. 84–93. There is a distinction between a basing and a common point. The latter is a competitive junction, to which rates are made on combination of locals. The basing point enjoys a still further advantage in that it gets even lower than the combination rates.

made by adding to the through rate into the basing point, the local from that city to the final destination. Since local rates in the South, based upon slender local traffic, are always exceedingly high, this appears to confer a very great advantage in the matter of charges on the cities thus favored. The way in which this system is opposed to the long and short haul principle in law has also been discussed in another connection. On the face of things it certainly appears unjust that goods should be transported directly through the place to which they are ultimately to go; and after being hauled to the basing point with a heavy charge for that haul, should thereafter be brought back again with the addition of a second high local rate for the service. And yet that very commonly occurs.

A number of economic defences for the basing point system have been urged by the carriers at different times. The most substantial one is that the basing points, historically, were originally important trade centres and are still intimately related to the business customs of the South.[2] These trade centres, it is alleged, were not made by the railroads: they were in existence before the railroads were constructed. They are an outgrowth of the agricultural system of the region. In the West a farmer may take a sample of his grain to the nearest town and sell the whole crop by that sample. No such transaction is possible with cotton and tobacco. Each shipment must be sampled, weighed and classified on its own merits. Such grading cannot take place at local stations. Convenient commercial centres are, therefore, a necessity, serving for the proper concentration of products. These trade centres, moreover, arising in connection with the sale of staple products of the soil, became natural distributing or jobbing points. The planters naturally buy in the places to which they resort to sell their crops, often employing the same merchant.[3] As such

---

[1] Page 474, *infra*.
[2] Senate (Elkins) Committee Hearings, Digest, App. III, pp. 73 and 78.
[3] *Cf.* chap. IV, p. 125, *supra*. Also I.C.C. Opinion, No. 861, 1906.

THE BASING POINT SYSTEM

natural trading centres, these southern towns are forced to compete with the older established distributing cities up north. At this point a second defence of the basing point system arises.[1] It is urged that a decentralization of jobbing trade in a sparsely settled or newly developed territory can be effected only by means of encouragement through peculiarly favorable rates to offset the strength of the remoter great cities. The plausibility of this defence, however, is considerably weakened by the fact that under the peculiar southern classification system, carload ratings are largely absent.[2] Therefore, as it appears, the local jobber in the South competes under a disability as compared with New York and Cincinnati which is no less at the basing point than in the small town. Still a third, and probably a valid, defense of this violation of the distance principle by the use of basing points, is the paucity of local business. It is alleged that in the North the competitive points are so near together, and the volume of competitive business is so large, that it pays to reduce the charges at immediate points. In the South, on the other hand, competitive points are so far apart and, relatively speaking, the local tonnage is so small, that the adoption of such a policy would be ruinous.[3]

The most prominent defence of the basing point system brought forward at all times, and greatly emphasized in proceedings before the Interstate Commerce Commission, is the widespread existence of water competition. Carriers allege that in order to secure any portion of the traffic at many points, low rates must be offered, quite irrespective of the charges to intermediate inland stations. They affirm that to lower all rates to this "compelled" competitive level, would deplete their revenues and lead to bankruptcy. This has been the main excuse for the persistent violation of the long and short

---

[1] H. R. Meyer's, Government Regulation of Railroad Rates, pp. 196 and 292–303.   [2] Page 310, chap. IX, *supra*.

[3] Senate (Elkins) Committee, 1905, p. 65: 80 per cent. of net earnings on the Louisville & Nashville in 1886 were from local business.

haul clause by carriers in the southern states down to the present time. The evidence goes to show, however, that on the lesser streams, at least, the steamers are so small, their service so irregular, and the incidental risk of damage, cost of insurance and other expenses of transhipment are so great, that the railroads practically control the business.[1] Furthermore, in many places it appears that the water lines were either owned by the railroads or appeared in league with them; or else that a division of the business had been effected by which the little river steamers were accorded a certain proportion of the low grade freight.[2] Such facts have been established before the Interstate Commerce Commission, for example, in the so-called Dawson case concerning the Chattahoochee river; on the Ocmulgee at Macon in the Griffin and Hawkinsville cases; at Montgomery in the Troy case; and on the St. Johns river at Palatka, Florida, in the Hampton case. A competent witness has declared in fact that there is "no more real water competition at many of these places than in the Rocky Mountains."[3] Probably the potentiality of competition is somewhat greater today with improvement of the larger navigable waterways. It seems to be real at Chattanooga since the construction of the Mussel Shoals canal; but that it has in late years been effective at Nashville seems open to question. The practical disappearance of the Mississippi river traffic also points to the decline in importance of the great rivers as rate regulators, except in respect of the carriage of ore, lumber, and coal. Whether the National Waterways movement will ever succeed in its revival is, it seems to me, open to serious question.[4]

[1] *Cf.* pp. 386, 591, 612 and 642, *infra*, for example.
[2] 24 I.C.C. Rep., 228, for Bowling Green, Ky., clearly establishes such a community of interest between rail and water lines.
[3] Senate Interstate Commerce Committee, Hearings, 1897. Twelfth Annual Rep. I.C.C., p. 59, well describes the situation.
[4] Compare chap. XX, p. 638, *infra*. Other references on internal waterways are as follows. 1905. Senate (Elkins) Committee, Digest, App. IV. — 1908. Report Inland Waterways Commission, 2 vols. — 1910. Reports U. S. National Waterways Commission, especially Document 11.

Analyzing these several grounds of defence, a distinction should be made at the start between three varieties of basing point. This is not clearly brought out in the numerous decisions upon rates in southern territory. In the first group are the old natural trading centres, usually once blessed with effective competition by water, even if at the present this is of limited character. Savannah and Montgomery, Alabama, are of this type. Then, secondly, there are the great railroad centres like Atlanta and Birmingham. These are modern creations without water competition of any sort, although the rivalry of railroads with one another is exceedingly keen. Until recently, moreover, this competition has been over such widely divergent routes that agreement has been difficult and consolidation impossible.[1] And, then, in the third place, there are the basing points which seem to be absolutely artificial. A number of these are to be found in the southeastern part of Georgia, such as Cordele, Americus, Albany, etc. In these cases the only criterion which seems to have been adopted is that the place shall have attained sufficient importance to enable it to compel some carrier to give it special privileges in the matter of rates. As was tersely stated in a leading case — Cordele at that time not having been made a basing point:[2]

"Cordele is not treated by defendant roads as a competitive point, because it is not a sufficiently large distributing point, and it is not such a distributing point because it is not treated as a competitive point. Hence it appears that the roads seek to excuse their wrong-doing by offering the results of the wrong in justification. Judged by its results, this system of rate making is at variance with all the equality provisions of the act to regulate commerce."

The subsequent experience in this last case is significant. One of the carriers at Cordele having afterwards discovered the

Traffic History of the Mississippi river. *Cf.* also, *Railway Age Gazette*, June 2 and 30, 1911 and Jan. 12, 1912: Bulletin 21, Bureau of Railway Economics; and the Bulletins of the U. S. Census.
    [1] Compare vol. II, on railroad consolidation in this territory, since 1900.   [2] 6 I.C.C. Rep., 343.

advantage to itself in making this town a basing point, all the other railroads were compelled to acquiesce. Such a thing has happened frequently throughout the South; with the result that many places have been given strongly preferential rates for no other reason than the arbitrary decision of some one of the carriers. Even the railroads themselves recognize this fact. They often deplore the necessity for reducing rates because of action by competitors at some particular point; but no option remains. It is with reference to this third class of purely artificial basing points that the most dissatisfaction among shippers arises.

The awkward and unreasonable situation is well exemplified in a very recent case, — important, also, because it was the first to be decided by the Interstate Commerce Commission under its new and enlarged powers. The location of Ashburn in southeastern Georgia, a county seat with a population of about 2,200, is shown with references to surrounding places by the map on opposite page.[1] It lies in the centre of an irregular quadrilateral, the corners of which are occupied by Cordele, Albany, Tifton and Fitzgerald. It has no commercial standing at present, but, being as large at least as Tifton, aspires to become a distributing centre in its immediate neighborhood. Yet from every direction its rates are made by a combination upon these surrounding towns. The disparity is illustrated by the charges from New York, which are $1.42 per hundredweight, first class, as compared with $1.17 to all the neighboring places. Examination of the history of these favored towns shows, however, that they have acquired their favored status as basing points, neither because they were originally important trading centres, nor because they enjoyed water competition. Two of them, actually, are as remote from streams as is Ashburn. The fact is that the competition of western and eastern dealers with one another, backed in each case by local railroads having routes or affiliations either northeast or northwest, has brought

[1] 23 I.C.C. Rep., 140.

THE BASING POINT SYSTEM

about their establishment as basing points. Neither is Ashburn today more of a local point than either Tifton or Cordele when they were first granted lower rates. As one examines further, it appears that this keenness of trade competition between East and West, — that is to say, from Baltimore and

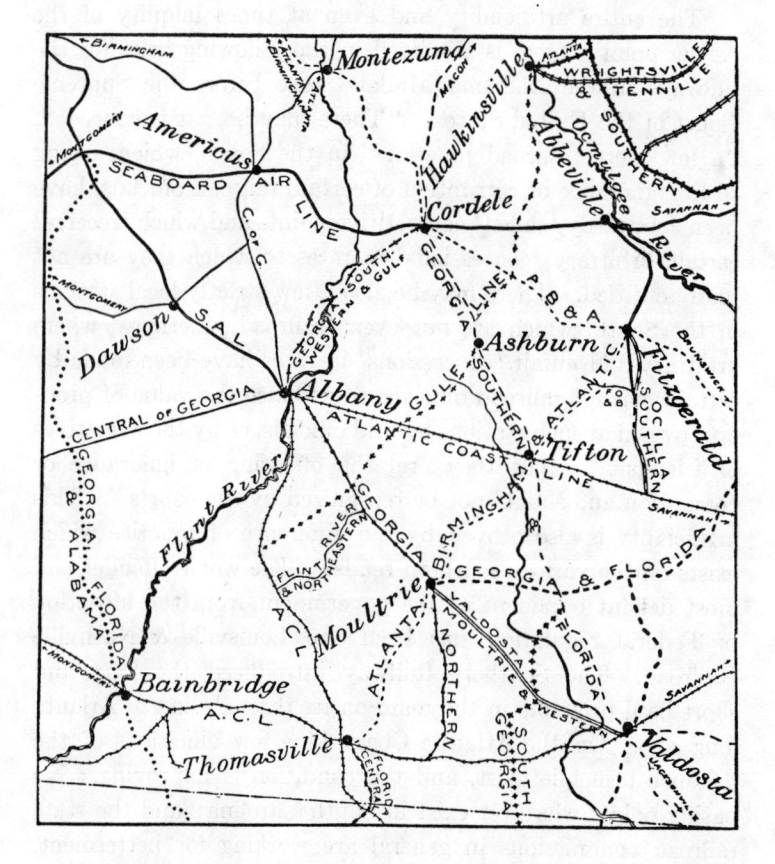

New York as against Cincinnati and Chicago, etc., — which has brought Atlanta into prominence and made it finally the key to the entire southern rate arch,[1] has in the same manner led to the special favors granted to one town as against another.

[1] *Cf.* p. 248, *supra.*

In this case the Interstate Commerce Commission ordered an equalization between all five points. It is to be hoped that this special case may be a point of departure for a general reform in the immediate future of the entire iniquitous scheme of local favoritism which has too long been allowed to exist.

The entire artificiality and even at times iniquity of the basing point system is admitted in the following brief for the railways in the Alabama Midland case before the Supreme Court of the United States. "There may be," it is conceded, "a few mere 'railroad junctions' in the South, which, owing to the ignorance or corruption of certain railroad officials, have been arbitrarily 'called' competitive points and which 'receive' certain arbitrary 'concessions' in rates to which they are not justly entitled. There may be also a few strictly local stations in the South, which are not even 'railroad junctions,' where arbitrary and unfair 'concessions' in rates have been made by certain corrupt railroad officials, to enhance the value of property owned at such stations by said officials, or by their relatives or friends . . . [but they are] the offspring of ignorance or corruption and should not be recognized by the courts." This artificiality is also proven by the difference of practice which exists on the various southern roads.[1] The worst offender and most defiant opponent of the government from the inception of Federal regulation, has been the Louisville & Nashville Railroad. The Southern Railway introduced the long and short haul principle in the main on its through line to Atlanta long ago. On the Atlantic Coast Line few violations of the distance principle exist, and the condition is improving. No basing points whatever exist in South Carolina; and the state railroad commissions in general are working for betterment. Neither the Chesapeake & Ohio nor the Norfolk & Western, operating alike in sparsely settled regions, find it necessary to violate the distance principle. One of the curses of the scheme,

---

[1] Senate (Elkins) Committee, 1905, Digest, App., III p. 93; gives a list of new basing points created since 1887.

however, is that irregularity of one carrier may compel its neighbors to adopt a policy which they recognize as unjust. Only by compulsion applied to all alike can a just solution be had.

A determined effort was made in 1880 by the carriers themselves to apply the trunk line rate system, based upon the distance principle, to the southern states.[1] A thoroughgoing scientific readjustment was proposed. The situation is significantly described in the following extract from this report:

"Your committee entered upon the performance of their duty entertaining the sentiment that experience and observation have rendered generally potent among those in charge of the revenue interest of transportation lines, namely, the necessity for more intelligent and defensible methods of making competitive freight rates than the following of figures, descending to us from tariffs named on arbitrary bases or conditions now obsolete, or by the assumption of differences between centres of trade now changed or junction points now no longer such, or other methods for which there are no reasons capable of satisfactory explanation."

Representatives of most of the important lines subscribed to this plan; but it fell through at the last because of the opposition of others, selfishly viewing their own particular interests rather than the general welfare of all. It is clear that while minor improvements may be introduced, no widespread reform can be effected without the interposition of Federal authority. It is to be hoped that this exercise of authority under the larger powers now conferred by Congress since 1906 may not long be withheld.

A third and essentially different problem respecting southern rates concerns the discrimination against western cities in favor of those along the Atlantic seaboard. This has been for years before the Interstate Commerce Commission in the Cincinnati and Chicago Freight Bureau cases.[2] The amount of this

---

[1] Southern Railway and Steamship Association Proceedings; Meeting of Aug. 12, 1880.
[2] Fully discussed at pp. 248 *supra* and 588 *infra*.

discrimination appears in the fact that at the time of the original complaint, the rate from Cincinnati to Atlanta was ninety-four per cent. of the rate from New York to the same point; although the distance from Cincinnati was scarcely more than half of that from New York. It appears as if this difference were largely the result of keen water competition by coastwise steamers, — a competition which affects rates for a considerable distance inland all along the coast as far as New Orleans. Where such water competition is absent, there seems to be a general arrangement as between East and West which is standardized by distance. Atlanta gives the keynote; and all rates from outside southern territory change with its fluctuations. The disability against western cities may be expressed, therefore, in another way, by the fact that New York, although so much farther north than Baltimore, — supposed theoretically to be kept on a par with Louisville as to rates, — reaches Atlanta on lower charges than are made to Cincinnati.

Fortunately an attempt at improvement of the southern rate system will be greatly aided by the wonderful industrial revival which has been under way during the last decade. The growth of population, and especially the development of manufactures, may render it possible for the carriers to endure the hardship which any traffic readjustment always entails. The growth of manufactures, measuring in a way the degree to which the South is learning to supply its own needs, appears in the fact that in 1907 it converted one-fifth of its cotton production into cloth, and reduced from its own ores one-half of its consumption of pig iron in its own local factories. Furniture shipments to the South were once large. At the present time High Point, North Carolina, is second only to Grand Rapids in this line of manufacture. Every new mill and mercantile establishment which springs up, is bound to help to a degree in the transition from a mediaeval scheme of rate making to a more defensible system.

The Texas "common point" system affords a valuable illustration of the influence of competitive forces in trade in bringing about an equalization of transportation charges over a wide area.[1] It also shows the danger of localization of interest through the exercise of piece-meal control by state commissions rather than the enforcement of broad-gauge regulation by the Federal government. The settlement of the great area of Texas naturally first took place by extension inland from the Gulf coast. All supplies came by sea from the north. Freight schedules were scaled from the seaboard according to distance, more or less, in competition with stage and wagon. Gradually, however, with the growth of St. Louis as a rival centre of distribution, railroads serving that city penetrated directly from the northeast. The St. Louis jobbers were at once brought into keen rivalry with merchants in North Atlantic states, served by coastwise steamship lines. This competition beginning at the points of contact of the two different sets of railroads, gradually extended all over the state. St. Louis lines, acting for local jobbers whose goods came from New York, might not charge more at any point in the aggregate than the total rate from the same initial city which applied by way of the Gulf steamers. Nor could the railroads in from the Gulf ask more for both steamer and rail carriage than the entire double charge from New York around by way of St. Louis. The natural stronghold of the Gulf lines was in the centre and the south; northern Texas was more naturally tributary to St. Louis; but gradually a compromise was effected whereby equality of rates was accorded either from New York or St. Louis to all stations throughout the state. Thus arose the so-called Texas Common Point Territory, to all parts of which Kansas City, Chicago, and finally all other distant cities were admitted on even terms.

Another feature of the Texas rate adjustment is suggestive.

[1] McPherson, Railroad Freight Rates, p. 92, is best on this. *Cf.* pp. 127 and 243, *supra*.

A vast territory, uniform in products and needs, might either be served by a few great distributing centres or by a larger number of smaller ones, each forming the natural focus of trade within a given district. Believing the latter arrangement to be better suited to local conditions, the Texas Railway Commission has arbitrarily prescribed such intra-state tariffs as to foster the development of a number of such jobbing points or mercantile centres. Local rates, more or less proportioned according to distance, are graded up to a maximum, all based principally upon the needs of the principal city, Houston, as served by its seaport, Galveston. The significant feature of these Texas local rates, however, is the fact that beyond a fixed maximum, — say 245 miles on classified tonnage, or 160 miles on cotton, — no further increase of rate occurs with extension of the haul. That is to say, beyond a certain radius fixed by the maximum rate, distributing centres are placed upon an entire parity with one another. Fort Worth, for example, within a distance of about two hundred miles, naturally has an advantage over all other competing centres, more distantly located; but outside of this zone, naturally tributary to it as a provincial trade centre, all others such as Dallas, Waco, or San Antonio enjoy equal opportunity. In only one respect is the distance principle violated: namely, in the preferential rates from the north to Houston and Galveston as compared with the higher charges to intermediate Texas points. These primary centres are encouraged by standing in a class by themselves.

This theoretically admirable Texas system is, however, unstable in several regards. It is artificial in that it is primarily adjusted to the needs of the state, without reference to the rights of other places lying beyond its borders.[1] The railroads naturally desire to contract the common point territory; the forces of trade rivalry seek to enlarge it. The growth of middle western cities and manufactures, supplying Texas from their own domestic plants rather than merely redistributing goods

[1] *Cf.* chap. XX on the conflict of state and Federal powers.

manufactured in the East, also tends to modify the scheme. Whether the common point system, therefore, can long withstand the force of these disintegrating influences remains to be seen. The conditions are not compact and homogeneous as they are in New England, which enjoys a similar flat rate system. And it may well be that ambitious cities along the northwestern border of the state, like Fort Worth, may finally succeed in forcing concessions in rates from the Middle West on the ground of their relative nearness as compared with competitors further south. On the other hand, distributing centres farthest away from the main sources of supply, like San Antonio, would naturally resist any infraction of the rule of parity. And then, again, it is becoming apparent that the decentralization of distribution through a number of secondrate jobbing towns rather than from one preëminent centre, is hindering the growth of a metropolis, able to compete on even terms in high grade products with the older centres of the East. Few dealers in Texas cities are able to purchase dry goods or boots and shoes in carload lots, that is to say, on the lowest terms as concerns freight rates; and the combination of shipments of different goods to make up a miscellaneous carload rate, thus overcoming this disadvantage, is open to serious objection.[1] All told, therefore, the experience of Texas is well worth attentive consideration, as a study in the intimate relationship between trade and transportation. The sharpness of contrast between such a common point scheme and the basing point system of the other southern states, brings the relative advantages and defects of each into strong relief.

Transcontinental freight rates have been brought into prominence of late in direct connection with the wonderful growth of population and trade on the Pacific slope.[2] Our

[1] *Cf.* chap. IX on carload rates as a problem in classification.
[2] This problem is discussed as a form of local discrimination at p. 245, chap. VII, *supra*, and as a long and short haul question at p. 610, chap. XIX, *infra*. The voluminous record in the pending Union Pacific-

territorial possessions in the Pacific and the development of Oriental trade, together with the general interest in the Panama Canal since 1900, have all conspired to direct attention to this complicated problem. The first point to notice is the relatively high level of rates, averaging very much more per mile than anywhere else in the United States. The following table of rates in 1905 is significant:

Miles	From	Class 1	Class 5
912	Chicago to New York	$0.75	$0.30
912	Chicago to New Orleans	1.10	0.47
2328	Chicago to San Francisco	3.00	1.65

These distance tariffs, however, as already explained in our chapter on Classification, need to be supplemented by additional details in order to bring into relief the relative amount of the charge. So far as these figures go, it will be observed that for a distance about two and one-half times as great as from Chicago to New York or the Gulf of Mexico, the rates to San Francisco are very much higher in proportion.

The unrest among shippers in far western territory is not due to the relatively high tariffs in force. It arises primarily from the nullification of the distance principle in rates. And, in the second place, it hinges upon the relation between carload ratings and the development of local jobbing business. The primary factor in the making of rates to the coast has always been the existence of water competition, either by way of Cape Horn or the Isthmus of Panama.[1] The facilities for cheap transportation over these routes have compelled the

Southern Pacific Merger case before the U. S. Supreme Court, No. 820, October term, 1911, is a primary source of material. It will be reviewed in the *Quarterly Journal of Economics* during 1912–13.

[1] Best described in 19 I.C.C. Rep., p. 245; and 21 *Idem*, pp. 345–354, 416–421.

all-rail lines to make low through rates which would enable them to secure a portion of the business. Inasmuch, also, as most of the competition of the steamships over these very long routes involves shipments in large quantity, competition with the railroads has mainly been felt in making rates by the carload. The result has been the existence for many years of a special transcontinental tariff, more or less uniformly adopted by all the roads, which consists in the main of commodity rates for carload shipments, the scale of these rates being sufficiently low to meet steamship competition as above described.

This simple situation has been complicated by the fact that all of the transcontinental lines, except the Southern Pacific with its eastern terminus at New Orleans, have had a particular interest in building up both manufacturing and jobbing business at their eastern terminals at Chicago or Missouri river points. For such a policy enabled them to secure the entire charge for the transportation of commodities to the Pacific coast, without the necessity of a pro-rating division, as when goods are hauled from the Atlantic seaboard cities. The situation then resolved itself practically into a competition of markets. Chicago, St. Louis, and St. Paul were pitted against New York, Philadelphia, and other Atlantic ports in rivalry for the trade of the Pacific coast. In order to benefit the cities in which they had a peculiar interest, the all-rail lines, therefore, gradually introduced what is known as the system of "postage-stamp rates."[1] That is to say, they gradually extended to one city after another east of the Mississippi river, the same rates to the Pacific coast as were enjoyed by the seaboard cities. As a consequence, for some years every city east of the Mississippi has been able to ship goods to San Francisco at the same rate which is paid from Boston and New York, which may be more than a thousand miles farther away.

[1] Historically discussed in 9 Int. Com. Rep., p. 318 and 19 I.C.C. Rep., p. 238 with map; both reprinted in our Railway Problems; and 21 *Idem*, pp. 352 and 418.

This system is justified in theory, even for rates from Chicago and St. Louis, as due to water competition; and it has been said that commodities are sometimes shipped from as far inland as this to the Atlantic seaboard, and thence to San Francisco by water. The latest phase of the controversy reveals the weakness of this argument. The inland cities, such as Chicago and St. Louis, having been accorded the same rate to San Francisco as New York and Philadelphia, demand lower rates than the Atlantic cities in proportion to their relative nearness to San Francisco. In other words, they demand that the rates, instead of being made upon the "postage-stamp basis" — absolutely the same from all cities, however remote — shall be graded. This would give Chicago, St. Louis, and St. Paul an advantage in laying down manufactures or in distributing products secondarily, in competition with the older centres at the East. To this policy the jobbing interests of the Pacific coast strenuously object. From their point of view, any grading of rates will enable the western cities to compete with them directly in local distributive business. They do not object to the low rates from the eastern seaboard, nor would it avail to do so because the natural conditions of water competition are beyond control. Moreover, the low rates from Atlantic points are all, as above said, on carload lots, and such low carload rates operate distinctly to the advantage of the Pacific coast jobber, enabling him to obtain goods in wholesale lots, and then to break bulk in order to distribute them up and down the coast.

The intimate relationship between the carload question and the grading of rates to interior centres, is plain from the foregoing paragraph. Viewed by itself alone, the carload question is not dissimilar to that presented in the southern states. Rivalry between jobbers in the East and provincial middlemen in a little developed territory is in evidence in either case. The St. Louis Business Men's League case best exemplifies this issue.[1]

[1] 9 Int. Com. Rep., p. 318; reprinted in our Railway Problems, chap. XVII.

Trade interests in this interior city wished to abolish all distinction between carload and less-than-carload lots, for the patent purpose of enabling them to sell direct throughout the Pacific coast territory in competition with San Francisco jobbers. The latter, on the other hand, demanded that all less-than-carload ratings should be abolished on transcontinental shipments; so that they might purchase their goods by the carload and resell them in parcels. The Commission, after fully weighing the evidence, decided that, so far as carload differentials were concerned, the existing scheme in 1902 was not abnormal as compared with other portions of the country. On the other aspects of the matter, such as the relativity of rates to Rocky mountain and Pacific terminal points, no ruling was made. But the dissenting opinion upon this point is significant, as we shall see, in that it put forth the suggestion of a scheme of rates graded according to distance, — a plan ten years later to be enforced by the Commission under its amplified powers at law.

The welfare of the entire Rocky mountain belt of population, and particularly its commercial centres, constitutes a second phase of the problem of transcontinental rates.[1] The whole chain of cities from Spokane on the north to the Mexican border has been long and vitally interested in this matter. Rates to these cities, elsewhere described,[2] as well as from these cities out in either direction, are very much higher than the rates for longer distances through them and beyond. Thus, for instance, in the case of Pueblo, it has been shown that bar iron was hauled 2,400 miles from Chicago to San Francisco, for fifty cents per one hundred pounds, and rails were hauled the

[1] 19 I.C.C. Rep., p. 238 with map, reprinted in our Railway Problems, voicing the complaint of the Nevada Railroad Commission, is thoroughly typical. The leading Kindel cases are in 8 I.C.C. Rep., p. 608; 9 *Idem*, p. 606 and 11 *Idem*, p. 495 (with a highly suggestive map); the San Bernardino cases are in 4 *Idem*, p. 104; and 9 *Idem*, p. 42; and for Salt Lake City, 19 *Idem*, p. 218. *Cf.* also University of Colorado, Economic Studies, Dec. 1909.   [2] Page 610 *infra*.

same distance for sixty cents; while for the haul from Pueblo, Colorado, to San Francisco, only 1,500 miles, the rate on both commodities was $1.60. Cotton piece goods were shipped from Boston to Omaha for fifty-two cents per one hundred pounds, with the added rate on to Denver of $1.25, giving an aggregate of $1.77. In face of this, the rate through Denver to California is only one dollar. The railways' defence for this situation was that the low through rates were compelled by water competition. But it is certainly difficult on this ground to justify lower rates to Missouri river points than to Denver or Salt Lake City. In other words, as urged in our chapter on local discrimination,[1] having once recognized the principle of blanket rates as far west as Kansas City, there seemed to be no reason why the limit should not be pushed further west. All of these allied cases, however, were left unsettled for years, owing to the lack of power on the part of the Interstate Commerce Commission to enforce its decisions under the law as then interpreted. With the new legislation since 1906, as will be shown,[2] a permanent and just solution of the matter is promised at last.

The relations between the Canadian railways and the transcontinental lines in the United States were for many years unsatisfactory; and were oftentimes a source of serious disturbance in the matter of rates. The Canadian Pacific claimed, and was in fact accorded for some years, a differential or a lower rate, in order to offset its disability in the matter of distance, extra-territoriality, etc. Thus, for instance, in 1888 the Canadian Pacific was allowed to quote rates thirty cents per one hundred pounds below those by the standard lines. The rates were afterwards increased on first-class traffic. The other roads refused, after a time, to continue differentials at this figure, and after a year the differential was reduced to twenty-eight cents from the Atlantic seaboard. The question was bitterly contested after that until 1892, when all agreements were aban-

[1] Page 342, *supra*.   [2] Chapter XIX, *infra*.

doned. Since that time the Canadian Pacific has acted independently, taking, as a rule, rates about ten per cent. less than its competitors in American territory. The whole question was submitted to arbitration in 1898, and by a divided opinion two out of three of the arbitrators decided that the Canadian Pacific Railway was not, nor should it be, entitled to a differential under the rates made by the United States lines.[1] The intricacy of the question is indicated by the non-concurrence in this conclusion of so well recognized an authority as J. W. Midgley. The railroads concerned having all agreed to acquiesce in this decision, the situation has been far more harmonious in this respect than for many years previous.

A difficulty often arises in connection with the interruption of a shipment of goods in order to subject it to some simple process of manufacture. Shall the entire journey from producer to consumer be considered as a unit in determination of the rate; or shall the two parts, before and after the change of form by manufacture, be considered as separate and distinct in this regard? This problem arises in connection with the so-called "milling-in-transit" system for grain.[2] Logs likewise may be stopped at some convenient point en route for cutting into lumber.[3] Cattle or hogs must sometimes be stopped on the way to market in order to fatten or otherwise prepare them for sale;[4] structural iron may be halted for the purpose of fitting, shearing, or punching;[5] transit privileges on wool or concentration points for other commodities may be involved;[6] or other goods may be substituted at an intermediate point.[7] And then, finally, there are the so-called "floating cotton"

[1] Board of Arbitration on Question of Canadian Pacific Differentials Proceedings and Decision, Oct. 12, 1898.
[2] Typical cases 8 Int. Com. Rep., p. 47; and 10 I.C.C. Rep., p. 675.
[3] The Central Yellow Pine case, No. 681, 1903; and Op. 705, 1906. Also in 1912, 22 I.C.C. Rep., p. 239.
[4] Best described by Bowes, Senate (Elkins) Committee, 1905, p. 2851.
[5] 14 I.C.C. Rep., 11.
[6] 23 I.C.C. Rep., 169 and 438.   [7] 18 *Idem*, p. 280; *cf.* p. 209, *supra*.

cases.[1] The principle at bottom is practically the same in all of these sets of cases. It may be worth while briefly to consider two of them.

The "milling in transit" system is simply that of according to grain which is unloaded and milled at an intermediate point, the low through rate from the point of origin to that of consumption. Thus, for instance, wheat grown in North Dakota may be unloaded and ground into flour at Minneapolis and thence shipped to New York at the through rate from its point of origin to New York. Oftentimes a very small charge, as, for instance, one cent per one hundred pounds, is made for the privilege. This system prevails throughout the southern states also. Grain is brought, for instance, from Kansas City to Nashville or Birmingham, milled there, and shipped farther south for consumption. The rate charged is based upon the entire haul from Kansas City to the local point where the flour is consumed. Obviously this system stimulates very greatly the development of the milling industry at intermediate points. It is opposed correspondingly by the large cities which otherwise enjoy special privileges in the matter of low rates.

Precisely the same principle is involved in what are known as "floating cotton" rates. In this case the system has developed of permitting cotton to be unloaded in transit and compressed at an intermediate point, it being thereafter reshipped to the point of destination at a through rate from its point of origin. Thus, for example, cotton may be hauled twenty to thirty miles to one of the larger towns. There it is unloaded, sorted and compressed, reloaded, and sent on as if it had not been interfered with at all. Obviously one rate for the entire shipment is much less than the local rate into the town — which is always very high — plus a second rate from that town on to destination. The system in respect to cotton has developed even further than that of milling in transit of grain; for in the latter case the grain must be unloaded at some point

[1] 8 Int. Com. Rep., p. 121, is typical of a large number.

on the line to destination; whereas in the case of cotton it may, under rulings of the Interstate Commerce Commission, be actually hauled *away* from its ultimate destination a number of miles and then reshipped back over the same line though at a lower rate than it could otherwise have enjoyed. Thus, in a leading case decided in 1899 it was held by the Interstate Commerce Commission that cotton could be hauled from Gattman, Mississippi, forty-one miles northwest to Tupelo, compressed there, and then hauled back again through Gattman and Birmingham to New Orleans.

Important centres, such as Memphis, which formerly enjoyed almost a monopoly of the compressing business, have strenuously opposed the development of this system. On the other hand, it offers a distinct advantage to the grower, because in place of selling the cotton through cotton factors at Memphis or other centres, it may be sorted and compressed at local stations. By this means much expense in the matter of drayage, handling and commissions is saved. This system is particularly advantageous because it tends to break up the pernicious basing point system, which tends to centralize all business at a few important points in the southern states. Almost a complete revolution in the matter of handling cotton has been effected during the last few years by the growth of this practice. Not only has the floating cotton system developed further than that of milling in transit by according the right of shipping even backward, away from the ultimate destination; it has also permitted of liberality in the handling of the product itself. It has been held that it is not even necessary for the same cotton to be reshipped from the point of compression. A carload started from the initial point for Boston, for example, may never reach there, other cotton being substituted for it. The destination of the car may be, and frequently is, changed. A few dozen grades of cotton being on the market, the original shipment into the point of compression may be entirely resorted and distributed to a dozen different points. Even the ownership of the cotton may change while it is in transit. Nevertheless, the system has been held as valid under the law, and its beneficial effects during the last few years have been observable, especially in the southern states. Of late the danger lurking in these systems of gross personal favoritism, have led to their careful examination in a number of cases. What the final policy regarding them is to be, cannot at this writing be affirmed.[1]

A problem of considerable difficulty, involving the relative shares of the various seaports in American export business, has occupied the attention of experts for more than a generation; and at this present writing, although before the Interstate Commerce Commission for the third time, seems to be almost as far from a satisfactory solution as ever.[2] It originated at the time of the rate wars in 1876. The first agreement between all the trunk lines concerning it was entered into in the following year. By this an attempt was made to equalize the aggregate cost of ocean and rail transportation between competing points in the West and all foreign and domestic points reached through Baltimore, Philadelphia, New York, and Boston. Under this agreement, Baltimore was allowed a rate of three cents below the rate from Chicago to New York; Philadelphia enjoyed a concession of two cents; while Boston had its rate fixed at a certain percentage of the Chicago-New York figure. There was considerable dissatisfaction expressed at various times with these differentials, and the whole matter was submitted to arbitration in 1882. The commercial interests of New York,

[1] 23 I.C.C. Rep., p. 448: U. S. Commerce Court, April session, 1912, No. 47. Ann. Rep., I.C.C., 1896, p. 78. Extensive investigations concluded July 6, 1912.

[2] The literature upon this subject, aside from the decisions specifically noted below, is voluminous. The Senate (Elkins) Committee, 1905, vol. V, devotes much attention to it as a constitutional difficulty in the way of amendment of the law. The admirable catalogue prepared by the Bureau of Railway Economics, 1912, at p. 126, well covers the field. *Cf.* chap. X, p. 361, *supra*.

as well as of the railroads centering in that city, have complained bitterly that these differences, once adjusted upon a very much higher scale of rates than at present, have become increasingly burdensome now that the Chicago-New York rate is perhaps not more than a third or a quarter of what it formerly was, while the differential has remained at a fixed figure. The recent decline of the export commerce of New York is, in fact, ascribed in a large measure to the operation of these differentials; and a leading case before the Interstate Commerce Commission, instituted by the Produce Exchange of New York, endeavored to secure their abolition. The Commission held, however, that the differentials — recognized by the Joint Traffic Association of 1896 — were legitimately based upon competitive relations of the carriers; and that consequently no unlawful preference or advantage had been accorded to the cities competing with New York for export business.

The result of pressure for a larger division of export business, particularly from Boston, led, in 1899, to a reduction by one-half of the differentials. The matter was finally submitted for arbitration to the Interstate Commerce Commission, which very fully examined the question and rendered a decision in 1905.[1] By this decision rates *via* Philadelphia on traffic for export were to be one cent less than by way of New York, while to Baltimore they were to be two cents less. This arrangement still left Boston subject to its former substantial disability. It was contended that the original purpose of the differentials, namely, equilibration of rates from western centres of production through the various ports to Liverpool, had been practically nullified. For a time the phenomenal development of the Gulf exports diverted attention, forcing all the Atlantic seaports to make common cause against their southern rivals.[2] But the passing of this danger once more revived interest in the struggle between the Atlantic cities. Opportunity for the collection of full data under the strengthened Federal law in

[1] 11 Int. Com. Rep., 13.   [2] Page 31 with diagram, *supra*.

1906, made it possible to reopen the case in 1912 before the Interstate Commerce Commission. But, in the meantime, both in 1909 and 1911, after an interval of twenty years, trunk line rate wars threatened to break out for the protection of Boston against its rivals. The latest decision by the Commission, just handed down,[1] still fails to satisfy Boston. No differential rate on export grain on the ground of distance as against New York is conceded; but those already in effect at Philadelphia and Baltimore are sanctioned. What the effect will be, remains for the future to determine.

The principle involved in the so-called import and export cases [2] is that of the reasonableness of charging lower rates on goods originally shipped from or destined to domestic points, than are charged for similar goods, over the same lines and for the same distances, when brought from or destined to foreign countries. Thus, for instance, in the case of cotton cloth shipped by way of Pacific ports to the Orient, the practice is not uncommon of charging a less rate to San Francisco for the transportation of goods ultimately destined for export, than is charged on similar goods which are to be unloaded for consumption at San Francisco or other California points. Or, reversing the case, this question touches the reasonableness of transporting goods from New York to Chicago at a lower rate, if they have been brought in from Europe, than is charged for similar service in the case of goods that have originated at or near New York. Cases of this description have become increasingly frequent during the last twenty years. The first and most important one, upon which both the Interstate Commerce

[1] 24 I.C.C. Rep., p. 55.
[2] The leading references are as follows: 4 I.C.C. Rep., p. 450; 10 *Idem*, p. 55; 13 *Idem*, p. 87; Rep. to the Senate by I.C.C., Feb. 28, 1903; Senate (Elkins) Committee, 1905, Digest, App. V. The leading export rate case, 8 I.C.C. Rep., p. 214, is reprinted in our Railway Problems. Johnson and Huebner, Railroad Traffic and Rates, vol. I, pp. 492–518. In this instance I have reproduced a portion of my report prepared for the U. S. Industrial Commission in 1900.

Commission and the United States Supreme Court have passed, originated in proceedings before the Interstate Commerce Commission, brought by the New York Board of Trade of Transportation against the Pennsylvania and other railroad companies. The case practically raised the ·general question whether, in the carriage of goods from American seaports, carriers subject to the act could lawfully charge less for the transportation of imported than of domestic traffic of like kind to the same destination. The Commission, after careful examination, held that such differences in rates constituted discrimination as against the domestic shipper. According to its view, the circumstances and conditions pertaining to the carriage of freight from a foreign port to the United States could not be considered as creating the dissimilarity of conditions which alone would justify a different rate for like service in the two cases. The Commission held that:

> One paramount purpose of the act to regulate commerce, manifest in all its conditions, is to give to all dealers and shippers the same rates for similar services rendered by the carrier in transporting similar freight over its line. Now, it is apparent from the evidence in this case that many American manufacturers, dealers, and localities, in almost every line of manufacture and business, are the competitors of foreign manufacturers, dealers, and localities for supplying the wants of American consumers at interior places in the United States, and that under domestic bills of lading they seek to require from American carriers like service as their foreign competitors. . . . The act to regulate commerce secures them this right. To deprive them of it by any course of transportation business or device is to violate the statute."

The Commission thereupon ordered the carriers to cease and desist from making such discrimination. This order, while obeyed by a number of carriers, was disregarded by the Texas and Pacific Railway, which operated an import line from New Orleans to San Francisco. Upon application by the Commission this case was carried to the Supreme Court of the United States for final adjudication. The Supreme Court decided that the interpretation of the law by the Commission was defective, although three members of the court, including the Chief Justice, dissented from this opinion. As an illustration of the discrimination which existed in this case it appeared that the domestic rate on books, buttons, carpets, etc., from New Orleans to San Francisco was $2.88 per one hundred pounds, while the total through charge on the same articles from Liverpool to San Francisco was only $1.07. The Supreme Court distinctly refrained from an opinion as to the reasonableness of these rates, and contented itself with passing upon the propriety of any difference in rates whatever. It held that the contention of the railroads was sound, namely, that all circumstances and conditions, whether within the United States or having regard for ocean rates and foreign competitive conditions, must be considered. In other words, they recognized the validity of the claim of the railroads that this import traffic must be taken at an extremely low rate if at all, since otherwise the goods would go by water around Cape Horn, or by another route. On the basis of such reasoning it would appear that any contribution from low import rates to the fixed charges of the railroad would enable that road to transport its domestic traffic at a lower rate than it otherwise might. What, however, the majority of the court did not add, although it was developed by the dissenting justices, was the fact that these conditions might exclude domestic purchasers entirely from certain markets, giving them over to importers who could control the market by reason of the low rates accorded. Since this decision in 1896 the railroads have still further developed this system of discrimination. The only safeguard for the domestic producer must lie, obviously, in some decision by a competent tribunal as to the amount of such differences which may reasonably exist. The Supreme Court has upheld their validity as a system, but it still remains for the amount of such difference which may be deemed reasonable, to be determined.

Identical in principle with the above described case,

although presenting reversed conditions, are the so-called export rate cases. These have to do mainly with the rates charged on products for domestic consumption as against like products for export. As an illustration of the extent of such differences, it was clearly shown before the Industrial Commission that at times the freight rate on wheat from Kansas City to Galveston was twenty-seven cents per one hundred pounds if for domestic consumption, while the proportion of an export rate for a similar service was ten cents.[1] The rate on wheat from the Mississippi river to New York for domestic consumption was at times twenty or twenty-one cents per one hundred pounds, while for the same service when the goods were to be exported, the rate would be thirteen cents per one hundred pounds. This system of stimulating foreign business by discriminatingly low rates seems to have attained large proportions only since 1897. The Interstate Commerce Commission took cognizance of the system in a decision rendered in 1899.[2] It was enabled to do so by virtue of the Import Rate decision above cited, whereby the United States Supreme Court authorized it to consider not only circumstances and conditions within the United States, but also those relating to ocean transport and foreign competition.

The railroads justify their action on the ground that only by making such concessions in export rates could they lay down grain in foreign markets in competition with other parts of the world. On the other hand, it was not made clear why such competition from foreign markets had become any more acute in the last few years than prior to that time. There appears to be much force in the argument of many shippers, and also of some railroad men, that this anomalous condition of rates was due, not so much to the keenness of foreign competition, as to the rivalry among the American carriers themselves. In

---

[1] *Cf.* Ann. Rep., I.C.C., 1899, p. 22.
[2] 8 Int. Com. Rep., p. 214; reprinted in our Railway Problems, chap. XVIII.

other words, it was said that the competition between the Gulf ports and the Atlantic ports was responsible for the abnormally low rates on export business. In line with this argument would seem to be the fact that it is the rates upon wheat and not upon flour for export, which have decreased more than in proportion to the decrease upon similar commodities for domestic consumption. The passing of the acutest phase of competition from the Gulf ports since 1906, has rendered these questions of lesser interest of late years. They may at any time be revived, but seem unlikely to regain the importance which they formerly assumed.

CHAPTER XII

THE MOVEMENT OF RATES SINCE 1870; RATE WARS

Contrast before and after 1900, 411.— Revenue per ton mile data, 412. — Their advantages and defects, 414. — Nature of the traffic, 416. — Low-grade traffic increasing, 416. — Growing diversification of tonnage, 418. — Present conditions illustrated, 419. — Length of the haul, 421. — The proportion of local and through business, 422. — Effect of volume of traffic, 424. — Proper use of revenue per ton mile, 425. — Index of actual rates, 426. — Its advantages and defects, 427. — Difficulty of following rate changes since 1900, 427. — Passenger fares, 429. — Freight rates and price movements, 430.

Improvement in observance of tariffs, 431. — Conditions in the eighties, 432. — The depression of 1893–1897, 433. — Resumption of prosperity in 1898, 436. — The rate wars of 1903–1906, 438. — Threatened disturbances in 1909–1911, 439.

THE course of freight rates in the United States during the last generation divides naturally into two periods, before and after 1900, respectively.[1] Prior to that date an almost uninterrupted decline took place, which has been followed by a strongly marked upward tendency during the last decade. In respect of freight rates this movement is commonly judged in either of two ways; by comparison of actual rates charged for specified service between given points through a series of years; or, secondly, by means of what is called the revenue per ton mile. Considering first the use of this latter index, the course of events is shown by means of the diagram opposite the next page, covering the period between 1867 and 1910. But before conclusions may safely be drawn from this showing, it is imperative that the true significance of revenue per ton mile statistics should be set forth. For a generation, and particularly in connection with the Roosevelt legislation in 1906, volumes of

[1] U. S. Industrial Commission, XIX, 1901, pp. 272–290; *Annals of the American Academy of Political Science*, 1898, pp. 324–352.

written and oral evidence upon moot questions were based upon such figures. Specious and misleading reasoning upon a public question was perhaps never more common in the course of our history.[1] It is most important to understand clearly the real significance of this common statistical unit. We shall then, only, be in position to interpret the diagram properly.

The revenue per ton mile for a given road, or for the railway system of the United States, is computed by dividing the total freight revenue for that service, whatever it may be, by the number representing the amount of freight in tons hauled one mile. Thus, for example, if the total freight revenue of a system of roads be $900,000,000, this having been received as compensation for hauling an equivalent of 90,000,000,000 tons of freight one mile, the compensation actually received for each ton hauled one mile is obviously one cent. All that is necessary in order to compute the average revenue per ton mile, then, is to know the total freight revenue and the amount of ton mileage service. Computed in this way the average revenue per ton per mile for the railways of the United States in 1867 was 1.92 cents. From this level a decline took place in 1890 to 0.941 cents — that is to say, the average amount received for each ton of freight hauled one mile had declined about one half. Since about 1897 there has been no considerable change, the corresponding figure for 1911 being 0.757 cents. In other words, at the present time the carriers of the United States receive about three-fourths of a cent for each ton-mile service. From a revenue point of view this unit may seem insignificant in amount; but it should be borne in mind, of course, that it is applied to an immense volume of traffic. Even the slight increase between 1900 and the present time, if applied to the volume of traffic now existing, would make a difference in freight revenue for the entire railway system of the United States of approximately $61,000,000.

[1] Revenue per ton mile in index to the Senate (Elkins) Committee Hearings, 1905, vol. IV.

RATES SINCE 1870 413

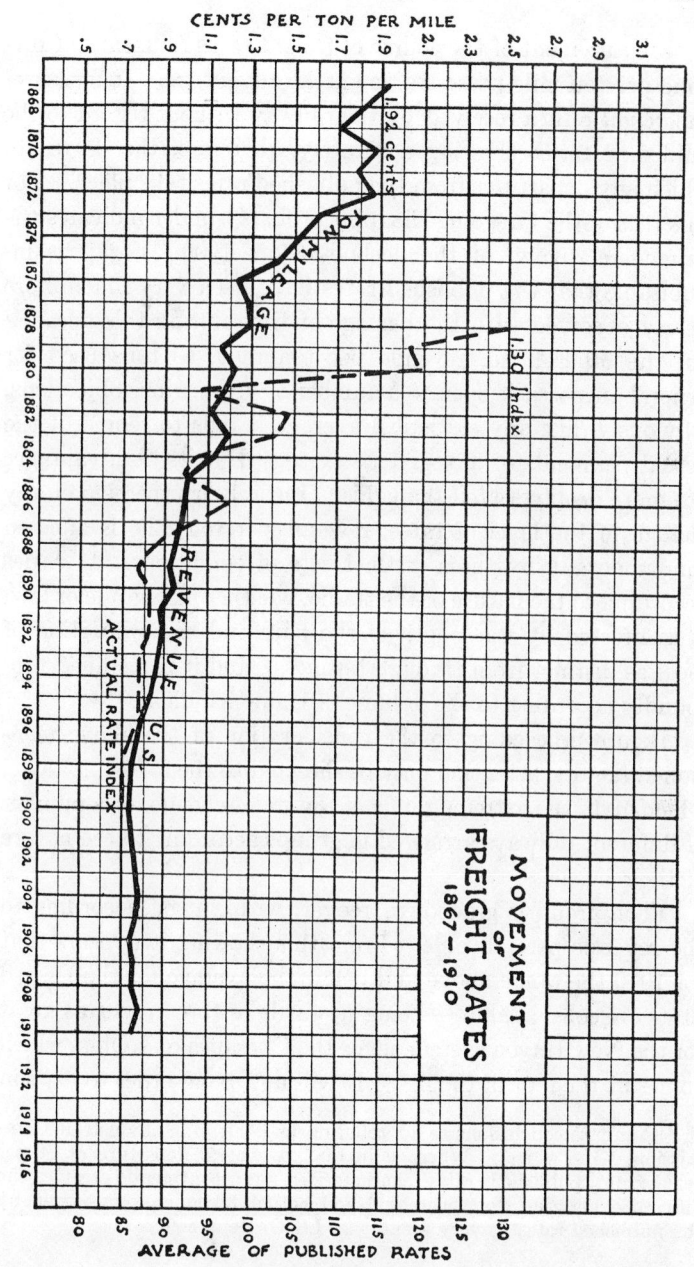

Measurement of the course of freight rates by means of revenue per ton mile possesses one great advantage. It measures the *actual* return received by the railway without regard to the published tariff, showing accurately, therefore, the degree to which any departures from the published rates take place. For this reason the foregoing diagram probably under-indicates the extent, relatively, of the decline before 1900. For it is indubitable that the published rates have been very much more nearly observed with the passage of time during this decade.[1] On the other hand, revenue per ton mile, as thus used for general purposes, is open to a number of very serious objections. Obviously, like any statistical average it fails to represent the actual payment for any given service. But its disadvantages are more deeply seated than this. Entirely irrespective of any change in the level of rates, revenue per ton mile is affected fundamentally by three distinct sets of conditions. It varies according to the nature of the traffic, whether high grade or low; it is affected by the length of the haul and the proportion of local as distinct from through business; and it is modified profoundly according to the volume of traffic handled.

Before proceeding to the consideration of the above mentioned factors, attention may be directed to the following table, which gives the extreme range of ton-mile revenue for a number of different railways arranged in groups according to the nature of their business.

Each group is graded, moreover, within itself according to the revenue per ton mile. From this showing it appears that for 1910 the range above and below the average for the United States is considerable — being upwards of three times as great for the New Haven system as for the Chesapeake & Ohio, which comes at the foot of the list. It will now be in order to explain

[1] Compare conclusions as to rebating in 1900; U. S. Industrial Commission, XIX, p. 285. When, as in 1887, a general departure of 50 per cent. from published rates characterized transcontinental traffic, the difference between the theoretical and actual revenue, as measured by the published rates, is very great. 21 I.C.C. Rep., 349.

RATES SINCE 1870

1910	Revenue per ton mile. (Cents)	Freight density.	Av. haul per ton. (Miles)
New England —			
New York, New Haven & Hartford	1.417	1,057,000	93.4
Boston & Maine	1.08	1,046,000	102.8
Southern —			
Atlantic Coast Line	1.273	365,000	145
Southern R.R.	.957	......	....
Louisville & Nashville	.751	1,124,000	170
Illinois Central	.589	1,445,000	238
Western and Transcontinental —			
Denver & Rio Grande	1,279	532,000	104
Southern Pacific	1.232	745,000	256
Union Pacific	1.011	1,091,000	364
Northern Pacific	.900	940,000	297
Great Northern	.822	814,700	244.1
Granger —			
Chicago & North Western	.891	729,000	141
Chicago, Milwaukee & St. Paul	.843	709,000	173
United States, all roads	.753	1,071,000	146
Trunk Lines —			
Erie	.626	2,808,000	146.
New York Central & Hudson River	.625	2,548,000	195
Pennsylvania Railroad	.580	5,139,000	168
Baltimore & Ohio	.577	2,711,000	191
Lake Shore & Michigan Southern	.515	3,911,000	171
Coal and Ore —			
Philadelphia & Reading	.765	4,506,000	97
Lehigh Valley	.646	3,288,000	174
Hocking Valley	.458	4,014,000	125
Bessemer & Lake Erie	.453	8,051,000	118
Norfolk & Western	.447	3,456,000	264
Chesapeake & Ohio	.407	3,161,000	267

the reasons for these wide variations, which are by no means, as is customarily assumed in public discussion, conditioned even primarily by the level or reasonableness of the freight rates charged. Until these attendant circumstances are fully understood, any conclusions as to relative freight rates for a given service based upon revenue per ton mile, are entirely misleading.

The nature of the traffic handled by a carrier is the most important consideration to be kept in mind in interpreting revenue per ton mile data. This is most clearly shown by comparison in the table between the group of coal and ore roads and the New England systems. The revenue per unit of service on a road whose traffic is largely of low grade most necessarily be low. Probably the lowest average ever reported in the United States was for the Chesapeake & Ohio in 1899 — the low point in the general movement of freight rates — when its ton-mile revenue touched 0.362 cents. Whenever the business of a carrier consists largely of coal, grain, lumber or other low-grade commodities on which the freight charges must necessarily be exceedingly low in order that the freight shall move at all, the revenue per ton mile must consequently stand at a low figure. Bald comparison of any such revenue with a corresponding figure for high-grade roads is obviously misleading and fallacious. It does not mean that the latter necessarily charges more for the same service; but its higher revenue per ton of freight moved one mile may be, and very likely is, merely due to the fact that much of its tonnage is capable of bearing higher charges. From this circumstance it also follows that comparisons from year to year either for single roads or for the entire railway net, must be made in the light of variations in the proportion of high and low grade tonnage. The trend seems to have been steadily downward in this regard year by year. A steady increase, relatively, in the volume of low-grade traffic has long been under way.[1]

The development of the last twenty years in the United States has certainly been in favor of a great increase in low-grade traffic. This is shown by the following table, giving the per cent. of tonnage in various classes upon the trunk lines from New York to and beyond Chicago.

[1] The movement of average trainloads in connection with ton-mile revenue bears upon this point. Thus in 1905, the increased trainload, accompanied by a lower ton-mile revenue, points specifically to an increase in low-grade traffic.

PER CENT. OF TONNAGE IN EACH CLASS OF FREIGHT ON TRUNK
LINES, WEST-BOUND [1]

Class	1878	1880	1885	1890	1892
1	30.4	26.4	24.8	21.0	19.9
2	6.9	6.7	7.1	6.4	5.4
3	4.8	4.4	4.2	12.3	11.3
4	57.9	50.1	29.3	12.7	10.4
5	0.0	10.6	34.6	10.0	9.6
6	0.0	0.0	0.0	37.6	43.4
Special	0.0	1.8	0.0	....	....
	100.0	100.0	100.0	100.0	100.0

From this it appears that "sixty per cent. of the tonnage is now (1893) carried in fourth, fifth and sixth classes. . . . Prior to 1886 no considerable number of articles were permanently assigned to the fifth and sixth classes; they embraced usually a few commodities which had been assigned a special rate." Further consideration of this table shows that first-class freight, forming thirty per cent. of the tonnage in 1878, declined to less than twenty per cent. in 1892; while at the same time sixth-class freight ran up from nothing to 43.4 per cent. in 1892. Fourth-class freight declined during the same period from 57.9 to 10.4 per cent. These figures simply mean that a great deal of traffic is now carried upon American railways for long distances which a generation ago it was believed could not be profitably moved at all. The utility of the railway service, once supposedly confined entirely to freight of the higher classes, has been gradually extended until today there is no commodity too cheap to be handled with the improved facilities. This vast increase in the amount of low-grade traffic is undoubtedly responsible to some degree for the apparent decline of freight rates so often instanced. Fortunately upon this point we have the specific testimony of traffic managers of long experience. On the other hand, in justice to the railways it must be admitted that the proportion of local business at high rates, which would tend to increase the average revenue per ton mile, has steadily increased with the growth of the country; and, moreover, as has

[1] Senate Finance Committee Report on Prices, 1893, Part I, p. 437.

already been shown, in times of exceptional prosperity the movement of high-grade freight has increased in more than its due proportion.[1] Nor are these facts adduced in criticism of American railway policy. They are simply intended to draw attention to the fact that, while changes of freight rates have undoubtedly been considerable, they have not been as great as is oftentimes plausibly stated. As for comparisons with foreign countries, they are practically invalidated by the difference in local conditions, as, for instance, in England where local delivery is involved. In the United States such service is charged in addition, either as drayage or express.

The increased diversification in the freight tonnage of American railways, always in the direction of a larger proportion of traffic from general business rather than from the movement of staple commodities, is also of great fiscal significance. It means not only more business, but better and more permanent traffic. The difference, moreover, between the charge which high-grade freight, such as merchandise, will bear by comparison with the highest rate upon grain or coal, is much greater than any difference in the cost of service. The profit, therefore, attendant upon the movement of traffic other than low-grade commodities is strikingly great; although, of course, profitableness is a question of relativity between operating cost and revenue. Heavy train loads of coal at 4 mills per ton mile may be better business than merchandise in light carloads at a rate five times as high. At all events the tendency toward higher grade tonnage has been notable, especially since 1900. Many western roads and even the trunk lines, formerly dependent in a great measure upon the movement of crops, are now affected only indirectly in this regard, by reason of their influence upon general business. The growing diversification of traffic because of its financial importance merits more concrete illustration.

[1] The effect of periods of depression, such as 1903 and 1908, upon the proportion of low-grade tonnage is a moot point.

The Lake Shore & Michigan Southern, during the calendar year 1900, increased its freight traffic by 1,760,000 tons. Of this only 194,000 tons were specified as products of agriculture and animals, while products of the forests actually declined by 84,000 tons. In other words, nearly all of this phenomenal increase in business in 1900 was due to the movement of manufactures, minerals and merchandise. A comparison made for the last three decades makes this point still more clear. Since 1880 there has been very little increase in agricultural tonnage upon this trunk line, with an actual decrease in the movement of grain. This, perhaps, may be in part explained by the great development of grain traffic upon the lakes, which, of course, absorbs much business formerly carried by this road. In other words, farm products and provisions transported by the Lake Shore rose from 3,465,000 tons in 1880 to only 3,843,000 tons in 1900. The movement of petroleum and lumber actually decreased, owing to the construction of pipe lines and the clearing of the forests. On the other hand, manufactures and merchandise increased three-fold in volume, rising from 3,754,000 tons in 1880 to 14,932,000 tons in 1900. Whereas agricultural products in 1880 formed over forty per cent. of the traffic upon the Lake Shore, they constituted in 1900 less than twenty per cent. Much the same tendency is manifested by other routes. Thus for the fiscal year 1901, the Chesapeake & Ohio reported substantial decreases in the actual tonnage of flour, grain, sand, stone, iron, etc.; but a largely augmented movement of general merchandise of the higher classes. Many of the soft-coal roads, such as the Cleveland, Lorain & Wheeling, which used to carry nearly two-thirds of their tonnage in the form of coal, now carry less than forty per cent. A feature of importance in the great prosperity of the anthracite coal roads has been a steady increase in the volume of their general traffic as distinct from coal tonnage. All over the country, in short, the steady growth of population and the decline in the proportion of grain for export is reducing, relatively, the importance of low-grade tonnage, supplanting it by a movement of supplies and merchandise in the contrary direction.

The classification of tonnage for the United States, as a whole and by main divisions, is shown by the following excerpt from *Statistics of Railroads for 1909:*

FREIGHT TRAFFIC MOVEMENT

Class of commodity	United States Tonnage Tons	Per Cent	Trunk Line Territory Tonnage Tons	Per Cent	Southern Territory Tonnage Tons	Per Cent	Western Territory Tonnage Tons	Per Cent
Products of agriculture	73,600,000	8.92	19,000,000	4.65	9,500,000	7.92	45,100,000	15.18
Products of animals	20,600,000	2.49	7.600,000	1.86	1,000,000	.83	11,900,000	4.03
Products of mines	459.500,000	55.60	256,200,000	62.71	63,000,000	52.20	140,200,000	47.22
Products of forests	97,100,000	11.75	21,500,000	5.28	25.300,000	20.95	50,200,000	16.92
Manufactures	108,600,000	13.15	70,000,000	17.15	13,300,000	11.09	25,100,000	8.48
Merchandise	33,900,000	4.11	13,500,000	3.31	4,800.000	3.98	15,600,000	5.26
Miscellaneous	32,800,000	3.98	20,500,000	5.04	3,600,000	3.03	8,600,000	2.19
Grand total	826,400,000	100.00	408,600,000	100.00	120,700,000	100.00	297,000,000	100.00

Conclusions from these figures are well worth noting. The importance, measured by traffic rather than revenue, of low-grade freight classed as products of mines, is notable. This forms more than half the aggregate tonnage for the United States, and has appreciably increased within the last ten years. In 1910 it constituted almost two-thirds of the business in trunk line territory and almost one-half in the West. Products of agriculture, on the other hand, even in western territory, amount to less than one-fifth of the total tonnage. These facts indicate clearly the diverse conditions under which railways operate in different parts of the country. The next table,[1] besides incidentally throwing more light upon the relative tonnage of staple commodities, will suffice to establish our main point —

[1] *U. S Statistics of Railways,* 1910, p. 64.

SUMMARY OF SELECTED COMMODITIES FOR THE YEAR ENDING JUNE 30, 1910[1]

Commodity	Freight carried in carload lots Tons	Ton-mileage of freight carried in carload lots Ton miles	Revenue from freight carried in carload lots	Average receipts per ton per mile from freight carried in carload lots Cents
Grain	31,947,009	7,067,690,568	$44,553,330	0.630
Hay	5,856,185	954,623,830	9,731,590	1.019
Cotton	3,400,316	689,594,719	12,573,674	1.823
Live stock	10,754,108	2,449,310,036	29,802,514	1.217
Dressed meats	2,407,454	724,239,606	6,548,955	.904
Anthracite coal	28,202,577	5,104,428,347	30,083,630	.589
Bituminous coal	192,479,389	22,228,778,428	110,139,107	.495
Lumber	68,482,732	11,891,569,514	87,225,470	.734

namely, that the nature of the traffic vitally affects all ton mile revenue statistics. It entirely, in fact, overshadows mere changes in the general level of freight rates. Any argument concerning the movement of such charges, which fails to correct fully for this factor, may be dismissed at once as valueless.

A second consideration in the interpretation of ton mile data, of equal importance with the nature of the traffic, is the length of the haul and the proportion of local as distinct from through business. This necessarily follows from the nature of a distance tariff. Only on condition that the rate augmented in direct proportion to the increase of distance, would the revenue per ton mile remain constant. The diagram at page 108 is instructive in this connection. The charges — denoted by the height of the curve at any given point — tend to grow much less rapidly than distance. In other words, the rate curve approaches a parabolic form, until after a certain point it becomes practically a flat rate, independent of distance. This fact of necessity causes ton-mile revenue to decrease steadily with the length of the haul. For ton-mile revenue is but the ratio of the abscissa to the ordinate of the curve at any given point; the former being the rate charged, the latter the distance.

[1] Mileage of roads represented on June 30, 1910 — 130,395.46 miles.

In practice, therefore, the longer the haul in general, the lower is the revenue per ton mile.[1] This is clearly shown by comparison of the two items for given roads, otherwise similarly circumstanced, in the table already discussed on page 415.

Closely akin to the length of haul in affecting ton-mile revenue, is the proportion of local traffic. This also is in practice vital. Obviously it costs much more to handle local business, the terminal expenses being far greater in proportion. And at the same time a larger proportion of the freight moves in small lots locally. This difference between revenue per ton mile for local business and through traffic is very great. On the Louisville & Nashville, for example, in 1886, it was 1.48 cents for the former, as against .99 cents for through business.[2] The Illinois Central in 1900 reported an average revenue per ton mile on through freight of 0.48 cents, while for local freight the corresponding figure was 1.17 cents, the average of both being 0.56 cents. It is apparent, therefore, that any accurate determination of the level of charges in general must take account of such facts as these.

Any carrier like the Southern Pacific, the Chesapeake & Ohio or the Erie, with relatively little local traffic and a business dependent largely upon the long haul, will conduct transportation for a materially lower figure than roads in a densely settled territory. This consideration was recently illustrated in Massachusetts experience.[3] The Fitchburg Railroad, devoted to long distance, low-grade business by the Hoosac tunnel route, was consolidated with the Boston & Maine in 1900. Its revenue per ton mile was formerly .818 cents based upon such traffic. When it was merged with the Boston & Maine, — considerably blessed as it is with local traffic, — the latter's ton-mile revenue fell from 1.44 cents in 1900 to 1.158 cents in the fol-

[1] *Cf.* Ripley Railway Problems, p. 509. *Cf.* also p. 103, *supra*.
[2] Senate (Elkins) Committee, Digest, App. III, p. 63, brings out the high proportion of local business in the South. On the L. &. N. 80 per cent. is thus classed.
[3] Mass. Commission on Commerce and Industry, 1908, p. 117.

lowing year. There had been no change whatever in freight rates.

A word may be interposed in this connection as to the peculiar movement of local as distinguished from through rates through a series of years. Local charges have decreased relatively little, probably because of the absence of competition in such cases. They have, moreover, decreased very unevenly in different parts of the country. Apparently one of the first and most beneficent results of the enactment of the Act to Regulate Commerce in 1887, was a reduction of local rates in various parts of the country, in order to bring the rate adjustment into conformity with the long and short haul clause. This was peculiarly the case in the northeastern or trunk line territory. It does not seem to have occurred in the southern states, where the long and short haul principle has never been accepted in its entirety. The most comprehensive report upon the subject concludes that local rates have in various parts of the country, during the last quarter century, been reduced from ten to fifty per cent.[1] Returns from various railway commissions interrogated by the Industrial Commission in 1900 upon the subject showed highly variable results. From Mississippi it appeared that "local freight rates in this state have been materially lowered in the last four years, especially in the lettered classes"; while in the adjoining state of Alabama "local rates on freight have decreased very little in the last five or six years, and have not decreased in proportion to the decrease made in interstate rates. In New England, comparison of actual freight rates did not indicate any very considerable reduction, the absence of competition in this section being, perhaps, in part responsible for this result. A comparison of published freight rates in southern territory, without making allowance for departures from such tariffs, apparently showed a very much smaller reduction than in other parts of the country. It is also apparently true that the reduction of cotton rates in this section, while

[1] McCain, in Senate Finance Committee Report on Prices, 1893.

considerable, had been much less rapid than that of the rates upon grain from Chicago to the seaboard in either direction. A few instances of an actual rise of local charges since 1900 may be cited.[1] But the fact that competition has been substantially eliminated in consequence of widespread consolidation since 1900, has rendered the movement of local and through freight rates more nearly alike all over the country than they were prior to that time.

The third consideration which must always be kept in mind in the interpretation of revenue per ton mile is the volume of the traffic handled. Any comparison of freight rates which is not made in the light of increase in the business transacted, is bound to be misleading. A reduction of cost of operation per unit, attending a growth in volume, has already been fully described in connection with the theory of rates. And it is but natural that a reduction in the rate should follow any lessening of cost. Moreover, a large volume of business usually implies a relatively greater amount of low-grade tonnage. In order to bring out this relationship the second column in the table on page 415 has been added. This permits a correlation between freight density — that is to say, ton miles per mile of line and revenue per unit of service. It will be noted that, in general, the revenue unit falls as the volume of traffic, measured by freight density, rises. This is strikingly shown by comparison of the groups of western and transcontinental roads with those concerned mainly with the carriage of coal and ore. The soft coal Hocking Valley road with its enormous density and very low revenue per ton mile, affords an excellent example. It is indubitable that the trunk lines and the coal roads are able to transact business for relatively low rates, not only because their tonnage is of low grade, long haul or both; but also because of its immense concentration per mile of line, permitting all of the economies incident to large-scale operation. In this connection, however, it should be noted as a general principle,

[1] I.C.C., Annual Rep., 1903, p. 150.

that oftentimes it is not the mere increase in the traffic of a particular sort which is significant; but rather the growth in the total volume of business of all kinds.[1]

The foregoing criticism of the use of revenue per ton mile as a means of showing the course of freight rates in general has been mainly destructive. This figure, nevertheless, will in many cases be found highly serviceable in the examination of particular rates. It may properly be used to determine whether a given commodity is contributing its due proportion to the general budget of the carrier. Revenue per ton mile can, of course, be computed for each particular service; inasmuch as both the income and the volume of that service are matters of independent record. The table on page 421 brings out this point. Or take a division of the Illinois Central for 1900. Its revenue per ton mile was 0.136 cents on wheat, 0.79 cents on flour, 4.267 cents on sugar-cane, 0.309 cents on soft coal, 1.148 cents on stone and sand, 2.238 cents on furniture, 3.165 cents on merchandise. On this basis one may properly inquire as to whether under all the circumstances wheat, coal or merchandise are doing their part, in the light of the particular expenses attached to their carriage, in maintaining the general burden of indivisible costs. When copper yields a revenue per ton mile of only 0.285 cents, the rate being only 1.6 per cent. of its market value, while on wheat for the same haul the corresponding unit of return is 0.4 cents per ton mile — equal to one-fifth of its worth — there is evidently a maladjustment favoring one commodity over another.[2] In a number of recent cases questions of this sort have been rather satisfactorily answered by resort to this unit of measurement.[3]

The curve of revenue per ton mile, as shown by diagram at the head of this chapter, certainly gives no indication of

[1] Emphasized in the case of wool rates. 23 I.C.C. Rep., 151.
[2] Samuel O. Dunn, *The American Transportation Question*, p. 65.
[3] 22 I.C.C. Rep., 617; 11 *Idem*, 296; 13 *Idem*, 418; 23 *Idem*, 7; 9 *Idem*, 382, etc.

the considerable increase of freight rates which has ensued since 1900. This follows from the fact that in at least two of the three respects, above mentioned, the trend of events, independent of any change in the level of freight rates, has operated to greatly dilute the revenue per ton mile. The growth of low-grade traffic and the immense augmentation in tonnage have both conspired to render this unit entirely useless for purposes of comparison year by year. The average length of haul alone seems to have remained much the same during the decade. Although the curve does not show it, there has been a notable upward movement all along the line, responsible, as we shall see, for much of the new Federal legislation. How may we, then, estimate the amount of these increases? Under such circumstances, it is necessary to turn to the movement of actual rates.[1] The course of these down to 1900 is best shown upon the same diagram above mentioned by means of the dotted curve, entitled Actual Rate Index, the scale for which is given at the right. This rate index is simply the average of the actual published rates for a number of specific commodities between certain given points. It differs in principle from the ton mileage revenue curve, in that it concerns merely the *published* rates, taking no account of rebates or departures from those rates in actual practice. A comparison of its course with that of the ton mileage curve shows a more abrupt decline from about 1878 to 1886, since which year the course of both lines is about parallel. Its irregularity is also significant as illustrating the violent fluctuations to which the published rates were sub-

[1] J. R. Commons, *Bulletin, Bureau of Economic Research*, No. 1, July, 1900; unfortunately not continued to date.

The best data giving actual rates and classifications is the *Forty Year Review*, etc., published by the Interstate Commerce Commission, as "Railways in 1902," part II, 1903; continued in Senate (Elkins) Committee, Digest, App. II, 1905; and 58 Cong. 2nd sess., Senate Doc. No. 257, savagely attacked in Bull. II, Chicago Bureau of Railway News and Statistics, 1904. The largest collection of material is in the Senate (Aldrich) Committee Report on Prices, 1890, I. pp. 397–658, covering the period 1852–1890. Also Bulletin 15, Misc. Series, Div. of Statistics, U. S. Dept. of Agriculture, 1898, pp. 1–80.

jected prior to 1887. Judged by this curve, the situation has been more settled since the enactment of the Act to Regulate Commerce in 1887.

Were data at hand for a continuation of this line to 1910 it would undoubtedly afford a fairly reliable measure, in general, of the substantial increase of rates which has taken place during the decade. The main objection to it would be that it did not weight the average according to the volume of the business carried for each of the thirty-seven concrete rates chosen.[1]

Tracing the rise of actual rates since 1900 is rendered peculiarly difficult, also, by reason of the fact that few of the changes took the form of an outright advance in charges. The end in view was more often accomplished surreptitiously. The sub-

[1] The continuation of Commons' index number of freight rates to date, seemed inadvisable on account of the changes in traffic conditions which have taken place. Originally well selected, the thirty-seven rates chosen in 1900 are not now representative. There are, for instance, no transcontinental quotations at all; none from the southern states, such as on raw cotton; none for the great staples elsewhere moving under commodity ratings, such as iron ore, chemical fertilizers, lumber, citrus fruit, etc. Moreover, twelve of the thirty-seven items chosen by Commons were rates on petroleum which now moves in bulk in pipe lines except locally. Several of the quotations for coal, and for all the other carload rates, as a matter of fact, have been so affected by changes in carload minimum rules, that the mere rate by itself has little significance.

Rejecting Commons' particular index number by reason of its inherent defects does not, however, lessen the desirability of choosing some other combination of rates which may be used as a standard for measurement of rate changes year by year. Yet the selection of such an index number is open to all the difficulties attaching to a similar index number of prices. Is the object, for example, an academic determination of rate changes *per se;* or is it intended to ascertain the financial burden of such charges upon the community? In the former case the volume of traffic affected would not be an important consideration. Local rates on indigo or millinery would be given the same weight as similar changes in the rate on wheat between Chicago and the Atlantic seaboard. The latter mode of approaching the question, on the other hand, would correspond to an index number of prices, weighted according to the volume of consumption. A doubled freight rate on hard coal to Perth Amboy would outweigh an equal change in the charge on castile soap in exact proportion to its commercial importance as measured by the total tonnage transported. Many such details would call for careful consideration before the final adoption of the rate items chosen to constitute the index number; but the Interstate Commerce Commission might well consider the initiation of such a statistical

stantial increases in 1900[1] which inaugurated the upward movement were mainly accomplished by changes of classification. Modification of the carload ratings brought about the same result. A notable instance appeared in the complaint of the dairy men in Wisconsin in 1909. An annual shipment of 38,000,000 lbs. of cheese to Chicago before 1899 moved at twenty cents per one hundred pounds, irrespective of the size of the consignment. Ten years later the rate had become twenty-eight cents for less-than-carload lots, and twenty-two and one-half cents for wholesale shipments. The relative disability of the small shipper under the new circumstances is as significant as the rise of rate for all.[2] The increase of charges might be brought about in another way without actually advancing rates by a withdrawal of commodity ratings, thereby subjecting the shipper to the higher scale of classified commodities. And, finally, a practical elimination of the rebate and the cessation of general rate wars has usually resulted in a very substantial increase in the revenue of the carriers as well as in the scale of charges imposed upon most shippers. Evidence upon this point is officially given in connection with the rate increases of 1903.[3] It thus appears that to follow step by step the movement of actual rates is an extremely complicated matter. Every factor entering into the determination of the charge must be considered; the distance tariff, the classification, minimum carload rules and a host of other specifications which enter into the final result. For our purposes it must suffice that the fact

project, endeavoring to do for railroad rates what the Federal Commissioner of Labor performs so satisfactorily in officially recording current changes in the price of commodities. Such a record of railroad rates extending over a series of years, supplemented by data for ton mileage revenue, would be invaluable in the determination of the reasonableness of rate advances in future; even as the rate increases of 1910 clearly pointed to the need of a similar standard for purposes of comparison from year to year in the past.

[1] U. S. Industrial Commission, XIX, pp. 281–291; 58th Cong., 2nd sess., Sen. Doc. 257.

[2] 16 I.C.C. Rep., 85. For other instances compare 12 I.C.C. Rep., 149, and 23 I.C.C. Rep., 158.   [3] 9 I.C.C. Rep., 382.

of a substantial rise of charges since the turning point in 1900 is beyond question.[1] On the other hand, it is indubitable that such increases as have occurred, arousing vehement protest among shippers, have been more widely advertised than changes in the opposite direction. Substantial reductions, especially on low-grade staples, have sometimes occurred. One is almost at a loss to strike a fair balance between the two, in the absence of dependable data.

The movement of passenger fares has been quite different from that of freight rates.[2] No marked decline during the last quarter of the nineteenth century took place. Growth in the volume of traffic was not accomplished by a reduction of charges. This is in consonance with the experience of foreign countries. Passenger business, while steadily growing, has increased less rapidly than freight tonnage. Generally, in other words, as measured by volume, freight business has become relatively more important with the progress of time. Fiscally the same thing is true. Only in New England does the revenue from this service approximate one-half of the total net earnings. The nature of railway competition explains why passenger fares have not decreased as rapidly as freight rates. Persons must necessarily be more or less directly transported from one point to another; while experience shows that competition in freight traffic may be exceedingly circuitous in route, goods even going hundreds of miles out of the direct-line for transportation by water. This narrowing of the sphere of competition in the case of passengers has consequently operated to lessen the

[1] For further examples supplementing our concrete instances above, the following citations are significant; For cattle, 11 I.C.C. Rep., 238, 296 and 381; 13 I.C.C. Rep., 418; 23 I.C.C. Rep., 7; for soft coal, 22 I.C.C. Rep., 617; for hay, 9 I.C.C. Rep., 246; for transcontinental rates in general, *U. S. v. Union Pacific Railroad*, etc., Supreme Court, 820. October Term, 1911, p. 558. The record, so far as the general advances of 1910 are concerned, will be considered in connection with the legislation of that date, in chapter XVIII.

[2] *Annals of the American Academy of Political Science*, 1898, pp. 324–352.

rate of decline. Another point to be considered in this connection is that no such increasing economies in the handling of passengers are possible as in the case of freight. Instead of decreasing the proportion of dead weight, which for passengers amounts to upward of ninety per cent., by any of the economies recently applied to freight traffic, it appears rather that the proportion of dead weight of equipment per passenger is increasing, owing to the necessity of providing more sumptuous accommodations. Bearing in mind all these facts, it appears not unreasonable that the progressive decline of passenger fares has continually lagged behind the decrease of freight rates. But the natural lethargy in the movement of passenger fares was rudely interrupted in 1908 in connection with the wave of legislation accompanying the Roosevelt campaign which culminated in the Mann-Elkins law. A widespread demand for lower passenger fares found expression in the passage by twenty-two states within five years of maximum fare laws. Eleven legislatures fixed the charge at two cents per mile, the others establishing it at less than three cents. Many appeals to the courts in connection with these statutes took place on the ground of confiscation, and sharp conflicts of authority between Federal and state governments arose.[1] Whether passenger rates would ever have declined without such exercise of authority is open to question, but the disturbance of established conditions at this time was extreme.

One further question with relation to the movement of rates merits consideration. In how far has the rise since 1900 been commensurate with the general upward movement of prices of other commodities than transportation — the particular commodity produced by railways? The evidence tends to show that prices in general have moved upward during the last ten years by approximately one-fourth, and it may be even one-third.[2] Have railway charges in general surpassed this rate or not?

[1] Discussed in chap. XX.
[2] *Quarterly Journal of Economics*, 1907, p. 618.

Some activity of railway experts has been devoted of late to the elucidation of this question.[1] But, after all, is this inquiry of basic importance as bearing upon the general reasonableness of railway rates? Here, as so often elsewhere in the discussion of these questions, the need is for the analysis of such problems with reference to particular services and not in connection with matters in general.[2] It is conceivable that railway rates might and properly ought to increase under certain circumstances much more than in proportion to the general change in freight rates; or that, on the other hand, they might fairly be compelled to lag behind. This introduces the larger question of reasonable rates in general which must remain for discussion in our second volume.

The general level of rates affects the ultimate consumer more than the shipper. Steadiness of rates, on the other hand, is vital to a healthy state of trade. It is important to examine the evidence from this point of view. The history of railroad rates shows a steady improvement in the direction of more general observance of published tariffs. Periods of abject demoralization incidental to the most furious rate wars, have alternated with periods of peace, characterized by more or less faithful observance of agreed rates. Viewed in a large way the intervals of disturbance have become less frequent and less intense with the passage of time. Present conditions are more satisfactory than any which have prevailed since 1850.

Rate wars are almost as old as railroading and are coincident with the appearance of competition. Among the earliest of note were the struggles between the Erie and the New York Central as soon as the former road was constructed to Dunkirk, Ohio, on the Great Lakes. But the most notorious rate wars

[1] Calculations of C. C. McCain on the Diminished Ratio of Railway Rates to Wholesale Commodity Prices, in connection with the increases in 1910.
[2] Well expressed in a recent soft coal case; 22 I. C.C. Rep., 617.

were those which prevailed between the trunk lines in respect of the carriage of grain to the seaboard. These wars began with the entrance of the trunk lines into Chicago in 1869.[1] The Baltimore and Ohio from the outset was the disturbing factor. Having no entry into New York except over the lines of the Pennsylvania Railroad, the refusal of the latter in 1874 to give proper facilities led to immediate retaliation by rate cutting on the Baltimore and Ohio. The details of these wars and their economic significance have become classics in our American industrial history. Suffice it to say that for intensity and persistence these contests which lasted for ten years after 1884, have been unequalled in our history since that time. A brief period of calm ensued after 1876. But soon the struggle broke out again in 1881, intensified by the construction of new parallel trunk lines like the West Shore and the Nickel Plate. These latter rate disturbances lasted for about three years.

The passage of the Act to Regulate Commerce in 1887 greatly improved the rate situation for a time;[2] but harmonious relations were rudely shaken by a bitter rate war in 1888 between the Grand Trunk Railway and the American Lines with reference to the rates upon dressed beef. Trouble over this traffic had occurred as far back as 1879, when the rate from Chicago to New York had been cut from one dollar to forty-five cents. In 1888, however, the rate on dressed beef for weeks was as low as six cents per hundred pounds. The Grand Trunk which had carried almost half of this business in 1887, had its proportion reduced to twenty-eight per cent. in the following year. At this time also extensive rate wars prevailed in the far western territory. The failure of the Atchison Road brought to light accumulated rebates for the four years prior to 1894 to the amount of $3,700,000. The prosperity of the early nineties led to a considerable improvement in rate observances. The

[1] Further details in our historical summary in chap. I.

[2] The main sources of the following chronicle have been the files of Annual Reports of the Interstate Commerce Commission and of the *Railway Age* and *Age-Gazette*.

only exception was the persistence of trouble from the Canadian carriers. The Soo line across the Straits of Mackinac, opening a short route from St. Paul and Minneapolis to the seaboard, was acquired by the Canadian Pacific Railroad in 1890. Combined lake-and-rail grain rates were sadly disturbed and the controversy over so-called ex-Lake grain between the lines from Buffalo to New York, which afterward cropped out in 1900, took its beginning. These Canadian Pacific rate wars were severe while they lasted. In 1892, for instance, the rate on boots and shoes from Boston to St. Paul dropped from one dollar and fifteen cents per hundredweight to forty-five cents.

The panic and subsequent depression of 1893 caused serious and widespread rate wars all over the country. Grain rates from Chicago to New York were openly reduced from twenty-five to fifteen cents. Two peculiarities of this rate war deserve mention. In the first place, every concession was publicly made, — that is to say, the cut rates were filed with the Interstate Commerce Commission; and, consequently, owing to the percentage-basis system to intermediate points, the rate war on Chicago-New York business automatically induced a rate war to every intermediate point in Central Traffic Association territory. Transcontinental rates were also badly upset at the same time. This was due not only to the prevalent hard times, but to complications arising from the independence of the Panama Railway. This line had been controlled since 1871 by the Union Pacific Railroad. The arrangement under which the Pacific Mail Steamship Company was also controlled came to an end in 1893, when the field was again opened to competition. The merchants of San Francisco established an independent line of steamships and for two years the most bitter and reckless rate war prevailed. During this conflict freight was carried from New York to San Francisco as low as thirty cents per hundredweight.[1] Matters were finally settled in

[1] A carload of bamboo steamer chairs across the continent for $9.40 is a cut to the bone indeed. 21 I.C.C. Rep., 349.

1898; but in the meantime the Union Pacific Railroad had gone into bankruptcy.

Entire demoralization in freight rates throughout the southern states occurred in 1894. Every carrier in this section was involved. Rates were cut for two months by as much as two-thirds. The first-class rate from New York to Atlanta dropped from $1.14 to forty cents per hundred pounds. The years 1894–1895 for the country as a whole were exceedingly unfortunate. Better conditions then supervened except for a rate war on grain at Missouri river points, so important that it was made the subject of special investigation.[1] The Chicago Great Western Railroad through the agency of a corporation known as the Iowa Development Company actually purchased on its own account large amounts of grain in order to secure its carriage. Grain was carried from Kansas City to Chicago under the system of rebating known as "protecting the through rate" for as low as two cents, when the open published rate was seventeen cents per hundredweight. Conditions then bettered somewhat largely through the activities of the Joint Traffic and Trans-Missouri Freight Associations. The prospect of legalization of pooling by Congress was bright. Rates seem to have been observed with more than usual faithfulness throughout the country, the only exception being another brief conflict in the southern states. But the Trans-Missouri decision by the United States Supreme Court in 1897, declaring these traffic associations illegal, once more precipitated most unsatisfactory conditions. And these were accentuated by the budding prosperity of the following year.

With the return of activity in business and agriculture in 1898 a frenzy for participation in the rapidly expanding traffic once more brought about extreme disorganization. The Interstate Commerce Commission reported that "a large part of the business at the present time is transacted upon illegal

[1] 54th Cong., 2nd sess., Sen. Doc. 115, is as fine a picture of utter rate demoralization as can be found.

rates ... in certain quarters the observance of the published rate is the exception." The commissioner of the St. Louis Traffic Bureau testified before the United States Industrial Commission that "there were fewer rates maintained in 1898 than at any other time within my knowledge of the railroad business, and I have been in the railroad business for twenty-eight years." At this point the Interstate Commerce Commission intervened by the proffer of its good offices. Conferences with the heads of the principal railroads were held. A decided change in the attitude of the Commission toward the carriers became evident. It wisely sought to arouse the railroads themselves to the enormity of the existing evils, being absolutely unable itself under the law either to prevent or correct the existing abuses. The result fully justified all expectations. The following year witnessed an almost complete restoration of published rates, although business continued to expand in volume. Naturally there was ample for all the railroads to handle. This condition lasted for some time. But during 1900 rate cutting again developed upon a large scale in westbound business. The great increase of eastbound shipments and the demand for return lading at any price was undoubtedly the cause. This condition lasted for some months.

Rate cutting between the trunk lines again broke out in the spring of 1901, grain being hauled as low as eleven cents per hundred pounds from Chicago to New York. Competition between the Lake line railroads seems to have been the cause. The problem of adjusting ex-Lake grain rates dates from this period. The community-of-interest plan of trunk line control was ineffective to prevent disturbance. In the same year a passenger rate war from the Missouri river to California was also threatened. The United States Industrial Commission sent out a number of inquiries concerning conditions in the summer of 1901. This indicated a firm and stable rate condition in the East but some disturbance on lines between Chicago and the Ohio river points. Trouble soon broke out, however.

The Atchison road suspecting its competitors of bad faith, cut its rates first-class from Chicago to the Missouri river from eighty cents to fifty cents per hundredweight. Agreements were repeatedly made and almost immediately violated, some of the strongest lines being the worst offenders. During the fall of that year export rates on flour and grain were badly slashed. The traffic manager of the New York Central lines testified that grain rates for export were not maintained for a number of months.

Apparently the general situation in 1900 was more satisfactory than at any previous time in the history of railroading in the United States. With few exceptions the published rates were observed. This commendable situation seems to have been due to several causes. Primarily an adequate appreciation by the railroads themselves of the losses of revenue to which they had voluntarily subjected themselves prevailed. An enormous volume of traffic incident to general prosperity, also, almost overtaxed the facilities of the carriers. And, in the third place, the spread of consolidation and the community-of-interest idea undoubtedly contributed to the same end. The determined attitude taken by important roads, notably the Southern Railway, contributed to the maintenance of rates. Even in the Far West and Northwest, rate conditions seemed to be in better shape than at almost any previous time. But it was too good to last; trouble soon broke out again. Grain rates from Kansas to Chicago during the summer dropped from nineteen cents to seven cents. Rates on packing-house products became utterly demoralized. So bad did conditions become that in March of 1902 the Interstate Commerce Commission intervened, seeking injunctions in the Federal courts against any departure from the published tariffs. This immediately bettered conditions; and in February of 1903 the passage of the Elkins law, as we shall see, contributed still further to this end. The enactment of this statute, passed at the solicitation of the carriers themselves and imposing much severer penalties upon departure from published rates, brought about conditions during the spring of 1903 unsurpassed for stability. The only exception was a minor disturbance concerning the carriage of ex-Lake grain from Buffalo to New York. Tariffs seem to have been faithfully maintained throughout the country with one exception, that is to say, concerning traffic to and from Missouri river points.

Since the passage of the Elkins Amendments in 1903, the phenomenal development of export trade through the Gulf Ports, principally New Orleans and Galveston,[1] has been mainly responsible for recurring and often ferocious rate wars, particularly during the years 1903–1906. These rate wars were usually precipitated in the first instance by struggles between the Gulf railroads and the trunk lines for the carriage of export corn. In 1904, for example, after a long period during which little surplus corn was available for export from Iowa, Kansas and Nebraska, much of it being locally consumed for stock feeding, a large surplus was left over. Rates were promptly cut during 1905 by both sets of lines. Thus the rate on export corn from Omaha to New Orleans was reduced from eighteen to eleven cents per hundred pounds. This cut was promptly met by a reduction of rates from Missouri river points to Chicago from twenty-four to thirteen cents. The rate from Omaha to New York dropped to the extraordinarily low figure of thirteen cents per hundred pounds. The Burlington and Missouri Pacific Railroads were particularly active in this contest; together securing over eighty per cent. of the corn traffic, although five other important roads were operating in this territory. All through the winter and spring of 1905 the struggle went on unabated. The Gulf ports during this period increased their exports of corn two and one-half times over. The struggle was not alone confined to the carriage of grain; although export flour being manufactured so far north, seems to have been immune from disturbance. The trouble extended over into

[1] Shown by diagram at p. 32, *supra*.

the field of packing-house products for export. It was long thought that this could not be shipped over the roundabout southern route, but its practicability was demonstrated at this time. The demand of the Gulf roads for a ten per cent. differential rate in their favor as an offset for the greater time requisite for transit, not being accorded, rates were again cut by one-third, sometimes being as low as twenty cents per hundred pounds.

The rate wars of 1905 in the carriage of export traffic immediately spread into the field of imports. Competition for transcontinental and far western business has always been keen by the Gulf routes. The notable Import Rate case already discussed, offers a good illustration of this fact. The great volume of tonnage moving outward through Galveston and New Orleans necessitated a correspondingly heavy northern and northwestern movement of empty cars. Hence the railroads leading from the Gulf ports, actively bid both against one another and in connection with the steamship lines against the trunk lines. Competition was particularly keen for the carriage of the large volume of sugar to the Middle West, particularly Missouri river points like St. Louis and Omaha. Carriers from every point of the compass were interested in this traffic. The trunk lines brought refined sugar from the seaboard cities where the West Indian product is concentrated. The Gulf lines brought the Louisiana product, partly as a back-load against exported grain. And the transcontinental lines brought the Hawaiian sugar, also as a back-load against a predominance of westbound tonnage. All hands thus directly took part.[1] For three years this sugar war persisted despite all attempts at harmony. Rates were constantly cut by fifty per cent., always of course to the profit of the large sugar refiners. Coffee, also constituting an important part of our import trade, and of course particularly adapted to entry through the Gulf ports, was carried at ruinous rates. Thus on green coffee during 1905, the rate from New Orleans

[1] Senate (Elkins) Committee, 1905, pp. 2730 and 2874.

to St. Paul was cut from forty to fifteen cents per hundred pounds, while coincidently the rate on sugar dropped from thirty-two to ten cents. The struggle for import business extended finally to all imports of merchandise from Europe. The Illinois Central, for example, actively bid for the imported plate glass business about this time. At a meeting of parties concerned in 1905, the fact developed that every one of the important lines had entered into contracts for the carriage of this traffic at rates approximately one-half those normally prevalent. The trunk lines of course had to meet this competition or lose the business. The Pennsylvania Railroad cut the rate on crockery from forty to eighteen cents; on imported seeds the rate dropped from fifty to twenty cents and on toys from seventy-five to twenty-five cents per hundred pounds. These rate wars it will be observed differed neither in extent nor degree from those of a generation earlier. One cannot avoid the conclusion that the utter demoralization of rates was ended only by the intervention of the Federal government; first by the sturdy and determined application of the Elkins Law under President Roosevelt's personal direction, and later by extension of the principle of supervision and regulation by the Hepburn Act of 1906.

The principal breach since the sugar wars was a rather persistent and locally interesting disturbance of westbound import rates, precipitated in the spring of 1909 by the Boston & Maine Railroad. Its object was to overcome the disability against the port of Boston in the matter of imports, due to the differentials allowed at Philadelphia and Baltimore.[1] This led to a general trunk line upset lasting about four months, in the course of which rates from Boston to Chicago were reduced from sixty-nine to fifty-eight cents. This obviously left little profit in the business. Yet it was a mild concession as compared with the struggles of earlier years. Two years later, in June, 1911, trouble threatened to break out again. This time it was

[1] *Cf.* p. 405, *supra.*

the Delaware & Hudson and Erie roads which filed reduced rates to the interior. But the solidarity of feeling between the trunk lines was such that an open breach was prevented at the last moment. The prompt intervention of the Federal authorities was a noticeable feature on this occasion. It may somewhat safely be predicated that further serious disturbance in future is unlikely to occur.

CHAPTER XIII

THE ACT TO REGULATE COMMERCE OF 1887 [1]

Its general significance, 441. — Economic causes, 442. — Growth of interstate traffic, 442. — Earlier Federal laws, 443. — Not lower rates, but end of discriminations sought, 443. — Rebates and favoritism, 445. — Monopoly by means of pooling distrusted, 446. — Speculation and fraud, 447. — Local discrimination, 448. — General unsettlement from rapid growth, 449. — Congressional history of the law, 450. — Its constitutionality, 451. — Summary of its provisions, 452. — Its tentative character, 453. — Radical departure as to rebating, 454.

DUE appreciation of the significance of the great body of Federal legislation concerning railroads which has accumulated during the last quarter century in the United States, depends upon a clear understanding of the economic events of the period. Great laws are not the figments of men's minds, conjured up in a day. They are a response to the needs of the time. Their true causes are thus immeasurably complex. Nor does a wholesale public demand for legislation arise overnight. From small beginnings the pressure steadily grows, oftentimes for years; until, perhaps through a conjuncture of particularly aggravating events, matters are at last brought suddenly to a head. Yet while this culmination of industrial or social pressure may finally result in legislation under some particularly strong political leadership, to assign such personal influence as even the remote cause of legislation, is to belie all the facts and experience of history. No clearer illustration of the close

[1] The following references are best: — 1866. Hudson, J. F. The Railways and the Republic. — 1877. Seligman, E. R. A. *Political Science Quarterly*, II, pp. 223-264 and 369-413. — 1887. Nimmo, J. Legislative history in *The Railway News*, currently reported. — 1887. Painter, U. H. Compilation from the Congressional Record. Privately published. — 1888-1889. Hadley, A. T. *Quarterly Journal of Economics*, II, pp. 162-187; III, pp. 170-187. In addition, the general works of Hadley, Charles Francis Adams and Haney; and the extensive list of magazine articles in the Bibliography on Railways of the Library of Congress, 1907.

relationship between economic causes and statutory results could perhaps be found, than in the field of our Federal legislation concerning common carriers. It forms one of the most important chapters in our industrial history.

Several of the economic causes of the Act to Regulate Commerce of 1887, are deep-rooted in the preceding decade. A few even run back to Civil War times. Foremost among these was the rapid expansion of the railway net; and particularly, as outlined in our introductory historical chapter, its phenomenal growth during the eighties. More new mileage was laid down in the year of the Act itself than at any other time in our entire history within a single twelvemonth. Of equal significance, however, was the far more than commensurate development of long distance, that is to say, interstate business. The through carriage of livestock and grain to the seaboard for export attained immense importance; and the settlement of the Middle West called for a corresponding westward movement of manufactured goods. The Windom Committee of 1874 on "Transportation Routes to the Seaboard"[1] bears eloquent testimony to the growing importance of this through traffic as a factor in legislative activity. According to the Cullom Committee Report twelve years later,[2] approximately three-fourths of the railway traffic of the country was already at that time interstate in character. On the trunk lines, excepting the Pennsylvania Railroad which still relied more largely on Pittsburg-Philadelphia tonnage, more nearly nine-tenths of the traffic consisted of through, as distinct from local, business. Obviously, this pointed to the assumption of authority by the Federal government, if any were to be exercised; inasmuch as the separate states, as will shortly appear, were held by the Supreme Court of the United States in 1886 to be powerless to deal with interstate commerce.

[1] 43d Congress, 1st session, Senate Report No. 307, 2 pts.
[2] 49th Congress, 1st session, Senate Report No. 46, 2 pts: pt. 1, pp. 16 and 137-166.

The growing disposition of Congress to assume control over interstate business had already been evinced in the passage of two Federal statutes. One in 1872 had dealt with abuses in the carriage of livestock. And another, even earlier, had sought to remove obstacles set up by local jealousy and monopoly to the through carriage of goods. Some railway charters actually prohibited railroads from making connections with other lines; or from allowing cars to leave their own rails. The Erie, for example, was thus hampered; lest the trade of southern New York be diverted to rival seaports. But the military necessity of through transport of troops, and the impediments to speedy and cheap carriage of mails and goods through delays at junction points, impelled Congress to authorize, though not as yet to compel, the formation of through routes and the issue of through bills of lading by the Act of 1866. The immediate response to this permissive legislation was the rise of the private car lines, elsewhere described, in connection with personal discrimination and also in the general historical review.[1]

No widespread demand for a general reduction of railroad rates seems to have existed in 1887. In this regard the situation is strikingly in contrast with that which prevailed during the protracted hard times succeeding the panic of 1873. Acute industrial depression during that period had aroused deep public feeling against the "extortions of soulless railway corporations." It was but natural that all the farmers in the newly settled states should actively participate in the Granger movement. The popular war cry in this agitation was lower freight rates. This demand is voiced in the President's message of 1872, calling for "more certain and cheaper transportation, of the rapidly increasing western and southern products, to the Atlantic seaboard." The proposals of the Senate to attain these objects are contained in the above-mentioned Windom Committee Report of 1874. Competition is to be stimulated by the development of waterways and new trunk lines. A bureau of

[1] Pp. 140 and 192

commerce is proposed. The long and short haul principle in rate making is to be enforced. Stock-watering is to be prohibited; and publicity of rates to be brought about. On the whole, reduced charges are to be secured rather by means of natural competition among carriers than through legislation. But the keynote of the Windom Report of 1874 is cheaper carriage of goods, — a general reduction of rates all along the line.

Many things happened during the next twelve years to modify this demand. By 1886, according to the Cullom Committee, "the paramount evil chargeable against the operation of the transportation systems of the United States, as now conducted, is unjust discrimination between persons, places, commodities, or particular descriptions of traffic." Purely economic events had brought about this change of opinion. The rate wars of the seventies; a revival of general prosperity in 1879; and great mechanical improvements and economies in operation, had brought about the desired decline of freight rates.[1] For the time the bogey of extortionate charges was laid at rest. The Act of 1887, elaborate as it was in form, seems not to have been intended to deal with rates in any general way. It was in the main aimed at the prevention of specific abuses. "The practice of discrimination in one form or another is the principal cause of complaint." Consequently, the long succession of bills introduced in the House of Representatives year after year for more than a decade by Judge Reagan of Texas and others, made no attempt to provide administrative machinery by which to fix rates in general; but sought merely to prohibit these specific abuses by statute.[2] The proposition for a permanent commission to deal with rates in a more comprehensive way, seems, as we shall see, to have emanated from the Senate at a later time. But this more statesman-like proposition from the upper chamber was essentially different from the response in the House of Repre-

[1] In detail at pp. 22 and 411, *supra*. [2] *Cf.* Haney, vol. II, p. 309.

sentatives to popular feeling against discriminatory practices, which slowly gathered force during more than a decade of agitation and debate.

What now were some of the specific "discriminations" which these various bills in Congress aimed to prevent? And why did the movement come to a head in 1887? The evidence is conclusive that personal favoritism as between rival shippers took first place. The indiscriminate and cut-throat competition of the carriers, particularly in connection with the trunk line rate wars, offered a golden opportunity to those in search of secret and preferential rates.[1] The chief offender, of course, was the Standard Oil Company under the direction of John D. Rockefeller. The Cassatt revelations in 1877 as to exclusive contracts with the great trunk lines for the carriage of oil, greatly stirred public opinion. Congressional attention had been directed to the subject some years before by complaints from the Pennsylvania field. But the abortive results of the investigation of 1875 demonstrated nothing beyond the shameful impudence of the chief offenders. According to the New York (Hepburn) Committee investigation in 1879, few shippers had ever seen printed tariffs. The Assistant General Freight Agent of the New York Central testified that one-half the business out of New York, and nine-tenths out of Syracuse went on special rates. At this time there was also unrest in the anthracite coal trade. Moreover, the activity of the "eveners" in the cattle business in 1875–1879[2] had laid the foundation for still other monopolies built up by means of rebates. But the constant irritant in the public eye was the Standard Oil Company.[3] The Lake Shore case, fought through every Ohio court and then on appeal up to the Supreme Court of the United States in 1886,

[1] *Cf.* pp. 22, and 431, *supra*.
[2] Select Senate Committee on Transportation of Meat Products, 1889, p. 2, etc.
[3] *Cf.* the chapter from Miss Tarbell's History of the Standard Oil Company, reprinted in our Railway Problems. Hudson, pp. 55–106, well summarizes the Hepburn Committee testimony.

widely advertised the discriminatory practices of the railroads. But the most spectacular disclosures of all took place in 1885-1888 in the George Rice cases in Ohio. The Cullom Committee in recommending publicity of rates as its primary remedy for the evils of the time, specifically cites "this most impudent and outrageous" proceeding.[1] In the protracted struggle in conference committee upon the provisions of the act, elimination of rebates was the only subject upon which both House and Senate conferees were in thorough accord from the start. Whatever the commercial crimes chargeable to the founder of the Standard Oil Company, he should, at least, be credited with the performance of a great public service in finally crystallizing public opinion in 1887 in favor of railroad legislation for the prevention of rebating.

Distrust of monopoly has always loomed up large in the public eye. The dread of it is voiced in every public document of the time. The Windom Committee in 1874, as we have seen, looked to the stimulation of railway competition as its chief remedy against high rates. Five years later, the Hepburn Committee in New York vehemently denounced railroad monopoly as an evil to be sternly repressed. But, in the meantime, the carriers, almost prostrated by the excesses of their rate wars, were slowly learning how to coöperate for the maintenance of more stable charges. Railroad pools and traffic agreements, first essayed about 1875, were gradually elaborated; until by 1886 nearly all parts of the country were covered by them.[2] From small beginnings in 1877, the Trunk Line Association under Albert Fink was in its heyday of activity. The Southern Railway Association was restoring order out of chaos, south of the Ohio river. By 1886 all competitive traffic north and west of Chicago was pooled. This was especially true of the highly competitive business between the Missouri and Mississippi rivers. Even in remoter regions, such agreements threatened

---

[1] *Op. cit.;* vol. I, p. 199.
[2] Pooling is discussed in detail in volume II.

to deprive the public of the benefits of rival railroad construction. In Colorado and New Mexico public sentiment was deeply aroused over the tripartite division of territory between the carriers then in the field.[1] The helplessness of independent railroads was made evident in connection with the attempt of the (now) Colorado & Southern road to gain a foothold. Its suits in both state and Federal courts, and the attempted remedial legislation by Colorado in 1885, disclosed the great power of monopoly over the public welfare in that region. In Texas, the Gould-Huntington apportionment of the field between the two systems in 1881,[2] was doubtless perceived as to its results, even if its precise terms were secret. The Texas Traffic Association, also, organized in 1875, embraced all the lines in that vicinity. May it not well be that the final inclusion in the Act of 1887 of the prohibition of pooling, upon direct insistence of the Texas representative in Congress against the protest of the Senate, had some connection with these events? It seems clear that the marked interest of the railways in eliminating competition all over the country at this critical time, carried great weight with Congress in shaping the law.

The years since the Civil War had witnessed an ever increasing volume of speculation and fraud in railway affairs, which reached its climax in the frenzied construction period of the eighties.[3] Jay Gould, "Jim" Fisk and their successors who contributed to the "railway panic" of 1884, had done their work well in arousing public hostility to the railroads. The Hepburn Committee Report in New York is symptomatic of the state of feeling in its vehement denunciation of these practices.[4] The Windom Committee, five years earlier, had officially registered its opinion that of all the abuses of the time, "none have contributed so much to the general discontent and indignation as

[1] University of Colorado Studies, V, 1908, pp. 137–148.
[2] Bulletin, University of Texas, No. 119, 1909, p. 73.
[3] Details in chapter I and in the discussion of speculation in volume II.
[4] Hudson, *op. cit.*, pp. 251–286, uses much of this testimony.

the increase of railway capital by *stock watering* and *capitalization of surplus earnings*. The murmurs of discontent have swollen into a storm of popular indignation. Your committee believe the evil to be of such magnitude as to justify and require for its prevention the coöperation of both Congress and the States." [1] Nor is the Cullom Committee less emphatic in 1886; although its condemnation is shifted from the trunk lines, particularly the New York Central and the Erie, to the newly constructed "unnecessary roads." "This practice (of stock watering) has unquestionably done more to create and keep alive a popular feeling of hostility against the railroads of the United States than any other one cause." [2] All were agreed that the remedy must be applied by the states, from which the companies derived their charters. But a powerful impulse toward publicity of accounts and operating details as well as of rates, to be enforced by the hand of the Federal government, was unquestionably imparted by the financial scandals of the time. It was hoped that fraudulent construction concerns, subsidiary companies for "milking" the main corporation, unnecessary paralleling of existing lines for purposes of blackmail, speculative bankruptcies and all similar practices of the period might be restrained in part by letting in the light of day upon their affairs.

Then again, there were the discriminations in rates, so vehemently denounced, against the small towns and local business, in favor of the large cities mainly interested in long distance traffic. Such jealousies and rivalries of course antedate the railroad. They are almost as old as trade. And yet the course of affairs since the panic of 1873, had lent peculiar force to them by the middle of the eighties. It had been a period of ruinous railroad competition all over the land, but especially in trunk line territory. Through rates had fallen tremendously; without any corresponding change in local charges.[3] The great western cities and the remote farmers were the immediate beneficiaries, of course. But there were the older communities

[1] Pp. 72 *et seq.* [2] Pp. 51 *et seq.* [3] Pages 22, 422, *supra*, and 456, *infra*.

of the East to be reckoned with,[1] — the farmers of New England and Middle New York and the secondary cities which had once been terminal points but were now become way stations. In the South, new towns were springing up, anxious to divide distributive trade with the older cotton concentration points. Nashville, soon to take first place in a celebrated case, was being built up by a favoring railway; and Atlanta, a purely railroad town, was in rapid growth at the expense of older rivals. The separate states had long sought to deal with this ancient evil of local discrimination in rates by means of long and short haul clauses; but to little effect. What wonder that the Cullom Committee in 1886, heads its long list of "complaints against the railroad system of the United States" by two forms of this alleged evil!

In brief, the contemporary evidence all goes to show that, — quite aside from evil intent, — the railroad business of the United States in the middle of the eighties, was in a highly disorganized state. Phenomenal economic development since the resumption of specie payments in 1879, had perhaps outstripped the capacity of managements to scientifically order their affairs. Collateral evidence as to this is the extraordinary wastefulness of operation which prevailed. Competition had run mad. All of the tricks and vagaries of roundabout routing of freight found place.[2] To keep pace with mere operating demands was a heavy enough task, — to say nothing of constructing well-ordered tariffs, keeping straight accounts, and providing adequate funds for growth. And out of this unsettled condition of affairs there had sprung the usual mushroom crop of speculation, fraud and corruption which is bound to flourish at such times.

And then, finally, in seeking to understand the economic situation in 1887, the intolerable arrogance of great railway managers must be kept in mind. Honorable exceptions there must have been, to be sure. But the "Public be damned"

[1] *Cf.* Hudson, *op. cit.*, pp. 41–46.   [2] *Cf.* chap. VIII.

attitude of the old Commodore Vanderbilt was evidently a general, although perhaps a somewhat exaggerated one. It is certain that there was no well-defined sense of responsibility to the public. All attempts at investigation or reform were treated as "interference with private business." The rising tide of popular feeling was increased by evidence of corrupt political practices, as well as of mere crude contempt for the rights of patrons. Read the congressional debates upon the Camden and Amboy monopoly in New Jersey; the special laws "jammed" through the state legislature by the New York Central Railroad;[1] and the revelations as to corruption in the Credit Mobilier and other proceedings in Congress.[2] Such things added fuel to the flames in the East, kindled and kept alive in the West by the Granger movement. The time for an attempt to curb the second great manifestation of corporate power in the United States was indeed at hand. The only question was as to the form which it should assume.

The congressional history of the Act of 1887 extends over a period of nearly fifteen years. The first general bill to pass the House of Representatives in 1874, had for its object a reduction of rates; but the movement for the elimination of discriminatory practices did not begin until two years later. Then in 1877, came the first of the long series of bills which finally led up to the statute in its final form, prepared by Representative Reagan of Texas. But it was not until 1884 that the Senate, ever tardy in its response to public sentiment, began to take the matter seriously. Its earlier interest in reduced rates had dissipated, ten years before, with the Windom Committee Report. Now, however, under the leadership of the Senator from Illinois, the Cullom Committee brought in a bill, the distinctive feature of which was provision for a permanent

---

[1] Chapters of Erie reprinted in part in our Railway Problems.
[2] *Cf.* Haney, Congressional History of Railways, vol. II, p. 256. The Credit Mobilier is also described by reprint in our Railway Problems.

THE ACT OF 1887

administrative commission. The various House bills, in their distrust of executive appointments and authority, had favored leaving the elimination of abuses, once clearly defined by law, to the Federal courts. A legislative deadlock between the two chambers resulted upon this point; as well as concerning the status of pooling. For the House sought to prohibit all traffic agreements; while the Senate would permit them under proper administrative supervision.

At this critical juncture the Supreme Court decision in the Wabash, St. Louis, and Pacific Railway case [1] was handed down. It specifically denied to the individual states, power to regulate the ever-increasing volume of interstate traffic. This decision put the match to the long train of influences making for action. The Senate and House bills were therefore taken up in conference committee, with the usual outcome of give and take. The Senate gained its point of administrative, rather than judicial, control. A commission was provided; but the courts were accorded power to entertain appeals. On the other hand, the House conferees insisted upon the prohibition of pooling and a more stringent long and short haul clause. All were agreed in respect to the publicity features. The series of votes at different times with steadily growing majorities, leading up finally to the passage of this compromise statute by both houses, is significant of the progress of public opinion upon the matter.

		House of Representatives	Senate
1874	Passed	121 to 116	—
1877	"	139 to 104	—
1884	"	161 to 75	43 to 12
1886	"	192 to 41	47 to 4
1887	"	219 to 41	37 to 12

The constitutionality of the Act to Regulate Commerce of 1887 need not long concern us.[2] Everything depended upon

[1] 118 U. S. 557.
[2] *Cf.* Cullom Committee, 1, pp. 28–40; and the summary of Congressional debates by Haney, *op. cit.*, vol. II, p. 231 *et seq.*

the interpretation of the clause in the Constitution conferring upon Congress power over commerce with foreign nations and among the states. A generation earlier the regulation of railroads by Federal statute might not have been sanctioned. But Lincoln and Grant had dealt a death blow to the old states' rights idea. And the positive legislation after the Civil War prior to this time, had already denoted a much more progressive and liberal point of view. The far-reaching decisions of the Supreme Court following *Munn v. Illinois* in 1876 had clearly upheld the power of the several states to regulate commerce. The situation called only for definition of the dividing line between state and Federal authority. This was accorded in the Wabash case, which, as has already been stated, terminated the congressional deadlock, and brought about an agreement upon the terms of the law. Nor is it without significance, in the light of subsequent events, that the Wabash case was an appeal by a common carrier to Federal authority for protection against a state statute.

A brief summary of the main provisions of the Act to Regulate Commerce, at this point, will be convenient for future reference.

Section 1. It applies to freight and passengers by land; or by land and water in cases of continuous or through shipment, even to foreign countries. All charges shall be reasonable and just; and every unjust and unreasonable charge is prohibited.

Section 2. Rebates and personal discrimination of every sort forbidden.

Section 3. Local discrimination forbidden; equal facilities for interchange of traffic with connecting lines prescribed.

Section 4. Long and short haul clause: "That it shall be unlawful for any common carrier subject to the provisions of this act, to charge or receive any greater compensation in the aggregate for the transportation of passengers or of like kind of property, under substantially similar circumstances and conditions, for a shorter than for a longer distance over the same line, in the same direction, the shorter being included within the longer distance; but this shall not be construed as authorizing any common carrier within the terms of this act to charge and receive as great compensation for a shorter as for a longer distance: *Provided, however,* That upon application to the Commission appointed under the provisions of this act, such common carrier may, in special cases, after investigation by the Commission, be authorized to charge less for longer than for shorter distances for the transportation of passengers or property; and the Commission may from time to time prescribe the extent to which such designated common carrier may be relieved from the operation of this section of this act."

Section 5. All pooling and traffic agreements prohibited.

Section 6. All rates and fares to be printed and posted for public inspection at all stations; and filed with the Commission at Washington. No advance in rates except after ten days notice. All charges, other than as published, forbidden.

Section 9. Procedure by complaint before the Commission or Federal courts. Power to compel testimony and production of papers.

Section 10. Penalty of $5000 for each offence in violation. (Amended in 1889, adding imprisonment.)

Section 11. Interstate Commerce Commission of five members established; by Presidential appointment; term six years.

Section 12. Powers of Commission to inquire, with right to obtain full information necessary to exercise of its authority. Power over witnesses and production of papers, to be sustained by U. S. Circuit Courts.

Sections 13-14. Procedure before Commission by complaint. Parties competent to appear. Decisions to include findings of fact upon which based, for courts on appeal.

Section 15. Duty of Commission to notify carriers to "cease and desist" from violation, or to make reparation for injury done.

Section 16. To enforce obedience, procedure by petition of Commission in Federal courts, which may issue writs.

Section 20. Annual detailed reports from carriers as to finance, operation, rates or regulations in prescribed forms as desired by the Commission.

Such is the substance of the statute which marks the real beginning of subjection of the railroads to control by the Federal government. It was avowedly tentative in character. It was a compromise, entirely satisfactory to no one. Many of its provisions were not new. Administrative commissions had already been in existence some time in several of the states. Pooling had also commonly been condemned. The long and short haul clause in the statute constitutes no innovation. It was based specifically upon a number of state laws, more or less similar to it in tenor.[1] In Vermont, for example, since 1850; in Virginia, since 1867; and in Massachusetts, since 1874, long and short haul clauses had been in force. Some seventeen states, prior to the enactment of the Interstate Commerce Act in 1887, had conceded the wisdom of such an adjustment between local and long hauls. Nor were such statutes disregarded, as a rule. Thus, in Massachusetts they were enforced to the extreme degree of prohibiting any concession in rates at Provincetown, on the point of Cape Cod, one hundred and twenty miles from Boston by land, while only thirty-six miles in a direct line by water, below the rates at any of the intermediate points on the roundabout rail line along the Cape. The debates in Congress at the time this section of the Act was under discussion show that the bill as finally passed was a compromise between an absolutely inflexible prohibition, in the House, and a more elastic measure, providing for exceptions, in the Senate.

In one respect the law of 1887 marks a profound revolution in both commercial theory and practice. Its provisions concerning equality of rates to all classes of shippers denote a great moral uplift in the business standards of the country. Prior to this time the English common law, while requiring reasonableness of charges by common carriers, by no means insured that such charges should be stable and uniform. This flowed perhaps from the circumstance that rebating was an essentially American abuse. Neither in England, nor on the continent for that matter, had business rivals ever made such use of the services of carriers to suppress fair competition in trade. With us, on the other hand, in the early free-and-easy days, entire freedom of contract between shipper and carrier had been the rule. Published tariffs were only the starting point for "higgle" and "dicker." It was not bad form for a shipper to "go shopping" freely among the freight agents of competing lines. The location of new enterprises, new opportunities for the

[1] 21 I.C.C. Rep., 340.

expansion of old ones, were all more or less conditioned by the special favors which were so readily obtainable on demand. Nor was the accompaniment of secrecy necessarily due to fear of moral condemnation by the community. Secrecy was an economic essential of the device, as has elsewhere been shown.[1] By this new statute all was suddenly changed. Rebating was made a crime, punishable as such. Is it any wonder that, almost from the outset and for nearly fifteen years, this part of the law was the storm centre of litigation; and that in respect of rebating, the need of supplementary legislation should first become apparent?

[1] Chapter XX.

CHAPTER XIV

1887–1905. EMASCULATION OF THE LAW

Favorable reception, 456. — First resistance from unwilling witnesses concerning rebates, 457. — Counselman and Brown cases, 458. — The Brimson case, 459. — Relation to Federal Courts unsatisfactory, 460. — Interminable delay, 461. — Original evidence rejected, 461. — The Commission's court record examined, 462. — Rate orders at first obeyed, 467. — The Social Circle case, 468. — Final breakdown in Maximum (Cincinnati) Freight Rate case, 469. — Other functions remaining, 472. — The long and short haul clause interpreted, 474. — The Louisville and Nashville case, 474. — The "independent line" decision, 476. — The Social Circle case again, 478. — "Rare and peculiar cases," 479. — The Alabama Midland (Troy) decision, 481. — Attempted rejuvenation of the long and short haul clause, 483. — The Savannah Naval Stores case, 484. — The dwindling record of complaints, 485.

THE first response to the new Federal law by the railroads was entirely favorable.[1] They sought to obey its mandates both in letter and spirit. The Commission reports in 1888 that the railroads "conformed promptly" to their orders; although in the South and West they were "moving more slowly." On the other hand, the new Commission under the leadership of Judge Cooley, an able jurist trusted by all parties concerned, was equally conciliatory in spirit. Many beneficent changes were brought about in railway practice. Attempts were made to remodel tariffs all over the country, particularly in the East, to conform to the long and short haul clause.[2]

The immediate effect of acquiescence in Section 4 was to compel, in many parts of the country, a reduction of the local rates in order to reduce them below the rates charged to terminal and competitive points. Thus, for example, throughout trunk

[1] *Cf.* Simon Sterne, Railways in the United States, 1912.
[2] *Cf.* Appendix C, Int. Com. Com. Annual Report, 1890.

line territory, they were almost uniformly adjusted to meet this requirement. Even in the southern states, where in some quarters the most persistent opposition to the law has from the first existed, there was a patent disposition shown to recognize the justice of such legislation. The Southern Railroad modified its tariff all along the line as far as Atlanta, although it claimed inability to make changes beyond that point. For nearly three years, in fact, the carriers conformed in an increasing degree to this requirement of the law.[1] A sincere effort toward uniform classification of freight, with substantial results in the direction of simplification of schedules, extended over several years. Many pools were disbanded; all were reorganized in conformity with the statute. And in the matter of uniformity and publicity of statistical returns, friendly coöperation between the railroads and the Commission, brought about great improvements in accounting practice. No considerable popular interest in the new commercial tribunal, to be sure, is indicated by the volume of its business. After five years experience, only thirty-nine formal complaints were filed in 1892. But this may have been due in part to the natural hesitancy of shippers to antagonizing the roads by coming out into the open with their grievances. Or, perhaps, it was merely because the people at large were as yet quite unfamiliar with the law and with the ease of procedure under it.

The earliest intimation of determined resistance by the carriers came in connection with prosecutions for rebating in 1890. This abuse was still widely prevalent. The Commission complained in that year of the "general disregard" of the law against personal discrimination; and set out to prosecute with vigor. But witnesses called upon to testify before grand juries as to such practices, proved recalcitrant.[2] Corporations could be made amenable to the law only through the instrumentality of persons in their employ. And guilt in such

[1] *Cf.* Brief of Counsel for Int. Com. Com. in the Danville case, p. 88.
[2] *Cf.* account in *Yale Review*, 1907, pp. 119–155.

matters could be detected only by the testimony of those who had directly witnessed, or participated in, the unlawful acts themselves. As one writer has put it, "Rebate contracts are not usually negotiated before large audiences nor are rebate payments commonly made upon street corners. An essential element in these practices, quite aside from their legality, is the secrecy with which they are conducted." It soon became apparent that unless this mantle of secrecy could be stripped off in preliminary proceedings, not even indictments could be had, — to say nothing of the proof needed for subsequent conviction.

The first ground for contesting the right of the government to extort testimony from unwilling witnesses arose, oddly enough, from an amendment of the law intended to increase its effectiveness. Originally punishable only by heavy fine, on recommendation of the Commission, Congress added in 1889 an amendment whereby departure from the published rate was made punishable also by imprisonment. By this change criminal, as well as civil, procedure was thus brought into play. The amendment, moreover, extended the punishment to shippers; the railroad official who gave rebates having alone been liable hitherto. An unexpected result speedily followed. In 1890 one Counselman, a shipper, questioned concerning his enjoyment of less than the open rate upon grain, declined to answer, taking refuge under the Fifth Amendment to the Constitution of the United States. This declared that "no person . . . shall be compelled in any criminal case to be a witness against himself." The witness persisted in his refusal to testify even before a district judge: and the case went on appeal through the Circuit Court which decided in favor of the Commission, up to the Supreme Court of the United States. This tribunal in 1892 held that the Revised Statutes of the United States which for twenty-five years had been held to protect the constitutional rights of witnesses when called upon to give testimony, against criminal proceedings based upon such evidence, did not in fact adequately afford such protection. Counselman was ordered discharged from the custody of the United States Marshal. It was held, furthermore, "that a statutory enactment to be valid, must afford absolute immunity for the offence to which the question relates." [1] Congress promptly passed a law to this effect in the following year. The matter did not, however, rest here. The validity of this later statute had now to be upheld. And, with discouraging defeat in 1894 in an Illinois Circuit Court, the issue had to be raised again a year later elsewhere, to be then carried on appeal a second time to the Supreme Court. This took place in the so-called Brown case.[2] The final outcome in 1896 was a complete denial of the right of witnesses to withhold material testimony. But it required six years of litigation to bring about the desired result.

During the pendency of the proceedings above described, a second line of resistance to the government developed. Not the merely negative personal right of witnesses to withhold testimony, but the positive legal authority of the Commission to exact it, was called in question. This struck at the very roots of all procedure. For it challenged the validity of the Act itself. In how far might an administrative body, independently, have power, hitherto resident alone in the courts and Congress, to compel the attendance and testimony of witnesses as well as the production of papers? Section 12 of the Act was evidently intended to confer such powers as were possessed and might be delegated by the Congress. But then there was the Constitution again to be considered! Certain witnesses declined to produce books and answer questions in 1892. One Brimson was selected for a test case. The first decision by the Circuit Court held these sections of the statute to be unconstitutional on the ground that "Congress cannot make the judicial department the mere adjunct or instrument of the other departments." But the Supreme Court of the United States in 1894 reversed this judgment; and, unreservedly,

[1] 142 U. S., 547.   [2] *Brown v. Walker*, 161 U. S., 591.

although by a bare majority opinion, affirmed the constitutionality of the procedure under the Act.[1] This Brimson opinion, together with the Brown decision two years later, were confidently believed to have so strengthened the arm of the government that rebating might at last be eliminated. But, as will shortly appear, an entirely new law was yet needed to eradicate the evil. For the moment, however, the right of Congress to legislate and of the Commission to act, had been upheld.

The relation of the Interstate Commerce Commission as an administrative body to the Federal courts under the provisions of the Act of 1887, proved unsatisfactory from the first. In order to understand the situation, it may be well to review the ordinary procedure. Formal complaint having been filed, the Commission heard the case and promulgated its decision in the form of an order to the carriers. If they chose to comply with it, well and good. Otherwise, the Commission must apply to a Federal court for the issuance of an injunction to compel obedience to the order. Thereupon the court proceeded to review the case; and upon the findings to issue an order of its own. From this order, however, appeal might be taken even up to the Supreme Court. Then, and then only, did the original mandate of the Commission have the force of law. Practically, two results followed, as shown by the experience of the succeeding years. There was intolerable delay in the redress of grievances; and, in the second place, all definitive proceedings were postponed until the case had gone on appeal to the courts. In other words the Commission instead of being a coördinate body with the courts, was reduced to an entirely subordinate position. Its function became merely to institute proceedings, and thereafter to appear as a complainant before other tribunals competent alone to decide the case. Intolerable delay in procedure was the constant complaint of shippers. Years

[1] 154 U. S., 447.

elapsed before final judgments were rendered. The average duration of cases appealed was not less than four years. Sometimes they extended over twice that period. Often, as in the Charleston, S. C., case in 1898, several years elapsed before the Commission itself rendered a decision. Knotty cases were sidetracked.

But the main source of delay was in the carriage of cases on appeal up to the Supreme Court of the United States. They had to await their turn in regular order, being given no priority on the crowded dockets. The Social Circle and Import Rate cases, soon to be discussed, consumed five years in litigation, even after the Commission had rendered its opinion. The Florida Fruit Exchange case involving rates on oranges, originally decided by the Commission in 1891, was for six years thereafter before the Federal Courts. The Georgia Railroad Commission cases were not settled for nine years. Nor did the tedious process end here. After the judicial review, which usually covered the law points, the entire question had to be remanded to the Commission for a new order in conformity with the findings of the court. After nine years of litigation in the Chattanooga case, back it went to the Commission to be re-tried after consideration of other commercial factors. First decided in 1892, it was reopened in 1904.[1] Is it any wonder that the number of formal proceedings instituted on complaint of shippers steadily dwindled year by year? In 1901 only nineteen petitions were filed. Business of this sort was almost at a standstill.

A second unsatisfactory feature of the relations of the Commission to the courts, lay in the refusal of the latter to accept the evidence taken before the Commission in the original proceedings as final. Trouble began in 1888 on the first appeal, known as the Kentucky and Indiana Bridge case.[2] The court

[1] The history of these cases up to 1900 will be found in 56th Congress, 1st session, Senate Document 319. Five years later they were more fully treated in Hearings before the Senate (Elkins) Committee on Interstate Commerce, 1905, vol. V, Appendix F, part 2, pp. 709–780.

[2] 37 Federal Reporter, 567.

treated it as an original proceeding, even as to questions of fact; and proceeded to consider it *de novo*. This of course involved a duplication of all expenses; which, in causes sufficiently important to appeal, were very heavy. Ten volumes of typewritten testimony, each as large as the Congressional Record, were taken, for instance, in the San Bernardino case.[1] Both shipper and railroad, therefore, commonly came to regard the proceedings before the Commission as merely a necessary formality to be observed prior to the conclusive adjudication of the matter by the courts. This placed the Commission in a most awkward predicament. It was compelled by law to render a decision upon an entirely imperfect presentation of facts. And this decision was thereafter liable to be reviewed upon the basis of entirely new testimony. Thus in the leading Alabama Midland case, involving the reasonableness of rates to Troy, Alabama, as compared with adjacent towns, much depended upon the existence of effective competition with the railroads from boat lines on the rivers at other places.[2] Before the Commission the evidence adduced by the carriers dwelt upon the navigability of the Chattahoochee river as compelling lower rates at Columbus and Eufaula than at Troy, an inland town. Yet, when the case was really opened up in appeal proceedings, it appeared that this magnificent waterway was really dry about half the year; that the channel was never deeper than three feet; and that boats were at all times of the year "embarrassed by the overhanging trees." How could the Commission be expected to pass upon vital questions wisely under such circumstances? Whether wilfully done or not, — and evidence is not lacking of a deliberate policy adopted in some cases, — the inevitable effect was to bring the Commission and the law itself into discredit. So accentuated did this evil become, that in the Social Circle case the Supreme Court distinctly discountenanced the practice, declaring it to be the

---

[1] 149 U. S., 264. [2] *Cf.* pp. 390, *supra*, and 481, *infra*; reprinted in full in our Railway Problems.

EMASCULATION OF THE LAW 463

intention of the law that all material facts should be disclosed in the original proceedings.[1] But it was not until 1906 that the mode of procedure on appeal was by statute clearly defined. In the meantime public interest in the work of the Commission was bound to wane.

In this connection it may not be out of place to refer to the persistent use made of the record of the Commission in court proceedings under these adverse circumstances, as a plausible argument by the railroads in later years against any augmentation of its powers. One brief, for example, recites that "since 1887, forty-three suits have been instituted to enforce final orders of the Commission as to rates. The net result of the action of the courts shows two affirmances and thirty reversals." It continues later, "as over ninety per cent. of the Commission's orders as to rates which have gone before the courts have been over-ruled, it is impossible to foretell what havoc would follow from the exercise of such powers." This statement is entirely true, but it is not the entire truth. We may profitably consider the cases of sufficient importance to have been passed upon by the Supreme Court of the United States. Between 1887 and 1905, sixteen such decisions were rendered on cases appealed for enforcement by the Interstate Commerce Commission. Fifteen of these were decided in favor of the carriers, while only one sustained in part the contention of the Commission. At first sight, this record certainly appears to warrant the condemnation of the Commission. A body so persistently on the wrong side of great questions as this record indicates, would surely invite distrust. There were two answers to this contention, however, which merit consideration before a final judgment can be rendered. One of these was the irregularity of procedure, above described. The other was that these court cases had nearly all involved, not so much the administrative application of the law to economic abuses, as the purely judicial interpretation of the law itself.

[1] 162 U. S., 184.

Only by means of concrete cases decided by the Commission as an administrative body, could the scope and meaning of the original law be determined. This was a most difficult task hinging upon the utmost legal technicalities and refinements. Even the most learned judges failed to agree among themselves. Thus in eight of the sixteen cases above mentioned, the decisions in the lower Federal courts failed of agreement with the final decree of the Supreme Court. In the Cartage case, — involving the legality of a railway giving one shipper free cartage of goods to a railway station as an inducement to ship over its line, while withholding the privilege from another, — the Commission was sustained in the Circuit Court and reversed in the two higher tribunals. In other instances, like the Social Circle case, — turning upon the discrimination in freight rates against small towns in favor of large competitive centres, — the first court ruled adversely, while the Circuit Court of Appeals and the Supreme Court sustained the Commission in part. Or yet again, as in the Chattanooga case, — wherein this city complained against a higher freight rate from New York than the rival city of Nashville enjoyed, although the goods for Nashville passed through Chattanooga and were hauled one hundred and fifty-one miles further, — both lower tribunals sustained the Commission only to be finally overruled by the Supreme Court. The fact that in only eight of these most important cases the courts could agree among themselves indicates the nicety of the legal issues comprehended. All parties were in fact working much in the dark, both as to the intention of the original law and as to the possible effects of its interpretation. The charge of incompetence, if it held good for the Commission, applied equally well to a large number of the most learned judges in the Federal courts.

Another indication of the extreme delicacy of the legal issues involved, is found in the lack of unanimity even among the justices of the Supreme Court itself. In nine of the sixteen Supreme Court cases the final decision was not rendered without dissent. As the lower courts were divided among themselves, so the justices of the Supreme Court were apparently somewhat at sea. The minority, to be sure, was small, in most cases being due to the failure of Justice Harlan to concur. But in the far-reaching Import Rates case,[1] the court was more evenly divided. The issue raised, concerned the legality of lower through rates on imports from Liverpool to San Francisco *via* New Orleans, than were granted on domestic shipments from New Orleans to the same destination. Thus the rate on books, buttons, and hosiery, from Liverpool to San Francisco through New Orleans was $1.07 per hundred pounds. At the same time the domestic shipper was compelled to pay $2.88, or two and one-half times as much, for a haul from New Orleans to San Francisco alone. In another important instance, tin plate was carried from Liverpool by steamer and rail through Philadelphia to Chicago for twenty-four cents per hundred pounds. For the American merchant in Philadelphia the rate to the same market was twenty-six cents. For the inland haul alone the Pennsylvania Railroad was receiving sixteen cents on the foreign goods, while coincidently charging American merchants ten cents more for the same service. Discrimination against the American merchant in favor of foreign competition, not infrequently more than sufficient to overbalance any supposed protection afforded by the tariff, has been repeatedly proved in such cases as this. The duty on imported cement was eight cents per hundredweight. In one instance, this duty with the total freight rate added amounted to only eighteen cents, as against a rate of twenty cents for the domestic producer from New York to the same point. There were reasons for this grievous discrimination against the domestic shipper, mainly concerned with the vagaries of ocean freight rates. Steamers must have ballast for the return trip to equalize out-going shipments of grain and

---

[1] 162 U. S., 197. Late data as to the extent of the practice are in App. V, Digest, Hearings (Senate) Committee on Interstate Commerce, 1905, pp. 1–29. *Cf.* also p. 406, *supra*.

other exports, and they will carry heavy commodities, such as salt, cement, crockery, and glass, at extremely low rates. Nevertheless, such imported commodities can be sold to advantage in competition with domestic goods only when the railways will contribute equally low rates to complete the shipment.

The Interstate Commerce Commission in these Import Rate cases originally held that such discriminations were unlawful. Two appellate courts, in turn, sustained this view. Finally, however, the Supreme Court decided, with three members, including the Chief Justice, dissenting, that the Interstate Commerce Law as phrased did not expressly prohibit the practice. Everything turned upon the interpretation of certain clauses in the law. No question was ever raised as to the economic issues involved, nor was it competent to these tribunals to pass upon such issues. The question was simply and solely this: When the Act to Regulate Commerce forbade inequality or discrimination between shippers, did it contemplate competition between shipments originating within the country and others from foreign ports? Was the Interstate Commerce Commission, in other words, empowered, in interpreting this act, to consider circumstances and conditions *without* as well as *within* the boundaries of the United States? If it was entitled to consider solely domestic conditions, it was certainly right and economically sound in forbidding such practices; if, on the other hand, it was required to take account of commercial conditions the world over, irrespective of the effect upon the domestic producer and internal trade, its decision should have been favorable to the railroads. To appreciate fully the extreme nicety of the legal points involved and the delicacy of the economic interests at issue, one must needs read the extended opinions both of the majority of the Supreme Court and of the three dissenting justices, including Chief Justice Fuller. But to interpret the reversal of the original decision of the Interstate Commerce Commission by this tribunal as in the slightest degree involving incompetence or judicial unfairness is a misrepresentation of all the facts involved. As in the preceding cases touching the interpretation of the long and short haul clause, it may fairly be said that the consensus of opinion among business men, and certainly among the professional economists of the country, was on the side of the Commission in condemning such practices. As to the law, that was decided otherwise by a narrow majority.

The final breakdown of the law of 1887 came, however, not from mere defects in procedure, but from the adverse construction placed by the Supreme Court of the United States upon its fundamental clauses, viz., those concerning the exercise of rate-making power by the Commission. Whether or not it was the intention of Congress to delegate such power, seems not to have been considered for some years. At all events, within two months after the law was passed the Commission certainly interpreted the law as giving it, not only power to investigate but to prescribe remedies for what it conceived to be unreasonable charges. The right to exercise general rate-making power in first instance was distinctly disclaimed.[1] But the right to prescribe a modification of existing rates on complaint was repeatedly affirmed, without question either by the carriers or the Federal courts.[2] The first order of the commission in *Evans vs. The Oregon Navigation Company* directed a reduction of the rate on wheat from Walla Walla, Washington, to Portland, Ore., from thirty to twenty-three and one-half cents. It was promptly complied with. Then came the Farmington-Red Wing, Minn., wheat case, touching not absolute but relative rates between two competing places. The order that the charge to one town should not exceed that to the other by more than one-third was likewise obeyed. Even freight classification, not specifically mentioned in the Act, was supposed to be fully subject to the Commission's control.

[1] Delaware and Hudson Canal case; 1 I.C.C. Rep., 152.
[2] Hearings before Committee on Interstate Commerce, U. S. Senate, Feb. 15, 1900 and May 18, 1905, vol. IV, pp. 2866 and 2880.

In the Reynolds case, railroad ties and lumber were ordered to be grouped together, without contest. The activity of the Commission at this time in promoting uniform classification elsewhere discussed,[1] was evidently based upon a similar belief in its legal competency to act. For nearly a decade attention seems to have been so concentrated upon matters of judicial procedure, that this more fundamental proposition was neglected. Moreover, all this time was needed to secure a final pronouncement from the Supreme Court, which was alone competent to settle it as a matter of law.

It was not, then, until almost ten years after the institution of the Commission, in fact, that its rate-making power was denied. The first shadow of doubt seems to have been expressed in the decision of the Supreme Court in the so-called Social Circle case.[2] This involved the reasonableness of rates from Cincinnati to the town of Social Circle, Georgia, as related to the rates to Atlanta and Augusta on either side. Disregarding other phases of the case which concerned the interpretation of the long and short haul clause, the Commission had, when the case was first decided in 1891, ordered a reduction of the rate from Cincinnati to Atlanta from $1.09 to $1 per hundred pounds. This case was carried to the Supreme Court, where decision was finally rendered in 1896. Purely as an *obiter dictum* the court discussed briefly the interpretation of the original act in respect to rate-making power. It expressed a reasonable doubt in the premises, even going further and confessing inability to find any provision of the act "that expressly or by necessary implication confers such powers." It does not seem clear whether by this statement the court had reference to the arbitrary prescription of rates in first instance to the carriers, or merely to action of the Commission in prescribing rates after complaint, in order to redress grievances.

Several decisions of circuit courts during 1896 reënforced the judicial doubt as to the validity of the rate-making power

[1] Chapter IX, *supra*.   [2] 162 U. S., 184: 4 I.C.C. Rep., 744.

of the Commission. Thus, for example, in the case of Coxe Brothers,[1] involving rates upon anthracite coal, which, by the way, had been pending since 1891, the Circuit Court of Appeals expressly declined to enforce an order of the Commission, stating that it "is not clothed with the power to fix rates which it undertook to exercise in this case." The court's reasoning in the Social Circle case was followed and expressly cited. During the same year, 1896, other cases, such as that of the Truck Farmers' Association, were decided in the same spirit. The final adjudication of this point, however, was reserved for the decision in the so-called Cincinnati Freight Bureau case. This had its origin in an application from the Commission to enforce an order issued in 1894 against the Cincinnati, New Orleans and Texas Pacific Railroad Company.[2] The case involved the adjustment of rates from eastern and western centres, respectively, into the southern states; and the Commission had decided that a reduction of the rates from the western cities was reasonable and necessary. This leading case, also known as the Maximum Freight Rate decision of 1896, is characterized by the Commission itself as perhaps "the most important since the enactment of the Act to Regulate Commerce." It merits consideration in some detail.

The reasoning in the Maximum Freight Rate case [3] cannot be better put than by the following excerpts from the opinion of the Supreme Court.

"It is one thing to inqure whether the rates which have been charged and collected are reasonable, — that is a judicial act; but an entirely different thing to prescribe rates which shall be charged in the future, — that is a legislative act.

* * * * * * * * * * *

"We have, therefore, these considerations presented: First. The power to prescribe a tariff of rates for carriage by a common carrier is a

[1] 32 Federal Reporter, 1002.   [2] Chapter VII, *supra*.
[3] 4 Int. Com. Rep., 592: 167 U. S., 479. Both the original opinion and final decision with a map are in our Railway Problems. *Cf.* also, p. 248, *supra*. The case revived in 1910 is in 18 I.C.C. Rep., 440. *Vide* p. 588, *infra*.

legislative, and not an administrative or judicial, function, and, having respect to the large amount of property invested in railroads, the various companies engaged therein, the thousands of miles of road, and the millions of tons of freight carried, the varying and diverse conditions attaching to such carriage, is a power of supreme delicacy and importance. Second. That Congress has transferred such a power to any administrative body is not to be presumed or implied from any doubtful and uncertain language. The words and phrases efficacious to make such a delegation of power are well understood, and have been frequently used, and, if Congress has intended to grant such a power to the Interstate Commerce Commission, it cannot be doubted that it would have used language open to no misconstruction, but clear and direct. Third. Incorporating into a statute the common-law obligation resting upon the carrier to make all its charges reasonable and just, and directing the commission to execute and enforce the provisions of the act, does not by implication carry to the commission, or invest it with the power to exercise, the legislative function of prescribing rates which shall control in the future. Fourth. Beyond the inference which irresistibly follows from the omission to grant in express terms to the commission this power of fixing rates is the clear language of section 6, recognizing the right of the carrier to establish rates, to increase or reduce them, and prescribing the conditions upon which such increase or reduction may be made, and requiring, as the only conditions of its action — First, publication; and, Second, the filing of the tariff with the commission. The grant to the commission of the power to prescribe the form of the schedules, and to direct the place and manner of publication of joint rates, thus specifying the scope and limit of its functions in this respect, strengthens the conclusion that the power to prescribe rates or fix any tariff for the future is not among the powers granted to the commission.

"These considerations convince us that under the interstate commerce act the commission has no power to prescribe the tariff of rates which shall control in the future, and therefore cannot invoke a judgment in mandamus from the courts to enforce any such tariff by it prescribed."

The immediate effect of this decision was to put an end to any enforcement of decisions relative to rates by the Commission. The carriers immediately refused to obey any orders which the Commission issued for the redress of grievances. This policy was manifested with increasing clearness during the five years subsequent to the decision. It became more and more certain that the denial of the right, not only to pass upon the reasonableness of a particular rate, but to prescribe what rate should supersede it, meant the abolition of all control whatever over the scale of charges. The entire inadequacy of making rate regulation dependent upon the mere determination of rates as applied *in the past*, without reference to the rates which should prevail *in the future*, was apparent on all sides. More than this, all remedy for the parties who had borne the burden of an unreasonable rate would seem to have been removed. This was clearly described in the report of the Commission for 1897. It was illustrated by the rates upon oranges. In 1890 there had been a sudden advance on rates from Florida to New York from thirty to forty cents. The Commission after investigation ordered that the rate be reduced to thirty-five cents. As a matter of fact, how could this action redress grievances of those who had already paid forty cents per box? It was difficult in the first place to discover who bore the burden of the unreasonable charge; and in the second place it was certain that some of those who suffered could not legally sue in court. The actual shipper who alone could sue for repayment of unreasonable charges was a middleman who recouped himself in any event, either from the grower, the consumer, or both. He lost nothing by reason of the unreasonable rate. As a matter of fact, not any single individual but the locality, had been mulcted by five cents per hundred pounds, supposing that a rate of forty cents were unreasonable. Experience showed that almost no shippers or other parties injured, actually attempted to secure the restitution of moneys already paid for unreasonable charges. In only five out of 225 cases down to 1897 was a refund actually sought; and in those cases $100 was the maximum sought to be recovered. As a matter of fact the damage inflicted by the existence of such an unreasonable rate could not be measured by hundreds or perhaps by hundreds of thousands of dollars. The bearing of this citation is to show that any effectual protection to the shipper must proceed from adjudication of the reasonableness of rates *before*, and not *after*, they have been paid; that is to say, in advance of their exaction by the carrier. Power to pass upon the reasonableness of such rates prior to their enforcement, as a consequence, constitutes practically the only safeguard which the shipping public may enjoy. It will be observed that in this discussion reference is made simply and solely to that class of cases where complaint is made against the unreasonableness of a rate *per se* as applied to all shippers alike, entirely distinct from the exercise of powers by the Commission in respect of unreasonable discrimination as between two or more persons or places. That other question of relative rates was to come up in another connection.

Despite this denial by the Maximum Freight Rate decision of power to prescribe future rates, in substitution for others held to be unreasonable, there were still certain things which the Commission might do in the matter of rate determination. The only question was as to whether they afforded an adequate remedy for the redress of grievances. Were they really worth while? Complaint as to a rate, once paid, might still be made. The Commission might still hold it unreasonable; and even pass upon the degree of its unreasonableness. And the complainant shipper might then institute proceedings for repayment of the excessive charges under that particular rate. But the difference between this range of powers and those which had been claimed by the Commission for ten years was simply this: That under the original interpretation of the law the Commission had not only decided whether rates were wrong; it had also prescribed a remedy by issuing an order as to what rates were right, believing that these would be enforced by the courts. Not even the power to prescribe maximum rates remained to the Commission after this interpretation. The only action open to it would be to declare one rate after another unreasonable until the carriers had been brought to terms. Its inadequacy as a practical remedy was the main factor in bringing about the passage of the new law of 1906.

EMASCULATION OF THE LAW 473

It must not be assumed that the Supreme Court in the Maximum Freight Rate decision intended to render the Commission an entirely superfluous body. But its functions, as set forth in the following quotation from the opinion, proclaimed the adoption of an entirely different policy concerning public control of rates from the one hitherto pursued. Whether it was adequate for the purpose in view will appear, as has just been observed, from the subsequent course of events.

"But has the commission no functions to perform in respect to the matter of rates, no power to make any inquiry in respect thereto? Unquestionably it has, and most important duties in respect to this matter. It is charged with the general duty of inquiring as to the management of the business of railroad companies, and to keep itself informed as to the manner in which the same is conducted, and has the right to compel complete and full information as to the manner in which such carriers are transacting their business. And, with this knowledge, it is charged with the duty of seeing that there is no violation of the long and short haul clause; that there is no discrimination between individual shippers, and that nothing is done, by rebate or any other device, to give preference to one as against another; that no undue preferences are given to one place or places or individual or class of individuals, but that in all things that equality of right, which is the great purpose of the interstate commerce act, shall be secured to all shippers. It must also see that that publicity which is required by section 6 is observed by the railroad companies. Holding the railroad companies to strict compliance with all these statutory provisions, and enforcing obedience to all these provisions, tends . . . to both reasonableness and equality of rate, as contemplated by the interstate commerce act."

The nadir of government regulation for the time being was reached in November, 1897, — six months after the Maximum Freight Rate decision. A second opinion from the Supreme Court of the United States in the Alabama Midland (Troy) case, with one blow practically nullified the long and short haul clause.[1] The first opinion had put an end to control over the

---

[1] The Congressional history of Section 4, is in Haney, *op. cit.*, p. 304; especially good in Brief for Appellees, by Ed. Baxter in the Alabama Midland Case, U. S. Sup. Court, Oct. term, 1896, No. 563, p. 98. All the leading English cases are reprinted (Gov. Printing Office) in "Extracts from the Parliamentary Papers relating to the Long and Short Haul Clause,"

reasonableness of rates in and of themselves. This second one denied the right to establish their reasonableness *relatively* as between competing places or markets. In order fully to appreciate the significance of this decision it will be necessary to review cursorily the tedious litigation which led up to this result, — the entire emasculation of the Fourth section. The final outcome may be best described by Justice Harlan in his dissenting opinion in this leading case:

"Taken in connection with other decisions defining the powers of the Interstate Commerce Commission, the present decision, it seems to me, goes far to make that commission a useless body for all practical purposes, and to defeat many of the important objects designed to be accomplished by the various enactments of Congress relating to interstate commerce. The Commission was established to protect the public against the improper practices of transportation companies engaged in commerce among the several States. It has been left, it is true, with power to make reports, and to issue protests. But it has been shorn, by judicial interpretation, of authority to do anything of an effective character."

The interpretation of the long and short haul clause [1] as applied to concrete cases by the Interstate Commerce Commission, was first enunciated in the decision known as the Louisville & Nashville case.[2] Immediately after the enactment of the law, a multitude of petitions were received from carriers all over the country praying that they be exempted

1895, pp. 1–83; with an "Analysis of American Cases" (National Publishing Co., Washington), 1895, pp. 1–39; both issued in connection with the C., N. O. and T. P. case, U. S. Sup. Court, Nos. 729 and 832. The complicated legal history is best detailed step by step in Annual Reports of the Commission; references are in Judson on Interstate Commerce. App. F, part II (Elkins), Senate Committee Hearings, 1905, pp. 65–130, gives a garbled outline, convenient for citations. 21 I.C.C. Rep., p. 405, summarizes well. Several of the leading cases are reprinted in our Railway Problems, as indicated by footnotes hereafter.

[1] For a few pages, I follow closely the line of my report on the subject for the U. S. Industrial Commission in 1900.

[2] 1 I.C.C. Rep. 31; First Annual Report, Int. Com. Com.; also Digest (Elkins) Committee, 1905. To be distinguished from the Supreme Court decision affirming the validity of the Kentucky long and short haul clause, 183 U. S., 503.

from the operation of this clause, which prohibited a greater charge for a lesser haul than for one over the same line between points more distant. The policy outlined in the Louisville & Nashville case, delivered by Judge Cooley, has practically remained unchanged to the present time. This railroad company operating a line parallel to the Mississippi, as well as intersected at various points by its tributary rivers, claimed that the existence of water competition compelled a rate to all competitive points, lower than rates which could be made to local and intermediate stations. It alleged that an adjustment of its local rates to the low level necessitated at competitive points, would prove disastrous from the point of view of revenue. The point at issue was as to the interpretation of the phrase "under substantially similar circumstances and conditions"; which, in the words of the Act, was necessary in order that the prohibition of the lesser charge for the longer haul should become operative. Without entering into the details of this decision, in the course of which the nature of railroad competition and of rate making were fully discussed, as well as the legislative history of this clause of the Act, it will suffice to note the conclusions. These were; firstly, that the prohibition against a greater charge for a shorter than for a longer distance over the same line in the same direction, the shorter being included within the longer distance, was limited to cases in which the circumstances and conditions were substantially similar; secondly, that carriers might judge in the first instance as to the similarity or dissimilarity of circumstances; but, thirdly, that this judgment was not final but was subject to review by the Commission and the courts. Perhaps the most important point, however, was the determination of the conditions which constituted such dissimilar circumstances and conditions as entitled the carrier to charge less for the longer than for the shorter haul. These conditions were the existence of water competition; the existence of other railroads not subject to the statute; and "rare and peculiar" cases of competition between railroads which were subject to the law. The Commission also held as a guiding principle in the interpretation of this clause that no distinction would be recognized between local traffic and so-called through business; and also that the expense to the carrier involved would not be recognized as a factor unless it happened to come under the case already cited as "rare and peculiar." Furthermore, the desire to encourage manufactures or to build up business or trade centres, was not recognized as a competent reason for claiming exemption from the prohibition in the Act.

The leading decision of the Interstate Commerce Commission, above mentioned, was rendered in 1887. It was not until October of 1892 that the first serious interference arose through judicial interpretation in the United States Courts. The first was the so-called "separate and independent line" decision.[1] This case arose respecting a suit for the repayment of $225 as over-charges on corn shipped by one Osborne from Scranton, Iowa, to Chicago. It was claimed that the charges were unjust and unreasonable, inasmuch as they were in excess of rates charged from Blair, Nebraska, a point more remote from Chicago. The United States Circuit Court of Appeals at St. Paul reversed the decision of the lower court, holding that the lesser rate from Blair with which the Scranton rate had been compared, was not a rate to Chicago, but part of an agreed through rate to New York and other eastern points. Under this interpretation, the aggregate charge for the longer distance from Blair to New York was not less than the charge for the shorter distance from Scranton to Chicago. To this point the decision was in conformity with the previous interpretation by the courts and the Commission; which had uniformly held that a portion of a joint through rate cannot be compared with local or individual rates in the determination of what constitutes the rate for the shorter or the longer haul. This decision went further, however, and therein profoundly affected

[1] 52 Federal Reporter, 912; Ann. Rep., I.C.C., 1892, p. 31.

the subsequent interpretation of the law. It proceeded to define the word "line" as used in the Act, by holding that the joint line formed by two roads is wholly independent of the two lines represented by the several roads taken separately and apart. Interpreted in this way, the decision held furthermore that the total joint rate over two roads, not being over the "same line," might for anything in the fourth section of the Act, not only be as low but even lower than the local rate of either. The effect of this decision was obviously to permit a railroad to engage in traffic agreements for through carriage of freight; and by so doing, legally to become a line separate and independent from the same physical property when engaged in the transportation of freight over its own line. Moreover, by every contract for through carriage of freight with different carriers, the road became a separate and independent line in the eyes of the law. As many lines could exist over one set of rails as there were traffic agreements for through haulage of freight between its terminal points.[1]

The apprehension of the Interstate Commerce Commission that this interpretation of the word line might render the Fourth section of the Act inoperative, was realized in the following year. Several decisions not only adopted the *obiter dictum* of the Osborne case, above described, but proceeded to expand upon it. Thus, for example, in the Georgia Federal Court, a case arose involving rates from the North to Atlanta as compared with the higher rates to intermediate points. The court held that traffic from Cincinnati to Augusta or Atlanta was carried over a different line than that which was used for transportation to points intermediate between Atlanta and Augusta; inasmuch as the several carriers agreeing upon the joint rate as far as Atlanta from the North, were different.

[1] The significance of this decision is fully discussed in the Sixth and Seventh Reports of the Interstate Commerce Commission, which early in 1887 had already defined the word "line" in the Central Vermont case, as meaning the physical line, and not mere traffic agreements or routing arrangements.

Moreover it held that the road from Atlanta to Augusta being wholly within the state of Georgia, might by making a local rate from Atlanta which was added to the through rate into Atlanta, constitute itself merely a state road, and therefore be exempted from the prohibition of the Act. Thus it appeared, to quote from the report of the Commission for 1893, "that in addition to the embarrassments proposed by the original 'line' decision, the very jurisdiction of the law itself is invaded by the extension of the line theory indulged in by the Georgia Federal court."

The interpretation put upon the Fourth section of the Act by the decision above cited, remained in force and largely nullified application of the Act itself until 1896. The next important interpretation came, in the decision by the Supreme Court of the United States in the so-called "Social Circle" case.[1] This decision fully discussed the interpretation placed upon the word "line" in the Act. The rates involved were those on buggies from Cincinnati, Ohio, to Social Circle, a local station between Augusta and Atlanta, Georgia. Following the practice of the carriers for some years, the Georgia Railroad Company, which alone served the town of Social Circle, had requested its connections at Atlanta not to name through rates to that place or any other local station on its road. The Circuit Court following the line of argument already described, had held that under such circumstances the Georgia railroad was only a local carrier and not a party to a joint or common arrangement, which would make it subject to the control of the Federal Commission. The Supreme Court reversed this opinion, however; and held that when goods are shipped on a through bill of lading, they constitute an interstate carriage subject to Federal supervision and control. The court held further that this state road became part of a continuous line, not by consolidation with other companies, but by a traffic arrangement for continuous carriage or shipment. The Supreme

[1] 4 I.C.C. Rep., 744; 162 U. S., 184. *Vide*, also, p. 468, *supra*.

Court interpreted the original Osborne decision as merely affirming that a railroad company doing business in one state could not be compelled to enter into any agreement with connecting carriers. For by so doing, it continued, the carrier might be deprived of its rights and powers to make rates on its own road. Viewed in this way a carrier might agree to form a continuous line for carrying foreign freight at a through rate without being prevented from charging ordinary local rates for state traffic. Stripped of legal verbiage, this interpretation by the Supreme Court, virtually overruled the previous decisions by lower courts, and rehabilitated the original interpretation of the word "line" by the Commission; namely, that when a continuous line for through traffic is formed by several railroads, the roads constituting that line and making use of it are merely parts of one through route and are not separate lines. In short, not being able to constitute themselves as separate lines by reason of traffic contracts, they must continue to conform their through charges to the rates which they have made upon local business. So far as the enforcement of the Fourth section was concerned, therefore, developments to this point had upheld the law as originally passed.[1] It remained, however, for a separate and distinct course of judicial interpretation to once more jeopardize both the practical operation of the law and the power of the Commission.

Reverting to the original Louisville & Nashville decision in 1887, it will appear that the Commission held at that time that competition between carriers subject to the Act, did not constitute such dissimilarity of circumstances and conditions as would justify the carriers in making their long distance rates lower than the rates between intermediate points. The only exception recognized at that time was to be found in certain "rare and peculiar" cases.[2] One of these will suffice

[1] Amendment of the law in 1910, precluded any further misunderstanding, also, by adding the word "route." P. 565, *infra*.

[2] Discussed, as an economic proposition in chap. VII, *supra*. Baxter's Brief in the Troy case, p. 117, proves it not peculiar.

as an illustration. There are two routes by which traffic from Youngstown, Ohio, may reach the East. One is by way of Pittsburg and the Pennsylvania Railroad; the other by an outlet to the north, at Ashtabula upon the Lake Shore and New York Central trunk lines. Between Youngstown, Ohio, and Pittsburg, two parallel lines exist, each having an interest in forwarding freight to the East by the two routes above mentioned. The peculiarity of the situation is that competitive traffic for the East may leave Pittsburg in either direction. If it goes around by Youngstown, that place becomes an intermediate point between Pittsburg and New York. If, on the other hand, it goes from Pittsburg directly east, Youngstown becomes not an intermediate point, but one more remote than Pittsburg from New York. Inasmuch as the Pennsylvania route from Pittsburg is the shorter, it makes the rate.[1] The other roundabout route is obliged to accede to this compelled rate or lose the business. The result is that the smaller indirect road is obliged to give a lower rate from Pittsburg round by way of Youngstown to New York than it gives to Youngstown itself. Any other course of action would deprive it of any participation in Pittsburg business. Such, then, is one of those "rare and peculiar" cases under which the Commission from the first recognized the necessity of exempting carriers, even where all are subject to the Act, from the prohibition of charging less for a shorter than for a longer haul over the same line.

The carriers from the outset had made a determined effort to show that the competition of carriers among themselves was sufficient to produce that dissimilarity of Circumstances and conditions which would justify exemption from the Act. This contention the Commission refused to recognize, and did so particularly in the important decisions of 1892 known as the Georgia Railroad Commission cases.[2] These again, like the

---

[1] Which line makes the rate? *Cf.* p. 255, *supra.*
[2] 5 I.C.C. Rep., 324. Decided by the Supreme Court in 1901; 181 U. S., 29; after the Alabama Midland decision.

Maximum Freight Rate case, involved rates from Cincinnati to various points throughout the South; and had reference particularly to the prevalent practice of granting low rates to certain important centres known as basing points. In this decision the Commission re-affirmed the principles set forth in the Louisville & Nashville case, except in one detail; namely, as to whether the carriers were justified in deciding for themselves in first instance whether a case of railroad competition was of that type already defined as "rare and peculiar" which would permit exemption from the long and short haul prohibition. Experience of five years had shown that the right of decision in this respect had led to manifold abuses; inasmuch as a strong disposition on the part of the carriers all over the country was shown to interpret all cases of railroad competition, however simple, as "rare and peculiar." The Commission, therefore, proceeded to overrule its earlier decision; and denied the right on the part of carriers to determine for themselves as to what constituted dissimilarity of circumstances and conditions, affirming that that right was its own.

All of the foregoing judicial interpretation is secondary in importance to the final decision of the United States Supreme Court in 1896 in what is known as the Alabama Midland case.[1] This once and for all overruled the interpretation placed upon the law by the Commission, that railroad competition did not constitute that dissimilarity of circumstances and conditions which would entitle a carrier to exemption from the prohibitions of the statute. This case, like almost all the others involving the interpretation of the Fourth section, arose upon complaint of a small town in the southern states that more important trade centres were securing advantages in the matter of rates which were denied to it. The Board of Trade of Troy, Alabama, complained that it was compelled to pay $3.22 a ton on phos-

[1] 6 I.C.C. Rep., 3; overruled by the Supreme Court in 168 U. S., 144. Both reprinted in our Railway Problems. Decisions of secondary importance down to 1905 are abbreviated in App. F, Senate Elkins Committee Hearings, 1905.

phate rock from Florida and South Carolina points, whereas the rate to Montgomery, a longer distance, was only $3.00 per ton. The rock was carried through Troy. It was also complained that rates on cotton discriminated against Troy as compared with Montgomery and other points; and that, thirdly, rates from Baltimore and New York were higher to Troy than to Montgomery, which was fifty-two miles further away. The

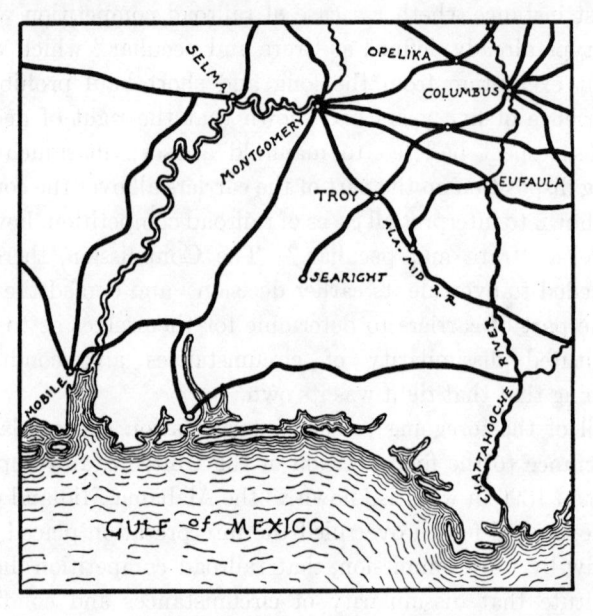

case was carried on appeal to the Supreme Court of the United States, where an opinion was handed down in 1896. The gist of this decision was that competition, whether of trade centres or of railroads, must be recognized as a factor in the determination of the similarity of circumstances and conditions under which the Fourth section of the clause should be applied. In other words, it recited that Montgomery being a larger place than Troy; and having been an important trade centre on a navigable river for many years, it was competent to the railroads centering at Montgomery to determine in part for themselves whether the existence of effective competition would warrant them in granting lower rates to Montgomery than to local stations like Troy. The court held, however, that such competition was only one of the elements which must be considered. It did not define it as the dominating one. The railroads, nevertheless, seized upon this interpretation of the law at once, making use of it to justify whatever departure they pleased to make from the practice originally contemplated in adjusting long and short haul charges.

After the discouraging reverse in the Alabama Midland decision, which the Commission interpreted to mean that if circumstances and conditions were different at the more distant point, that fact, of itself, removed the case from the inhibition of the Fourth section; certain inferior Federal court opinions somewhat modified this view.[1] The question as to whether the discrimination at bar was or was not justifiable, was permitted to be considered; in addition to inquiring merely whether circumstances and conditions were different at the more distant point. The Commission somewhat reanimated by these decisions, sought to apply this judicial modification of the Alabama Midland reasoning to several then pending complaints as to local discrimination. Both in the Danville[2] and Hampton cases[3] the carriers were ordered to desist from discriminating against the nearer point under this interpretation of the law. But the Supreme Court put an end to it all by condemning this line of reasoning in its last leading decision upon the Fourth section rendered in 1901, finally disposing of the so-called Chattanooga case. This dealt the final death blow to the long and short clause.[4] The complaint in this case

[1] 21 I.C.C. Rep., 407. Elkins Committee Digest. Judson on Interstate Commerce, etc.
[2] Reprinted in our Railway Problems. Sustained by the lower courts in 1903; 122 Fed. Rep., 800.
[3] 8 I.C.C. Rep., 503; 120 Fed. Rep., 934.
[4] Facts are given in chap. VII, p. 228, *supra;* and in full in our Railway Problems. The law is in 181 U. S., 1. The only later decisions, not changing the law, are in 190 U. S., 273.

arose from the fact that freight rates to Chattanooga, Tennessee, from eastern cities were higher than to Nashville, although the latter was the more distant point. The Commission found that there was no water competition at Nashville compelling the lower rate; but that there was competition of railways and of markets. The Supreme Court reversed the Commission in its final attempt thus to revivify the moribund Fourth section, and fully confirmed its original view as to the meaning of the Alabama Midland decision. If such circumstances and conditions as competition of markets or railways at the two points were dissimilar, carriers might without restraint depart from the long and short haul rule. Thus the Fourth section of the law was to all intents and purposes repealed. Complaint after complaint was perforce set aside by the Commission. For practical purposes this part of the law was rendered absolutely nugatory. The chapter was closed. For twenty years, in face of the litigation above outlined, no order of the Commission respecting local discrimination was enforced. Only with its amendment in 1910, as subsequently described,[1] did the long and short haul clause once more resume its due importance upon the statute books.

One special case may be cited in this general connection, as typical of the arbitrary action of carriers particularly in the South. It was this sort of thing which went far to arouse public opinion and focus attention upon the need for real regulation.[2] The situation appears upon the accompanying map. The planters in a certain southern territory served by the Louisville & Nashville railway had been accustomed to ship out their cotton to the North by various routes. It might go by way of New Orleans, *via* Pensacola, up the main line along the Mississippi valley, or be hauled eastward to Savannah and other Atlantic ports, and thence go by vessel to New

[1] Pp. 564 and 601, *infra*.
[2] Known as the Savannah Naval Stores case. 8 Int. Com. Rep., 376. It is reprinted in full in our Railway Problems.

England. Inasmuch as the through rate was the same by all routes, no monetary issue to the planter was involved. But not so to the railway. For by the first routes it secured a long haul; while by the last it not only was limited to short carriage of the goods, but was compelled to accept an even smaller fraction of the joint through rate. In this case the Louisville & Nashville railway — which, by the way, more persistently denied the existence of abuses than any other road in the country — advanced the Savannah cotton rate arbitrarily in 1899 from $2.75 to $3.30 a bale. This effectually dammed up

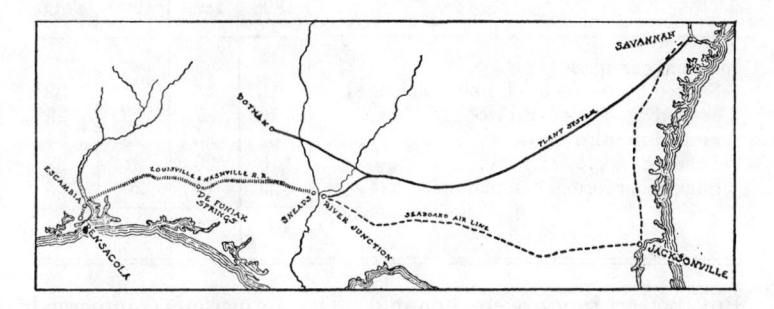

the eastern outlet and jeopardized the interests of the port of Savannah to that degree. Doubtless the Louisville & Nashville was not oblivious to the welfare of that great seaport. It could not afford to be, for Savannah's growth must indirectly accrue to its benefit. It did not love Savannah less; but it loved its own particular seaport, Pensacola, or the long haul *via* Louisville, more. Maybe it was better that traffic should go out this way — who knew best? The real point to be made is that no competent tribunal or process for impartially determining the question was provided by the now emasculated law.

The work of the Commission during these discouraging years was naturally affected most profoundly by these limitations placed upon its activity by the Federal courts. The number of formal complaints, never large, steadily dwindled year by year. Thirty-nine were filed in 1892; but in 1900 and the following year only nineteen were presented annually.[1] The Commission persisted in its statistical work with marked success. Important independent investigations continued to be made, in pursuance of the only policy remaining open to it, that of publicity. But even the informal complaints, representing mainly the grievances of individual shippers rather than of competing cities or commercial bodies, were few in number, as the following official figures show.

	1898	1899	1900	Total
Informal complaints:				
Settled by payment of amount claimed ..	18	5	9	32
Settled by change of rates	10*	7	12	29
Settled in other ways	32	30	22	84
Pending	16	20	31	67
Suggesting formal complaints	29	14	20	63
	105	76	94	275

But better times were coming. The return of commercial prosperity brought with it new problems. Old abuses, quiescent during the long industrial depression of 1893–1897, once more made their appearance. New constructive legislation followed, based as before upon the economic needs of the time, as they made themselves manifest; but a great campaign of education, led by the vigorous personality of Theodore Roosevelt, was necessary, as we shall see, to compel Congress to act.

[1] *Cf.* the chart at p. 523, *infra.*

CHAPTER XV

THE ELKINS AMENDMENTS (1903): THE HEPBURN ACT OF 1906

New causes of unrest in 1899, 487. — The spread of consolidation, 487. — The rise of freight rates, 488. — Concentration of financial power, 490. — The new "trusts," 491. — The Elkins amendments concerning rebates, 492. — Five provisions enumerated, 493. More general legislation demanded, 494. — Congressional history 1903-1905, 495. — Railway publicity campaign, 496. — President Roosevelt's leadership, 498. — The Hepburn law, 499. — Widened scope, 499. — Rate-making power increased, 500. — Administrative *v.* judicial regulation, 501. — Objection to judicial control, 503. — Final form of the law, 505. — Broad *v.* narrow court review, 506. — An unfortunate compromise, 507. — Old rates effective pending review, 508. — Provisions for expedition, 511. — Details concerning rebates, 512. — The commodity clause, 513. — History of its provisions, 514. — Publicity of accounts, 515. — Extreme importance of accounting supervision, 516. — The Hepburn law summarized, 520.

THE new incentives to rehabilitation of the Interstate Commerce law by Congress, becoming year by year more insistent after 1899, were four in number. Most of the old long-standing grievances were still on the docket. New sources of dissatisfaction and danger were now added in plenty as a result of important industrial changes. The most far-reaching of these was the spread of consolidation among railroads. This, as we shall see,[1] led within a few years to a partition of the entire railway net of the country into a few large systems, each controlled financially, although seldom by actual majority investment, by powerful individuals or banking groups, mainly located in New York. Many small local roads, long closely identified with the welfare of particular communities, were now merged in great systems under entirely different and probably absentee ownership and management. Boston, Baltimore,

[1] Exhaustively described in volume II.

New Orleans, St. Paul, Cincinnati, not to mention a host of other smaller places, seemed commercially cast adrift. The welfare of railroads and of the particular communities in which they lay, — long supposed to be indissolubly linked together, — was now seen by concrete experience to be separable, often into conflicting parts. The New Haven monopoly in New England might be managed rather in the interest of New York than of the port of Boston. The Illinois Central, once devoted whole-heartedly to the upbuilding of New Orleans, must now, as a part of the Union Pacific system, comprehend San Francisco and even Savannah within the scope of its plans. New systems implied new traffic arrangements. Railroad policy must of necessity involve a choice, not between two evils, perhaps, but between a resultant good and a necessarily attendant evil. All these corporate changes made inevitably for much commercial re-adjustment. And each re-adjustment left a trail of real or alleged grievances; for the settlement of which no competent tribunal existed. There can be no doubt, therefore, that the significant changes in the railroad map after 1899 had much to do with the demand for new legislation.

The second new and general cause of dissatisfaction among the public was the great and almost continuous rise of freight rates which began about 1900. This was of course a direct outcome of the spread of railroad consolidation. The movement of freight rates has been elsewhere described in detail.[1] It has appeared that the steady decline which ensued for almost a generation after the panic of 1873, was sharply reversed when combination succeeded competition as a fundamental policy of railroading. This striking reversal of the course of railway charges was not, of course, an isolated phenomenon. It took place in a period of marked and general rise of prices, not unconnected with changes in the value of gold. But the upward trend was more accentuated, and apparently more irresistible,

[1] Chapter XII, *supra*, and chap. XVIII, *infra*.

in the charges for transportation than in the prices of commodities. Prior to 1899, not even the most astute railroad managers ever anticipated any such change. The Boston & Maine Railroad even permitted the inclusion of a prohibition of any higher rates in future than were then in force, to be incorporated in the acts of the New Hampshire legislature authorizing its leases of important lines. Attorneys sought to prove that railroads were not subject to the law of increasing returns, because it was *inevitable* as an economic law that with growth in the volume of business, rates should progressively decline.[1] If there was often public dissatisfaction at the scale of charges under these conditions, how irresistible might the unrest among shippers become when rates actually began to move so strongly upwards!

A single illustration of the class of complaints thus engendered may not be out of place.[2] It concerned the reasonableness of an increase of two cents per hundred pounds on lumber from Georgia points to the Ohio river. From 1894 to 1903 these rates had been already raised by three or four cents, to a level of thirteen or fourteen cents; so that prosperity had been already discounted by a rise of thirty or forty per cent. On top of this, and despite an enormous increase in the tonnage, came a further raise of two cents per hundred pounds in April, 1903. This was too much. To this exaction, involving not less than $132,000 per year additional freight rates, the lumbermen of Georgia objected. The Interstate Commerce Commission upheld their contention; and in July, 1905, more than two years afterward, the Circuit Court sustained the Commission. Appeal was then taken to the Supreme Court which rendered a decision in 1907, more than four years after the increase had occurred; and during which time the railroads

[1] *Journal of Political Economy*, VI, 1898, pp. 457–475.
[2] Central Yellow Pine Association, etc., 10 I.C.C. Rep., 505 and 549; 206 U. S., 428. Other cases dating from this time are given in chap. XVI as they reached the Supreme Court.

had been collecting the added charge. The shippers had naturally at once shifted the burden upon the public so far as the competition of other lumber-producing centres, each championed by its own railroad or set of roads, would permit. No recovery of this tax, now held to be unjust by the highest court in the land, could possibly be had. The loss was irreparable. The frequency of complaints of this sort, involving the absolute reasonableness of rates, proves conclusively how potent a factor in furthering legislation the rise of the scale of charges had become.

The demonstration of the menace to public welfare of an inordinate concentration of financial power in the hands of a few privileged individuals, served a useful end in bringing about new legislation. The general rise of rates had been a direct outcome of the substitution of combination for competition among railroads. The danger of absolute dominion over all trade, commerce and finance without accountability to the law, was a concomitant of the growth of great railroad systems.[1] A special investigation in 1905 showed, for example, that the majorities of the boards of directors of practically all of the roads east of the Mississippi river might be selected from a group of only thirty-nine persons. The spectacular career of Edward H. Harriman with the Union Pacific and other companies was a convincing argument in itself. The disclosures in the New York insurance investigation of 1905 as to the intricate ramifications of financial power came, as will shortly appear, at a most opportune time for promoting congressional activity. The need of it was, perhaps, never more clearly shown than in the following frank admission by Mr. Harriman in December, 1906, — only a few months after the law had been amended, — made in the course of a general investigation of railroad consolidations by the Interstate Commerce Commis-

[1] *Cf.* data on concentration of railway control in the United States App. VI, Digest of Hearings before Senate (Elkins) Committee on Interstate Commerce, 1905, pp. 1–56.

sion.[1] Questioned as to where his policy of acquisition was to end, the following colloquy ensued:

"A. I would go on with it. If I thought we could realize something more than we have got from these investments I would go on and buy some more things.

* * * * * * * * * * * *

"Q. Supposing that you got the Santa Fe?
"A. You would not let us get it.
"Q. How could we help it?
"A. How could you help it? I think you would bring out your power to enforce the conditions of the Sherman anti-trust act pretty quick. If you will let us, I will go and take the Santa Fe to-morrow.
"Q. You would take it to-morrow?
"A. Why, certainly I would; I would not have any hesitation; it is a pretty good property.
"Q. Then it is only the restriction of the law that keeps you from taking it?
"A. I would go on as long as I live.
"Q. Then after you had gotten through with the Santa Fe and had taken it, you would also take the Northern Pacific and Great Northern, if you could get them?
"A. If you would let me.
"Q. And your power, which you have, would gradually increase as you took one road after another, so that you might spread not only over the Pacific coast, but spread out over the Atlantic coast?
"A. Yes."

Was there ever a clearer case of megalomania, menacing the welfare of a great people?

But it was not alone the dangers incident to monopoly in transportation which excited popular alarm. There was the ever increasing danger of abuse of monopolistic power by the newly created industrial combinations. Most of these had sprung up overnight in the great promotion movement of 1899–1901. The general public had long been aware of the gross favoritism in transportation, which had created the Standard Oil Company. It knew something of the power of the beef packers' monopoly, built up by the use of private car lines. But with the publication of Miss Tarbell's History of the Standard Oil

[1] 12 I.C.C. Rep., 1.

Company in 1903-1904, followed by the reports of the United States Commissioner of Corporations in 1906, its attention was newly directed to the evil.[1] Even the carriers themselves were now roused to protest by the pressure for secret favors by large shippers. The Elkins amendments to the law in 1903, as we shall see, enabled the government to convict many offenders. But even this new law was not enough. The rebating still went on, under new and ingenious forms. If the United States Steel Corporation, the "Sugar Trust," the International Harvester Company, the Colorado Fuel and Iron Company and a host of others were not restrained, monopoly in transportation would soon be followed by monopoly in manufacture. Each new disclosure verified the suspicions of the public as to the magnitude of these abuses. The necessity of a special corrective was first applied to rebating; but this action in turn only served to reënforce the popular conviction that more general legislation was necessary. The Elkins amendments of 1903 surely paved the way for the Hepburn law three years thereafter.

The so-called Elkins amendments to the Act of 1887, — the first changes of importance in its substantive clauses, — were made in 1903, in response to a demand of the carriers. Educated to a sense of the grave losses of revenue incident to rebating and general rate cutting, prominent railroad men united in urging Congress to act. The ease and decorum with which this legislation was passed is, in itself, eloquent testimony to the organized influence of the railroads over Congress, which made itself felt during the next few years in opposition to further changes in the law for the benefit of the public. The entire inadequacy of the original act to prevent rebating had been proven time and again. The Interstate Commerce Commission had done its best. The Department of Justice had attempted to apply the equity processes of injunction without

[1] Chapter VI gives details as to these events.

much result. Other Federal laws had been invoked in vain. When the carriers themselves asked for more stringent legislation, it was accorded by Congress with commendable despatch. No opposition whatever appeared. Nor was there much debate. The machinery of legislation moved expeditiously and almost without noise to the desired end.

These Elkins amendments dealt solely with the provisions of law concerning observance of published tariffs. They in no wise affected the determination of what those tariffs should be. That problem of reasonableness was the bone of contention in the great struggle in Congress, hardly as yet under way but soon to follow. The changes in 1903, therefore, had mainly to do with penalties and legal procedure. They were, as elsewhere outlined, five in number. The railroad corporation itself, — and not merely its officers and agents as heretofore, — was made liable to prosecution and penalty. This put an end to the anomalous immunity hitherto enjoyed by the principal and beneficiary of a guilty transaction. Secondly, the penalty of imprisonment for departure from the published tariff, — added to the law in 1889 in the hope of rendering it more effective, — was removed. It had been hoped that the reluctance of witnesses to become parties to such condign punishment of associates might thus be somewhat overcome; especially since the liability to fines now ran to the corporation rather than to the individual. The third change in the law was of great importance, as it had been construed by the courts. Preferential treatment of shippers had been made to depend upon proof; first, that rates lower than as published in the tariff had actually been allowed; and, in the second place, that these full tariff rates, or, at least, higher rates, had been paid by others on like shipments at the same time. Such proof had turned out to be practically impossible in any general rate war; inasmuch as, at such times, rates were cut more or less substantially for all shippers alike. In other words, there might well be departure from the published rates, without preferential treatment. And it was the object of the law to put a stop to both of these abuses. The Elkins law, therefore, explicitly made the published tariff the standard of lawfulness. Any departure from it, proven by itself alone, was declared a misdemeanor. In the fourth place, the new law made shippers or any other interested parties defendants; whereas formerly only the giver of rebates, not the recipient, could be prosecuted. This change rendering the guilty shipper liable, was an eminently proper one. And then, finally, the new law provided for the issuance of injunctions, — viz., peremptory orders punishable by contempt of court, — by any Federal judge whenever the Interstate Commerce Commission had reasonable ground for belief that any common carrier was deviating from the published tariff, "or is committing any discrimination forbidden by law." A summary prohibition from this judicial source, it was hoped, would act as a powerful deterrent.

The enactment of more general remedial legislation than the Elkins amendments was a far more serious matter. That statute has not inaptly been described as "not even a preliminary skirmish. It was a truce of the principals to abolish piracy." The original law of 1887 was avowedly experimental and imperfect. With this in view the statute had specifically directed that there should be transmitted to Congress in its annual reports "such recommendations as to additional legislation . . . as the Interstate Commerce Commission may deem necessary." This duty was conscientiously performed year by year. One may find, therefore, in these documents, especially after 1896, the most convincing presentation of the need for amendment of the law. Yet despite its importance, Congress was for some years so intent upon more pressing public business, that no action was taken in the matter. Currency legislation, the Spanish War and the Philippines, the Isthmian Canal, pure food and the trusts quite engrossed public attention. And, oddly enough, when the campaign opened seriously in 1899, activity was for a time confined mainly to the Senate. This was in sharp contrast with the situation both before 1887 and after 1905, when the upper house was the obstructive member.

As early as 1894 the Senate Committee on Interstate Commerce had reported favorably a bill; but nothing came of it. Five years later, both Senators Cullom of Illinois, — sponsor for the original law, — and Chandler of New Hampshire introduced bills. All these measures aimed to confer rate-making power upon the commission and to expedite judicial procedure upon appeal. In the meantime important organizations, especially in the West, such as the National Board of Trade and the Conventions of State Railroad Commissioners, had taken the matter up. Much evidence was heard by the United States Industrial Commission which dealt with it in an elaborate report in 1901.[1] The chances seemed favorable for action. The Senate Committee on Interstate Commerce in that year added several progressively inclined members. The general freight rate increases of 1900 had greatly stirred the people. But at this juncture the powerful new financial influences, concerned with the formation of the great transportation systems, came into play. Effective regulation might interfere with some of these plans. The matter was becoming serious. Railroad opposition began to organize. It became clear that a bitter contest would be needed to secure legislation.

Renewed pressure from the public came in 1902. Senator Chandler had been retired by direct railroad influence in New Hampshire. But Senator Cullom again brought in a bill,[2] which was consolidated with another by Senator Nelson of Minnesota. Public interest was plainly rising; yet these measures all died in committee. And the House of Representatives was too busy with other concerns. But in 1903,

[1] The evidence is in vols. IV and IX. Our final report on the subject is in vol. XIX.
[2] B. H. Meyer, Railway Legislation in the United States, 1903, is best on this period.

for the first time, the lower house devoted some attention to the so-called Cooper-Quarles bill;[1] although no vote was taken. It did, however, with little debate, as we have seen, grant what the railroads asked for the suppression of rebating in the passage of the Elkins amendments. The necessity of general legislation on the subject was not yet strongly felt. The trusts, floundering in the panic of 1903, seemed more threatening to public order than the railroads. Only in a few communities like Wisconsin under the able leadership of Governor La Follette, had public opinion become sufficiently aroused to achieve definite results.

Matters were finally brought to a head by the determined attitude of President Roosevelt. In his annual message to Congress in 1904 he made railroad regulation "a paramount issue." The remedies proposed differed little from those of the bills above mentioned. The cardinal point was that the Interstate Commerce Commission was to be given power to prescribe actual rates, to be effective until reversed by the courts. Under this spur, the House of Representatives passed the so-called Esch-Townshend bill — an administration measure — by the impressive majority of 326 to 17. It was now the Senate's turn to delay. It, however, authorized its Interstate Commerce Committee to sit during the spring and summer, and to report in December.[2] A mass of testimony was taken, which despite the activity of a powerful body of paid railroad attorneys, proved to be most convincing. But even more cogent proof of the need of control was the outrageous attempt of the carriers to influence popular opinion through so-called publicity bureaus.[3] An extensive service, regardless of cost, was set up with headquarters at Washington and with branches

[1] Fully discussed in Haines, Restrictive Railroad Legislation, 1905, p. 265 *et seq.*
[2] Hearings before the Committee on Interstate Commerce, Senate of the United States, Dec. 16, 1904 to May 23, 1905; 5 vols., appendices, digests, etc.; commonly known as the Elkins Committee.
[3] The *Chicago Tribune* and the *Record-Herald* effectively exposed the affair. *Cf. Colliers Weekly*, May 4, 1907, for a good résumé.

in all the leading cities, headed by the President of the Southern Railway. Bogus conventions, packed for the purpose, — such as the "Alabama Commercial and Industrial Association," — passed resolutions unanimously, to be scattered broadcast by free telegraphic despatches all over the country. "Associations for the Maintenance of Property" held conventions; the fact being duly advertised. Palpably garbled news items from Washington were distributed without cost, especially during the hearings of the Senate Committee. Even more insidious and misleading methods were employed. An elaborate card catalogue of small newspapers throughout the United States was made; in which was noted all of the hobbies, prejudices, and even the personal weaknesses of the editors. One of the cards is reproduced on this page. Magazine sections or "ready

Town	Name of Paper	Circulation	Date of Issue	Politics
		600	Wkly	Dem
1167		Infl. small	Sat	Anti-beef
				Anti-oil
	Owner & Nd	2nd paper	6-	Anti-harvestor
				Anti-corp
10870		Farmers		Anti-Rep Machine
C M St P		Weak Eds		Pro-R R
				Pro-Roosevelt
		1.50		

S D ——— is weak and bibulous man. Tractable to R R suggestions. Many Bohemians in region. Rich county. Junction town.

Duplicate copied from a card in the Chicago Publicity Bureau's index of newspapers. These cards furnish, in the last column, detailed information as to the position of the editor on public questions. At the bottom they indicate by what opening he could be persuaded to accept railroad "doctrine." The data which would identify the paper and editor on this card have been erased.

to print" insides were also made up, in which appropriate and subtle references to railroad issues were concealed in a mass of general reading matter. Two or three weekly letters were sent gratis to minor newspapers without regular Washington correspondents, containing "good railroad doctrine," together with spicy local news items. Dakota farmers got suggestions as to the danger of the proposed legislation affecting their rates. Kentucky planters were warned of the probable effect upon tobacco prices. As an indication of the formidable proportions of this campaign of education, the Chicago office, alone, employed some forty highly paid experts. Regular reports were rendered by this news service to the railroads' committee, as to the results achieved; setting forth the number of columns of news matter distributed and the changes effected in the proportion of "pro" and "con" items published. It was indeed a most astounding demonstration of the lengths to which organized corporate power would go to defeat regulative legislation. That it proved upon exposure to be a boomerang for the railroad cause, is to be inferred from the entire absence of all such political methods from the succeeding campaigns dealing with further amendment of the law.

The President again insisted upon action in the annual message of 1905, this time recommending control over maximum, not absolute, rates.[1] Executive pressure was brought to bear heavily upon Congress. The public was plainly becoming insistent; with the result that the so-called Hepburn bill was passed by 346 votes to 7. Whether the Senate, under the influence of one of the most powerful lobbies ever let loose upon a legislative body, would have yielded even then, had it not been for an extraordinary conjuncture of economic events, one dare not surmise. The general causes of dissatisfaction, already described, such as the spread of combination, the growth of autocratic power, the steady rise of freight rates and the abuses of personal favoritism had been long at work. But

[1] Senator La Follette in his Autobiography, *American Magazine*, June, 1912, p. 185, avers that the president's main insistence at first was upon discriminations, not absolutely unreasonable charges; but the consumer is mainly interested in the latter point. The claim is made that the suggestion of thorough going control came from this personal source. La Follette's three-day speech on April 19–21 was certainly the ablest presentation made of the progressive policy of regulation.

now at the psychological moment came the general breakdown and congestion of railroad service all over the country;[1] the insurance investigation in New York; the Pennsylvania Railroad coal car scandal;[2] the Atchison rebate disclosures, with "barefaced disregard of the law," besmirching a member of the President's cabinet;[3] and the exposure of the outrageous publicity campaign methods of the carriers. The evidence was cumulative and overwhelming as to the need of action. The Senate was forced to acquiesce in a conference committee bill, passing it at the end with only three dissenting votes.[4] On June 29, 1906, the Hepburn bill became law. The fundamental principle of governmental control over the most powerful corporations in the country had been fully affirmed. It was an historic event, — the most important, perhaps, in Theodore Roosevelt's public career, — and a not insignificant one in our national history.

The Hepburn law of 1906, in the first place, greatly broadened the field of Federal regulation.[5] This was now extended to cover both express and sleeping-car companies. Pipe lines, — such powerful factors in the creation of monopoly in the oil business as opportunely showed by the Report of the Commissioner of Corporations in 1906, — were expressly included. "Transportation" was now broadly defined as comprehending among other things, "all services in connection with the receipt, delivery, elevation, and transfer in transit, ventilation, refriger-

[1] Chapter II, pp. 62 and 80, *supra*.
[2] Chapter VI, p. 199, *supra*. [3] P. 195, *supra*.
[4] *Munsey's Magazine* for March, 1912, has a good review of the Congressional battle; with details of the defeat of the Aldrich-Cannon contingent.
[5] The best references on the Hepburn Act are as follows: Dixon, F. H., *Quarterly Journal of Economics*, XXI, 1906, pp. 22–51; Smalley, H. S., *Annals American Academy of Political Science*, 1907, pp. 292–309. The course of events is currently well reported in the file of the *Railway Age Gazette*. *Cf.* also, *Review of Reviews*, May and July, 1906; and the magazine references in the Bibliography on Railroads of the Library of Congress.

ation or icing, storage, and handling of property transported." Whether certain of these powers, especially over pipe lines, are practically enforcible as well as legally sound, remains yet to be seen. The inclusion of all switches, spurs, and terminal facilities, with appurtenances of all sorts, was an added detail of importance, in view of the complicated uses made of them in connection with rebating, as elsewhere described. And the express power to require facilities for shipment, as well as to regulate joint rates and services in every detail, was yet another notable extension of Federal authority. Part-rail and part-water transportation was included; but coastwise and inland traffic exclusively by water, was left out. In view of its intimate relation to rates and services by rail, this omission was unfortunate. The notorious instability of water rates and the difficulties incident to the enforcement of the long and short haul clause, render such water-borne traffic of great importance in the proper regulation of carriers on land.

The significance of the Hepburn law, however, was not primarily in the wider scope of Federal control. The heart of it consisted of its more intensive character. The rate-making power of the Commission was greatly increased. Two other points were contested with equal vigor, viz., the scope of judicial review of decisions of the Commission, and the question as to whether its orders in cases appealed should take effect at once, or only upon final judgment by the Federal court. Viewed in a large way, however, all three of these propositions depended upon the determination of a basic issue. A clear separation of powers between the legislative, executive and judicial branches of government was a fundamental principle in our Federal Constitution. It was generally agreed that a considerable confusion of functions, laid upon the Commission by the original law, must in future be avoided. Here, it was said, was a body which, if empowered to make rates, would be exercising a legislative function; if applying and enforcing them, would be acting administratively; and if hearing complaints, would be serving as a court. It was generally conceded, nevertheless, except by a few extremists, that the time had now come when some competent tribunal must be provided for the effective and prompt settlement of transportation disputes. To which one of these three branches of the government should this important duty be assigned? In other words, disregarding mere matters of detail, should the Interstate Commerce Commission or the Federal courts be charged with the real control of the common carriers of the country?

The alignment upon this question was clearly defined. The administration and the representatives of the shippers and the general public, were unanimously agreed that control of rates and regulations, to be effective must be through an administrative agency, — a body, that is to say, attached to the executive branch of the government. Their reasons will be set forth in due time. On the other hand every railroad proposition was based upon the exercise of real control by the judiciary. The Commission, as an administrative body, was not to be abolished; but in all matters of rate regulation it was to be subordinated to the courts. The motives for this policy will also appear shortly. Senator Foraker of Ohio, — soon retired because of his uncompromisingly pro-railroad attitude, — proposed to strip the Commission of all rate-making power whatsoever; and to reduce it to an initiating body which should merely certify all complaints to the Federal courts for settlement. Senator Elkins of West Virginia, — an equally ardent railroad representative, — introduced a bill to create a special transportation court, subordinate only to the Supreme Court of the United States on questions of law. Until this tribunal had heard the cause, and had sanctioned interference on the ground of unreasonableness, the Interstate Commerce Commission might not intervene.[1] And in any event its functions were

[1] Compare this with the plans proposed by W. C. Noyes, American Railroad Rates, 1905, p. 255; and A. N. Merritt, Federal Regulation of Railway Rates, 1907, p. 193.

to be mainly connected with the enforcement, not the promulgation, of orders as to rates or service. These plans favoring the carriers' interests, as we shall see, were all based upon the proposition that Congress could not constitutionally delegate general rate making, that is to say, legislative power to an administrative body.

The constitutionality of clothing an administrative body with large regulative power by act of Congress, was, of course, essential to the administration's plan. It was urged that there was one exception to the general rule that power delegated to Congress to legislate under the Constitution could not be further delegated. "There may be such delegation where the purpose in the original conferring of the power can be subserved only by its delegation to an agent. Obviously Congress cannot spend time and labor upon rate making, even were it economically competent to do so. If the power is to be exercised at all, practically, it can be done only through an agency like the Commission." Congress certainly could not delegate such legislative power, viz., power to make rates, to the courts. That would even more flagrantly transgress the constitutional rule. In brief, any plan for judicial control meant the exclusion of rate regulation in any thorough-going way. And that, of course, was the reason why the "railroad Senators" all insisted upon such a plan. Other support for the administration plan was found in the *dictum* of the court in the Maximum Rate case;[1] and in opinions cited by the Attorney-General in a special message on the subject to the Senate.[2] These and other points, such as the bearing of the so-called "preference clause" of the Federal Constitution requiring equality of treatment in commerce between all ports of the United States, need not detain us further. The constitutionality of the amendments have

[1] Chapter XIV, p. 468, *supra*.
[2] Hearings, Senate Committee on Interstate Commerce, 1905, II, pp. 1662–1674. *Cf.* also Digest, pp. 84–87; and *Review of Reviews*, May, 1906.

now been duly upheld. But, inasmuch as the particular form which the law assumed was the outcome of these debates, it is essential that they be reviewed. Other questions of interpretation at a later time, also follow the same line of cleavage in debate.

Judicial regulation of common carriers, as proposed by the railroad advocates, was open to many objections; so controlling that they fortunately turned the scales in favor of the administration plan. The first of these was in itself so fatal that it is almost a work of supererogation to state the others. Judicial control, as we have seen, had been the outcome under the old law. It was the desperate plight from which escape was sought. No decisions could be rendered until the rate or practice had been put into effect. The denial of power to make rates for the future had broken down the old law. The stable door might indeed be closed, but only some years after the horse had been stolen. Therein lay the primary defect of all judicial processes. When the bituminous coal-carrying roads and water lines were collecting fifty cents a ton additional on 10,000,000 tons of coal annually, destined for New England alone, as a result of the practical elimination of monopoly since 1904, the only effective way to prevent irreparable loss to consumers, would be to veto the increase before it went into effect. For a Federal judge to hold it an unreasonable exaction, four years or even six months after it had been paid, would be of no benefit to the coal-consuming public, upon which the incidence of the tax really fell.

The entire futility of judicial control was well exemplified in the Colorado Fuel and Iron Company case of 1895. This corporation complained of excessive rates from Pueblo, Colorado, to San Francisco on iron and steel. The Interstate Commerce Commission ordered the rates on steel rails not to exceed forty-five cents per one hundred pounds, or seventy-five per cent. of the Chicago-San Francisco rate on the same commodity, whatever that might be. The Southern Pacific, under pressure, complied with this order for about two years; and then in 1898 advanced the rate one-third, to sixty cents per one hundred pounds. Thereupon the Iron Company obtained an injunction from the United States Circuit Court prohibiting the violation of the Commission's order. The case went to the Circuit Court of Appeals, which reversed this decree. Meantime, proceedings before a master had fixed the amount of damages under the rate increase at $35,300. The court held that these damages, if due, could be recovered before a jury which should establish the unreasonableness of the rates in force. But while this was being done, what became of the California business of the Colorado Fuel and Iron Company? The Pacific coast was one of its most important markets. The price of steel rails for competitors from Pittsburg or Europe, who ship by water, would remain quite undisturbed. It would be difficult to recover trade when once lost. No damages, based upon mere increased freight rates, actually paid, would begin to measure the possible loss. And, moreover, even if this sum were recovered after prolonged litigation, the situation would not be remedied. Precisely the same rates which gave rise to the damages would still be in effect. An indefinite series of litigations might result, which would harass the company and perhaps drive it from the field altogether. The outcome of this Southern Pacific case sufficiently proves, even where the shipper is a powerful corporation, the futility of seeking redress through judicial proceedings. Again and again one is forced back to the same conclusion: that the only remedy for an unjust rate is not to continue an unfair one and pay damages, but as speedily as possible to substitute a reasonable charge. How much greater force has this conclusion for the small shipper, if the remedy fails even for an industrial combination, powerful enough to extort secret rebates of $1,000 a day from the Atchison railroad, as proved in the now celebrated Morton case of 1906!

Other serious objections to judicial control may be briefly stated. The functions of a court, acting judicially, permit of reliance as to reasonableness upon only one standard, viz., that the rate or practice under consideration will lead to confiscation of property. The courts can set this maximum limit to charges; but above that point they are powerless to intervene. Rates for the future must be judged with the same freedom exercised by the traffic officials who promulgated them in first instance. Correction can be applied only by an expert tribunal, possessed of the same sort of knowledge had by those who issued the tariff or ordered the practice at the outset. Of course, the objection of lack of technical knowledge on the part of judges, might be readily enough overcome by means of a specialized professional personnel. But the objection that judicial control, in contradistinction to administrative regulation, is necessarily intermittent rather than steady and constant is one not so easily met. As has been recently well said of our Federal policy toward the trusts, "Government by a series of explosions is rarely effective." There are too many and too long intervals between decisions. And then again, there is the slowness of formal court proceedings and the necessarily conservative attitude of judges, in matters concerning vested property rights. These arguments were all unanswerable in the end. It was inevitable that control should be exercised by a distinct enlargement of the powers of the Interstate Commerce Commission, as an adjunct of the executive arm of the government.

The law of 1906[1] authorized the Commission upon complaint to "determine and prescribe" just and reasonable maximum rates, regulations or practices to be thereafter observed; and to order conformity thereto. Such orders, except for money payments, were to become effective after thirty days; and were to remain in force for two years, unless suspended, modified, or set aside by a court of competent jurisdiction. In addition the Commission might order an apportionment of joint rates, when the carriers are unable to agree upon a division; establish

[1] Amendment of Section 15 of the law of 1887; see p. 453, *supra*.

through routes; and fix reasonable charges for services or instrumentalities rendered or provided by shippers. This covers the case of charges for icing refrigerator cars or for the use of special equipment.

Fairly general rate-making power was thus conferred upon the Commission; limited, however, to the adjudication of specific complaints. But the carriers being routed at this point, promptly fell back upon a second line of defences. Their representatives took a stand upon the directly consequent point of broad review by the Federal courts of the Commission's orders. It was yet possible to practically nullify administrative control by according indefinite limits to the appellate jurisdiction of these courts. Might they pass upon law points alone; or were they to be empowered to review the entire order of the Commission? A most brilliant constitutional debate again took place in the Senate.[1] The first detail concerned the power of Congress to restrict the right of the lower Federal Courts to suspend the Commission's orders by writ of injunction. Any limitation upon this power would, of course, lessen interference with the Commission's mandates, and greatly promote a speedy settlement of transportation disputes. Were these injunctions to be freely issued, holding up the Commission's orders and thereby leaving the old rate or practice in effect pending final adjudication, the carriers would, of course, then have everything to gain and nothing to lose by their issuance. Every order might be attacked, not with any serious expectation of final success, but merely to secure the benefit of the delay. And if, after this delay, the widest possible scope of review were allowed in the formal trial of the case, judicial instead of administrative regulation might still be brought about.

The first essential in the conservative programme, then, was

---

[1] Professor Dixon in the *Quarterly Journal of Economics*, XXI, 1906, p. 544, has succinctly reviewed this. *Cf. American Political Science Review*, IV, 1910, p. 547.

to ensure the most comprehensive right of review for all cases appealed. But could Congress by statute limit or define the exercise of this judicial power on the equity side? There was no doubt as to its right under the Constitution to create or abolish Federal courts, other than the Supreme Court. But could it restrict their judicial functions, legal or equitable, including primarily the power to issue injunctions? Practically, the alternative lay either in omitting all reference to the subject in the amended act, leaving the scope of the courts' powers to be determined by judicial construction of the statute; or in attempting to define it specifically, item by item. The carriers' representatives would not agree to the former course, lest silence upon this matter, as they averred, might imperil the constitutionality of the law. Nor could the progressive reformers refuse a definition of the matter, under suspicion of bad faith. For if, as they had so stoutly maintained, the constitution amply safeguarded the rights of appellants without further prescription, a mere re-affirmation of these rights could do no harm. The result was a clause so worded as virtually to satisfy the conservatives; while ostensibly being a compromise. Power is expressly conferred upon the Circuit Courts,[1] by suit to "enjoin, set aside, annul or suspend" orders or requirements of the Commission. But this power is limited by the condition that five days' notice must be given to enable the Commission to prepare its case for protest. And the hearing must be had before three Federal judges instead of one. These details were intended to prevent the issuance of restraining orders for frivolous or merely obstructive reasons.

The unfortunate feature of this compromise, arrived at only after weeks of bitter controversy, was its entire indefiniteness as to the grounds upon which the courts might base their review of the Commission's orders. It thus stopped short of

[1] By Amendment of Section 16; see p. 453, *supra*. The attempt to insert the words "fairly remunerative" in place of "reasonable" so as to invoke new judicial tests is discussed by Smalley, *op. cit.*, 1906, p. 59.

conferring more liberal powers of review for railroads than those enjoyed under the constitution by all other classes of persons and property.[1] In so far the railroads lost their case. It is evident that Congress intended to create a really competent administrative board, with whose orders the courts might interfere only when those orders were *ultra vires*, or unconstitutional. The courts under the law must accord the same consideration to such decisions, "if regularly made and duly served," as to an act of Congress, with the presumption always in favor of validity. Judicial interference might be expected only when the railroads had a good case. This, at least, was a clear gain. There was yet another even more important one. Under the old law the burden of initiative or proof on all cases appealed, rested upon the Commission. This might now be reversed. Penalties formerly did not begin to run until the final decision of the highest court to which appeal was taken, had affirmed the validity of the Commission's order. Carriers might continue to disobey with impunity throughout the period of protracted litigation. But now a penalty of $5,000 a day for each day's violation of the order, began at the expiration of thirty days. The initiative to secure relief from this order must now come from the carrier. It, and not the Commission, became the petitioner before the courts. A speedier adjudication of contested cases might far more confidently be expected under such conditions. But the grounds, legal or economic, upon which such determination of the reasonableness of the Commission's orders must rest, were, unfortunately, as we have seen, left open for judicial interpretation in the course of time.

The railroads won a decided victory in one other bitterly contested detail of the relation of the Commission to the courts. The new law still left the old rate or practice of which complaint had been made, in effect without penalty pending the review

[1] *Annals, American Academy of Political Science*, March, 1907, p. 302, deals with this point. Also, the able discussion by Professor Smalley, reprinted in our Railway Problems, chapter XXIV.

of the case. The administration bill would not have permitted restraining orders to issue until the Commission's decision had been held unreasonable in formal review. The point appears to have been decided by Congress upon economically unjustifiable grounds. The interval of time between the Commission's decision and the final settlement of the case might be considerable. Under the old conditions, the carriers had imposed the burden of disputed rates upon the public. The importance of this point may be illustrated by the fact that during the protracted litigation in the Chicago Terminal Charge case, finally settled in 1909, the sum involved for this period alone amounted to $3,000,000. Was this fair? The real disputants after all were not the government and the railway company. The Commission was supposedly acting impartially as an umpire. Such being the case, unless it were shown that greater injustice would result from the change, the natural condition would seem to be this; that in cases of dispute the decision of the umpire, and not of the bigger contestant, should prevail until final settlement of the cause. This would seem to be the obvious, the natural and the just conclusion from the premises.

But, the railroads contended, suppose the Commission should order a rate reduced, as in the Maximum Freight Rate case; put a lower tariff into effect; and then the courts should ultimately decide that the original rate ought not to have been disturbed at all. The railroad meantime would have suffered a corresponding loss of revenue on all traffic carried at the low rate. This would certainly be a hardship, and incontrovertibly unjust. But would it be more so than that the shipper should unjustly have borne the burden in the contrary case? As matters then stood, the public was compelled to pay the high rate, even if the courts afterward decided it to have been unreasonable. The railway as an interested party enjoyed the benefit of the doubt, and imposed the burden of proof upon the public at all times. Would it not have been more in consonance with justice, that the government, an impartial umpire, should temporarily lay the burden upon that party against whose contention the greatest reasonable doubt existed?

The only just remedy would seem to be one which would insure final recovery for unreasonable rates, by whichever party paid, during the uncertain period of adjudication. One of the principal objections of the railways to the proposed change arose at this point. Large corporations are more responsible parties at law than most individual shippers. Suppose, through an unjustly low rate, a railway had suffered loss of revenue; could it as readily recoup itself by suits for damages against scores of shippers, large and small, as could the latter, in the contrary case, recover back from the railway company? This cogent argument suggested a compromise measure. Why not permit the original railroad rate to continue in force, as before, pending final adjudication; but require the carriers to give bond for prompt repayment of any surplus charges over those finally sanctioned by the courts?[1] This would have left the business of rate making in railway hands; and yet have afforded a substantial remedy for the disputatious shipper.

The railways would not accede to such a compromise measure, with all the financial burdens thereby entailed. Unfortunately even this scheme is woefully short of a just solution. The whole matter looms up larger at this point. Enter again the interests of the real consumer! In most cases freight rates to some degree affect the price of commodities. Has the shipper, having paid a freight bill afterward adjudged unreasonably high, any right to sue for recovery of the amount? Has he not, with his fellow merchants, probably shifted the burden upon the public? Evidence shows that carload rates on cattle from Texas to South Dakota have been increased within ten years after 1898, from sixty-five dollars to one hundred dollars. Probably part of this thirty-five dollars increase has been taken from

---

[1] This procedure has been actually adopted in several cases, Ann. Rep., I.C.C., 1908, 61.

the profits of the cattlemen; but can there be doubt that a part of it has been added to the price of beef?[1] No, tackle it as you will, from whatever point of view, you return to the same proposition: that the damage of an unreasonable freight rate, once paid, is irreparable. Particular shippers may recover what seem to be damages; but which are likely not to have been so to them individually at all.[2] By standards of abstract justice, the real solution should distribute the temporary burdens incident to the delays of legal procedure, as nearly evenly as the laws of chance will permit. A compilation in 1905 showed that, of 316 freight rate cases decided by the Interstate Commerce Commission, fifty-four per cent. — practically one half — turned in favor of the complainant. Inasmuch as these complaints were practically all brought on behalf of shippers against the railroads, this shows how evenly balanced the issues have been. Were the orders of the Commission to become effective at once, the losses incident to errors afterward corrected by the courts, would be distributed in about equal proportions. Under the law even as amended in 1906, all the penalty of a mistake falls upon the shipper and the public; the railway always goes scot free. An impartial commission should be clothed with power to distribute these onerous burdens by prescribing the temporary rate. Quite possibly the limitation of the equity power of Federal judges to protect the railroads in their constitutional rights, might have been overthrown by the Supreme Court; but the advantage in the contrary case would have been well worth the risk.

The only remedy left for the public under the circumstances of compromise above outlined, was to forward the course of judicial procedure in every way. The Expedition Act of 1903 had done much. The new amendments went still further, by

[1] 17 I.C.C. Rep., 317, is a case in point where cotton-oil mills refused to protect an advance in rates.
[2] *Cf.* 13 Int. Com. Com. Rep., 668; 190 Fed. Rep. 659; and U. S. Commerce Court, 1911, 193 Fed. Rep., 667.

providing for appeal directly to the Supreme Court with the privilege of precedence upon its docket. Other details served the same purpose. Formerly it had taken much time for the Commission to prepare its formal orders and its *prima facie* case for the courts. All the evidence had to be duly set forth.[1] Except for damage suits, all this was now changed. The Commission in its orders need only state its conclusions in the premises, without the delays, labor and expense incident to formal re-examination of witnesses and the preparation of extended records of evidence. This has materially expedited the settlement of contested cases. It has yet another advantage. The Commission was stripped of one of its semi-judicial functions; always an anomaly under our plan of government. And the assignment of the duty of formal prosecution of cases on appeal to the Attorney-General of the United States, was yet another improvement along the same line.

In the matter of personal discrimination, the disheartening persistence of illegal practices, despite the provisions of the Elkins law of 1903, rendered it necessary to specifically extend jurisdiction of the Commission over private car lines; and to confer authority over all incidental services at terminals. Separate publication of storage, icing and other charges was called for; and railroads were held responsible for the provision of special equipment when requested. Industrial railroads, "tap lines," spurs and sidings, so ingeniously employed in discrimination,[2] were expressly included under the Commission's authority. Passes for individuals, a fruitful source of favoritism and political corruption in the past, were even more particularly prohibited. The only exceptions were for employees and their families, the poor or unfortunate, and persons engaged in religious or philanthropic work. In this connection, it may be added that the law of 1910 somewhat modified this rule by enlarging the meaning of "employees" to include caretakers of

---

[1] *Cf.* conditions under the old law; p. 461, *supra*.
[2] See pp. 195 and 213, *supra*.

milk and other commodities. It also dealt with the issuance of franks by express, telegraph and telephone companies in some detail. Superannuated or pensioned employees and the bodies of persons killed in service might also be carried free. Such details are significant as illustrating the extreme nicety of definition required by the drastic character of the prohibitions.

An important change was also made by the law of 1906 in re-imposing the penalty of imprisonment, as well as of fine, for departure from the published tariff. Its removal from the original law of 1887, in the interest of effective enforcement, was recognized as a mistake. With the complete affirmance by the courts of power to compel the production of evidence, recalcitrant witnesses were now under control. It was hoped that vigorous prosecution with this criminal punishment added, might put an end to the abuse.

An entirely new feature was added to the law by the so-called "Commodity Clause." This sought to divorce transportation entirely from all other lines of business. The experience of years had shown that corporations, especially in the coal-fields, by combining both the service of carrier and shipper, might most effectively stifle competition of independent producers. Rank discrimination might be concealed by means of ingeniously framed systems of inter-company accounts. And denial of equal facilities such as cars or sidings might operate to drive competitors out of the business. While the Hepburn law was before Congress, several events drew attention forcibly to the existence of such abuses. The Interstate Commerce Commission in April, acting under the Tillman-Gillespie resolution, uncovered flagrant violations of law on the Pennsylvania system.[1] Equally important was the decision handed down in February by the Supreme Court in the Chesapeake and Ohio Railroad case.[2] This dealt with discriminatory rates on soft coal for the New Haven road, given by means of manipulation

---

[1] *Cf.* p. 199, *supra.*
[2] 200 U. S., 613: 20th Ann. Rep. I.C.C., p. 42.

of the pro-rating division between the various companies interested. The general public was also greatly concerned over the growth of monopoly in the anthracite fields and the coincident rise in the price of coal. The independent producers in the soft coal regions were at the same time roused over the grievous discriminations practised against them, especially in West Virginia.[1] Senator Elkins of that state, — usually a strong railroad partisan, — introduced the amendment under pressure from his constituents. It was warmly supported by the most radical administration representatives. For it was apparent at once that a withdrawal of railroads from all such correlated businesses was not only proper in itself, but would also greatly promote the enforcement of many other provisions of the law. Yet the radical character of the proposition was perhaps scarcely appreciated. Some railroads, like the Lackawanna, were dependent for nearly three-fourths of their tonnage upon the anthracite coal traffic; much of it from their own mines. The Chesapeake and Ohio in the eastern fields and the 'Frisco in the Middle West, relied upon soft coal for more than half of their tonnage. A great many other carriers were interested to a lesser degree. To compel them all to give up their coal properties was indeed a serious matter.

The "commodity clause" provided that "after May 1, 1908, it shall be unlawful for any railroad company to transport from any state . . . to any other state . . . any article or commodity other than timber and the manufactured products thereof, manufactured, mined, or produced by it, or under its authority, or which it may own in whole or in part, or in which it may have any interest, direct or indirect, except such articles or commodities as may be necessary and intended for its use in the conduct of its business as a common carrier."

The original proposition was even more drastic. It was to apply to all common carriers, such as the pipe lines in the

[1] *Cf.* 10 I.C.C. Rep., 473 and p. 640; 11 *Idem* Rep., 538; 13 *Idem* Rep., p. 70; 19 *Idem* Rep., 356.

oil business. But it was soon considerably modified in the course of passage.[1] First, it was limited to railroads. Then the western senators, on behalf of the lumber industry, secured its special exception. And, finally, an attempt to prohibit specifically the control of subsidiary industrial companies through stock ownership was defeated. But, as thus limited, the clause finally passed the Senate, — the stronghold of the railroad interests, — by a vote of 67 to 6. This affords a good indication of the extent of popular feeling on the subject. It was fortunate indeed that the prohibition was not to take effect for two years, in view of the litigation necessary for its precise interpretation. For in any event it was bound to lead to much corporate readjustment. The course of these proceedings will be considered in the next chapter.

There remains for consideration one of the most important provisions of the Hepburn law, namely that dealing with publicity of accounts.[2] Section twenty of the law of 1887 called for the filing by all carriers of annual reports with the Interstate Commerce Commission. These reports were to be standardized; and the Commission was empowered, in addition, to demand specific information whenever it was so desired. But the absence of express authority to enforce these orders, except by means of tedious equity proceedings in the courts, made improvements in accounting almost entirely dependent upon the tact and resourcefulness of the statistician. The Commission was most fortunate in the services of Prof. Henry C. Adams, who succeeded in bringing about cordial coöperation between the accounting officials of the railroads and the government. Great improvements in the line of uniformity resulted; but the need of positive control became increasingly apparent.

[1] An excellent account of the debates and early litigation is in the *Journal of Political Economy*, vol. XVII, 1909, pp. 448–460.
[2] Fully described in *Quarterly Journal of Economics*, vol. XXII, 1908, pp. 364–383. For comparison with foreign countries; *ibid.*, vol. XXIV, 1910, pp. 471–500.

Many officials were unwilling to certify by oath to the correctness of their returns. With the increasing size of the roads, it became more and more difficult to secure promptness. The annual Statistics of Railways had almost to await the pleasure of the carriers in filing their statements. And vitally important information was often withheld. In the case of the Lake Shore road, for example, which for years had charged all its improvements to operating expenses, it positively declined to state what portion of those improvements were permanent additions to the property, properly chargeable to capital account, and what were in the nature of renewals and repairs. And the Supreme Court had found no authority in the law to compel the furnishing of this information.[1] With the growth of extended systems of railroads, characterized by the most involved methods of inter-corporate accounting, the need of precise data became ever more imperative. Something more was evidently necessary than a mere expression by Congress of an opinion favorable to publicity. The mandatory provisions added in 1906 to the Twentieth Section are, therefore, vital, not only in themselves; they are essential to the administrative enforcement of nearly every other part of the regulative law. A determined effort was made in 1908 to defeat the purpose of this clause by restricting appropriations for carrying it into effect.[2] But it emerged unscathed — thanks to President Roosevelt — and stands today as one of the best features of the new statute.

One may readily distinguish no less than five distinct and important special services to be rendered by full publicity of accounts. The earliest to be fully appreciated was its serviceableness in securing equality of treatment of all shippers. In the good old freebooters' days, rebates were probably openly entered as such on the books. But with the need of concealment, they came to be covered up in all sorts of ways; often-

---

[1] 197 U. S., 536.
[2] *Munsey's Magazine*, March, 1912, well outlines it.

times under such guises, as in the notable Atchison case, in such manner that not even the directors knew what they meant. With full standardization of accounts, such abuses may readily be detected and the offenders traced and punished. In the second place, open standardization of the books makes strongly for more efficient and honest operation.[1] The comparative method in statistics may be readily applied; so that the president of a railroad may have at command a complete statement of operations in detail, which is comparable not only with his own results in preceding years but with other roads similarly circumstanced. The haphazard and unscientific methods of operation in the British Isles are largely a resultant of the absence of any logical and uniform system of public accounts.[2]

Detailed cost keeping in the management of great systems of inter-related railroads, being absolutely essential to efficiency, makes also for honesty in operation. Such gross frauds as developed upon the Illinois Central in 1910, variously estimated to have cost the road from $2,500,000 to $5,000,000 through overcharges for equipment repairs, might readily enough have been detected under an efficient and honest management. This instance immediately suggests a third advantage of full publicity of accounts, namely the protection of investors. Flagrant manipulation of maintenance accounts, "skinning" or "fattening" roads in the interest of inside speculators, has always been dependent upon secrecy. Assurance of a stable market for railroad securities, based upon entire frankness as to the degree to which these properties are being kept whole or improved, is one of the prime advantages which may be expected to flow from such governmental prescription of accounts. And general public confidence in railway invest-

[1] *Cf.* Scientific Management in Railroad Operation; *Quarterly Journal of Economics*, vol. XXV, 1911, pp. 539–562. Our second volume, it is hoped, will afford some idea of this comparative method.
[2] *Quarterly Journal of Economics*, 1912, p. 536, outlines the new law.

ments cannot conceivably be better encouraged than by such publicity. In no other detail than this, does the Act to Regulate Commerce more directly benefit the general body of stockholders in railroads, as well as the corporations themselves.

The three foregoing advantages of publicity had been long appreciated. These recent changes introduced in the Federal law brought two others into special prominence. One is the newly assumed responsibility by the government in the matter of rate making. The other is its intervention in cases of dispute between the carriers and their employees. In both cases it is imperative that there should be available data for a just determination of the issues at stake. There must be assurance that every essential feature of the situation is fully and fairly set forth upon the books. Otherwise, as in disputed rate cases, every fact as to cost of service, — a primary basis of measurement, — is vitiated. Absurd and misleading calculations may be presented in evidence, which greatly hamper the government in deciding the case.[1] And now with the projected physical valuation of properties as an element in rate making, all of the factors of maintenance, betterment and depreciation, of joint facilities, rentals and sinking funds must be taken into account. In labor disputes, the same considerations apply.[2] Under the requirements of the Erdman Act, every mediation, — and the need for it is more frequent every year, — calls for critical analysis by the chairman of the Commission and the Federal commissioner of labor of the statements from both sides as to the reasonableness of the action to be taken respecting wages or conditions of employment.[3] The notable arbitration in 1912 is the most important instance as yet. Having all of these services in mind, it seems likely that the account-

[1] The Meeker case in 1911, concerning the cost of transporting coal to tidewater by the Lehigh Valley, is a good illustration. 21 I.C.C. Rep., 144.
[2] *Cf.* Bulletin U. S. Bureau of Labor, No. 98, 1912.
[3] *Cf.* Standardization of Wages of Railroad Trainmen; *Quarterly Journal of Economics*, XXV, 1910, pp. 139–160.

ing provisions added to the law in 1906 will be second to none in bringing about the elimination of existing evils, and in standardizing and improving operation, finance and traffic practice.

Under the new law monthly and special as well as annual reports, might be required under oath; with appropriate penalties of fine and imprisonment for delay or mis-statement. All accounts must be kept according to forms, general and detailed, prescribed by the Interstate Commerce Commission. Such rules applied of course to all carriers subject to the law, such as express and sleeping-car companies, pipe lines and even water carriers where operated in connection with railroads. Moreover, the Commission was to have access to the books at all times. For this purpose, it might employ special examiners.[1] In other words, the system employed for years in connection with the regulation of national banks, was now extended to the interstate carriers. An additional safeguard was provided in the clause which made it unlawful to keep any other accounts books or memoranda than those approved; with the same penalties for violation. In brief, the policy was now perfectly definite. Carriers were rendered public service companies in every sense of the word. Mere indefinite publicity was replaced by specific regulation. This policy was not only clearly written in the law; but the Commission in promulgating its orders relative to accounting, laid upon every officer concerned, full personal responsibility for the statements rendered. Minor officials, made scapegoats for chief offenders, were no longer to be tolerated. The relation between agent and principal was clearly defined. It was assumed that so far as accounts were concerned, such officials were representatives of the Commission in carrying out the law. A new principle was introduced in the regulation of carriers which could not fail to be productive of great good. In this respect the Hepburn amendments

[1] *Munsey's Magazine*, March, 1912, p. 7, outlines the attempt in 1908 to defeat this provision by withholding appropriations.

granted all that the most ardent advocates of publicity demanded.[1]

A summary view of this important legislation, — in form merely an amendment of the original law of 1897, but in reality constituting an entirely new departure, — may now be had. The gains for effective regulation were considerable. Among them may be noted its enlarged field, the separation of transportation from other businesses, elimination of the iniquitous railroad passes, control over joint rates and prorating, the expedition of judicial procedure, full publicity of accounts, enhancement of the dignity and compensation of the Commission, and, most important of all, the grant in so many words of administrative rate-making power. The carriers — and the administration also — failed to obtain the much-desired repeal of the prohibition of pooling. On the other hand, as against these gains for reform should be set the following concessions to the railroads. Rate-making control was still subject to broad court review. No one as yet knew what this might bring forth. Maximum rates only might be prescribed. And much as to the proper relativity of rates, involved both in matters of freight classification and of enforcement of the long and short haul clause, was left untouched. Rate advances were still possible without determination of their reasonableness in advance. Suspension of orders pending judicial review, still remained. There was as yet no control over physical operation, such as furnishing cars, although switches might be ordered. Many of the states had long since undertaken this work. And the great body of independent carriers on our inland waters were still left beyond the reach of the Federal law. In the main, the administration had won a notable victory, although at some considerable cost. The principle of effective regulation of public-service carriers

[1] The affirmance of these powers by the Supreme Court in 1912 is described at p. 586, *infra*.

had been, indeed, vigorously affirmed in no mistakable terms. But the task was not yet completed. Many details of law were needed to "Clinch the Roosevelt policies." Nevertheless, it was probably better that a brief experience with the new law, both among the people and in the courts, should precede further legislation. Great reforms should not be too suddenly effected, else reaction is certain to take place. For the time being a positive step forward had been taken.

CHAPTER XVI

EFFECTS OF THE LAW OF 1906; JUDICIAL INTERPRETATION, 1905–'10

Large number of complaints filed, 522. — Settlement of many claims, 524. — Fewer new tariffs, 525. — Nature of complaints analyzed, 526. — Misrouting of freight, 527. — Car supply and classification rules, 527. — Exclusion from through shipments, 529. — Opening new routes, 530. — Petty grievances considered, 530. — Decisions evenly balanced, 532. — The banana and lumber loading cases, 532. — Freight rate advances, 534. — General investigations, 536.

Supreme Court definition of Commission's authority, 538. — The Illinois Central car supply case, 538. — Economic *v.* legal aspects considered, 540. — The Baltimore and Ohio decision, 541. — The Burnham, Hanna, Munger case, 542. — The Pacific Coast lumber cases, 543. — Decisions revealing legislative defects, 546. — The Orange Routing case, 546. — The Portland Gateway order, 547. — The Commission's power to require testimony affirmed, 549. — The Baird case, 549. — The "Immunity Bath" decision and the Harriman case, 550. — Interpretation of the "commodity clause," 552. — Means of evasion described, 553.

THE first direct effect of the new law was a great increase in the volume of business of the Interstate Commerce Commission. Within two years over nine thousand appeals were made to it in one form or another for the adjustment of transportation disputes. The overwhelming majority of these complaints were settled informally out of court; and in this work of conciliation one of the most conspicuous and beneficial functions of the new commission appears. But, nevertheless, an increasing number of grievances seem to have required a formal hearing and decision of record. Some indication of the public relief sought is afforded by the fact that within approximately the first two years and a half, — up to August 28, 1908, — 1053 cases on the formal docket were disposed of, leaving over five hundred issues still undecided. As compared with this total of over fifteen hundred formal complaints under the new law, the number filed under the old statute amounted to only 878 throughout the long period of eighteen years.[1] Moreover, the number of complaints filed, steadily increased for several years.

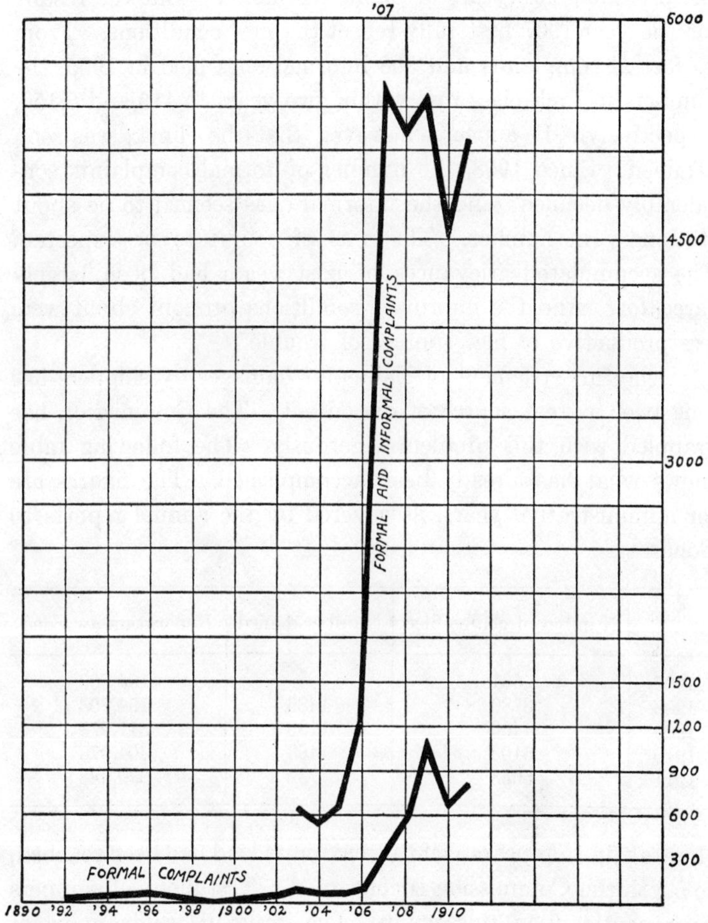

The accompanying diagram well illustrates the great revival of interest which took place. The two curves show respectively the number of formal complaints by administrative years since

[1] *Cf.* the record for 1898–1900 at p. 486, *supra.*

1892, and the total of both formal and informal ones since 1903. The sudden increase after the new law went into effect in 1906, is, of course, presaged by some accession of business during the preceding two years of public discussion. But the results for the year 1907 first fully reflect the new conditions. From 65 formal complaints and 568 informal ones filed in 1905, the numbers in each class rose within two years to 415 and 5,156, respectively. It appears, however, that the climax was soon attained. Since 1908, the number of formal complaints considerably declined; and the informal ones seemed to be about stationary in number. This was of course to be expected. The accumulated grievances of past years had been largely cared for. And the improved conditions brought about were less productive of new sources of trouble.

Delay in settlement of claims for damages by shippers has long been a great source of discontent. The Commission has grappled with this problem vigorously. The following table shows what has already been accomplished. The figures are for administrative years, as covered by the annual reports to Congress.

	Number of claims filed	Number denied	Reparation awarded
1907	561	—	$104,700
1908	3789	1486	154,703
1909	4406	1199	311,978
1910	5103	1463	404,976
1911	5653	739	329,388

Here, again, it appears as if the maximum load had been reached, so far as the Commission is concerned. Testimony of shippers is emphatic upon this point.[1] One railroad traffic manager stated that the number of overcharge claims against his line, — one of the most important in the country, — was twenty-five per cent. less in 1909 than two years earlier; and that loss and

[1] Annual Report I.C.C., 1909, p. 11.

damage claims were reduced approximately one-third. A very large shipper compared his former "claims suspense account," sometimes amounting to $100,000, with $7,500 for 1909. The number of such overcharge claims was 1,008 in 1905. For nine months of 1909 it was 205. And yet these damages paid are but a trifle, as compared with the aggregate of claim settlements made by the roads directly. For the fiscal year to June 30, 1910, such settlements made to shippers directly by steam roads amounted to $21,941,232. How much of this sum was a legitimate allowance for loss or damage incurred in transit, one cannot discover. But it appears likely that an appreciable fraction served as a cover for personal discrimination. Compulsory reference to the government of all such claims would speedily determine the true facts. In the meantime it is a satisfaction to know that a competent tribunal now exists, to which appeal with a minimum of expense may be made by aggrieved shippers. Furthermore, it should also be noted in this connection, that the situation as respects claims has been benefited by a detail of the law of 1906, not heretofore mentioned. The so-called Carmack amendment provided that carriers must issue a through receipt or bill of lading, and thereby become liable for the shipment throughout its entire journey; that is to say, whether upon the initial road or a later connection. The legal principles accepted in England since 1841 are thus adopted. There is no doubt that great improvement in the relation between the roads and the shipping public may be anticipated as a result.

The great improvement in respect of standardization of rates, evidenced primarily through reduction in the number of separate tariffs issued by the railroads, has been elsewhere described[1] in connection with classification. From 193,900 separate schedules in 1906 to less than half that number five years later is a notable achievement, — so notable indeed that it merits repetition in this connection. The course of complaints, of claims

[1] P. 324, *supra*.

and of new rates filed at Washington, affords cumulative evidence of the great improvement in conditions which the new legislation has brought about.

This activity of the Interstate Commerce Commission, it is almost needless to mention, affords no true measure of the benefits resulting from the law. Like every other sound piece of legislation, it was intended to be preventive, not punitive. The number of arrests by the police affords no indication of the effectiveness of a criminal statute. Not the violations of law, but the breaches forestalled, are of real significance. And similarly in this instance, one surely finds the primary benefit of legislation, not in the complaints preferred, but in the fact that, under the improved relationship between the principals concerned, many long-standing causes of irritation and misunderstanding are being removed. The real gain, not to be measured by figures, is to be found in the improved spirit of the intercourse now prevalent between railway officials and their customers. The shipper — especially if he be a small one — having business to transact, may now be sure of courteous treatment and a prompt and probably just outcome. In the old days he was too often made to feel his utter economic dependence. As a high traffic official recently put it: "One reason we do not like this law is because we have to stop and think twice what we are about. We must be ready to explain and show a warrant for every act. An attack of indigestion cannot any longer serve as an excuse for an arbitrary, off-hand ruling." This improved spirit has permeated the whole staff of railway officials who have seen a new light on the public aspect of their calling.[1]

The nature of the complaints before the Interstate Commerce Commission, with its amplified powers under the new

[1] 16 I.C.C. Rep., 276, is a typical instance of voluntary correction of a mal-adjustment of rates, as soon as attention was officially called to it. Also, 21 *Idem* where several railroads being unable to agree upon the classification of live and dead locomotives, appeal to the Commission to decide the matter.

law, affords the best indication of the most important feature of its work, namely the settlement of disputes between the railroads and their clients.[1] And it will be apparent that a large number of these only indirectly raise the issue of the actual freight rate. Oftentimes they concern rather the manner of conducting business. An attentive perusal of these decisions of the Commission offers interesting evidence of the range of a carrier's activities. Every little station all over the country between Aaron and Zuwash, and every conceivable commodity, from "mole-traps in crates" to "jewelers' sweepings," is comprehended. The fact that these disputes, often pecuniarily insignificant, could not be amicably adjusted by the good offices of the Commission informally, but necessitated formal hearing and decision, is the strongest possible proof that some competent tribunal of this sort was greatly needed in the interest of industrial peace.

One of the commonest petty complaints is of misrouting of freight. Goods are carried by a roundabout way, or by one not enjoying the lowest through rate. Thus, to be specific, in 1908 six carloads of print-paper were shipped from Little Falls, Minnesota, to Boisé, Idaho.[2] Three routes were open, the rates being respectively $1.30, $1.36, and $2.17 per hundred pounds. The Northern Pacific road, in absence of instructions, sent the goods by the third route, — presumably the one most profitable to itself, — the result being a freight rate $1,760.62 greater than it otherwise might have been. Reparation to this amount was granted within three months by order of the Commission.

Another frequent difficulty concerns the supply of suitable cars for the needs of the shipper. Carload rates are always proportionately lower than charges for package shipment.[3] The carriers very properly prescribe a certain minimum lading as a requisite for the grant of these proportionately lower whole-

[1] L. G. McPherson, Railroad Freight Rates, 1909, pp. 275–300, examines these topically, but without individual detail.
[2] 12 I.C.C. Rep., 626. [3] *Cf.* p. 325, *infra*, on classification.

sale rates. The shipper at carload rates must, however, pay for the full capacity of the car, whether his shipment fills it or not. No exception can be taken to this practice, unless the carrier is unable or unwilling to supply cars of a suitable size. This sometimes happens. For instance, in 1908 a lumberman in Oregon, having a shipment of 39,500 pounds to make to a point in Pennsylvania, requested of the Southern Pacific a car of 40,000 pounds capacity.[1] Not having one at hand, a much larger car was furnished, having a minimum capacity of 60,000 pounds. Following the standing rule as to carload rates, the shipper was compelled to pay sixty-two and one-half cents per hundred pounds on the marked capacity of the car, that is to say, on 20,000 pounds more freight than he actually shipped. This made a difference of $128.12 in the freight bill — nearly fifty per cent. in excess of the charge based upon the actual shipment. The Commission issued its order for reparation within five weeks of the filing of the complaint.

A flagrant case of the misapplication of similar rules was recently decided.[2] A retail druggist at Douglas, North Dakota, bought a sheet of plate glass eight feet square at St. Paul for forty-six dollars. Usually such large sheets have to lie flat on the car floor; and, occupying so much space, are properly assessed at a minimum weight of five thousand pounds, regardless of the actual lading. But in this instance the glass was carried upright, screwed to the end of the car, along with a lot of miscellaneous freight. Applying the standard rule made the freight bill for a distance of 587 miles, $9.50 more than the *entire cost* of the glass at St. Paul. It appears strange that the carrier should have permitted so clear a case to come to a formal hearing at all. Presumably it contested it as much for the protection of its standard rules as for the sake of the actual revenue involved. No exception can be taken to these shipping rules as a whole; but these cases make it evident

[1] 14 I.C.C. Rep., 561. Another case of this sort decided for the railroad is in 15 I.C.C. Rep., 160.   [2] 15 I.C.C. Rep., 301.

that their application may be at times too harsh and rigid. The tribunal established by the new law performs a much-needed service to the community in tempering their application in exceptional instances.

Attempts at arbitrary exclusion from participation in through shipments, in order to stifle competition, not infrequently crop out in these decisions. In 1905 the Enterprise line, capitalized at four hundred thousand dollars, put three steamers into commission from Fall River to New York.[1] This independent line was of the utmost importance to the cotton manufacturers, as it was expected that at New York connection could be made with competing rail and water lines to every part of the United States. But all these lines, presumably at the behest of the New York, New Haven and Hartford Railroad, which had hitherto enjoyed a monopoly of the business and which, with its enormous tonnage of high-grade freight to be parcelled out among connecting lines at New York, was a formidable factor, promptly declined to join in making any through rates. All their local rates from New York on, were, of course, prohibitory. In one instance, while the through rate accorded to the shipper over the New Haven road was sixteen and five-eighths cents per hundredweight from New York on, the patron of the Enterprise line was charged twenty-five and one-half cents for the same service.

This case recalls a similar one in 1897, when the independent Miami line of steamers from New York tried to break the monopoly held by the steamship lines owned by the railroads out of Galveston, Texas. The roads not only refused to prorate, but actually demanded prepayment of freights from Galveston on, as local rates. The Federal courts tinkered with the subject for a while, until the Circuit Court of Appeals, while recognizing a probable violation of law, affirmed that suit could be legally instituted only by the United States.[2] Meantime,

[1] 21st Annual Report, I.C.C., p. 71: 12 I.C.C. Rep., 326.
[2] 86 Fed. Rep., 407.

of course, the company was forced out of that business; and rates have steadily risen ever since. In this later instance of the Enterprise line, the Commission promptly ordered an extension of the same privileges to the independent line that were enjoyed by its powerful rival.[1]

The frequency of complaints as to the supply of equipment needed for the regular operation of mills or mines, has already been noted. There may be enough cars; but they may be supplied too irregularly.[2] And petitions for the issuance of through rates or the opening of new routes became so common that a substantial amplification of the law in 1910, as we shall see, was effected in this regard. The carriers, of course, always prefer in case of a choice of routes, to take the longest possible haul over their own lines. This operates to close the more direct way. The northern transcontinental lines got more revenue from traffic which went east over their lines a thousand miles by way of Spokane, than when it was turned over to a rival line at Portland, Oregon, after a haul by them of only one hundred and fifty miles.[3] Even in 1907, at the time of extreme congestion of the Northern Pacific main line, when it was literally overwhelmed with business, the lumbermen complained that they could find no relief by these other routes.[4] Much the same question was raised in another way in 1909, by a complaint from growers and shippers of grain against the rate adjustment which forced or attracted Kansas grain to the Kansas City market, instead of permitting it to move on lower rates directly from the point of origin to the Gulf ports for export, and to Texas milling and consuming points.[5] In this instance, however, the shippers failed to make out a good case; so that the complaint was dismissed.

No grievance is too petty to receive consideration. A peach-

[1] 21 I.C.C. Rep., 651; is an odd instance of a broken deadlock between carriers as to furnishing equipment for completing a shipment.
[2] 15 I.C.C. Rep., 160. *Cf.* p. 538, *infra*.
[3] 12 I.C.C. Rep., 21, and 23 *Idem*, 263.
[4] 14 I.C.C. Rep., 51.   [5] 15 I.C.C. Rep., 491.

canner in Martinsdale, Georgia, is awarded reparation of $8.91 on a shipment of three cars of his wares.[1] The sum of $11.84 is awarded to a complainant for an overcharge on eleven rolls of old worn-out canvas, assessed for freight rates as cotton goods instead of junk, which it properly was.[2] Or in another case, where a small boiler was shipped from Kalamazoo to Blue Mounds, Michigan, on a combination of local rates, when it was properly entitled to a joint through rate, an award of $6.87 to the shipper followed.[3] It makes no difference whether the welfare of a great territory or the smallest dealer is concerned. It is all one to the government. The Hope Cotton Seed Oil Company [4] in the South, shipped seventeen carloads of one season's product in 1907 out over a certain road, on a low through rate. The railroad agent was then informed that these shipments interfered with the policy of establishing new industries of this sort on another line; and the through rate was cancelled. This jumped the charges from seventeen and one-half cents per hundredweight to sixty-seven cents, — almost the entire worth of the cotton-seed. Since the new law went into effect, the Commission has prescribed a new rate of thirty cents; and industrial peace is the result.

Thus has the work of this tribunal gone on, with its daily grist of opinions on almost every conceivable phase of the transportation business. It might be to prescribe that, even though inflammable, small-lot shipments of petroleum must be accepted by a carrier at least twice every week, instead of on only one day; that structural iron might be stopped off *en route* at Indianapolis,[5] as it is at Chicago and St. Louis, to be sheared, fitted and punched, without losing the benefit of a low through rate, just as cotton is halted at the compressor, or grain is milled in transit; that a definite rate must be quoted on jewelers' sweepings,[6] — the dirt and waste laden with particles of gold

[1] 16 I.C.C. Rep., 523.
[2] 15 I.C.C. Rep., 551.
[3] 16 I.C.C. Rep., 41.
[4] 12 I.C.C. Rep., 307.
[5] 15 I.C.C. Rep., 370.
[6] 15 I.C.C. Rep., 7.

destined to the smelter, — even though it expose the carrier to the risk of exorbitant claims for damage in case of accident; that the railroad was properly entitled to charge storage after six months on brewer's rice left on a wharf pending piecemeal shipment to purchasers;[1] or that two different rates were contemporaneously charged on nitrate of soda, according to whether it was to be used in the manufacture of fertilizer or gunpowder.[2] But whatever the issue, one has the satisfying conviction, after reading the *pros* and *cons* in the decisions, not only that the matter has been settled by a disinterested and supposedly impartial third party, but that the decision is endowed with the beneficent force of public authority. As one reads these decisions, there is no evidence of political log-rolling, or of legal quibbling. They go straight to the point on the economic and common-sense issues involved. It is gratifying, moreover, to note occasionally that the dispute has already been informally settled before the Commission has time to render its opinion.

By no means are all these decisions in favor of the shipper. In fact, during the first fourteen months, only forty-six out of one hundred and seven formal cases were thus settled. The railroads enjoy no monopoly of unfair practices. Indeed, many of the rules, the exceptional application of which works hardship, were originally provided to meet some attempt at fraud by shippers. They might be underclassifying; seeking free storage on wheels pending sale of their goods; claiming exorbitant damages; or perpetrating any one of a thousand petty meannesses to which human nature is liable. One or two instances of shippers' complaints set aside as unreasonable may not be out of place.

The Topeka banana dealers in 1908 complained that bananas *en route* from New Orleans were subject to an appreciable shrinkage in weight, amounting to about six hundred pounds per car.[3] Inasmuch as about fourteen thousand cars were

[1] 15 I.C.C. Rep., 280.   [2] 13 I.C.C. Rep., 620.   [3] 13 I.C.C. Rep., 651.

being moved annually, it is clear that the aggregate loss of weight was considerable. The practice had been to weigh the bananas when transferred from the steamers at New Orleans to the cars, and to levy the freight rate upon this weight. To this the dealers objected, instancing among other things the practice, long prevalent in the cattle business where a similar loss of weight in transit occurs, of charging according to the weight of the shipments, not at the initial point, but at the point of delivery. At first sight the complaint appears to be well founded. Surely one should not be compelled to pay freight on a greater lading than is carried. But the Commission on examination decided in favor of the roads. It was shown that the service was most exceptional as to the shipment, handling and speed; and it was held that the charges were on the whole reasonable and just.

One of the most important issues in which the railroads have won their contention concerned the loading of lumber on flat cars.[1] For half a century the practice has been that the shipper should provide his own lumber-stakes and pay freight on them as on the lumber itself. In 1905 the National Lumbermen's Association tried to change all this, and to impose upon the carriers the legal duty of securing the loads in place as they do with many other commodities. The carriers offered a compromise, agreeing to allow five hundred pounds per car free for the weight of the stakes; but refused to accept responsibility for safely stowing the goods. The Commission, finally, after prolonged inquiry by experts, relieved the carriers of this care and expense.

It is undeniable also that the carriers have found solace in certain unforeseen ways under the amended law. The rigid prohibition of all favors and rebates has substantially raised the general level of charges, so general was the practice of cutting rates a few years ago. To be sure, this increase has affected principally the large shippers, thus tending to equalize oppor-

[1] 14 I.C.C. Rep., 154.

tunity between all grades of competitors. But over and above this, the prohibition of any act tainted with favoritism has enabled the carriers successfully to withstand many leakages of revenue. Claims for damages can be plausibly denied on the ground that their settlement might arouse suspicion, and possibly lead to prosecution for the grant of individual favors. Many roads have also actually augmented their revenues by this same line of argument. The custom of charging a merely nominal rental of one dollar for freight-sheds, other buildings or land used for side-tracks or elevators, was formerly general. It would have been awkward to place these contracts on a strictly commercial basis, especially where the tenants were shippers with the option of resorting to a rival line. But on the plea that a continuance of these nominal rentals might be considered a criminal act of favoritism, substantial increases of revenue have been obtained. On one road alone over three thousand of these nominal rentals have been raised to strictly commercial figures. The aggregate increase of revenue from this source has been by no means inconsiderable.

A very important group of cases brought before the Interstate Commerce Commission under the new law concerned the reasonableness of the various freight-rate advances which were occurring all along the line.[1] This raised a question as to the absolute fairness of the new rates as against the interest of the general public. One conclusion is certain. The new law did not prevent the carriers from persisting in a policy, adopted nearly ten years earlier, after a generation of steadily declining rates, of quite generally putting up their charges. Unfortunately, the law of 1906 was defective in making no provision for dealing adequately with such cases. The Interstate Commerce Commission was limited in its scope to the consideration only of specific complaints. It could not on its own initiative pass upon the reasonableness of an entire new schedule of rates in advance of its taking effect. It must take the matter up, if

[1] Economic Review, 1911, pp. 766–789, reviews this whole movement.

at all, bit by bit, as individual shippers chanced to complain, after the rates have become operative. This abridgment of its power to pass upon the reasonableness of tariffs as a whole was effected in the Senate. It was not contemplated either by President Roosevelt or by the House of Representatives. The result, as predicted, was that little protection was afforded to the public in any large way. Judging by results, the railroads were as free as they ever were, to increase their tariffs whenever they saw fit so to do.

The imperative need of amending the law, and of granting power to suspend such rate advances, not merely in particular cases on complaint, but as to entire schedules of rates prior to their taking effect, was in fact met by the next set of amendments in 1910. The experience of the intervening years amply proved the need of some such amendment.

The extent of the changes after the new law went into effect may be indicated by a few typical instances. Few commodities are of greater importance to the United States than chemical fertilizers, used in enormous quantities all over the country. The basis of these is phosphate rock. The freight rate on this from Tennessee to Chicago in 1907 was $3.40 per ton. It was increased to $3.95, until the Commission ordered its reduction to the old figure.[1] At the same time the Oregon lumbermen had their rates to the East increased about one quarter, after a period of quiescence of six years. From the Willamette valley to San Francisco — a test case soon to run a long course before the courts [2] — lumber rates were $3.10. In 1907 they were put up to five dollars. The Commission held that $3.40 was an adequate rate. The last general increase had occurred in January, 1909, particularly in transcontinental rates, where the fruit of the Harriman monopoly made itself felt. Not unduly great in the East, considering the increased cost of operation, — twenty-five cents per ton on pig iron and iron pipe, for instance, — the Pacific Coast rates from New York rose

[1] 15 I.C.C. Rep., 79.   [2] 219 U. S., 433: *Cf.* p. 545, *infra.*

often as high as fifty per cent. The rate on dry goods went up by one-third. Therein lay a part of the motive power for Union Pacific speculative finance.[1] Among the most persistently contested schedules was that concerning rates from the southwestern cattle ranges to the markets of the Middle West.[2] In 1897 the rate on steers was twenty-seven cents per hundredweight. Step by step it went up to the level of thirty-six and one-half cents in 1903, — a rise of more than one-third within six years.

Occasionally one strikes an exorbitant rise in the East, however, as in one instance where on imported iron pyrites used in making sulphuric acid, the rate, which in 1903 was $1.56, became $2.72 four years later.[3] And the hardship often lay in the fact that these increases were most marked in the case of the small shipper, — the very one who, in these days of large enterprises, we can least afford to spare. The rate on cotton goods from the South to the Pacific Coast rose only fifteen per cent. between 1896 and 1907 by the carload; for smaller lots it rose sixty-five per cent.[4] In 1907, 38,000,000 pounds of cheese were produced in southwestern Wisconsin. The shipper to Chicago by carload paid only about ten per cent. more in 1907 than eight years earlier; but the shipper in smaller lots was compelled to pay forty per cent. more.[5] As always, the change was along the line of least resistance. Such a policy made for larger dividends; but did it tend to the perpetuation of equality of opportunity as between great and small concerns? That was a social question of the very first importance, which had much to do with the demand for still further increase of the regulative power of the Federal government in 1910.

Under the new powers conferred by law, it was now possible to investigate scientifically many matters which heretofore

[1] Much data is in *U. S. v. Union Pacific*, etc., Supreme Court, No. 820, Oct. term, 1911, Appellants Brief of Facts, p. 558 *et seq.*

[2] All the Cattle Raisers Association of Texas cases, especially 11 I.C.C. Rep., p. 296. *Cf.*, also, pp. 70 and 167, *supra*, and 567, *infra*.

[3] 13 I.C.C. Rep., 357. [4] 12 I.C.C. Rep., 149. [5] 16 I.C.C. Rep., 85.

had been privately governed by rule of thumb. For instance the reasonableness of the charges for refrigeration in the movement of citrus fruit is dependent in practice upon the methods employed in gathering and packing them for market.[1] Was it better business practice to ship oranges and lemons in ice-cooled refrigerator cars, or was it better to adopt the so-called pre-cooling process, combined with great care in handling? The former was the long-standing practice of the fruit-growers, while the latter, substantially supported by the investment of more than a million dollars in plant, was advocated by the carriers. One had been tested in practice, the other was yet in the experimental stage. But aside from rivalry of method, were not the shippers entitled to pre-cool or refrigerate their fruit privately if they so desired? The determination of this question meant an elaborate investigation with careful records in detail as to the results obtained in either case. The decision upheld the carriers in their charges for the older methods of treatment; but pre-cooling charges had to be reduced by seventy-five per cent. It appears, therefore, that authority to deal with one of the most serious grievances voiced before the Elkins Committee in 1905, may now be fairly and scientifically exercised for the public benefit.

A similar technical investigation concerned the methods of transporting the products of "creameries."[2] Shall dairy products be centralized at favored points, possessed of a sufficient supply from the surrounding territory to permit of large-scale manufacture; or shall the older local creamery method prevail, whereby the product is taken directly from country stations to the great centres of consumption like Chicago? The particular rate adjustment makes all the difference between creameries scattered throughout the countryside or, on the other hand, located in the great cities. One of the prime difficulties is in the sparcity and uneven distribution of the cow population. Here was an order requiring a very careful investigation of the

[1] 20 I.C.C. Rep., 106. [2] 15 I.C.C. Rep., 109.

entire business, followed by a nice judgment as to the economic merits of the case. The history and development of the dairy business in the West had to be thoroughly looked into. Quite irrespective of the resulting order, it is apparent that the public is certain to benefit from an exhaustive inquiry. Yet other general investigations of the same sort might be cited to the same end. The wool business was examined thoroughly in 1911.[1] The entire New England rate system as well as the conditions of operation were overhauled in the following year, and a general inquiry into the hard coal situation is just now under way. A general improvement of conditions is bound to flow from the free exercise of such general powers.

The leading Supreme Court decision construing the Hepburn law, — and, constitutionally, one of the most important in recent years, — was rendered in 1910 with reference to the relation between the exercise of power over transportation by the Interstate Commerce Commission and the right of review of such action by the courts.[2] The details of the controversy are indicative of the nicety of economic adjustment required in such cases. There was a shortage of equipment for the carriage of soft coal on the lines of the Illinois Central Railroad. This commodity, practically speaking, cannot be stored. It must be disposed of at once, so that the available supply of cars determines the output of each mine. If, in this case, all the cars had belonged to the Illinois Central Railroad to be used indiscriminately by the mine owners, it would have been a simple matter to have allotted the equipment among all the operators along its lines upon the basis of the established capacity of each. Unfortunately, diversity of ownership of these cars had brought about, all over the country, special rules for effecting the allotments. Some cars belonged to the railroad;

[1] 23 I.C.C. Rep., 151.
[2] 215 U. S., 452; also *Ibid.*, 481. The original order of the Commission is in 13 I.C.C. Rep., 451.

others to the mine company, to other private parties, or to foreign railways. Certain railroads first deducted all fuel carried by other equipment than their own from the estimated capacity of each mine, and then divided up their own available cars *pro rata* among all the mines according to the net capacity thus fixed. Others allotted their cars according to the gross mine capacity, taking no account of the private or outside equipment which any particular coal mine possessed or might obtain. This second practice evidently favored the larger concerns, supplied with abundant capital for investment in cars or for renting equipment. For, in addition to their own cars, they could still demand as many more from the railroad on daily allotment as if they were entirely dependent upon it for the movement of all their coal. Which was the fairer practice? A nice economic question was thus raised. Has a shipper the right to exclusive use of all his own fuel cars, and, in addition thereto, a full share of the system cars of the railroad? Disputes of this sort have been before the Commission and the courts for years.

In this Illinois Central case, a colliery company complained of even a more minute detail of the rule employed by the railroad in making its daily allotment, affirming it to be discriminatory in effect. There was a shortage of cars and of coal. The railroad was employing many of its own cars in the special service of carrying fuel for its own use. The particular grievance was its insistence upon treating these special Illinois Central cars, for the purposes of allotment, as if they were merely ordinary private cars; that is to say, by supplying them in practice regardless of and outside of the daily allotment, otherwise agreed upon. It thus appears that the economic issue was highly technical in character. Similar complaints had been already variously decided by other tribunals. The Commission, moreover, was bound to consider this complaint with several others of a like sort. Exercising its best business judgment under all the circumstances, it decided against the practice, ordering the Illinois Central, under the powers conferred by the new law of 1906, to include all cars, however owned or for whatever purpose used, in figuring its daily allotments in time of shortage of equipment. The case went to the Supreme Court upon petition of the railroad to set aside the order of the Commission.

By contrast with the economic intricacy of this case, the fundamental legal question was simple. How broad was the right of review of the Commission's order, as conferred by the amendments adopted in 1906? Were the courts to rest content merely to pass upon the regularity and lawfulness of the forms of procedure adopted by the Commission, or might they go further, and, hearing all the evidence as to fact, proceed to settle the economic controversy as well as the law points, in entire independence of the Commission? In the former case administrative control would result. In the latter, regulative power would really reside in the judicial branch of the government. It was the same old controversy which by adoption of the second alternative had practically emasculated the law of 1887, and had necessitated its amplification by amendment in 1906.[1] A momentous issue was presented. To go forward would make for logical definition and separation of the powers of the Federal government; to retreat would be to precipitate anew the inevitable conflict in Congress, from which, it was hoped, we had emerged for good!

The importance of the Illinois Central decision is such that the conclusion should be stated by direct quotation, with our italics as to the main point.

"Beyond controversy, in determining whether an order of the Commission shall be suspended or set aside, we must consider, *a*, all relevant questions of constitutional power or right; *b*, all pertinent questions as to whether the administrative order is within the scope of the delegated authority under which it purports to have been made; and, *c*, a proposition which we state independently, although in its essence it may be contained in the previous one, viz., whether, even

[1] P. 502, *supra*.

JUDICIAL INTERPRETATION

although the order be in form within the delegated power, nevertheless it must be treated as not embraced therein, because the exertion of authority which is questioned has been manifested in such an unreasonable manner as to cause it, in truth, to be within the elementary rule that the substance, and not the shadow, determines the validity of the exercise of the power. *Postal Telegraph Cable Co. v. Adams*, 155 U. S., 688, 698. Plain as it is that the powers just stated are of the essence of judicial authority, and which, therefore, may not be curtailed, and whose discharge may not be by us in a proper case avoided,[1] *it is equally plain that such perennial powers lend no support whatever to the proposition that we may, under the guise of exerting judicial power, usurp merely administrative functions by setting aside a lawful administrative order upon our conception as to whether the administrative power has been wisely exercised. Power to make the order and not the mere expediency or wisdom of having made it, is the question.*"

On this cogent reasoning the Supreme Court, therefore, quite independently of its opinion upon the economic merits, declined to permit interference with the order of the Commission.

Immediately following the Illinois Central decision another was rendered concerning somewhat the same economic issue, namely methods of supplying coal cars on the Baltimore and Ohio.[2] The following quotation is significant of what promises to be the line of reasoning in future.

"In . . . the . . . case just decided, it was pointed out that the effect of the section was to cause it to come to pass that courts, in determining whether an order of the Commission should be suspended or enjoined, were without power to invade the administrative functions vested in the Commission, and, therefore, could not set aside an order duly made on a mere exercise of judgment as to its wisdom or expediency. Under these circumstances it is apparent, as we have said, that these amendments of 1906 add to the cogency of the reasoning which led to the conclusion in the Abilene Case, that the primary interference of the courts with the administrative functions of the Commission was wholly incompatible with the act to regulate commerce. This result is easily illustrated. A particular regulation of a carrier engaged in interstate commerce is assailed in the courts as unjustly preferential and discriminatory. Upon the facts found, the complaint is declared to be well founded. The administrative powers of the Commission

---

[1] *Italics are ours.*   [2] 215 U. S., 481.

are invoked concerning a regulation of like character upon a similar complaint. The Commission finds, from the evidence before it, that the regulation is not unjustly discriminatory. Which would prevail? If both, then discrimination and preference would result from the very prevalence of the two methods of procedure. If, on the contrary, the Commission was bound to follow the previous action of the courts, then it is apparent that its power to perform its administrative functions would be curtailed, if not destroyed. On the other hand, if the action of the Commission were to prevail, then the function exercised by the court would not have been judicial in character, since its final conclusion would be suceptible of being set aside by the action of a mere administrative body. That these illustrations are not imaginary is established not only by this record, but by the record in the case of the *Illinois C. R. Co. v. Interstate Commerce Commission.*"

These opinions, expressly recognizing the constitutionality of the free and full exercise of legislative power delegated by Congress beyond the power of the courts to review, are of fundamental importance. Had they been rendered a few days earlier, as we shall see, they might have prevented the supposed necessity of setting up a new commerce court by law in 1910. They would certainly have abridged the Congressional debates over points of law. Under these decisions, only authority and constitutional rights may be reviewed. The same issues were raised in the Portland Gateway opinion in 1910, soon to engage our attention, concerning the Commission's right to designate through routes for passenger travel. Over-ruling the Commission in this instance, however, the narrow right of review by the courts, as laid down in the Illinois Central case, is somewhat widened by an apparent refusal to treat the Commission's findings as to fact as conclusive in determining its jurisdiction; however conclusive it may regard them in other respects. A shady byway of judicial encroachment is thus rather surreptitiously indicated.

A more satisfactory re-affirmation of the disposition of the Supreme Court to allow a wide field and a free hand to the Commission in the exercise of its offices, is to be found in a third opinion, the so-called Burnham, Hanna, Munger case, also rendered in 1910.[1] Certain Missouri river cities complained that rates from the Atlantic seaboard were unduly high by comparison with those to cities in Central Traffic territory, namely between the Mississippi river and Buffalo. The Commission held the complaint well founded; and ordered a readjustment, by reduction of that portion of the rate west of the Mississippi. Thus, by leaving the rates to the Central Traffic Association cities unchanged, it materially benefited those along the Missouri river by comparison. Omaha and Kansas City were brought substantially closer to the seaboard as compared with Chicago and similar trade centres. The western roads, alone affected by this order, attacked it in the courts as an assertion by the Commission of power "artificially to apportion out the country into zones tributary to given trade centres to be pre-determined by the Commission, and non-tributary to others." The Supreme Court, in upholding the order, held that it would indeed be an abuse of power to raise or lower rates for the sole purpose above-outlined. Nevertheless, if the Commission were seeking primarily to correct rates inherently unreasonable, such action would not be invalidated by incidental effects upon trade conditions. The Supreme Court found, therefore, that the order in question was within its power, as thus defined, and, governed by the reasoning in the Illinois Central case, held that the Commission's decision could not be judicially reviewed upon the merits.

The line of judicial interpretation preceding the Mann-Elkins law of 1910 has been even more rigidly followed by the Supreme Court since that time. Perhaps the most important was rendered in January, 1912. This concerned the absolute reasonableness of rates on fir lumber from the northern Pacific forests to the Middle West.[2] But it involved the additional consideration that the transcontinental roads had in a measure

[1] 218 U. S., 88; 14 I.C.C. Rep., 299. Also, 16 *Idem*, 56; 21 *Idem*, 546; and 23 *Idem*, 195. Ann. Rep. I.C.C., 1909, p. 33, discusses it fully.
[2] 32 Supreme Court Rep., 109. Economic details in chap. V, p. 150, *supra*.

guaranteed an economic status to lumbermen under which they had made large investments, which, as they claimed, were jeopardized by an increase of freight rates in 1907. Two points were raised. One concerned the reasonableness of the new rates *per se;* the other their reasonableness in the light of their effects upon an established yet dependent industry. It was the old issue, in brief, between cost of service and value of service. A decision upon the latter basis alone might have resulted, as in a similar action in the Burnham, Hanna, Munger case, just outlined, in decreeing an extension of authority over commerce by the Commission. Fortunately the court found otherwise in these lumber cases. It was able to uphold the order of the Commission, without deviation from the path of reasoning laid down in the Illinois Central opinion. The decision concludes as follows:

"Considering the case as a whole, we cannot say that the order was made because of the effect of the advance on the lumber industry, nor because of a mistake of law as to presumptions arising from the long continuance of the low rate when the carrier was earning dividends, nor that there was no evidence to support the finding. If so, the Commission acted within its power, and, in view of the statute, its lawful orders cannot be enjoined."

The unsatisfactory element in this decision is its implication that the Commission must be governed by cost of service principles in fixing reasonable rates. For to admit the plea of the lumbermen, that their industry could not stand the increase, would obviously lend an ear to the principle of value of service. May the railroads properly adopt either of the two principles in fixing their tariffs, while the Commission is confined to cost of service alone? Any such conclusion would tend to paralyze regulation. And Congress would certainly in a moment fly to the rescue with amplification of the statute.

This Pacific coast lumber opinion also contains the following succinct statement of the grounds upon which alone the Federal courts may review the orders of the Commission:

"There has been no attempt to make an exhaustive statement of the principle involved, but in cases thus far decided, it has been settled that the orders of the Commission are final unless (1) beyond the power which it could constitutionally exercise; or (2) beyond its statutory power; or (3) based upon a mistake of law. But questions of fact may be involved in the determination of questions of law, so that an order, regular on its face, may be set aside if it appears that (4) the rate is so low as to be confiscatory and in violation of the constitutional prohibition against taking property without due process of law; or (5) if the Commission acted so arbitrarily and unjustly as to fix rates contrary to evidence, or without evidence to support it; or (6) if the authority therein involved has been exercised in such an unreasonable manner as to cause it to be within the elementary rule that the substance, and not the shadow, determines the validity of the exercise of the power."

Quite like the preceding case was another concerning the reasonableness of advances of rates upon fir lumber from the Willamette valley to San Francisco. The Commission had ordered a reduced rate, from which the Southern Pacific appealed to the Supreme Court.[1] This tribunal set aside the order on the ground that, while seeking to protect an investment in lumber mills, it had not been governed by considerations as to the intrinsic reasonableness of the rates. The lumbermen then went back to the Commission with a new complaint, in response to which a slight advance was permitted to the railroad, apparently as a token of compliance with the opinion of the Supreme Court. But the Southern Pacific, not yet content, promptly appealed a second time under the Mann-Elkins law to the new Commerce Court. On June 4, 1912, this tribunal fully sustained the Commission in a most suggestive declaration of the obligation of a carrier, having once induced capital to embark in a new enterprise under promise of low rates, being subsequently estopped from charging to the full limit of what the traffic will bear.[2] This is a gratifying evidence of acquiescence of this new tribunal in the main line of interpretation laid down by the Supreme Court.

[1] 219 U. S., 433; 14 I.C.C. Rep., 61. Economic details at p. 150, supra. [2] U. S. Commerce Court, No. 59, April session, 1912.

Federal decisions construing the law of 1906 during this period under review, revealed various shortcomings and defects which could be repaired only by additional legislation. They are to be considered among the causes contributing to the passage of the Mann-Elkins Act of 1910, shortly to engage our attention. Two in particular, the Orange Routing case and the Portland Gateway order, merit discussion. Neither directly involved monetary considerations, but a conflict between the rights of shippers and carriers. And both alike went on appeal to the Supreme Court of the United States.

The Orange Routing case against the Southern Pacific Railroad touched the right of the shipper to name the particular railways over which his fruit should reach Eastern markets.[1] Rates were the same by whatever route; but the railways denied the right of the shipper not only to name, but even to know, the route taken by his goods in transit. The same issue came up some years ago, concerning the right of cotton shippers at Memphis to designate the particular connecting railroads which should haul their goods. The purpose of the carriers in seeking to control this matter is obvious, and may be praiseworthy. Secret rebates cannot often be secured by shippers from the initial carriers, especially if, as in California, no railway competition exists. For the Atchison and the Southern Pacific have done away with that by pooling their fruit business. Secret rebates, if secured by shippers at all, must be wrung from the connecting lines, which bid for it at the great junction points, like Kansas City and Chicago. The initial road, by reserving the right to route the freight, is able most effectively to nullify all such pernicious contracts. But, on the other hand, this practice denies to the owner of the goods, control, or even supervision, over his own. Market conditions may easily change while the goods are in transit. It may be desirable to stop them off at Chicago, or divert them to New Orleans. And, moreover, damages for delay on such perishable goods as fruit are refused

[1] 200 U. S., 536.

by the terms of the contract. The routing road exercises power without assuming responsibility. On these grounds, and in consonance with the long-established principles of common law, the Interstate Commerce Commission held that the shippers' rights were jeopardized. It was shown that freight was often diverted from one road to another in order to secure more valuable percentages of the through rate for the initial carrier. The Circuit Court in September, 1904, provisionally sustained the Commission; but its opinion was reversed by the Supreme Court in 1906. The court of last resort failed to find in the law any prohibition of such regulations concerning routes by the railroads. Incidentally it held that the Federal courts might enforce orders of the Commission, even although for reasons differing from those which governed the original order.[1]

The Portland Gateway case in 1910, before the Supreme Court,[2] also disclosed a defect in the law of 1906. It dealt with the right of the Commission to designate through passenger routes. Seattle, Washington, may be reached from the Middle West either by various lines to St. Paul and from thence due west by the "Hill lines," or by various railroads to Kansas City and thence by the Burlington and the Northern Pacific, also "Hill lines." There are also many routes first proceeding westward *via* the Union Pacific to Portland, Oregon, and from thence up to Seattle. By these latter routes most of the journey would be over the "Harriman lines," whereas by the former it would be by way of their competitors for the control of the northwest. Passengers all the way over the "Hill lines" were afforded every facility for through travel in the way of tickets and baggage; but if they chose the Portland route, great inconvenience followed from the refusal of the Hill lines to coöperate in facilities at the transfer point. In brief the "Hill lines" were working for the long haul over their own rails, as against the merely local haul from Portland to Seattle, which would follow the choice of the Harriman route.

[1] The resulting change in the law at p. 572, *infra*. [2] 216 U. S., 538.

The Commission upon its own motion investigated this situation, and, as a result, ordered the Northern Pacific to join with its rivals in establishing through routes *via* Portland to Seattle. This was done under authority in the law of 1906 to establish through routes and joint rates, provided "no reasonable or satisfactory through route exists." The Northern Pacific claimed, and was upheld therein by a dissenting opinion from the Commission, that there was already in existence such a route. Quick and comfortable travel *via* St. Paul already existed. Some eight thousand persons annually for one reason or another preferred, nevertheless, to go through Portland. The Commission held that this preference was reasonable, and that accordingly, with respect to such travellers, there was indeed no reasonable through route in effect. Passenger traffic, involving the element of personal choice, in other words, was different in law from freight business. The Circuit Court set aside this order upon the ground that a satisfactory alternative route over the Northern Pacific did actually exist. This decree was affirmed by the Supreme Court of the United States in 1910. But it was a hard-won victory for the carriers, inasmuch as Congress within six months specifically authorized the Commission to regulate such matters in future, without limitation as to the existence of other satisfactory routes.

The bitter rivalry between the Hill and Harriman systems for the control of the Northwest, as affecting the routing of freight traffic as well as of passengers through Portland, resulted in carrying a second case of the same sort before the Supreme Court. May temporary delay and congestion of business by way of any given line afford the Commission authority to designate another through route! In this instance, the Supreme Court has affirmed the order of the Commission.[1] It would appear, therefore, that this issue, for the present at least, is closed. The regulative power of the Federal government

[1] Rendered January, 1912. The Commission's order is in 14 I.C.C. Rep., 51.

over routes and the division of joint rates is satisfactorily upheld.

Several Supreme Court decisions defining the power of the Commission to require testimony, both oral and documentary, in relation to matters which came before it, were rendered about this time. Its prestige and authority in this regard, — already affirmed in the late nineties,[1]— were considerably enhanced by an opinion delivered in April, 1904.[2] In the course of the proceedings, upon complaint of William R. Hearst against the Reading and other coal roads, certain contracts between the Lehigh Valley Coal Company and independent operators were called for. One Baird and others, including President Baer of the Reading company, declined to produce these coal purchase contracts. Others refused to testify concerning methods of fixing the price for anthracite coal at tidewater. Disregarding certain purely legal details, these refusals were based upon the contention that neither the Commission nor Hearst, — a well-known owner of various newspapers, — had shown any legal interest in the complaint. The court held, however, that the want of direct damage to the complainant was not essential to his standing before the Commission. Moreover, in this case, the Supreme Court overruled the Federal Circuit Court, which had held that the details of the contracts for purchase of coal by railroads from independent operators related wholly to intrastate transactions, — that, in other words, the selling of coal in Pennsylvania had nothing to do with interstate commerce. The Supreme Court adjudged that all the details of these transactions had a bearing upon the general question of the degree of monopoly in the coal business, and could not properly be withheld from examination as evidence by the Commission. In conclusion the court said: "To unreasonably hamper the Commission by narrowing its field of inquiry beyond the requirements of the due protection of rights of citizens, will be to

[1] Pp. 457–460, *supra*.   [2] 194 U. S., 25.

seriously impair its usefulness and prevent a realization of the salutary purposes for which it was established by Congress." This sweeping decision by the court of last resort well buttressed the former decisions of that tribunal in the Brimson and Brown cases.

The so-called "Immunity Bath" Supreme Court decision in 1906 materially affected, not so much the scope of authority of the Commission as its mode of procedure in eliciting testimony in railroad cases.[1] A resolution of the House of Representatives in 1904 had directed the Commissioner of Corporations to conduct an investigation into the affairs of the so-called "Beef Trust." In the course of this inquiry, Federal officials from the bureau held interviews in Chicago with prominent members of the beef-packing establishments. Important evidence was obtained, with the understanding that this was merely a general investigation having no relation to the Department of Justice, nor intended to be used in the prosecution of any suits at law. At the same time, agents examined the books of these companies. The accountants, however, in all cases refused to certify to their accuracy under oath. The material thus secured was incorporated in a report of the bureau in the following year. Not long afterward, when the prosecution of this combination was undertaken by the Department of Justice, the attorneys for the government made use of data in this report of the Bureau of Corporations in presenting their case. Consequently, on behalf of the packers under indictment under the provisions of the Sherman Anti-Trust Act, it was urged that the interdictions of this law were inoperative as to them, inasmuch as they had virtually been made to testify against themselves. The Supreme Court affirmed this immunity from prosecution under the provision of the Constitution forbidding any person from being compelled in a criminal case to be a witness against himself.[2]

[1] 142 Fed. Rep., 808.

[2] This immunity was expressly limited to natural persons. Corporations had been made directly liable by the Act of 1903. This point was brought out in the Henkel and Nelson cases; 201 U. S., 43, 90, 147.

The direct bearing of this decision upon subsequent prosecutions for rebating, as in the notable Chicago and Alton case in the following year, is apparent. No general investigation of any subject, evidently, should be undertaken either by Congress or the Interstate Commerce Commission, in the course of which testimony shall be elicited under pressure, if it is intended that criminal prosecution by the Department of Justice is subsequently to take place. The eagerness of witnesses to secure the privileges of the "Immunity Bath" by frank avowal of material facts might otherwise thwart the government in the pursuance of its ends.

Another important decision of the Supreme Court touching the right of the Commission to compel testimony was rendered in 1908 in connection with the investigation of the Union Pacific system.[1] Mr. Harriman, the dominant factor in the management of this system, had caused the Union Pacific to purchase certain stocks of the Atchison and a number of other railroads in different parts of the country. The purchase price being known, the witness was asked whether he had a personal interest in the securities thus acquired by the road under his control. He declined to answer, on the ground that the power to require testimony was limited to the only cases where the sacrifice of privacy was necessary, namely those where the investigation concerned a specific breach of the law. The court, with three justices dissenting, sustained Harriman in his refusal, on the ground that this particular investigation was undertaken, not in pursuance of a complaint of specific violation of the law, but merely for the sake of general information as to the manner and method in which the business of common carriers was being conducted. No question was raised as to the right of the Commission to undertake general investigations of this sort; it was merely held that in the course of such investigations there was a limit to the inquisitorial power of this administrative body.

[1] 211 U. S., 407. This decision is critically examined with reference to the policy of the Commission in its Annual Report, 1908, p. 17.

It may be added in this connection that the amendments added by the Mann-Elkins Act of 1910 most specifically defined the authority of the Commission in this regard.

The "commodity clause" of the Hepburn amendments to the Interstate Commerce Law, because of its unfortunate ambiguity, has already twice been before the Supreme Court.[1] The first interpretation was given in a decision concerning the Delaware and Hudson Railroad, handed down in May, 1909.[2] This affirmed the constitutionality of the statute at all points; but, at the same time, emasculated it most effectually. For, in order to harmonize the opinion with prior ones holding that ownership of stock in a corporation did not constitute legal ownership of the property of the company, it was necessarily held that a railroad by owning the share capital of a coal company did not thereby possess an interest, direct or indirect, in the coal mined. Moreover, a railroad which was the legal owner of coal at the mine might escape the interdiction of the law by selling the coal before transportation began. A handy means of evading the intent of the law could not have been more plainly indicated.

An attempt specifically to prohibit stock ownership in coal mines by railroads, — thus meeting in part the situation arising out of the foregoing decision, — was made in connection with the Mann-Elkins Act in 1910; but to no avail. The Senate, by a vote of twenty-five to thirty-one, rejected an amendment proposed by Senator Bailey of Texas, to prohibit stock ownership so clearly "that not even a judge of the Supreme Court could fail to understand it." The negative votes were all cast by the so-called "regular" Republicans. In the meantime, the clause had been carried to the Supreme Court for further interpretation in a suit against the Lehigh Valley Railroad.[3] The

[1] Congressional History at p. 513, *supra*. The coal combination will be fully described in vol. II.
[2] *United States v. Delaware and Hudson Railroad*, etc.; 213 U. S., 257.
[3] 200 U. S., 257; decided April, 1911.

government in the lower court had already been defeated in an attempt to raise questions of fact as to the pecuniary interest of the road in the coal transported, irrespective of the technicalities as to legal ownership. The outcome in this case was more satisfactory. The Circuit Court was held to have erred in ruling out these considerations. It was unanimously decided by the Supreme Court that it was in violation of the law to use stock ownership for the purpose of destroying the entity of a producing corporation, while still so "commingling" its affairs in administration with the affairs of the railroad as to make the two corporations virtually one. This was a distinct gain for the government. It necessitated a compliance with the law in good faith. Upon the basis of this decision the Department of Justice instituted a new action against the Lehigh Valley Road, which was promptly met, however, by a readjustment of its corporate affairs.

The economic results under the "commodity clause" have been quite different from those doubtless anticipated by Congress. A salutary separation of coal mining from transportation is being effected; but in the case of the anthracite properties at least, in such manner as to hold out small hope of any direct benefit to the general public.

Absolute alienation of their coal properties by the railroads was subject to two difficulties. Some roads, like the Reading and the Lehigh Valley, had heavy issues of bonds outstanding, based upon the security, jointly, of both the railroad and the coal properties. The two could not readily be separated without retirement of these general mortgage bonds. In the second place, the operating relations between the railroads and their subsidiary coal companies, had for years been fixed upon the general principle of concentrating all profit from the two conjoined transactions of mining and carriage upon the transportation service alone. In other words, freight rates were established at so high a percentage of the selling price of coal that mining was necessarily conducted at a nominal profit, if any.

This made no difference to the carriers, owning both mines and roads, but it had the desired effect of making it impossible for coal operators, independent of the railroads, to engage in the business. Without a modification of this plan the coal companies, already separately organized for the business by most of the railroads, could hardly be disposed of to advantage, either to the general public or even to their own shareholders. The only coal companies controlled by railroads which independently showed a considerable book-keeping profit were those owned by the Jersey Central and the Delaware and Hudson roads. The Lehigh Valley Coal Company had never paid dividends to its railroad corporation, but had contented itself with providing a very profitable tonnage. The Philadelphia and Reading Coal and Iron Company had likewise never been allowed to show a book-keeping profit sufficient to meet the interest upon its bonds and to provide for a sinking fund against exhaustion of its assets under ground.

Despite these practical obstacles, a general legal separation of hard-coal mining from transportation is in a fair way to be effected.[1] The Delaware, Lackawanna, and Western in 1909 was the first to act. With no joint mortgages and a charter right to mine coal directly, it merely organized a separate corporation, the Delaware, Lackawanna and Western Coal Company. The capital stock of this concern was then distributed gratis as a special dividend among its own shareholders. This coal company at once purchased all of the railroad's coal in stock, leased its mining appurtenances, and agreed henceforth to purchase all of its coal at the mine mouth for sixty-five per cent. of the tidewater price. The railroad continued to mine coal, but thus disposed of it before accepting it again for carriage. The Delaware and Hudson likewise entered into a contract with a coal company organized in 1901, which, after June, 1909,

[1] A monograph by Mr. Eliot Jones of Harvard University on the anthracite coal business, soon to be published, will afford every detail of these transactions.

agreed to purchase all of its future output. The Lehigh Valley Railroad rearrangement was more complicated. It already had a coal company of the same name, the capital stock of which was pledged under its general railroad mortgage. Ownership was thus indissoluble. So the Lehigh Valley *Coal Sales* Company was organized in January, 1912. Its capital of $10,000,000 was provided by the railroad, which declared a stock dividend to its own shareholders, sufficient in amount to enable them to subscribe to the capital of the new concern. This company, then, like the others above mentioned, thereupon agreed to purchase all the coal mined by the railroad's subsidiary coal corporation.

At this writing great speculative interest attaches to the probable plan to be adopted by the Reading. Its intricate organization,[1] whereby both the railroad and the coal companies are owned by a purely finance or holding company, renders the problem of dissociation unique. A large volume of joint bonds are outstanding, with complicated provisions for sinking funds. The railroad actually owns no coal lands. The coal company, independently, is not profitable under existing traffic arrangements. Its operating ratio in 1911 was 98.7 per cent. It is "land poor"; carrying vast reserves of coal purchased by bond issues. The only asset sufficiently profitable by itself to make it attractive as a gift to shareholders, is the subsidiary coal company of the Jersey Central Railroad, which is itself controlled by means of stock ownership. The formation of a third coal sales company, whose stock could be distributed to shareholders of the Reading, as was done by the Lehigh Valley, would seem to be the only feasible plan.

But is there not danger, financially, for these and other railroads, that they may place this lucrative traffic in jeopardy by thus distributing their coal properties among shareholders by means of stock dividends? While, for a time, community of

[1] Intercorporate Relations of Railways, Special Report, Int. Com. Com., 1906, p. 24.

interest between railroad and coal mine may be assured through lodgment of stock ownership of both companies in the same persons, is it not likely that the two may become widely dissociated in the course of time? This contingency has been guarded against by an ingenious provision. The contracts providing for purchase and shipment of coal by the coal sales companies are terminable at the will of the railroad. So that if conflict of interest should arise in future, through transfers of stock of the coal sales company to outsiders, the carriers would be free to cancel the arrangement; create another corporation; distribute its shares among their stockholders once more; and thereafter go on as before. Manifold and ingenious, indeed, are the devices of the law for purposes of circumvention!

Whether the "commodity clause" is to bring about a further separation of transportation from activities of carriers in other lines of business remains to be seen. It was doubtless intended to have a general application. Some roads, other than those in the anthracite coal fields, have taken steps to set off their subsidiary concerns. The Louisville & Nashville, for example, has distributed among its stockholders all the shares of the Louisville Properties Company. This is a Kentucky corporation to which the railroad had transferred its holdings of coal and other lands. It was expected at the time that its capital stock of $600,000 would be worth par. The Union Pacific has done even better. It voluntarily reconveyed to the United States considerable tracts of coal lands, where title had been called in question in the course of investigations as to such railroad ownership. While there has been no sign of the Pennsylvania Railroad disposing of its investments in the Cambria and Pennsylvania Steel Companies, made prior to 1906, it is clear that the interdiction of the law will render any further outside operations of this sort difficult if not impossible.

CHAPTER XVII

THE MANN-ELKINS ACT OF 1910

Prompt acquiescence by carriers, 557. — Opposition begins in 1908, 557. — Political developments, 558. — President Taft's bill, 559. — Three main features of the new law, 560. — Suspension of rate changes, 561. — Former defective injunction procedure remedied, 562. — The new long and short haul clause, 564. — Provision for water competition, 566. — The new Commerce Court, 566. — Congressional debates, 567. — Jurisdiction of the new Court, 568. — Its defects, 569. — Prosecution transferred to the Department of Justice, 570. — Liability for rate quotations, 571. — Wider scope of Federal authority, 572. — Its report analyzed, 574. — The Railroad Securities Commission, 573. — The statute summarized, 578.

THE course of events after 1906, so far as acquiescence in the law was concerned, was precisely like that of twenty years earlier. For some time the railroads seemed submissive, — in almost a chastened mood. The Commission also exercised its new powers rather timidly. Up to July 1, 1908, only a single appeal to the Federal courts had been taken by the carriers against orders of the Commission. A sudden change of front supervened at this time. During the second half of that year, sixteen suits to set aside orders of the Commission were filed. Nine more were entered in the following year, and thirteen during 1910; with the result that the dockets were greatly congested with proceedings of this sort. No less than thirty-six were before the circuit courts, when in 1910 they were all transferred to the newly constituted Commerce Court, soon to be described. This accumulation of unfinished business, with the consequent delay in settlement of important transportation disputes, contributed greatly to the movement in Congress in favor of further amendment of the law.

There were several reasons for this sudden shift of attitude toward the law in 1908 on the part of the carriers. The political atmosphere had suddenly cleared so far as popular hostility to railroads was concerned. A change of administration had ensued, with a marked preponderance of professional legal talent in the Cabinet. And several important decisions of the Supreme Court, once threatening, had now been rendered in favor of the carriers. Among these may be mentioned the first interpretation of the "commodity clause," — on the one hand upholding the constitutionality of the law, and on the other, pointing the broad and easy way to its evasion; the Harriman decision, protecting witnesses from disclosure of details as to their personal participation in the finances of companies under their control; and the exculpation of the Standard Oil Company by the aid of eminent counsel and the technicalities of the law, with escape from the extreme penalties of the statutes for rebating and personal favoritism. Things seemed indeed to be going at last the railroads' way.

The brightening financial outlook also gave better heart to the carriers. The panic of 1907, with its forced postponement of ambitiously constructive plans, seemed to have passed. The revival of these projects might be hampered by a further extension of government regulation and publicity. Railroad labor, moreover, was becoming restive. Demands for increased wages were imminent; and the carriers evidently proposed to shift the incidence of these wage increases, if granted, upon the public by means of an advance of rates. Such increases were bound to be disputed. It was deemed important to test the law at every point. This need was the more imperative as the Commission itself was bound to pass upon several questions of fundamental importance, such as the adjustment of transcontinental freight schedules and others soon to be described.

A presidential campaign took place in 1908. Both political parties committed themselves in their platforms to still further amendment of the Interstate Commerce Law. The Republican party, however, modestly confined its recommendations to authorization of traffic agreements and the regulation of stock and bond issues by railroads for the prevention of over-capitalization. The Democrats offered a much broader program providing for real amplification of the power of the Commission over rates. President Taft, — well in advance of his party, controlled as it was by the so-called "regulars," — offered soon after election a more definite policy. Its main feature was the establishment of a Court of Commerce to which all judicial review of orders of the Commission should be submitted, in lieu of revision by the regularly constituted Federal judiciary. He evidently proposed to seriously amend the law; but, beyond the foregoing proposition, most of the other details of his plan seemed to be either half-way measures or else ill-designed to meet the real difficulties of the case. Thus the proposal to give power over mere rules and regulations in advance of their taking effect, without at the same time conferring a like power to pass upon the reasonableness of rates themselves, seemed to miss the main point. The same criticism was applicable to the plan of conferring authority to postpone the taking effect of a new classification until it had been approved by the Commission. Other excellent details were such as conferred authority to compel through routes and to forbid stockholding by one road in other competing lines, set forth in speeches in the fall of 1909.

A special presidential message of January 7, 1910, contained the specific program recommended for legislation to Congress. It consisted merely of a tentative bill, which was introduced in both houses and properly referred.[1] By this time the influence of the Interstate Commerce Commission in strengthening the proposals was apparent. More positive provisions were added, such as the right to suspend rate increases pending determination of their reasonableness. Serious consideration was given this bill in appropriate committees both of the House and

[1] Characterized somewhat heatedly by Senator La Follette in his Autobiography (*American Magazine*, 1912, p. 189), as "in all the history of railroad legislation, the rankest, boldest betrayal of public interest ever proposed in any legislative body."

Senate. It was, in fact, with the consent of the Attorney-General, amended out of all semblance to its original form. The most serious changes were made in the Committee on Interstate Commerce of the House of Representatives. The coalition of Democrats and "insurgent" or "progressive" Republicans, succeeded in striking out the authorization of traffic agreements, as well as a proposition permitting a railroad owning a majority of stock in other non-competing lines to purchase the balance of their shares. Several radical amendments of the Commerce Court plan were likewise effected, especially those giving the power of appointment to the Chief Justice instead of the President. The hands of the "progressives" in all this work were considerably strengthened, without doubt, by the course of events during the spring months of 1910, especially the impending general increase of freight rates all over the country.

The strength of political sentiment in favor of the measure appears in the fact that the radical House bill was passed unanimously; while the Senate bill was adopted by a solid Republican vote with the aid of six Democrats, — the total vote being fifty to eleven. Reference to a conference committee, which considered it for ten days, still further modified the original plan. Pooling was dropped entirely; stockwatering and details of inter-corporate finance between non-competing lines were also thrown out as favoring the carriers unduly. Physical valuation, as provided in the House bill, was considerably restricted. Prompt approval of the conference bill followed in both houses. And the signature of the President was added on June 18. Thus did the Mann-Elkins "Amendments" become law.

The three most important features of the Mann-Elkins Act [1] were: the grant of power to suspend changes in rates for ex-

[1] The best references are the following: — F. H. Dixon, *Quarterly Journal of Economics*, vol. XXIII, 1910, pp. 593–633; reprinted in the

amination as to their reasonableness; resuscitation of the long and short haul clause; and the creation of the Commerce Court for review of the Commission's orders. Of these, the first two represent substantial extension of the regulative power of the government; the third being a mere modification of procedure on appeal.

The proposition to so amend Section 15[1] of the Act of 1887 as to confer power upon the Commission to suspend proposed changes in rates, seems to have been a feature added at the behest of the insurgent-Democratic coalition in Congress. It was neither in the President's first unofficial program nor in the formal bill drawn up by the Attorney-General. The intolerable obstructions in the way of prompt determination of transportation disputes incident to the practical working of the law, even since 1906, had created a renewed demand for relief. Great force was added to this demand among shippers by the rate advances which had been occurring all along the line for two years; and particularly by the rumors of a general rate advance by the western and trunk line roads during the progress of the debate upon the bill. The President, to be sure, blocked this advance by means of a clever legal and political move. On May 31 an injunction was issued against twenty-four carriers, temporarily restraining them from putting into effect higher tariffs, as they had planned on June 1. This action was taken upon the allegation that the simultaneous action of all these roads in so doing constituted a violation of the Anti-Trust Law. The injunction, which as a weapon had been turned mainly by the carriers against enforcement of the orders of the Commission, was now invoked against the railroads. Regardless as to whether a *bona fide* prosecution was contemplated, the effect of these equity proceedings was to secure

---

Railway Age Gazette, vol. XLIX, p. 688 *et seq; American Political Science Review*, vol. IV, 1910, pp. 537–554. Our other sources are the files of the Annual Reports of I.C.C.; the Congressional Record, *Railway Age Gazette*, and daily press reports. [1] P. 452, *supra*.

postponement of the advance in rates; and, of course, at the same time forcibly to attract the attention of Congress to the necessity of control. The carriers withdrew their tariffs in some discomfiture; the injunctions were dissolved; and all proceedings were stopped.

It is unnecessary, perhaps, to repeat the demonstration that a loss by shippers once incurred through payment of an unreasonable rate, is irretrievable. The manner in which transportation costs enter into the profitableness of contracts by the shipper for future delivery is well known.[1] Any change of rates during a period for which shippers have contracted to deliver at fixed prices, must seriously affect the chances of profit. It was recognized as essential, therefore, that adequate protection for the shipper could be given only through suspension of any change in rates until the reasonableness of that change had been determined.

The extent to which the aid of the courts had been invoked by the carriers to set aside orders of the Commission has already been described. Proceedings on the equity side in the courts had also, although in a most unsatisfactory manner, been undertaken to restrain advances in rates. But in all cases the exercise of this power had been bitterly contested, and proved at best to be so cumbersome as to be almost futile. The utmost confusion resulted in some cases. For example, in 1908 the carriers filed notice of an advance in rates on boots and shoes from New England to the South. An injunction was obtained prohibiting such advance, on condition that application be immediately made to the Commission for a ruling upon the reasonableness of the proposed change. This would have left the carriers without choice except to collect one rate while continuing to publish another. They therefore withdrew their schedules, leaving the old rates in effect. As a result no complaint could be filed with the Commission, the new rate not having come into operation. To meet this situation, the court then so modified

---

[1] Concrete instance in 17 I.C.C. Rep., p. 317. Also p. 510, *supra*, and 587, *infra*.

its injunction that carriers might publish the advanced schedule, but were restrained from collecting it. This was manifestly an absurd situation. Moreover, supposing that the Commission could immediately take up the question, no order could become effective until after thirty days. In the meantime, the whole matter must remain in suspense. Considering that 15,000 tariffs advancing rates in trunk line territory alone, were filed in July, 1910, the necessary delay incident to such roundabout procedure would render it intolerable. Other complications might be mentioned, such as the localization of injunctions within the territorial jurisdiction of the enjoining court; legal technicalities touching the filing of bonds; and the status of non-petitioning shippers. Speedy relief must be had: that was clear beyond question.

Aside from the practical unworkableness of the injunction process as a protection against unreasonable rate advances, reform might well be demanded on grounds of fairness. No reduction of rates ought to be compelled without opportunity for protest by the carrier. Contrariwise, no new burden should be laid upon the shipper without a hearing. The burden of proof against disturbance of a long-standing adjustment ought properly to rest upon the party responsible for the change. Such delay as was requisite for determination of the reasonableness of the change could not constitute a serious burden; and even if it did, it was but just under the attendant circumstances.

The new law yielded to these arguments by a radical extension of the authority of the Commission. It was authorized to suspend the taking effect of any new rate or regulation for not more than one hundred and twenty days, to afford opportunity for hearing and decision as to its reasonableness. If necessary, a further period of six months' suspension might be had. Moreover, the burden of proof that the change was just and reasonable was laid upon the carrier. Beyond the ten months' period thus allowed, postponement might not extend. Thereafter the rates became effective automatically. This control fell short of the demand of the "insurgents" that downright approval of the Commission for all changes should be required; but it was, nevertheless, a substantial increase of power. It remains to be seen what the practical result of this great extension of government control may be. It was predicted that its greatest benefit would come from those suspensions of rate advances which ultimately brought about their withdrawal.[1] This prophecy was fulfilled, as will be seen in the next chapter, in the first great test to which the law was put, almost immediately after its passage.

Resuscitation of the long and short haul clause of the Act of 1887 was the second important feature of the new legislation. The long and tedious process of judicial interpretation, by means of which this section of the statute was nullified for so many years, has already been set forth.[2] Dissatisfaction with the local discrimination prevalent throughout the southern states and in the Rocky mountain region had been steadily increasing for a long time. Public opinion in these districts urgently demanded the relief which the original law sought to afford. Chairman Knapp fairly described the situation in 1905 before the Elkins Committee as follows:[3] — "No one, I think, can read the Fourth section . . . . and be in doubt that Congress intended to provide some actual and potential restraint upon that particular form of discrimination. And, I may say, it remains today much as it was then, not the greatest evil, but the most irritating and obnoxious form of discrimination that has been encountered." No distributing business could hope to become established in the West or South without vitalizing this section of the law. The larger cities, and particularly the manufacturing districts in the East, on the other hand, viewed with alarm any encroachment upon the far distant markets

[1] The suspension of increased rates on Maine potatoes in October, 1912, long enough to permit the entire season's crop to be marketed on the old tariffs is a case in point.
[2] P. 474, *supra*.   [3] Volume IV, p. 3293.

which they were able to hold by reason of peculiarly low rates. The railroads' coöperation with eastern representatives in Congress had successfully prevented any change in 1906. But four years later it became apparent early in the debates that something would have to be done for the relief of the West and South.

The long and short haul clause was amended by the influence of the Progressive Republicans in the House.[1] Four changes were made. The first was the total elimination of the clause "under substantially similar circumstances and conditions," which had been responsible for almost all of the trouble in the courts. This change made it necessary in all cases in future for permission to be secured in advance from the Commission for any lesser charge for a long haul than for a shorter one, no matter what the local circumstances might be. Secondly, the prohibition was specifically made to cover "routes" as well as "lines." Although the Osborne case[2] had already virtually made it clear that the clause applied to a series of connecting railways as well as to a single company, this addition placed the matter beyond dispute. The third change, practically legalizing a standing rule of the Commission for many years, prohibited a higher through rate than the sum of the local charges over the

---

[1] The following is the form in which the Fourth Section now stands:

"SECTION 4. That it shall be unlawful for any common carrier subject to the provisions of this act to charge or receive any greater compensation in the aggregate for the transportation of passengers, or of like kind of property, for a shorter than for a longer distance over the same line or route in the same direction, the shorter being included within the longer distance, or to charge any greater compensation as a through route than the aggregate of the intermediate rates subject to the provisions of this act; but this shall not be construed as authorizing any common carrier within the terms of this act to charge or receive as great compensation for a shorter as for a longer distance: Provided, however, That upon application to the Interstate Commerce Commission such common carrier may in special cases, after investigation, be authorized by the Commission to charge less for longer than for shorter distances for the transportation of passengers or property; and the Commission may from time to time prescribe the extent to which such designated common carrier may be relieved from the operation of this section: Provided, further, That no rates or charges lawfully existing at the time of the passage of this amendatory act shall be required to be changed by reason of the provisions of this section prior to the expiration of six months after the passage of this act, nor in any case where application shall have been filed before the Commission, in accordance with the provisions of this section, until a determination of such application by the Commission.

Whenever a carrier by railroad shall in competition with a water route or routes reduce the rates on the carriage of any species of freight to or from competitive points, it shall not be permitted to increase such rates unless after hearing by the Interstate Commerce Commission it shall be found that such proposed increase rests upon changed conditions other than the elimination of water competition."

[2] P. 476, *supra*.

same line.[1] An addition covering an entirely new point constituted the fourth modification of the section. It is suggestive as an indication of the determined spirit which animated Congress. This last detail was borrowed from the then recently submitted report of the National Waterways Commission, which in turn had borrowed it from the state constitution of California. It was intended to meet the tactics so often adopted by land carriers in competition with water lines, of drastically reducing rates until the competition by water had been killed, after which the losses were recouped by even higher tariffs than before.[2] Under the new law, no railroad, having once reduced its rates in competition with a water route, was permitted to increase those charges until the Interstate Commerce Commission should have found that such proposed increase rested upon changed conditions other than the elimination of water competition.

Improvement of the procedure on appeal, by the establishment of the Commerce Court, was the third important feature of the new law. It was not only the delay of which complaint was made, but the illogical process of review as well. For this

[1] *Cf.* the example on p. 590, *infra*.

[2] The following account, by W. M. Acworth in the *Railway Age Gazette*, of a conversation with the late Collis P. Huntington illustrates the possible abuse:

"The Southern Pacific built two fine steamers to run between San Francisco and Sacramento, Cal. They gave a daily service, each boat running up one day, and down the next, and the passenger fare was $2. A private individual thought he saw his way to compete with advantage, and bought a smaller boat, which only gave a service every other day, but, on the other hand, only charged $1 for this service.

"The Southern Pacific began to lose money, and when Mr. Huntington next came to California the position was put before him. 'Would you like to leave me to run this fight?' said he to the local manager. 'Certainly, sir,' was the reply. 'Is there an old boat you can buy that could give a service?' Being told that there was, Mr. Huntington bought it, ordered the two first-class boats to be laid up, and announced that the new purchase would run alongside the rival boat at a fare of 50 cents. 'Why, sir,' said the local manager, '50 cents won't pay for the coal.' 'No, I do not suppose it will,' was the answer, 'but when you go to war you have got to fight!'"

"Before long the owner of the rival boat came to Mr. Huntington and asked him what he was prepared to do about it. Mr. Huntington replied that he would buy his boat for $10,000 — I think the sum was. 'But, Mr. Huntington, the boat cost me $20,000, and she is worth it.' 'Very likely, but I am only going to give you $10,000.' So the fight went on for a while longer. When the spring came Mr. Huntington was on the point of returning to New York. He sent word to his rival that he was leaving California the following week, and that if the matter was not settled before he left, his 50-cent boat would continue to run till his return the following winter. Whereupon his competitor at once threw up the sponge and then sold his boat for $10,000. 'Since then,' concluded Mr. Huntington, 'there has been no competition with the Southern Pacific on the Sacramento river.'"

permitted the orders of a technically expert commission of seven men to be set aside by the order of a single judge who, in fact, relied upon subordinates for an examination of the evidence as to economic fact. This may be illustrated by two recent cases. In 1907 the transcontinental railroads substantially increased their rates on lumber. The Commission held that this advance was unreasonable; but permitted one half of it to take place. The carriers appealed to the Federal Circuit Court. All the evidence, involving great money and commercial considerations, was taken for the court by a master. Upon the findings of this single individual, without opportunity for the court to critically examine the evidence, the deliberate judgment of the Interstate Commerce Commission was set aside. The same thing happened in the Texas Cattle Raisers' case in 1910, involving rates on live stock from the southwest to northern ranges. In this instance, to be sure, the Circuit Court declined to enjoin the Commission. That did not, however, alter the fact that the decision was based upon hearings by a master, extending over sixty-three days and rolling up a voluminous record which the court did not have time even to peruse cursorily. To standardize procedure, as well as to eliminate delay, was the purpose of the President in the plan for the Commerce Court.

Many objections were advanced in the course of debate in Congress against the creation of a special tribunal. It was urged that such a court with limited jurisdiction would be open to political influence, as well as exposed to the danger of narrowness. It was said to be foreign to our judicial organization, which heretofore had known only courts of general jurisdiction. It was stated that no necessity for a commerce court existed, so small would be the number of cases which might be brought before it. Objection was also raised to it on the ground of expense. The problem of court review was, of course, complicated rather than made more simple by the Hepburn Act of 1906. Prior to that time no administrative orders took effect other than through enforcement by the courts. But this law provided that rates and regulations of the Commission should take effect *proprio vigore* within thirty days. The contest over broad *v.* narrow court review has already been described, with the outcome at the time regarded as a victory for broad review. The situation was entirely changed, however, by the Illinois Central decision in 1910,[1] which appeared to put a restraint upon judicial review, except when the order of the Commission was either beyond its legal powers or else unconstitutional. This decision did not, as might have been expected, put an end to the plan for a new transportation court; but it did bring about a specific restriction of the powers of this tribunal to those possessed by the regular circuit courts.

The Commerce Court, as finally constituted in 1910, was composed of five judges, each to serve for five years, designated and assigned thereto by the Chief Justice of the Supreme Court from among the circuit judges of the United States. No member might serve continuously for more than one term, but might be reappointed after an interval of one year. The court was to sit at Washington, and was to be always open for the transaction of business. From it, direct appeal to the Supreme Court might be taken, with as simple a mode of procedure as possible to eliminate delay. The original record, for example, was to be transmitted; and agents of every carrier must be designated at Washington upon whom process might at any time be served. Whatever may be said of other details of this judicial experiment, it certainly sought in good faith to promote promptness in procedure.

The jurisdiction of this Commerce Court was expressly conferred over four kinds of cases:[2]

First, those for enforcement of any order of the Interstate Commerce Commission, other than the payment of money.

---

[1] Page 538, *supra*.
[2] Opinion No. 44, 1911, is the first Commerce Court case to interpret this jurisdiction. *Cf.*, also, p. 587, *supra*.

Second, cases brought to enjoin, set aside, annul or suspend, in whole or in part, any order of the Commission.

Third, all proceedings on appeal under the Elkins amendments of 1903 with reference to rebates or departure from the published tariffs.

Fourth, all proceedings concerning the enforcement of the law in respect of publicity of accounts, the furnishing of facilities, or compulsion in the movement of traffic.

Proceedings in the first class above mentioned, for enforcement of orders of the Commission, remained practically unchanged in form, except that they were to be prosecuted in the Commerce Court instead of in the ordinary circuit courts. Cases of the second sort, wherein the carrier sought to enjoin or set aside orders of the Commission, were somewhat modified in procedure. The Administration bill provided that the Commerce Court should not issue injunctions, except in cases where irreparable damage would follow. In this regard, the Senate succeeded in somewhat amplifying judicial control. Five days' preliminary notice to the Commission, secured in 1906 after a bitter contest, was now cut down to three days; and the full court might extend the temporary stay of sixty days granted by a single judge, over the entire period necessary for final decision by the Supreme Court. With this exception, the new law held all the ground gained by the Hepburn Act as judicially interpreted in the Illinois Central case.

The principal criticism which may be directed against the Commerce Court, as thus organized, is that, instead of being an unchanging body of judges, becoming expert in the details of transportation by long experience, its membership must change year by year. Fortunately, at the outset the court was favored by the appointment, as presiding justice, of the Chairman of the Interstate Commerce Commission; but it seems likely that the lack of experience and technical knowledge in this ever-changing body may render it an obstruction rather than an assistance in fixing the responsibility for the settlement of these important cases. Specialization ought to be as beneficial here as in all other departments of government. It is a pity that the original plan of a permanent court should finally have been changed, through the insistence of the carriers' representatives, to a tribunal, each of whose members no sooner becomes proficient in the details of his work than he is marked for transfer to other fields of activity.

Next to the creation of the Commerce Court, the most important change in procedure introduced in 1910 was the transfer of the task of prosecuting suits on appeal cases from the Interstate Commerce Commission to the Federal Department of Justice. The confusion of governmental powers in the past, through permitting the Commission to prosecute cases in the Federal courts in which it already had an interest, has already been described. It was obviously illogical that a body having once rendered an opinion should then appear in court in defence of its own order. The jealousy of the Department of Justice in this regard was probably responsible also for the change effected in the law. The amendment of 1910 provides that hereafter all cases and proceedings, either in the Commerce Court or the Supreme Court, shall be brought in the name of the United States under the charge and control of the Attorney-General. It was provided also that the Commission or "any party or parties in interest" might appear of their own motion and as of right, and might be represented by counsel. Communities, associations, or individuals interested in the controversy were authorized to intervene, and the Attorney-General was forbidden to discontinue any proceedings over the objection of such parties in interest.[1] This apparently reasonable procedure was authorized after vehement protest of shippers against the original administration program. The Senate objected to it on the ground that it "would introduce intolerable confusion in legal proceedings and subordinate the general interests of all the people to the selfish concerns of one or more

[1] 191 Fed. Rep., 37, first interprets this clause. P. 587, *infra*.

parties." And the Commission insisted throughout that it must participate in such suits, else no competent parties would be at hand to guide the prosecution in complicated proceedings.

Several provisions in the law were aimed at specific abuses which had been revealed in the course of prosecutions under the criminal provisions of the Act. The original law provided for the posting of tariffs in public places, in order that shippers might inform themselves as to the scheduled rates. But the possibilities of concealment of special favors, as well as the mere mechanical difficulty of ascertaining the facts in so complicated a maze of descriptions and rules with all sorts of exceptions, made it necessary that the shipper should rely upon information obtained from the agent. Nor could the shipper recover for losses incurred through misquotation of the rate by this agent inasmuch as the carriers must collect according to the tariff, under severe penalties for departure therefrom. Even a mistake by the agent in quoting the wrong rate did not permit of recovery. The new law met this contingency by the requirement that the railroad should quote the rate upon written request; and should be liable to a penalty of $250 for mis-statement from which loss to the shipper should result. The requirement that both the request and the reply as to rates should be written, it was hoped, would facilitate detection of rebating in the future. Another clause added a penalty of $1000 and made it a misdemeanor for any carrier or its agent to disclose information concerning either the route or destination of any shipment, when such information might be used to the injury of a competing shipper. Solicitation of such information was also penalized. The abuse against which this provision of law was directed is well illustrated in the prosecution of the so-called Powder Trust in 1911. It appeared in one instance that a freight agent had been paid from $15 to $18 a month for furnishing weekly statements of the shipments, with addresses of consignees, made by a competing concern in Chattanooga.[1] Such

[1] *Quarterly Journal of Economics*, XXVI, 1912, p. 444.

outrageous espionage, long practised by the Standard Oil Company, it is to be hoped will be eliminated in future by this provision of law.

Certain details of the act may be dismissed with mere mention. The scope of regulation was extended to include telegraph, telephone, and cable companies. The Commission was specifically authorized to establish and enforce reasonable classification of freight. Such authority, to be sure, had been continuously exercised for years; but this clause put it beyond dispute. A leaf was taken from the experience before the Supreme Court in interpretation of the authority over through routes and joint rates in the "Portland Gateway" case, described in the preceding chapter. Other "reasonable or satisfactory routes" were more specifically defined; although the complicated phraseology adopted was of doubtful value. It may well be that the clause, under judicial interpretation, limited rather than amplified the Commission's power as compared with the law of 1906. But the added requirement that every carrier must provide reasonable facilities for the operation of through routes, proper rules for the interchange of cars, etc., was bound to promote the efficiency of through business. The experience in the "Orange Routing" cases, also, brought about a clear affirmation in the new statute of the right of a shipper to designate the route which he preferred for shipment over connecting lines. The shipper might also demand a bill of lading conformable to his instructions. Whether this freedom of choice to the shipper, with the incidental assumption of responsibility for all consequences, regardless of strikes, blockades, or acts of God, will work to his advantage in the long run remains to be seen. He may probably rely upon strict enforcement of the so-called Carmack amendment of 1906, which makes the initial carrier liable for damage, even if it occurs off its own line. And, finally, among the minor changes in 1910 was the authorization of the Commission to institute inquiries upon its own initiative. Such power had frequently been exercised;

THE ACT OF 1910

but in the enactment of the Hepburn Act four years before, certain verbal inconsistencies were introduced into Section 15. It was deemed best to remedy this error by complete authorization to undertake investigations either with or without complaint.[1]

In place of regulation of the issues of stocks and bonds by Federal authority, as pledged in the political platforms, the almost unanimous opposition in the Senate to such a plan, brought about the substitution of a Railroad Securities Commission to investigate the subject. This, after all, was probably wise; inasmuch as many details as to conflicting state and Federal powers in such matters, were yet to be determined judicially. Moreover, the plans proposed, as it appeared, were so complicated that their adoption might result in the validation of all capitalization then outstanding without reference to its real value. The question certainly merited further investigation at the hands of experts.

Under the authority above mentioned, the President appointed an able although distinctly conservative commission, headed by President Hadley of Yale University. This body rendered its report in November, 1911.[2] The document was concise, cogent in reasoning (with the exceptions noted below), wise in its general conclusions and eminently conciliatory in spirit. It was obviously intended to promote good relations between the government and the carriers. The dominant note was complete publicity as a corrective for all financial abuses of the time. The adequacy of this remedy was probably exaggerated. The wise accounting provisions of the Acts of 1906–1910 [3] were certainly already far-reaching in effect. The Securities Commission proposed, however, that they be elaborated to cover fully all phases both of promotion and of subsequent finance.

[1] *Cf.* p. 537, *supra.*
[2] Report of the Railroad Securities Commission, Nov. 1, 1911.
[3] Page 515, *supra.*

Not less important and wise than the insistence upon financial publicity, was the recommendation that, until the Supreme Court had clearly defined the relations between Federal and state authority, the Federal government should refrain from attempting to regulate the issue of securities. Too many difficult legal complications remained to be cleared up.

There certainly should have been a more enthusiastic commendation of the efforts of states like Massachusetts, Wisconsin, Texas and New York to cope with their local problems of financial control.[1] The apparent absence of a due appreciation of the importance of the work of the various public service commissions all over the country may perhaps be accounted for on the ground that it lay outside the scope of the work of a purely Federal commission. Yet a word of encouragement to these state administrations would have done something to offset the rather negative character of its conclusions. Someone must exercise financial control. If inadvisable for the Federal government to undertake it at this time, as might well be, then it was important to emphasize the fact that the states must do it as best they could. On the other hand, the recommendations concerning physical valuation as an element in rate regulation were sufficiently progressive to impart an aspect of judicial balance and general fairness to the report as a whole.

Two specific conclusions of the securities commission, however, were surely open to debate. One was the contention that little relation obtains between capitalization and rates. The statement is, of course, largely true; but like most generalizations of the sort fails to state the whole truth. It is probably absolutely true as to *particular* rates. No one would claim for a moment that the heavily capitalized Wabash, operating in trunk line territory alongside the Pennsylvania system, could charge any higher rates because of its financial disabilities.

[1] These will be fully described in our second volume in connection with stockwatering, valuation and allied financial problems.

THE ACT OF 1910

Rather the reverse. But while true of particular rates, capitalization does exert an *indirect* but nevertheless a very appreciable influence upon the *general* level of rates. For this point I have argued elsewhere at some length.[1] Was it surprising that the pressure for advanced rates in 1910–1911 in trunk line territory should come from the heavily capitalized New York Central, with substantial aid and comfort from the Erie? Was it a mere coincidence that the Lackawanna road, with its stock quoted above $500, was a less prominent factor in the agitation than some of its neighbors? True enough, no direct relation between rates and capitalization exists; but that a positive incentive to higher charges in general may be found in the need of supporting a large capitalization seems reasonably clear in the light of experience. This point was certainly neglected or glossed over in the report.

A most debatable and, as I hold it, dangerous proposition in this report was the proposed abolition of the "dollar mark" upon capital stock. However desirable it might be for mining companies and the lesser industrials, as in Germany, to do away with any stated par value for share capital in order to disabuse the public mind of its purely artificial character, the proposition is quite different when applied to an industry like a railroad. There is all the difference in fact between purely private and competitive conditions of a more or less speculative character, and those under which monopoly privileges are conferred by gift of the public. Space does not permit a criticism of this proposition in detail. I have elsewhere discussed it more at length.[2] Many objections occur at once, none of them mentioned in this report which, almost jauntily, as it seems, proposed to revolutionize all of our customary habits of financial thought. Among these objections there is the fact that abolition of par value removes the restraint upon the promoter or management, for liability to creditors in case of part-paid shares. The experience

---
[1] Volume II, in the chapter on Valuation.
[2] Volume II, in the chapter on Capital Stock.

of the Asphalt Company of America is illuminating in this regard. May we trust mere publicity to provide corresponding safeguards for honest promotion with this liability removed? Then again, how about the issue of stock in exchange for property acquired, as had frequently occurred in the course of railway consolidation? Was it immaterial whether the absorbing company put out 500,000 "participating shares," with a market value of $100 each, or twice that number of "certificates of participation" commanding half that figure per unit in exchange for the property acquired? And still further, there is the inevitable effect upon speculation. One of the primary needs of the time was to effect a separation of our common carriers from Wall Street influence. Did it make no difference whether the Southern Railway "participating shares" were traded in around $25; or those of the Louisville & Nashville commanded a price of $150? Low quotations always offer a great stimulus to speculative manipulation — as any student of Rock Island affairs must concede. To do away with par, which means permission to emit, without reproach, at any figure "below par" — how hard it is, indeed, to get rid of that conception of some standard of normality — could not but exert a malign influence. And then, finally, over and above all other considerations there was the need of some general standard of comparison for all sorts of purposes — some base from which to judge of normality. The proposal to wipe out all such standards, with the mere warning to public and investors alike to beware, seemed like a step backward.

This brings us to the insistence of the commission upon the need of the railroads for more capital for development; and the difficulty of financing new enterprises under regulative provisions of law, such as the prohibition of the issue of shares at a discount. Massachusetts had recently passed through an experience of probably excessive regulation. But simple modifications of its anti-stockwatering laws seemed to have solved the difficulty. Of course the developmental problems of the West and South are quite different from those of New England. Yet there was the experience of Texas to fall back upon. Complaint had been made, of course, especially by the Gould roads, of the insufficiency of capital for new work. But the growth of mileage seemed, nevertheless, to compare not unfavorably with progress in other states. Were the Gould roads, for example, any better off in other states where greater liberality of laws prevails? The fact was that much new construction and improvement remained to be done all over the country, as this report duly emphasized; but much of it would probably have to be done by companies already in the field. Not many new steam railroad companies are now needed even in the West. It must be confessed that the recently authorized extension of the Grand Trunk Railway into the heart of New England shows how persistent is the demand for new roads even in the East. But whoever may build, let them learn the lesson, so often forgotten, that honest management and conservative financing, to the end that solid credit be first established, has far more to do with facilitating development than non-interference by law. This was probably a time when encouragement to the railroads in a period of stress should properly be given. But let it not be forgotten that good faith to the public and to stockholders, together with prudent financing, must be the primary source of credit.

Many admirable features of this report deserve mention, did space permit. The clear exposition of the distinction between stocks and bonds, and especially the discussion of intercorporate financing, occupied a prominent place. The document promised to play a large part in the determination of governmental policy in future. It well merited the most careful perusal by legislators, financiers and economists. In the nature of things so conservative a document could never hope for a popular reception. But many of its financial platitudes were probably in need of reiteration for the good, both of the carriers and the public.

The Hepburn Act of 1906, despite the agitation over its enactment in Congress, "came in like a lion and went out like a lamb," imitating thereby the month of March in which its crucial changes were effected. In the end it proved to be a much less drastic measure than the railroads feared. This Mann-Elkins law, four years later, on the other hand, introduced by the presidential bill as a merely supplementary piece of legislation,[1] "rounding out the Roosevelt policies," emerged from Congress really radical in character. Every change made was "progressive"; and yet there was little public interest manifested on either side. No publicity campaign was carried on by the carriers. No extended discussion took place in the press. There were several reasons for this contrast. It is partly true, as one writer has suggested, that "the marrow had already been extracted from railroad regulation as a political issue; and that it had become merely a bone of contention in a factional strife." Moreover, the fundamental principle of effective governmental regulation had been indisputably affirmed in 1906. The Act of 1910 had for its purpose a firmer intrenchment of the position already occupied. Debate centred largely upon uninteresting technical questions. The broader issues were relegated to second place. Even the carriers on their part were extremely reserved in stating their position. It was conceded on all sides that the less public opinion in general was aroused, the lighter would be the sentence passed upon the prisoners at bar. It is difficult to determine in how far the marked advance made in this statute was due to contemporary happenings, like the general advances of freight rates, the Illinois Central scandals and the like; or to a deep-seated conviction on the part of the progressive element in Congress. But that the law, as a whole, was a surprise in the end even to its proponents is beyond doubt.

A word may be added concerning the omissions in the

[1] *Cf.* Senator La Follette's characterization of it. Footnote, p. 559, *supra*.

Mann-Elkins law. The most important was the elimination of the administration plan for authorizing agreements between carriers as to rates, subject to supervision by the Commission. The Republican platform had definitely promised relief of this sort to the railroads. The Democratic party had somewhat equivocally promised an amendment of the law prohibiting pooling "to make it unlawful, unless approved by the Commission." The plan, however, met with persistent opposition on all sides, largely on the ground that it conflicted with the Sherman Anti-Trust law. Other details which fell by the way concerned proposals to extend jurisdiction over water carriers on inland waterways.[1] Whether the Commission might exercise any control over those which formed parties to a through line still remained an open question.[2] And then at the last there was the omission of Congress to deal with the question of fixing minimum rates or differentials between rates. This was responsible, as will shortly appear, for much of the difficulty encountered in the application of the long and short haul clause to the transcontinental rate problem.

[1] The National Waterways Commission Report of 1912 urged this strongly. And the attempts in connection with fixing the tolls for the Panama Canal in the same year, to prohibit all railway ownership or interest in coastwise steamships, were significant of legislation yet to come. *Cf.* pp. 591 and 638, *infra.*
[2] *Cf.* the Goodrich Transit Co. case. Page 586, *infra.*

CHAPTER XVIII

THE COMMERCE COURT: THE FREIGHT RATE ADVANCES OF 1910

The Commerce Court docket, 581. — The Commerce Court in Congress, 582. — Supreme Court opinions concerning it, 583. — Legal v. economic decisions, 586. — Law points decided, 586. — The Maximum (Cincinnati) Freight Rate case revived, 588. — Real conflict over economic issues, 590. — The Louisville & Nashville case, 590. — The California Lemon case, 592. — Broad v. narrow court review once more, 593. The freight rate advances of 1910, 594. — Their causes examined, 595. — Weakness of the railroad presentation, 596. — Operating expenses and wages higher, 597. — The argument in rebuttal, 598. — "Scientific management," 598. — The Commission decides adversely, 599.

THE three vital features of the Mann-Elkins law of 1910 were: the creation of the Commerce Court, for the purpose of expediting the judicial review of cases appealed from the Interstate Commerce Commission; the grant of power to suspend rate advances pending examination as to their reasonableness; and the rehabilitation of the long and short haul clause. The law was passed on June 18, 1910. Within the brief period of two years it successfully emerged from a supreme test respecting rate advances; enough experience had already been had with the new Commerce Court to warrant an opinion as to its merits as a special tribunal for the review of transportation decisions; and, finally, an opinion by the Interstate Commerce Commission was rendered, and is at this writing under review by the Supreme Court of the United States, in the most important case ever likely to arise under the long and short haul clause. Predictions were freely made in 1910 that certain shortcomings in the revised law, particularly the failure to grant control over minimum rates and the establishment of differentials between rates, would soon have to be remedied. Experience promptly threw light upon these questions also.

The present is thus an opportune time to review the entire situation respecting Federal railroad regulation.

When the Commerce Court was created, fears were entertained that there would not be enough business to employ its time. This prediction was far from being realized, judging by the record of the first year.[1] Including thirty-six cases transferred to it from the various Federal circuit courts, a total of fifty-seven suits were placed upon its docket up to December 20, 1911. Fifty-four of these cases directly concerned orders of the Interstate Commerce Commission, the large majority — forty-four — being suits brought by carriers to set aside such orders. The Commission appealed to the court but once for enforcement of its mandates, the remaining nine cases being appeals of shippers for relief. But a number of these suits were withdrawn or dismissed, or else lay outside the class of what may fairly be called contested cases. Only thirty-eight of them were in reality of significance as throwing light upon the function of the court as an appellate tribunal, standing between the Interstate Commerce Commission and the Supreme Court of the United States. Thirty of these were disposed of up to December 20, 1911. That the court took itself seriously as a check upon, rather than a coördinate body with the Commission, was evidenced by the fact that restraining orders or final decrees in favor of the railroads and against the shippers and the Commission were issued in all but three really important cases out of the entire thirty. And even of these three cases the Commerce Court held two to be outside its jurisdiction, while in the third the carriers had already joined in the view of the Commission, so that there was really no contest.[2]

[1] Interstate Commerce Commission, Annual Report 1911, pp. 53, 57, 59 and 206.
[2] Since this time a number of decisions have been rendered, on the whole more favorably to the Commission. Notably in the Willamette lumber case, for example, it was fully upheld: no. 59, April session, 1912;

A bitter campaign for the abolition of the Commerce Court, as a result of the tendency of its decisions, was waged in Congress during the session of 1911–1912. The House of Representatives, in response to popular feeling, promptly passed a bill abolishing it forthwith, the vote standing 120 to 49, with many Republicans joining the Democrats in its condemnation. A sharp contest was precipitated in the Senate over "the legislative recall of judges," as the matter was not inaptly termed. The Administration, through the Attorney-General, ably defended the imperilled court.[1] Evidence was adduced to show that the Commission had been sustained in a larger proportion of cases than under the old circuit court system;[2] that injunctions had not issued with greater freedom than formerly and that none of them turned upon questions of fact; and, finally, that the Administration plan had been very much more expeditious. But so far as Congress was concerned this evidence seems not to have been convincing. The Senate soon followed the House of Representatives, by a vote of thirty-six to twenty-three defeating an amendment to the Legislative, Executive and Judicial Appropriation Bill that made provision for further maintenance of the court. So strong was the feeling that only by a close vote was an amendment prevented which sought to legislate the justices out of office as well as out of the Commerce Court. For without such provision, of course, they would, under the law of 1910, be reassigned to service in the circuit courts, from which most of them were drawn. The final conference agreement between the two houses, appended to the appropriation bill above mentioned, definitely abolished

and also concerning southern rates: no. 40, February session, 1912. In June several petitions were dismissed for lack of jurisdiction. In the Shreveport case, notable as involving conflict of Federal and state authority, the Commission's order was enjoined in June on the ground of confiscation of property.

[1] 62nd Cong., 2nd sess., House Rep., no. 472: Hearings on H. R. 1907–1908 before the House Committee on Interstate Commerce, March 14, 1912: Hearings on H. R. 25596 and 25572, July–August, 1912, pp. 1–298.

[2] *Cf.* p. 460, *supra.*

the court, but followed the House plan of reassignment of the justices to duty in the circuit courts. This bill was twice vetoed by the President; but the second time, it failed of re-passage in the Senate over his veto by a narrow margin. In the House the popular view was expressed by re-passing the abolition measure by a vote of 149 to 53. These details are highly significant as indicating the impatience of Congress with any attempt at interference with the positive program of administrative control of railroads decreed in 1906–1910. The fate of the court then rested in the hands of the President, its original sponsor. A delicate situation, concerning the relations between Congress and the executive in the matter of legislative "riders" to appropriation bills, resulted. Whether such summary proceedings as those initiated by Congress were warranted by the facts, depended upon the final disposition of the contested cases by the Supreme Court, before which tribunal most of them were then pending on appeal. If it appeared that the court had in reality, as alleged, sought to usurp powers legitimately exercised by the Commission, the case for abolition would be greatly strengthened. But in any event, the certainty of a presidential veto of any law affecting this pet project of the Administration rendered the attack upon the Commerce Court for the time being abortive. As the matter was finally left, Congress acceded to the President's wishes, continuing the appropriation for maintenance of the court until March 4, 1913. What will happen in the meantime after Congress reassembles, remains to be seen.

The determination of the proper scope and function of judicial review was substantially forwarded by several decisions of the Supreme Court of the United States in June, 1912. The general effect of these was substantially to curtail the overweening ambition of the Commerce Court as an intermediate judicial body. Following the Goodrich Transit Company opinion[1] which first reversed the Commerce Court, all three of

[1] Discussed *infra*, p. 586.

these latest opinions on appeal again favored the Interstate Commerce Commission as against its judicial reviewer. In two instances, the assumed jurisdiction of the new court was denied; while in the third, although jurisdiction was recognized, its decision was reversed. Because of their bearing upon subsequent developments, a brief review of these cases may not be out of place.

The Proctor and Gamble Company, well-known soap manufacturers, had complained of certain regulations concerning demurrage upon their tank cars. The Commission upheld the carriers, affirming that their rules were proper and lawful. The complainants thereupon appealed to the Commerce Court, which claimed jurisdiction to award pecuniary relief, although in this instance it declined so to do, on the ground that the Commission had rightfully decided the matter in the first instance. Appeal then followed to the Supreme Court, with the odd circumstance that the Commission and the railways joined issue against the shippers. The question was largely a legal one, involving definition of the jurisdiction of the new tribunal. The Supreme Court in this instance,[1] — and, it may be added, in the Cincinnati Freight Bureau case,[2] which similarly involved the relative powers of the court and the Commission, — unanimously affirmed the right of the Commission to decide such matters of fact finally.

To recognize the existence in the court below [the Commerce Court] of the power which it deemed it possessed, would result in frustrating the legislative public policy which led to the adoption of the act. The act creating the Commerce Court was intended to be but a part of the existing system for the regulation of interstate commerce. . . . It was not intended to destroy the existing machinery or method of regulation, but to cause it to be more efficient. . . . Wholly irrespective of the general considerations stated, we think the conclusion of the [Commerce] Court, as to its possession of jurisdiction over the subject referred to, was clearly repugnant in other respects to the express terms of the act.

[1] 32 Supreme Court Rep., **761.**
[2] 188 Fed. Rep., 242. At p. 588, *infra.*

THE COMMERCE COURT 585

Such a pronouncement, following the line of decisions headed by the Illinois Central Car Distribution case,[1] must make for concentration of responsibility and more effective regulation in the years to come.

The third decision of the Supreme Court, above referred to, was known as the "Restrictive Rate case."[2] Might railway companies — the Baltimore & Ohio and others — charge a different rate for the carriage of coal to railways than to other shippers, the coal being intended for the use of the railways as fuel? In this instance the Commission forbade the practice. Its order was then promptly enjoined by the Commerce Court. Jurisdiction of the Commerce Court was conceded by the Supreme Court in this instance also, but its opinion was again flatly reversed. The issue at bottom was really one of value of service as against cost of service in the determination of reasonable rates. Obviously the cost of carrying railway-fuel coal between two given points is practically the same as that of carrying commercial coal. The Commission, supported now by the Supreme Court in frowning upon any difference in the charge, was thus according priority to this consideration of cost. The view of the Commerce Court, which was here reversed, tended, on the other hand, to emphasize such facts as that the two sorts of coal were intended for different purposes and did not come in competition with one another as to price. In other words, value of service — what the traffic would bear — was given greater weight than mere considerations of cost. The Supreme Court declined to accept this view, preferring to regard transportation as a matter of physical carriage of goods, rather than to look beyond this essential service "to the greater or less inducement to seek the service" — that is to say, to regard its commercial aspects.

The last of this batch of Supreme Court decisions was mainly a question at law, namely the right of the Commerce Court to enjoin the enforcement of an order of the Commission

[1] P. 538, *supra*.   [2] 32 Supreme Court Rep., 742.

concerning certain allowances for lighterage and terminal service on sugar in New York harbor.[1] The judicial poise of the Supreme Court was here evidenced in its affirmation of the right of the Commerce Court to issue the injunction. The plain purpose of the law in setting up this intermediate tribunal as a safeguard against abuse of administrative authority was given effect; but it was ordered, nevertheless, that the case be remanded, to be disposed of on its merits before the Interstate Commerce Commission, the forum selected by Congress for that purpose.

The grist of cases appealed to the Commerce Court may profitably be divided for discussion into two groups, namely, those which clearly concerned questions of law and those in which matters of fact, or economic conclusions based thereon, were primarily at stake. The first group of purely law cases need detain us but briefly. There could be little doubt about the necessity of judicial review of law findings of the Commission. The best illustration is afforded by the first decision of the Commerce Court to be reviewed by the Supreme Court of the United States.[2] Inland water carriers were not placed under the jurisdiction of the Act to Regulate Commerce by the Mann-Elkins amendments of 1910, except in so far as they were joined in control with railroads or might enter into arrangements for continuous shipments with carriers by land. But the Commission, having always required railroads to file accounts covering both their local and interstate business, called upon the carriers on the Great Lakes to render similar statements as to their entire traffic, whether subject to Federal control or not. This the water lines refused to do. The Commerce Court, in overruling the Commission, did not question the power of Congress to require such accounts, but held that it was its intention to confine publicity to that portion of the lake traffic over which the jurisdiction of the Commission actually

[1] 32 Supreme Court Rep., 817.
[2] *Goodrich Transit Company v. I.C.C.*; Commerce Court, nos. 21–24, April term, 1911. Decided by the Supreme Court, April 1, 1912; 32 Supreme Court Rep., 436; 190 Fed. Rep., 943.

THE COMMERCE COURT 587

extended. It thus appears that the law point was doubly important, inasmuch as its determination affected not alone the enforcement of publicity for water lines but also of all carriers by land, so far as their intrastate business was concerned. Fortunately the Supreme Court, in sustaining the Commission, held that the Commerce Court had erred in confusing "knowledge" of intrastate business with its "regulation." As to the former, the authority of the Commission was fully upheld. This and the important question upon which the entire Intermountain rate controversy rested, namely, as to the authority of the Commission to prescribe relativity of rates,[1] were the most important points of law at first raised before the new tribunal. Other legal questions decided by the Commerce Court — generally in favor of the railroads, be it observed — were: whether reparation might be claimed for an unreasonable rate when the burden had been already passed on to the consumer;[2] whether the Nashville Grain Exchange might lawfully intervene in proceedings before the Commission under the liberal terms of the law of 1910;[3] whether "separately established rates" applied by a carrier to through traffic when there is a through rate but no joint rate are matters of interstate commerce or not;[4] as to the limitations by law of the right of carriers to refund overcharges to shippers;[5] and whether the Union Stockyards Company was a common carrier engaged in interstate commerce, and thus subject to control as to preferential treatment of shippers.[6] However these cases might be finally decided by the court of last resort, there could be no conflict of powers between the Commerce Court and the Commission in regard to such matters of law. The real bone of contention between the two bodies — administrative and judicial, respectively — was the question of their respective powers outside the field of law.

[1] Cf. p. 624, infra.
[2] 193 Fed. Rep., 678.
[3] 191 Fed. Rep., 37.
[4] 195 Fed. Rep., 968.
[5] 193 Fed. Rep., 667.
[6] 192 Fed. Rep., 330.

Before leaving the disputes over law points, we may profitably consider one further case, important because of its bearing upon the determination of reasonable rates. This occurred in 1911 through a revival of the old Maximum (Cincinnati) Freight Rate case of 1896.[1] It will be recalled that this involved the relative rates to southern centres from eastern and middle western cities.[2] In the original case in 1894, the Commission held that the rates from Cincinnati were too high by comparison with the rates from New York; ordering those for first-class freight, for example, to be reduced from seventy-six cents to sixty cents per hundred pounds. The Supreme Court directed a dismissal of the bill of complaint, on the ground that the Commission had no authority to establish rates for the future. This defect in the law being remedied by the amendment of 1906, the Commission, upon a new complaint, made a second order in 1910. This differed from its earlier decision in prescribing a reduction of the rate from Cincinnati from seventy-six cents to only seventy cents, whereas the first decision had ordered it reduced to sixty cents per hundred pounds. The Cincinnati shippers, not content with this reduction, then promptly appealed to the Commerce Court for a review of the case. The proceeding was unique, therefore, in that the appeal to the Commerce Court was taken, not by the carriers but by shippers who complained that the rates *established by the Commission were too high*. The Commerce Court in sustaining the order of the Commission, therefore, in reality acted in favor of the railroads, being thereby consistent with its general attitude of conservatism. But its right to take cognizance of such questions was denied by the Supreme Court. Thus, in all probability, this famous and protracted litigation was brought to a close.

The specific law point in this Cincinnati case was as to whether the reasonableness of a rate should be determined in the light solely of its effect upon the particular carrier con-

[1] 32 Supreme Court Rep., 769.   [2] Pp. 248 and 391, *supra*.

cerned; or whether the result for other competing lines and for the entire territory served, should also be taken into consideration. The Cincinnati Southern Railroad extended as a short and direct route 336 miles due south to Chattanooga. It was neither expensive to construct, to maintain or to operate. It was the first in the field; having been constructed by the city of Cincinnati to reach the southern markets. It was not burdened by unremunerative branch lines. Its net earnings amounted to over forty per cent. upon the capital stock. Other competing railroads between the same points were one-third longer and were otherwise burdened by the necessity of maintaining unprofitable branches. These other roads could not be so economically operated. But they had voluntarily entered the field in competition *after* this direct line was constructed, and they had elected to continue therein. The rates established, however, for the Cincinnati Southern, — the short line, — naturally fixed the rates at which these others had to participate in the traffic. At the rate of seventy cents, prescribed in this second order of the Commission, all the carriers concerned could make a living. The short line alone, presumably, could have endured the rate of sixty cents as prescribed at first. Was it lawful, however, to decide a complaint preferred against a particular most-favored railroad by a city which built it to attain a certain object, upon the basis of the effect of such rates, not upon this road but upon others subsequently built and less fortunately situated? To do so would, of course, enable the most-favored carrier to prosper exceedingly; even more so than it did then. But these higher rates would, most unfortunately, thwart the very purpose animating its construction. The Commission, sustained by the majority of the Commerce Court, adopted the latter view.[1] A dissenting minority, on the other hand, presented strongly the opinion that under such special circumstances, in the determi-

[1] Other cases similarly decided are as follows: 9 I.C.C. Rep., 382; 15 *Idem*, 376 and 555.

nation as to reasonableness, no right existed for considering the effect of a rate upon other roads than the particular one against which the complaint lay. The Supreme Court in affirming the sole authority of the Commission to pass upon such issues, nevertheless, left this detail concerning the determination of reasonableness of rates for possible reargument in future.

Attention may be now directed to the controversy as to the seat of authority, not over law points, but concerning distinctly economic issues. A typical case before the Commerce Court concerned rates from New Orleans to several

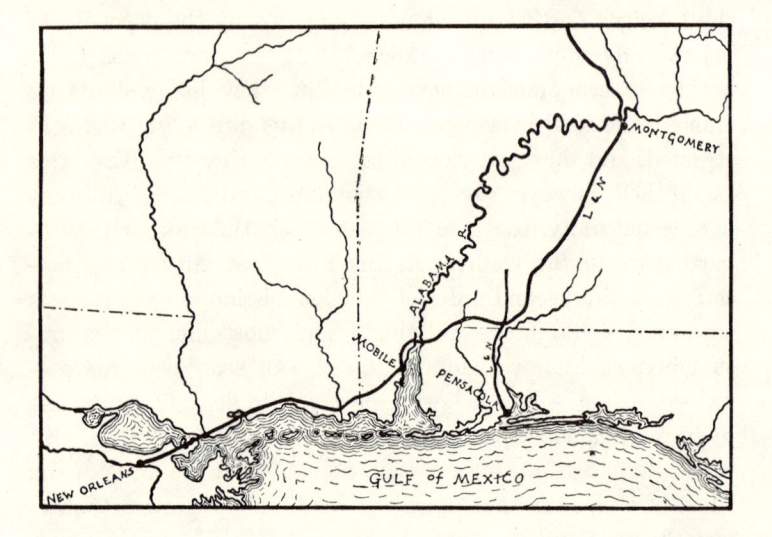

competing cities on the line of the Louisville & Nashville Railroad.[1] An interesting phase of local discrimination appeared. The accompanying map discloses the situation. Normally the through rate from New Orleans to Montgomery (the long-distance point) would be less than the sum of the

[1] 195 Fed. Rep., 541, *L. & N. R. R. v. I.C.C.* In this case there was no dispute as to facts, but only as to the conclusion to be drawn therefrom. A straight difference on points of fact was raised in the Pacific Coast Switching cases (188 Fed. Rep., 229). The dissenting opinion as to usurpation of the rights of the Commission is significant.

local rates from New Orleans to Mobile (the intermediate point) and then from Mobile on to Montgomery. This would conform to the general rule, which is based on the simple fact that through rates, being competitive, are usually forced below the level of local charges, commonly unaffected by such competition. In this case the situation was reversed. Water competition affected the local rates, both into Mobile from New Orleans by sea on the one side, and then up the Alabama to Montgomery by river steamer on the other. But such water competition did not apply to the through rate, probably because through shipment by water would necessitate a transfer *en route* from a gulf steamer to a river boat at Mobile. Thus in this case it came about that local competition was keener than the rivalry as to through traffic. The Louisville & Nashville, nevertheless, had secured the bulk of the business to Mobile by reason of the low local rates by rail which had been in effect for many years, even after practical elimination of the water lines. The situation was certainly anomalous, from the viewpoint of cost of service by rail alone; in that the freight rate was higher on goods sent to Montgomery direct than when shipped on a combination of local rates on Mobile. This situation, it is apparent, enabled Mobile jobbers to buy goods in New Orleans and actually lay them down in Montgomery for less than the freight charges to the Montgomery dealers who were on the spot. The same situation prevailed at Pensacola.

The immediate cause of dispute was the promulgation by the Commission in 1907, under the new powers conferred by the Hepburn Act, of a rule that through rates must not exceed the combination of locals between the same points. To comply with this rule, the Louisville & Nashville, in this instance, faced the alternative either of reducing the through rate from New Orleans to Montgomery to the sum of its local charges or else of raising one or both of the latter. The railroad naturally chose the latter course — now enabled to do so with safety as the boat lines had long since been put out of business. It advanced its local rates from New Orleans to Mobile sufficiently to make the new combination of local charges equal the through rate to Montgomery. The Commission, on complaint of Montgomery, suspended this advance,—seeking to compel the railroad to even things up, not by advance of the local charges but by a reduction of the through rate. This, it is obvious, would relieve Montgomery of the discrimination as against Mobile of which it complained. As to none of the facts above outlined, was there dispute between the court and the Commission. The controversy turned solely upon which of the two remedies should be chosen to meet the situation. Were the through rates unreasonably high? This was the Commission's contention. If so, equalization should be attained by their reduction. Or, on the other hand, were the local rates unreasonably low? If so, they might be evened upward with propriety. This was the contention of the Commerce Court, leading it to set aside the order of the Commission. Which was the body competent to pass upon such an issue? The Supreme Court had to be called upon to decide. And in the meantime there was the same old story of delay, while irreparable loss to shippers went on.

In another instance,—the California lemon case,—[1] the issue was even more sharply drawn between the Commission and the Commerce Court. The latter, it was averred, not even content to draw its own conclusions in matters of fact, had made an "attempt to look into the mind of the Commission for the purpose of ascertaining the reasons on which its order was based." The case dated from 1909, when the blanket rate from the entire territory east of the Rocky mountains was advanced by the railroads from $1.00 to $1.15. This action followed the imposition of a high protective duty on lemons in the Payne-Aldrich tariff. After careful investigation the Commission, reviewing the whole matter of rates upon citrus

[1] 190 Fed. Rep., 591. Second opinion in 22 I.C.C. Rep., 149.

fruits, ordered the lemon rate to be reduced once more to $1.00. Appeal was promptly taken to the Commerce Court, which set aside the order as beyond the scope of authority delegated by Congress. The court held that the Commission had sought so to adjust rates as to afford protection to the California lemon industry against foreign competition, especially from the growers in Sicily; in place of confining its attention to the "intrinsic reasonableness" of the transportation charge. The gage thus thrown down was promptly taken up by the Commission in a second opinion, rendered within two months of the injunction granted by the Commerce Court. This time it exhaustively considered all phases of the cost and manner of transportation for oranges and lemons and re-affirmed its opinion that the rate of one dollar per hundred pounds was reasonable. At this writing the matter rests there. What the Commerce Court will do, remains to be seen. The case, as re-stated by the Commission, is masterly in its discussion of the responsibilities laid upon it by the law. "Is the country to be treated as a whole for commercial purposes, or shall it be infinitely divided?"

The Intermountain Rate cases, discussed in the next chapter as a phase of the long and short haul question, illustrate even more clearly these conflicts between the court and the Commission on matters of economics. But they introduced no new legal technicalities. They merely emphasized the critical nature of the controversy, so far as it concerned the larger constitutional question of separation of powers between the three main branches of our government.

The situation, as revealed by these typical cases, reduced itself, in brief, to this: it was the same old question of broad *versus* narrow court review all over again. The Commerce Court held it to be its proper function, as a court of law, to review in the broadest way all cases which came before it on appeal. The Commission, on the other hand, maintained that not only all matters of fact, but all inferences as to economic facts, of necessity lay solely within the range of its own authority. And it was certainly true that, without some such limitation upon the right of review, the Commission might about as well have retired from the field of regulation entirely, and contented itself with enforcing the safety appliance laws, collecting statistics and serving as a general publicity office.[1] Fortunately the situation promised to be saved by the line of Supreme Court decisions flowing from the Illinois Central case.[2] The making of a rate for the future being a legislative and not a judicial function, the power to determine that a particular rate was or was not reasonable for the future, or that a particular discrimination was or was not undue, was a discretionary legislative power which could not be reviewed by the judiciary. If the Supreme Court in due time applied this reasoning to these later cases, the Commerce Court might confidently be expected to take its proper place in the Federal scheme of things. Until it was forced to do so, much of the railroad legislation of recent years would fail to ensure that full measure of certainty and promptitude of relief to which the country was entitled, and which it was bound to have.

The decision of the Interstate Commerce Commission in 1910 in the matter of freight rate advances [3] was of prime importance; not alone because of the great monetary and commercial interests involved, but also because it might afford a forecast of the policy of the government in such matters in future. Public interest was quickened also because of the novelty of resting the burden of proof upon the railroads rather

---

[1] Precisely like the situation following the earlier emasculation of the law. P. 473, *supra*.
[2] 215 U. S., 452. P. 538, *supra*.
[3] 61st Cong., 3rd sess., Senate doc., p. 725, 1911, 10 vols. Admirably summarized in *American Economic Review*, I, 1911, pp. 766–789. *Yale Review*, 1910, pp. 268–288. Haines Problems in Railway Regulation, 1911, pp. 143–154; and files of the *Railway Age Gazette*, especially 1910, p. 1108. H. A. Bullock in *Boston Transcript*, Nov. 12, 19, and 21, 1910, offers suggestive comment.

than upon the shippers, as in the past. The effect of this change in procedure was apparent throughout. The representatives of the shippers were, in most cases, content to point out the inadequacy of the reasons advanced by the carriers. The railroads, on the other hand, were forced to come forward aggressively with positive arguments favoring their side of the case. The only exception to the negative task of appearing in rebuttal against the carriers' arguments was in the somewhat spectacular presentation of the novel issue of "scientific management," shortly to be discussed.

The movement of freight rates since 1900 was insistently upward. On two separate occasions prior to 1910, as we have seen,[1] general advances by concerted action of the carriers took place, namely in 1903 and 1907. These earlier changes had been mainly confined to commodity rates. All the great staples, such as iron and steel, grain, coal and coke, glass, brick and cement, were affected. The rate increases of 1910, on the other hand, which gave rise to the first important test of the Mann-Elkins law, were mainly confined to advances in class rates, — that is to say, the rates upon merchandise and the better grades of freight. It was doubtless true, as alleged, that the steady decline throughout a generation before 1900 had unduly depressed the scale of charges for transportation service; and that prices in general, and especially wages and costs of operation, had greatly enhanced since that time. To meet this situation, the carriers had proceeded either to get together by an understanding not to compete; or else they had permanently put an end to competition by downright consolidation. After the first upward movement which paused about 1904, some time elapsed without further efforts in this direction. Then, after postponement of a concerted attempt in 1908 matters went on quietly enough until 1910. Many changes were unostentatiously made in individual instances by modification of traffic rules or classification;[2] but no widespread

[1] Pp. 411 and 488, *supra*.   [2] P. 427, *supra*.

action took place. The occasion for the renewal of the upward movement in 1910 was an insistent demand of railroad employees all over the country for a rise in wages. And the acquiescent attitude of the railroad managers toward their employees, suggested a tacit understanding that wages were to be raised on condition that the brotherhoods support the movement to recover this advance from the public through an increase in freight rates.

The trunk lines filed their new tariffs in 1910, even while Congress was in the throes of debate over the Mann-Elkins Act. These schedules substantially increased all class rates, — by from eight to twenty per cent —; and affected about half the commodity rates, mainly of the lesser sort. The western railroads promptly followed suit, filing higher tariffs by about ten per cent. for approximately 200 commodities. In response to vehement protest from all over the country, Congress, as we have seen,[1] promptly conferred authority upon the Interstate Commerce Commission by the Mann-Elkins amendments to suspend such rate advances temporarily for examination as to their reasonableness. By virtue of this authority the Commission took testimony for several months and rendered its decisions both for the eastern and western railroads on February 22, 1911.[2] The strongest impression which one gains from examination of the testimony, is that the case for the railroads was imperfectly organized and inadequately presented. There was no division of the field in argument, with intensive cultivation in each case; but all of the railway representatives traversed much of the same ground, so widely scattering their effort that but superficial treatment of each point was possible. The shippers, on the other hand, evidently laid out their plan of campaign with more system and had correspondingly better results.

The railroads in the presentation of their case were somewhat embarrassed by several complications, some applicable

[1] P. 561, *supra*.   [2] 20 I.C.C. Rep., 243 and 307.

to all the roads alike, while others arose from the diversity of financial and operating conditions on different lines. All alike were denied resort to the main argument advanced in favor of the general rate advances in earlier years, particularly in 1900. It had been expected that stress might be laid upon the increased cost of materials used in construction or operation; but the fact that, largely as an aftermath of industrial depression, prices of many commodities were actually lower in 1910 than they had been on the average for a decade, deprived the railroads of this powerful argument. The main exceptions in this respect were in the prices of fuel and lumber. Owing to the diversity of operating conditions among the carriers, difficulty was also experienced in adducing the wage increases of 1910 as a warrant for advancing freight rates. Considering the entire railroad net affected, it appeared that the augmentation in revenue from the proposed advances would be $27,000,000; whereas the already conceded wage increases were in excess of $34,000,000, — in each case calculations being based upon the same volume of traffic and employment as in the preceding year. The wage argument, generally applied, was thus valid. But taking the carriers one by one, it appeared that the changes in wages and revenue which might result, varied greatly. On the New York Central, the increase in revenue would just about cover the rise in wages; on the Pennsylvania, it was less than half of the enlarged payroll. It was thus apparent that emphasis upon the increase in wages would not be equally valid for argument by all roads alike. The possible advantage of a united front was thereby denied.

Broader ground for rate increases was taken by the carriers, in the argument that operating expenses had greatly augmented in recent years, not so much because of higher prices or even wages, but because of the exactions of the public in the way either of better facilities and service or of greater safety. It was alleged that vast expenditures had been necessarily made for such purposes without a commensurate increase in revenue.[1] The main proof of this point lay in statistical presentation of the greatly increased operating ratio within recent years; that is to say, the higher percentage of gross revenue which it was necessary to expend in operation. Here again, the carriers failed to agree in the particular margin of safety above a reasonable return upon the investment, paid in dividends, which should be put back into the property. It was also urged by the carriers that the necessary funds for constructive development in future could be obtained only by such improvement in railroad credit as would result from a substantial margin of net earnings above reasonable dividends. Such were, in the main, the arguments presented by the railroads on behalf of their plea that the proposed rate advances should not be suspended.

The case in rebuttal, as presented by representatives of commercial organizations, was carried aggressively into the enemy's territory in only one line of argument. It was alleged that sufficient economy in operation could be effected by means of "scientific management" to more than offset the increase in wages together with the general demand for better service and improvements by the public.[2] On the whole the arraignment of the carriers in this regard failed to establish its point. Whatever results from "efficiency" had been obtained in manufacturing establishments, the limited experience in railroading outside of shop management, while generally satisfactory, had not been altogether convincing. Essential differences between railroads and factories, particularly in respect of minute supervision of labor scattered over hundreds of miles of line, tended to render impracticable many of the improvements in process advocated by efficiency engineers. The

[1] This point has since been well presented in Suffern, *Railroad Operating Cost*, New York, 1911. *Cf.* chap. II, *supra*.

[2] This argument is critically examined in the *Quarterly Journal of Economics*, XXV, 1911, pp. 539–562. *Cf. Railway Age Gazette*, 1912. p. 287.

demands incident to the operation of public-service companies are also different from those applicable in private business. Railroads must consider not only profit-making, but adequate and satisfactory service. And, finally, the thorough organization of labor among carriers was a bar to the untrammelled introduction of new methods. Nevertheless, the publicity which was derived from the presentation of this case before the Commission could not fail to draw attention to the need of determined and general application of such sound and businesslike methods as were found practicable.

The shippers attempted, in general, to meet the railway arguments point by point. Thus the plea of steadily increasing operating ratios absorbing an ever larger proportion of gross earnings, was met by statistical evidence showing that gross revenues had so rapidly augmented during the decade as, nevertheless, to permit of a steady increase in net revenue year by year. In this regard, the time was certainly opportune for establishing this point. Recovery from the depression following 1907 was actively under way during 1909–1910. Not even the indications that a less rosy future was to ensue in 1911, — judged by the then course of net earnings, — sufficed to offset statistical evidence in this regard. Even if for all the roads taken together the wage increases would more than absorb the increasing revenues, the fiscal year 1910 had produced so large an increase in net earnings, — $55,000,000, — as to still leave the carriers better off than they were before, even without the increased freight rates for which they were asking.[1]

The decisions of the Commission in both cases, covering advances east and west, was unanimously against the railroads.[2] It was held that the carriers had failed to prove their case at practically every point. While it was true that cost

[1] Data as to gross and net earnings at this time by comparison with former years will be found at p. 79, *supra*.
[2] 20 I.C.C. Rep., 243 and 307.

of operation had increased for various reasons, it was also plain that the growth of the business had more than absorbed these additional outlays. And as to the contention that a fair return upon the value of the property was not being earned, the entire field of argument concerning the reasonableness of railroad rates as related to investment, was necessarily held in abeyance pending more positive data than was then at hand. The decisions, however, contained a ray of hope for the carriers in the promise that while this general increase would not be upheld, particular changes in future would be considered on their merits in each case.[1] The railroads accepted the decision as final, and withdrew the proposed tariffs with surprisingly little protest.[1] Whether the great increase in prices in 1912 over preceding years, operating indirectly through insistent pressure for wage increases to enhance costs of operation, will necessitate a reopening of this issue in a large way, seems likely to depend upon the rate at which the volume of traffic augments in the immediate future. It is clear, in any event, that a sufficient surplus earning power must be permitted to insure a continuance in favor of railway securities as compared with other forms of investment.

[1] *Cf. Railway Age Gazette*, LIV, 1912, pp. 10–14, and 803. A peculiarly suggestive instance is the allowance of increases on soft coal. Not a mere motive, — the need of more revenue, — but proof of reasonableness in detail was offered in evidence. 23 I.C.C. Rep., 617.

CHAPTER XIX

THE LONG AND SHORT HAUL CLAUSE: TRANSCONTINENTAL RATES

"Substantially similar circumstances and conditions" stricken out in 1910, 601. — Debate and probable intention of Congress, 602. — Constitutionality of procedure, 603. — Nature of applications for exemption, 604. — Market and water competition, 605.
The Intermountain Rate cases, 610. — The grievances examined, 611. — The "blanket rate" system, 611. — Its causes analyzed, 612. — Previous decisions compared, 615. — Graduated rates proposed by the Commission, 616. — The Commerce Court review, 620. — Water v. commercial competition again, 620. — Absolute v. relative reasonableness, 622. — Legal technicalities, 625. — Minimum v. relative rates, 624. — Constitutionality of minimum rates, 625.

THE original long and short haul clause, as we have seen, forbade a greater charge for a short than for a long distance over the same line under "substantially similar circumstances and conditions." The principal amendment in 1910 was the elimination of this troublesome clause, "substantially similar circumstances and conditions"; — responsible, as experience had shown for the practical nullification of the entire fourth section of the law of 1887 through the interpretation placed upon it in 1896 by the courts.[1] The insertion of a new provision in 1910 prohibiting carriers from charging "any greater compensation as a through route than the aggregate of the intermediate rates," concerned a somewhat different question, and may be omitted from consideration in this connection. The Commission was given authority under the amended law to relieve carriers from the prohibition of the statute, which, in this regard, did not become effective until February 17, 1911. It was uncertain at the time how extensive was the violation of the distance principle; although a comprehensive investigation by

[1] The history of the clause will be found at pp. 473 and 564, *supra*.

the Elkins Committee in 1905[1] showed the existence of many irregular tariffs all over the country. Within the first ten months after the law took effect, 5723 applications for relief under this section were filed. Of this number only two hundred and ninety concerned passenger fares: making it clear that the problem was mainly one of adjustment of freight rates. Inasmuch as the Commission held that each application should be treated as a formal complaint to be separately passed upon, it will be seen that these applications for relief considerably outnumbered the total of 4570 formal complaints which had otherwise been filed since 1887. Amendment of the fourth section obviously imposed a heavy additional burden upon this administrative arm of the Federal government.

The proposition to amend the long and short haul clause in 1910 called forth the same divergence of opinion in Congress as to regulation which characterized the original debate twenty years before. One party wanted an absolute long and short haul clause, permitting of no departure from the distance principle. The other stood for a more elastic plan, whereby carriers under certain economic justification should be allowed to make a higher charge at the intermediate point. The prime difficulty lay in defining these exceptional cases. Had Congress left this solely to the discretion of the Commission without such definition, the law might be held unconstitutional, as involving a complete delegation of legislative power. The situation was clearly stated at the time by the Chairman of the House Committee on Interstate Commerce. "Practically what we do here is to give the Commission power to say what, in a particular case, shall be a just and reasonable rate; although we declare as a general proposition that it shall be unjust and unreasonable to charge more for a short haul than for a long haul." In brief, it is clear that Congress intended that the general language of

---

[1] Digest of the Hearings, Appendix III, Dec. 15, 1905, pp. 1–244. An excellent body of unworked economic data on rate making is here afforded.

the statute should furnish the rule which the Commission was to adopt in applying this section of the law.

Was there any further intention of Congress in thus amending the long and short haul clause? The carriers contended that the only effect was to deny the railways the right to decide for themselves whether they might disregard the rule of the section: in other words, that they must conform to the interpretation laid down by the Commission itself in the Georgia Railroad Commission cases in 1892.[1] The Commission, on the other hand, at once interpreted the amendment, as defining the purpose of Congress differently. It held that the railroads must assume the burden of justification. The carriers, therefore, must become the advancing party in proving that violation of the distance principle was warranted by the necessities of the case. It is obvious that, without this interpretation placed upon the amendment, Congress would not be providing a remedy for local discrimination, but would be merely giving power to declare the existence of a wrong.

The constitutionality of the amended section seemed likely to depend upon the manner in which it was applied administratively. If construed as conferring unrestricted power to grant or deny applications for relief, it would probably be held void, as already observed, as an unfettered delegation of legislative authority. Rate making being a legislative function, this attribute of the Congress could not constitutionally be vested in entirety in an administrative body. The Commission must, in other words, be restricted and guided by certain rules and standards set by the legislature. This point had been well established respecting the exercise of control over the issue of capital stock by railroads by the state commissions. It was clear, also, that the long and short haul clause did not impose an inviolable rule to be enforced against all carriers. This had been the contention of complainants against the railroads in the Spokane case, soon to be

[1] P. 240, *supra*.

considered. It seemed clear that the proper function of the Commission under the law, was to investigate each case by itself in the light of the first three sections of the Act in general. After such investigation, if it appeared that a departure from the distance principle would result neither in unreasonable rates nor in due discrimination, permission therefore must be granted. Under such circumstances it could not lawfully be withheld. And in the contrary case deviation from the long and short haul principle must likewise be refused.

The Commission in enforcing the new long and short haul clause, in the first place laid down certain general rules for its own guidance.[1] Perhaps the most important of these was that the different rates or fares to be compared, must apply to the same classes of transportation. It would be obviously unjust to compare a one-way fare with either excursion or commutation rates. Export and import freight rates, usually lower than regular domestic rates, must each be dealt with in a class by themselves, in determining whether the more distant point by having a higher rate prejudiced the rights of intermediate ones. Congress certainly did not intend to make the charging of a commodity or carload rate in transcontinental traffic unlawful, merely because it happened to be lower than local rates or less-than-carload classified shipments from intermediate points. Violation of the distance principle must properly always be determined by comparison between rates of the same kind. A number of similar rules were promulgated for the sake of duly standardizing practice.

Applications from the carriers for exemption from the long and short haul clause in freight tariffs fell into four distinct groups. The largest number of petitions, — more than one-fourth of the total filed, — had to do with the necessities of circuitous lines in meeting through rates made over more direct routes.[2] In such cases the lowest through rate was often

---

[1] 25th Ann. Rep. I.C.C., 1911, discusses the matter fully.
[2] *Cf.* p. 255, *supra*, as to which line makes the rate.

made by the longer line, which might, at the same time, conceivably be operated at a lower cost. Permanent relief was granted by the Commission in comparatively few of such instances; and then only when it appeared either that the short line had observed the distance principle throughout, or else that the intermediate rates upon the long line were apparently reasonable and just, in and of themselves. Under such conditions the Commission sometimes permitted the circuitous route, especially if it were manifestly so, to meet, not only the prevailing rate over the short line, but also any future rate which it might put into effect.

Next in importance, measured by the number of applications for relief from the long and short haul clause in freight tariffs, were those based upon the exigencies of market competition. The familiar case of the rivalry of Florida and California orange growers in the eastern markets may illustrate the situation.[1] The growers must be put into that market and held there in each case in competition with one another, each served by the carriers who profited by their traffic. Should it be said that because such market competition compelled a low through rate, irrespective of distance, that no higher rate at any intermediate point where such market competition did not exist, should be allowed? The difficulty and danger, however, of accepting the justification of market competition was, of course, the fact that exemption from the distance principle might deny to the intermediate points the advantage to which they were justly entitled by reason of their geographical location.[2] The compelling force of market competition is exemplified also in the transportation of pine lumber from all along the southern tier of states to the consuming territory of the treeless Middle West. The mills in Mississippi, Louisiana, Arkansas, and Texas are so much nearer than those in Florida or Georgia, that

[1] 14 I.C.C. Rep., 476.

[2] *Cf.* instances cited by Judge Knapp before the Senate (Elkins) Committee, 1905, IV, p. 3294. Hammond, Rate Theories of the I.C.C., also marshals these cases.

exceptionally low rates per mile must be put in from these latter states to enable them to hold their own. Such exceptionally low rates, if applied to all intermediate points, would, of course, prove ruinously unprofitable to the railroads concerned. There were certainly contingencies of this sort entitled to relief.

Closely akin to market competition in compelling departure from the long and short haul clause, were the practices arising in connection with commodity rates to meet special circumstances in production or consumption. A public building, perhaps, was to be erected at a given point; and active competition arose from quarrymen in different parts of the country for supplying the cut stone. A carrier serving such a quarry put in a special carload rate in order to enable the shipper on its line to compete for the contract. No similar commodity rates, as a fact, were called for from intermediate stations, inasmuch as no other quarries on the line were interested in this particular job. The Commission ruled in such cases that no tariffs from intermediate points need be filed, unless desired for the benefit of some other shipper. Such cases are obviously analogous in principle to those above mentioned under the heading of market competition.

The third and perhaps, as it may appear in the future, the most substantial ground for seeking relief from the long and short haul clause in freight rates was the force of water competition. For example, all along the Atlantic seaboard the low rates of coastwise steamships were absolutely compelling in their effect upon through rates by rail. Obviously the railroads could not share in the business, unless they met the low water rate, — a low water rate which, very properly, ought not to affect the higher charges at interior intermediate points not enjoying such competition by water. On the other hand, it was evident that the utmost care needed to be exercised in accepting this excuse for the lower rate at the more distant point; or, otherwise stated, for higher rates at the intermediate

LONG AND SHORT HAUL CLAUSE 607

points not in the enjoyment of water competition. It was unquestionable, as experience all over the country had demonstrated, that the force of such competition upon internal waterways had been greatly exaggerated by the railroads for their own purposes. The steamboats had disappeared from the Mississippi and all its branches, and from the smaller rivers of the southern states, not because they were surpassed either in speed or in economy, but by reason of the superior organization and certainty of through shipments by land.[1] The railroad always beat the steamboat, mainly because it was not hampered by the difficulty of breaking bulk at transfer points. The river boat served relatively few places, while the railroad could make connections everywhere. And, finally, the water lines, being open at all times to competition for the worth-while business from rivals who needed merely to assemble enough capital to buy a boat, could not distribute their margin of profit according to the pressure of competition at different points along every line.[2] Whether a revival of commerce upon our inland waterways will ever change the nature of this competition between water and land transportation remains to be seen. But, in the meantime, it was indubitable that the plea of competition by water required careful examination before being accepted at its face value. The importance of this consideration appears clearly in connection with the Intermountain rate cases, soon to be discussed.

The petition of the Southern Pacific Railroad for exemption from the prohibition of the amended long and short haul clause in 1912,[3] as to rates between San Francisco points and Portland, Oregon, presented a concrete problem in the fair adjustment of distant and intermediate rates under the force of coastwise water competition. There was no question as to the force of this rivalry; more than three-fourths of the traffic

[1] *Cf.* F. H. Dixon, A Traffic History of the Mississippi River; Doc. 11, Report National Waterways Commission, 1911.
[2] *Cf.* pp. 385, 566, *supra*, and 638, *infra*.   [3] 22 I.C.C. Rep., 366.

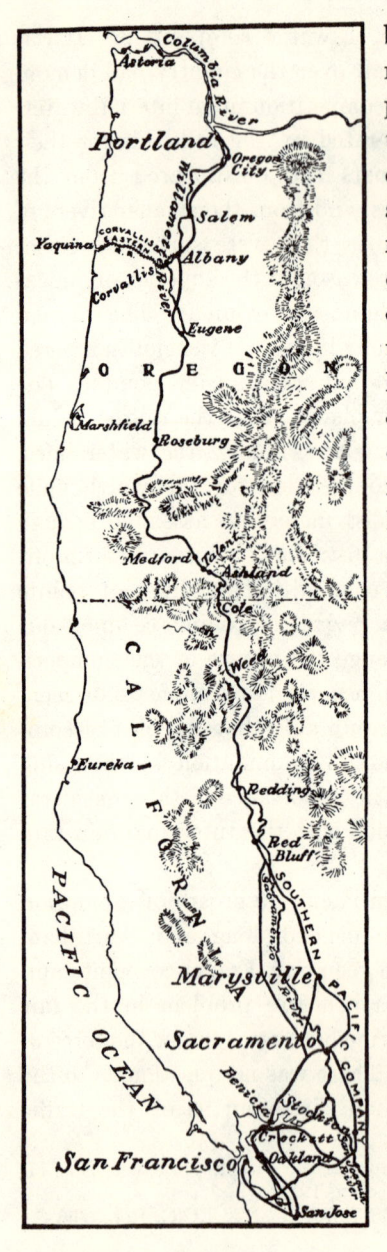

between the distant seaports moving by boat. The geographical situation is shown by the map herewith. But the difficult point to decide was as to whether the intermediate rates were not too high by comparison, — being made, in other words, to compensate unduly for the low rates and loss of traffic at the two ends of the line. The high intermediate point was Talent. The first-class San Francisco-Portland rate for 746 miles was 51 cents per hundred pounds, as against a San Francisco-Talent rate for 409 miles of $1.66, — more than three times the charge for about one-half the haul. Moreover, the inadequacy of water competition as a full explanation appeared at many points. Albany, for example, was no farther from Portland than Sacramento was from San Francisco. Yet while Sacramento enjoyed the low water rate north bound, neither Albany nor other places much nearer Portland were given the same advantage in southerly shipments. This case, left open for further examination as to facts, is also interesting as to points at law. The carrier, as in the Intermountain rate cases, contended that under the amended long and short haul clause, the Commission need consider only the force of water competition; and need not concern itself with the reasonableness of the intermediate rates. The Commission held this not to be a right construction of the law.

The reasons for seeking exception from the long and short haul clause in passenger business, judging by the petitions filed by carriers under the new law, had to do mainly with complications following the establishment of mileage schedules by law in the different states. Some of these states had also enacted two-cent fare laws, in which case it often happened that intrastate fares were arbitrarily higher than those which applied on interstate business. But the main reason for seeking exemption from the Fourth Section was the desire of circuitous routes to meet the charges made by the short lines. Obviously, as in freight traffic, the long line could not charge more than the short line, and usually the short line made the rate. Practically under such circumstances, the long line carrier could not well maintain a higher fare to the intermediate point, since in passenger traffic, unlike freight, the traveller could if he pleased buy his ticket to the more distant point and then get off at the intermediate one. The Commission, in view of this fact, naturally found less flagrant violations of the distance principle in passenger fares than in freight rates.

What economic reasons among all these advanced by the railroads, should be accepted by the Commission as warranting a departure from the distance principle? Originally, as we have seen, it was held that competition either with carriers by water, with railroads not subject to the Act, or other rare and peculiar cases, created such dissimilarity of circumstances and conditions as to warrant a modification of the distance principle.[1] In the first great case under the amended law, the Commission held, more broadly, that other factors than these might properly be

[1] P. 473, *supra*.

taken into account. It considered itself authorized not merely to decide whether circumstances in respect of competition at the two points were dissimilar, but also whether, and to what extent, that dissimilarity justified a departure from the rule. In other words, as interpreted by the Commission, modification of the rule might be permitted to just the degree which would seem to be called for by consideration of the whole situation. The best way to understand the bearing of these considerations, however, will be to examine this first great case in detail.

The Intermountain rate cases, affording the first crucial test of the long and short haul amendments of 1910, were doubly significant. They afforded a prime example of the struggle for supremacy between the administrative and the judicial branches of the government. And they also stood foremost among all the transportation controversies of the last generation.[1] The grievances were long-standing. They had been before the Interstate Commerce Commission since 1889.[2] They comprehended geographically a range of interests covering the entire northern half of the United States. While the Rocky mountain territory and the Pacific coast terminals were most directly concerned, the rights in trade of every factory and distributing point east of Denver were indirectly involved, in so far as they participated in commerce with the Far West. Not even the inevitable conflict over remodelling the southern basing point system by enforcement of the new fourth section of the Mann-Elkins law, was equal to this one, either in geographical scope or commercial importance. And at the same time the fact that the new Commerce Court was in 1912 on trial for its life — this being one of its leading cases on appeal — endowed the controversy with an even greater significance. Both in the eyes of the law and of commerce and finance, the issue was plainly of the first importance.

[1] Already discussed in other connections in chapters VII and XI.
[2] 5 I.C.C. Rep., 478, 510.

The transportation grievance of the tier of Rocky mountain communities from Washington to Arizona, although simple, divided naturally into two parts. The first was that the freight rates from all eastern territory to these localities were from one-quarter to over one hundred per cent. higher than to the Pacific coast, although the goods in transit passed their very doors and might be hauled a distance greater by one-fourth. A carload of glassware from Pittsburg to Spokane, Washington, paid a freight rate of $649.44; while the charge to Seattle, four hundred miles farther west, was only $393.60. A first-class commodity (carload) rate from Omaha to Reno, Nevada, was $858. If the goods were delivered 154 miles farther west, at Sacramento, passing through Reno *en route*, the freight bill amounted to but six hundred dollars. But this discrimination was less than half the indictment, inasmuch as the compelling force of ocean competition at the coast was conceded by all. It might well be that San Francisco and its sister terminal points were unreasonably favored, rather than that the intermountain rates were unduly high in themselves. The carriers by land might indeed be, as they alleged, powerless in the face of a water competition beyond their control. And if they were thus impotent, surely the government could not account their tariffs unlawful, however irregular they might be.

The second item in the complaint of the intermountain cities showed the cloven hoof of the transcontinental carriers. These mountain rates, relatively so high by comparison with more remote terminals, were equally high from every point east of Denver over a territory two thousand miles in width.[2] In other words, entirely regardless of distance, the freight rate to Spokane or Reno, whether from New York, Chicago, St. Paul, Omaha, or even Denver, was the same. It was indeed a blanket

[1] For Spokane, 15 I.C.C. Rep., 376 (1909); 19 *Idem*, 162 (1910); 21 *Idem*, 400 (1911). For Nevada: 19 *Idem*, 238 (1910) and 21 *Idem*, 329 (1911). The latest Denver case is 15 *Idem*, 555. For Salt Lake City 19 *Idem*, 218.

[2] Shown by a map in 19 I.C.C. Rep., 241.

rate, like the fixed charge of two cents for postage. And it made no difference how near any point in this wide zone might be, the disparity in rates a ainst the intermountain points was relatively the same. Thus our two concrete examples, above cited, were for shipments from Pittsburg and Omaha, respectively; but in any case, were the point of origin as remote as Portland, Maine, or even as near as Colorado "common points," the disparity of rates was unchanged. They were always very much higher to the intermountain cities than on to the Pacific coast; although the carriers east of the Missouri river got no more for their portion of the haul when the goods were bound for Spokane than if they went on to Seattle for a much lower through charge. This latter fact, of course, narrowed the complaint down to the policy of the western lines. The discrimination, if it were one, was clearly of their making. Whatever trouble there was, originated west of the Missouri river. However much the other railroads all over the country might have joined in transcontinental business, they remained impartial onlookers in this particular contest.

Some of the causes of the apparently abnormal western rate adjustment are perfectly plain. The low rates to the coast were due to water competition, which, while now under some measure of railroad control — partially "neutralized" in fact[1] — was always present and potentially great. It will be even more controlling when the Panama Canal is opened.[2] To meet this situation, the carriers had established a series of through commodity rates which practically covered all transcontinental business. For all this traffic exposed to water competition, it was averred, the intermountain territory was more remote, if not geographically, at least for purposes of rate making. The railroads consequently added the charge for the local haul back from the coast to the low transcontinental or through rate

[1] 19 I.C.C. Rep., 250; 21 *Idem*, 351, 416–421; Dunn, The American Transportation Question, pp. 178–221. *Railway Age Gazette*, LIII, p. 202.
[2] *Cf.* chap. XX, *infra*.

in determining the charge to all the intermediate cities. Thus, they alleged, a discrimination was forced upon them, not of their own creation. They could not grade all their intermediate rates down to a through tariff thus fixed at the farther end. It would mean bankruptcy. Thus far the situation is analogous to Hadley's classic oyster car case.[1] The main difficulty arose in satisfactorily explaining the second half of the scheme. How did the blanket or "postage stamp" rate zone arise, permitting exactly the same rates, whether to Spokane or Seattle, from points scattered over a territory covering practically two-thirds of the United States? Was it an artificial scheme, modifiable at the will of the carriers or of the government; or, like the law of gravitation, was it beyond the control of either?

The truth was that westbound rates from New York, Chicago, Omaha and St. Paul had come to be fixed at the same level, not by water competition primarily, but by the forces of commercial rivalry between centres bidding for the far western market. They were originally graded somewhat according to distance in the early days.[2] And it is plain that water competition, at first confined to the Atlantic seaboard, gradually extended inland. In order to secure the business to San Francisco by steamer or clipper ship, rail charges from Pittsburg or Buffalo back to Philadelphia or New York had been absorbed in the through rate, thus gradually extending the benefits of water competition farther and farther west from the seaboard cities.[3] And, of course, as population and manufactures grew in the Middle West, the narrow fringe of such competition steadily and inexorably spread in from the Atlantic coast over a wide zone of blanket rates, all based on New York. The direct all-rail carriers, naturally, met this competition at all points. Manufactures and population continued to spread

---

[1] P. 217, *supra*.
[2] 9 I.C.C. Rep., 318 *et seq.* Reprinted in our Railway Problems.
[3] *Cf. U. S. v. U. P.*, etc., Evidence, I, p. 295.

toward the West; but, imperceptibly, a new competitive factor appeared. As the force of direct water competition lessened with ever-widening distance inland from the Atlantic, market competition began to gather strength. One need not go so far as to concede that "market competition is a euphemism for railroad policy," in order to realize that artificial rather than natural influences gradually came to bear in the westward extension of the blanket rate. The trans-Missouri lines, getting the *whole* rate on shoes made in St. Louis for the Pacific slope, while only getting a part of it if the goods came from New England, had a direct motive to put St. Louis into the western market and thereafter to hold it there at all cost. Every increment in the St. Louis traffic, moreover, was surely theirs for ever. It could not be stolen away by Canadian railways or ocean steamship lines, as it might if it originated at Boston. It became a settled policy of these western lines, therefore, to meet even the water-compelled seaboard rates at all points, no matter how far inland. The blanket zone thus steadily widened, out of all semblance to its originally modest proportions as based upon water competition alone. A competition originally natural, gradually merged into another of an entirely artificial sort.

The importance of both the intermountain and Pacific coast traffic originating along the western confines of the blanket zone, steadily increased. One record showed that three-fourths of the business at Reno, Nevada, originated west of Chicago.[1] It all moved on the same rate as freight from Portland, Maine, whether destined to Nevada or to the Pacific coast. The disparity against Nevada remained absolutely the same in either case. It was to hold this traffic, originating west of Chicago, against all eastern competitors, that the blanket zone was so abnormally widened by the trans-Missouri railroads.

For years the transcontinental rate scheme had been before the Interstate Commerce Commission. A number of

[1] *Cf. Railway Age Gazette*, LIII, p. 201.

decisions [1] were rendered prior to 1910, under the old long and short haul clause, emasculated as it was by the Alabama Midland decision of 1896. The Hepburn amendments of 1906 had so far strengthened the hands of the Commission that it made several attempts to deal with the question. But the orders in these cases were confined to classified tonnage, although it was clear that most of the transcontinental business moved under commodity rates. Such carload or wholesale tonnage, of course, was the only sort actually affected by the competition by sea. This fact greatly aggravated the discrimination against which the intermountain cities complained. For, in absence of such water competition, they enjoyed relatively fewer commodity ratings. And their youthful, though ambitious, jobbing trade was dependent upon just such special carload rates in competition with middlemen on the Pacific coast. If "tin boxes and lard pails, nested" moved in carloads, Seattle got them from "anywhere east" for a commodity rate of eighty-five cents, as against the regular fourth-class rate to Spokane of $1.90 per hundred pounds. The Commission grappled with the problem of such discrimination manfully; but made little headway until the new law of 1910 put it in better case. Then for the first time it tackled the heart of the matter, in revising the commodity rates in the great cases now under review. There is evidence that the railroads were already endeavoring to remodel their tariffs, under pressure in some degree from the Commission even before the amendment of the law in 1910. It was recognized that some modification of the existing scheme was needed.[2] And it was relatively easy to re-arrange mere class rates.[3] They were little affected by water competition. But the commodity schedules, concerned in these later cases, were far more important commercially.

[1] Best reviewed in Brief for the United States in *U. S. v. Atchison, Topeka and Santa Fe Railway*, etc.: Supreme Court, October term, 1911, p. 10.
[2] *Railway Age Gazette*, May 14, 1909, and November 25, 1910.
[3] Brief for U. S., *loc. cit.*, p. 12.

Two plans were possible to mitigate the violation of the distance principle.[1] The rates to intermediate points might be lowered conformably to the long-distance standard. This would enable the railroads to hold the coast traffic against the water lines, but would decrease the revenues from "way" business. Or, on the other hand, the coast rates might be put up, regardless of water competition, in the expectation that much through business would still go by rail. Tariffs by land were already considerably higher than by the sea routes. Possibly the rail rates might be increased somewhat further. Some coast business would be lost to the water lines, but on what remained a higher return would accrue. Moreover, a considerable development of interior distributing centres would be bound to ensue. And, best of all, the grievances of the interior places would be somewhat mitigated.[2] Unfortunately the Pacific coast points were in an uproar at this threat against their supremacy in the jobbing business. And, in the meantime, the new powers under which the present proceedings were taken had been conferred by the Mann-Elkins law. The carriers unaided could probably not have greatly bettered matters. But the government, at all events, chose to deal with it; so that these private attempts came to naught. Subsequently such action as the carriers took, naturally assumed the form of increases at terminals rather than reductions at intermediate points.

The new orders[3] were radically different from the preceding ones, not only in applying to commodity rates, under which most of the tonnage really moved, but also in respect of the form of remedy proposed. In order to correct the discrimination,

[1] 191 Fed. Rep., 861.

[2] The plan is in *Railway Age Gazette*, June 4, 1909, p. 1182. New tariffs are described in *ibid*. *Cf*. also *Boston Transcript*, November 28, 1910, for other plans.

[3] 21 I.C.C. Rep., 329, 400. Both the Spokane and Nevada cases are combined in the appeal to the Supreme Court; as is also the independent order of the Commission denying relief from the fourth section to the Union Pacific and other roads.

the previous decisions prescribed the absolute rates to be put into effect at various points. The new orders did not establish absolute rates at all, but endeavored, instead, to set up a system of relative rates or differentials. All the former decisions had held the intermountain rates inherently unreasonable. The new opinions treated them as only relatively so. A clear distinction was drawn between real water competition and that *pseudo* water competition which, as has been said, resolved itself practically into a mere competition of markets with one another. The guiding principle adopted was that the force of water competition, — the only one entirely beyond the carriers' control, — of necessity increased with the proximity of the shipping-point to the Atlantic seaboard. Business from New York to Seattle by rail had to go at rates compelled by the rivalry of steamship lines. Traffic from Omaha to Reno, Nevada, was surely free from it. Yet under the then existing system no distinction whatever was made between the two sets of circumstances. All rates were blanketed, regardless of remoteness from the eastern seaports. The new governmental order substituted a series of zones suggestive of those so long prevalent in trunk line territory.[1] These are shown by the map on page 618. As one passed westward from zone IV, with water competition under full pressure at New York, the influence of the roundabout carriers by sea progressively diminished; until, at last, beyond the Missouri it became *nil*. Such water competition affording the only pretext for a grant of lower rates to the Pacific terminals than to intermountain points, it followed, logically, that the disparity in charges between such interior and coastal places should decrease *pari passu* with the westward movement of the originating point. A substantially lower rate from New York to San Francisco than from New York to Nevada might be permitted; but no such difference, relatively, ought to obtain from St. Paul or Omaha to San Francisco as compared with Rocky mountain territory. For these inland

[1] Chap. X, *supra*, especially the map facing p. 365.

initial points were practically beyond the range of steamship rivalry.

Specifically, the Commission in these orders forbade any higher charge to the mountain points from any part of zone I than applied to the Pacific terminals. From zone II, lying

four hundred miles more to the east, there would probably never be any considerable traffic coming back to New York in order to go round by sea, but in rare instances there might be some. From this zone, therefore, intermountain rates might be not more than seven per cent. above those to the Pacific terminals. And so on as one went east. Rates from zone III might be not more than fifteen per cent. higher to Spokane

INTERMOUNTAIN RATE CASES 619

than to Seattle. From zone IV to Rocky mountain territory they might be twenty-five per cent. above those to San Francisco; but the disparity against the intermountain territory, even from here with water competition in full effect, must never exceed this percentage.

This ingenious plan certainly commends itself in principle to the economic student. It restored in a measure the gradations existing in 1887.[1] It did not create the zones out of whole cloth. It utilized a scheme for division of territory already adopted by the transcontinental lines for other purposes.[2] And, most important of all, it was elastic, not prescribing absolute rates, but resting content with laying emphasis upon the need of gradation. Yet it granted a substantial measure of relief from the present disparity of rates. For, whereas the former intermountain tariffs from the East were from fifty to one hundred per cent. above those to the Pacific coast, the difference under this order might never exceed twenty-five per cent. The new scheme was cleverly planned, also, from a legal-strategic point of view. It could scarcely be attacked under the Fourteenth Amendment as confiscatory, inasmuch as it left so much latitude to the carriers in the readjustment of their tariffs.[3] To overset it on this ground, they must prove that disaster would result from the particular rates which they had chosen to adopt. This would be an impossible task. The only choice remaining to the carriers, therefore, would be to

[1] 9 I.C.C. Rep., 318. The first suggestion I find of graded rates is in the dissenting opinion in this St. Louis Business Men's League case. Reprinted in our Railway Problems.

[2] Brief for U. S., *loc. cit.*, p. 55. Annual Report I.C.C., 1911, p. 31.

[3] A compromise offered by the railways and accepted by commercial bodies pending the Supreme Court decisions was filed June 18, 1912. It is estimated to save Spokane shippers alone about $500,000 annually. Class rates are the Commission's from the seaboard, but from interior points are somewhat lower. The acceptance of the distance principle is the significant point.

"As the distance, St. Paul to Spokane, approximately 1500 miles, is 150 per cent. of the distance Omaha to Salt Lake, approximately 1000 miles, a reasonable rate from St. Paul to Spokane would not be less than 130

attack the order on the ground that the Commission was exceeding its powers, delegated by Congress. This, in effect, was what was done.[1]

The opinion of the Commerce Court,[2] setting aside the intermountain rate orders of the Interstate Commerce Commission, will shortly be reviewed by the Supreme Court of the United States, to which tribunal appeal was promptly taken. Disregarding the dissenting opinion that the entire long and short haul clause, as amended in 1910, was unconstitutional, the significant differences between the two tribunals were three in number.

The first point at issue between the court and the Commission concerned the differentiation of water competition from so-called market competition.[3] The Commerce Court refused to recognize any distinction between the cause of lower rates to the Pacific coast from Omaha or from New York, respectively. It ascribed the disparity in all cases to competitive forces entirely beyond the railroads' control "If the carrier from St. Paul, in order to meet new water competition from New York," etc. The Commission, on the other hand, clearly set apart market competition, applicable to western cities, from that due to carriage by water, which controlled rates from the Atlantic seaboard. The railways, it said, must conform in their rate-making policies to the latter. They were not bound by the

per cent. of the rate from Missouri river to Salt Lake, and in the proposed tariff rates from St. Paul to Spokane would be made accordingly.

"From Mississippi common points as defined by current tariffs, the rates would be 112½ per cent. of the St. Paul rates.

"From Chicago and common points, the rates would be 116⅔ per cent. of St. Paul rates.

"From Detroit and common points, 125 per cent. of the St. Paul rates.

"From Buffalo, Pittsburg and common points, 130 per cent. of St. Paul rates.

"From New York, Boston and common points, 130 per cent. of St. Paul rates.

"From Colorado common points, 90 per cent. of St. Paul rates."

[1] *Cf. Railway Age Gazette*, July 28, 1911, p. 162.
[2] 191 Fed. Rep., 856.
[3] Market competition as such is discussed at p. 118, *supra*.

former. For market competition (as already quoted) "is a euphemism for railroad policy."[1] And, speaking as an economist ignorant of the technicalities of the law, I venture to affirm that the Commission in this contention was absolutely right.[2] Even as far west as South Bend, Indiana, wagons may go to California by the direct rail route; or, with a change of ten cents in the rate, they may come back to New York and thence go round by sea. Such is the delicacy of adjustment even as far west as Chicago. Hence the failure to recognize that low rates to the Pacific coast from points west of the Missouri river were due to an entirely different cause — namely, the arbitrary determination of the transcontinental lines to hold the fort for their local clients against all odds — was to commit an egregious economic blunder. Furniture goes from Chicago to San Francisco on rates as low as if compelled by water competition.[3] But steamships never carry commodities of this bulky sort, even from New York. How much less, then, could water competition apply so far inland? The carriers were bent on keeping Chicago in the Pacific market. That was the real reason. The Commerce Court clearly missed the main point.

Equally sound economic evidence that water competition alone was not responsible for the entire present transcontinental rate system, was afforded by the fact that the wide blanket zone, already described, covering two-thirds of the United States for westbound rates, found no counterpart in the scheme under which rates were made up in the opposite direction.[4] It is a poor rule which will not work both ways. And surely water competition, when present, should be potent in either direction. It was undeniable that the absence of pushing cities along the

[1] 21 I.C.C. Rep. 355, 367: the Transcript of Testimony in the Supreme Court record is especially illuminating. *Cf.* also Twenty-fifth Annual Report I.C.C., pp. 30–40.
[2] S. O. Dunn in *Railway Age Gazette*, November, 25, 1910.
[3] *Railway Age Gazette*, 1910, p. 1005.
[4] 21 I.C.C. Rep., 418–423 is best on this. *Cf.* also p. 608, *supra*.

Pacific slope, desirous of developing trade relations with the Atlantic states, discouraged even the slightest extension of terminal rates inland. The ironclad monopoly enjoyed by the Harriman and Hill lines would probably have prevented this in any event. But the significant point was that there was no demand for a blanket zone for eastbound traffic. Hence water-compelled rates staid where they belonged; that is to say, closely confined to the Pacific seaboard cities. Thus it would also have been in the eastern half of the country, had it not been for "market competition" — this artificial factor which the Commerce Court failed utterly to recognize as in a class by itself.

The second vital difference of opinion between the Commerce Court and the Commission was economico-legal. The economist in the office of critic here stands upon less firm ground. And yet, whatever the law may be, the reasoning rests upon the interpretation of the facts.[1] The Commerce Court held that "when the rate for the longer haul is forced unreasonably low by competition, the only elements that can enter into the consideration of the rate for the shorter haul are its reasonableness," etc.[2] The controlling idea, in other words, in the reviewing judicial mind, was that, so long as the rate at Spokane or Reno was reasonable *in itself*, it was a matter of indifference to that locality what rate might be made to Seattle. All that the Commerce Court needed to do, therefore, was to consider the "intrinsic reasonableness"[3] of the intermediate rate. Not so, held the Commission. Whether this charge was reasonable or not was a question of relativity. It depended upon what rate was made to other points all around it and competitive with it. In other words, the intermediate could not be dissociated from the long-distance point. Railroads as public carriers owed a common duty to both points. No intermediate rate,

---

[1] As analyzed in chapter VII, *supra*.
[2] Brief for the U. S., *loc. cit.*, p. 37; Annual Report I.C.C., 1911, p. 36.
[3] In the Lemon rate cases also; 190 Fed. Rep., 593. *Cf. supra*, p. 592.

however low *per se*, could be reasonable, if the carrier was voluntarily offering a lower rate to points beyond. If its lower rate beyond was accorded under compulsion, that of course was a different matter. But in so far as these low Pacific terminal rates were due to an artificial railroad policy, any discrimination against the nearer points was unwarranted.

The analogy is clear between this difference of opinion of Commission and court and that between the two schools which would base judicial determination of rates in general upon inherent or relative reasonableness, respectively. The "remuneration" test, which the carriers' representatives sought to insert in the law of 1906, seeks to discover innate reasonableness of rates; not affected, that is to say, by the revenue which may accrue from them in the aggregate. The other standard declares such reasonableness to be always dependent upon circumstances; notably upon the amount of the investment and the resultant earning power arising out of the volume of business carried at the rates in question.[1]

The third difference of opinion between court and Commission was purely one of law.[2] Had the latter exceeded its powers delegated by Congress in attempting to fix a *relation* of rates, instead of prescribing certain maximum rates applicable to particular points?[3] The reasoning followed was apparently derived from the Supreme Court opinion in the Chattanooga case.[4] This reasoning, the government now contended in its argument on appeal to that tribunal, was inapplicable to the since amended law. Limits of space and the natural diffidence of an economist, alike forbid extended discussion of this nice point at law. The Commission alleged that, except by the

[1] H. S. Smalley in *Annals of the American Academy of Political Science*, March, 1907, pp. 299–304. *Cf.* also our Railway Problems, chap. XXIV. The point will be more fully discussed in vol. II, dealing with matters of finance, valuation, etc.

[2] Annual Report I.C.C., 1911, p. 38. Brief for U. S. Supreme Court, no. 883 *et seq.*, pp. 23–37. Also Brief for I.C.C. in the same case.

[3] Commerce Court opinion, p. 15. *Cf.* p. 507, *supra*.

[4] 181 U. S., I. *Cf.* also p. 592, *supra*.

exercise of such authority to prescribe relativity of rates, it would be powerless to remedy such discriminations in future. In consequence, inasmuch as Congress evidently intended to enable it to afford such remedy, authority over relativity of rates must be derived by necessary implication. And it is certain, economically speaking, that in this position the Commission was once more perfectly right. Whether it was legally so remained yet to be decided.[1] In this connection, it seems odd that none of the briefs for the government mentioned an important instance of the undisputed exercise of such power to establish relativity of rates. The Commission had for years, even in absence of any express authorization by law until 1910, freely prescribed details of freight classification in a large number of important cases.[2] It had never done more than to fix relativity; and the constitutionality of its orders had never been attacked.

An entirely new issue arose at this point. Prescribing relativity of rates implied determination of minimum rates. For if, as in this transcontinental case, the freight rate to Nevada points from New York might never be more than twenty-five per cent. greater than to San Francisco, a lower limit as well as an upper one was thereby prescribed for the latter point, and *vice versa*. The rate to one point once fixed by the carrier, voluntarily if you please, the minimum rate to the other might be necessarily determined thereby. If a dollar rate prevailed at Spokane, the Seattle rate must not fall below seventy-five cents. Was this not something new? Did it not suggest fixing, not maximum rates alone, but absolute rates as well? And if an attempt to fix absolute rates, was it not unconstitutional? There could be no two minds about the need of conferring power upon the Interstate Commerce Commission

---

[1] Of significance on this point is Commissioner Lane's dissent in the Lemon rate case. P. 592, *supra*.

[2] For details, *Cf.* Hammond, Rate Theories of the Interstate Commerce Commission (1911) and J. Strombeck, Freight Classification (1912). Also p. 468, *supra*.

over minimum or differential rates, if effective government regulation were ever to be attained. This had been my contention for years.[1] It had the best possible expert support from the side of the carriers.[2] Discriminatory rates could never be corrected until such power was delegated by Congress or conferred by judicial interpretation of the law. Kansas City now enjoys lower rates to Chicago on packing-house products than are accorded to Omaha. On every sound principle of rate making, the two cities ought to be placed on a parity. But the Commission could not rectify the abuse; for the roads from Kansas City promptly reduced their rates *pari passu* with any reduction of the charge at Omaha.[3] There was no bed rock below which rates could not go. The Omaha railroads as well as the government were powerless in face of the situation.

May power to fix minimum rates, so necessary to an adequate program of control, be constitutionally delegated by Congress? The question has never been squarely presented to the Supreme Court.[4] But the language in many cases has been such as to indicate that maximum rates alone may be lawfully established. Is the reiteration of the word "maximum" intentional? Or may it be that the judicial mind has never yet contemplated the need of regulating the minimum rate? Surely it seems an anomaly that the government should ever seek to

[1] *Atlantic Monthly*, September and October, 1905. On shortcomings of the later amendments of the law, *cf.* F. H. Dixon, in *Quarterly Journal of Economics*, vol. XXIII, 1910, p. 630.

[2] *Railway Age Gazette*, editorial, January 12, 1912, p. 41; and S. O. Dunn, The American Transportation Question, 1912.

[3] *Cf.* the Fort Worth case decided June 6, 1912; also the Eau Claire case, 5 I.C.C. Rep., 264. The latest case in which the Commission held that it had power to suspend a proposed reduction in rates arose from just such a condition of affairs, 22 I.C.C. Rep., 160.

[4] I am indebted to Professor Smalley of Ann Arbor, certainly the best authority among economists, for many citations on this point; as well as to Professor F. H. Dixon for suggestions. *Cf.* also 21 I.C.C. Rep., 415; Annual Report I.C.C., 1911, p. 34; and the Commerce Court opinion under discussion. Commissioner Harlan in his dissent in the Shreveport case asserts a clearer right over minimum than over maximum rates as against state authority. 23 I.C.C. Rep., 54.

fix such a lower limit, *below* which compensation may not be had. And yet many cases show that it is absolutely necessary, to the end that justice may be done. Or may the unconstitutionality of fixing minimum rates depend upon the fact that, if thus prescribed along with maximum rates, it will amount, practically, to determination of the absolute rate — the bogey which the carriers seem most of all to hold in dread? Interesting and inviting possibilities of judicial interpretation are indeed suggested along this line, were there opportunity to pursue them further.

CHAPTER XX

THE CONFLICT OF FEDERAL AND STATE AUTHORITY; OPEN QUESTIONS

History of state railroad commissions, 627. — The legislative unrest since 1900, 628. — New commissions and special laws, 629. — The situation critical, 630. — Particular conflicts illustrated, 631. — The clash in 1907, 632. — Missouri experience, 633. — The Minnesota case, 634. — The Governors join issue, 634. — The Shreveport case, 635. Control of coastwise steamship lines, 638. — Panama Canal legislation, 641. — The probable effect of the canal upon the railroads, especially the transcontinental lines, 643.

HISTORICALLY, the attempt of the separate American states to control railways began with a law after the English model in New Hampshire establishing a commission in 1844.[1] Three other New England states then followed suit prior to the Civil War.[1] But these early experiments were mainly concerned with matters of safety rather than of rates. The first real step was taken by Massachusetts in 1869. The Railroad Commission created in that year has served ever since as a model of the so-called "weak" or "advisory" type of regulation. Others of this sort were more common in the eastern states. Such commissions, in Massachusetts for example,

[1] On state commissions and the conflict with the Federal government, consult as follows:
1900. Hendrick, F., Railway Control by Commissions.
1900. McLean, S. J., *Economic Journal*, pp. 22–42.
1903. Meyer, B. H., Railway Legislation in the United States.
1903. Railways in the United States in 1902, part II. United States Interstate Commerce Commission.
1905. Dixon, F. H. *Political Science Quarterly*, XX, pp. 612–624.
1908. Huebner, G. G. *Annals Amer. Acad. Pol. Sci.*, pp. 138–155.

In a List of References on Railways, published by the Congressional Library, 1907, special articles on experience by states, such as Dixon on Nebraska, Meyer on Wisconsin, Million on Missouri, etc., will be found under the names of states. Even more comprehensive is the collective catalogue prepared by the Bureau of Railway Economics, Chicago, 1912.

rely mainly upon public opinion for the enforcement of their decisions. They possess very limited authority over rates, although they are empowered to recommend such changes as may be deemed advisable. Back of this authority, of course, lies the legislative power of the General Court, invoked on special occasions. But, in general, the activities of the Massachusetts type of commission have been mainly confined to supervision, either of construction or of capitalization.[1] New York and several other states conformed in the main to this type, although none of them had any authority over matters of finance. A second variety of the older railroad commissions dates from the period of the Granger Movement in the West. Maximum rate laws were passed by a number of commonwealths in the seventies, notably Illinois, Minnesota, Iowa, and Wisconsin. The outcome of this legislation was the decision of the Supreme Court of the United States, elsewhere discussed,[2] holding that state legislatures had the power to fix rates. The so-called "strong" commissions had their rise in connection with these events. Railway boards of this second type exercised control over rates in two ways; namely, by means of the promulgation of freight classifications and the prescription of maximum distance tariffs. For the purposes of such regulation most of the western states grouped the carriers according to their earning capacity, with a different schedule in each case. In certain of the southern states these older commissions adopted even more drastic policies which brought about prolonged litigation. The peculiar case of Texas, adding financial legislation to the direct prescription of rate schedules, has been discussed by itself.[3]

A new chapter in railroad regulation by the separate states dates from the general public unrest and Congressional activity of the Roosevelt period. An almost frenzied activity after

[1] Financial regulation will be discussed in vol. II.
[2] P. 452, *supra*. Also chaps. XXIII *et seq.* in our Railway Problems.
[3] Vol II, in connection with capitalization and stock-watering.

1900 culminated in 1907 in a legislative wave which swept over the entire country. No less than fifteen new or remodelled commissions were created in the two years 1905–1907, bringing the total number by 1908 to thirty-nine. Practically all of these were of the so-called "strong" type; that is to say, possessing the most extensive powers over all matters of rate operation and in many cases of finance as well. The most notable of these, of course, were the so-called Public Utility Commissions of Wisconsin (1905) and New York (1907). The subjugation of the formerly, dominant railway interests in New Jersey and Pennsylvania was also highly significant.[1] The movement even invaded the New England States, — so long a sanctuary of the "weak" or advisory commission. Vermont and New Hampshire set up powerful boards, and Massachusetts (1912) almost extended the powers of its commission in harmony with the general movement. Several features of this new lot of state commissions contrast markedly with even the old-fashioned "strong" type. Many of them permit the fixing of absolute rates. The majority now provide for appointment rather than election of the commissioners; and also by salary and in other ways enhance the dignity of the office. This operates naturally to lift these boards out of a semi-political atmosphere formerly too characteristic in many cases; and to bring them more to a par with the state courts.

The "Wisconsin Idea," achieving its full flower under the remarkable leadership of Governor La Follette in 1905, ably seconded by a number of prominent University of Wisconsin men, notably Hon. B. H. Meyer, now a member of the Interstate Commerce Commission, most completely realizes the progressive policy of sane state regulation.[2] The principle is

[1] On the new Pennsylvania commission consult the *Quarterly Journal of Economics*, August, 1912.
[2] "The Wisconsin Idea," by Charles McCarthy, described by Van Hise in "Concentration and Control," 1912, p. 236.

laid down "that it was as much the duty of the state to furnish transportation facilities as it ever had been to make roads or build bridges; and that if the function was delegated to any one, it was the duty of the state to regulate it so that the agent should be required to furnish adequate service, reasonable rates, and practise no discrimination." And, it is added, that this procedure should be "so simple that a man can write his complaint on the back of a postal card, and if it is a just one, the state will take it up for him." The three fundamental principles of the Wisconsin programme, now happily incorporated in the Federal law, were full authority over future rates; secured without expense to the complainant; and with the burden of proof laid upon the railroad in cases of appeal. In short, the Wisconsin plan provided for thoroughgoing administrative control, that is to say, with strict limitation of judicial review to the determination of points at law. The issues were in no wise different from those already discussed heretofore in connection with the development of the recent Federal policy; except possibly in respect of the persistency of opposition, which has had to be overcome more gradually in the Senate of the United States, — the natural stronghold of corporate influence.

The creation of powerful state commissions since 1905 has, oddly enough, been accompanied by a great activity of the state governments in the enactment of statutes aiming independently to regulate common carriers. Laws of this class are not new. As far back as 1890 there were twenty-two maximum rate and fare statutes. A period of quiescence, marked by only four such laws in twelve years, was followed by the passage within five years to 1907 of no less than twenty-two maximum fare laws and nine maximum rate schedules.[1] To these may be added a large grist of statutes dealing with almost every detail of operation or service. Demurrage, provision for terminals, train service and connections, distribution of

[1] Huebner, *op. cit.*, p. 147 has carefully tabulated all these laws.

cars, industrial and spur tracks, and hours of labor, may be cited among a host of others.

The activities of state governments in recent years in the creation of powerful railroad commissions, with the added grist of drastic independent statutes, have greatly emphasized the eternal conflict of authority between the state and Federal governments, as well as between the different states. Problems akin to those raised by the diversity of our laws respecting marriage, labor, and bankruptcy have been forced upon the attention of Congress and the Federal courts. Reasonable coöperation might be counted upon to accomplish something; but the course of events since 1905 points to the necessity of a final settlement of this important issue as far as common carriers are concerned, so authoritatively that a greater measure of political and industrial peace may prevail in future. The situation respecting railroads was well described by Justice McKenna of the United States Supreme Court in an opinion annulling the North Carolina law requiring railroads to receive goods for interstate transportation whether they had published rates for the proposed shipment or not; — "if the carrier obeys the state law, he incurs the penalty of the Federal law; if he obeys the Federal law, he insures the penalty of the state law. Manifestly, one authority must be paramount, and when it speaks, the other must be silent." It may be added that in this recent case, following the inevitable trend of events it was the state law upon which the penalty of silence was visited.

The ultimate ramifications of a state law under the complexities of modern railway rate adjustment and operation can never be foreseen. It is not simply a question of avoiding conflict between distance tariffs and classifications.[1] Often-

[1] The effect of Missouri distance tariffs upon rates over a large part of the Middle West is best instanced in the Missouri-Mississippi rate scheme. *Cf.* p. 128, *supra*, and especially chap. XX in our Railway Problems, rev. ed. *Cf.* also local and through tariffs at p. 394, *supra;* the Wabash decision, p. 451, *supra;* and the two-cent fare laws, p. 429, *supra.*

times the most modest rules and regulations may lead to results affecting commerce over a wide area. The great increase in large cars throughout the West, by contrast with other parts of the country, as traceable to the establishment by Missouri of minimum carloads,[1] is a case in point. We have also already observed how the revised milk laws of Massachusetts opened up an issue covering all of New England.[2] And then there are the various attempts of the railroad commissions, notably Texas[3] and Minnesota, to set up schemes of rates which shall concentrate the distributive business of the community in local cities as against the competition of jobbers at a distance. The extreme confusion introduced in matters of classification by conflicting authorities has already reached a point where demand for the substitution of a single uniform schedule for the United States has become wellnigh irresistible.[4] There are also conflicts respecting laws regulating service, illustrated by the Supreme Court decision in 1907, holding that the attempt of North Carolina to require through fast mail trains to stop at small way stations, was unconstitutional;[5] and finally, some agreement as to division of accounts between interstate and intrastate business will at once be recognized as an essential to the determination of reasonable rates for through and local service respectively.[6] From every side, in short, the need of a clear separation of state and Federal powers is becoming more and more insistent.

The conflict between general and local authority came to a head in 1907, resulting in a violent clash between the Federal and state courts.[7] The worst complication arose in the South, particularly in North Carolina and Alabama. Certain rail-

---

[1] P. 335, *supra*. [2] P. 329, *supra*.
[3] *Cf.* p. 394, *supra*, the Texarkana, I.C.C. case, May, 1900; and 11 *Idem*, 180, for Arkansas. Also 13 *Idem*, 48; and 18 *Idem*, 415. For later cases, 22 *Idem*, 110; and 23 *Idem*, 404 and 688.
[4] *Cf.* p. 338, *supra*.   [5] 207 U. S., 328.   [6] P. 586, *supra*.
[7] *Economic Bulletin*, of the Amer. Econ. Ass., I; Annual Rep. I.C.C., 1907, p. 93; and *Idem*, 1908, pp. 71 and 76.

roads brought suit in the Federal courts to annul rates fixed by the state legislatures; and temporary Federal injunctions were at once issued suspending the statutes until determination of their constitutionality. Popular feeling was much aroused, and local officials sought vigorously to defend states' rights. Ticket agents collecting more than the state prescribed fare, were condemned to the chain gang and the president of the railroad company was arrested. Federal judges promptly released all parties by writs of *habeas corpus*. A truce was finally patched up, pending determination of the matter at issue by the Supreme Court of the United States. The final and inevitable outcome, of course, was a decision by this tribunal, upholding the authority of the general government.[1] Technically, the question in these cases concerned the power of the Federal courts to issue temporary injunctions suspending state laws; or, in other words, raising the nice distinction as to whether a suit against a state officer was a suit against the state or not. Various other legal technicalities were involved both in North Carolina and Alabama. The main issue has been dealt with for the future by a special clause of the Mann-Elkins law of 1910. This provides that a petition for an injunction suspending a state law, shall be heard by three Federal judges, one at least of a superior court. Five days' notice is required; and there is a direct appeal to the Supreme Court of the United States. But an injunction, thus issued, is given clear precedence over any statute regarding common carriers emanating from authority of an individual state.

The state of Missouri has had a trying experience. This occurred in connection with a statute of 1907 reducing passenger rates from three to two cents a mile. Federal judges promptly granted injunctions against the enforcement of this statute. The state's Attorney-General in the meantime cited the railroads into the state courts to show cause for failing to obey. The compromise in this case took the form of an agree-

[1] 209 U. S., 123, 205.

ment to give the new law a trial of several months in order to test the financial effect of the reduction in fares. Then followed an interchange of injunctions, quite characteristic of the old days of the Erie Railroad, save for the integrity of the judges concerned. To this there then succeeded a decision by the Federal Circuit Court that the rates were confiscatory; although for some reason the two-cent fares and other reduced charges remained practically in effect. Controversies similar to this have arisen since 1907 in some seven different states. Oregon and West Virginia took issue as to the validity of two-cent passenger fare laws. In the latter case, the state supreme court held that the statute was not confiscatory. In Oregon the lower Federal court upheld the state law. The contest from Kentucky involved the constitutionality of a state railroad commission act, already held unconstitutional in the United States Circuit Court. The Arkansas appeal had mainly to do with maximum rate laws in relation to physical valuation of property; and in Ohio, the validity of a state rate on coal to Lake Erie was in dispute. The railroad contended that the traffic was interstate commerce, a contention denied by the state authorities.[1] The Minnesota case, — perhaps the most voluminous in its record of all, — had primarily to do with the confiscatory nature of reductions of intrastate rates: and this in turn hinged upon the mode of separating accounts.[2] A distinct affirmation of Federal supremacy has also been had by a Circuit Court opinion in 1911. All these cases are at this writing (1912) before the Supreme Court of the United States for decision. The main issue is pooled by agreement between the governors of the seven commonwealths concerned. The outcome cannot fail to be of the utmost importance, — far-reaching in its effect not only upon the

[1] The similar controversy in Minnesota regarding iron ore shipments seems to have been settled by voluntary abandonment of the claim to regulate by the state on Nov. 20, 1911. *Cf.* Minn. R. R. Com., Rep.

[2] To be discussed in vol. II.

regulation of railways but throughout the entire field of constitutional law. Such decisions as the Supreme Court has already rendered in connection with these matters having been entirely favorable to Federal authority, undoubtedly in this instance induced the joint action of the state executives for mutual protection and support. There can be no doubt that a sweeping decision, upholding Federal authority, will go far to solidify control by the Interstate Commerce Commission. It will also clear the air and greatly simplify the problem of operation by the managements of the railroads, not only in these seven states but all over the United States as well.

The delicate balance between state and Federal authority over commerce is also in a way to be tested in what promises to become an historic case before the Interstate Commerce Commission, — historic in the sense that its final adjudication by the Supreme Court of the United States will add a positive contribution to the body of our fundamental law.[1] It may best be understood by first gaining a clear idea of the nature of the economic grievance. Shreveport, Louisiana, is situated on the Red river, an important tributary of the Mississippi, some 190 miles distant from Dallas and 231 miles from Houston, — both of the latter being important and ambitious provincial distributing points in Texas. Shreveport, enjoying the benefits of water competition, — probably more keen historically than at present, — was granted correspondingly low carload rates by rail on merchandise from the north and east. These favorable rates were not extended to the two Texas cities, inasmuch as water competition was entirely absent. Naturally, therefore, an advantage was given to the Louisiana city in competition for distributive business in all the intermediate territory and even over in the *Hinterland* in Texas. In pursuance of a long-standing policy of encouraging the growth of provincial jobbing points within its own borders,[2]

[1] Railroad Commission of Louisiana, etc.; 23 I.C.C. Rep., 31.
[2] *Cf.* p. 394, *supra*.

the Texas Railroad Commission proceeded to overcome this disability by prescribing relatively low rates out of Dallas and Houston as compared with the rates from Shreveport to the same points. It seems even to have gone further and to have interposed positive barriers against the competition of Shreveport jobbers in Texas territory, by somewhat more than compensating for the low water rates at Shreveport. The disparity thus set up may be best illustrated by the following table of charges for approximately equal distances.

Rates in cents per hundredweight

		Class 1	E
From Dallas to Big Sandy, Texas	101 miles	44	13
From Shreveport, La., to Crow, Texas	100 miles	95	18
From Houston to Renova, Texas	103 miles	45	14
From Shreveport, La., to Angeline, Texas	104 miles	68	15

Stated in another way, sixty cents would carry one hundred pounds of first-class traffic some 160 miles out of Dallas into eastern Texas; while an equal rate out of Shreveport into the same Texas territory, west bound, was exacted for a haul of only fifty-five miles, — about one-third the distance.

The Commission decided upon the evidence by a bare majority that these Texas tariffs were unduly preferential; and ordered them to be so readjusted that the charges should be the same for equal distances from all three cities regardless of state lines. Concerning the minor point that it was lawful for a carrier to equalize conditions as between two competing places by imposing high local rates upon one point in order to offset the advantages as to inbound through rates enjoyed by the other, the Commission merely reaffirmed its belief that natural advantages of geographical location could not lawfully thus be nullified.[1]

The opinion rendered in this case is remarkable, less in its economic aspects, concerning which there seems not to have

[1] *Ibid.*, p. 34. A number of other cases are cited and compared by Hammond, Rate Theories, etc., 1911, p. 82 *et seq.*

been any great diversity of view, than as regards the divergent views expressed as to the legal authority of the Commission to interfere in the matter at all. Was undue preference and advantage in the eyes of the law, — the decision being rendered under the third section of the act, — created by the set of circumstances above described? At this point the Commission divided, with no fewer than two concurring and two dissenting opinions added to the majority view. According to this last, not only was the power of Congress to legislate in such matters paramount, but it was also held that this supreme power to put an end to all forms of local discrimination, — even those created by the act of state authorities, — had been delegated by Congress to the Interstate Commerce Commission. And in such instances, wherein conflict arose between Federal and state authority, the only rational and possible course, it was held, was for the national government through its administrative agent "to assume its constitutional right to lead."

The three separate dissenting opinions are of interest as expressing the need of a definitive pronouncement upon this great question by the Supreme Court of the United States. Not alone as to whether Congress intended to delegate authority to the Commission to settle such issues, but even the right of Congress itself to pass upon them under the Federal constitution, were called in question by the members of this administrative board. Two dissenters were content to submit the matter to "the august tribunal of the people which is continually sitting" to choose between submitting to such grievances as an alternative for virtually legislating state authority out of existence. The third dissentient view was more thoroughgoing. It not only discovered, legally speaking, no undue discrimination in the circumstances. It pointed out that on reducing the Shreveport local tariff "we fix interstate rates by the Texas yardstick," whereby "the national government therefore *leads* by *following*." It concluded by affirming that the Commission "should confine itself within the four corners of the law of its creation, usurping neither the legislative function of the Congress nor the judicial power of the courts." From all of which it is clear, first, that the Supreme Court of the United States, having once clearly defined the jurisdiction of the Federal government in such matters, it may, in the second place, well be that further amendment of the Act to Regulate Commerce will be in order.

In conclusion, it is pertinent, apropos of the approaching completion of the Panama Canal and the intensified interest in a more complete utilization of our internal waterways, to discuss briefly the relation between railroads and carriers by boat. The most stupendous canal projects are being brought forward, in the expectation that they will not only provide for a vast amount of low-grade traffic in themselves, but also that through the forces of competition they will bring about a substantial lowering of charges by railway. The most ambitious of these enterprises is the plan for a "Lakes to the Gulf" ship canal, even comprehending the dream of a twenty-four foot channel down the course of the Mississippi. Another and more modest proposition, probably practicable, is the construction of a canal from Lake Erie to the Ohio river. Altogether it has been credibly estimated[1] that the entire scheme for internal improvements of this sort would call for an outlay of not less than $2,000,000,000. Before engaging in any experiments upon such a magnificent scale, it is certainly proper to enquire whether the results will be in any way commensurate with their cost.

The cost of water carriage, like that of transportation by rail, should at the outset be divided into two distinct parts; one of which varies more or less in proportion to the volume of traffic, while the other, concerned with fixed charges on the

[1] The most careful examination of this subject is in H. G. Moulton's Waterways *Versus* Railways, 1912.

investment, maintenance and depreciation, is constant. The latter in other words bears little or no relation to the tonnage transported.[1] A careful distinction between these two great groups of expenditures is of fundamental importance in any comparison between rail and water carriage. The failure to so distinguish is responsible for much of the fallacious reasoning upon the subject both in and outside of the halls of Congress. It is indisputable that mere operating expenses are very much less by boat than by rail, especially when the economies of large craft can be had. The phenomenal development of commerce upon the Great Lakes, especially for the carriage of iron ore, coal and lumber, is due to this fact.[2] But, on the other hand, it is equally clear that the second great group of expenditures, particularly the fixed charges due to the enormous first cost of construction, are very much greater by artificial waterways than by rail. The balance between low operating costs and heavy fixed charges, of course, will be struck according to the nature of the particular enterprise. And canals, being entirely artificial, offer the least advantageous opportunity for realization of the economies incident to movement of freight by water.[3]

Improved riverways are economical by comparison with canals just in proportion to their lessened first cost; but, on the other hand, mere movement expenses, maintenance and depreciation are apt to be higher according to the strength of the current. In each instance everything depends upon first cost and the consequent burden of fixed charges. This point is almost totally neglected in popular discussion of the subject. Internal waterways being, without exception, public enterprises, the burden of interest charges is generally put aside as of no consequence. Naturally therefore, these being elimi-

[1] *Cf.* p. 45, *supra*.
[2] *Cf.* the Final Report of the U. S. Industrial Commission, 1901, vol. XIX.
[3] *Cf.* the data published by the Bureau of Railway Economics, in *Bulletin* 21, 1911, on the relative cost of transportation upon the Erie Canal.

nated, the apparent economy of carriage by water is mirrored forth with great effect.[1]

The experience of Germany, so often adduced in favor of water carriage, when examined in the light of the foregoing economic principles, is peculiarly illuminating. Much traffic, to be sure, moves apparently with greater cheapness than by rail upon both canals and rivers. Considering the tariffs which are based upon movement expenses alone, excluding, that is to say, any adequate return upon the total investment, such methods of transportation seem very economical and highly effective. But when *total* costs, rather than merely partial ones, are considered, the picture is completely reversed. The Dortmund-Ems canal, for instance, certainly the most important in Germany, represents an investment per mile fifty per cent. greater than the average for German railways.[2] For the single year 1905, the contributions from the states and cities interested, amounted to a subsidy of about $900,000. This financial burden, if distributed over the total tonnage, would make the entire cost of operation nearly one-fourth greater than the average by rail.

Rivers, as we have seen, possess certain advantages over canals, mainly in proportion to the lessened first cost of their improvement. The Rhine is often cited as an example of what the Mississippi should be as a great channel of commerce; but again that fatal objection of the first cost and, in the case of the Mississippi, of maintenance must always be kept in mind. The Rhine like the Hudson river or the St. Lawrence is, indeed, naturally adapted for carriage by water. Its firm banks, gentle gradient and constancy of level, are all elements in its favor. But it is certainly futile to anticipate similar results on the Mississippi or its tributaries, — huge and inconstant leviathans as they are, traversing a great alluvial plain devoid of solid foundations of any sort. The fact that today with a

---

[1] *Cf.* p. 386, *supra*, on competition by river in the South.
[2] *Cf.* Moulton, *op. cit.*

nine foot channel, Pittsburg makes no use of the Ohio river for its shipments of iron and steel, but sends them to the Pacific coast by way of New York, certainly does not augur well for the success of even an enlarged riverway in future, except possibly as to coal. Of course, if the government is to write off all the original investment, shifting the incidence to the general taxpayers of the country, that is a different matter. But unless the state thus chooses to subsidize the enterprise entirely, the total cost of transportation by rail will continue to be in future as it has been in the past, substantially lower than by the older and now antiquated methods of transportation. If the end in view be the attainment of the lowest possible rates, why not subsidize the railroads directly by this same amount? or even buy them up and operate them for cost? The expense to the taxpayers would be no more; and this plan would unquestionably give far better results. Even the electrically-towed canal boat is not to be compared for efficiency in reaching all parts of the country without transhipment, with giant locomotives, low grades, heavy rails and large train loads.

The ownership or control of water carriers by railroads constitutes a troublesome feature of present day conditions. Peculiar prominence, legislatively speaking, was given to it because of the attempt in 1912 to combine legislation dealing with this possible evil with the matter of Panama Canal tolls and regulations. Such control of water lines in competition with railways is matter of public record.[1] Much of the coastwise traffic is thus tied up. The Long Island sound service of the New Haven system, the Old Dominion Company, jointly owned by eastern railroads, and the Morgan Line and Pacific Mail Company, both parts of the Southern Pacific system, are notable instances. The same thing is true upon the Great

[1] *Cf.* pp. 386, 590 and 612, *supra*. Data will be found in the U. S. Industrial Commission Report, 1900–1901, and the Senate (Elkins) Committee, 1905.

Lakes, where a practical monopoly of eastbound transportation has been long held by the trunk lines. By refusal to grant through routes and joint rates to the Lake lines at Buffalo, these railroads have practically throttled the independent water service.[1] Even on the lesser rivers this phenomenon of neutralization of water competition occurs. Oftentimes where the bulk of the tonnage, as in transcontinental business, moves by rail, the water lines simply follow the railroads as to rates with a modest differential dependent upon circumstances. But the fact of practical elimination of competition by boat line is well recognized.

The concrete shape in which this matter arose in Congress was in the form of amendments to the Panama Canal law of 1912. In the House a bill providing for free passage of all American coastwise vessels was passed by a vote of 206 to 61, this measure at the same time prohibiting all railroads from owning stock in or otherwise controlling directly or indirectly, any competing steamship lines. The overwhelming nonpartisan majority is significant of public sentiment on the question. The Senate took a less radical stand in limiting the prohibition of railroad ownership to vessels making use of the Panama Canal. After prolonged discussion in the conference committee, the more drastic measure was, fortunately, eliminated.

From several points of view absolute prohibition of financial relationship between railway and water carriers seems unwise. A practical objection is that it may seriously handicap American roads in competition with Canadian carriers. The Grand Trunk, for example, reaching tidewater on Long Island sound might lawfully operate a boat line extending its service into New York; whereas the New Haven Railroad would be forced to dispose of its water lines to the same point, because

---

[1] The so-called Flour City case, recently decided in 1912 by the I.C.C. (not yet reported), held it to be the duty of these railroads to provide facilities for the handling of flour on through shipments of this sort.

they were in competition with its railroad service. And it is indisputable that similar injustice to American railroads might elsewhere be brought about. Moreover, the undoubted evil of water competition thus neutralized by railroads, might be remedied in other ways. One of these, embodied in recommendations of the Port Directors of Boston in 1912, opposing the more drastic legislation above mentioned, is the prevention of monopoly through public ownership or control of docks and wharfs. For railway ownership or lease of these, as at Philadelphia, San Francisco, Boston and elsewhere, is one of the easiest methods of preventing water competition. The water lines find it physically impossible to secure suitable terminals. And then, finally, there is always the possibility under the now amplified Interstate Commerce law, of enforcing both reasonable rates and facilities for through shipments, part rail and part water, as exemplified in the Flour City case above mentioned. It is not improbable that further amplification of the law, as recommended by the National Waterways Commission in 1912, may be necessary. Probably, in the light of bitter Southern Pacific experience, it was wise to restrict Panama Canal traffic to water lines not under railroad control. But any attempt to go farther and absolutely to divorce rail and water lines without provision, even, for the approval of the Interstate Commerce Commission in exceptional cases, might be productive of great harm both to the railroads and the public.

What will be the probable effect of the opening of the Panama Canal upon the railroads of the United States? One must consider the nature and volume of transcontinental traffic. The most important fact is that nearly nine-tenths of all transcontinental business at the present time moves by rail.[1] The tonnage by vessel west bound either around Cape

[1] An excellent review of the situation in *Railway Age Gazette*, LIII, pp. 199 and 249.

Horn or by the Isthmian routes has, to be sure, doubled within five years to 1911. But by far the larger proportion of the business moves by railroad direct. Secondly, it is important to note that a large part of transcontinental traffic consists of an exchange of commodities between the Middle West and the Pacific coast. Over one-half of the rail shipments west bound to Pacific terminals comes from west of Chicago. Less than one-quarter of the through traffic of one of the principal transcontinental roads originated at Atlantic coast points. And, inasmuch as water competition is still mainly confined to eastern seaboard territory, the diversion of this middle western business from the rail routes will not be disastrous in amount. In the opposite direction probably an even higher proportion of business is carried by rail, the principal reason being that much of the bulky freight of the Pacific slope,—lumber for example,—is consumed throughout the treeless Mississippi valley. None of this traffic naturally ever moves by water. It is apparent, therefore, that the effect of opening the Panama Canal, although great, will be for the most part localized as to results.

Specifically stated, four distinct changes seem likely to be brought about in the transcontinental situation. The first will probably be a considerable stimulation to the merchants and cities along the Atlantic seaboard throughout a zone extending inland, perhaps, as far as Cleveland and Pittsburg. A substantial drop in steamship rates will be followed, of course, by a corresponding reduction in through rates to the Pacific coast. But, on the other hand, it must be borne in mind that at best this tonnage is even today relatively unimportant to the transcontinental railroads. More than two-thirds of their through traffic, as we have just seen, now comes from the Middle West. These railways will probably prefer to lose a portion of this Atlantic seaboard business rather than to reduce their rates upon perhaps four-fifths of the other traffic, as they would otherwise have to do under the present system of postage stamp rates, from the Atlantic seaboard to the west of the Missouri river.[1] The eastern trunk lines, moreover, may probably be relied upon to extend the low seaboard rates somewhat farther inland than at present, rather than to divide low or even lower through all-rail rates from the Atlantic to the Pacific.

Next to the Atlantic seaboard territory, the so-called Intermountain or Rocky mountain region, may be expected to benefit substantially from the opening of the canal. It will surely get lower direct rates than at present on all its supplies from the East. Atlantic seaboard cities will doubtless also seek to regain some of the business throughout this region, which has been lost to them because of the growth of manufactures in the Middle West. The transcontinental railroads will seek to protect their clients in St. Louis and Chicago as against the merchants in New York and Boston, who gain an entrance to Denver and Spokane through the backdoor, so to say. Not only will lower rates prevail, therefore, but there will also probably be a larger proportion of supplies for these mountain states drawn directly from the eastern seaboard.

The foregoing prognostication, at first glance, seems to indicate that the Middle West is likely to profit less by the opening of this great waterway than other parts of the country. But it should be borne in mind that their hold upon west coast trade is now most firmly established. A part, but certainly only a part, of Pacific terminal business may be lost, but this will be more than offset by the growth of intercourse with the intermountain states. Surely the transcontinental railroads west from St. Paul, Chicago, and St. Louis may be relied upon to protect the direct exchange of goods of their constituents with the intermountain communities. Transcontinental railway rates will, of course, be lowered somewhat. The railways will, however, probably prefer to surrender the lesser portion of their present traffic in order to maintain profitable charges

[1] *Cf.* pp. 397 and 611, *supra.*

upon the major share of their tonnage. The profit of these railways will doubtless for the moment be lessened; but there can be little question that an enhancement of their prosperity will follow in the long run. The opening of this great new avenue of commerce by sea is bound to stimulate immensely the growth and prosperity of the entire country. And it is beyond question that in any such large development in future, they will all share to a large degree.

APPENDIX I

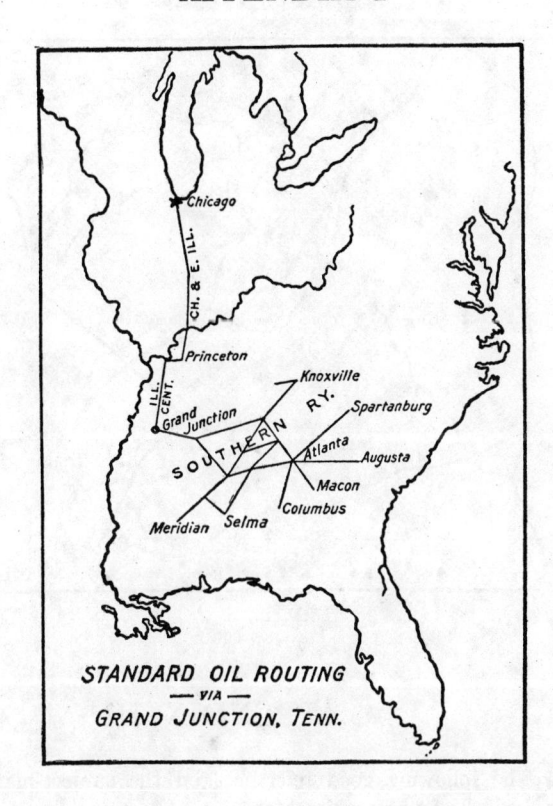

STANDARD OIL ROUTING
— VIA —
GRAND JUNCTION, TENN.

APPENDIX II

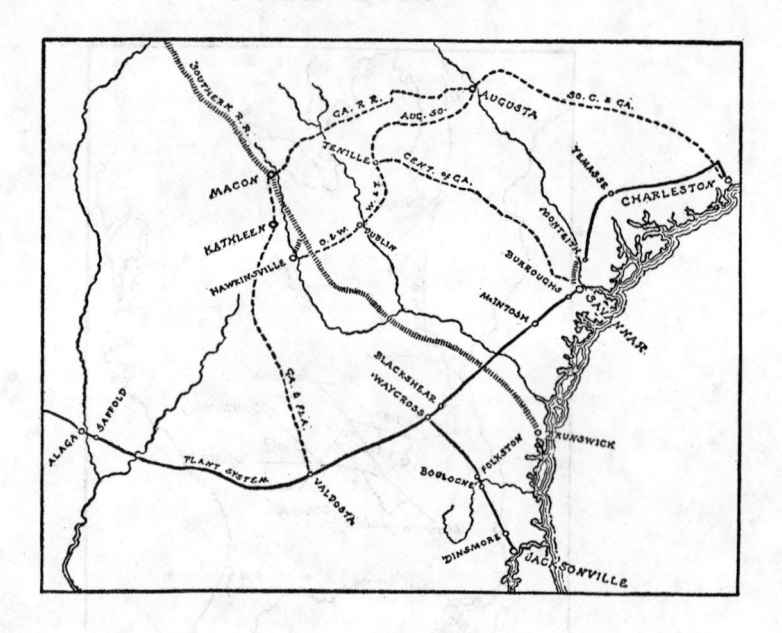

APPENDIX III

The following good references on the subject-matter of chapter I will be found serviceable:

1907. BISHOP, A. L. The State Works of Pennsylvania; Trans., Connecticut Academy of Arts and Sciences, XIII, pp. 1–298; and *Yale Review*, 1907, pp. 391–411.
1904. PAINE, A. E. The Granger Movement in Illinois (Bibliography); Studies, University of Illinois, I, pp. 1–53. With this should be compared, The Effects of the Granger Acts, *Journal of Political Economy*, 1903, pp. 237–256.

INDEX

A

Accounts, 515, 586 (*See also* PUBLICITY)
Act to Regulate Commerce (*See* contents of chapters as follows: original law, XIII; emasculation, XIV; Hepburn Amendments, XV and XVI; Mann-Elkins Act, XVII; and subsequent details, XVIII, XIX), congressional history, 450; outline, 452
Acworth, 65, 168
Adams, H. C., 44, 515
Agreements (*See* POOLS)
Alabama, and Federal laws, 632
Alabama Midland case, 270 (map), 390, 462, 473, 481, 482 (map)
Anthracite coal (*See also* COAL), tonnage and ton-mile revenue, 1910, 421; Federal case, 549
Arkansas, and Federal laws, 632
Ashburn case, (map) 388
Atchison, rebates, 190
Attorney-General, 570
Average train load (*See* TRAIN LOAD)

B

Back loading (*See also* DIRECTION), 287
Baltimore, 404
Baltimore & Ohio, railroad, 7, 18; car supply case, 541
Banana rates, 532
Basing point system (*See also* contents of chapter XI, South, etc.), compared with transcontinental basing line system, 239; main objections to, 242; citation of cases, 380; economic defence, 384

Basing points, enumerated and defined, 383; distinction between natural and artificial, 383, 387
Beef, exports in 1870, 21; and cattle rates, 139
Beef Trust, 550
Betterments, 83
Bishop, A. L., 648
Bituminous coal (*See also* COAL), tonnage and ton-mile revenue, 1910, 421
Blanchard, S. R., 257
Blanket rates (*See* POSTAGE STAMP RATES, FLAT RATES, etc.), 611
Board of Uniform Freight Classification, 338
Bogue differentials, 162
Bond, 510
Bonds, 553, 573
Books and papers (*See* WITNESSES)
Boston, 404
Boston & Albany Railroad, 11
Brimson case, 459
Brown case, 459
Buffalo, competition with Duluth, 145
Burnham, Hanna, Munger case, 442
By-products, marketing of, 142

C

California, wheat and Kansas flour, 138; raisin culture and rates, 178; fruits, 537; lemon case, 592; coastwise competition, 607
Camden and Amboy, 450
Canadian Pacific Differentials, 262
Canadian railroads, 33, 400
Canals (*See also* contents of chapter XX), early interest in, 2; early construction of, 3; in the West, 6, supersession in '70s, 24, 638

650　INDEX

Capital investment, as affecting operating costs, 65, 257
Capitalization, and rates, 574
Capital stock, 575
Carload rates (*See* contents of chapter IX), few in South, 311; theoretical basis, 326; mixed, 331, 340; in transcontinental system, 398
Carmack amendment, 572
Cars, larger in '80s, 24; economy of large, 95; capacity and classification, 334; complaints as to supply, 527
Car supply cases, 199, 538
Cartage case, 191, 257, 464
Cattle (*See* TEXAS, etc.), exports in 1870, 21, 401; and beef rates, 139; legislation as to carriage, 443; eveners, 445; rates, 510, 536
Centralization, 162
Central Pacific, 41
Central Traffic Association, 377
Central Yellow Pine Association case, 489
Chandler, 495
Chanute, 103
Charging what the traffic will bear (*See* VALUE OF SERVICE)
Chattanooga case, 228 (map), 240, 461, 464, 483
Cheese, 428
Chesapeake and Ohio Canal, 5
Chesapeake & Ohio Railroad case, 513
Chicago Terminal Charge case, 509
China, rates on, 183
Cincinnati Freight Bureau case, (*See also* MAXIMUM FREIGHT RATE CASE), 248; as a part of southern problem, 392; Supreme Court opinion, 469; Commerce Court revival, 588
Circuitous competition, 604
Cities, relative size in 1850, 12; rivalry between, 127; competition of large, 278; location in trunk-line zones, 368
Citrus fruit, 537

Civil War, effect on transportation, 16; primitive conditions, 17
Classification (*See* contents of chapter IX), and relativity of rates, 180; and use of commodity, 183; cost *v.* value of service, 183; historical development, 306; according to use, 318; in practice empirical, 319; and tariffs interlock, 347
Classification committees, conflicting rules and territory, 340
Coal (*See also* COMMODITY CLAUSE), early shipments by river, 14; rates, 469, 513, 585
Coal Car cases, 199
Coastwise traffic, 274, 608
Colorado Fuel and Iron case, 503
Commerce Court (*See* contents of chapters XVII, XVIII), 566; jurisdiction, 568; docket, 581; congressional history, 582; Intermountain rate decision, 620
Commercial competition (*See* COMPETITION OF MARKETS), in the oyster case, 234; in trunk-line system, 372
Commission, Federal *v.* state, 627
Commodities, increase in ratings, 309
Commodity clause, 513, 552
Commodity rates, 108; and law of joint cost, 266, 322, 324, 606; *v.* class rates in transcontinental traffic, 615
Common point system, 393
Company cars, 539
Competition, as affecting rate sheets, 104; three sorts of, 114; of routes, 114; of facilities, 116; of markets, 118; differences between trade and transportation, 136; Hadley's illustration, 164; no abandonment of field, 165; nature of, in local discrimination, 219; of routes, which line makes the rate? 255; between eastern and western cities, 391; less for passenger fares, 429
Competition of markets, two vari-

INDEX

eties of, 118; as applied to jobbing business, 124; as distinct from rivalry of routes, 242; in transcontinental rates, 613, 620

Complaints decline in number, 485; under Hepburn Act, 523; nature under Hepburn Act, 526; none too petty, 531

Concentration points, 537

Conducting transportation, in operating costs, 47, 53; declining cost of, as related to capital investment, 65

Conflict (*See* contents of chapter XX), of state and Federal authority, 631

Congestion of traffic, in 1903–'05 and in 1906–'07, 62, 80, 548

Consolidation, 487

Constitutional questions, as to Act of 1887, 451; in Hepburn Act, 502, 506; as to amended long and short haul clause, 603; as to minimum rates, 625

Constructive mileage, 275

Cooley, T. M., 140, 456

Cordele, Alabama case, 387

Corn, and flour rates, 143

Cost keeping, 517

Cost of carriage, by highway heavy, 3; declining by 1860, 16; as affected by distance 103, 108

Cost of service, and value of service compared, 166–184; objections to, 169; but essential, 170; not mere distance important, 256; in coal cases, 585

Cotton piece goods, rates, 345, 346, 348, 400, 536

Cotton, rate controversy in 1900, 153; rates, 356, 384, 401; tonnage and ton-mile revenue, 1910, 421

Counselman case, 458

Courts, relation to Commission in 1887, 453; original law, 460; unsatisfactory after 1887 as to evidence, 461; record in appeal cases, 463; judicial review in 1905, 503; objections to judicial control, 504; indefinite basis of review, 507; futility of procedure, 562; new mode of procedure on appeal, 570; broad *v.* narrow review again, 593

Coxe Brothers Coal case, 469

Creameries, 537

Credit Mobilier, 450

Cullom Committee, 442, 444, 448, 450

Cullom, S. M., 495

Cumberland Road, 3

D

Dairy products, 537

Damage claims, 524, 534

Danville case, 227, 483

Decade 1840–'50, 11; 1870–'80, 85

Decentralization, 385

Delaware and Hudson, 554

Delaware, Lackawanna and Western Coal Company, 554

Density of traffic, 86

Denver, 242

Des Moines Committee, 344

Detroit, 373

Differentials (*See also* contents of chapter XI), 22; Bogue, 162, 262, 361; Canadian, 400, 404, 579; in Intermountain rate cases, 617

Direction of traffic, 287, 374

Discriminations (*See* contents of chapters VI and VII), complaints in 1887, 445

Distance, as a factor in tariff construction, 102; subordinated in United States, 133; disregard of, produces inelasticity, 161; subordinated to cost of service, 256; relative unimportance, 264; excessive transportation, 277; attempt to reform southern system, 391; nullified in transcontinental rates, 396

Distributing business (*See also* JOBBING BUSINESS), in Texas, 394

Dixon, F. H., 499, 506, 625

INDEX

Dollar mark, 575
Dortmund-Ems canal, 640
Dressed meats, tonnage and ton-mile revenue, 1910, 421
Duluth, competition with Buffalo, 145
Dumping, 158
Durham, N. C., case, 210

E

Earnings, during panic of 1907, 75; statistics of gross and net since 1890, 79; as affected by level of rates, 82; gross and net compared, 84; comparison with decade 1870-'80, 85; monthly variation, 100
Eaton, J. S., 66
Eau Claire lumber case, 162, 254
Economic wastes, theory and practice, 268
Elkins, S., 501
Elkins Committee, 496
Elkins law (*See* contents of chapter XV), application to Standard Oil cases, 205; prosecutions under, 208; main provisions, 493
Equipment, supply, 527
Erie Canal, 4, 7, 15; still important in 1865, 18; decline after 1872, 24; plans for enlargement, 31, 358
Erie Railroad, early importance, 16
Esch-Townshend bill, 496
Eveners, 445
Evidence (*See also* WITNESSES), powers as to, 461; as to rebates, 493; immunity bath, 550
Ex-Lake grain, 145
Expedition Act, in 1903, 511
Expenditures (*See also* FIXED CHARGES, MAINTENANCE OF WAY, etc.), earliest classification of, 44; primary division into constant and variable, 45, 55; revised grouping in 1906, 46; statistical distribution, 49; as affected by seasons and circumstances 56-57; according to nature of road, 58; dependent on density of traffic, 60; constant and variable ever changing, 61; under curtailment of traffic, 63; inseparable as between freight and passengers, 68; affected by betterment charges, 83
Expenses, 64; separation of freight and passenger, 68; comparison with tonnage and revenue, 80
Export grain, beginning after Civil War, 18; after 1870, 20; *via* Gulf ports, 31
Export rates, on wheat and flour, 135, 404-406
Exports (*See* BEEF, CATTLE, WHEAT, etc.)

F

Facilities, competition of, 116
Federal authority (*See* contents of chapter XX)
Federal courts (*See* COURTS)
Fertilizer rates, 535
Fines, 451, 493, 513
Fink, Albert, 357, 367, 446
Fixed charges, 45; *v.* operating expenses, 257
Flat rates, example, 127; evils in, 132, 243-247
Flour, and wheat rates, 135; for export, 135; domestic, 138; and corn, 143
Foraker, J. H., 501
Fort Worth, 394
Fourteenth Amendment, 619
Freight tonnage (*See* TONNAGE)
Fuel cost, 59
Furniture rates, 621

G

Galveston, 31, 32, 33, 394, 437; cotton meal case, 186
General Expenses, 48, 54
Georgia Railroad Commission cases, 240
Germany, unified operation in, 294, 640
Glass, 351, 528

INDEX

Goodrich Transit Co., case, 586
Gould-Huntington, agreement, 447
Gould, Jay, in 1866–1869, 17, 28
Grain elevator cases, 211
Grain rates (*See* CORN, WHEAT, etc.), 402
Grain, tonnage and ton-mile revenue, 1910, 421
Grand Junction, Tennessee, case, 203
Grand Trunk Railway, 33, 432
Granger movement, 443, 628, 648
Great Western Railroad, 434
Green lines, 12, 15
Gross Revenue (*See* EARNINGS), 79
Gulf Ports, 437

H

Hadley, A. T., 105, 164, 217, 573
Harlan, Justice, 465
Harriman, E. H., 490, 551
Harriman system, 547
Hay, tonnage and ton-mile revenue, 1910, 421
Hearst case, 549
Hepburn Act (*See* contents of chapters XV and XVI), congressional history, 497; provisions, 499; effects, 522
(Hepburn) Committee, 445, 447
Hides, 320
Highways, early interest in, 2
Hill Lines, 547
Hillsdale ice case, 221 (map)
Hogs, 401
Hoosac Tunnel, 18
Household goods, 350
Houston, 394
Huebner, 627, 630
Hutchinson salt case, 195

I

Illinois Central car supply case, 538, 568
Illinois Central Railroad, construction, 14
Immunity Bath, 550
Import rates, 406, 409, 438, 464
Imprisonment, 451, 493, 513
Improvements, in operation, 93
Increasing returns, law as applied to railroads, 71–75; law of, qualified, 76; as tested practically, 77; law of, obscured since 1906, 84; final conclusion as to, 98
Industrial Combinations, and rebates, 213, 491
Industrial railroads (*See also* TERMINAL RAILROADS), 195, 212–213, 512
Injunction, 561, 562, 569, 586, 633, 634
Ink, 302
Intermountain rate case (*See also* TRANSCONTINENTAL RATES and contents of chapter XIX), 610; history, 614; new orders, 616; Commerce Court opinion, 620
Internal waterways (*See also* contents of chapter XX, CANALS, RIVERS, etc.), 640
International Harvester case, 196
Interstate Commerce Act (*See* ACT TO REGULATE COMMERCE)
Interstate Commerce Commission (*See also* chapters XIV, XV, XVI, XVII, XVIII, XIX, COURTS, PROCEDURE, etc.), reduction in tariffs filed, 324; created by law, 453; record on appeal cases, 460; rate-making power demanded, 468; complaints analyzed since 1906, 526; dissenting opinions in Shreveport case, 636
Intrinsic reasonableness, 622
Iowa Development Company, 434
Iron pyrites, 536
Iron rates, 399

J

Jobbing business, market competition in, 124; car load rates, 327–329; in the South, 384; decentralization, 385; in transcontinental rates, 397; and Pacific rates, 616
Joint cost, 67; two limitations upon the law, 265
Joint Rate Committee, 367
Joint rates, 529
Judicial review (*See* COURTS)

K

Kansas, wheat and California flour, 138; meal and Texas corn, 143
Keeping everyone in business, 119, 149
Kentucky and Indiana Bridge case, 461
Kindel case, 399

L

La Follette, 498, 559, 629
Lake Shore road, 419
Lake traffic, 358
Lakes to the Gulf canal, 638
Land grants, Illinois Central, 14; others, 35
Lemons, rates on, 345, 537; rate case, 592
Lighterage cases, 586
Lime, rates, 336
Lincoln, Nebraska, case, 147
Live stock (*See also* CATTLE, etc.), tonnage and ton-mile revenue, 1910, 421
Local Discrimination (*See* contents of chapters VII and XIX and *also* LONG AND SHORT HAUL CLAUSE), definition, 215; before 1887, 448
Local rates, in the South, 383; in Texas, 394; and revenue per ton mile, 421; reduced after 1887, 456, 591; the Shreveport case, 635
Local traffic, as affecting averages, 91; proportion of, 259; in basing point system, 385
Locomotives, 24; increased power of, 94
Logging in transit, 401
Long and Short haul clause (*See* LOCAL DISCRIMINATION and *also* contents of chapter XIX), tariff structure, obviating waste, 295; final text, 452, 565; congressional history, 473; English cases, 473; emasculation by courts, 476; amendment in 1910, 564
Long line, defined, 256; competition, 604

Louisiana rates, 634
Louisville & Nashville, 590
Louisville & Nashville case, 223, 244, 296, 474, 479
Louisville Properties Company, 556
Lumber, competitive rates for, 142; and wood pulp rates, 148, 181; tonnage and ton-mile revenue, 421; stakes, 533
Lumber rates, Pacific coast cases, 150, 535, 543, 581; tap line case, 212; logging in transit, 401; from Georgia, 489

M

MacGraham, 360
Maintenance of Equipment, 47, 52; 64
Maintenance of Way, expenses analyzed, 47, 51, 74
Mann-Elkins Act (*See* contents of chapter XVII), congressional history, 558; provisions, 562
Manufactures, westward drift in '80s, 30
Market, definition of, 119
Markets, competition of, 118, 605; consuming capacity as affecting carload rules, 336
Massachusetts Railroad Commission, 627, 629
Maximum Freight Rate case (*See also* CINCINNATI FREIGHT BUREAU CASE), 248, 469–473, 502
Maximum rates, constitutionality of, 623; state laws, 630
Memphis, 403
Meyer, B. H., 495, 629
Meyer, H. R., 385
Middlemen (*See* JOBBING BUSINESS)
Midnight tariffs, 197
Mileage, statistics since 1890, 79
Milk rate cases, in New York, 243, 255; in New England, 329
Milling in transit, 402
Minimum carload rates (*See* contents of chapter IX), 332
Minimum rates, 254, 624
Minnesota, and Federal laws, 632
Misquotation of rates, 571

INDEX

655

Misrouting, 527
Mississippi river, tonnage on 1845, 13; declining traffic in '80s, 26
Missouri, carload minimum rates, 335; and Federal laws, 632
Missouri-Mississippi rate scheme, 128, 442, 543
Mixed carloads, 331, 340
Monopoly, resulting from rebates, 187; distrust of, in 1887, 446
Montgomery, Alabama, case, 590 (map)
Morawetz, V., 165
Munn case, 452

N

Nashville, 342
Nashville Grain Exchange, 587
Natural market and territory, 158
Net Earnings (*See* EARNINGS), 79
Nevada, 611
Newcomb, H. T., 73
New England, oil rates, 202; milk rates, 329; common point system, 395
New Orleans, 31, 32, 33, 437
New York Board of Trade case, 306, 325, 407
New York Central railroad, construction, 15; importance in '80s, 30; compared with Pennsylvania Railroad, 58
New York city (*See also* DIFFERENTIALS, EXPORTS, etc.), importance in export trade, 30; supremacy threatened, 31
Nickel Plate line, 29
North Carolina, and Federal laws, 632
Northern Pacific railroad, 28

O

Official classification committee, 304
Ohio river, tonnage in 1845, 13
Open car system, 330
Operation (*See also* EXPENDITURES, etc.), improvement in '80s, 23; recent technical improvements in, 93; in 1910, 597

Orange rates, 345, 471, 537
Orange Routing case, 546, 572
Osborne case, 476
Oyster case, 217

P

Pacific coast (*See also* TRANSCONTINENTAL RATES, etc.), early trade with, 19; rapid development in '80s, 28; lumber cases, 150; routes by sea and rail, 276
Panama Canal, 638, 643
Panic, of 1857, 16; of 1907, 75; of 1893, 433
Par value, 575
Parallelling, 29
Passenger traffic, 429, 609
Passes, 512
Pennsylvania, internal improvements, 8; state works, 648
Pennsylvania Railroad, 8, 11; illustration of theory of rates, 62; coal supply scandals, 199; and steel companies, 556
Performance, of equipment improved, 96
Periodicity of expenditures, 61
Personal Discrimination (*See* contents of chapter VI), 185; philosophy of, 185; as creating monopoly, 187–189; distinction from general rate cutting, 188
Philadelphia (*See* DIFFERENTIALS, EXPORTS, etc.), 404
Physical valuation, 518
Pools, before 1887, 23, 446; obviating waste, 293; prohibited, 453, 579; after 1887, 457
Population, westward drift in '80s, 30
Portland Gateway case, 547, 572
Portland, Oregon, 608
"Postage-stamp rates" (*See* FLAT RATES), 397, 611
Powder Trust, 571
Prices, and rates, 172, 430, 471, 510, 587, 597
Primary commercial competition, 121
Private car lines, 140, 192

Procedure (*See* COURTS, WITNESSES, etc., and *also* COMMERCE COURT), under Hepburn Act, 505, 511
Proctor and Gamble case, 584
Produce Exchange case, 405
Pro-rating, 281, 514, 529, 543, 547
Public aid, 35
Publicity, 515, 574
Pueblo, 399
Pulp rates, 148

R

Railroad Construction, early in southern states, 9; sudden expansion in 1848, 13; new north and south lines, 14; decline during Civil War, 16; rapid during the '70s, 18; climax in '80s, 27; since 1890, 34; comparison with Europe, 35
Railroad mileage (*See* MILEAGE)
Rails, steel introduced, 17, 24, 93
Rate advances, complaints since 1906, 534; suspension in 1910, 561
Rate-making power, 467, 468; under Hepburn law, 500; constitutional aspects, 502, 506; suspension of tariffs, 560
Rates (*See also* PRICES, etc., and contents of chapter XII), decline in '70s, 21; intricacy of, 134; on raw and finished materials, 134; export wheat and flour, 135; domestic wheat and flour, 138; beef and cattle, 139; as between by-products, 142; cases of substitution, 143; general protective policy, 146; under changing conditions, 147; insurance function, 149; elasticity of, 152; rigidity, 153; as promoting economic unrest, 156; stability desirable, 157; use of classification in advances, 301; growing distinction between C. L. and L. C. L., 310; lime, 336; glass, 351; trunk line system, 354; cotton, 356; high level in the South, 382; no demand for reduction in, 1887, 443; movement since 1870, 411; actual index, 426; and prices, 430, 471, 510, 528; rise of, 488, 534; and capitalization, 574; advances of 1910, 594; absolute *v.* relative, 623; prescribing minimum, 624
Rate wars (*See* contents of chapter XII), during the '70s, 22; during the '80s, 23; dressed beef, 33; historical survey of, 431
Reagan, Judge, 444, 450
Reasonable rates (*See* contents of chapter VII), 588; in Inter-mountain rate case, 622
Rebates (*See* PERSONAL DISCRIMINATION and *also* ELKINS AMENDMENTS), 185, 280, 286; Standard Oil cases, 446; novelty of prohibition, 454; first prosecutions after 1887, 457, 512
Red Rock Fuel case, 199
Refrigerator cars, 140
Rentals, 534
Reports (*See* ACCOUNTS), 519
Restrictive Rate case, 585
Revenue (*See* EARNINGS), and rates in 1910, 599
Revenue per ton mile (*See* contents of chapter XII), decline during rate wars, 23; as related to earnings and expenses, 85, 99; Dilution of, 289; how computed, 412; advantages, 414; on different roads, 415; as influenced by nature of traffic, 416; as affected by distance, 421; and volume of traffic, 423
Review by courts (*See* COURTS)
Rice cases, 446
Rivers (*See* contents of chapter XX), early improvement of, 3; still important in 1850, 12; tonnage in 1845, 13; declining importance in '70s, 26, 382; competition in the South, 386, 640
Rockefeller, John D., 445
Roosevelt, President, 486, 496
Roundabout routing, 116, 269
Routes, competition of, 114; new law as to, 572

INDEX

Routing (*See also* contents of chapter VIII), complaints, 530, 546
Rules, growing complexity in classification, 312

S

St. Cloud case, (map) 235
St. Louis Business Men's League case, 125, 241, 246, 398
St. Louis, rates under three classifications, 348
Salt Lake City, 400, 611
Savannah Fertilizer case, 224
Savannah Naval Stores case, (map) 484
Sax, 168
Scientific Management, 517, 598
Seaboard differentials (*See* DIFFERENTIALS), 404
Secondary commercial competition, 122
Securities Commission, 573
Sherman Anti-Trust Act, 561, 579
Shoes, 320
Short line, defined, 256
Shreveport, Louisiana, case, 635
"Similar circumstances and conditions" (*See* LONG AND SHORT HAUL CLAUSE), 475
Smalley, H. S., 499, 507, 625
Social Circle case, 380, 462, 464, 468, 478
South (*See* contents of chapter XI), system of rates into, 248; high local rates, 260; classification conditions, 311; commodity rates, 323; jobbers in, 327
South Carolina Railroad tariff, 307
Southern Basing Point (*See* BASING POINT SYSTEM)
Southern Classification (*See* contents of chapter IX)
Southern Classification Committee, 304
Southern Pacific Railroad, construction, 28; water competition, 1912, 607
Southern Railway & Steamship Association, 23
Special rates (*See also* COMMODITY

RATES), as distinct from class rates, 113; and joint cost, 266, 280
Speculation, rampant in '80s, 29
Spokane, 226, 303, 611
Standard Oil Company, rebates on tank cars, 192; allowances on sale of supplies, 198; later forms of rebates, 198, 200, 200–206, 445, 491
State railroad commissions, 574, 627
Stock, 552, 573
Stock-watering, 444, 448
Stockwatering laws, 576
Storage, 191
Subsidies and public appropriations, 37
Sugar, rate war, 439; rates, 586
Sunday Creek Coal case, 209
Supreme Court (*See also* COURTS), delay in appeal cases, 461; divided opinions, 464
Surplus, statistics since 1890, 80
Suspension of rates, 561

T

Taft, President, 559
Tank cars, 192
Tap line decision, 212
Tarbell, Miss, 491
Tariffs, construction of, 101; too complex and numerous, 155; concealment of rebates in, 198; as distinct from classification, 301; classification as affecting, 321; reduction in number filed, 324; as interlocked with classification, 347; and rates, 407; new law concerning, 571
Taussig, F. W., 67
Tax, economic waste, 291
Telegraph companies, 572
Telephone companies, 572
Terminal cost, 101
Terminal railways, as means of rebating, 195; complicated phases of, 213, 512
Testimony (*See* WITNESSES)
Texas Cattle Raisers case, 70, 167, 567

Texas, cornmeal and Kansas corn, 143; rate system, 393, 635
Theory (*See* contents of chapters II and III), of classification, 314
Through freight lines, 23
Through rates, 359, 442, 529, 587, 588
Tobacco, 384
Tobacco Trust, 210
Ton mileage, statistics since 1890, 78
Ton-mile revenue (*See* REVENUE PER TON MILE), 364
Tonnage, statistics since 1890, 77; distribution by years, 417; increasing diversification, 418; classified for 1909, 420
Traffic Density (*See* DENSITY OF TRAFFIC), 86
Traffic Expenses, 48
Traffic (*See* TONNAGE), trunk line conditions in 1882, 357; nature of, as affecting ton-mile revenue, 416; by Panama canal, 643
Train load, 88; limit to economy of, 92
Train mile, cost and revenue per, 98
Transcontinental classification committee, 304
Transcontinental rates (*See* contents of chapters XI and XIX), rigidity, 154; compared with basing point system, 239, 245; general high level, 396; demoralization after 1893, 433; commodity *v.* class rates, 615; future traffic, 643
Troy case (*See* ALABAMA MIDLAND CASE), (map) 270, 390, 462, (map) 481
Trunk Line Rate System (*See* contents of chapter X), as related to separate line tariffs, 111
Trusts, and rebates, 213; 491, 571
Two-for-one-rule, 343

U

Underclassification, 190
Uniform classification (*See* contents of chapter IX), 338; objections and advantages, 345
Uniform Classification Committee, 339
Union Pacific Railroad, 19, 40
Union Stockyards Company, 587

V

Valuation, 518
Value of service, and cost of service compared, 166–184; objection to, 172; dynamic force in, 177; inadequate alone, 179; in classification, 315; in coal cases, 585
Vanderbilt, Commodore, 450
Volume of traffic (*See* TONNAGE, etc.), as an element in cost, 261

W

Wabash, St. Louis, & Pacific Railway case, 451
Wages, 518
Wagons, 109, 621
Wars (*See* RATE WARS)
Waste (*See* contents of chapter VIII, in transportation, 268; six causes of, 280; five results, 288; remedy for, 292
Water carriage, circuitous routing, 273; cost compared with rail, 638; controlled by railways, 641
Water carriers, failure to regulate, 579
Water competition, by coastwise steamers to Chattanooga, 232, 359, 475; in the South, 382, 385, 387, 392; by sea in Pacific coast traffic, 396; new law covering, 566, 591; and new long and short haul clause, 606; neutralized in Pacific rates, 612; *v.* market competition in Pacific cases, 620
Waterways (*See* contents of chapter XX and *also* CANALS, RIVERS, etc.), 638
West, classification conditions, 311
Western & Atlantic road, 12
Western classification committee, 304
West Shore railroad, 29

INDEX

What the traffic will bear (*See* VALUE OF SERVICE), illustrated by rate sheets, 107
Wheat, and flour rates, for export, 135; domestic, 138; rates, 467
Wichita cases, 232
Willamette lumber case, 535, 545
Windom Committee, 442, 443, 446, 447
Wisconsin, Two Cent Fare decision, 69; investigation as to rebates, 206; the "Wisconsin idea," 629
Witnesses, 451, 455, 457, 549
Wooden pipe rates, 303
Wool rates, 333, 352, 401

Y

Youngstown case, 223, 244, 296, 480

Z

Zone rates, trunk line territory, (map) 365; transcontinental, (map) 618

Big Business
Economic Power in a Free Society
An Arno Press Collection

Alsberg, Carl L. **Combination in the American Bread-Baking Industry:** With Some Observations on the Mergers of 1924-25. 1926

Armes, Ethel. **The Story of Coal and Iron in Alabama.** 1910

Atkinson, Edward. **The Industrial Progress of the Nation:** Consumption Limited, Production Unlimited. 1889

Baker, John Calhoun. **Directors and Their Functions:** A Preliminary Study. 1945

Barron, Clarence W. **More They Told Barron:** Conversations and Revelations of an American Pepys in Wall Street. 1931

Bossard, James H. S. and J. Frederic Dewhurst. **University Education For Business:** A Study of Existing Needs and Practices. 1931

Bridge, James H., editor. **The Trust:** Its Book. Being a Presentation of the Several Aspects of the Latest Form of Industrial Evolution. 1902

Civic Federation of Chicago. **Chicago Conference on Trusts.** 1900

Clews, Henry. **Fifty Years in Wall Street.** 1908

Coman, Katharine. **The Industrial History of the United States.** 1910

Crafts, Wilbur F. **Successful Men of To-Day:** And What They Say of Success. 1883

Davis, John P. **The Union Pacific Railway:** A Study in Railway Politics, History, and Economics. 1894

Economics and Social Justice. 1973

Edie, Lionel D., editor. **The Stabilization of Business.** 1923

Edwards, Richard, editor. **New York's Great Industries.** 1884

Ely, Richard T. **Monopolies and Trusts.** 1912

Ford, Henry. **My Life and Work.** 1922

Freedley, Edwin T. **A Practical Treatise on Business.** 1853

Hadley, Arthur Twining. **Standards of Public Morality.** 1907

Hamilton, Walton, et al. **Price and Price Policies.** 1938

Haney, Lewis H. **Business Organization and Combination.** 1914

Hill, James J. **Highways of Progress.** 1910

Jenks, Jeremiah Whipple and Walter E. Clark. **The Trust Problem.** Fifth Edition. 1929

Keezer, Dexter Merriam and Stacy May. **The Public Control of Business.** 1930

La Follette, Robert Marion, editor. **The Making of America:** Industry and Finance. 1905

Lilienthal, David E. **Big Business:** A New Era. 1952

Lippincott, Isaac. **A History of Manufactures in the Ohio Valley to the Year 1860.** 1914

Lloyd, Henry Demarest. **Lords of Industry.** 1910

McConnell, Donald. **Economic Virtues in the United States.** 1930

Mellon, Andrew W. **Taxation:** The People's Business. 1924

Meyer, Balthasar Henry. **Railway Legislation in the United States.** 1909

Mills, James D. **The Art of Money Making.** 1872

Montague, Gilbert Holland. **The Rise and Progress of the Standard Oil Company.** 1904

Mosely Industrial Commission. **Reports of the Delegates of the Mosely Industrial Commission to the United States of America, Oct.-Dec., 1902.** 1903

Orth, Samuel P., compiler. **Readings on the Relation of Government to Property and Industry.** 1915

Patten, Simon N[elson]. **The Economic Basis of Protection.** 1890

Peto, Sir S[amuel] Morton. **Resources and Prospects of America.** 1866

Ripley, William Z[ebina]. **Main Street and Wall Street.** 1929

Ripley, William Z[ebina]. **Railroads:** Rates and Regulation. 1912

Rockefeller, John D. **Random Reminiscences of Men and Events.** 1909

Seager, Henry R. and Charles A. Gulick, Jr. **Trust and Corporation Problems.** 1929

Taeusch, Carl F. **Policy and Ethics in Business.** 1931

Taylor, Albion Guilford. **Labor Policies of the National Association of Manufacturers.** 1928

Vanderlip, Frank A. **Business and Education.** 1907

Van Hise, Charles R. **Concentration and Control:** A Solution of the Trust Problem in the United States. 1912

The Wealthy Citizens of New York. 1973

White, Bouck. **The Book of Daniel Drew.** 1910

Wile, Frederic William, editor. **A Century of Industrial Progress.** 1928

Wilgus, Horace L. **A Study of the United States Steel Corporation in Its Industrial and Legal Aspects.** 1901

[Youmans, Edward L., compiler] **Herbert Spencer on the Americans.** 1883

Youngman, Anna. **The Economic Causes of Great Fortunes.** 1909